Textbook Trialware

Free 180-day Trial of Crystal Ball Software. Compliments of the Crystal Ball Education Initiative

KEEP THIS CARD!!
See instructions on back to download
Oracle Crystal Ball
software

1. Visit http://www.oracle.com/technetwork/middleware/crystalball/downloads/index.html

2. Accept the OTN License Agreement and choose the correct version of Crystal Ball

3. Sign Up for a free Oracle Web Account- After all information is entered, hit the Create button at the bottom of the page

4. Choose Crystal Ball from the dropdown list and after download and after running the Set Up file: Enter the information below to license

Username: Meredith9781119369110
Serial Number: 3B2EB63A-8898AF2A-2FC637A5-E43369E6

Project Management

A Strategic Managerial Approach

Tenth Edition

Project Management

A Strategic Managerial Approach

Tenth Edition

JACK R. MEREDITH

**Broyhill Distinguished Scholar and Chair in Operations, Emeritus
Wake Forest University**

SCOTT M. SHAFER

**Associate Dean and Professor of Management
Wake Forest University**

SAMUEL J. MANTEL, JR. (DECEASED)

**Previously the Joseph S. Stern Professor Emeritus of Operations Management
University of Cincinnati**

WILEY

DEDICATION

To the memory of Sam Mantel, Jr.: Scholar, author, mentor, friend.

J. R. M. and S.M.S

VICE PRESIDENT AND EXECUTIVE PUBLISHER	George Hoffman
EXECUTIVE EDITOR	Darren Lalonde
SENIOR MANAGER	Karen Staudinger
ASSOCIATE DEVELOPMENT EDITOR	Courtney Luzzi
SENIOR EDITORIAL ASSISTANT	Ethan Lipson
CONTENT MANAGER	Nichole Urban
SENIOR CONTENT SPECIALIST	Nicole Repasky
SENIOR DESIGNER	Maureen Eide
EXECUTIVE MARKETING MANAGER	Chris DeJohn
PRODUCTION EDITOR	Kavitha Balasundaram
ACCOUNT MANAGER	Shiv Singh Bisht
PHOTO EDITOR	Alicia South

This book was set in 10/12 pt STIX-Regular by SPi Global

Founded in 1807, John Wiley & Sons, Inc. has been a valued source of knowledge and understanding for more than 200 years, helping people around the world meet their needs and fulfill their aspirations. Our company is built on a foundation of principles that include responsibility to the communities we serve and where we live and work. In 2008, we launched a Corporate Citizenship Initiative, a global effort to address the environmental, social, economic, and ethical challenges we face in our business. Among the issues we are addressing are carbon impact, paper specifications and procurement, ethical conduct within our business and among our vendors, and community and charitable support. For more information, please visit our website: www.wiley.com/go/citizenship.

ISBN: 978-1-119-58608-1 (PBK)
ISBN: 978-1-119-36906-6 (EVALC)

Library of Congress Cataloging-in-Publication Data:

Names: Meredith, Jack R., author.
Title: Project management : a strategic managerial approach / JACK R. MEREDITH, Broyhill Distinguished Scholar and Chair in Operations, Emeritus, Wake Forest University, SCOTT M. SHAFER, Associate Dean and Professor of Management Wake Forest University, SAMUEL J. MANTEL, JR. (DECEASED), Previously the Joseph S. Stern Professor Emeritus of Operations Management, University of Cincinnati.
Description: Tenth Edition. | Hoboken : Wiley, [2017] | Revised edition of Project management, 2015. | Includes index. |
Identifiers: LCCN 2017036857 (print) | LCCN 2017040295 (ebook) | ISBN 9781119369080 (pdf) | ISBN 9781119369110 (epub) | ISBN 9781119586081 (pbk.) | ISBN 9781118947029
Subjects: LCSH: Project management.
Classification: LCC HD69.P75 (ebook) | LCC HD69.P75 M47 2017 (print) | DDC 658.4/04—dc23
LC record available at https://lccn.loc.gov/2017036857

The inside back cover will contain printing identification and country of origin if omitted from this page. In addition, if the ISBN on the back cover differs from the ISBN on this page, the one on the back cover is correct.

Printed in Great Britain by TJ International Ltd, Padstow, Cornwall, UK

10 9 8 7 6 5 4 3 2 1

Approach

We have come a long way in project management since our cavemen ancestors formed a project, as our former colleague Sam Mantel used to say, "to gather the raw material for mammoth stew." However, its use has virtually exploded since the mid-1990s. Businesses now regularly use project management to accomplish unique outcomes with limited resources under critical time constraints. In the service sector of the economy, the use of project management to achieve an organization's goals is even more common. Advertising campaigns, voter registration drives, weddings, and even management seminars on the subject of project management are organized as projects.

But a relatively new growth area is the use of projects as a way of accomplishing strategic organizational changes such as new ways of providing services, typically in conjunction with new software programs and other advanced technologies. Transformational change on this level is a major step beyond the delivery of a project's outputs like a road, a building, a new product, or a computer program. The difference is that much more attention is directed toward both the initiation of the project, including the business case and its non-monetary justifications, and the utilization of the project, involving possibly customers or other stakeholders. Moreover, the scope of strategic transformational projects frequently involves dynamic perturbations, meaning that the project manager and other stakeholders have to alter course throughout the duration of the project.

When we wrote the first edition of this textbook in 1983, there weren't any textbooks for those interested in learning project management, only professional (typically engineering) books, so we adopted a *managerial* perspective for the book following the "life cycle" of the project. That is, it addresses project management from the perspective of what the project manager and other stakeholders will encounter, both chronologically during the initiation, implementation, and utilization of the project's output, as well as practically, in the sense of what senior managers and the project manager need to know and do.

This managerial life-cycle perspective, we believe, addresses the basic nature of managing all types of projects—public, business, engineering, information systems, and so on—as well as the specific techniques and insights required to carry out this unique way of getting things done. It also discusses the demands made on the project manager and the nature of the manager's interaction with the rest of the parent organization. And the book covers the difficult problems associated with conducting a project using people and organizations that represent different cultures and may be separated by considerable distances. Finally, it even covers the issues arising when the decision is made to close or terminate a project.

The book is primarily intended for use as a college textbook for teaching project management at the advanced undergraduate or master's level. The book is also intended for both senior managers as well as current and prospective project managers who wish to share our insights and ideas about the field. We have drawn freely on our personal experiences working with senior and project managers and on the experience of friends and colleagues who have spent much of their working lives serving in what they like to call the "real world." As well as being a text that is equally appropriate for classes on the management of service, product, or engineering projects, we have found that information systems/technology (IS/IT) students in our classes find the material particularly helpful for managing their projects.

Organization and Content

Given our managerial perspective, in this tenth edition we have kept the previous organization which demarks more clearly the activities that occur before the launch of the project, setting up those activities that have to do with the *context* (or *initiation*) of the project in the first part of the book, and those that have to do with the *planning* for the project in the second part. Actually *executing* the project and then utilizing the outputs constitutes the third part of the book. Each part consists of four chapters, which seems to be a comfortable and easy framework for the reader.

Following an introductory chapter that comments on the role and importance of projects in our society and discusses project management as a potential career for aspiring managers, the book covers the context, events, and issues arising during the management of projects in the order in which they usually occur in the life of a project. *Part I, Project Initiation* concerns the context of the project, which is crucial for the project manager to understand if he or she is to be successful in executing the project. It begins with a description of how projects are selected for implementation based on their tie to the organization's strategy and goals. Part I also covers the many roles and responsibilities of the project manager, the skills the project manager needs for handling conflict, and the various ways the project may be set up within the organization's reporting structure (including how different ways of organizing projects tend to create different problems for project managers and their teams).

Part II, Project Planning then moves into the planning processes starting with the major tools used in project activity planning. This is followed by project budgeting and risk planning, project scheduling, and finally, resource allocation among the activities. *Part III, Project Execution* finally gets into the action, beginning with monitoring the activities, largely through information systems, and then controlling them to assure that the results meet senior management's expectations. Evaluating and possibly auditing the project at its major milestones or phase-gates is another, though separate, control action that senior management often employs, and last, the project must be closed and its outputs utilized to achieve the benefits desired from the project.

We have relegated the discussion of two important aspects of projects that usually occur very early in the project life cycle—creativity/idea generation and technological forecasting—to the book's Web site. Although few project managers engage in either of these tasks (typically being appointed to project leadership after these activities have taken place), we believe that a knowledge of these subjects can make the project manager more effective.

In writing this text we assume that all readers have taken an elementary course in management or have had equivalent experience, and are familiar with some basic principles of probability and statistics. (Appendix A on the Web site (http://www.wiley.com/college/meredith) can serve as an initial tutorial on the subject or as a refresher for rusty knowledge.)

Any approach chosen to organize knowledge carries with it an implication of neatness and order that rarely occurs in reality. We are quite aware that projects almost never proceed in an orderly, linear way through the stages and events we describe here. The need to deal with change and uncertainty is a constant task for the project manager. We have tried to reflect this in repeated references to the organizational, interpersonal, economic, and technical glitches that create crises in the life cycle of every project, and thus in the life of every project manager.

Finally, although we use a life-cycle approach to organization, the chapters include material concerning the major areas of the *Project Management Body of Knowledge* (PMBOK®) as defined by the Project Management Institute. (See Bibliography for Chapter 1.) Anyone wishing to prepare for PMI certification (see Chapter 1) in some of these areas may have to go beyond the information covered in this text.

Pedagogy

Because this book is primarily a textbook, we have included numerous pedagogical aids to foster this purpose. As in earlier editions, *short summaries* appear at the end of the text of each chapter, followed by *glossaries* defining key terms and concepts introduced in the chapter. End-of-chapter materials also include *review questions* and *exercises* revisiting the materials covered in the chapter. There are also sets of conceptual *discussion questions* intended to broaden the students' perspectives and to force them to think beyond the chapter materials to its implications. The answers (though not the detailed solutions) to the even-numbered problems are on the book's website. To keep our attitude in perspective, we occasionally offer *Dilbert*® cartoons appropriate to the topic under discussion. Finally, there are questions covering the many Project Management in Practice application examples found throughout the chapters.

As in the past, we include *incidents for discussion*, which are brief "caselettes" oriented primarily toward the specific subjects covered in the chapter, but sometimes materials and concepts covered in earlier chapters. We also offer a *continuing integrative class project* for those users who prefer a running case throughout the chapters that builds on the chapter materials as students progress through the book. And at the very end of each chapter, we typically offer a *reading* and/or a *case*, with potential discussion questions at the end of each.

What's New

In this edition, we have made many updates, additions, and changes.

- One of the major changes in this edition has been the introduction of Organizational Project Management in Chapter 2, including the strategic issue of governance, especially for mega-projects, as they are now called. We describe the internal stakeholders involved in each of the four phases of a project and their roles and responsibilities and conclude this discussion with a public sector example.

- Due to the increased length of Chapter 2, we cut out some of the quantitative project selection material, rewrote an example to focus on project selection, and moved the last section on Project Bids and RFPs into the section Better Cost Estimating and Bidding in Chapter 7.

- Two significant changes are the addition of a major section on Agile project management in Chapter 6 and a new Reading on the Evolution of Agile.

- Due to the increased length of Chapter 6, we moved the issues of risk planning to Chapter 7 to join the existing section there on risk simulation. Chapter 7 also has a new reading on resilience, risk, and agility.

- Chapter 7 also has a new Case on Fuddruckers project budgeting.

- We enhanced the existing case in Chapter 8, now titled Nutristar Energy, Inc.

- A new follow-on case was written for Chapter 11 based on the Chapter 10 case: The Project Manager/ Customer Interface (B).

- A new section on Benefit Realization was added in Chapter 13 to close the project in accordance with the concepts of organizational project management.

- With all the aforementioned changes, we added some new questions and moved summary items, questions, glossary items, exercises, and bibliography entries, to their new chapters.

- To supplement the new material, we added new references to the bibliography and deleted most of the older references before 1990, except for a few classics.

- In the Excel spreadsheet examples, we replaced the algebraic calculations with Excel functions.

- Finally, we updated the Dilbert cartoons.

As before, a student version of Crystal Ball®, an Excel® add-in, again comes with the book. This software makes simulation reasonably straightforward and not particularly complicated. The use of simulation as a technique for risk analysis is demonstrated in several ways in different chapters. (Because relatively few students are familiar with simulation software, step-by-step instructions are included in the text.)

Microsoft Project® has become the dominant application software in the field, outselling its closest competitor about 4 to 1. Our coverage of software tends, therefore, to be centered on Microsoft Project® (and on Crystal Ball®), but includes a brief discussion of the many "add-ons" that are now available to supplement Microsoft Project® and its competitors. Because the various versions of Microsoft Project® are quite similar in the way that they perform most of the basic tasks of project management, we generally do not differentiate between the versions, referring to any and all simply as Microsoft Project (MSP). We have also added some exercises to the end-of-chapter material that can utilize computer software. Similar materials are also available on the Web site.

There is, of course, the danger that human nature, operating in its normal discrete mode, will shift the task of learning project management to that of learning project management software. Projects have often failed because the project manager started managing the software instead of the project. Instructors need to be aware of the problem and must caution students not to fall into this trap.

Online Supplements

The *Instructor's Resource Guide* on the Web site www.wiley.com/college/meredith provides additional assistance to the project management instructor. In addition to the answers/solutions to the problems, questions, readings, and cases, this edition includes teaching tips, a computerized test bank, additional cases, and PowerPoint slides. All of these valuable resources are available online (http://www.wiley.com/college/meredith). In addition, the student Web site contains Web quizzes, PowerPoint® slides, Appendix A: Probability and Statistics, Appendix B: Answers to Even-Numbered Problems, Appendix C: Technological Forecasting, Appendix D: Creativity and Idea Generation, Chapter 3 Appendix: Primer on Effective Time Management, and a Microsoft Project Manual.

Acknowledgments

We owe a debt of gratitude to all those who have helped us with this book. First, we thank the managers and students who helped us solidify our ideas about proper methods for managing projects and proper ways of teaching the subject. Second, we thank the project teams and leaders in all of our project management classes. Third, we thank the adopters and reviewers of the many editions of this book, many who contacted us personally to convey improvements and corrections. Finally, we thank the staff at Wiley for their help in the production of this book, and Suzanne Ingrao of Ingrao Associates for her work as our personal production editor *par excellence.*

Special thanks are due to those who have significantly influenced our thinking about project management or supplied materials to help us write this book: Jeffrey Camm, James Evans, Martin Levy, John McKinney, and William Meyers, all of the Univ. of Cincinnati; S. J. Mantel III, PMP; Jeffrey Pinto, Pennsylvania State Univ. at Erie; Stephen Wearne, Univ. of Manchester; and the Staff of the Project Management Institute.

We owe a massive debt of gratitude to the reviewers for this and previous editions: Steve Allen, Truman State Univ.; Kwasi Amoako-Gyampah, Univ. of North Carolina at Greensboro; Nicholas Aquilano, Univ. of Arizona; Bob Ash, Indiana Univ., Southeast; Bud Baker, Wright State Univ.; Robert J. Berger, Univ. of Maryland; Robert Bergman, Univ. of Houston; William Brauer, Bemidji State Univ.; Tyson Browning, Texas Christian University; Maj. Mark D. Camdle, Air Force Inst. of Tech.; Howard Chamberlin, Texas A&M Univ.; Chin-Sheng Chen, Florida International Univ.; Murugappan Chettiar, Farleigh Dickinson University; Susan Cholette, San Francisco Univ.; Denis Cioffi, George Washington Univ.; Desmond Cook, Ohio State Univ.; the late Larry Crowley, Auburn Univ.; Catherine Crummett, James Madison Univ.; Edward Davis, Univ. of Virginia; Burton Dean, San Jose State Univ.; Michael H. Ensby, Clarkson Univ.; Abel -Fernandez, Univ. of the Pacific; Bruce Fischer, Elmhurst College; Bertie M. Geer, Northern Kentucky Univ.; Erin Gerber, University of Louisville; Richard E. Gunther, California State Univ., Northridge; William Hayden, Jr., SUNY, Buffalo; Jane E. Humble, Arizona State Univ.; Richard H. Irving, York Univ.; Roderick V. James, DeVry Univ.; Homayoun Kahmooshi, George Washington Univ.; David L. Keeney, Stevens Inst. of Tech.; Ted Klastorin, Univ. of Washington; Erich Kreidler, University of

Southern California; David Kukulka, Buffalo State Univ.; Young Hoon Kway, George Washington Univ.; Chung-Shing Le, Pacific Lutheran University; William Leban, DeVry Univ.; Ardeshir Lohrasbi, Univ. of Illinois, Springfield; Bil Matthews, William Patterson University; Sara McComb, Univ. of Massachusetts, Amherst; Abe Meilich, Walden Univ.; Mary Meixell, Quinnipiac Univ.; Jaindeep Motwani, Grand Valley State Univ.; William Moylan, Eastern Michigan University; Barin Nag, Towson Univ.; John E. Nicolay, Jr., Univ. of Minnesota; David L. Overbye, Gregory Parnell, University of Arkansas, Fayetteville; DeVry Univ.; Pat Penfield, Syracuse Univ.; Ed Pohl, Univ. of Arkansas; Michael Poli, Stevens Inst. of Tech.; Amit Raturi, Univ. of Cincinnati; David J. Robb, Univ. of Calgary; Arthur C. Rogers, City Univ., Washington; David Russo, Univ. of Texas, Dallas; Boong-Yeol Ryoo, Florida International Univ.; Thomas Schuppe, Milwaukee School of Engineering; Ruth Seiple, Univ. of Cincinnati; John Shanfi, DeVry Inst. of Tech., Irving, TX; Wade Shaw, Florida Inst. of Tech.; Richard V. Sheng, DeVry Inst. of Tech., San Marino, CA; Bill Sherrard, San Diego State Univ.; Joyce T. Shirazi, Univ. of Maryland, Univ. College; Chris Simber, Stevens Inst. of Tech.; Gene Simons, Rensselaer Polytech. Inst.; Kimberlee Snyder, Winona State Univ.; Herbert Spirer, Univ. of Connecticut; Eric Sprouls, Univ. of Southern Indiana; Peter Strunk, Univ. of Cincinnati; Samuel Taylor, Univ. of Wyoming; Tony Trippe, Rochester Inst. of Tech.; Jerome Weist, Univ. of Utah; William G. Wells, Jr., The George Washington Univ.; Susan Williams, Northern Arizona State Univ.; James Willman, Univ. of Bridgeport; James Yarmus, Stevens Institute of Technology; and Charles I. Zigelman, San Diego State Univ.

JACK MEREDITH
Broyhill Distinguished Scholar and Chair in Operations, Emeritus
Wake Forest University, P.O. Box 7659
Winston-Salem, NC 27109
meredijr@wfu.edu
http://business.wfu.edu/directory/jack-meredith

SCOTT M. SHAFER
Associate Dean and Professor of Management
Wake Forest University, P.O. Box 7659
Winston-Salem, NC 27109
shafersm@wfu.edu
http://business.wfu.edu/directory/scott-m-shafer/

Brief Contents

Please visit http://www.wiley.com/college/meredith for Appendices.

Contents

CHAPTER 1

Projects in Contemporary Organizations

Growth and new developments in project management continue to accelerate in our society, in practice, and in our research publications. Beyond the attention previously (and still) paid to project management, program management, project portfolios, project maturity, project management offices (PMOs), Agile, and other such project issues, we are now seeing attention also directed to mega-projects, organizational project management, project governance, strategic projects, benefit realization, the duties of the project sponsor, the meaning of executive commitment, and other such issues. Projects are getting much more sophisticated and complex, involving multiple organizations and billions of dollars. And even though our knowledge of how to successfully execute standard projects has resulted in much better success rates in practice, the rates of success for less traditional projects, such as strategic and multiorganizational projects, are still poor. Part of the reason for this is just now becoming clear that projects are only the middle portion of a set of activities involving the recognition of a need, the selection of a project to meet it, designing a governance structure for the project, executing the project, and the tasks needed to ensure the benefits of the project are realized. These activities are now also being focused on and we hope to thereby see better success rates for our strategic and more complex projects.

The past several decades have been marked by rapid growth in the use of project management as a means by which organizations achieve their objectives. In the past, most projects were external to the organization—building a new skyscraper, designing a commercial ad campaign, launching a rocket—but the growth in the use of projects lately has primarily been in the area of projects internal to organizations: developing a new product, opening a new branch, implementing a new enterprise software system, improving the services provided to customers, and achieving strategic objectives. As exhilarating as outside projects are, successfully executing internal projects is even more satisfying in that the organization has substantially improved its ability to execute more efficiently, effectively, or quickly, resulting in an agency or business that can even better contribute to society and simultaneously enhancing its own competitive strength. Fundamentally, project management provides an organization with powerful tools that improve its ability to plan, implement, and control its activities as well as the ways in which it utilizes its people and resources.

In this introductory chapter to project management, we begin by defining precisely what a project is. Both the objectives and characteristics of projects are also discussed to help further define them. Next, we address the emergence of project management, the forces that have fostered project management, and recent trends in project management. Following this, we describe the project life cycle. Finally, the chapter concludes with an overview of the structure of the remainder of the text. In later chapters, we will get into the newer topics of benefit realization, mega-projects, project governance, and other such issues.

Glossary

1.1 The Definition of a "Project"

Formally, a project may be defined as "A temporary endeavor undertaken to create a unique product, service, or result" (**PMBOK**®, Project Management Institute, 2013, p. 417). Consistent with this definition, there is a rich variety of projects to be found in our society. Although some may argue that the construction of the Tower of Babel or the Egyptian pyramids were some of the first "projects," it is probable that cavemen formed a project to gather the raw material for mammoth stew. It is certainly true that the construction of Boulder Dam and Edison's invention of the light bulb were projects by any sensible definition. Modern project management, however, is usually said to have begun with the Manhattan Project. In its early days, project management was used mainly for very large, complex research and development (R&D) projects like the development of the Atlas Intercontinental Ballistic Missile and similar military weapon systems. Massive construction programs were also organized as projects, including the construction of dams, ships, refineries, and freeways.

As the techniques of project management were developed, mostly by the military, the use of project organization began to spread. Private construction firms found that organizing work on the basis of projects or a project-based organization was helpful on smaller projects, such as the building of a warehouse or an apartment complex. Automotive companies used project organization to develop new automobile models. Both General Electric and Pratt & Whitney used project organization to develop new jet aircraft engines for airlines, as well as the Air Force. Project management has even been used to develop new models of shoes and ships. More recently, the use of project management by international organizations, and especially organizations producing services rather than products, has grown rapidly. Advertising campaigns, global mergers, and capital acquisitions are often handled as projects, and the methods have spread to the nonprofit sector. Weddings, SCOUT-O-RAMAS, fund drives, election campaigns, parties, and recitals have all made use of project management. Most striking has been the widespread adoption of project management techniques for the development of computer software.

To add to our vocabulary in discussions of project management, it is sometimes useful to make a distinction among terms such as *project, program, task*, and *work packages*. The military, the source of most of these terms, generally uses the term *program* to refer to an exceptionally large, long-range objective that is broken down into a set of projects. These projects are divided further into *tasks*, which are, in turn, split into *work packages* that are themselves composed of *work units*. Of course, exceptions to this hierarchical nomenclature abound. For example, the Manhattan Project was a huge "program," but a "task force" was created to investigate the many potential futures of a large steel company. In the broadest sense, a project is a specific, finite task to be accomplished. Whether large- or small-scale or whether long- or short-run is not particularly relevant. What is relevant is that the project be seen as a unit. There are, however, some objectives that all projects share and some attributes that characterize projects.

Three Project Objectives: The "Triple Constraint" or "Iron Triangle"

While multimillion-dollar, 5-year projects capture public attention, the overwhelming majority of all projects are comparatively small—though nonetheless important to doer and user alike. They involve outcomes, or deliverables, such as a new floor for a professional basketball arena, a new insurance policy to protect against a specific casualty loss, a new website, a new casing for a four-wheel-drive minivan transmission, a new industrial floor cleanser, the installation of a new method for peer review of patient care in a hospital, even the development of new software to help manage projects. The list could be extended almost without limit. These undertakings have much in common with their larger counterparts. Importantly, they have the same general objectives—specified deliverables (also commonly known as *scope*[1]), a specific deadline (time), and budget (cost). We refer to these as "direct" project objectives or goals.

There is a tendency to think of a project solely in terms of its outcome—that is, its scope. But the time at which the outcome is available is itself a part of the outcome, as is the cost entailed in achieving the outcome. The completion of a building on time and on budget is quite a different outcome from the completion of the same physical structure a year late or 20 percent over budget, or both.

Indeed, even the concept of scope is perhaps more complex than is apparent. In particular, it is important to recognize that the expectations of the client are an inherent part of the project specifications, which unfortunately tend to evolve over time. To consider the client's desires as different from the project specifications is to court conflict between client and project team. All too often projects begin with the client specifying a desired outcome. Then the project team designs and implements the project. Then the client views the result of the team's ideas. In following this approach, differences between the client's expectations and the project team's designs commonly develop as a project proceeds due to both changing expectations on the client's part as they learn new information and limitations on the team's part about what they can deliver. As a result, meeting the client's latest desires may not be well reflected by the initially specified scope of the project. The expectations of client and project team therefore need to be continuously realigned and integrated throughout the entire project, but they frequently are not. As a result, we believe in making an effort upfront and throughout the project to ensure that the nebulous elements of the client's evolving expectations and desires are identified and realigned with the client's latest scope (though possibly at additional cost). We discuss these issues in more detail in the coming chapters.

The three direct project objectives are shown in Figure 1.1, with the specified project objectives on the axes. This illustration implies that there is some "function" that relates them, one to another—and so there is! Although the functions vary from project to project, and from time to time for a given project, we will refer to these relationships, or trade-offs, throughout this book. The two primary tasks of the project manager (the "PM") are to manage these trade-offs and to anticipate and address risks to the project. In addition to the direct project goals, organizations often have a unique set of ancillary project objectives/goals that are often unarticulated but nevertheless important to the success of the project.

Ancillary goals include improving the organization's project management competency and methods, developing individuals' managerial experience through project management, gaining a foothold in a new market, and similar goals. In a more basic sense, those with a stake in the project (the PM, project team, senior management, the client, and other project stakeholders) have an interest in making

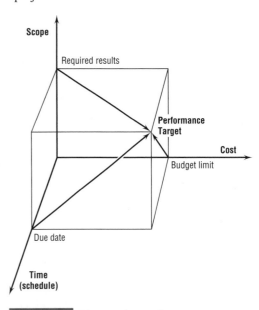

FIGURE 1.1 Direct project goals—scope, cost, and time.

----

[1]The term "scope" is typically used when differentiating between what is included and what is excluded in something, but in project management the term has come to mean the specified deliverables. The Project Management Institute's Project Management Body of Knowledge (**PMBOK**®) defines Scope as follows: "The sum of the products, services, and results to be provided as a project." We will refer to the **PMBOK** guide frequently throughout this book and use the icon seen here in the margin to draw the student's attention to this important reference (see the PMI reference in the "Bibliography" section). If particular **PMBOK** figures, tables, sections, or chapters are relevant to the discussion, we note this under the icon as, for example, Section 3.2.

Glossary

the project a success. Shenhar et al. (1997) have concluded that project success has four dimensions: (1) project efficiency, (2) impact on the customer, (3) the business impact on the organization, and (4) opening new opportunities for the future. The first two are clearly part of what we have defined as the project's direct objectives; the last two are typical of what are frequently unspecified ancillary goals.

One other crucial, but unstated, trade-off that a PM must consider is the health of the project team as well as the rest of the organization. The PM cannot burn out the team in an attempt to achieve the direct objectives, nor destroy the organization's functional departments in an attempt to meet the project's goals. Another factor in making project trade-offs is the project's *environment*, that is, those things or persons outside the project, and often outside the sponsoring organization, that affect the project or are affected by it. Examples of this environment might be environmental groups, trade unions, competitive firms, and the like. We will deal with these issues in more detail in Chapter 12.

From the early days of project management, the direct project objectives of time, cost, and scope (as generally agreed to by the client and the organization actually doing the project) have been accepted as the primary determinants of project success or failure. In the past 25 years or so, other direct and ancillary objectives have been suggested. These did not replace the traditional time, cost, and scope, but were added as also relevant. For the most part, however, Chapters 1 through 11 will focus mainly on the traditional direct objectives.

Characteristics of Projects

There are three characteristics that all projects share and a number of other characteristics that are common to projects but not universal. We begin our discussion with the three universal characteristics and then direct our attention to several of the common characteristics.

The first universal characteristic of projects is that every project is unique. Though the desired end results may have been achieved elsewhere, every project has some unique elements. No two construction or R&D projects are precisely alike. Though it is clear that construction projects are usually more routine than R&D projects, some degree of customization is a characteristic of projects. In addition to the presence of risk, as noted earlier, this characteristic means that projects, by their nature, cannot be completely reduced to routine. The PM's importance is emphasized because, as a devotee of *management by exception*, the PM will find there are a great many exceptions to manage by.

The second universal characteristic is that a project is a one-time occurrence with a well-defined and specific set of desired end results. (We discuss poorly defined, or "quasi-" projects a bit later.) These end results are referred to as the "scope," or sometimes required "performance," of the project. The project can be divided into subtasks that must be accomplished in order to achieve the project goals. The project is complex enough that the subtasks require careful coordination and control in terms of timing, precedence, cost, and scope. Often, the project itself must be coordinated with other projects being carried out by the same parent organization.

The third universal characteristic of projects is that they have a finite duration. There is a clear date when the project is launched and a corresponding due date or deadline. Furthermore, like organic entities and their growth curve, projects have life cycles. Often starting with a slow beginning and progressing to a buildup of size, then peaking, beginning a decline, and finally must be closed by some due date. (Also like organic entities, they often resist closure.) Some projects end by being phased into the normal, ongoing operations of the parent organization. The life cycle is discussed further in Section 1.3, where an important exception to the usual description of the growth curve is mentioned. There are several different ways in which to view project life cycles. These will be discussed in more detail later.

Interdependencies

While not universally true, projects often interact with other projects being carried out simultaneously by their parent organization. Typically, these interactions take the form of competition for scarce resources between projects, and much of Chapter 9 is devoted to dealing with these issues. While such interproject interactions are common, projects

Project Management in Practice

A Unique Method for Traveler-Tracking at Copenhagen Airport

IT University of Copenhagen, Denmark, was working with Copenhagen Airport to improve both the efficiency and effectiveness of the management of their airport through a new approach: traveler-tracking, but without invading people's privacy. The 3-year project focused on a unique, low-cost approach—capturing the Bluetooth signals from passengers' phones with two electronic readers that cost only $30 each. At the time, not everyone had a smartphone that emits signals, of course, but about 7 percent of the passengers did, enough to provide a random sample for tracking. To ensure travelers' privacy, a crucial stakeholder in this project, they collected only a portion of each signal and deleted the addresses. They also informed the public about the project on the airport's website and on-site as well. To encourage positive traveler response to the project, they provided alerts to passengers willing to synchronize their Bluetooth to receive information regarding when their plane was boarding and a map to the gate.

Knowing when people were entering and leaving Security allowed the airport to balance the staff at Security so lines didn't build up, thereby shortening the time passengers

must wait, while also reducing over- and understaffing of screeners. In addition, the information allows them to post wait times at the check-in gates. The data also lets the airport to determine which shops and areas are getting the most traffic so they can shift usage of facility space to better serve the travelers and the friends and families accompanying them. Moreover, when construction and rerouting changes traffic flows, they can determine the impact on passengers and take action to reduce the inconvenience.

Questions

1. Are the triple constraints of this project clear? What are they?

2. What was unique about this project? What was the main conflict?

3. Why are the travelers themselves a stakeholder in this project, since most of them won't even know they are being tracked?

4. How widespread do you think this technology will become? What uses will be garnered from it? Do any of them concern you?

Source: S. F. Gale, "Data on the Go," *PM Network*, Vol. 24.

always interact with the parent organization's standard, ongoing operations. Although the functional departments of an organization (marketing, finance, operations, and the like) interact with one another in regular, patterned ways, the patterns of interaction between projects and these departments tend to be changeable. Marketing may be involved at the beginning and end of a project, but not in the middle. Operations may have major involvement throughout. Finance is often involved at the beginning and accounting (the controller) at the end, as well as at periodic reporting times. The PM must keep all these interactions clear and maintain the appropriate interrelationships with all external groups.

Projects also typically have limited budgets, both for personnel and other resources. Often the budget is implied rather than detailed, particularly concerning personnel, but it is strictly limited. The attempt to obtain additional resources (or *any* resources) frequently leads to the next attribute—conflict.

More than most managers, the PM lives in a world characterized by conflict. Projects compete with functional departments for resources and personnel. More serious, with the growing proliferation of projects, is the project-versus-project conflict for resources within multiproject organizations. The members of the project team are in almost constant conflict for the project's resources and for leadership roles in solving project problems. The PM must be expert in conflict resolution, but we will see later that there are helpful types of conflict. The PM must recognize the difference.

Conventional thinking suggests that different stakeholders (e.g., clients, the parent organization, the project team, and the public) define success and failure in different ways. For example, the client wants changes and the parent organization wants profits. Likewise, the individuals working on projects are often responsible to two bosses at the same time: a functional manager and the PM. Under such conditions, conflict can arise when the two bosses have different priorities and objectives.

While the conventional view tends to regard conflict as a rather ubiquitous part of working on projects, more recently others have challenged this view. For example, John Mackey, cofounder and co-CEO of Whole Foods Market, suggests in his recent book *Conscious Capitalism* (2013) that satisfying stakeholder needs is not a zero-sum game where satisfying one stakeholder must come at the expense of another. Rather, Mackey suggests a better approach that is to identify opportunities to satisfy all stakeholder needs simultaneously. One way to accomplish this is to identify ways to align the goals of all stakeholders with the purpose of the project. As was mentioned earlier, the primary role of the PM is to manage the trade-offs. However, as Mackey warns, if we look for trade-offs we will always find trade-offs. On the other hand, if we look for synergies across the stakeholder base, we can often find them too. The clear lesson for project managers is to not be too quick to assume trade-offs exist among competing project objectives and stakeholder groups.

Nonprojects and Quasi-Projects

If the characteristics listed earlier define a project, it is appropriate to ask if there are nonprojects. The use of a manufacturing line to produce a flow of standard products is a nonproject. The production of weekly employment reports, the preparation of school lunches, the delivery of mail, the flight of Delta 1288 from Dallas to Dulles, checking your e-mail all are nonprojects. While one might argue that each of these activities is, to some degree, unique, it is not their uniqueness that characterizes them. They are all *routine*. They are tasks that are performed over and over again. This is not true of projects. Each project is a one-time event. Even the construction of a section of interstate highway is a project. No two miles are alike and constructing them demands constant adaptation to the differences in terrain and substructure of the earth on which the roadbed is to be laid. Projects cannot be managed adequately by the managerial routines used for routine work.

Project Management in Practice

The Smart-Grid Revolution Starts in Boulder, Colorado

© ermingut/iStockphoto

Boulder's utility company, Xcel Energy, decided that it was time to create a roadmap for a 3-year, $100 million "smart-grid" electrical system that would span the entire city. There were no standards, benchmarks, or tested procedures for converting a city from a conventional electric-grid system to a fully integrated smart one, though it was known that if customers can monitor the true cost of their energy, they will automatically reduce their usage, by up to 30 percent in some cases. Of course, the smart grid would also allow Xcel to reroute power around bottlenecked lines, detect power outages, identify service risks, cut its use of road crews, read customer meters remotely, reduce outages, and identify false alarms more quickly.

Xcel brought in a mass of partners on the project, such as Accenture consulting for engineering, energy industry consultants, leading technologists, business leaders, IT experts, and, of course, Boulder city managers, leaders, and user-citizens. The public and private partners were divided into eight teams, all led by a senior PM working with a PMO. With all these different stakeholders, with different objectives and interests, it was crucial to have steady, reliable communication to keep everyone up to date and the project on track. Security and privacy were high-priority items on the project, and communication with the community was facilitated through town hall meetings, the local media, tours of project sites, and even a touring trailer allowing citizens to get a hands-on demonstration of the smart-grid technology. With the completion of the project, Xcel is now measuring its many benefits and expects it will take a year to collect and analyze all the data across all the seasons. The project partners have also created an industry consortium to establish industry standards for future, larger smart-grid projects. They now see Boulder as a living laboratory from which they can continue to learn and thereby successfully deploy smart grids across the entire country.

Questions

1. **Are the triple constraints of this project clear? List each of them.**
2. **Given the range of benefits listed for the new technology, what interdependencies and conflicts do you suspect smart grids will create for utilities?**
3. **A major portion of this project had to do with carefully managing all the stakeholders. List those mentioned in the article and divide them into the four groups mentioned above. Do any stakeholders fall into more than one of the groups?**
4. **What conflicts do you suspect might have occurred among all the different stakeholders in this project?**
5. **Why do you think Xcel agreed to invest $100 million in this risky experiment? What might have been their ancillary goals?**

Source: S. F. Gale, "A Closer Look," *PM Network*, Vol. 24.

In addition to projects and nonprojects, there are also quasi-projects: "Bill, would you look into this?" "Mia, we need to finish this by Friday's meeting." "Samir, can you find out about this before we meet with the customer?" Most people would consider that they have just been assigned a project, depending on who "we" and "you" is supposed to include. Yet there may be no specific task identified, no specific budget given, and no specific deadline defined. Are they still projects, and if so, can project management methods be used to manage them? Certainly! The scope, schedule, and budget have been implied rather than carefully delineated by the words "this," "meet," and "we" (meaning "you") or "you" (which may mean a group or team). In such cases, it is best to try to quickly nail down the scope, schedule, and budget as precisely as possible, but without antagonizing the manager who assigned the project. You may need to ask for additional help or other resources if the work is needed soon—is it needed soon? How accurate/thorough/detailed does it need to be? And other such questions.

One common quasi-project in the information systems area is where the project includes discovery of the scope or requirements of the task itself (and possibly also the budget and deadline). How can you plan a project when you don't know the scope requirements? In this case, the project is, in fact, determining the scope requirements (and possibly the budget and deadline also). If the entire set of work (including the discovery) has been assigned to you as a project, then the best approach is to set this determination as the first "milestone" in the project, at which point the resources, budget, deadline, capabilities, personnel, and any other matters will be reviewed to determine if they are sufficient to the new project requirements. Alternatively, the customer may be willing to pay for the project on a "cost-plus" basis, and call a halt to the effort when the benefits no longer justify the cost.

Project Management in Practice

The Olympic Torch Relay Project

Getting the Olympic Flame, known as the Olympic Torch Relay, to the Olympic Games is no simple matter. Generally, the Torch Relay has gotten longer and more complex with every Olympic event. In the 1936 Olympics, the torch left from the original site of the Olympics, the Temple of Hera in Olympia, Greece, and traveled through seven countries to reach its final destination at the games in Berlin. For the Beijing 2008 Olympics, the flame traveled 137,000 kilometers (about 85,000 miles)! This increasing length and complexity are driven by the realization of host country citizens that it is a rare opportunity to have the Olympic torch pass through your hometown and the corresponding goal of the Olympic Committee to touch as many lives as possible in a positive way.

As an example, the planning for the 1996 Atlanta Olympic Torch Relay (see figure) took 2 years, cost over $20 million, and involved an 84-day, 42-state campaign using 10,000 runners to carry the torch for 15,000 miles! Accompanying the runners was a 40-vehicle caravan carrying security officers, media personnel, medical personnel, computers, telecommunications gear, clothing, food, and spare lanterns with extra flames in case the original torch went out. The caravan included: 50 cell phones; 120 radios; 30 cars; 10 motorcycles; and clothing for 10,000 runners, 10,000 volunteers, as well as 2,500 escort runners.

The Torch Relay is also a major marketing campaign, primarily for the relay's sponsors. Thus, accompanying the Atlanta-bound caravan were trucks hawking Olympic memorabilia: t-shirts, sweatshirts, baseball caps, tickets to the soccer matches, and on and on. In addition to retail commercialism, a number of companies were piggybacking on the

Torch Relay to further their own commercial interests: IBM, Motorola, BellSouth, Texaco, BMW, Lee, Coca-Cola, and so on. We can only wonder how far and complex the Torch Relay will be in the next Olympics!

Questions

1. Which of the three universal and three common characteristics of projects are displayed in the regular torch relay?

2. Since this is such a regular project—every 4 years since 1936—would you consider it a nonproject, or a quasi-project? Why, or why not?

3. Is the Torch Relay another part of the Olympics themselves, perhaps a subproject?

Sources: G. Ruffenach, "Getting the Olympic Flame to Atlanta Won't Be a Simple Cross-Country Run," *The Wall Street Journal*, 1996; http://olympics.india-server.com/torch-relay.html; www.bladesplace.id.au/olympic-games-candidates.html.

1.2 | Why Project Management?

It is popular to ask "Why can't they run government the way I run my business?" In the case of project management, however, business and other organizations learned from government, not the other way around. A lion's share of the credit for the development of the techniques and practices of project management belongs to the military, which faced a series of major tasks that simply were not achievable by traditional organizations operating in traditional ways. NASA's Apollo space program and, more recently, Boston's "Big Dig" tunnel and freeways project and the development of Boeing's 787 "Dreamliner" are a few of the many instances of the application of these specially developed management approaches to extraordinarily complex projects. Following such examples, nonmilitary government sectors, private industry, public service agencies, and volunteer organizations have all used project management to increase their effectiveness. For example, most firms in the computer software business routinely develop their output as projects or groups of projects.

Project management has emerged because the characteristics of our contemporary society demand the development of new methods of management. Of the many forces involved, three are paramount: (1) the exponential expansion of human knowledge; (2) the growing demand for a broad range of complex, sophisticated, customized goods and services; and (3) the evolution of worldwide competitive markets for the production and consumption of goods and services. All three forces combine to mandate the use of teams to solve problems that used to be solvable by individuals. These three forces combine to increase greatly the complexity of goods and services produced plus the complexity of the processes used to produce them. This, in turn, leads to the need for more sophisticated systems to control both outcomes and processes.

The basic purpose for initiating a project is to accomplish specific goals. The reason for organizing the task as a project is to focus the responsibility and authority for the attainment of the goals on an individual or small group. In spite of the fact that the PM often lacks authority at a level consistent with his or her responsibility, the manager is expected to coordinate and integrate all activities needed to reach the project's goals. In particular, the project form of organization allows the manager to be responsive to (1) the client and the environment, (2) identify and correct problems at an early date, (3) make timely decisions about trade-offs between conflicting project goals, and (4) ensure that managers of the separate tasks that comprise the project do not optimize the performance of their individual tasks at the expense of the total project—that is, that they do not suboptimize.

Actual experience with project management (such as through Six-Sigma projects) indicates that the majority of organizations using it experience better control and better customer relations and apparently an increase in their project's return on investment (Ibbs and Kwak 1997). A significant proportion of users also report shorter development times, lower costs, higher quality and reliability, and higher profit margins. Other reported advantages include a sharper orientation toward results, better interdepartmental coordination, and higher worker morale.

On the negative side, most organizations report that project management results in greater organizational complexity. Many also report that project organization increases the likelihood that organizational policy will be violated—not a surprising outcome, considering the degree of autonomy required for the PM. A few firms reported higher costs, more management difficulties, and low personnel utilization. As we will see in Chapter 5, the disadvantages of PM stem from exactly the same sources as its advantages. The disadvantages seem to be the price one pays for the advantages. On the whole, the balance weighs in favor of project organization if the work to be done is appropriate for a project.

The tremendous diversity of uses to which project management can be put has had an interesting, and generally unfortunate, side effect. While we assert that all projects are to some extent unique, there is an almost universal tendency for those working on some specific types of projects to argue "Software (or construction, or R&D, or marketing, or machine maintenance, or . . .) projects are different and you can't expect us to schedule (or budget, or organize, or manage, or . . .) in the same way that other kinds of projects do." Disagreement with such pleas for special treatment is central to the philosophy of this book. The fundamental similarities between the processes involved in managing all sorts of projects, be they long or short, product- or service-oriented, parts of all-encompassing programs or stand-alone, are far more pervasive than are their differences.

There are also real limitations on project management. For example, the mere creation of a project may be an admission that the parent organization and its managers cannot accomplish the desired outcomes through the functional organization. Further, conflict seems to be a necessary side effect. As we noted, the PM often lacks the authority-of-position that is consistent with the assigned level of responsibility. Therefore, the PM must depend on the goodwill of managers in the parent organization for some of the necessary resources. Of course, if the goodwill is not forthcoming, the PM may ask senior officials in the parent organization for their assistance. But to use such power often reflects poorly on the skills of the PM, and while it may get cooperation in the instance at hand, it may backfire in the long run.

We return to the subject of the advantages, disadvantages, and limitations of the project form of organization later. For the moment, it is sufficient to point out that project management is difficult even when everything goes well. When things go badly, PMs have been known to turn gray overnight and take to hard drink! The trouble is that project organization is the only feasible way to accomplish certain goals. It is literally not possible to design and build a major weapon system, for example, in a timely and economically acceptable manner, except by project organization. The stronger the emphasis on achievement of results in an organization, the more likely it will be to adopt some form of project management. The stake or risks in using project management may be high, but no more so than in any other form of management; and for projects, it is less so. Tough as it may be, it is all we have—and it works!

All in all, the life of a PM is exciting, rewarding, at times frustrating, and tends to be at the center of things in most organizations. Project management is now being recognized as a "career path" in a growing number of firms, particularly those conducting projects with lives extending more than a year or two. In such organizations, PMs may have to function for several years, and it is important to provide promotion potential for them. It is also common for large firms to put their more promising young managers through a "tour of duty" during which they manage one or more projects (or parts of projects). This serves as a good test of the aspiring manager's ability to coordinate and manage complex tasks and to achieve results in a politically challenging environment where negotiation skills are required.

Forces Fostering Project Management

First, the expansion of knowledge allows an increasing number of academic disciplines to be used in solving problems associated with the development, production, and distribution of goods and services. Second, satisfying the continuing demand for more complex and customized products and services depends on our ability to make product design an integrated and inherent part of our production and distribution systems. Third, worldwide markets force us to include cultural and environmental differences in our managerial decisions about what, where, when, and how to produce and distribute output. The requisite knowledge does not reside in any one individual, no matter how well educated or knowledgeable. Thus, under these conditions, teams are used for making decisions and taking action. This calls for a high level of coordination and cooperation between groups of people not particularly used to such interactions. Largely geared to the mass production of simpler goods, traditional organizational structures and management systems are simply not adequate to the task, unlike project management.

The organizational response to the forces noted above cannot take the form of an instantaneous transformation from the old to the new. To be successful, the transition must be systematic, but it tends to be slow and tortuous for most enterprises. Accomplishing organizational change is a natural application of project management, and many firms have set up projects to implement their goals for strategic and tactical change.

Another important societal force is the intense competition among institutions, both profit and not-for-profit, fostered by our economic system resulting in organizational "crusades" such as "total quality management," "Six-Sigma,"[2] and particularly prominent these days: "supply chain management." The competition that these crusades engenders puts extreme pressure on organizations to make their complex, customized outputs available as quickly as possible. "Time-to-market" is critical. Responses must come faster, decisions must be made sooner, and results must occur more quickly. Imagine the communications problems alone. Information and knowledge are growing explosively, but the time permissible to locate and use the appropriate knowledge is decreasing.

In addition, these forces operate in a society that assumes that technology can do anything. The fact is, this assumption is reasonably true, within the bounds of nature's fundamental laws. The problem lies not in this assumption so much as in a concomitant assumption that allows society to ignore both the economic and noneconomic costs associated with technological progress until some dramatic event focuses our attention on the costs (e.g., the global financial crisis, the Gulf oil spill). At times, our faith in technology is disturbed by difficulties and threats arising from its careless implementation, as in the case of industrial waste, but on the whole, we seem remarkably tolerant of technological change, such as the overwhelmingly easy acceptance of communication by e-mail and shopping on the Internet.

Finally, the projects we undertake are large and getting larger. The modern advertising company, for example, advanced from blanket print ads to regionally focused television ads to personally focused Internet ads. As each new capability extends our grasp, it serves as the base for new demands that force us to extend our reach even farther. Projects increase in size and complexity because the more we can do, the more we try to do.

The projects that command the most public attention tend to be large, complex, and multiorganizational endeavors. Often, such endeavors are both similar to and different from previous projects with which we may be more or less familiar. Similarities with the past provide a base from which to start, but the differences imbue every project with considerable risk. The complexities and multiorganizational aspects of projects require that many parts be put together so that the project's objectives—deliverables, time (or schedule), and cost—are met and desired benefits achieved.

In his fascinating book, *Rescuing Prometheus* (Hughes, 1998), technology historian Thomas Hughes examines four large-scale projects that required the use of a nontraditional management style, a nontraditional organizational design, and a nontraditional approach to problem solving in order to achieve their objectives. These huge projects—the Semi-automatic Ground Environment (SAGE) air defense system, the Atlas Intercontinental Ballistic Missile, the Boston Central Artery/Tunnel (better known as "the big dig"), and the Department of Defense Advanced Research Projects Agency's Internet (ARPANET)—are all characterized by extraordinarily diverse knowledge and information input requirements.[3] The size and technological complexity of these projects required input from a large number of autonomous organizations—governmental, industrial, and academic—that usually did

---

[2]Six-sigma (see Pyzdek and Keller, 2009) itself involves projects, usually of a process improvement type that involves the use of many project management tools (Chapter 8), teamwork (Chapters 5 and 12), quality tools such as "benchmarking" (Chapter 11), and even audits (Chapter 12).
[3]Hughes's term for this is "transdisciplinary" (across disciplines), which is rather more accurate than the usual "interdisciplinary" (between disciplines).

not work cooperatively with other organizations, were sometimes competitors, and could be philosophical and/or political opponents. Further, any actions taken to deal with parts of the total project often had disturbing impacts on many other parts of the system.

Obviously, these projects were not the first complex, large-scale projects carried out in this country or elsewhere. For example, the Manhattan Project—devoted to the development of the atomic bomb—was such a project. The Manhattan Project, however, was the sole and full-time work for a large majority of the individuals and organizations working on it. The organizations contributing to the projects Hughes describes were, for the most part, working on many other tasks. For example, Massachusetts Institute of Technology (MIT), the Pentagon, IBM, Bell Labs (now Lucent Technologies), RAND Corporation, the Massachusetts Department of Highways, and a great many other organizations were all highly involved in one or more of these projects while still carrying on their usual work. The use of multiple organizations (both within and outside of the sponsoring firm) as contributors to a project is no longer remarkable. Transdisciplinary projects are more the rule than the exception.

These revolutions and modifications in the style of management and organization of projects will be reflected throughout this book. We will identify the specific tasks facing top management, project executives, and PMs. We investigate the nature of the projects for which the PM is responsible; the trade-off, risk analysis, and other skills that must be used to manage projects; and the means by which the manager can bring the project to a successful conclusion.

The Project Manager and Project Management Organizations

While managing the trade-offs, the PM is expected to integrate all aspects of the project, ensure that the proper knowledge and resources are available when and where needed, and above all, ensure that the expected results are produced in a timely, cost-effective manner. The complexity of the problems faced by the PM, taken together with the rapid growth in the number of project-oriented organizations, has contributed to the professionalization of project management. In the early days of projects, being a PM was known as the "accidental profession." There was no training or career path in project management; you just became one by accident. That has now all changed and the role has become "professionalized."

One of the major international organizations dedicated to this professionalization is the Project Management Institute (PMI®, www.pmi.org), established in the United States of America in 1969. By 1990, the PMI had 7,500 members, and by 2017, it had exploded to 450,000 members in more than 190 countries (see Figure 1.2). This exponential growth is indicative of the rapid growth in the use of projects, but also reflects the importance of the PMI as a force in the development of project management as a profession. Its mission is to foster the growth of project management as well as "building professionalism" in the field through its many worldwide chapters, its meetings and seminars around the globe, and its journals, books, and other publications. However, there are many other project management organizations as well, such as the Association for Project Management (APM; www.apm.org.uk) headquartered in the United Kingdom, which started in the early 1970s and serves all of Europe. As well, there is the International Project Management Association (IPMA; www.ipma.ch) headquartered in Switzerland, which began in 1965 and serves a global constituency.

Another major objective of these organizations is to codify the areas of knowledge required for competent project management. As a result, the APM has its APM Body

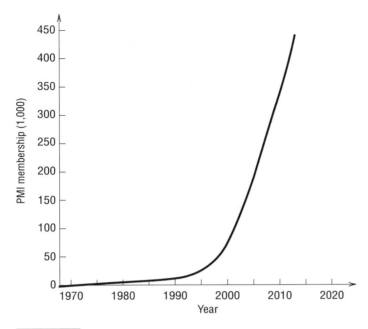

FIGURE 1.2 Project Management Institute growth history.

of Knowledge, PMI has its project management body of knowledge, **PMBOK**® (Project Management Institute, 5th edition, 2013), as well as a new 3rd edition of *Standard for Program Management* and a new 3rd edition of *Standard for Portfolio Management*. Other groups have similar project management bodies of knowledge, as well as credentials (see the following text), such as PRINCE2 (**PR**ojects **IN** **C**ontrolled **E**nvironments) used primarily in the information systems industry and employed extensively by the UK government. Table 1.1 illustrates the difference between the APM BOK and **PMBOK**®.

All these compilations of knowledge are meant to serve as the fundamental basis for education for PM. To certify that active PM understand and can competently apply these bodies of knowledge, various associations offer credentials certifying to this proficiency. For example, PMI offers a certificate called the Project Management Professional (PMP®) that includes a group of education, experience, and testing requirements to obtain. More recently, PMI has added seven more certificates, including one for advanced program managers, called the Program Management Professional (PgMP®), another for developing PMs, the Certified Associate in Project Management (CAPM®), which has less educational and experience requirements, and five more specialized certificates, including one in Agile project management. (More information on these certificates is contained in the Appendix to this chapter.) As a result of all this activity, the profession has flourished, with the result that many colleges and universities offer education and training in project management, and some offer specialized degree programs in the area.

Although obtaining more education in the field is always desirable, and being certified or credentialed verifies that knowledge to a potential employer, the recipient of such proof must avoid preaching the "body of knowledge" bible excessively lest they find themselves again seeking employment. As one employer stated (Starkweather and Stevens, 2011, p. 37): "It is useful background info, but fresh PMPs® want to ram that knowledge down clients' throats and clients are not willing to pay for it." It turns out that although recruiters like to see certification on a resumé, executives are much less interested in it and wish to see performance instead (pp. 36, 38, 39): "There is no correlation between a good PM and certification based on my 15 years of experience," and "Would like the PMP® program to

TABLE 1.1 Comparison of APM's BOK (5th ed., ©2006) and PMI's PMBOK® (5th ed., ©2013)

APM's BOK: This 179-page book consists of 1½ page introductions, definitions, and references for 52 major project management areas of knowledge divided among 7 sections	PMI's PMBOK®: This 589-page book tries to capture the basic knowledge of project management, consisting of 10 knowledge areas (Chapters 4–13) and 5 process groups: initiating, planning, executing, monitoring/controlling, and closing. It aims to describe the norms, methods, processes, and practices of PM. There are now over four million copies of PMBOK in circulation	
Section 1: Project Mgt. in Context—projects, programs, portfolios, sponsors, PMO, project context	**Chapter 1: Introduction**—projects, programs, portfolios, role of the project manager, environment, **PMBOK**	**Chapter 8: Project Quality Management**—plan quality, perform quality assurance, control quality
Section 2: Planning the Strategy—success, stakeholders, value, risk, quality, environment, health, safety	**Chapter 2: Organizational Influences and Project Life Cycle**—life cycle, routine work, stakeholders, organization	**Chapter 9: Project Human Resource Management**—develop HRM plan, acquire and develop team
Section 3: Executing the Strategy—scope, schedule, resources, budgets/cost, changes, earned value, information	**Chapter 3: Project Management Processes**—interactions, process groups: initiating, planning, executing, monitor/controlling, closing	**Chapter 10: Project Communications Management**—identify stakeholders, plan communications, distribute information, manage expectations, report performance
Section 4: Techniques—requirements, development, estimates, technology, value engr., modeling, testing, configuration management	**Chapter 4: Project Integration Management**—charter, plan, execution, monitor/control, change, close	**Chapter 11: Project Risk Management**—identify, qualitative risk analysis (RA), quantitative RA, plan response, monitor/control risks
Section 5: Business and Commercial—business case, marketing, sales, financing, procurement, legal	**Chapter 5: Project Scope Management**—collect requirements, define scope, create work breakdown structure, verify scope, control scope	**Chapter 12: Project Procurement Management**—plan, conduct, administer, close procurements
Section 6: Organisation and Governance—life cycles, implementation, handover, closeout, reviews, org. structure, org. roles, methods, procedures, governance	**Chapter 6: Project Time Management**—define activities, sequence, resources, durations, schedule, control schedule	**Chapter 13: Plan Stakeholder Management**—identify stakeholders, analyze stakeholder expectations, develop strategies to engage stakeholders
Section 7: People and the Profession—communication, teamwork, leadership, conflicts, negotiation, HRM, behavior, learning, development, professionalism, ethics.	**Chapter 7: Project Cost Management**—estimate costs, determine budget, control costs	

more rigorously measure understanding of the methodology rather than memorization. I've seen very little correlation between having a PMP® and having a deep understanding of how to apply the methodology, how to tailor it for a specific situation."

Clearly, rapid growth in the number of PMs and the membership in these project management associations were the result, not the cause, of tremendous growth in the number of projects being carried out. The software industry alone has been responsible for a significant percentage of the growth. Another major source of growth has been the need to control project activity in large organizations. As the number of nonroutine activities increases in an organization, there is an increased need in senior management to understand and control the system. Project management, with its schedules, budgets, due dates, risk assessments, statements of expected outcomes, and people who take responsibility, is a way to meet this need. These forces have combined and led to the creation of a project-organized firm. Much more will be said about project-oriented organizations in Chapter 4.

As we note in the coming chapters, the PMs job is not without problems. There is the ever-present frustration of being responsible for outcomes while lacking full authority to command the requisite resources or personnel. There are constant problems of dealing with the stakeholders involved in any project—senior management, client, project team, and public—all of whom seem to speak different languages and have different objectives. There are ceaseless organizational and technical "fires to be fought." There are vendors who cannot seem to keep "lightning-strike-me-dead" promises about delivery dates. This list of troubles only scratches the surface.

Difficult as the job may be, most PMs take a considerable amount of pleasure and job satisfaction from their occupation. The challenges are many and the risks significant, but so are the rewards of success. Project managers usually enjoy organizational visibility, considerable variety in their day-to-day duties, and often have the prestige associated with work on the enterprise's high-priority objectives. The profession, however, is not one for the timid. Risk and conflict avoiders do not make happy PMs. Those who can stomach the risks and enjoy practicing the arts of conflict resolution, however, can take substantial monetary and psychological rewards from their work.

Trends in Project Management

Many new developments and interests in project management are being driven by quickly changing global markets, technology, and education. Global competition is putting pressure on prices, response times, and product/service innovation. Computer and telecommunications technologies along with greater education are allowing companies to respond to these pressures, pushing the boundaries of project management into regions where new tools are being developed for types of projects that have never been considered before. In addition, the pressure for more and more products and services has led to initiating more projects, but with faster life cycles. We consider a variety of trends in turn.

Achieving Strategic Goals   There has been a greater push to use projects to achieve more strategic goals and filtering existing major projects to make sure that their objectives support the organization's strategy and mission. Projects that do not have clear ties to the strategy and mission are terminated and their resources are redirected to those that do.

Achieving Routine Goals   On the other hand, there has also been a push to use project management to accomplish routine departmental tasks that would previously have been handled as a functional effort. This is because lower level management has become aware that projects accomplish their scope objectives within their budget and deadline and hope to employ this new tool to improve management of their functions. As a result, artificial deadlines and budgets are created to accomplish specific, though routine, tasks within the functional departments, a process called "projectizing." However, as reported by Jared Sandberg (2007) in the *Wall Street Journal*, there is an important danger with this new tactic. If the deadline isn't really important and the workers find out it is only artificial (e.g., either by meeting it but getting no appreciation or by missing it but with no penalty), this will destroy the credibility of any future deadlines or budgets, much like "the boy who cried wolf."

Improving Project Effectiveness   A variety of efforts are being pursued to improve the results of project management, whether strategic or routine. One well-known effort is the creation of a formal *Project Management Office* in many organizations, which is responsible for the evaluation and improvement of an organization's project management "*maturity*," or skill and experience in managing projects. Other measures to improve project effectiveness are better liaison with the project's stakeholders, especially the client, through improved governance procedures, and implementing more innovative risk-sharing win—win contracts.

Virtual Projects With the rapid increase in globalization, many projects now involve global teams with team members operating in different physical geographic locations and different time zones, each bringing a unique set of talents to the project. These are known as virtual projects because the team members may never physically meet before the team is disbanded and another team reconstituted. Advanced telecommunications and computer technologies allow such virtual projects to be created, conduct their work, and complete their project successfully.

Dynamic and Quasi-Projects Led by the demands of the information technology/systems departments, project management is now being extended into areas where the final scope requirements may not be understood, the time deadline unknown, and/or the budget undetermined. When any one or all of the three primary project objectives are ill-defined, we call this a "quasi-project." Such projects are extremely difficult to manage and are often initiated by setting an artificial due date and budget, and then completed by "de-scoping" the required deliverables as the project progresses, to meet those limits. However, new tools for these kinds of quasi-projects are now being developed—prototyping, Agile project management, and others—to help these teams achieve results that satisfy the customer in spite of all the unknowns. Similarly, when change happens so rapidly that the project is under constant variation, other approaches are developed such as "emergent planning" (also known as "rolling wave"), environmental manipulation, alternate controls, competing experiments, and collaborative leadership (Collyer et al., 2010).

1.3 | The Project Life Cycle

Most projects go through similar stages on the path from origin to completion. We define these stages, shown in Figure 1.3, as the project's *life cycle*. The project is born (its start-up phase) and a manager is selected, the project team and initial resources are assembled, and the work program is organized. Then work gets under way and momentum quickly builds.

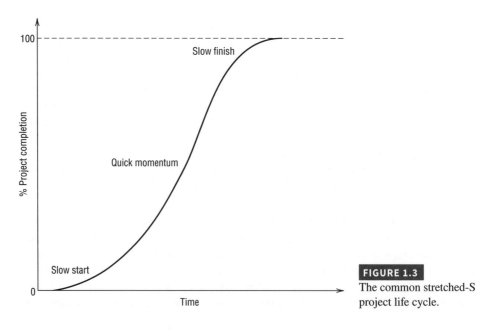

FIGURE 1.3
The common stretched-S project life cycle.

Progress is made. This continues until the end is in sight. But completing the final tasks seems to take an inordinate amount of time, partly because there are often a number of parts that must come together and partly because team members "drag their feet" for various reasons and avoid the final steps.

This "stretched-S" pattern of slow–rapid–slow progress toward the project goal is common. Anyone who has watched the construction of a home or building has observed this phenomenon. For the most part, it is a result of the changing levels of resources used during the successive stages of the life cycle. Figure 1.4 shows project effort, usually in terms of person-hours or resources expended per unit of time (or number of people working on the project) plotted against time, where time is broken up into the several phases of project life. Minimal effort is required at the beginning, when the project concept is being developed and subjected to project selection processes. (Later, we will argue that increasing effort in the early stages of the life cycle will improve the chance of project success.) Normally, there is a strong correlation between the life-cycle progress curve of Figure 1.3 and the effort curve of Figure 1.4 because effort usually results in corresponding progress (although not always). Hence the mathematical derivative of the former tends to resemble the latter (Cioffi, personal communication, 2004). Moreover, since the effort curve is generally nonsymmetrical, the progress curve will in general not be symmetrical either.

Activity increases as planning is completed and execution of the project gets underway. This rises to a peak and then begins to taper off as the project nears completion, finally ceasing when evaluation is complete and the project is terminated. While this rise and fall of effort always occurs, there is no particular pattern that seems to typify all projects, nor any reason for the slowdown at the end of the project to resemble the buildup at its beginning. Some projects end without being dragged out, as is shown in Figure 1.5. Others, however, may be like T. S. Eliot's world, and end "not with a bang but a whimper," gradually slowing down until one is almost surprised to discover that project activity has ceased. In some cases, the effort may never fall to zero because the project team, or at least a cadre group, may be maintained for the next appropriate project that comes along. The new project will then rise, phoenix-like, from the ashes of the old.

The ever-present goals of meeting scope, time, and cost are the major considerations throughout the project's life cycle. It was generally thought that scope took precedence early in the project's life cycle. This is the time when planners focus on finding the specific methods required to meet the project's scope goals. We refer to these methods as the project's *technology* because they require the application of a science or art.

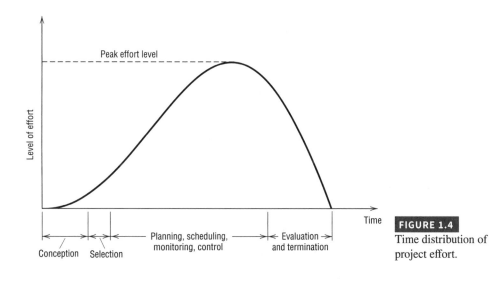

FIGURE 1.4
Time distribution of project effort.

bounded at 100 percent completion. In Chapter 7, we will see that the distinction between these types of life cycles plays a critical role in developing budgets and schedules for projects. It is not necessary for the PM to estimate the precise shape of the life-cycle curve, but the PM must know which type of project life cycle applies to the project at hand. It is also important to point out that other life-cycle patterns such as a linear life cycle are possible.

There is another comparison between the two types of project life cycles that is instructive. For the stretched-S life cycle in Figure 1.3, percentage of project completion is closely correlated with cost, or the use of resources. In fact, this is the basis for the use of "earned value," a technique for monitoring project progress that we will describe in more detail in Chapter 10. However, for the stretched-J progress curve in Figure 1.5, the expenditure of resources has little correlation with progress, at least in terms of final benefit.

Risk During the Life Cycle

It would be a great source of comfort if one could predict with certainty, at the start of a project, how the scope, time, and cost goals would be met. In a few cases, routine construction projects, for instance, we can generate reasonably accurate predictions, but often we cannot. There may be considerable uncertainty about our ability to meet project goals due to various risks to the project during its life cycle. The shaded portion of Figure 1.6 illustrates that uncertainty.

Figure 1.6 shows the uncertainty as seen at the beginning of the project. Figure 1.7 shows how the uncertainty decreases as the project moves toward completion. From project start time, t_0, the band of uncertainty grows until it is quite wide by the estimated end of the project. As the project actually develops, the degree of uncertainty about the final outcome is reduced (e.g., see the estimate made at t_1). A later forecast, made at t_2, reduces the uncertainty further. It is common to make new forecasts about project scope, time, and cost either at fixed intervals in the life of the project or when specific technological milestones are reached. In any event, the more progress made on the project, the less uncertainty there is about achieving the final goal.

Note that the focus in Figures 1.6 and 1.7 is on the uncertainty associated with project cost—precisely, the uncertainty of project cost at specific points in time. However, the same applies to the scope and schedule also, with the result that there is uncertainty in all three of these direct objectives due to risks to each of them during the project. As a result, the uncertainty over time if plotted in three-dimensional space is more of an ellipsoid

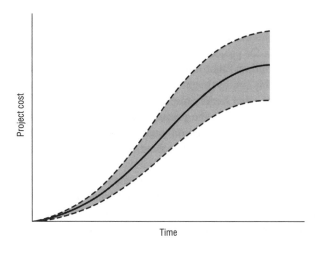

FIGURE 1.6 Estimate of project cost: estimate made at project start.

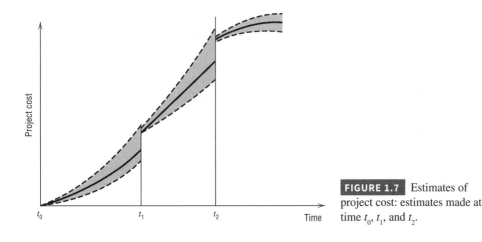

FIGURE 1.7 Estimates of project cost: estimates made at time t_0, t_1, and t_2.

(or partially flattened football) with differing uncertainties in each of scope, cost, and schedule. Dealing with the risk that brings this uncertainty is a major responsibility of the PM. **PMBOK**® devotes an entire chapter to the subject of risk management.

Chapter 11

1.4 The Structure of This Text

This book, a project in itself, has been organized to follow the life cycle of all projects. It begins with the creative idea that launches most projects and ends with closing out the project. This approach is consistent with our belief that it is helpful to understand the entire process of project management in order to understand and manage its parts. Another characteristic of the book also relates to the process of project management: some topics, such as "procurement," can largely be treated as stand-alone issues, discussed in a single appropriate place in the book, and then dispensed with. Other topics, however, such as "risk" or "planning," arise throughout the book and are treated wherever they are relevant, which may be quite often. To attempt to treat them in a single section, or chapter, it would be misleading. In addition, although this book is intended primarily for the student who wants to study project management, we feel it can also be of value to the prospective or acting PM and to senior managers who initiate projects and select, work with, or manage PMs. Therefore, our interests often go beyond the issues of primary concern to beginning students.

Most actual projects will not be of the size and complexity addressed in many of our discussions. Though our intent was not to confine our remarks only to large engineering-oriented projects, these are typically the most complex and place the greatest demands on project management. Smaller, simpler projects may therefore not require the depth of tools and techniques we will present, but the student or manager should be aware that such tools exist.

Project management actually begins with the initial concept for the project. We feel that this aspect of project management is so important, yet so universally ignored in books on project management, that we included two appendices covering this area in previous editions of this book. In one paper, we discussed *creativity* and *idea generation*. In another, we described some of the techniques of *technological forecasting*. While our notion about the importance of these subjects is unchanged, the location of the two appendices has been moved from the end of this work to the Internet. The complete text of both appendices now appears in *www.wiley.com/college/meredith* (along with other items noted in the preface to this edition). One of the major factors making for successful projects is having a clear set of goals for the project in the beginning, so it is critical that top management makes these goals completely clear to all involved in the project, including the PM, the team, and the users of the project.

Before undertaking a journey, it is useful to know what roads are to be traveled. While each individual chapter begins with a more detailed account of its contents, what follows is a brief description of chapter contents along with their organization (Figure 1.8) into three general areas: project initiation, project planning, and project execution.

Part I: Project Initiation

Following this current introductory chapter, the material in Part I focuses on the *context* for initiating the project. We realize that many instructors (and students) would rather get right to the basics of managing projects and that can be done by moving directly to Part II of the text. However, we believe that without understanding the context of the project—why it was selected and approved, what project managers are responsible for and their many roles (such as leading a team and negotiating for resources), the importance of the PMO, and where (and why) the project resides in the organization's hierarchy—a PM is courting disaster. Chapter 2 covers the initiation of a project, whether tactical or strategic, and the evaluation and selection of a project from a portfolio of potential projects. It also covers the governance mechanisms needed for ensuring projects deliver the benefits to the organization that were intended by the funder of the project, including its use by the intended final customers of the project. The topics of project success factors; the meaning of top management commitment to a project; project management "maturity"; the role of the PMO; and the duties of all the managers involved in running projects, such as the project owner, the sponsor, and the program manager, are also covered. Chapter 3, "The Project Manager," concerns the PM's roles, responsibilities, and some personal characteristics a PM should possess. It also discusses problems a PM faces when operating in a multicultural environment. Next, Chapter 4 covers a subject of critical importance to the PM that is almost universally ignored in project management texts: the art of negotiating for resources. The chapter also includes some major sources of interpersonal conflict among members of the project team. Concluding Part I of the book, Chapter 5 concentrates on

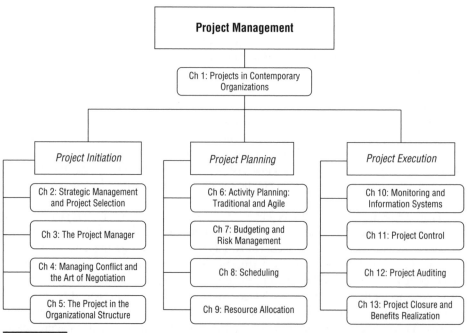

FIGURE 1.8   Organization chart of the parts and chapters of the text.

establishing the project organization. Different project organizational forms are described, as well as their respective advantages and disadvantages. The staffing of the project team is also discussed.

Part II Project Planning

This part of the text discusses the essentials of planning the project in terms of activities, costs, risks, and schedule. Chapter 6 deals with project activity planning, both traditional and Agile, and presents tools useful in organizing and staffing the various project tasks and assessing and prioritizing risks to the project. It also contains a short discussion of phase-gate management systems and other ways of dealing with the problems that arise when multidisciplinary teams work on complex projects. Because costs and risk are important elements of project planning, the topics of budgeting and risk management, including techniques such as simulation to estimate costs and risks, are addressed next in Chapter 7. Scheduling, a crucial aspect of project planning, is then described in Chapter 8, along with the most common scheduling models such as the Program Evaluation and Review Technique (PERT), and precedence diagramming. Concluding Part II, resource allocation is covered in Chapter 9, where the Critical Path Method (CPM) of applying resources to speed up projects is explained. For single projects, we also discuss how the resource allocation problem can be addressed through resource *leveling* to minimize the cost of the resources.

Part III: Project Execution

Finally, we can address how to actually run a project. Chapter 10 examines the information requirements of a project and the need for monitoring critical activities, particularly through the concepts of time and cost variances and "earned value," and projecting the final cost and time of the project. Chapter 11 then describes the control process in project management. This chapter covers standards for comparison and tools to help the manager keep the project in control. Chapter 12 deals with methods for both ongoing and terminal audits and evaluations of a project, as well as identifying factors associated with project success and failure. Chapter 13 describes the different forms of project closure, such as outright shutdown, integration into the regular organization, or extension into a new project. Each of these forms presents unique problems for the PM to solve. Finally, though the project itself may be closed, there is still the issue of realizing the full benefits from the project's outputs and the tasks involved with this effort.

With this introduction, let us begin our study, a project in itself, and, we hope, an interesting and productive one.

Summary

This chapter introduced the subject of project management and discussed its importance in our society. It defined what we mean by a "project," discussed the need for project management, and described the project life cycle. The final section explained the structure of this text and gave an overview of the material to be described in the coming chapters.

The following specific points were made in the chapter:

- The Project Management Institute (PMI) was founded in 1969 to foster the growth and professionalism of project management.

- Project management is now being recognized as a valuable "career path" in many organizations, as well as a way to gain valuable experience within the organization.

- Project management, initiated by the military, provides managers with powerful planning and control tools.

- The three primary forces behind project management are (1) the growing demand for complex, customized goods and services; (2) the exponential expansion of human knowledge; and (3) the global production–consumption environment.

- The three prime objectives of project management are to meet specified scope within budget (cost) and on schedule (time).

- The two primary tasks of the PM are to manage trade-offs among the three prime objectives and to manage risks.

- Our terminology for size follows in this order: program, project, task, work package, and work unit.
- Projects are characterized by their uniqueness, singular occurrence, desired end results, and finite duration.
- Projects are only the middle portion of a set of activities involving the recognition of a need, the selection of

a project to meet it, designing a governance structure for the project, executing the project, and the tasks needed to ensure the benefits of the project are realized.
- Projects often start slowly, build up speed while using considerable resources, and then slow down as completion nears.

Glossary

Deliverables The desired elements of value, outcomes, or results that must be created for a project to be considered complete.

Interdependencies Relations between organizational functions where one function or task is dependent on others.

Life Cycle A standard concept of a product or project wherein it goes through a start-up phase, a building phase, a maturing phase, and a termination phase.

Program Often not distinguished from a project, but frequently meant to encompass a group of projects oriented toward a specific goal.

Project "A temporary endeavor undertaken to create a unique product, service,

or result" (Project Management Institute, 2013, p. 417).

Project Management The means, techniques, and concepts used to run a project and achieve its objectives.

Risk The chance that project processes or outcomes will not occur as planned.

Stakeholder Individuals or groups with a special interest in a project, usually the project team, client, senior management, and specific public interest groups that impact or are impacted by the project.

Suboptimize Doing the best within a function or area but at a cost to the larger whole.

Task A subset of a project, consisting of work packages.

Technology The means for accomplishing a task.

Trade-off Taking less on one measure, such as scope, in order to do better on another, such as schedule or cost.

Uncertainty Having only partial or no information about the situation or outcomes, often due to ambiguity or complexity. Greater uncertainty translates into increased risk.

Work Package A sub-element of a task used to assign costs and values.

Questions

Material Review Questions

1. Name and briefly describe the societal forces that have contributed to the need for project management.

2. Describe the life cycle of a project in terms of (1) the degree of project completion and (2) required effort.

3. Describe the limitations of project management.

4. List the main characteristics of a project and briefly describe the important features of each.

5. Name and briefly describe the three primary goals of a project.

6. Discuss the advantages and disadvantages of project management.

7. How do projects, programs, tasks, and work packages differ?

8. How would you define a project?

9. What are some of the interdependencies related to a project?

10. What are some sources of conflict the PM must deal with?

11. Differentiate between direct and ancillary project goals. Would learning a new skill through the project be a direct or ancillary goal? Entering a new market?

12. Describe the characteristics of quasi-projects.

Class Discussion Questions

13. Give several examples of projects found in our society, avoiding those already discussed in the chapter.

14. Describe some situations in which project management would probably not be effective.

15. How does the rate-of-project-progress chart (Fig. 1.3) help a manager make decisions?

16. Expound on the adage, "Projects proceed smoothly until 90 percent complete, and then remain at 90 percent forever."

17. Would you like to be a PM? Why or why not?

18. Discuss why there are trade-offs among the three prime objectives of project management.

19. Why is the life-cycle curve often "S" shaped?

20. How might project management be used when doing a major schoolwork assignment?

21. Why is there such a pronounced bend in the curve of Figure 1.2?

22. Describe a project whose life cycle would be a straight line from start to finish. Describe a project with an inverse-S life cycle.

23. How does the recognition that projects are only the middle portion of a longer chain of activities help improve the effectiveness of a project?

24. Why do project managers frequently not understand the purpose of the project they are responsible for?

Incidents for Discussion

Blanka Transport, Inc.

After several years of driving long-haul trucks, Joe Blanka founded his own trucking company, Blanka Transport Inc. (BTI), which specialized in less-than-truckload shipments in the midwestern part of the United States. Joe developed a successful method for scheduling BTI's runs that met or exceeded the delivery expectations of its customers. As a result, BTI shipments were growing at a rate between 15 and 20 percent per year. The growth, however, was not evenly distributed across BTI's territory. On some routes, capacity was overloaded in one direction and underloaded in the other.

Joe noticed that the imbalance problem was not stable across time. In some months, capacity was short in one direction, and in other months, it was short in another direction. He thought that one way of solving the problem would be through marketing, by offering incentives to customers whose shipments would improve load balance. Another approach to the problem was to analyze and restructure the route–equipment combinations. He also thought that it might be possible to warehouse some less-urgent shipments for short periods in order to help the balance.

Joe's son, the first member of the Blanka family to attend college, was a senior in engineering school. He had just completed a course in project management, and after briefly describing some of the basic concepts to his father, he suggested that a process improvement project might be a good way to deal with the balance problem. He thought that the Marketing Manager and the Route Manager could serve as project co managers. He also felt that some of the older, more experienced drivers might be helpful. The objective of the project would be to decrease the size of the route imbalances by 75 percent in a 1-year period.

Questions

Is this a proper approach to the problem? Is this a "project"; if so, what are the three triple constraints? What, if any, helpful suggestions would you make to Joe?

Maladroit Cosmetics Company

The plant manager of the Maladroit Cosmetics Company must replace several of her filling machines that have become obsolete. She is about to take delivery of six machines at a total cost of $4 million. These machines must be installed and fully tested in time to be used on a new production line scheduled to begin operation in 6 months. Because this project is important, the plant manager would like to devote as much time as possible to the job, but she is currently handling several other projects. She thinks she has three basic choices: (1) she can handle the project informally out of her office; (2) she can assign the project to a member of her staff; or (3) the company that manufactures the machines can handle the installation project for a fee close to what the installation would cost Maladroit.

Questions

Would you classify the work of installing the six machines as a project? Why or why not? Explain how the PM might trade off one of the primary objectives for another. What type of life cycle would you envision the machine installation work would follow? Why?

Continuing Integrative Class Project

It often helps in communicating the process, difficulties, and satisfactions of project management if the class can do a team project together during the term of the course. The instructor may have a prechosen project for the class to work on, perhaps in a local organization, or the school itself (where there are many excellent projects: the cafeteria, parking, library, counseling, class scheduling, etc.), but if not, the following project is offered as an alternative.

The project is to prepare a "Student Study Guide" for this course, due (time requirement) on the last day of the course *before* the final examination. The purpose of the guide is to help the students learn the material of the course, both by preparing the guide and by using it to study for the final examination. The requirements (scope) for the guide are as follows:

- A professional-looking appearance.
- A consistent approach throughout the chapters.
- A copy for every student, as well as the Instructor.
- Presented in hard copy CD, flash memory, or electronic (e.g., web) form (check with your Instructor).
- Everyone in class must participate, with one exception noted further below.
- If subteams are used, they must not be organized to operate independently of each other (e.g., by doing all the work on one of the chapters).
- The project plans can be constructed manually or in Microsoft Project® or another software program (check with your Instructor).

In addition, one student will be appointed as "Historian," whose job is to monitor and prepare a written report on the progress of the project over its duration. This includes both the tasks to be accomplished and also the attitude and spirit of the PM, the project team and/or subteams, and the various stakeholders in the project (team members, Instructor, future students who may use the Guide) as well as the culture and environment of the project. The main task of the Historian is to compare the reality of the class project to that described in the textbook and point out in the written report similarities and differences that will be recognizable by the PM and team members. The Historian will have no work to do on the project itself, but will need to sit in on meetings, confer with the PM and subteam heads, talk to team members occasionally, confer with the Instructor, and other such activities as needed to properly monitor task progress. The role of this person is especially critical for the class to learn how closely their project followed the typical path of a normal project, what problems arose and how they should have been handled, and so forth. As a result, this person should probably be selected by the Instructor right at the beginning of the course.

There may also be some expenses (budget requirement), such as photocopying costs and travel expenses, that may require assistance from the Instructor. Usually, these costs are minor, but it depends on the project. Of course, in a real project the major cost would be the labor/personnel costs of the team members doing the work, a cost that is essentially "free" here.

In future chapters, we will continue to develop the various elements of the project, such as selecting the PM, organizing the team, scheduling the deliverables, and monitoring progress. However, executing the requisite tasks of the project takes the most time in a real project but is a topic that is outside the scope of this text, which concerns only the generic tasks of project *management*. (Every project will have different tasks associated with it, many with very technical requirements.) Therefore, it will be necessary to forge ahead and do all the preparatory project elements, particularly in Parts I and II of the book, so that progress on the project tasks can begin right away. It would, of course, be best if the class could read all the material up to Chapter 10, which initiates Part III: Project Execution, where the work begins, before actually starting the project. Unfortunately, the course would be almost over by then and it would be too late to start a project. As a result, the PM and the class will have to skip ahead and read the Continuing Integrative Class Project assignments, at least for Chapters 2–10 now; hopefully, they will discover in retrospect how they could have conducted each of the various elements of the project better.

But for right now, it is most important to cover the project elements in Chapters 2 and 3—what the project will be and who will be the PM, respectively, so the project can get underway ASAP. It is best to do these two elements in the very first class, the first one in consultation with the Instructor and the second one with the Instructor ABSENT from the room but with instructions for where to find him or her once the class has selected the PM, hopefully within 20 minutes but most certainly by the end of the class. Good luck!

Bibliography

Collyer, S., C. Warren, B. Hemsley, and C. Stevens. "Aim, Fire, Aim—Project Planning Styles in Dynamic Environments." *Project Management Journal*, September 2010.

Gido, J., and J. P. Clements. *Successful Project Management (with Microsoft Project 2010)*. Cincinnati, OH: South-Western, 2011.

Hughes, T. P. *Rescuing Prometheus*. New York: Pantheon, 1998.

Ibbs, C. W., and Y. H. Kwak. "Measuring Project Management's Return on Investment." *PM Network*, November 1997.

Ibbs, C. W., and Y. H. Kwak. "Assessing Project Management Maturity." *Project Management Journal*, March 2000.

Kerzner, H. *Project Management: A Systems Approach to Planning, Scheduling, and Controlling*, 11th ed. New Jersey: Wiley, 2013.

Larson, E. W., and C. F. Gray. *Project Management: The Managerial Process*. New York: McGraw-Hill, 2010.

Mackey, J., and R. Sisodia. *Conscious Capitalism*, Boston, MA: Harvard Business Review Press, 2013.

Project Management Institute. *A Guide to the Project Management Body of Knowledge*, 5th ed. Newtown Square, PA: PMI, 2013.

Project Management Institute. *Pulse of the Profession Report: The Strategic Impact of Projects—Identify Benefits to Drive Business Results*. Newtown Square, PA: PMI, 2016.

Pyzdek, T., and P. Keller. *The Six Sigma Handbook*, 3rd ed., New York: McGraw-Hill, 2009.

Sandberg, J. "Rise of False Deadline Means Truly Urgent Often Gets Done Late." *Wall Street Journal*, January 24, 2007.

Shenhar, A. J., O. Levy, and D. Dvir. "Mapping the Dimensions of Project Success." *Project Management Journal*, June 1997.

Starkweather, J. A., and D. H. Stevens. "PMP® Certification as a Core Competency: Necessary but Not Sufficient." *Project Management Journal*, February 2011.

Appendix: PMI Certifications

We discuss here only the CAPM® and PMP® certifications. For information on the other credentials, please visit the PMI website at www.pmi.org.

Certified Associate in Project Management (CAPM®)

This is the "entry level" credential, which typically leads to qualifying for the full Project Management Professional (PMP®) credential, although a candidate can maintain their CAPM® certification by retaking the exam every 5 years. It is mainly for project team members with 1500 hours of documented experience or for those who can verify they have taken 23 face-to-face hours of project management classroom education or training. The exam is 3 hours to complete 150 questions and costs $225 ($300 for non-PMI members) to sit for the exam.

Project Management Professional (PMP®)

This is the longstanding standard certification that a person is fully competent in project management and regularly lead and direct project teams. The credential is maintained by gaining 60 PDUs every 3 years. To sit for the exam, a candidate must have a high school education plus 5 years of documented project management experience and can verify they have taken 35 hours of face-to-face project management classroom education or training. Alternatively, a candidate can demonstrate that they have a bachelor's degree (or global equivalent) plus 3 years of documented project management experience and can verify they have taken 35 hours of project management classroom education or training. The exam is 4 hours to complete 200 questions and costs $405 (or $555 for non-PMI members, based on 2017 rates) to sit for the exam.

CHAPTER **2**

Strategic Management and Project Selection

As we noted in Chapter 1, projects are now being used extensively for implementing strategic initiatives in both private and public organizations, often coming directly from the top executive teams in those organizations. Although our success with projects has improved substantially in the last few decades, it has mostly been with the smaller, tactical, shorter, technical, and/or straightforward projects where the triple constraints (iron triangle) were relatively clear at the outset, and the complexity and number of stakeholders in the project were minimal. But our success with strategic initiatives, which often are complex, multi-stakeholder, inter-related (with other projects), longer-duration, mega-sized, or organizational-change projects, has been much poorer.

Projects focusing on strategic initiatives are critical to an organization's competitiveness and long-term success. Indeed organizations spend about $100 billion a year on creating competitive strategies (Morgan et al., 2007, p. 1), yet 90 percent of them (thousands) fail due to poor execution of these projects. Unfortunately, the report card on organizational success with strategic projects has not been stellar. For example, an early research study (Thomas et al., 2001) found that 30 percent of all such projects were canceled midstream, and more than half of the completed projects were up to 190 percent over budget and 220 percent late. This same study found that the primary motivation of organizations to improve and expand their project management processes was due to major troubled or failed projects, new upcoming mega-projects, to meet competition, or to maintain their market share.

More recent research (Alderton, 2013; Economist, 2013) shows little progress. Less than half of firms considered their strategically important projects a success, over a quarter of all firms lacked a sponsor and detailed implementation processes for their strategic projects, only two out of five had adequately skilled personnel for their strategic projects, and only one out of five thought hiring skilled staff was a high priority. Note also that we are talking here about strategic projects specifically. Of course, not all of an organization's projects will be strategy implementation or organizational change projects, but all of the projects in the organization's portfolio should be consistent with the organization's strategic goals.

There has also been extensive research on how to improve this situation. There is uniform agreement (Alderton, 2013; Economist, 2013; Derby and Zwikael, 2012; Zwikael et al., 2015) that projects, programs, and project portfolios are crucial to organizations' future competitiveness. The best firms have the most top management involvement, get the most feedback, dedicate the most resources, and have the most robust processes for their projects. Also, it is now recognized that implementation, not formulation, is the critical skill in strategic and competitive success. One researcher noted that all organizations now have the same data and information but not all can execute effectively.

As Mihalic (2013) points out, project success these days isn't just meeting the triple technical constraints of scope, schedule, and budget but also meeting the strategic goals that result in a desired benefit for the project. Organizations need to link the strategic elements with the tactical to streamline decision making, increase efficiencies, and better align organizational goals. Program and project managers today have to cope with unheard-of levels of ambiguity and complexity (Pitsis et al., 2014), especially in terms of the number of stakeholders and their power to delay and even stop a project. As well, the pace of technology and interdependency of systems has created tremendous levels of uncertainty. Leadership and strategic management of these challenges are now just as important as technical management.

For these more complex strategic projects where the benefits of the project do not automatically result when the technical details of the project are completed, the problem seems to be due to two factors. The first involves a concept known as *agency theory* (Müller et al., 2005), also sometimes called principle-agent theory, which in the case of strategic projects relates to the fact that the funder of the project (the principle) has no representative (the agent) guiding the execution and application of the project to attain the benefits the funder desired. The second factor is *governance theory* (Turner et al., 2001) and concerns the people, groups, and procedures that are needed to ensure the project achieves the strategic aims intended. Both theories are embedded in a perspective; we consider next, called *organizational project management* (Aubry et al., 2012; Drouin et al., 2005), which is particularly appropriate to the management of strategic projects.

2.1 Organizational Project Management and Governance

According to Wikipedia (2017), the term "organizational project management" (OPM) was coined by John Schlichter in 1998 at a PMI Standards Committee meeting and does not denote project management generically but rather as a framework for executing strategies through projects by combining the systems of portfolio, program, and project management. It then was incorporated into PMI's *Organizational Project Management Maturity Model* (OPM3; see PMI, 2013) in 2003 and later adopted as an ANSI (2008) standard. Over the intervening years, OPM has been gaining adherents for its attention to the difficulties of realizing the benefits of many of today's projects which typically involve large sums of money, multiple stakeholders, dozens of subcontractors, extensive organizational change, and/or years of effort. Current thinking has fleshed out some initial concepts of OPM to the point that there is now substantial agreement on many of the groups, roles, and duties involved, though some are still under debate, and, of course, different organizations structure the groups and roles according to their own situation and preferences (PMI, 2014). Figure 2.1 illustrates the general thinking about the groups and roles involved in OPM.

Figure 2.1 illustrates the flow of activity from conception of a project to its final routine use by some "users" of the project, whereby the benefits anticipated from the project are realized. We will give a detailed example of an actual real project (name is disguised) a bit later to illustrate. The roles indicated within the blocks in the figure are all "stakeholders" in the project, but there may be other stakeholders (Dick et al., 2015) as well, primarily outside the organization such as regulatory agencies, the local populace, interested or affected organizations, public authorities, and so on, as shown by the dashed and dotted lines. Be aware that different stakeholders have different levels of clout (Eskerod et al., 2016a, 2016b), and the project owner should take this into consideration when dealing with them. If there are changes in the project along the way, it may even be necessary to get the signoff approval of particularly powerful stakeholders.

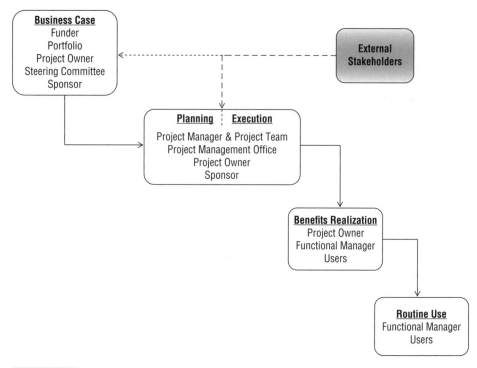

FIGURE 2.1   Governance structure for strategic projects.

A project begins with a Business Case (Kopmann et al., 2015) being presented to a funding entity (called the "funder" here) by some group or person within the organization. If it is a person, then this role is commonly called the project's "champion" (not shown in the figure). The business case typically includes monetary cost and benefit elements as well as nonmonetary factors such as the strategic justification for the project, expected behavioral impacts (e.g., resistance), increases in efficiency, service improvements, competitiveness effects, and so on. It often happens, especially for strategic projects, that the nonmonetary effects are more important than the monetary ones. Pinto et al. (1987) found that the most important project success factor was a clearly defined goal and direction for the project in the business case; the second was top management support by providing the needed resources and authority. Zou et al. (2014) found the same two critical success factors except they were reversed, with top management commitment first and clearly defined objectives second.

There have been several names used in the literature for the funder, such as "client," "customer," "owner," and others. The problem with these other names is that they can often be misinterpreted, depending on the project situation. For example, the "customer" could be either the funder or perhaps the user of the output of the project and may be either internal or external to the funding organization. And the "owner" may be misinterpreted also, especially if this is the end user of the project output. The name "funder," of course, clearly provides the funds with some anticipated benefit expected from the project. There usually is some set of projects that the funder has initiated, called the "portfolio," and the business case must sufficiently justify any project's purpose and cost to be included in the portfolio (discussed further in Section 2.3). The selection of projects to include in the portfolio is a complex process, discussed in detail in the following sections. Also, the project may be part of a larger set of projects, known as a "program" (Dunn, 2014), which has a "program manager" (not shown) who oversees all the projects that are expected collectively to achieve some particular result.

For each project, there is an agent employed by the funder known as the "project owner" (or PO) who is accountable for working with all parties to make sure the business case and expected benefits of the project are realized. There is also a "sponsor" employed by the funding entity, usually a senior level manager, whose responsibility is to politically "protect" the project and help get the resources the project needs to be successful. The PO's role begins with understanding the need and helping develop the business case in the first place, then helping select a project manager (PM) and working with him or her and the sponsor to ensure that the project plan is viable and will achieve the outputs expected from the project. But the PO's job doesn't end there; it also includes working with the "functional manager" and final "users" who will use the project outputs and thereby achieve the benefits desired by the funder. Although this in itself is a long, involved process, it is even more complex because every project plan, especially for strategic projects, seems to change multiple times over the duration of the project due to changes in the economy, government regulations and laws, competition, new information that is gained as the project progresses, and especially changes in the leadership of the organization. This is the main source of frustration for project managers, but with the help of the PO and sponsor, such changes can be more easily accommodated in the project plan, and it is pointless to complete a project that no longer provides the benefits for the funder that were anticipated.

There is usually some oversight committee, typically called a "steering committee" or such, for every project, of which the PO is usually a member, or perhaps the Chair, unless the steering committee also oversees the entire portfolio of projects. One more entity influencing the initiation of the project is the impact of external stakeholders who, depending upon their power, may alter the nature, direction, timing, cost, or benefits of the project and its business case, shown with a dotted line in the figure. The main impact of these external stakeholders is usually on the actual project planning and execution itself however, as indicated by the dashed line (Nieto-Rodriguez et al., 2014).

From the Business Case initiation of the project, we now move to the project's planning and execution. These are two separate, important activities indicated in the middle block of the figure by the dotted vertical line but executed by the same group of participants shown in the block. (In this text, Planning constitutes Part II and Execution Part III.) It should be noted that the project itself may be conducted either by an internal group or by a contractual external group. If external, then the contractor may also have a "sponsor" for the project whose job is similar to that of the funder's sponsor but who works with internal resources, while the contractor's sponsor works with external resources. The PM usually creates the project plan, which is overseen and approved by the project owner and sponsor. Zwikael et al. (2007) found that the best tool for warding off risks to the project was the development of a well-thought out project plan that all stakeholders bought into. And Pinto et al. (1987) found this to be the third most important project success factor.

There is usually a Project Management Office (PMO, discussed in more detail in Chapter 5) charged with improving the "maturity" (Aubry, 2015) or overall effectiveness of the organization's project management processes, which will help the PM and team with their activities, and it will become involved as well at this time. Following the preparation and acceptance of the project plan, the PM and project team then execute the project using their special expertise and the help of the PMO. Meanwhile, as noted earlier, there will usually be changes in the plan as events unfold.

While the PM and team are executing the project, the PO will be monitoring the project's progress and any changes needed due to scope or other changes required by the funder, designing trade-offs with the PM to accommodate the changes. The PO will also be managing the demands of the stakeholders and searching for other strategic risks to the realization of the benefits from the project. In addition, the PO needs to be working with the functional manager and final customers to make sure that the project outputs will be accepted by the manager and customers in order to achieve the benefits intended. This may well involve training, education, reorganization, motivation, engagement, procedural changes, responsibility changes, and myriad other impacts on the function, which may also change as the project plan changes. Once the project outputs have been successfully completed, the PO will help with the project shutdown, transfer of personnel and resources, and preparation of the closeout and lessons learned report. Then, the Benefits Realization phase begins in full and continues until the benefits have been permanently achieved, operational responsibility handed off to the functional manager and customers, if appropriate, and the function has moved on to Routine Use of the project's outputs.

A School Library Example

The Oakville City School District some years ago converted their five elementary school libraries from a card catalog to a computerized system. The funder was the Oakville School Board, financed primarily by city and county taxes, who decided to initiate this project based on a business case presented to them by the Superintendent of Oakville Schools, the Project Owner (PO), who also acted in this case as the Sponsor for the project. The business case highlighted the speed of checking books in and out, plus better controlling and locating of books. Monetary benefits included reduction of lost books, minimized book purchasing through better awareness of both required and popular books based on usage data, less space for the storage of unneeded books, and reduced labor costs through increased library efficiency.

A project manager (PM) was selected from among the faculties at the five schools based on their efficiency, literary expertise as a Reading Specialist, technological adeptness, and high regard among the school staff. The project team consisted of the vendor representative of the library computer system, and the librarians, assistant librarians, volunteers from the PTA (Parent–Teacher Association), and student helpers from each of the schools. The functional managers were the five librarians at the five schools and the customers were the librarians, schoolteachers, and students. External stakeholders included parents of the schoolchildren, the principals of the schools, book publishers, and the city and county tax authorities.

The PM worked with the Superintendent/PO, the vendor, and the librarians to develop a logical project plan for the transition to the computerized system. The transition was projected to take about 5 months, beginning after the start of the spring semester when the libraries would be shut down for 3 weeks while the books were being prepared for computer barcode scanning; the labeling barcodes and other book labels were prepared in advance by the vendor for each library. The project plan also included policies for who could use the new system, which students would be allowed to check out books, what to do in case of a computer malfunction, and other such anticipated matters. Training sessions for the librarians and other users were planned as well, relying heavily on the vendor representative for the skills and the Superintendent for the resources.

When the project was completed, the PM returned to their classroom teacher duties. But the Superintendent/PO continued to monitor the implementation of the system, watching for when additional training might be needed for some users and developing policies for unanticipated events such as if a librarian wasn't available some particular day; if parents or teachers objected to something about the new system or policies; if some students couldn't seem to learn how to use the new system; and other such practical matters. It was critical, however, that users not be discouraged from using the system as intended. One example of an unanticipated event was when the records showed that parents, rather than students, were much more likely to be excessively tardy in returning books on time, so the policy on who could check out books had to be modified to exclude parents. It was suspected that the reason for this was that the parents gave the books to their children who, having not checked them out, didn't feel any responsibility for returning them.

A few comments on this real-world example:

- Note how the project governance was adjusted to suit the existing organizational entities in this specific situation; some specific examples follow.
- The Superintendent in this case was the most appropriate person to be the PO, but given his normal duties, was also the most appropriate sponsor. It is common and completely acceptable for some of these roles, but not that of the PM, to be combined.

- In this case, the external contractor/vendor did not take over and execute the project for the School Board, which might have been the situation if the Board wanted a new building constructed, but instead worked within the internal governance structure set up by the Board.

- Note that project plan was not limited to just the physical project elements but also organizational policies regarding the new system, how it should work, and who could use it.

- The PM for this project was a functional (classroom) manager, although not directly in the area where the system was to be employed, and when the project was completed went back to their functional position.

- Note that the PO continued to monitor the utilization of the system and kept adjusting policies and training as needed to realize the benefits desired from the system. In this case, the PO, being the sponsor as well, could then bring the resources to bear to assure the benefits were fully realized.

2.2 Project Selection Models

Project selection is the process of evaluating proposed projects or groups of projects, and then choosing to implement some set of them so that the strategic objectives of the organization will be achieved. This same systematic process can be applied to any area of the organization's business in which choices must be made between alternatives. For example, a TV station can select which of several syndicated comedy shows to rerun in its 7:30 P.M. weekday time-slot; a construction firm can select the best subset of a large group of potential projects on which to bid; or a hospital can find the best mix of psychiatric, orthopedic, obstetric, and other beds for a new wing. Each project will have different costs, benefits, and risks. Rarely are these known with certainty. In the face of such differences, the selection of one (or more) project out of a set is a difficult task. Choosing a number of different projects, a *portfolio*, is even more complex (discussed later). Despite this difficulty, selecting the appropriate portfolio of projects is critical as it is the portfolio of projects that determines an organization's success, not the completion of an individual project.

In the paragraph just above, note that some projects are "internal" to the organization and others are "external," either doing something for an external client (e.g., the construction firm's bid), or engaging an external supplier. Whether for inside or outside clients, as in the case of the construction firm, the projects will use the organization's own resources, and both types of projects are usually dealt with as "competing" for the same pool of resources.

Only rarely will a project manager be involved in the process by which projects are selected for inclusion in the set of projects the parent organization adopts for investment. It is, however, critically important to the success of the PM that he or she fully understands the parent organization's objectives in undertaking a project that the PM is expected to lead. As we will see, most of the decisions that the PM is forced to make will have an impact on the degree to which the project contributes to those objectives the parent organization expected from the project. Indeed, effectively executing the PM's primary role of managing trade-offs requires that the PM make trade-offs in a way that best supports the organization's overall strategy.

In what follows, we discuss several techniques that can be used to help senior managers select projects. The proper choice of investment projects is crucial to the long-run survival of every firm. Daily we witness the results of both good and bad investment choices. In our daily newspapers, we read of Procter and Gamble's decision to invest heavily in marketing its products on the Internet and through social media; or problems faced by school systems when they update student computer labs—should they invest in Microsoft® based systems or stick with their traditional choice, Apple®? But can such important choices be made rationally? Once made, do they ever change, and if so, how? These questions reflect the need for effective selection models.

There are two basic types of project selection models, *numeric* and *nonnumeric*. Both are widely used. Many organizations use both at the same time, or they use models that are combinations of the two. Nonnumeric models, as the name implies, do not use numbers as inputs. Numeric models do, but the criteria being measured may be either objective or subjective. It is important to remember that the *qualities* of a project may be represented by numbers and that *subjective* measures are not necessarily less useful or reliable than *objective* measures.

A paper by Åstebro (2004) reports on a study of more than 500 strategic R&D projects. He found that four project characteristics were excellent predictors of a project's commercial success: (1) expected profitability, (2) technological opportunity, (3) development risk, and (4) appropriateness, the degree to which a project is appropriate for the organization undertaking it. This finding is particularly important because the experimental design was free of the hindsight bias that is so common in studies of project success and failure. The model correctly predicted almost 80 percent of the project failures and almost 75 percent of the project successes.

A primary cause for the failure of strategic projects is insufficient care in evaluating the proposal before the expenditure of funds. What is true for strategic projects also appears to be true for other kinds of projects, and it is clear that product development projects are more successful if they incorporate user needs and satisfaction in the design process (Matzler et al., 1998). Careful analysis of a potential project is mandatory for profitability in the construction business. There are many horror stories about firms that undertook projects for the installation of a computer information system without sufficient analysis of the time, cost, and disruption involved.

Once again, we must emphasize that the tendency of many organizations to depend on profitability models to the exclusion of nonfinancial costs and benefits is a serious mistake. It is not uncommon for the "minor side-effects" of a new product or process to have major impacts on the parent organization. Often, projects intended to alter the organization's infrastructure—extending engineering software to include new analytic methods or installing a day-care facility for preschool children of employees—can have significant positive effects on worker morale and productivity. On the other hand, replacing workers with new technology may make financial sense but could hurt morale and productivity so much that the change substantially reduces profitability. Of the two basic types of selection models (numeric and nonnumeric), nonnumeric models are older and simpler and have only a few subtypes to consider. We examine them first.

Nonnumeric Models

The Sacred Cow   In this case the project is suggested by a senior and powerful official in the organization. Often the project is initiated with a simple comment such as, "If you have a chance, why don't you look into...," and there follows an undeveloped idea for a new product, for the development of a new market, for the design and adoption of a global data base and information system, or for some other project requiring an investment of the firm's resources. The immediate result of this bland statement is the creation of a "project" to investigate whatever the boss has suggested. The project is "sacred" in the sense that it will be maintained until successfully concluded, or until the boss, personally, recognizes the idea as a failure and terminates it.

The Operating Necessity If a flood is threatening the plant, a project to build a protective dike does not require much formal evaluation. XYZ Steel Corporation has used this criterion (and the following criterion also) in evaluating potential projects. If the project is required in order to keep the system operating, the primary question becomes: Is the system worth saving at the estimated cost of the project? If the answer is yes, project costs will be examined to make sure they are kept as low as is consistent with project success, but the project will be funded.

The Competitive Necessity Using this criterion, XYZ Steel undertook a major plant rebuilding project in its steel bar manufacturing facilities near Chicago. It had become apparent to XYZ's management that the company's bar mill needed modernization if the firm was to maintain its competitive position in the Chicago market area. Although the planning process for the project was quite sophisticated, the decision to undertake the project was based on a desire to maintain the company's competitive position in that market.

In a similar manner, many business schools are restructuring their undergraduate and MBA programs to stay competitive with the more forward-looking schools. In large part, this action is driven by declining numbers of tuition-paying students and the need to develop stronger programs to attract them.

Investment in an *operating necessity* project takes precedence over a *competitive necessity* project, but both types of projects may bypass the more careful selection analysis used for projects deemed to be less urgent or less important to the survival of the firm.

The Product Line Extension In this case, a project to develop and distribute new products would be judged on the degree to which it fits the firm's existing product line, fills a gap, strengthens a weak link, or extends the line in a new, desirable direction. Sometimes careful calculations of profitability are not required. Decision makers typically act on their beliefs about what will be the likely impact on the total system performance if the new product is added to the line.

Comparative Benefit Model In this situation, an organization has many projects to consider, perhaps several dozen. Senior management would like to select a subset of the projects that would most benefit the firm, but the projects do not seem to be easily comparable. For example, some projects concern potential new products, some concern changes in production methods, and still others propose to create a daycare center for employees with small children. The organization may have no formal method of selecting projects, but members of the Selection Committee think that some projects will benefit the firm more than others, even if they have no precise way to define or measure "benefit."

The concept of comparative benefits, if not a formal model, is widely adopted for selection decisions on all sorts of projects. Of the several techniques for ordering projects, the Q-Sort is one of the most straightforward. First, the projects are divided into three groups—*good, fair,* and *poor*—according to their relative merits. If any group has more than eight members, it is subdivided into two categories, such as *fair-plus* and *fair-minus*. When all categories have eight or fewer members, the projects within each category are ordered from best to worst. Again, the order is determined on the basis of relative merit. The rater may use specific criteria to rank each project, or may simply use general overall judgment (see Figure 2.2 for an example of a Q-sort).

The process described may be carried out by one person who is responsible for evaluation and selection, or it may be performed by a committee charged with the responsibility. If a committee handles the task, the individual rankings can be developed anonymously, and the set of anonymous rankings can be examined by the committee itself for consensus. It is common for such rankings to differ somewhat from rater to rater, but they do not often

Steps	Results at Each Step
1.	
2.	
3.	
4.	
5.	

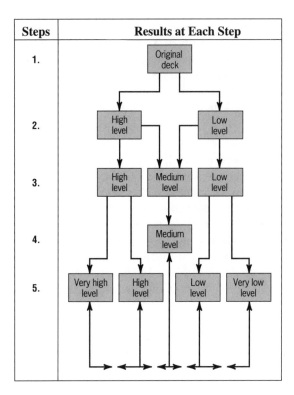

FIGURE 2.2 Q-sort method.

vary strikingly because the individuals chosen for such committees rarely differ widely on what they feel to be appropriate for the parent organization. Projects can then be selected in the order of preference, though they are usually evaluated financially before final selection. Although it is easy to dismiss nonnumeric models as unscientific, they should not be discounted casually. These models are clearly goal-oriented and directly reflect the primary concerns of the organization. The sacred cow model, in particular, has an added feature; sacred cow projects are visibly supported by "the powers that be." Full support by top management is certainly an important contributor to project success. Without such support, the probability of project success is sharply lowered.

Sustainability

The December 2009 issue of *PM Network* is devoted to "sustainability." The discussion begins with the following (Gale, 2009): "Somewhere along the line, sustainability became interchangeable with that *other* buzzword; green. There's just one small problem. It's not really accurate. Sustainability does, of course, call for incorporating environmental concerns into project decision-making, but it also covers social issues—and the bottom line."

More and more organizations are building sustainability into the set of criteria that must be met for proposed projects to be selected for funding. Jewelry companies avoid the use of "blood diamonds," and manufacturing firms avoid purchasing inputs from suppliers that use child labor. The sale of a pharmaceutical of questionable purity or serious side-effects is commonly far more costly in the long run than the cost of better quality control or the research needed for better drug design. In other words, sustainability focuses on long-run profitability rather than short-run payoff. To integrate sustainability into the organization's decision-making requires the appointment of a senior manager with responsibility for the task. Metrics must be developed to measure the results of policy changes to increase sustainability, and this often requires developing the "soft" measures that we will discuss later in this chapter.

Project Management in Practice

Taipei 101: Refitted as World's Tallest Sustainable Building

The owners of Taiwan's Taipei 101 tower, the tallest building in East Asia, wanted to show the world that it is possible to make an existing building sustainable by winning a LEED (Leadership in Energy and Environmental Design) certification. When the building was constructed in 1998, advanced elements of sustainability were included, such as low-emissivity windows, energy-efficient HVAC systems, and smart controls on its double-deck elevators. The new $1.8 million effort will extend these green elements to include eco-friendly processes (cleaning, solid-waste management, purchasing), healthy office environments (air-quality testing, environmental inspections), energy consumption (optimizing operating and maintenance programs, automatic turnoff of lighting in unoccupied restrooms), water usage (replacing toilet and urinal flush valves, reducing washbasin faucet flow rates), and tenant recycling, waste management, and office fit-outs.

However, the engineering aspects of the tower refitting were the easy parts of the project. More difficult was getting all 85 organizations occupying the tower, comprising over 10,000 people, on board with the recycling (including purchase of recycled supplies) and other sustainability routines. The project manager notes that changing people's attitudes is by far the greatest challenge for sustainability.

Questions

1. **Why did the owners pick such a big building for sustainability refitting?**

2. **What aspect of the tenant's habits and routines relates to sustainability, as opposed to "green?"**

3. **In what ways does refitting the tower enhance long-term profitability?**

Source: S. A. Swanson. "The Sky's the Limit," *PM Network*, 24.

Numeric Models: Profit/Profitability

As noted earlier, a large majority of all firms using project evaluation and selection models use profitability as the sole measure of acceptability. We will consider these models first, and then discuss more comprehensive models. Cost aspects of profitability are covered in the fourth knowledge area of the **PMBOK®**.

Chapter 7

Payback Period   The payback period for a project is the initial fixed investment in the project divided by the estimated annual net cash inflows from the project. The ratio of these quantities is the number of years required for the project to repay its initial fixed investment. For example, assume a project costs $100,000 to implement and has annual net cash inflows of $25,000. Then

$$\text{Payback period} = \$100,000 / \$25,000 = 4 \text{ years}$$

This method assumes that the cash inflows will persist at least long enough to pay back the investment, and it ignores any cash inflows beyond the payback period. For some managers, this method also serves as a proxy for risk (discussed later in this section). The faster the investment is recovered, the less the risk to which the firm is exposed.

Discounted Cash Flow   Also referred to as the net present value (NPV) method, the discounted cash flow method determines the NPV of all cash flows by discounting them by the required rate of return (also known as the *hurdle rate, cutoff rate*, and similar terms) as follows:

$$\text{NPV (project)} = A_0 + \sum_{t=1}^{n} \frac{F_t}{(1 + k + p_t)^t}$$

where

F_t = the net cash flow in period t,
k = the required rate of return, and

A_0 = initial cash investment (because this is an outflow, it will be negative)

p_t = the predicted rate of inflation (or deflation) during period t.

Early in the life of a project, net cash flow is likely to be negative, the major outflow being the initial investment in the project, A_0. If the project is successful, however, cash flows will become positive. The project is *acceptable* if the sum of the NPVs of all estimated cash flows over the life of the project is positive. A simple example will suffice. Using our $100,000 investment with a net cash inflow of $25,000 per year for a period of 8 years, a required rate of return of 15 percent, and an inflation rate of 3 percent per year, we have

$$\text{NPV (project)} = -\$100,000 + \sum_{t=1}^{8} \frac{\$25,000}{(1+0.15+0.03)^t}$$
$$= \$1,939$$

Because the present value of the inflows is greater than the present value of the outflow—that is, the NPV is positive—the project is deemed acceptable.

Several comments are in order about all the profit-profitability numeric models. The commonly seen phrase "return on investment," or ROI, does not denote any specific method of calculation but usually involves some form of NPV calculation. There are a number of advantages of numeric profitability models: they are simple to use and understand, the accounting data is usually available (though possibly inaccurate), and they can often be adjusted to account for project risk. But there are many disadvantages as well: they ignore all nonmonetary factors (which are often the most important), models that do not use discounting ignore the time value of money, but models that do discount are strongly biased toward short-term solutions, and all of the models are highly sensitive to data errors in the early years of a project.

Numeric Models: Real Options

A more recent approach to project selection employs financial analysis that recognizes the value of positioning the organization to capitalize on future opportunities. It is based on the financial options approach to valuing prospective capital investment opportunities. Through a financial option an organization or individual acquires the right to do something but is not required to exercise that right.

To illustrate the analogy of financial options to project selection, consider a young biotech firm that is ready to begin clinical trials to test a new pharmaceutical product in humans. A key issue the company has to address is how to produce the drug both now in the low volumes needed for the clinical trials and in the mass quantities that will be needed in the future should the new drug succeed in the clinical trial phase. Its options for producing the drug in low volumes for the clinical trials are to invest in an in-house pilot plant or to immediately license the drug to another company. If it invests in an in-house pilot plan, it then has two future options for mass producing the drug: (1) invest in a commercial scale plant or (2) license the manufacturing rights. In effect then, investing now in the pilot plant provides the pharmaceutical company with the option of building a possibly highly profitable commercial scale plant in the future, an option it would not have if it chose to license the drug right from the start.

In addition to considering the value of future opportunities a project may provide, the cost of *not* doing a project, and thus foregoing a potential future opportunity, should also be considered. This approach to project selection is based on the well-known economic concept of "opportunity cost." Consider the problem of making an investment in one of

Ceramic Sciences, Inc.

Ceramic Sciences, Inc. (CSI), a large producer of decorative ceramic pots, is considering the installation of a new marketing software package that will, it is hoped, allow more accurate sales information concerning the inventory, sales, and deliveries of its pots as well as its vases designed to hold artificial flowers.

The information systems (IS) department has submitted a project proposal that estimates the investment requirements as follows: an initial investment of $125,000 to be paid up-front to the Pottery Software Corporation; an additional investment of $100,000 to modify and install the software; and another $90,000 to integrate the new software into the overall information system. Delivery and installation are estimated to take 1 year; integrating the entire system should require an additional year. Thereafter, the IS department predicts that scheduled software updates will require further expenditures of about $15,000 every second year, beginning in the fourth year. They will not, however, update the software in the last year of its expected useful life.

The project schedule calls for benefits to begin in the third year, and to be up to speed by the end of that year. Projected additional profits resulting from better and more timely sales information are estimated to be $50,000 in the first year of operation and are expected to peak at $120,000 in the second year of operation, and then to follow the gradually declining pattern shown in the table at the end of this box.

Project life is expected to be 10 years from project inception, at which time the proposed system will be obsolete for this division and will have to be replaced. It is estimated, however, that the software can be sold to a smaller division of CSI and will thus have a salvage value of $35,000. CSI has a 13 percent hurdle rate for capital investments and expects the rate of inflation to be about 2 percent over the life of the project. Assuming that the initial expenditure occurs at the beginning of the year and that all other receipts and expenditures occur as lump sums at the end of the year, we can prepare the Net Present Value (NPV) analysis for the project as shown in the table below.

The NPV of the project is positive, and, thus, the project can be accepted. (The project would have been rejected if the hurdle rate were 14 percent.)

Just for the intellectual exercise, note that the total inflow for the project is $759,000, or $75,900 per year on average for the 10-year project. The required investment is

= B5 − C5 [Copy to D6:D15]

	A	B	C	D
1	**Hurdle Rate**	13.0 %		
2	**Inflation Rate**	2.0 %		
3				
4	**Year**	**Inflow**	**Outflow**	**Net Flow**
5	20X0*	$0	$125,000	−$125,000
6	20X0	$0	$100,000	−$100,000
7	20X1	$0	$90,000	−$90,000
8	20X2	$50,000	$0	$50,000
9	20X3	$120,000	$15,000	$105,000
10	20X4	$115,000	$0	$115,000
11	20X5	$105,000	$15,000	$90,000
12	20X6	$97,000	$0	$97,000
13	20X7	$90,000	$15,000	$75,000
14	20X8	$82,000	$0	$82,000
15	20X9	$100,000	$0	$100,000
16	**Total**	**$759,000**	**$360,000**	**$399,000**
17	**NPV**			**$17,997**
18				
19	*t = 0 at the beginning of 20X0.			

= $65,000 cost savings + $35,000 salvage value

= D5 + NPV(B1 + B2, D6:D15)

$315,000 (ignoring the biennial overhaul charges). Assuming 10-year, straight line depreciation, or $31,500 per year, the payback period would be

$$PB = \frac{\$315,000}{\$75,900 + 31,500} = 2.9$$

A project with this payback period would probably be considered quite desirable.

only two projects. An investment in Project A will force us to forgo investing in Project B, and vice versa. If the return on A is 12 percent, making an investment in B will have an opportunity cost of 12 percent, the cost of the opportunity forgone. If the return on B is greater than 12 percent, it may be preferred over selecting Project A.

Occasionally, organizations will approve projects that are forecast to lose money when fully costed and sometimes even when only direct costed. Such decisions by upper management are not necessarily foolish because there may be other, more important reasons for proceeding with a project, such as to:

- Acquire knowledge concerning a specific or new technology
- Get the organization's "foot in the door"
- Obtain the parts, service, or maintenance portion of the work
- Allow them to bid on a lucrative, follow-on contract
- Improve their competitive position
- Broaden a product line or line of business

Of course, such decisions are expected to lose money in the short term only. Over the longer term they are expected to bring extra profits to the organization. It should be understood that "lowball" or "buy-in" bids (bidding low with the intent of cutting corners on work and material, or forcing subsequent contract changes) are unethical practices, violate the PMI Code of Ethics for Project Managers (www.pmi.org or **PMBOK**, p. 2, 2013), and are clearly dishonest.

The real options approach acts to reduce both technological and commercial risk. For a full explanation of the method and its use as a strategic selection tool, see Luehrman (1998a and 1998b). An interesting application of real options as a project selection tool for pharmaceutical R&D projects is described by Jacob et al. (2003). Real options combined with Monte Carlo simulation is compared with alternative selection/assessment methods by Doctor et al. (2001).

Numeric Models: Scoring

In an attempt to overcome some of the disadvantages of profitability models, particularly their focus on a single decision criterion, a number of evaluation/selection models that use multiple criteria to evaluate a project have been developed. Such models vary widely in their complexity and information requirements. If the models include both monetary and qualitative factors, they are generally known as cost–benefit analyses. If the element of risk is added to this mix, we believe these models come closest to how managers actually evaluate investments. The following example illustrates one type of numeric scoring model.

Weighted Factor Scoring Model When numeric weights reflecting the relative importance of each individual criterion (or factor) are added, we have a weighted factor scoring model. In general, it takes the form

$$S_i = \sum_{j=1}^{n} s_{ij} w_j$$

where

S_i = the total score of the ith project,
s_{ij} = the score of the ith project on the jth criterion, and
w_j = the weight of the jth criterion.

The weights, w_j, may be generated by any technique that is acceptable to the organization's policy makers. There are several techniques available to generate such numbers, but the most effective and most widely used is the classic Delphi method. The Delphi method (Dalkey, 1969) is a technique for developing numeric values that are equivalent to subjective, verbal measures of relative value. The use of experts to develop weightings is nicely demonstrated by Jolly (2003) who applies the technique to the development of weights to a technology portfolio. When numeric weights have been generated, it is helpful (but not necessary) to scale the weights so that

$$0 \leq w_j \leq 1 \quad j = 1, 2, 3, \ldots, n$$

$$\sum_{j=1}^{n} w_j = 1$$

The weight of each criterion can be interpreted as the "percent of the total weight accorded to that particular criterion."

A special caveat is in order. It is quite possible with this type of model to include a large number of criteria. It is not particularly difficult to develop scoring scales and weights, and the ease of gathering and processing the required information makes it tempting to include marginally relevant criteria along with the obviously important items. Resist this temptation! After the important factors have been weighted, there usually is little residual weight to be distributed among the remaining elements. The result is that the evaluation is simply insensitive to major differences in the scores on trivial criteria. A good rule of thumb is to keep the number of factors to eight or less because the higher weights, say 20 percent or more, tend to force the smaller weights to be insignificant with weights less than 2 percent or 3 percent. (If elements are discarded, and if you wish $\Sigma w_j = 1$, the weights must be rescaled to 1.0.) It is not particularly difficult to computerize a weighted scoring model by creating a template on Excel® or one of the other standard computer spreadsheets. An example of a weighted factor scoring model to select a project is illustrated next.

Gettin' Workin'

The Project Council of WorkinFerYa Corporation, Inc. is trying to select an initial strategic project to improve their customer service processes. They have five proposals to evaluate and they want to select the one that has the most promise to lead off with and then may select one of the others to follow on later. Various departments have proposed different projects, but these five have been identified as the most promising. They will use the weighted factor scoring model to make the choice and then review the selection again in a full council discussion.

The scoring model must have the following elements:

1. A set of criteria on which to judge the value of each alternative
2. A numeric estimate of the relative importance (i.e., the "weight") of each criterion in the set
3. Scales by which to measure or score the performance or contribution to value of each alternative on each criterion

The criteria weights and measures of performance must be numeric in form, but this does not mean that they must be either "objective" or "quantitative." Criteria weights, obviously, are subjective by their nature, being an expression of what the decision maker thinks is important. The development of performance scales is more easily dealt with in the context of our example, and we will develop them shortly.

Assume that we have chosen the criteria and weights shown in Table A to be used in our evaluations.* The weights represent the relative importance of the criteria measured on a 10-point scale. The numbers in parentheses show the proportion of the total weight carried by each criterion. (They add to only .99 due to rounding.) Raw weights work just as well for decision making as their percentage counterparts, but the latter are usually preferred because they are a constant reminder to the decision maker of the impact of each of the criteria.

Prior to consideration of performance standards and sources of information for the criteria we have chosen, we

TABLE A   **Criteria and Weights for Project Selection**

Customer response	4	(.10)
Revenue increase	3	(.07)
Employee response	7	(.17)
Cost, operating	5	(.12)
Cost, original	10	(.24)
Competitiveness	7	(.17)
Risk	5	(.12)
Total	41	.99

*The criteria and weights were picked arbitrarily for this example.

must ask, "Are there any characteristics that must be present (or absent) in a candidate for it to be acceptable?" Assume, for this example, that to be acceptable, an alternative must not endanger the image of the company or threaten its finances. If an alternative violates these conditions, it is immediately rejected.

For each criterion, we need some way of measuring the estimated performance of each alternative. In this case, we might adopt the measures shown in Table B. Our purpose is to transform a measure of the degree to which an alternative meets a criterion into a score, the s_{ij}, that is a general measure of the utility or value of the alternative with respect to that criterion. Note that this requires us to define the criterion precisely, as well as to specify a source for the information.

Figure A shows the scores for each criterion transformed to a 5-point scale, which will suffice for our ratings. Using the performance scores shown in Figure A, we can evaluate the projects we have identified as our alternatives: providing all service reps with a specially developed service app for their cellphone, implementing a new Customer Relationship Management software package, reorganizing the Sales and Service groups for increased intercommunication and efficiency,

installing an incentive plan for the service reps, and give upper management more time to interact with the service and sales groups in their meetings and more resources to support their activities. Each project is scored on each criterion according to the categories shown in Figure A. Then each score is multiplied by the criterion weight and the result is entered into the appropriate box in Figure B. Last, the results for each alternative are summed to represent the weighted score.

According to this set of measures, we prefer the Exec Presence, but while it is a clear winner over Service Rep App and Sales/Service Reorg, and scores about 8 percent better than Incentive Plan, it rates only about 0.13 points or 4 percent above CRM Software. Note that if we overrated Exec Presence by one point on Employee response or Competitiveness, or if we underrated the CRM Software by one point on either of these criteria, the result would have been reversed. (We assume that the original cost data are accurate.) With the scores this close, we might want to evaluate these two projects by additional criteria (e.g., Opening new markets or Sustainability) prior to making a firm decision.

All in all, if the decision maker has well-delineated objectives, and can determine how specific kinds of performance contribute to those criteria, and finally, can measure those kinds of performance for each of the alternative courses of action, then the scoring model is a powerful and flexible tool. Beyond incorporating multiple criteria into the decision-making process, another reason that the scoring model is so powerful is the complementary sensitivity analysis that can be performed on the model. In particular, the model readily lends itself to exploring how the rankings change as alternative criteria weightings and/or alternative scores are used for the options under consideration. Such sensitivity analysis can provide important insights into the decision-making situation that are often as useful, if not more useful, than simply developing a simple ranking of the options. Of course, to the extent that criteria are not carefully defined, performance is not well linked to the criteria, and is carelessly or wrongly measured, the scoring model rests on a faulty foundation and is merely a convenient path to error.

TABLE B	Project Selection Criteria, Measures, and Data Sources
Customer response	Subjective judgment, anticipated
Revenue increase	Anticipated percentage, based on survey of sales managers
Employee response	Subjective judgment
Cost, operating	Software maintenance costs
Cost, original	Hardware, software, and training costs
Competitiveness	Based on marketing department's input
Risk	Based on Risk Committee's input

Scores					
Criteria	1	2	3	4	5
Customer response	Ugh	Poor	Adequate	Good	WOW
Revenue increase	None	<1/2%	1/2–1%	1–2%	2–3%
Employee response	Bad	Poor	Adequate	Good	Excellent
Cost, operating*	>$2.5	$2.1–2.5	$1.9–2.1	$1.6–1.9	<$1.6
Cost, original*	>$32.5	$26–32.5	$21–26	$17–21	<$17
Competitiveness	No change	Up a bit	Up some	Up a lot	Way up
Risk	Worst	Poor	Adequate	Good	Excellent

*Cost data in $1,000s

FIGURE A Performance measures and equivalent scores for selection of an automobile.

	Criteria and Weights							
Alternatives	Customer Response (0.10)	Revenue Increase (0.07)	Employee Response (0.17)	Cost, operating (0.12)	Cost, original (0.24)	Competi- tiveness (0.17)	Risk (0.12)	$\Sigma\ s_{ij}w_j$
Service rep app	3×0.10 $= 0.30$	1×0.07 $= 0.07$	4×0.17 $= 0.68$	2×0.12 $= 0.24$	1×0.24 $= 0.24$	2×0.17 $= 0.34$	3×0.12 $= 0.36$	2.23
CRM software	3×0.10 $= 0.30$	3×0.07 $= 0.21$	2×0.17 $= 0.34$	5×0.12 $= 0.60$	4×0.24 $= 0.96$	2×0.17 $= 0.34$	4×0.12 $= 0.48$	3.23
Sales/service reorg	2×0.10 $= 0.20$	1×0.07 $= 0.07$	4×0.17 $= 0.68$	4×0.12 $= 0.48$	3×0.24 $= 0.72$	1×0.17 $= 0.17$	3×0.12 $= 0.36$	2.68
Incentive plan	5×0.10 $= 0.50$	4×0.07 $= 0.28$	3×0.17 $= 0.51$	2×0.12 $= 0.24$	2×0.24 $= 0.48$	5×0.17 $= 0.85$	2×0.12 $= 0.24$	3.10
Exec presence	4×0.10 $= 0.40$	5×0.07 $= 0.35$	5×0.17 $= 0.85$	2×0.12 $= 0.24$	1×0.24 $= 0.24$	4×0.17 $= 0.68$	5×0.12 $= 0.60$	3.36

As was the case with profitability models, scoring models have their own characteristic advantages and disadvantages. The advantages are:

1. These models allow multiple criteria to be used for evaluation and decision making, including profit/profitability models and both tangible and intangible criteria. Furthermore, the models allow the inclusion of both objective and subjective criteria.

2. They are structurally simple and therefore easy to understand and use.

3. They are intuitive and reflect the way we think about making choices: what are our options, what are the important criteria, what is the most important criterion, and how do the options compare on the criteria.

4. They are a direct reflection of managerial policy.

5. They are easily altered to accommodate changes in the environment or managerial policy.

6. Weighted scoring models allow for the fact that some criteria are more important than others.

7. These models allow easy sensitivity analysis. The trade-offs among the several criteria are readily observable.

The disadvantages are the following:

1. The output of a scoring model is strictly a relative measure. Project scores do not represent the value or "utility" associated with a project and thus do not directly indicate whether or not the project should be supported.

2. In general, scoring models are linear in form and the elements of such models are assumed to be independent.

3. The ease of use of these models is conducive to the inclusion of a large number of criteria, most of which have such small weights that they have little impact on the total project score.

4. To the extent that profit/profitability is included as an element in the scoring model, this element has the advantages and disadvantages noted earlier for the profitability models themselves.

Numeric Models: Window-of-Opportunity Analysis

In the early stages of new product development, one may know little more than the fact that the potential product seems technically feasible. Just because one can develop and/or install a new technology does not necessarily imply that the new technology is worth implementing, or will be economically profitable. Fundamentally, the decision to invest in the development of a new process or product depends on an estimate of cash flows and other benefits expected to result if the innovation is successful—a difficult problem at best.

Given some idea for a new product or process, we can attempt to determine the cost, timing, and performance specifications that *must* be met by this new technology *before* any R&D is undertaken. (This is called the *window of opportunity* for the innovation.) The method for conducting such an analysis is as follows. Given a potential production process innovation, for example, the current production process is analyzed in detail and baseline data on the current process are collected (e.g., its cycle time, its cost). Following this, the level of improvement needed from the process improvement project is determined. Finally, if estimates of the benefits from the process improvement project meet the required level of improvement in a resource effective way, the process improvement project is approved. For an example of such an approach, see Evans et al. (1985).

Numeric Models: Discovery-Driven Planning

Like the window-of-opportunity analysis, discovery-driven planning (McGrath et al., 1995; Rice et al., 2008) also reverses the expensive and risky traditional approach of trying out the technology to determine its benefits. This approach funds enough of the project to determine if the initial assumptions concerning costs, benefits, etc. were accurate. When the funds are gone, the assumptions are reevaluated to determine what to do next.

The idea isn't to implement the project but rather to *learn* about the project. The assumptions about the project are written down and analyzed carefully to determine two aspects about them: (1) which are the critical assumptions that will make or break the desirability of the project, and (2) how much will it cost to test each of the assumptions. The high-priority, deal-killer assumptions that will cost the least then are ranked at the top, with the lesser and more expensive assumptions following. If a critical assumption proves to be invalid, management must rethink its strategy and the project. This process is not just a one-time exercise, however; the process continues as the stages of the project are executed so that at any point in the project, management can step in and terminate it if conditions change and the project looks less promising. And conditions are always changing: the economy gets worse, the market moves toward or away from the promise of the project, a key team member of the project leaves the company, the strategy of the organization changes with a new executive, a new government regulation impacts the project, and so on. Project failure is more often management's failure to consider an important problem or question than it is a technical failure within the project.

Choosing a Project Selection Model

Selecting the type of model to aid the evaluation/selection process depends on the philosophy and wishes of management. Swanson (2011b) reports on an airline that previously considered only ROI in prioritizing projects but now also considers strategic contributions, resource limitations, and nonnumeric factors such as regulatory mandates and operating necessities. Other organizations are considering the real options their projects offer.

We strongly favor weighted scoring models for three fundamental reasons. First, they allow the multiple objectives of all organizations to be reflected in the important decision about which projects will be supported and which will be rejected. Second, scoring models are easily adapted to changes in managerial philosophy or changes in the environment. Third, they do not suffer from the bias toward the short run that is inherent in profitability models that discount future cash flows. This is not a prejudice against discounting and most certainly does not argue against the inclusion of profits/profitability as an important factor in selection, but rather *it is an argument against the exclusion of nonfinancial factors* that may require a longer-run view of the costs and benefits of a project. Finally, they support performing detailed sensitivity analyses of the criteria and scores, which in turn provides further insights into the decision-making situation.

Nonetheless, the actual use of scoring models is not as easy as it might seem. Decision makers are forced to make difficult choices and they are not always comfortable doing so. They are forced to reduce often vague feelings to quite specific words or numbers. Multiattribute, multiperson decision making is not simple.

The use of any project selection model assumes that the decision-making procedure takes place in a reasonably rational organizational environment. Such is not always the case. In some organizations, project selection seems to be the result of a political process, and sometimes involves questionable ethics, complete with winners and losers (Baker et al., 1995). In others, the organization is so rigid in its approach to decision making that it attempts to reduce all decisions to an algorithmic process in which predetermined programs make choices so that humans have minimal involvement—and responsibility.

Whether managers are familiar with accounting systems or not, it is useful to reflect on the methods and assumptions used in the preparation of accounting data. Among the most crucial are the following:

1. Accountants live in a linear world. With few exceptions, cost and revenue data are assumed to vary linearly with associated changes in inputs and outputs.

2. The accounting system often provides cost–revenue information that is derived from standard cost analyses and equally standardized assumptions regarding revenues. These standards may or may not accurately represent the cost–revenue structure of the physical system they purport to represent.

3. The data furnished by the accounting system may or may not include overhead costs. In most cases, the decision maker is concerned solely with cost–revenue elements that will be changed as a result of the project under consideration. Incremental analysis is called for, and great care should be exercised when using pro forma data in decision problems. Remember that the assignment of overhead cost is always arbitrary. The accounting system is the richest source of information in the organization, and it should be used—but with great care and understanding.

4. **Warning!** A great many organizations utilize project cost data as the primary, *and the only* routine measure of project performance. In Chapter 1 we emphasized that projects should be measured on three dimensions, time, cost, and scope. Without including information on the schedule and the physical completion of work, cost measurements have no useful meaning. We will repeat this warning throughout this book.

Finally, no matter what method is used for project selection, as time goes by the selection model's inputs must be constantly updated. The world does not stand still—things change! What was a promising project yesterday may be a loser today—and yesterday's loser may be today's winner.

Risk Considerations in Project Selection

In our previous discussion of factors to consider when selecting projects, we emphasized costs and benefits, with only a side reference to the inherent uncertainty associated with both of these, though benefits are usually more uncertain than costs. However, both are uncertain, and can be greater or less than expected. In the case of being worse than expected, the organization is exposed to some, perhaps substantial, level of risk. There are many more ways of dealing with project risk besides using a shorter payback period. Although our major discussion of techniques to handle risk will come in Chapter 7 when we discuss budgeting and risk management, the topic is highly relevant to project selection as well, and we will briefly comment on it here. PMI (2011) reports that risk management is used significantly more by high-performing project organizations than low-performing organizations.

Chapter 11

During the past several years, increasing attention has been paid to the subject of managing some of the risks inherent in most projects. The subject first appeared in PMI's 1987 edition of **PMBOK** (PMI, 2008). For the most part, risk has been interpreted as being unsure about project task durations and/or costs, but uncertainty plagues all aspects of the work on projects and is present in all stages of project life cycles. The impact of imperfect knowledge on the way a project is organized and on its budget and schedule will be discussed in the chapters devoted to those subjects.

In the real world of project management, it has been common to deal with estimates of task durations, costs, etc. as if the information were known with certainty. In fact, a great majority of all decisions made in the course of managing a project are actually made under conditions of uncertainty. However, we can still make some estimates about the *probabilities* of various outcomes. If we use appropriate methods for doing this, we can apply what knowledge we have to solving project decision problems. We will not always be correct, but we will be doing the best we can. Such estimates are called "subjective probabilities" and are dealt with in most elementary courses on probability and statistics. While such probabilities are no more than guesses, they can be processed just as empirically determined probabilities are. In the world of project management, a best guess is always better than no information at all. Then it is possible to examine some of the effects of uncertainty on project selection.

At times, an organization may wish to evaluate a project about which there is little information. R&D projects sometimes fall into this general class. But even in the comparative mysteries of R&D activities, the level of uncertainty about the outcomes of R&D is not beyond analysis. As we noted earlier, there is actually not much uncertainty about whether a product, process, or service can be developed, but there can be considerable uncertainty about *when* it will be developed, at *what* cost, and *whether* it will be viable.

As they are with R&D projects, time and cost are also often uncertain in other types of projects. When the organization undertakes projects in which it has little or no recent experience—for example, investment in an unfamiliar business, engaging in international trade, and myriad other projects common enough to organizations, in general, but uncommon to any single organization—there are three distinct areas of uncertainty. First, there is uncertainty about the timing of the project and the cash flows it is expected to generate. Second, though not as common as generally believed, there may be uncertainty about the direct outcomes of the project—that is, what it will accomplish. Third, there is uncertainty about the side effects of the project—its unforeseen consequences.

Typically, we try to reduce such uncertainty by the preparation of *pro forma* documents. *Pro forma* profit and loss statements and break-even charts are examples of such documents. The results, however, are not very satisfactory unless the amount of uncertainty is reflected in the data that go into the documents. When relationships between inputs and outputs in the projects are complex, Monte Carlo simulation (Meredith et al., 2002) can handle such uncertainty by exposing the many possible consequences of embarking on a project. With the great availability of microcomputers and user-friendly software (e.g., Crystal Ball®), simulation for assessing risk is becoming very common. A thorough discussion of methods for handling risk and some simulation examples will be given in Chapters 7 and 8.

2.3 | Project Portfolio Management (PPM)

Although up to now we have primarily talked about the selection of a project in competition with other projects, in reality organizations typically maintain a *portfolio* of projects, and trying to keep a proper balance among this portfolio is the real task of upper management. With limited resources, management must choose between long-term and short-term projects, safe and risky projects, manufacturing and marketing projects, and so on. To help choose between the myriad project proposals, in competition with ongoing projects as well as each other, management needs some overarching measures to evaluate each of the projects, and those measures are commonly related to the organization's mission, goals, and strategy. Project portfolio management is briefly defined and compared to project and program management in Chapter 1 of **PMBOK®**.

We will assume here that the organization has already identified its mission, goals, and strategy and that these are well known throughout the organization. If this is not the case, then any attempt to tie the organization's projects to its goals is folly and PPM will have little value. In an attempt to identify the characteristics of "great" projects, Dvir et al. (2011) used four criteria to select potential projects for further analysis: (1) a major undertaking of strategic importance to the organization; (2) the outcome contributed substantially and over a long duration to the performance of the organization and well-being of its clients; (3) highly innovative from a scientific, technological, design, or operational perspective; and (4) the outcome had a major impact on its industry and stimulated others to follow. Based on this, they then analyzed 15 great projects and identified 7 common characteristics of *highly* successful strategic projects:

PMBOK

1.4.2

1. It creates a unique competitive advantage and/or exceptional value for its stakeholders.
2. It requires a long period of project definition dedicated to defining a powerful vision, a clear need, and a successful execution approach.
3. It creates a revolutionary project culture.
4. It needs a highly qualified project leader who is unconditionally supported by top management.
5. It maximizes the use of existing knowledge, often in cooperation with outside organizations.
6. It uses integrated development teams with fast problem-solving capability and the ability to adapt to business, market, and technology changes.
7. Its project team has a strong sense of partnership and pride.

In contrast to these seven characteristics, Deloitte Consulting (McIntyre, 2006) found that only 30 percent of surveyed organizations insisted on knowing the value a project would add to the organization's strategy before granting approval. Deloitte also identified the following eight symptoms of a misaligned portfolio:

- Many more projects than management expected
- Inconsistent determination of benefits, including double-counting
- Competing projects; no cross-comparison of projects
- "Interesting" projects that don't contribute to the strategy
- Projects whose costs exceed their benefits
- Projects with much higher risks than others in the portfolio; no risk analysis of projects
- Lack of tracking against the plan, at least quarterly
- No identified "client" for many projects

If the goals and strategies have been well articulated, however, then PPM can serve many purposes, as articulated by Swanson (2011a):

- To identify proposed projects that are not really projects and should be handled through other processes
- To prioritize the list of available projects
- To intentionally limit the number of overall projects being managed so the important projects get the resources and attention they need
- To identify the real options that each project offers
- To identify projects that best fit the organization's goals and strategy
- To identify projects that support multiple organizational goals and cross-reinforce other important projects
- To identify codependent projects
- To eliminate projects that incur excessive risk and/or cost
- To eliminate projects that bypassed a formal selection process and may not provide benefits corresponding to their risks and/or costs
- To keep from overloading the organization's resource availability
- To balance the resources with the needs
- To balance short-, medium-, and long-term returns

PPM attempts to link the organization's projects directly to the goals and strategy of the organization. This occurs not only in the project's initiation and planning phases but also throughout the life cycle of the projects as they are managed and eventually brought to completion. In the reading "From Experience: Linking Projects to Strategy" at the end of this chapter, Hewlett-Packard, a firm that is highly dependent on successful new-product projects, found that through their version of PPM they could reduce their portfolio of projects by about two-thirds. This resulted in better funding and executing those projects that were most strategically important to the company and thereby substantially improving the chances of project success.

Thus, PPM is also a means for monitoring and controlling the organization's strategic projects. On occasion, and particularly during recessions and difficult economic times, this will mean shutting down projects prior to their completion because their risks have become excessive, their costs have escalated out of line with their expected benefits, another (or a new) project does a better job of supporting the goals, or any variety of similar reasons. It should be noted that a significant portion of the administration of this process could be managed by the Project Management Office, a concept to be discussed in Chapter 5.

As was mentioned earlier, there has been more research on project portfolio management recently, including the application of strategic management theories (Killen et al., 2015). For example, Sanchez and Robert (2010) suggested using a system of key performance indicators (KPIs, such as contribution to the strategic objectives and progress toward meeting the triple constraint) to identify interdependencies between projects, risks, and opportunities across projects, and the effect of any given project on overall portfolio performance. Martinsuo (2013) found that portfolio management was not a straightforward rational process but required intuition, negotiation, and bargaining in a very context-dependent environment. In a later paper, Martinsuo (2014) also found that managers typically stressed the commercial value of their strategic projects but obtained more value through organization measures such as knowledge development, knowledge sharing, stakeholder satisfaction, and employee satisfaction. Beringer et al. (2013) concluded in a study of internal stakeholders that project managers should be responsible for operational results, but not strategic, concurring with Derby and Zwikael (2012) who suggested the project owner or sponsor should be responsible for strategic and business results of the project.

Project Management in Practice

Using a Project Portfolio to Achieve 100 percent On-Time Delivery at Decor Cabinet Company

Décor Cabinets, a custom cabinet maker in Canada, adopted the strategic goal of 100 percent on-time delivery of their cabinets to achieve long-term customer loyalty and create added value that enhances their profitability. Having such a clear objective helped them assemble a project portfolio uniquely focused on their goal, although it also meant declining some seemingly profitable project ideas requested by customers. However, if demand increased for the requested products, it could have had a serious negative impact on their delivery goals. It was difficult to resist pressure from different areas of the company to support these kinds of projects, "You can easily lose focus," the CEO admitted. "Sometimes when ROI drives all decision-making you miss the bigger picture."

Questions

1. **Might it not make sense to include a least a few of the more promising new product projects in their portfolio?**

2. **If ROI isn't the big picture, what do you think is?**

Source: S. F. Gale, "The Bottom Line," *PM Network*, 21.

Finally, some studies even looked at uncertainty and risk in portfolio management. Petit and Hobbs (2010) studied the impact of uncertainty and project interdependence on portfolios and identified four sources of change, two of which were significant (actual portfolio performance and changes in project scope). Teller and Kock (2013) studied the impact of risk management on portfolio success in terms of two primary measures: portfolio risk transparency (formalizing the risk management process and instilling a risk management culture) and portfolio risk coping capacity (e.g., risk prevention, monitoring, and inclusion in the PPM process), both of which help prevent risks and thereby enhance portfolio success. Last, Kopmann et al. (2015) studied the control of the project business cases in the portfolios of 183 firms through initial reviews, monitoring during execution, and postproject tracking, finding that all three led to better portfolio success.

There are eight steps in the PPM process, which generally follow those described in Longman et al. (1999) and Englund et al. (1999).

Step 1: Establish a Project Council

The main purpose of the project council is to establish and articulate a strategic direction for those projects spanning internal or external boundaries of the organization, such as cross-departmental or joint venture. Thus, senior managers *must* play a major role in this council. Without the commitment of senior management, the PPM will be incapable of achieving its main objectives. The council will also be responsible for allocating funds to those projects that support the organization's goals and controlling the allocation of resources and skills to the projects.

In addition to senior management, others who should be members of the project council are

- all program managers
- project owners or sponsors of major projects
- the head of the Project Management Office
- particularly relevant general managers
- those who can identify key opportunities and risks facing the organization
- anyone who can derail the progress of the PPM process later on

One example of this type of strategic council was developed by Blue Cross/Blue Shield, as described in the sidebar.

Implementing Strategy through Projects at Blue Cross/Blue Shield

Since strategic plans are usually developed at the executive level, implementation by middle level managers is often a problem due to poor understanding of the organization's capabilities and top management's expectations. However, bottom-up development of departmental goals and future plans invariably lacks the vision of the overall market and competitive environment. At Blue Cross/Blue Shield (BC/BS) of Louisiana, this problem was avoided by closely tying project management tools to the organizational strategy. The resulting system provided a set of checks and balances for both BC/BS executives and project managers.

Overseeing the system is a newly created Corporate Project Administration Group (CPAG) that helps senior management to translate their strategic goals and objectives into project management performance, budget, and schedule targets. These may include new product development, upgrading information systems, or implementing facility-automation systems. CPAG also works with the project teams to develop their plans, monitoring activities and reports so they dovetail with the strategic intentions.

The primary benefits of the system have been that it allows

- senior management to select any corporate initiative and determine its status;
- PMs to report progress in a relevant, systematic, timely manner;
- all officers, directors, and managers to view the corporate initiatives in terms of the overall strategic plan; and
- senior management to plan, track, and adjust strategy through use of financial project data captured by the system.

Questions

1. **Do you think that all projects will be monitored by the CPAG or just the strategic projects?**
2. **Will all tactical projects be terminated in the future? Where could these be handled or tracked?**
3. **Do you think the CPAG will substantially improve the achievement of BC/BS's strategic goals?**

Source: P. Diab, "Strategic Planning + Project Management = Competitive Advantage," *PM Network*, 12.

Step 2: Identify Project Categories and Criteria

In this step, various project categories are identified so the mix of projects funded by the organization will be spread appropriately across those areas making major contributions to the organization's goals. In addition, within each category, criteria are established to discriminate between very good and even better projects. The criteria are also weighted to reflect their relative importance. Identifying separate categories not only facilitates achievement of multiple organizational goals (e.g., long term, short term, internal, external, tactical, strategic) but also keeps projects from competing with each other on inappropriate categories.

The first task in this step is to list the goals of each existing and proposed project: What is the mission, or purpose, of this project? Relating these to the organization's goals and strategies should allow the council to identify a variety of categories that are important to achieving the organization's goals. Some of these were noted above, but another way to position some of the projects (particularly product/service development projects) is in terms of their extent of product and process changes.

Wheelwright et al. (1992) have developed a matrix called the *aggregate project plan* illustrating these changes, as shown in Figure 2.3. Based on the extent of product change and process change, they identified four separate categories of projects:

1. **Derivative projects**   These are projects with objectives or deliverables that are only incrementally different in both product and process from existing offerings. They are often meant to replace current offerings or add an extension to current offerings (lower priced version, upscale version).
2. **Platform projects**   The planned outputs of these projects represent major departures from existing offerings in terms of either the product/service itself or the process used

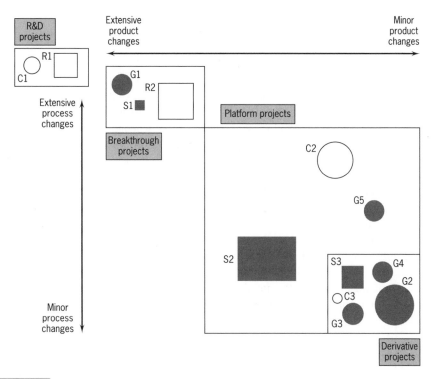

FIGURE 2.3   Aggregate project plan.

to make and deliver it, or both. As such, they become "platforms" for the next generation of organizational offerings, such as a new model of automobile, a tablet computer,
or a new type of insurance plan. They thus form the basis for follow-on derivative projects that attempt to extend the platform in various dimensions.

3. **Breakthrough projects**   Breakthrough projects typically involve a newer technology than platform projects. It may be a "disruptive" technology that is known to
the industry or something proprietary that the organization has been developing over
time. Examples here include the use of fiber-optic cables for data transmission, cash-
balance pension plans, and hybrid gasoline–electric automobiles.

4. **R&D projects**   These projects are "blue sky," visionary endeavors oriented toward
using newly developed technologies, or existing technologies in a new manner.
They may also be for acquiring new knowledge, or developing new technologies
themselves.

   The size of the projects plotted on the array indicates the size/resource needs of the
project and the shape may indicate another aspect of the project, for example, internal/
external, long/medium/short term, or whatever aspect needs to be shown. The numbers
indicate the order, or time frame, in which the projects are to be (or were) implemented,
separated by category, if desired.
   The aggregate project plan can be used to

1. View the mix of projects within each illustrated aspect (shape)

2. Analyze and adjust the mix of projects within each category or aspect

3. Assess the resource demands on the organization, indicated by the size, timing, and
   number of projects shown

4. Identify and adjust the gaps in the categories, aspects, sizes, and timing of the projects

5. Identify potential career paths for developing project managers, such as team member of a derivative project, then team member of a platform project, manager of a derivative project, member of a breakthrough project, and so on

Next, the council should develop separate criteria and cost ranges for each category that determine those projects that will support the organizational strategy and goals. Example criteria might include alignment with the organization's goals/strategy, riskiness of the project, financial return, probability of success, and knowledge acquisition. Scales also need to be determined for each criterion to measure how different projects score on each of them. The scales should also serve as an initial screen, to start the process of winnowing out the weakest projects by including limits on their extremes, maximum probability of technical failure given proposed budget and schedule, or minimum acceptable potential market share. Finally, the council needs to set an importance weighting for the various criteria in each category.

The model we have described above is a "weighted factor scoring model," as described earlier. There are some standard, well-known tools to help develop the weights, scales, and criteria such as the simplified method by Frame (2002), and even software such as *Expert Choice*®. (Frame's method is illustrated in the Reading section at the end of this chapter.) Regardless of the approach used to define the weights, there is considerable value in the process of discussing the weights and ultimately gaining consensus on them.

Step 3: Collect Project Data

For each existing and proposed project, assemble the data appropriate to that category's criteria. Be sure to update the data for ongoing projects and not just use the data from the previous evaluation. Then document any assumptions made so that they can be checked in the future as the project progresses. If the project is new, you may want to fund only enough work on the project to verify the assumptions or determine the window-of-opportunity for the proposed product or process, holding off full funding until later. Similarly, identify any projects that can be deferred to a later time period, those that must precede or follow other projects, those that support other projects or should be done in conjunction with them, those that can be outsourced, and other such special aspects of the projects.

Next, screen out the weaker projects: Have costs on existing projects escalated beyond the project's expected benefits? Has the benefit of a project lessened because the organization's goals have changed? Does a competitor's new entry obviate the advantages of a project? Does a new (or old) project dominate an existing or proposed project in terms of its benefits, furtherance of organizational goals, reduced costs? Also, screen *in* any projects that do not require deliberation, such as projects mandated by regulations or laws, projects that are operating or competitive necessities, projects required for environmental or personnel reasons, and so on. The fewer projects that need to be compared and analyzed, the easier the work of the council.

Step 4: Assess Resource Availability

Next, assess the availability of both internal and external resources, by type, department, and timing. Note that labor availability should be estimated conservatively, leaving time for vacations, personal needs, illness, holidays, and, most important, regular functional (nonproject) work. After allowing for all of these things that limit labor availability, add a bit more, perhaps 10 percent, to allow for the well-known fact that human beings need occasional short breaks to rest or meet other human needs. Timing is particularly important, since project resource needs by type typically vary up to 100 percent over the life cycle of projects. Needing a normally plentiful resource at the same moment it is fully utilized elsewhere may doom an otherwise promising project. Eventually, the council will be trying to balance aggregate project resource needs over future periods with resource availabilities so timing is as important as the amount of maximum demand and availability. This is the major subject of Chapter 9.

Step 5: Reduce the Project and Criteria Set

In this step, multiple screens are employed to try to narrow down the number of competing projects. As noted earlier, the first screen is each project's support of the organization's goals. Other possible screens might be criteria such as the following:

- Whether the required competence exists in the organization
- Whether there is, or will be, a market for the offering
- How profitable the offering is likely to be
- How risky the project is
- If there is a potential partner to help with the project
- If the right resources are available at the right times
- If the project is a good technological/knowledge fit with the organization
- If the project uses the organization's strengths, or depends on its weaknesses
- If the project is synergistic with other important projects
- If the project is dominated by another existing or proposed project
- If the project has slipped in its desirability since the last evaluation

The result of this step may involve canceling some ongoing projects or replacing them with new, more promising projects. Beware, however, of the tendency to look more favorably upon new, untested concepts than on current projects experiencing the natural problems and hurdles of any promising project.

Step 6: Prioritize the Projects within Categories

Apply the scores and criterion weights to rank the projects within each category. It is acceptable to hold some hard-to-measure criteria out for subjective evaluation, such as riskiness, or development of new knowledge. Subjective evaluations can be translated from verbal to numeric terms easily by the Delphi or other methods and used in the weighted factor scoring model. It should be remembered that criteria such as riskiness are usually composite measures of a set of "risks" in different areas. The same is true for criteria like "development of new knowledge."

It is also possible at this time for the council to summarize the "returns" from the projects to the organization. However, this should be done by category, not for each project individually since different projects are offering different packages of benefits that are not comparable. For example, R&D projects will not have the expected monetary return of derivative projects; yet it would be foolish to eliminate them simply because they do not measure up on this (irrelevant, for this category) criterion.

Step 7: Select the Projects to Be Funded and Held in Reserve

The first task in this step is important: determining the most appropriate mix of projects across the various categories and time periods. Ultimately, the organization's strategy drives the appropriate mix of projects. For example, a company that competes on the basis on being first to market with new products would expect to have a larger percentage of breakthrough projects while a company that competes in mature markets would likely have more derivative projects.

Next, be sure to leave some percent (often 10–15 percent) of the organization's resource capacity free for new opportunities, crises in existing projects, errors in estimates, and so on. Then allocate the categorized projects in rank order to the categories according to the mix desired. It is usually a good practice to include some speculative projects in each category to allow future options, knowledge improvement, additional experience in new areas, and such.

Overall, the focus should be on committing to fewer projects but with sufficient funding to allow project completion. Document why late projects were delayed and why some, if any, were defunded. One special type of delayed project mentioned earlier is sometimes called an "out-plan" project (in contrast to the selected "in-plan" projects) (Englund et al., 1999). Out-plan projects are those that appear promising but are awaiting further investigation before a final decision is made about their funding, which could occur in the next PPM cycle or sooner, if they warrant the use of some of the 10–15 percent funding holdout. The result of this step (and most of the project portfolio process) is illustrated in Figure 5 in the Reading section.

Step 8: Implement the Process

The first task in this final step is to make the results of the portfolio analysis widely known, including the documented reasons for project cancellations, deferrals, selections, and non-selections as was mentioned earlier. Top management must now make their commitment to the PPM process totally clear by supporting the process and the results. This may require a PPM champion near the top of the organization. As project proposers come to understand the workings and importance of the PPM process, their proposals will more closely fit the profile of the kinds of projects the organization wishes to fund. As this happens, it is important to note that the council will have to concern itself with the reliability and accuracy of proposals competing for limited funds.

Senior management must fully fund the selected projects. It is neither appropriate nor ethical for senior management to undermine PPM and the council as well as strategically important projects by playing a game of arbitrarily cutting X percent from project budgets. The council needs to be wary of interpersonal or interdepartmental competition entering the scene at this point also. In some organizations, individuals with their own particular agenda will ignore committees and processes until implementation time rolls around, and then they attempt to exercise their political power to undermine the results of others' long labors. If this does occur, it is indicative of serious organizational problems and the PPM process will fail until the problems are corrected.

Of course, the process will need to be repeated on a regular basis. The council should determine how often this should be, and, to some extent, it depends on the speed of change in the industry the organization is in. For some industries, quarterly analysis may be best while in slow-moving industries, yearly may be fine. Swanson (2011a) warns, however, that too-frequent reprioritizing of projects can result in confusion and frustration, particularly if resources suddenly are unavailable.

Finally, the process should be flexible and improved continuously. Instinct may suggest ways that the process may be altered to better match the competitive environment, or to reflect more closely the organization's goals. The process should be changed when it is found appropriate to do so, including categories, criteria, steps, the order of tasks, and so on.

Before leaving the subject of project portfolios, it is important to consider the problem of decreasing the size of the organization's investment in projects. The sharp economic downturn of 2008–2009 required a great many firms to do just that, and many were simply not prepared to handle the problem. Senior management, or the project council, should also develop a set of criteria for removing projects from the portfolio. In an interesting short paper, Wheatley (2009) notes that issues such as the size of the expected ROI may be of less importance than the timing of cash in- and outflows. The organization's tolerance for risk is very likely to change during downturns. Some projects are luxuries. Others may be major drivers of future profits and growth. Some may be oriented to cost savings that could have almost immediate benefits. Even projects aimed at meeting legal mandates may have a cost that is significantly higher than the possible legal penalties if the mandates are ignored for a time. Many firms are choosing to pay the penalty instead of implementing costly federal mandates. Some projects can be stopped midway without doing much damage to the project's expected success. Others cannot, and if delayed must start from scratch, or be cancelled.

Developing a list of possible criteria for cutting or eliminating the funding for a project is complicated. To be useful, each item in the list should be prioritized. This is a job that demands close attention from senior management.

A recent summary of PMI's Thought Leadership Series concerning The Power of Portfolio Management (PMI, 2015) concluded with the following points:

- Successful portfolio management requires effective communication and cooperation between those who formulate the strategy and those who execute it.
- Yet, survey respondents also reported that 20 percent of current projects should be terminated, 29 percent receive too few resources, and 19 percent receive too many.
- At a majority of firms, the degree to which C-suite executives follow their own interests and pet projects undermines formal portfolio management.
- Portfolio management maturity correlates to firm success.
- Leading firms connect project execution to strategy fulfillment by aligning projects and programs to the strategy.
- Leading firms also seek simplicity, finding that the less complicated the approach to portfolio management, the more likely the firm can sustain its success.
- Leading firms create a portfolio-oriented culture and develop strong capabilities in portfolio management.

In the next chapter we consider the selection of the appropriate manager for a project and what characteristics are most helpful for such a position. We also address the issue of the project manager's special role, and the demands and responsibilities of this critical position.

Summary

This chapter initiated our discussion of the project management process by first describing organizational project management and the different roles and entities it encompasses. This included the initiation phase, the planning and execution of the project phase, and, finally, the benefit realization and routine use phases. Next, we described procedures for strategically evaluating and selecting projects. We then outlined some criteria for project selection models and discussed the general nature of these models. The chapter described the types of models in use and their advantages and disadvantages. Considering the degree of uncertainty associated with many projects, a section was devoted to evaluating the impact of risk and uncertainty. Concluding the discussion, some general comments were made about data requirements, the use of these models, and how to implement the project portfolio process.

The following specific points were made in this chapter:

- The role of projects in achieving the organization's goals and strategy is critical.

- The eight-step project portfolio process is an effective way to select and manage projects that are tied to the organization's goals.
- Preparatory steps in using a model include (1) identifying the firm's objectives; (2) weighting them relative to each other; and (3) determining the probable impacts of the project on the firm's competitive abilities.
- Project selection models can generally be classified as either numeric or nonnumeric; numeric models are further subdivided into profitability, scoring, window-of-opportunity analysis, and discovery-driven planning categories.
- Nonnumeric models include (1) the sacred cow; (2) the operating necessity; (3) the competitive necessity; and (4) comparative benefit.
- The weighted factor scoring model is the most flexible of the models since it can include monetary, numeric, and nonnumeric factors.

Glossary

Delphi A formalized method for transforming the opinions of a group of individuals into quantitative measures that can be aggregated to use in decision making.

Governance Designing the entities and roles involved in initiating, planning, executing, and routinizing projects.

Maturity The sophistication and experience of an organization in managing multiple projects.

Model A way of looking at reality, usually for the purpose of abstracting and simplifying it, to make it understandable in a particular context.

Organizational project management The systematic management of projects, programs, and portfolios to achieve the strategic goals of an organization.

Portfolio A group or set of projects with varying characteristics.

Pro forma Projected or anticipated, usually applied to financial data such as balance sheets and income statements.

Project portfolio management A procedure for selecting, implementing, and reviewing projects that will help an organization achieve its strategic goals.

Simulation A technique for emulating a process, usually conducted a considerable number of times to understand the process better and measure its outcomes under different policies.

Questions

Material Review Questions

1. Who in the governance structure has the longest serving role?
2. Contrast the competitive necessity model with the operating necessity model. What are the advantages and disadvantages of each?
3. What is a sacred cow? Give some examples.
4. Give an example of a Q-Sort process for project selection.
5. What are some of the limitations of project selection models?
6. Contrast the real options selection approach with profitability models.
7. How does the discounted cash flow method answer some of the criticisms of the payback period method?
8. What are some advantages and disadvantages of the profit/profitability numeric models?
9. What is the desired result of applying project portfolio management? What do firms usually find happens?
10. Describe the discovery-driven planning approach.
11. Describe the project portfolio management process.
12. Describe the various phases of governance for strategic projects and their purpose.
13. Why do many researchers consider the first governance phase to be the most important?

Class Discussion Questions

14. Which of the many purposes of project portfolio management are most important to a firm with a low project management maturity? Which to a firm with high maturity?
15. On what basis does the real options model select projects?
16. What is the difference between profitability and scoring models? Describe a model that could fit both categories.
17. Contrast the window-of-opportunity approach with discovery-driven planning.
18. Discuss how the following project selection models are used in real-world applications. (a) Capital investment with discounted cash flow. (b) Simulation models.
19. Why do you think managers underutilize project selection models?

20. Would uncertainty models be classified as profitability models, scoring models, or some other type of model?

21. Recent research on strategic projects has found that "scope" is much more important than either time or cost. Why do you think so?

22. Are there certain types of projects that are better suited for nonnumeric selection methods as opposed to numeric ones?

23. What important comparisons does the aggregate project plan in Figure 2.3 allow?

24. Which roles in the governance structure do you think are the most well-defined and the least well-defined?

25. If sustainability focuses on long-run profitability, why is it classified as a "nonnumeric" model?

Exercises

1. Two new Internet site projects are proposed to a young start-up company. Project A will cost $250,000 to implement and is expected to have annual net cash flows of $75,000. Project B will cost $150,000 to implement and should generate annual net cash flows of $52,000. The company is very concerned about their cash flow. Using the payback period, which project is better, from a cash flow standpoint?

2. Sean, a new graduate at a telecommunications firm, faces the following problem his first day at the firm: What is the average rate of return for a project that costs $200,000 to implement and has an average annual profit of $30,000?

3. A 4-year financial project has net cash flows of $20,000; $25,000; $30,000; and $50,000 in the next 4 years. It will cost $75,000 to implement the project. If the required rate of return is 0.2, conduct a discounted cash flow calculation to determine the NPV.

4. What would happen to the NPV of the above project if the inflation rate was expected to be 4 percent in each of the next 4 years?

5. A 4-year financial project has estimates of net cash flows shown in the following table:

Year	Net Cash Flow
1	$20,000
2	25,000
3	30,000
4	35,000

It will cost $65,000 to implement the project, all of which must be invested at the beginning of the project. After the fourth year, the project will have no residual value.

Using the most likely estimates of cash flows, conduct a discounted cash flow calculation assuming a 20 percent hurdle rate with no inflation. (You may use either an Excel® or a paper-and-pencil calculation.) What is the discounted profitability index of the project?

6. Use a weighted score model to choose between three projects (A, B, C) for updating an important internal process.

The relative weights for each criterion are shown in the following table as are the scores for each project on each criterion. A score of 1 represents unfavorable, 2 satisfactory, and 3 favorable.

Criterion	Weight	Project A	Project B	Project C
Cost	20	1	2	3
Risk	20	2	3	1
Opportunity	10	2	1	3
Profitability	10	3	3	2
Sustainability	10	2	1	1
Safety	25	1	2	3
Competitiveness	10	2	2	2

7. Develop a spreadsheet for Exercise 6
   a. What would your recommendation be if the weight for the safety went down to 10 and the weight of profitability went up to 25?
   b. Suppose instead that method A received a score of 3 for safety. Would your recommendation change under these circumstances?
   c. The vice president of finance has looked at your original scoring model and feels that tax considerations should be included in the model with a weight of 15. In addition, the VP has scored the methods on tax considerations as follows: method A received a score of 3, method B received a score of 2, and method C received a score of 1. How would this additional information affect your recommendation?

8. Nina is trying to decide in which of four shopping centers to locate her new boutique. Some locations attract a higher class of clientele than others, some are in an indoor mall, some have a much greater customer traffic volume than others, and, of course, rent varies considerably from one location to another. Because of the nature

of her store, she has decided that the class of clientele is the most important consideration, the higher the better. Following this, however, she must pay attention to her expenses and rent is a major item, probably 90 percent as important as clientele. An indoor, temperature-controlled mall is a big help, however, for stores such as hers where 70 percent of sales are from passersby slowly strolling and window shopping. Thus, she rates this as about 95 percent as important as rent. Last, a higher traffic volume of shoppers means more potential sales; she thus rates this factor as 80 percent as important as rent.

As an aid in visualizing her location alternatives, she has constructed the following table. A "good" is scored as 3, "fair" as 2, and "poor" as 1. Use a weighted score model to help Nina come to a decision.

	Location			
	1	2	3	4
Class of clientele	Fair	Good	Poor	Good
Rent	Good	Fair	Poor	Good
Indoor mall	Good	Poor	Good	Poor
Traffic volume	Good	Fair	Good	Poor

9. Referring to Exercise 8, develop a spreadsheet to help Nina select a location for her boutique. Suppose Nina is able to negotiate a lower rent at location 3 and thus raise its ranking to "good." How does this affect the overall rankings of the four locations?

Incidents For Discussion

Portillo, Inc.

Portillo, Inc. is a manufacturer of small household appliances and cooking utensils. Working with Johanna Portillo, the CEO of the firm, her executive team has developed a scoring model to analyze and select new items to be added to the product line. The model is also used to select old items to be dropped from the line. It employs both objective and subjective estimates of scores for the financial and nonfinancial elements that make up the model. The model is used by a Drop/Add Committee she appointed.

Ms. Portillo is pleased with the construct of the model and feels that it includes all of the factors relevant to the drop/add decision. She is also comfortable with the factor weights developed by her executives.

Following a review of the past year's meetings of the Drop/Add Committee, Ms. Portillo discovered that several managers made significant errors when estimating costs and benefits of many projects. After a careful study of the estimates, she noticed that the sponsors of a product seemed to overestimate its benefits and underestimate its costs. It also appeared that other managers might be underestimating benefits and overestimating costs.

She was not sure about her suspicions and wondered how to find out if her notions were correct. Even if they were correct, she wondered what to do about it.

Questions

How can Ms. Portillo find out if her suspicions are correct? What are her options if her idea is supported?

L & M Power

In the next 2 years, a large municipal gas company must begin constructing new gas storage facilities to accommodate the Federal Energy Regulatory Commission's Order 636 deregulating the gas industry. The vice-president in charge of the new project believes there are two options. One option is an underground deep storage facility (UDSF) and the other is a liquefied natural gas facility (LNGF). The vice-president has developed a project selection model and will use it in presenting the project to the president. For the models, she has gathered the following information:

	Initial Cost	Operating Cost/Cu. Ft.	Expected Life	Salvage Value
UDSF	$10,000,000	$0.004	20 years	10%
LNGF	25,000,000	0.002	15	5

Since the vice-president's background is in finance, she believes the best model to use is a financial one, NPV analysis.

Questions

Would you use this model? Why or why not?

Continuing Integrative Class Project

The task for the class here is to select an appropriate project for the course, if one wasn't already selected. Consideration should be given to the fixed end-of-term deadline, the limited monetary but large personnel resources available, the irrelevance of financial returns, and the availability of contacts and good project possibilities outside the classroom. As indicated in Chapter 1, there are often many excellent projects on a college campus, such as in the residence halls, the library, the cafeteria, the medical care office, and so on. When evaluating these situations for potential projects, consider factors such as whether the class has a good inside contact to sponsor the project, whether data will be easily accessible for the class, how many students the organization or department can handle at a time, how extensive the project is, how clear the problem/opportunity is, when they will need an answer, and other such important issues. Design an appropriate governance structure for the project.

Bibliography

Alderton, M. "Anchoring Projects to Strategy." *PM Network*, August 2013.

ANSI/PMI 08-004-2008.

Åstebro, T. "Key Success Factors for Technological Entrepreneurs' R & D Projects." *IEEE Transactions on Engineering Management*, August 2004.

Aubry, M. "Project Management Office Transformations: Direct and Moderating Effects that Enhance Performance and Maturity." *Project Management Journal*, November, 2015.

Aubry, M., H. Sicotte, N. Drouin, H. Vidot-Delerue, and C. Besner. "Organisational Project Management as a Function Within the Organisation", *International Journal of Managing Projects in Business*, Vol. 5, No. 2, pp. 180–194, 2012.

Baker, B. "The Fall of the Firefly: An Assessment of a Failed Project Strategy." *Project Management Journal*, September 2002.

Baker, B., and R. Menon. "Politics and Project Performance: The Fourth Dimension of Project Management." *PM Network*, November 1995.

Beringer, C. D., D. Jonas, and A. Kock. "Behavior of Internal Stakeholders in Project Portfolio Management and Its Impact on Success." *International Journal of Project Management*, Vol. 31, 2013.

Cicmil, S., and D. Hodgson. "New Possibilities for Project Management Theory: A Critical Judgement." *Project Management Journal*, December 2006.

Dalkey, N. C. *The Delphi Method: An Experimental Study of Group Opinion* (RM-5888-PR). Santa Monica, CA: The Rand Corporation, June 1969.

Derby, C., and O. Zwikael. "The Secret of Defining Success." *PM Network*, August 2012.

Dick, B., Sankaran, S., Shaw, K., Kelly, J., Soar, J., Davies, A., and Banbury, A. "Value Co-creation with Stakeholders Using Action Research as a Meta-methodology in a Funded Research Project." *Project Management Journal*, Vol. 46, No. 2, pp. 36–46, 2015.

Doctor, R. N., D. P. Newton, and A. Pearson. "Managing Uncertainty in Research and Development." *Technovation*, February 2001.

Dunn, K. "Research Working Session–Program Management." *PMI Today*, January 2014.

Drouin, N., and K. Jugdev. Standing on the Shoulders of Strategic Management Giants to Advance Organizational Project Management. *International Journal of Managing Projects in Business*, Vol. 7, No.1, pp. 61–77, 2014.

Dvir, D., and A. J. Shenhar. "What Great Projects Have in Common." *MIT Sloan Management Review*, Spring 2011.

Economist, The. *Why Good Strategies Fail: Lessons for the C-Suite*. U.K.: The Economist Intelligence Unit, Ltd., 2013.

Englund, R. L., and R. J. Graham. "From Experience: Linking Projects to Strategy." *Journal of Product Innovation Management*, Vol. 16, No. 1, 1999.

Eskerod, P., M. Huemann, and G. Savage. "Project Stakeholder Management–Past and Present." *Project Management Journal*, December/January, 2015/2016a.

Eskerod, P., M. Huemann, and C. Ringhofer. "Stakeholder Inclusiveness: Enriching Project Management with General Stakeholder Theory." *Project Management Journal*, December/January, 2015/2016b.

Evans, J. R., and S. J. Mantel, Jr. "A New Approach to the Evaluation of Process Innovations." *Technovation*, October 1985.

Frame, J. D. *The New Project Management: Tools for an Age of Rapid Change, Corporate Reengineering, and Other Business Realities*. San Francisco, CA: Jossey-Bass, 1997.

Gale, S. F. "The Real Deal." *PM Network*, December 2009.

Githens, G. "Financial Models, Right Questions, Good Decision." *PM Network*, July 1998.

Ibbs, C. W., and Y. H. Kwak. "Assessing Project Management Maturity." *Project Management Journal*, March 2000.

Jacob, W. F., and Y. H. Kwak. "In Search of Innovative Techniques to Evaluate Pharmaceutical R & D Projects." *Technovation*, April 2003.

Jolly, D. "The Issue of Weightings in Technology Portfolio Management." *Technovation*, May 2003.

Killen, C. P., K. Jugdev, N. Drouin, and Y. Petit. "Advancing Project and Portfolio Management Research: Applying Strategic Management Theories." *International Journal of Project Management*, Vol. 30, No. 5, 2012.

Kloppenborg, T. J., D. Tesch, and C. Manolis. "Project Success and Executive Sponsor Behaviors: Empirical Life Cycle Stage Investigations." *Project Management Journal*, February/March 2014

Kopmann, J., A. Kock, C. P. Killen, and H. G. Gemuenden. "Business Case Control in Project Portfolios: An Empirical Investigation of Performance Consequences and Moderating Effects." *IEEE Transactions on Engineering Management*, Vol. 62, No. 4, 2015.

KPMG, "Global IT Project Management." < http://www.kpmg.com/ >, 2005.

Liberatore, M. J., and G. J. Titus. "The Practice of Management Science in R & D Project Management." *Management Science*, August 1983.

Longman, A., D. Sandahl, and W. Speir. "Preventing Project Proliferation." *PM Network*, July 1999.

Lubianiker, S. "Opening the Book on the Open Maturity Model." *PM Network*, March 2000.

Luehrman, T. A. "Investment Opportunities as Real Options: Getting Started on the Numbers." *Harvard Business Review*, July–August 1998a.

Luehrman, T. A. "Strategy as a Portfolio of Real Options." *Harvard Business Review*, September–October 1998b.

Martinsuo, M. "Portfolio Project Management in Practice and Context." *International Journal of Project Management*, Vol. 31, 2013.

Martinsuo, M., and C. P. Killen. "Value Management in Project Portfolios: Identifying and Assessing Strategic Value." *Project Management Journal*, Vol. 45, October/November 2014.

Matzler, K., and H. H. Hinterhuber. "How to Make Product Development Projects More Successful by Integrating Kano's Model of Customer Satisfaction into Quality Function Deployment." *Technovation*, January 1998.

McGrath, R. G., and I. MacMillan. "Discovery-Driven Planning." *Harvard Business Review*, July–August 1995.

McIntyre, J. "The Right Fit." *PM Network*, November 2006.

Meade, L. M., and A. Presley. "R & D Project Selection Using the Analytic Network Process." *IEEE Transactions on Engineering Management*, February 2002.

Meredith, J. R., S. M. Shafer, and E. Turban. *Quantitative Business Modeling.* Cincinnati, OH: Southwestern, 2002.

Mihalic, J. "From the Board: Leading the Way with Thought Leadership." *PMI Today*, September 2013.

Morgan, M., R. E. Levitt, and W. Malek. Executing Your Strategy: How to Break It Down and Get It Done. Boston: Harvard Business Review Press, 2007.

Müller, R., and J. R. Turner. "The Impact of Principle-Agent Relationship and Contract Type on Communication Between Project Owner and Manager." *International Journal of Project Management*, Vol. 23, p. 348–403, 2005.

Nieto-Rodriguez, A., and Waite, C. J. W. "Requirements Management–Critical to Project Success." *PMI Today*, September 2014.

Patanakul, P., and A. J. Shenhar. "What Project Strategy Really Is: The Fundamental Building Block in Strategic Project Management." *Project Management Journal*, Vol. 43, February 2012.

Pennypacker, J. S., and K. P. Grant. "Project Management Maturity: An Industry Benchmark." *Project Management Journal*, March 2003.

Petite, Y., and B. Hobbs. "Project Portfolios in Dynamic Environments: Sources of Uncertainty and Sensing Mechanisms." *Project Management Journal*, Vol. 41, September 2010.

Pinto, J. K., and D. P. Slevin. "Critical Factors in Successful Project Implementation." *IEEE Transactions on Engineering Management*, February 1987.

Pitsis, T.S., Sankaran, S., Gudergan, S., and Clegg, S. "Governing Projects Under Complexity: Theory and Practice in Project Management." *International Journal of Project Management*, Vol. 32, No. 8, p. 1285–1290, 2014.

Project Management Institute. "The Power of Portfilio Management." *PMI Today*, December 2015.

Project Management Institute. *Implementing Organizational Project Management: A Practice Guide.* Newtown Square, PA: Project Management Institute, 2014.

Project Management Institute. *A Guide to the Project Management Body of Knowledge*, 5th ed. Newtown Square, PA: Project Management Institute, 2013.

Project Management Institute. "Survey Reveals How Organizations Succeed." *PMI Today*, February 2011.

Remy, R. "Adding Focus to Improvement Efforts with PM[3]." *PM Network*, July 1997.

Rice, M. P., G. C. O'Connor, and R. Pierantozzi. "Implementing a Learning Plan to Counter Project Uncertainty." *Sloan Management Review*, Winter 2008.

Ross, S. A., R. W. Westerfield, and B. D. Jordan. *Fundamentals of Corporate Finance*, 8th ed. New York: Irwin/McGraw-Hill, 2008.

Saaty, T. S. *Decision for Leaders: The Analytic Hierarchy Process.* Pittsburgh, PA: University of Pittsburgh, 1990.

Sanchez, H., and B. Robert. "Measuring Portfolio Strategic Performance Using Key Performance Indicators." *Project Management Journal*, Vol. 41, December, 2010.

Swanson, S. A. "Perfect Alignment." *PM Network*, November 2011a.

Swanson, S. A. "All Things Considered." *PM Network*, February 2011b.

Teller, J., and A. Kock. "An Empirical Investigation on How Portfolio Risk Management Influences Project Portfolio Success." *International Journal of Project Management*, Vol. 31, 2013.

Thomas, J., C. L. Delisle, K. Jugdev, and P. Buckle. "Mission Possible: Selling Project Management to Senior Executives." *PM Network*, January 2001.

Turner, J. R., and A. Keegan. "Mechanisms of Governance in the Project-Based Organization: Roles of the Broker and Steward." *European Management Journal*, Vol. 19, No. 3, 2001.

Turban, E., and J. R. Meredith. *Fundamentals of Management Science*, 6th ed. Homewood, IL: Irwin, 1994.

Wheatley, M., "Making the Cut." *PM Network*, June 2009.

Wheelwright, S. C., and K. B. Clark. "Creating Project Plans to Focus Product Development." *Harvard Business Review*, March–April 1992.

Wikipedia. https://en.wikipedia.org/wiki/Organizational_project_management (accessed January 2017).

Zou, W., M. Kumaraswamy, J. Chung, and J. Wong. "Identifying the Critical Success Factors for Relationship Management in PPP Projects." *International Journal of Project Management*, Vol. 32, No. 2, p. 265–274, 2014.

Zwikael, O., and J. Smyrk. "Planning Effort as an Effective Risk Management Tool." *Journal of Operations Management*, Vol. 25, p. 755–767, 2007.

Zwikael, O., and J. Smyrk. "Project Governance: Balancing Control and Trust in Dealing with Risk." *International Journal of Project Management*, Vol. 33, p. 852–862, 2015.

The following case concerns a European firm trying to choose between almost a dozen capital investment projects being championed by different executives in the firm. However, there are many more projects available for funding than there are funds available to implement them, so the set must be narrowed down to the most valuable and important to the firm. Financial, strategic, and other data are given concerning the projects in order to facilitate the analysis needed to make a final investment recommendation to the Board of Directors.

Case

Pan-Europa Foods S.A.*   C. Opitz and R. F. Bruner

It was early January, and the senior-management committee of Pan-Europa Foods was to meet to draw up the firm's capital budget for the new year. Up for consideration were 11 major projects that totaled over €208 million (euros). Unfortunately, the board of directors had imposed a spending limit of only €80 million; even so, investment at that rate would represent a major increase in the firm's asset base of €656 million. Thus the challenge for the senior managers of Pan-Europa was to allocate funds among a range of compelling projects: new-product introduction, acquisition, market expansion, efficiency improvements, preventive maintenance, safety, and pollution control.

The Company

Pan-Europa Foods, headquartered in Brussels, Belgium, was a multinational producer of high-quality ice cream, yogurt, bottled water, and fruit juices. Its products were sold throughout Scandinavia, Britain, Belgium, the Netherlands, Luxembourg, western Germany, and northern France (see Exhibit 1 for a map of the company's marketing region).

The company was founded in 1924 by Theo Verdin, a Belgian farmer, as an offshoot of his dairy business. Through keen attention to product development, and shrewd marketing, the business grew steadily over the years. The company went public in 1979 and by 1993 was listed for trading on the London, Frankfurt, and Brussels exchanges. Last year Pan-Europa had sales of almost €1.1 billion.

Ice cream accounted for 60 percent of the company's revenues; yogurt, which was introduced in 1982, contributed about 20 percent. The remaining 20 percent of sales was divided equally between bottled water and fruit juices. Pan-Europa's flagship brand name was "Rolly," which was represented by a fat, dancing bear in farmers' clothing. Ice cream, the company's leading product, had a loyal base of customers who sought out its high butterfat content, large chunks of chocolate, fruit, nuts, and wide range of original flavors.

Recently, Pan-Europa sales had been static (see Exhibit 2), which management attributed to low population growth in northern Europe and market saturation in some areas. Outside observers, however, faulted recent failures in new-product introductions. Most members of management wanted to expand the

*Reprinted with permission. Copyright Darden Graduate Business School Foundation, Charlottesville, Virginia.

company's market presence and introduce more new products to boost sales. These managers hoped that increased market presence and sales would improve the company's market value. Pan-Europa's stock was currently at eight times earnings, just below book value. This price/earnings ratio was below the trading multiples of comparable companies, but it gave little value to the company's brands.

Resource Allocation

The capital budget at Pan-Europa was prepared annually by a committee of senior managers who then presented it for approval by the board of directors. The committee consisted of five managing directors, the *président directeur-général* (PDG), and the finance director. Typically, the PDG solicited investment proposals from the managing directors. The proposals included a brief project description, a financial analysis, and a discussion of strategic or other qualitative considerations.

As a matter of policy, investment proposals at Pan-Europa were subjected to two financial tests, payback and internal rate of return (IRR). The tests, or hurdles, had been established by the management committee and varied according to the type of project:

Type of Project	Minimum Acceptable IRR	Maximum Acceptable Payback Years
1. New product or new markets	12%	6 years
2. Product or market extension	10%	5 years
3. Efficiency improvements	8%	4 years
4. Safety or environmental	No test	No test

The most recent estimated weighted-average cost of capital (WACC) for Pan-Europa was 10.5 percent. In describing the capital-budgeting process, the finance director, Trudi Lauf, said, "We use the sliding scale of IRR tests as a way of recognizing differences in risk among the various types of projects. Where the company takes more risk, we should earn more return. The payback test signals that we are not prepared to wait for long to achieve that return."

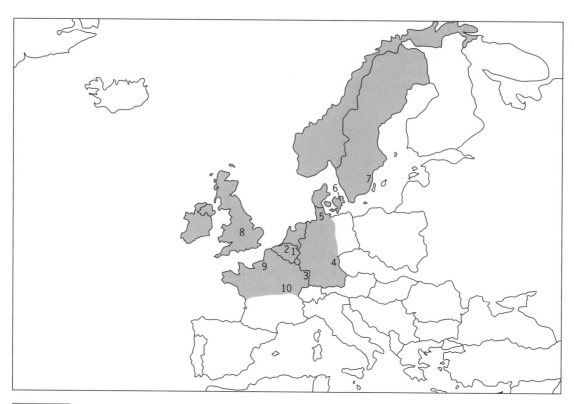

EXHIBIT 1 Pan-Europa Foods S. A. Nations Where Pan-Europa Competed

Note: The shaded area in this map reveals the principal distribution region of Pan-Europa's products. Important facilities are indicated by the following figures:

1. Headquarters, Brussels, Belgium
2. Plant, Antwerp, Belgium
3. Plant, Strasbourg, France
4. Plant, Nuremberg, Germany
5. Plant, Hamburg, Germany
6. Plant, Copenhagen, Denmark
7. Plant, Svald, Sweden
8. Plant, Nelly-on-Mersey, England
9. Plant, Caen, France
10. Plant, Melun, France

Fiscal Years Ending December 31			
	Previous Year	Last Year	This Year
Gross sales	1,076	1,072	1,074
Net income	51	49	37
Earnings per share	0.75	0.72	0.54
Dividends	20	20	20
Total assets	477	580	656
Shareholders' equity (book value)	182	206	235
Shareholders' equity (market value)	453	400	229

EXHIBIT 2 Summary of Financial Results (all values in € millions except per-share amounts)

Ownership and the Sentiment of Creditors and Investors

Pan-Europa's 12-member board of directors included three members of the Verdin family, four members of management, and five outside directors who were prominent managers or public figures in northern Europe. Members of the Verdin family combined owned 20 percent of Pan-Europa's shares outstanding, and company executives owned 10 percent of the shares. Venus Asset Management, a mutual-fund management company in London, held 12 percent. Banque du Bruges et des Pays Bas held 9 percent and had one representative on the board of directors. The remaining 49 percent of the firm's shares were widely held. The firm's shares traded in London, Brussels, and Frankfurt.

At a debt-to-equity ratio of 125 percent, Pan-Europa was leveraged much more highly than its peers in the European consumer-foods industry. Management had relied on debt financing significantly in the past few years to sustain the firm's capital spending and dividends during a period of price wars initiated by Pan-Europa. Now, with the price wars finished, Pan-Europa's bankers (led by Banque du Bruges) strongly urged an aggressive program of debt reduction. In any event, they were not prepared to finance increases in leverage beyond the current level. The president of Banque du Bruges had remarked at a recent board meeting,

> *Restoring some strength to the right-hand side of the balance sheet should now be a first priority. Any expansion of assets should be financed from the cash flow after debt amortization until the debt ratio returns to a more prudent level. If there are crucial investments that cannot be funded this way, then we should cut the dividend!*

At a price-to-earnings ratio of eight times, shares of Pan-Europa common stock were priced below the average multiples of peer companies and the average multiples of all companies on the exchanges where Pan-Europa was traded. This was attributable to the recent price wars, which had suppressed the company's profitability, and to the well-known recent failure of the company to seize significant market share with a new product line of flavored mineral water. Since last year, all of the major securities houses had been issuing "sell" recommendations to investors in Pan-Europa shares. Venus Asset Management in London had quietly accumulated shares during this period, however, in the expectation of a turnaround in the firm's performance. At the most recent board meeting, the senior managing director of Venus gave a presentation in which he said,

> *Cutting the dividend is unthinkable, as it would signal a lack of faith in your own future. Selling new shares of stock at this depressed price level is also unthinkable, as it would impose unacceptable dilution on your current shareholders. Your equity investors expect an improvement in performance. If that improvement is not forthcoming, or worse, if investors' hopes are dashed, your shares might fall into the hands of raiders like Carlo de Benedetti or the Flick brothers.[1]*

At the conclusion of the most recent meeting of the directors, the board voted unanimously to limit capital spending in the next year to €80 million.

Members of the Senior Management Committee

The capital budget would be prepared by seven senior managers of Pan-Europa. For consideration, each project had to be sponsored by one of the managers present. Usually the decision process included a period of discussion followed by a vote on two

to four alternative capital budgets. The various executives were well known to each other:

Wilhelmina Verdin (Belgian), PDG, age 57. Granddaughter of the founder and spokesperson on the board of directors for the Verdin family's interests. Worked for the company her entire career, with significant experience in brand management. Elected "European Marketer of the Year" in 1982 for successfully introducing low-fat yogurt and ice cream, the first major roll-out of this type of product. Eager to position the company for long-term growth but cautious in the wake of recent difficulties.

Trudi Lauf (Swiss), finance director, age 51. Hired from Nestlé to modernize financial controls and systems. Had been a vocal proponent of reducing leverage on the balance sheet. Also had voiced the concerns and frustrations of stockholders.

Heinz Klink (German), managing director for Distribution, age 49. Oversaw the transportation, warehousing, and order-fulfillment activities in the company. Spoilage, transport costs, stock-outs, and control systems were perennial challenges.

Maarten Leyden (Dutch), managing director for Production and Purchasing, age 59. Managed production operations at the company's 14 plants. Engineer by training. Tough negotiator, especially with unions and suppliers. A fanatic about production-cost control. Had voiced doubts about the sincerity of creditors' and investors' commitment to the firm.

Marco Ponti (Italian), managing director for Sales, age 45. Oversaw the field sales force of 250 representatives and planned changes in geographical sales coverage. The most vocal proponent of rapid expansion on the senior-management committee. Saw several opportunities for ways to improve geographical positioning. Hired from Unilever to revitalize the sales organization, which he successfully accomplished.

Fabienne Morin (French), managing director for Marketing, age 41. Responsible for marketing research, new-product development, advertising, and, in general, brand management. The primary advocate of the recent price war, which, although financially difficult, realized solid gains in market share. Perceived a "window of opportunity" for product and market expansion and tended to support growth-oriented projects.

Nigel Humbolt (British), managing director for Strategic Planning, age 47. Hired 2 years previously from a well-known consulting firm to set up a strategic-planning staff for Pan-Europa. Known for asking -difficult and challenging questions about Pan-Europa's core business, its maturity, and profitability. Supported initiatives aimed at growth and market share. Had presented the most aggressive proposals in 1992, none of which were accepted. Becoming frustrated with what he perceived to be his lack of influence in the organization.

---

[1]De Benedetti of Milan and the Flick brothers of Munich were leaders of prominent hostile-takeover attempts in recent years.

The Expenditure Proposals

The forthcoming meeting would entertain the following proposals (*see summary table also*):

1. **Replacement and expansion of the truck fleet** Heinz Klink proposed to purchase 100 new refrigerated tractor trailer trucks, 50 this year and another 50 next year. By doing so, the company could sell 60 old, fully depreciated trucks over the two years for a total of €1.2 million. The purchase would expand the fleet by 40 trucks within two years. Each of the new trailers would be larger than the old trailers and afford a 15 percent increase in cubic meters of goods hauled on each trip. The new tractors would also be more fuel and maintenance efficient. The increase in number of trucks would permit more flexible scheduling and more efficient routing and servicing of the fleet than at present and would cut delivery times and, therefore, possibly inventories. It would also allow more frequent deliveries to the company's major markets, which would reduce the loss of sales caused by stock-outs. Finally, expanding the fleet would support geographical expansion over the long term. As shown in Exhibit 3, the total net investment in trucks of €20 million and the increase in working capital to support added maintenance, fuel, payroll, and inventories of €2 million was expected to yield total cost savings and added sales potential of €7.7 million over the next seven years. The resulting IRR was estimated to be 7.8 percent, marginally below the minimum 8 percent required return on efficiency projects. Some of the managers wondered if this project would be more properly classified as "efficiency" than "expansion."

Project	Expenditure (€ millions)	Sponsoring Manager
1. Replacement and expansion of the truck fleet	22	Klink, Distribution
2. A new plant	30	Leyden, Production
3. Expansion of a plant	10	Leyden, Production
4. Development and introduction of new artificially sweetened yogurt and ice cream	15	Morin, Marketing
5. Plant automation and conveyor systems	14	Leyden, Production
6. Effluent water treatment at four plants	4	Leyden, Production
7. Market expansion eastward	20	Ponti, Sales
8. Market expansion southward	20	Ponti, Sales
9. Development and roll-out of snack foods	18	Morin, Marketing
10. Networked, computer-based inventory-control system for warehouses and field representatives	15	Klink, Distribution
11. Acquisition of a leading schnapps brand and associated facilities	40	Humbolt, Strategic Planning

2. **A new plant** Maarten Leyden noted that Pan-Europa's yogurt and ice-cream sales in the southeastern region of the company's market were about to exceed the capacity of its Melun, France, manufacturing and packaging plant. At present, some of the demand was being met by shipments from the company's newest, most efficient facility, located in Strasbourg, France. Shipping costs over that distance were high, however, and some sales were undoubtedly being lost when the marketing effort could not be supported by delivery. Leyden proposed that a new manufacturing and packaging plant be built in Dijon, France, just at the current southern edge of Pan-Europa's marketing region, to take the burden off the Melun and Strasbourg plants.

The cost of this plant would be €25 million and would entail €5 million for working capital. The €14 million worth of equipment would be amortized over seven years, and the plant over ten years. Through an increase in sales and depreciation, and the decrease in delivery costs, the plant was expected to yield after-tax cash flows totaling €23.75 million and an IRR of 11.3 percent over the next ten years. This project would be classified as a market extension.

3. **Expansion of a plant** In addition to the need for greater production capacity in Pan-Europa's southeastern region, its Nuremberg, Germany, plant had reached full capacity. This situation made the scheduling of routine equipment maintenance difficult, which, in turn, created production scheduling and deadline problems. This plant was one of two highly automated facilities that produced Pan-Europa's entire line of bottled water, mineral water, and fruit juices. The Nuremberg plant supplied central and western Europe. (The other plant, near Copenhagen, Denmark, supplied Pan-Europa's northern European markets.)

The Nuremberg plant's capacity could be expanded by 20 percent for €10 million. The equipment (€7 million) would be depreciated over seven years, and the plant over ten years. The increased capacity was expected to result in

Project	1	2	3	4	5	7	8	9	10	11
	Expand Truck Fleet (note 3)	New Plant	Expanded Plant	Artificial Sweetener	Automation and Conveyer Systems	Eastward Expansion (note 5)	Southward Expansion (note 5)	Snack Foods	Inventory-Control System	Strategic Acquisition (note 6)
Investment										
Property	20.00	25.00	10.00	15.00	14.00	20.00	20.00	15.00	15.00	30.00
Working Capital	2.00	5.00					20.00	3.00	15.00	10.00
Year					EXPECTED FREE CASH FLOWS (note 4)					
	(11.40)	(30.00)	(10.00)	(5.00)	(14.00)	(20.00)	(20.00)	(18.00)	(12.00)	(15.00)
1	(7.90)	2.00	1.25	(5.00)	2.75	3.50	3.00	3.00	5.50	(20.00)
2	3.00	5.00	1.50	(5.00)	2.75	4.00	3.50	4.00	5.50	5.00
3	3.50	5.50	1.75	3.00	2.75	4.50	4.00	4.50	5.00	9.00
4	4.00	6.00	2.00	3.00	2.75	5.00	4.50	5.00		11.00
5	4.50	6.25	2.25	4.00	2.75	5.50	5.00	5.00		13.00
6	5.00	6.50	2.50	4.50	2.75	6.00	5.50	5.00		15.00
7	7.00	6.75	1.50	5.00	2.75	6.50	6.00	5.00		17.00
8		5.00	1.50	5.50		7.00	6.50	5.00		19.00
9		5.25	1.50	6.00		7.50	7.00	5.00		21.00
10		5.50	1.50	6.50		8.00	7.50	5.00		59.00
Undiscounted Sum	7.70	23.75	7.25	22.50	5.25	37.50	32.50	28.50	4.00	134.00
Payback (years)	6	6	6	7	6	5	6	5	3	5
Maximum Payback Accepted	4	5	5	6	4	6	6	6	4	6
IRR	7.8%	11.3%	11.2%	17.3%	8.7%	21.4%	18.8%	20.5%	16.2%	28.7%
Minimum Accepted ROR	8.0%	10.0%	10.0%	12.0%	8.0%	12.0%	12.0%	12.0%	8.0%	12.0%
Spread	−0.2%	1.3%	1.2%	5.3%	0.7%	9.4%	6.8%	8.5%	8.2%	16.7%
NPV at Corp. WACC (10.5%)	−1.92	0.99	0.28	5.21	−0.87	11.99	9.00	8.95	1.16	47.97
NPV at Minimum ROR	−0.13	1.87	0.55	3.88	0.32	9.90	7.08	7.31	1.78	41.43
Equivalent Annuity[2]	−0.02	0.30	0.09	0.69	0.06	1.75	1.25	1.29	0.69	7.33

[1]The effluent treatment program is not included in this exhibit.

[2]The equivalent annuity of a project is that level annual payment over 10 years that yields a net present value equal to the NPV at the minimum required rate of return for that project. Annuity corrects for differences in duration among various projects. For instance, project 5 lasts only 7 years and has an NPV of 0.32 million; a 10-year stream of annual cash flows of 0.05 million, discounted at 8.0 percent (the required rate of return) also yields an NPV of 0.32 million. In ranking projects on the basis of equivalent annuity, bigger annuities create more investor wealth than smaller annuities.

[3]This reflects €11 million spent both initially and at the end of year 1.

[4]Free cash flow = incremental profit or cost savings after taxes + depreciation − investment in fixed assets and working capital.

[5]Franchisees would gradually take over the burden of carrying receivables and inventory.

[6]€15 million would be spent in the first year, 20 million in the second, and 5 million in the third.

EXHIBIT 3 Free Cash Flows and Analysis of Proposed Projects[1] (all values in € millions)

additional production of up to €1.5 million per year, yielding an IRR of 11.2 percent. This project would be classified as a market extension.

4. **Development and introduction of new artificially sweetened yogurt and ice cream** Fabienne Morin noted that recent developments in the synthesis of artificial sweeteners were showing promise of significant cost savings to food and beverage producers as well as stimulating growing demand for low-calorie products. The challenge was to create the right flavor to complement or enhance the other ingredients. For ice-cream manufacturers, the difficulty lay in creating a balance that would result in the same flavor as was obtained when using natural sweeteners; artificial sweeteners might, of course, create a superior taste.

€15 million would be needed to commercialize a yogurt line that had received promising results in laboratory tests. This cost included acquiring specialized production facilities, working capital, and the cost of the initial product introduction. The overall IRR was estimated to be 17.3 percent.

Morin stressed that the proposal, although highly uncertain in terms of actual results, could be viewed as a means of protecting present market share, because other high-quality ice-cream producers carrying out the same research might introduce these products; if the Rolly brand did not carry an artificially sweetened line and its competitors did, the Rolly brand might suffer. Morin also noted the parallels between innovating with artificial sweeteners and the company's past success in introducing low-fat products. This project would be classed in the new-product category of investments.

5. **Plant automation and conveyor systems** Maarten Leyden also requested €14 million to increase automation of the production lines at six of the company's older plants. The result would be improved throughput speed and reduced accidents, spillage, and production tie-ups. The last two plants the company had built included conveyer systems that eliminated the need for any heavy lifting by employees. The systems reduced the chance of injury to employees; at the six older plants, the company had sustained an average of 75 missed worker-days per year per plant in the last 2 years because of muscle injuries sustained in heavy lifting. At an average hourly wage of €14.00 per hour, over €150,000 per year was thus lost, and the possibility always existed of more serious injuries and lawsuits. Overall cost savings and depreciation totaling €2.75 million per year for the project were expected to yield an IRR of 8.7 percent. This project would be classed in the efficiency category.

6. **Effluent water treatment at four plants** Pan-Europa preprocessed a variety of fresh fruits at its Melun and Strasbourg plants. One of the first stages of processing involved cleaning the fruit to remove dirt and pesticides. The dirty water was simply sent down the drain and into the Seine or Rhine rivers. Recent European Community directives called for any waste water containing even slight traces of poisonous chemicals to be treated at the sources and gave companies 4 years to comply. As an environmentally oriented project, this proposal fell outside the normal financial tests of project attractiveness. Leyden noted, however, that the water-treatment equipment could be purchased today for €4 million; he speculated that the same equipment would cost €10 million in 4 years when immediate conversion became mandatory. In the intervening time, the company would run the risks that European Community regulators would shorten the compliance time or that the company's pollution record would become public and impair the image of the company in the eyes of the consumer. This project would be classed in the environmental category.

7. **and** 8. **Market expansions eastward and southward** Marco Ponti recommended that the company expand its market eastward to include eastern Germany, Poland, Czechoslovakia, and Austria and/or southward to include southern France, Switzerland, Italy, and Spain. He believed the time was right to expand sales of ice cream, and perhaps yogurt, geographically. In theory, the company could sustain expansions in both directions simultaneously, but practically, Ponti doubted that the sales and distribution organizations could sustain both expansions at once.

Each alternative geographical expansion had its benefits and risks. If the company expanded eastward, it could reach a large population with a great appetite for frozen dairy products, but it would also face more competition from local and regional ice-cream manufacturers. Moreover, consumers in eastern Germany, Poland, and Czechoslovakia did not have the purchasing power that consumers did to the south. The eastward expansion would have to be supplied from plants in Nuremberg, Strasbourg, and Hamburg.

Looking southward, the tables were turned: more purchasing power and less competition but also a smaller consumer appetite for ice cream and yogurt. A southward expansion would require building consumer demand for premium-quality yogurt and ice cream. If neither of the plant proposals (i.e., proposals 2 and 3) were accepted, then the southward expansion would need to be supplied from plants in Melun, Strasbourg, and Rouen.

The initial cost of either proposal was €20 million of working capital. The bulk of this project's costs was expected to involve the financing of distributorships, but over the 10-year forecast period, the distributors would gradually take over the burden of carrying receivables and inventory. Both expansion proposals assumed the rental of suitable warehouse and distribution facilities. The after-tax cash flows were expected to total €37.5 million for eastward expansion and €32.5 million for southward expansion.

Marco Ponti pointed out that eastward expansion meant a higher possible IRR but that moving southward was a less risky proposition. The projected IRRs were 21.4 percent and 18.8 percent for eastern and southern expansion, respectively. These projects would be classed in the new market category.

9. **Development and roll-out of snack foods** Fabienne Morin suggested that the company use the excess capacity at its Antwerp spice and nut-processing facility to produce a line of dried fruits to be test-marketed in Belgium, Britain, and the Netherlands. She noted the strength of the Rolly brand in those countries and the success of other food and

beverage companies that had expanded into snack food production. She argued that Pan-Europa's reputation for wholesome, quality products would be enhanced by a line of dried fruits and that name association with the new product would probably even lead to increased sales of the company's other products among health-conscious consumers.

Equipment and working-capital investments were expected to total €15 million and €3 million, respectively, for this project. The equipment would be depreciated over 7 years. Assuming the test market was successful, cash flows from the project would be able to support further plant expansions in other strategic locations. The IRR was expected to be 20.5 percent, well above the required return of 12 percent for new-product projects.

10. Networked, computer-based inventory-control system for warehouses and field representatives. Heinz klink had pressed for three years unsuccessfully for a state-of-the-art computer-based inventory-control system that would link field sales representatives, distributors, drivers, warehouses, and even possibly retailers. The benefits of such a system would be shortening delays in ordering and order processing, better control of inventory, reduction of spoilage, and faster recognition of changes in demand at the customer level. Klink was reluctant to quantify these benefits, because they could range between modest and quite large amounts. This year, for the first time, he presented a cash-flow forecast, however, that reflected an initial outlay of €12 million for the system, followed by €3 million in the next year for ancillary equipment. The inflows reflected depreciation tax shields, tax credits, cost reductions in ware-housing, and reduced inventory. He forecasted these benefits to last for only three years. Even so, the project's IRR was estimated to be 16.2 percent. This project would be classed in the efficiency category of proposals.

11. **Acquisition of a leading schnapps brand and associated facilities** Nigel Humbolt had advocated making diversifying acquisitions in an effort to move beyond the company's mature core business but doing so in a way that exploited the company's skills in brand management. He had explored six possible related industries, in the general field of consumer packaged goods, and determined that cordials and liqueurs offered unusual opportunities for real growth and, at the same time, market protection through branding. He had identified four small producers of well-established brands of liqueurs as acquisition candidates. Following exploratory talks with each, he had determined that only one company could be purchased in the near future, namely, the leading private European manufacturer of schnapps, located in Munich.

The proposal was expensive: €15 million to buy the company and €25 million to renovate the company's facilities completely while simultaneously expanding distribution to new geographical markets.[2] The expected returns were high: after-tax cash flows were projected to be €134 million, yielding an IRR of 28.7 percent. This project would be classed in the new-product category of proposals.

Conclusion

Each member of the management committee was expected to come to the meeting prepared to present and defend a proposal for the allocation of Pan-Europa's capital budget of €80 million. Exhibit 3 summarizes the various projects in terms of their free cash flows and the investment–performance criteria.

Questions

1. Strategically, what must Pan-Europa do to keep from becoming the victim of a hostile takeover? What rows/categories in Exhibit 2 will thus become critically important this coming year? What should Pan-Europa do now that they have won the price war? Who should lead the way for Pan-Europa?

2. Using NPV, conduct a straight financial analysis of the investment alternatives and rank the projects. Which NPV of the three should be used? Why? Suggest a way to evaluate the effluent project.

3. What aspects of the projects might invalidate the ranking you just derived? How should we correct for each investment's time value of money, unequal lifetimes, riskiness, and size?

4. Reconsider the projects in terms of:
   - are any "must do" projects of the nonnumeric type?
   - what elements of the projects might imply greater or lesser riskiness?
   - might there be any synergies or conflicts between the projects?
   - do any of the projects have nonquantitative benefits or costs that should be considered in an evaluation?

5. Considering all the above, what screens/factors might you suggest to narrow down the set of most desirable projects? What criteria would you use to evaluate the projects on these various factors? Do any of the projects fail to pass these screens due to their extreme values on some of the factors?

6. Divide the projects into the four project categories of derivative, platform, breakthrough, and R&D. Draw an aggregate project plan and array the projects on the chart.

7. Based on all the above, which projects should the management committee recommend to the Board of Directors?

The following reading describes the approach Hewlett-Packard uses to select and monitor its projects for relevance to the firm's strategic goals. The article describes the behavioral aspects of the process as well as many of the technical tools, such as the aggregate project plan, the plan of record, and the software aids they employed. In addition, the authors give tips and identify pitfalls in the process so anyone else implementing their approach will know what problems to watch out for.

---

[2]Exhibit 3 shows negative cash flows amounting to only €35 million. The difference between this amount and the €40 million requested is a positive operating cash flow of €5 million in year 1 expected from the normal course of business.

Reading

From Experience: Linking Projects To Strategy*   R. L. Englund and R. J. Graham

Growth in organizations typically results from successful projects that generate new products, services, or procedures. Managers are increasingly concerned about getting better results from the projects under way in their organizations and in getting better cross-organizational cooperation. One of the most vocal complaints of project managers is that projects appear almost randomly. The projects seem unlinked to a coherent strategy, and people are unaware of the total number and scope of projects. As a result, people feel they are working at cross-purposes, on too many unneeded projects, and on too many projects generally. Selecting projects for their strategic emphasis helps resolve such feelings and is a corner anchor in putting together the pieces of a puzzle that create an environment for successful projects [6].

This article covers a series of steps for linking projects to strategy. These steps constitute a process that can be applied to any endeavor. Included throughout are suggestions for action as well as guidelines to navigate many pitfalls along the path. Process tools help illustrate ways to prioritize projects. The lessons learned are from consulting with many firms over a long time period and from personal experiences in applying the lessons within Hewlett-Packard Company (HP), a $40 billion plus company where two-thirds of its revenue derives from products introduced within the past 2 years.

The Importance of Upper Management Teamwork

Developing cooperation across an organization requires that upper managers take a systems approach to projects. That means they look at projects as a system of interrelated activities that combine to achieve a common goal. The common goal is to fulfill the overall strategy of the organization. Usually all projects draw from one resource pool, so they interrelate as they share the same resources. Thus, the system of projects is itself a project, with the smaller projects being the activities that lead to the larger project (organizational) goal.

Any lack of upper management teamwork reverberates throughout the organization. If upper managers do not model desired behaviors, there is little hope that the rest of the organization can do it for them. Any lack of upper management cooperation will surely be reflected in the behavior of project teams, and there is little chance that project managers alone can resolve the problems that arise.

A council concept is one mechanism used at HP to establish a strategic direction for projects spanning organizational boundaries. A council may be permanent or temporary, assembled to solve strategic issues. As a result, a council typically will involve upper managers. Usually its role is to set

directions, manage multiple projects or a set of projects, and aid in cross-organizational issue resolution. Several of these council-like activities become evident through the examples in this article.

Employing a comprehensive and systematic approach illustrates the vast and important influence of upper management teamwork on project success. Increasingly evident are companies who initiate portfolio selection committees. We suggest that organizations begin by developing councils to work with project managers and to implement strategy. These councils exercise leadership by articulating a vision, discussing it with the project managers, asking them their concerns about and needs for implementing the strategy, listening carefully to them, and showing them respect so they become engaged in the process. In this way, upper managers and project managers develop the joint vision that is so necessary for implementation of strategy.

Process for Project Selection and Prioritization

Once the upper management team is established, they can follow a process to select sets of projects that achieve organizational goals. They are then ideally positioned to implement consistent priorities across all departments. Figure 1 represents a mental model of a way to structure this process. Outputs from the four steps interrelate in a true systems approach. This model comes from experience in researching and applying a thorough approach to all the issues encountered in a complex organization. It is both simple in concept and complex in richness. The authors use the model both as an educational tool and to facilitate management teams through the process.

What the Organization Should Do and How to Know When You Are Doing It

First, identify who is leading the process and who should be on the management team. More time spent here putting together a "mission impossible" team pays dividends later by getting up-front involvement of the people who will be affected by the decisions that will be made. Take care not to overlook any key-but-not-so-visible players who later may speak up and jeopardize the plan. This team may consist solely of upper managers or may include project managers, a general manager, and possibly a customer. Include representation of those who can best address the key opportunities and risks facing the organization. Ideally they control the resources and are empowered to make decisions on all projects. The leader needs to get explicit commitment from all these people to participate actively in the process and to use the resulting plan when making related decisions. Be aware that behavioral issues become super urgent. This process hits close to home and may have a severe impact on projects that people care personally about. Uncertainty and doubt are created if management does not tread carefully and pay attention to people concerns.

The team begins by listing all projects proposed and under way in the organization. Many times this step is a revelation

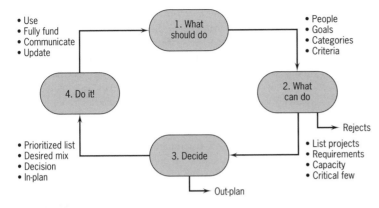

FIGURE 1 A systematic approach to selecting projects.

in itself. A usual reaction is, "I didn't realize we had so many projects going on." The intent is to survey the field of work and begin the organizing effort, so avoid going into detailed discussion about specific projects at this point.

The team clarifies or develops the goals expected from projects. Be careful not to get constrained through considering only current capabilities. Many teams get sidetracked by statements such as "We don't know how to do that," effectively curtailing discussion on whether the organization ought to pursue the goal and develop or acquire the capability. Rather, the discussions at this stage center around organizational purpose, vision, and mission. This is a crucial step that determines if the rest of the project selection process can be successful. In the authors' experience, those organizations with clear, convincing, and compelling visions about what they should be doing move ahead rapidly. Any lack of understanding or commitment to the vision by a member of the team leads to frustration, wheel spinning, and eventual disintegration of the whole process. This pattern is so prevalent that clarity of the goal or strategy is applied as a filter before agreeing to facilitate teams through the process.

Organize the projects into categories that will later make it easier to facilitate a decision-making process. Wheelwright and Clark [14] suggest using grids where the axes are the extent of product change and the extent of process change. Some organizations use market segments. The benefit to this effort is that seeing all projects and possible projects on a continuum allows checking for completeness, gaps, opportunities, and compliance with strategy. This might also be a good time to encourage "out-of-the-box" thinking about new ways to organize the work. Use creative discussion sessions to capture ideas about core competences, competitive advantage, and the like to determine a set of categories most effective for the organization. For example, the categories might be:

Evolutionary or derivative—sustaining, incremental, enhancing.

Platform—next generation, highly leveraged.

Revolutionary or breakthrough—new core product, process, or business.

The actual products in Figure 2 were introduced to the market over time in alphabetical order and positioning shown. Although the figure represents a retrospective view, it illustrates a successful strategy of sequencing projects and products. There is a balanced mix of breakthrough products, such as A, followed by enhancements, B through E, before moving on to new platforms, F through H, and eventually developing a new architecture and product family with L. At the time, this strategy was improvisational [1]; it now represents a learning opportunity for planning new portfolios. No one area of the grid is overpopulated, and where large projects exist there are not too many of them.

Another reason to organize projects into these "strategic buckets" is to better realize what business(es) the organization is in. Almost every group the authors work with get caught in the "tyranny of the OR" instead of embracing the "genius of the AND" [1997]. In trying to do too many projects and facing the need to make trade-offs among them, the decision becomes *this* OR *that*. In reality, most organizations need a balanced portfolio that creates complete solutions for their customers. They need to do *this* AND *that*. The way to achieve this goal is to set limits on the size of each category and then focus efforts on selecting the best set of projects within each category. The collective set of categories becomes the desired mix, a way of framing the work of the organization. The ideal percentage that constitutes the size of each category can be determined from the collective wisdom of the team or perhaps through experimentation. The organization can learn the right mix over time but only if it makes a concerted effort to do so.

Within each category, determine criteria that can assess the "goodness"—quality or best fit—of choices for the plan. A criterion is a standard on which a comparative judgment or decision may be based. Because the types of projects and the objectives within categories may be quite different, develop unique criteria for each category or have a core set of criteria that can be modified. Many teams never get to the point of developing

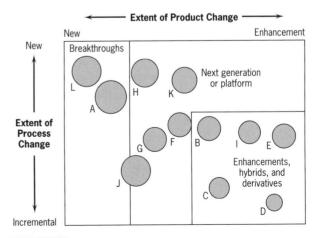

FIGURE 2 Bubble diagram of a product grid for one HP division. Size of bubble = size of project.

or clarifying criteria, and they usually want to discuss projects before agreeing on criteria; reversing the order is much more effective.

Several works on research and development project selection [8, 9, 12] provide a robust set of criteria for consideration. Examples include strategic positioning, probability of success, market size, and availability of staff. Most important is to identify the criteria that are of greatest significance to the organization; fewer are better. However, teams usually need to brainstorm many criteria before focusing on the few.

The role of each criterion is to help compare projects, not specify them. Select criteria that can measurably compare how projects support the organizational strategy. For example, one criterion may be degree of impact on HP business as interpreted by a general manager. On a scaling model from 1 to 10, small impact scores a 2, strong a 6, critical to the success of one business an 8, and critical to the success of multiple businesses a 10. Most likely all proposed projects meet meaningful specifications and provide value to the organization. The task is to develop tough criteria to select the best of the best.

Some organizations use narratives to describe how each project contributes to the vision; others use numerical scores on whether one project is equal, moderate, or strongly better than another. It is also helpful to set thresholds or limits for projects that will be considered for the plan. These help to screen out projects so that later prioritization efforts can focus on fewer projects.

Writing a thorough description of each criterion helps ensure understanding of the intent and expectations of data that must be supplied to fulfill it. One team of three or four people at HP spent 5 days working only on the criteria they were to use for decision-making. And this was only the beginning; they next involved customers in the same discussion before reaching consensus and beginning to evaluate choices. An "Aha" occurred when people found they were wrong to assume that everyone meant the same thing by terms such as packaging; some used wider definitions than others did, and the misunderstanding only surfaced through group discussion. Asked if the selection process ever failed the team, its leader replied, "If the results didn't make sense, it was usually because the criteria weren't well defined." Unfortunately, most teams do not exhibit the same patience and discipline that allowed this team to be successful.

Before moving to the next step, the team should establish relative importance among criteria. Assign a weighting factor for each criterion. All criteria are important but some more so than others. The example in Figure 3 is the result of one team's brainstorming session that ultimately led to selecting four criteria. Breakout groups subsequently defined each criterion with subcriteria. They also devised scoring methods to apply the criteria. Collectively they then determined the respective weighting or importance of each criterion (see the Process Tools section for how they did this). Unlike threshold criteria that "gate" whether a project is go or no-go, all projects have to satisfy selection criteria to some extent. Weighting of criteria is the technique that can optimize and determine the best of the best. Another "Aha" that helped teams get through the hurdle to develop effective criteria is when they realized the task at this point is "weighting, not gating."

It is the authors' experience that criteria, while universally desired, are usually lacking or not formalized. One benefit of effective criteria is the shaping effect it has on behavior in the organization. When people know how projects will be scored, they tend to shape proposals in positive ways to meet the criteria better. A pitfall is when people play games to establish criteria that support personal agendas. Then it is up to the leader to identify and question these tactics. Remind people to support the greater good of the organization. Significant effort could be devoted to the behavioral aspects that become relevant when deciding upon criteria; suffice to say, be warned that this is a touchy area to approach with sensitivity and persuasiveness.

Customer Satisfaction (28%)
- Improves service levels
- Results in more consistent and accurate information/transactions
- Helps ensure services are delivered as expected

Employee Satisfaction (7%)
- Improves employee knowledge
- Increases employee efficiency or effectiveness
- Improves work/life balance promised
- Positive impact to employee survey
- Helps balance workload

Business Value (46%)
- Achieves results that are critical for a specific window of opportunity
- Minimizes risk for implementation and ongoing sustainability
- Improves integration and relationships with partners
- Provides a positive ROI in < 2 years
- Aligns with business goals

Process Effectiveness (19%)
- Enables employees to do things right the first time
- Increases the use of technology for service delivery
- Reduces manual work and non-value added activities
- Increases employee self-sufficiency

FIGURE 3   Sample criteria and weighting, plus subcriteria, developed by one HP team.

What the Organization Can Do

The next step for the team is to gather data on all projects. Use similar factors when describing each project in order to ease the evaluation process. Engage people in extensive analysis and debate to get agreement on the major characteristics for each project. This is a time to ask basic questions about product and project types and how they contribute to a diversified set of projects. Reexamine customer needs, future trends, commercial opportunities, and new markets. The person consolidating the data should challenge assertions about benefits and costs instead of accepting assumptions that may have been put together casually. It is important for each member of the team to assess the quality of the data, looking closely at sources and the techniques for gathering the data. When putting cost figures together, consider using activity-based costing models instead of traditional models based on parts, direct labor, and overhead. Activity-based costing includes the communications, relationship building, and indirect labor costs that usually are required to make a project successful.

The team needs to constantly apply screening criteria to reduce the number of projects that will be analyzed in detail. Identify existing projects that can be canceled, downscaled, or reconceived because their resource consumption exceeds initial expectations, costs of materials are higher than expected, or a competitive entry to the market changed the rules of the game. The screening process helps eliminate projects that require extensive resources but are not justified by current business strategies; maybe the projects were conceived based on old paradigms about the business. The team can save discussion time by identifying must-do projects or ones that require simple go/no-go decisions, such as legal, personnel, or environmental projects. These fall right through the screens and into the allocation process. Determine if some projects can be postponed until others are complete or until new resources or funding become available. Can project deliverables be obtained from a supplier or subcontractor rather than internally? Involve customers in discussions. The team constantly tests project proposals for alignment with organizational goals.

It is not necessary to constrain the process by using the same criteria across all categories of projects. In fact, some teams found that different criteria for each category of projects were more effective. Also, consider adjusting the weighting of criteria as projects move through their life cycles. Kumar et al. [7] documented research showing that the most significant variable for initial screening of projects is the extent to which "project objectives fit the organization's global corporate philosophy and strategy." Other factors, such as available science and technology, become significant later during the commercial evaluation stage. A big "Aha" experienced by some teams when confronted with this data is that they usually did it the other way around. That explains why they got into trouble—by focusing on technology or financial factors before determining the link to strategic goals.

Cooper (and others before him) report that top-performing companies do not use financial methods for portfolio planning. Rather, they use strategic portfolio management methods where strategy decides project selection [3]. This lesson is still a hotly debated one, especially for those who cling to NPV as the single most important criterion. The difficulty lies in relying upon forecast numbers that are inherently fictitious. The authors' experience is that teams get much better results tapping their collective wisdom about the merits of each project based upon tangible assessments against strategic goals. Using computed financial numbers more often leads to arguments about computation methods and reliability of the data, resulting in unproductive team dynamics.

The next part of gathering data is to estimate the time and resources required for each potential and existing project. Get the data from past projects, statistical projections, or simulations. The HP Project Management Initiative particularly stresses in its organizational initiatives to get accurate bottom-up project data from work breakdown structures and schedules. Reconcile this data with top-down project goals. Document assumptions so that resource requirements can be revisited if there are changes to the basis for an assumption. For new or unknown projects, make a best estimate, focusing first on the investigation phase with the intent to fund only enough work to determine feasibility. The team can revisit the estimates when more information becomes available. Constantly improve estimation accuracy over time by tracking actuals with estimated task durations.

Next, the team identifies the resource capacity both within and outside the organization that will be available to do projects. Balance project with nonproject work by using realistic numbers for resource availability, taking into account other projects, vacations, meetings, personal appointments, and other interruptions. Tip: a wise planner consumes no more than about 50 percent of a person's available time.

One assessment about the quality of projects in a portfolio is to look at the rejects. In a story attributed to HP founder Bill Hewlett, he once established a single metric for how he would evaluate a portfolio manager's performance. He asked to see only the rejects. He reasoned that if the rejects looked good, then the projects that were accepted must be excellent.

All the actions in this step of the process are intended to screen many possible projects to find the critical few. The team may take a path through multiple screens or take multiple passes through screens with different criteria to come up with a short list of viable projects. Figure 4 represents one scenario where Screen 1 is a coarse screen that checks for impact on the strategic goal. Subsequent screens apply other criteria when more data are available. Any number of screens may be applied, up to the number n, until the team is satisfied that the remaining projects relate to compelling business needs. These steps actually save time because the next section on analysis can get quite extensive if all possible projects go through it.

It usually is necessary to go through several validation cycles before finishing the next step: the upper management team proposes project objectives, project teams provide preliminary estimates based on scope, schedule, and resources back to management, management is not happy with this response and makes adjustments, and so on. This exercise in due diligence is a healthy negotiation process that results in more realistic projects getting through the funnel.

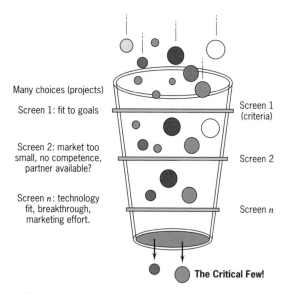

Many choices (projects)

Screen 1: fit to goals — Screen 1 (criteria)

Screen 2: market too small, no competence, partner available? — Screen 2

Screen *n*: technology fit, breakthrough, marketing effort. — Screen *n*

The Critical Few!

FIGURE 4   Application of criteria screens during a funneling process eliminates the *trivial many projects* from the *critical few* that the organization can realistically complete.

Analyze and Decide on Projects

The next step is to compare estimated resource requirements with available resources. A spreadsheet is useful to depict allocation of resources according to project priority.

Part of the analysis is qualitative: Consider the opportunity costs of committing to short-term, opportunistic, or poorly conceived projects that take resources away from future prospects that may be a better fit strategically. Also, avoid selecting "glamorous" new ideas over addressing the tough issues from ongoing projects. Some people lack the stamina to deal with the details of implementation and so are ready to jump to a new solution at the slightest glimmer of hope from the latest technology. This is a recipe for disaster. Also, be careful to balance the important projects rather than giving in to urgent, but not so important, demands.

Documenting all the findings and supportive data using a common set of descriptive factors makes it easier to compare similar factors across projects. Use a "project charter" form or a template where all information about each project, its sponsors, and key characteristics is recorded.

The team can now prioritize the remaining projects. Focus on project benefits before costs; that way the merits of each project get full consideration. Later include costs to determine the greatest value for the money. Compute overall return from the set of projects, not from individual projects, because some projects may have greater strategic than monetary value. Requiring each and every project to promise a high financial return actually diminishes cooperation across an organization. Also, optimize return over time and continuity or uniformity of revenue from the projects. Some future projects must be funded early to ensure a revenue stream when current projects taper off.

Using previously agreed-upon criteria and weighting factors, the team compares each project with every other one within a category. Repeat the process for each criterion. See the discussion and example later in this article about using an analytical hierarchy process (AHP) to facilitate this step. Consider using software to compute results—an ordered list of projects within each category. A pitfall to avoid that engenders fear among the team is showing one list that prioritizes all projects from top to bottom. People get concerned when their project is on the line. It is not fair to compare internal development projects with high grossing products; keep them separated and within their respective categories.

Finally, the team is ready to decide which projects to pursue. Be prepared to do fewer projects and to commit complete resources required by projects that are selected. Decide on a mix of projects consistent with business strategy, such as 50 percent platform projects, 20 percent derivative projects, 10 percent breakthrough projects, and 10 percent partnerships. Note that these total only 90 percent; taking some lessons from financial portfolio management, diversify the set of projects by investing in some speculative projects. The team may not be sure which markets or technologies will grow, so buy an "option" and make a small investment to investigate the possibilities. Include experimental projects. It is also important to leave a small percent of development capacity uncommitted to take advantage of unexpected opportunities and to deal with crises when they arise.

Wheelwright and Clark [14] cite an organization that reduced the number of its development projects from 30 to 11: "The changes led to some impressive gains . . . as commercial development productivity improved by a factor of three. Fewer products meant more actual work got done, and more work meant more products." Addressing an internal project management conference, an HP Executive Vice President emphasized the need to focus on doing fewer projects, especially those that are large and complex: "We have to be very selective. You can manage cross-organizational complex programs if you don't have very many. If you have a lot of them with our culture, it just won't work. First of all, we need to pick those opportunities very, very selectively. We need to then manage them aggressively across the company. That means have joint teams work together, strong project management and leadership, constant reviews, a framework, a vision, a strong owner—all those things that make a program and project successful." Subsequently, a number of organizations sought help from the HP Project Management Initiative to systematically reduce 120 projects down to 30. Another organization went from 50 projects down to 17. It appears counter-intuitive, but by prioritizing and more carefully selecting projects, organizations actually get more projects completed.

Figure 5 illustrates a document that captures the output of this process. Record projects that are fully funded in an aggregate project plan (*in-plan*). In a separate section or another document, list projects for future consideration (*out-plan*); also capture and communicate reasons for delaying or not funding projects. The *plan of record* (POR) is both a process and a tool used by some organizations at HP to keep track of the total list of projects. It lists all projects under way or under consideration by the entity. If a project is funded and has resources assigned, it has achieved *in-plan status*. Projects below the cutoff line of

ID	Strategic Category	Priority	Project	Head Ct	Feb	Mar	Apr	May	Jun	Jul	Aug	Sep
1	**Platform (Mix = 40%)**											
2	In Plan	1	Proj F	2								
3		2	Proj G	2								
4		3	Proj H	4								
5		4	Proj J	5								
6		5	Proj K	3								
7	Out Plan		Next Step									
8												
9	**Enhance (Mix = 20%)**											
10	In Plan	1	Proj B	2								
11		2	Proj C	1								
12		3	Proj D	1								
13		4	Proj E	2								
14		5	Proj I	1								
15	Out Plan		Fat City									
16												
17	**R & D (Mix = 30%)**											
18	In Plan	1	Proj A	7								
19		2	Proj L	5								
20												
21												
22												
23	Out Plan		Blue Sky									
24												
25	**Infrastructure (Mix = 10%)**											
26	In Plan	1	Bus. Plan	1								
27		2	Portfolio	1								
28		3	Update plan	1								
29												
30												
31	Out Plan		Corner Office									

FIGURE 5 An example plan of record showing the mix of projects in priority order and the time line for each project.

available resources or that have not yet achieved priority status are on the *out-plan*. The figure also categorizes the projects and specifies the desired mix.

Project managers at HP describe one benefit of the POR process as identifying gaps between required and actual resources. For flexible changes, the process gets all people into the communications loop. If people want to add something, the management team has to decide what should be deleted. The process helps two divisions that work together agree on one prioritized list instead of two. They utilize direct electronic connections for bottom-up entry of projects and resources by all project managers into a centralized administration point.

Implement the Plan

No job is complete until it is acted upon. The team needs to "evangelize" all others in the organization to use the aggregate project plan or POR to guide people who plan work, make decisions, and execute projects. Although it may be countercultural to do so, do not starve committed projects of the resources they need. The team or the responsible upper managers need to enforce the plan by fully staffing committed projects; that now becomes possible because fewer projects are happening simultaneously. Also, use the plan to identify opportunities for leverage across projects or for process reengineering. Match people skills to project categories to tap their strengths and areas for contribution.

The team or a program management office needs to maintain the plan in a central place, such as a project office or online. Make it known to, and accessible by, all people in the organization doing projects, subject to confidentiality requirements. All the work to this point may go for naught if the process, the steps, and the results are not widely communicated.

The same people who develop the plan are also the ones who can best update it periodically, perhaps quarterly or as changes occur. Use tools such as an online shared database to gather data directly from project managers about resources needed for each project. This system can be used both to gather data when developing the plan and to update it. View the plan as a "living document" that accurately reflects current realities.

The challenge for HP and many companies is to "master both adaptive innovation and consistent execution . . . again and again and again . . . in the context of relentless change. . . . Staying on top means remaining poised on the edges of chaos and time . . . These edges are places of adaptive behavior. They are also unstable. This instability means that managers have to work at staying on the edge" [1]. The advice is clear: the plan is indispensable as a strategic guideline, but don't fall in love with it! Be prepared to adapt it and to communicate the changes.

Process Tools

One tool that can assist in the decision-making process is the AHP [10]. Because of the interactions among many factors affecting a complex decision, it is essential to identify the important factors and the degree that they affect each other before a clear decision can be made. The AHP helps structure a complex situation, identify its criteria and other intangible or concrete factors, measure the interactions among them in a simple way, and synthesize all the information to obtain priorities. The priorities then can be used in a benefit-to-cost determination to decide which projects to select. The AHP organizes feelings and intuition alongside logic in a structured approach to decision-making—helpful in complex situations where it is difficult to comprehend multiple variables together. An individual or team focuses on one criterion at a time and applies it step by step across alternatives. A number of sites across HP find value in using AHP.

In another example, a team got together to choose among a set of services they will offer to customers. More choices were available than the organization had capacity to support. After defining organizational strategy or product goals, the first task was to identify which criteria to enter into the decision-making process. After give-and-take discussion, they decided that the criteria were customer satisfaction, business value, process effectiveness, and employee satisfaction.

Next, the criteria were ranked according to priority by making pairwise comparisons between them. Which is the more desirable criterion and by how much, customer satisfaction or business value? Process effectiveness or employee satisfaction? Business value or process effectiveness? These questions were asked about all possible pairs.

Each potential project or service then was scored underneath each criterion, and decisions were made about which projects to include in the portfolio, based upon existing resources. This team went on to create a POR similar to Figure 5.

A detailed explanation for computing the priority scores and the final rank ordering list can be quite complex, involving eigenvalues and eigenvectors, so it is much easier to get a software package (Expert Choice [4]) that does the computations. As an alternative, a spreadsheet could be constructed to normalize the numbers.

This process appears complex and analytical but is easy when the software handles the computations, and the management team concentrates on the comparisons. It is thorough in guiding the team to consider all criteria, both emotional and logical, and to apply them to all projects. One team rejected the process as too analytical, so be aware that it does not work for everyone.

The key benefit in doing this process is the improved quality of dialogue that occurs among the management team members. In facilitating a number of teams at HP through this process, each one achieved far more progress than they thought possible. People admit that they become addicted to the AHP process. They immediately buy the software. The systematic approach is feasible whether selecting products for a product line, projects that comprise a portfolio, or the best supplier or candidate for a job. In reality, the discussions are more valuable than the analysis. The process in this case provides the discipline that makes the dialogue happen.

Frame [5] offers an alternative "poor man's hierarchy." He puts selection criteria along the side as well as across the top of a grid. If the criterion on the side is preferred to the one on the top, put a 1 in the cell. If the criterion on top is preferred, put a 0 in the cell. Diagonals are blanked out where criteria would be compared to themselves. Below the diagonal, put the opposite

	Business	Customer	Technology	Employee		Total Votes	%
Business	***	16	16	18	=	50	46
Customer	2	***	13	15	=	30	28
Technology	2	5	***	14	=	21	19
Employee	0	3	4	***	=	7	7

FIGURE 6   A simplified hierarchy used by one HP team to weight criteria.

value from corresponding cells above the diagonal. Then add up the numbers across the rows to get total scores, which provide a rank order. One team at HP modified this process to replace the 1s and 0s with an actual count of how 18 people voted in each pairwise comparison of alternatives. Again, they added up the rows and normalized the results for a priority order and weighted ranking (Figure 6).

This simplified hierarchy is especially helpful for weighting criteria. It can be used for prioritizing projects when applied to one criterion at a time. It becomes bulky and less useful when applied to multiple projects over multiple criteria.

Barriers to Implementation

Now for a reality check. The model depicted in this article is thorough, and it integrates objective and subjective data. When all is said and done, however, people may throw out the results and make a different decision. Sometimes the reason is a hunch, an instinct, or simply a desire to try something different. Sometimes people have a pet project and use the process to justify its existence, or a hidden agenda may be at play—perhaps the need to maneuver among colleagues, trading projects for favors. Politics at this stage cannot be ignored, nor are they likely to-disappear. It is imperative for leaders to become skilled in the political process. Any attempt at leading change in how an organization links projects to strategy is bound to meet resistance. The concept receives almost unanimous intellectual support. Implementing it into the heart and soul of all people in the organization is another story. It goes against the cultural norms in many organizations and conjures up all kinds of resistance if the values it espouses are not the norm in that organization. The path is full of pitfalls, especially if information is presented carelessly or perceived as final when it is work in process.

Some people resist because the process is too analytical. Some want decision-making to be purely interactive, intuitive, or the purview of a few people. A complete process cannot be forced upon people if the organization has more immediate concerns or unresolved issues. Resistance occurs when there is no strategy, the strategy is unclear, or people are uncomfortable with the strategy. Work on the process may come to a standstill when people realize how much work is involved to fully link projects to strategy. If the pain is not great enough with the status quo, people are not going to be ready to change.

And if people sense that the leader does not authentically believe in the elements, such as the goals, the process, or the tools, they are hesitant to follow with any enthusiasm. When the leader lacks integrity and exhibits incongruity between words and actions, people may go through the motions but do not exert an effort that achieves meaningful results.

Enablers for Effective Implementation

It is possible to lead people through this change process if the leader asks many questions, listens to the concerns of all people involved, and seeks to build support so that people feel they have an active role in developing the process [9]. A flexible process works better than a rigid one. Cultivate "champions" who have the credibility and fortitude to carry the process across the organization. Believe that change is possible.

When the effort appears too massive, one approach is to go after the low-hanging fruit. Start with one of the more pressing issues and use the general concepts of this model to address it. Still have a vision for what the organization ultimately can achieve but understand that patience and pacing are necessary to get there. Consider also that this process is hierarchical—it can be applied singularly or collectively, up or down the organization.

For people who get frustrated when all linkages are not present, the authors urge teams and individuals to "just do it." Small changes in initial conditions have enormous consequences. Eventually successes or small wins are noticed. The practices start to permeate an organization. This can happen in the middle, move up, and then over to other organizations. Incidentally, a corporate group such as HP's Project Management Initiative helps facilitate this transformation. We do this by acting as a conduit for success stories and best practices.

Over the long run, we believe that organizations that follow a process similar to the one described increase their odds for greater success. This happens because teams of people following a systematic process and using convincing data to support their arguments more often produce better results than individuals. Their projects have more visibility, and the quality of dialogue and decision-making improve. The power of using criteria that are tightly linked with strategy and known by everyone in the organization is the mitigating effect it has to guide behavior in constructive ways. Having a process means it can be replicated and improved over time until it is optimized. It also means other people can learn the process and coach others, thereby creating a learning organization.

References

1. Brown, S. L., and K. M. Eisenhardt. *Competing on the Edge: Strategy as Structured Chaos*. Boston: Harvard Business School Press, 1998.
2. Collins, J. C., and J. I. Porras. *Built to Last: Successful Habits of Visionary Companies*. New York: HarperCollins, 1994.
3. Cooper, R. G., S. J. Edgett, and E. J. Kleinschmidt. *Portfolio Management for New Products*. Reading, MA: Addison-Wesley, 1998.
4. "Expert Choice," Pittsburgh, PA: Expert Choice Inc. (see *www.expertchoice.com*).
5. Frame, J. D. *The New Project Management: Tools for an Age of Rapid Change, Corporate Reengineering, and Other Business Realities*. San Francisco: Jossey-Bass Publishers, 1994.
6. Graham, Robert J., and Randall L. Englund. *Creating an Environment for Successful Projects: The Quest to Manage Project Management*. San Francisco: Jossey-Bass Publishers, 1997.
7. Kumar, V., et al. "To Terminate or Not an Ongoing R&D Project: A Managerial Dilemma." *IEEE Transactions on Engineering Management* 279 (1996).
8. Martino, J. *R & D Project Selection*. New York: Wiley, 1995.
9. O'Toole, J. *Leading Change: Overcoming the Ideology of Comfort and the Tyranny of Custom*. San Francisco: Jossey-Bass Publishers, 1995.
10. Saaty, T. L. *Decision Making for Leaders*. Pittsburgh, PA: RWS, 1990.
11. Stacey, R. D. *Managing the Unknowable: Strategic Boundaries Between Order and Chaos in Organizations*. San Francisco: Jossey-Bass Publishers, 1992, p. 62.
12. Turtle, Q. C. *Implementing Concurrent Project Management*. Englewood Cliffs, NJ: Prentice Hall, 1994.
13. Westney, R. E. *Computerized Management of Multiple Small Projects*. New York: Dekker, 1992.
14. Wheelwright, S., and K. Clark. "Creating Project Plans to Focus Product Development." *Harvard Business Review*, March–April (1992).

Questions

1. Why are successful projects so important to Hewlett-Packard?
2. How far should an evaluation team go in trying to quantify project contributions to the firm's mission or goals? What is the role of financial selection criteria in HP's project selection process?
3. Considerable attention is paid to the measures HP uses to evaluate its projects. Is the aim of carefully defining these measures to simplify the project selection process or something else?
4. What do the aggregate project plan and the plan of record illustrate to upper management?
5. When should out-plan projects be reconsidered for inclusion?
6. What was your impression of the impact that HP's project selection process had on the number of projects underway? How do you expect HP would score on project management maturity?
7. How did the new project selection process handle nonnumeric type projects? Risk? How did this new process alter new project proposals at HP?

CHAPTER 3

The Project Manager

Chapters 3 and 4 discuss topics relevant to **PMBOK** knowledge area 6, *Human Resource Management*. In the previous chapter, we described how projects are evaluated and selected for development. Before more progress can be made, a project manager (PM) must be appointed. Not only the appointment of a PM (the project "leader") is important to initiate any project, but also the PM is probably the major resource input to the project compared to the team, the capital, the materials, and any other inputs—hence our extensive discussion here. As the leader, this person will take responsibility for planning, implementing, and completing the project, beginning with the job of getting things started. Actually, the way to get things started is to hold a meeting. We will delay the discussion of the initial project meeting, however, until Chapter 5 because it is the first step in the process of planning the project.

1.7, 4.3, 9

The PM can be chosen and installed as soon as the project is selected for funding or at any earlier point that seems desirable to senior management. If the PM is appointed prior to project selection or if the PM originated the project, several of the usual start-up tasks are simplified. On occasion, a PM is chosen late in the project life cycle, usually to replace another PM who is leaving the project for other work. For example, a large agricultural products firm regularly uses a senior scientist as PM until the project's technical problems are solved and the product has been tested. Then it replaces the scientist with a middle manager from the marketing side of the firm as marketing becomes the focal point of the project. (The transition is difficult and, according to firm spokespeople, the results are sometimes unsatisfactory.)

Usually, a senior manager briefs the PM on the project so that the PM can understand where it fits in the general scheme of things in the parent organization and its priority relative to other projects in the system and to the routine work of the organization. The PM's first set of tasks is typically to prepare a preliminary budget and schedule, to help select people to serve on the project team, to get to know the client (either internal or external), to make sure that the proper facilities are available, to ensure that any supplies required early in the project life are available when needed, and to take care of the routine details necessary to get the project moving.

As people are added to the project, plans and schedules are refined. The details of managing the project through its entire life cycle are spelled out, even to the point of planning for project closure when the work is finally completed.

Mechanisms are developed to facilitate communication between the PM and top management, the functional areas, and the client. As plans develop still further, the PM holds meetings and briefings to ensure that all stakeholders who will affect or be affected by the project are prepared in advance for the demands they will have to meet as the project is implemented.

In this chapter, we discuss the unique nature of project management and some of the ways project management differs from *functional* management. Our emphasis is on the role and responsibilities of the PM. We concentrate on the demands placed on the PM, particularly on those unique to project management. We then identify the skills required by the PM and link them to the nature of the task faced by the PM.

It is best to describe the PM's job relative to some assumptions about the nature of projects and the organization within which the project must function. We assume that the parent firm is functionally organized and is conducting many projects simultaneously with its ongoing, routine operations. We also assume a fairly large firm, a project that has some technical components, with an output to be delivered to an "arm's-length" customer. Clearly, not all, and possibly even not most, projects operate under these circumstances, but these are the most demanding, and we address the most difficult problems a PM might have to face. Smaller, simpler projects may not require the tools we will present here, but the PM for these projects should be aware that such tools exist.

Thus far, we have had in mind a PM with reasonably normal skills and operating under reasonably normal circumstances. In the last sections of this chapter, we will discuss a major complication for PM—managing a project being carried out in a *multicultural* environment. We emphasize the word multicultural, a word that is not synonymous with (but includes) projects whose member organizations and geographical locations may transcend national boundaries. In fact, it is not the differences in national boundaries that matter; it is differences in *cultures*. Moreover, it is not merely the differences in cultures that matter, it is also differences between the *environments* within which the projects are conducted— economic, political, legal, and sociotechnical environments.

In this chapter, two conditions receive special attention. Both have a profound effect on the outcome of the project, and neither is under the complete control of the PM—though the PM can greatly influence both by dealing with the conditions early in the project life. The first of these concerns the degree to which the project has the support of top management. If that support is strong and reasonably unqualified, the project has a much better chance of success (Pinto et al., 1989; Zimmerer et al., 1998).

The second condition concerns the general orientation of the project team members. If they are highly oriented toward their individual, functional disciplines, as opposed to the project itself, project success is threatened. If, on the other hand, they are oriented toward the project (i.e., problem oriented rather than discipline oriented), the likelihood of success is much greater. As Thomas Hughes (1998) writes about the SAGE and Atlas projects:

> *"Teams of engineers, technicians, and scientists polarized around problems rather than disciplines. As a result, new discipline-transcending organizational forms . . . presided over system-building projects rather than discipline-bound departments. The transdisciplinary team approach is still considered front-edge management almost half a century later."*

3.1 Project Management and the Project Manager

The Functional Manager Versus the Project Manager

The best way to explain the unique role of the PM is to contrast it with that of a functional manager in charge of one of a firm's functional departments such as marketing, engineering, or finance. Such department heads are usually specialists in the areas they manage. Being specialists, they are analytically oriented and they know something of the details of each operation for which they are responsible. When a technically difficult task is required of their departments, they know how to analyze and attack it. As functional managers, they are administratively responsible for deciding how something will be done, who will do it, and what resources will be devoted to accomplish the task.

A PM generally starts his or her career as a specialist in some field who is blithely informed by a senior manager that he or she is being promoted to the position of PM on the Whizbang Project. The PM must now metamorphose from technical caterpillar into generalist butterfly. (For an excellent set of instructions for the transformation, see Matson (1998).) The PM, new or experienced, must oversee many functional areas, each with its own specialists (see Figure 3.1). Therefore, what is required is an ability to put many pieces of a task together to form a coherent whole—that is, the PM should be more skilled at synthesis, whereas the functional manager should be more skilled at analysis. The functional manager uses the *analytic approach*, and the PM uses the *systems* (or synthesis) *approach*.

The analytic method focuses on breaking the components of a system into smaller and smaller elements. We are not saying that this is wrong; it is merely inadequate for understanding a complex system. Regardless of the dissector's skill or the degree to which, say, a frog is dissected, the dissection allows only a partial understanding of the total animal "frog." The systems approach maintains that to understand a component, we must understand the system of which the component is a part. And to understand the system, we must understand the environment (or larger system) of which it is a part.

Adoption of the systems approach is crucial for the PM. Consider, if you will, the problem of managing a project devoted to the development of software that will create and maintain a database, and to undertake this task without knowing anything about the decision support system in which the database will be used, or the operating system of the computers that will contain the DSS, or the purposes for which the information in the database will be used, and so forth.

Our comparison between the PM and the functional manager reveals another crucial difference between the two. The functional manager is a direct, technical supervisor. The PM is a facilitator and generalist. These simple statements, while true, are misleading. Both require specialized technical knowledge. The functional manager's knowledge must be in the technology of the process being managed. The PM should be competent in the science of project management (Sahlin, 1998; Zimmerer et al., 1998), but this is not sufficient. In our opinion, there is strong evidence that the PM should be both generalist and facilitator and have a reasonably high level of technical competence in the science of the project.

Three major questions face PMs in their task of synthesis: What needs to be done, when must it be done (if the project is not to be late), and how are the resources required to do the job to be obtained? In spite of the fact that the PM is responsible for the project, the functional managers will probably make some of the fundamental and critical project decisions. For example, they usually select the people who will actually do the work required to carry out the project. They may also develop the technological design detailing how some tasks will be accomplished. And they frequently influence the precise deployment of the project's resources.

FIGURE 3.1 Project management organization showing typical responsibilities of a project manager.

This separation of powers between functional and PMs, which may aid in the successful completion of the project, is also a source of considerable "discomfort" for both. Note here that the PM is responsible for organizing, staffing, budgeting, directing, planning, and controlling the project. In other words, the PM "manages" it, but the functional managers may affect the choice of technology to be used by the project and the specific individuals who will do the work. (It is not uncommon, however, for the PM to negotiate with functional managers about the assignment of special individuals to carry out certain project work.) Arguments about the logic or illogic of such an arrangement will fall on deaf ears. The PM cannot allow the functional manager to usurp control of the project. If this happens, work on the project is likely to become secondary to the work of the functional group and the project will suffer. But the functional manager cannot allow the PM to take over authority for technical decisions in the functional area or to control the assignment of functional area personnel.

At times, a senior manager (often the PM's immediate superior) will, in effect, take over the PM's job by exercising extremely close supervision over every action the PM takes or will actually tell the PM precisely what to do. All of the powers normally delegated to the PM are withdrawn, and the PM's boss runs the project. This condition is known as *micromanagement*. It stamps out any creativity or initiative from the PM or project workers, frustrates almost everyone connected with the project, and generally ensures mediocre performance, if not failure. To be frank, we do not know how to cure or prevent micromanagement. It is practiced by individuals who have so little trust in their coworkers that they must control everything. Our considered advice to PMs who are micromanaged is to request a transfer.

At the other end of the spectrum, the relationship between the PM, the functional managers, the project team, and the PM's superior may be characterized as "collegial," and the organization may be populated by talented people. In such organizations, conflict is minimized, cooperation is the norm, no one is terribly concerned with who gets the credit, and the likelihood of success is high. We will have more to say later in this chapter and in other chapters about building and maintaining teams. Effective teams tend to operate in a collegial mode. It is worth noting, however, that collegiality without talent leads to failure—even if the project team smiles a lot while failing.

The Project Manager's Responsibilities

The PM's responsibilities are broad and fall primarily into three separate areas: responsibility to the parent organization, responsibility to the project and the client, and responsibility to the members of the project team. Responsibilities to the firm itself include proper conservation of resources, timely and accurate project communications, and the careful, competent management of the project. It is very important to keep senior management of the parent organization fully informed about the project's status, cost, timing, and prospects.

It is also a major, and ethical, responsibility of the PM to inform senior management if the viability of the project has become doubtful due to its inability to achieve the organization's strategic objectives (Starke, 2012). This may happen due, for example, to deficiencies in the project, changes in the market, or changes in the strategic direction of the organization. Continuing on with the project under such circumstances would be a waste of financial and human resources for the organization.

Senior managers should also be warned about likely future problems. The PM should note the chances of running over budget or being late, as well as methods available to reduce the likelihood of these dread events. Reports must be accurate and timely if the PM is to maintain credibility, protect the parent firm from high risk (risk management is covered in detail in Chapter 7), and allow senior management to intercede where needed. *Above all, the PM must never allow senior management to be surprised!*

The PM's responsibility to the project and client is met by ensuring that the integrity of the project is preserved in spite of the conflicting demands made by the many stakeholders who have legitimate interests in the project. The manager must deal with the engineering department when it resists a change advised by marketing, which is responding to a suggestion that emanated from the client. In the meantime, contract administration says that the client has no right to request changes without the submission of a formal Request for Change order. Manufacturing says that the argument is irrelevant because marketing's suggestion cannot be incorporated into the project without a complete redesign.

The PM is in the middle of this turmoil. The PM must sort out understanding from misunderstanding, soothe ruffled feathers, balance petty rivalries, and cater to the demands of the client. One should, of course, remember that none of these strenuous activities relieves the PM of the responsibility of keeping the project on time, within budget, and up to specifications.

In Chapter 5, it will become evident that it is very common for the PM to have no direct subordinates in spite of the fact that several, perhaps many, people "work for him/her" on the project. These people form what we have been referring to as the "project team." In spite of the strange circumstance where people are said to work for someone who is not their boss, the PM's relationship to the team may be considerably closer than one might expect, particularly when individuals are assigned to spend much or all of their time working on the project.

The PM's responsibilities to members of the project team are dictated by the finite nature of the project itself and the specialized nature of the team. Because the project is, by definition, a temporary entity and must come to an end, the PM must be concerned with the future of the people who serve on the team. If the PM does not get involved in helping project workers with the transition back to their functional homes or to new projects, then as the project nears completion, project workers will pay more and more attention to protecting their own future careers and less to completing the project on time.

One final note on this subject: If we have made the process of project management seem orderly and rational, we apologize. If any single descriptor could be used to characterize project management, the adjective would be "messy." In an excellent, classic article that should be read by anyone interested in understanding the reality of management, Kotter (1982) has shown that general managers are less organized, less formal, and less structured than college students are led to believe. The same is undoubtedly true of PMs. This fundamental lack of organization and structure makes it all the more important that PMs implement good planning and organizational skills where possible, or the chaos becomes unmanageable.

PM Career Paths

Many firms have a wide variety of types and sizes of projects in progress simultaneously. Of these, it is typical to find that many are not large enough or sufficiently complex to require a full-time manager. Quite a few PMs are in charge of several projects simultaneously. The firm may be planning and building a new factory (3 years), undertaking several dozen R&D projects (1–7 years), improving the landscape surrounding its factory in Mussent Point (2 months), considering the acquisition of another firm (6 months), upgrading the equipment in its thiotimolene plant (2 years), buying artworks produced by artists in each city in which the firm operates for display in corporate offices (1 year), planning the annual stockholders' meeting (3 months), and doing a large number of other things, many of which are organized as projects.

Who manages these projects? Where does the company find people competent to manage such a wide variety of projects? In Chapter 1, we referred to the professionalization and rapid growth of project management, to **PMBOK** (the project management body of knowledge), as well as to the development of college- and university-level courses and degree programs available in the field. Although the percentage of PMs who are academically trained is increasing rapidly, many current PMs have no college-level training in the field. A rapidly growing number of private consulting firms offer instruction in project management as well as programs preparing individuals for the PMI's examination for certification as Project Management Professionals (PMPs—see Chapter 1 Appendix).

The great number of fairly small, short-term projects being carried out, when managed by an experienced PM, serve a purpose beyond the output of the projects themselves. They provide an excellent training ground for new PMs who frequently begin their preparation with involvement in some major aspect of a small project. A number of firms, Procter & Gamble for one, often take management trainees and give them some project-management responsibility; for instance, the guidance of a new cosmetic through test procedures to ensure that it is not toxic to users. Such experience serves to teach trainees many things, not the least of which are the importance of an organized plan for reaching an objective, of "follow-through," of negotiation with one's coworkers, and of sensitivity to the political realities of organizational life. The skills and experiences gained from managing a project, even a small one, are a scaled-down version of what it is like to run a full-sized organization. Thus, projects provide an excellent growth environment for future executives and for developing managerial skills.

The career path of a PM often starts with participation in small projects, and later in larger projects, until the person is given command over small and then larger projects. For example, the path could be tooling manager for small Project U, project engineer for larger Project V, manufacturing manager for large Project W, deputy PM for large Project X, PM for small Project Y, and PM for large Project Z.

The actual establishment of multiple career paths to the top of organizations is more talked about than acted on. Wishful thinking aside, with a very few notable exceptions,[1] we know of no *specific* career paths that can take PMs to CEO positions. In a great many firms, however, experience as a PM is seen as a desirable (sometimes mandatory) step on the way up the corporate ladder. The logic of such a view is obvious. The capability of a PM to meet the demands of senior management positions is clearly evidenced by the PM's ability to achieve the project's goals without the need for explicit authority while operating in an environment typified by uncertainty, if not chaos.

The global recession in the late 2000s and accompanying unemployment have put pressure on the project management profession as much as any other profession. Recent comments in the media (Zupek, 2010) seem to indicate that "the days of a 'generic' project manager are numbered" and that firms are now looking for PMs who have "specific experience and understand the nuts and bolts" of the technology or project being implemented. As a result, it's important that PMs not only continue to develop their project management skills and gain their PMP® certifications but keep themselves trained in the latest technologies. If true, then it would appear that gaining a wide range of experience would also be more likely to win a job or promotion than gaining depth in one particular area.

---

[1] For example, Eli Lilly and Co., the pharmaceutical firm, finds that projects involving new drugs often last 8–12 years. No PM would be willing to manage a project that long without the opportunity for promotion. Lilly, therefore, has established a career path for their PMs that potentially leads to the top of the firm. They already had career paths progressing through "administration" or "R&D" to the top and have clearly demonstrated the reality of both paths.

Project Management in Practice

The Project Management Career Path at AT&T

1889

1900

1939

1964

1969

1984

2006

As a result of the many organizational and technological changes in the telecommunications industry, AT&T realized that the old ways of doing business would not be competitive in the new market they now faced and decided to revamp their whole process of providing technology to the market. They decided that organizing by project management would give them better control over their business and bring them a competitive advantage. Thus, they set the goal of becoming the leader in project management in the industry.

AT&T had previously used project managers in many of its activities but in a significantly different way. For instance, it was more a project coordination responsibility that could be successfully completed through achieving the activities on a task list. However, the position was of low status and seen as only a temporary activity serving to carry someone on to a better functional manager position. Thus, the reward for doing a good job was to move into a functional position and get out of project management.

AT&T realized it would have to change the whole nature of the project management role, and the entire structure of the organization as well, if it were to be successful in this strategy. They needed to develop professional project managers, plus a support system to maintain their abilities and careers in project management. The managerial mentality of two or three years on a project and then moving on to a functional job had to be changed to an attitude of professional pride in project management and staying in the field for the remainder of their careers. Equally important, the organizational mentality of admiring heroic rescues of projects in trouble had to be replaced with admiration for doing a competent job from the beginning and time after time.

The reorganization for project management was a major project in itself, including the areas of candidate selection, education and training, compensation, career development, organizational restructuring, and methods development. In terms of organizational structure, a National Project Management (NPM) organization was created at the corporate level, reporting to the service operating vice president. Reporting to the director of NPM were three project directors spread across the United States, a systems support organization, and a methods and support staff. Program managers, project managers, and their subordinates reported to the project directors. This structure provided an integrated, self-contained project management group.

The project management career path now consists of:

- Trainee: a 6-month position to learn about project management.
- Cost Analysis/Schedule Engineer: a 6–18-month team position reporting to a project manager.
- Site Manager: a 6–12-month position responsible for a large site and reporting to a program manager.
- Small Project Manager: sole responsibility for a $1M to $3M revenue project.
- Project Manager: responsible for $3M to $25M projects.
- Program Manager: responsible for multiyear projects and programs over $25M.

Candidates for the project manager career track are selected from AT&T's Leadership Continuity Plan, a program to identify the people with the most potential to progress to middle and senior management levels of responsibility, as well as from career people within the organization. Particular skills sought are interpersonal leadership skills; oral and written communication skills; a presidential, big-picture perspective; political sensitivity; delegating, problem-solver orientation; optimistic, can-do attitude; planner mentality; kaizen (continuous improvement) spirit; and administrative, in-charge credibility.

AT&T's Project Management organization now includes a staff in Denver and groups of project managers in the major cities throughout the nation. These groups now manage over $500 million in a range of telecommunications projects, ranging in size from $1M to $92M. Their project management approach is deemed the most capable in the industry, setting the pace for AT&T's competitors.

Questions

1. How difficult is it to change a culture where project management is perceived as of low status and something to get out of, to one where project management is respected? How would you approach such a task?

2. What was the problem with the mentality of admiring heroic rescues of projects in trouble?

3. Compare the skills sought for project managers among AT&T's Leadership Continuity Plan with those listed in the chapter.

Source: D. Ono, "Implementing Project Management in AT&T's Business Communications System," *PM Network*, Vol. 4.

3.2 | Special Demands on the Project Manager

A number of demands are unique to the management of projects, and the success of the PM depends to a large extent on how capably they are handled. These special demands can be categorized under the following headings.

Acquiring Adequate Resources

It was noted earlier that the resources initially budgeted for a project are frequently insufficient to the task. In part, this is due to the natural optimism of the project proposers about how much can be accomplished with relatively few resources. Sometimes, it is caused by a deliberate, unethical understatement of resource requirements to ensure that a project is accepted for funding. At times, it is caused by the great uncertainty associated with a project. Many details of resource purchase and usage are deferred until the PM knows specifically what resources will be required and when. For instance, there is no point in purchasing a centrifuge now if in 9 months we will know exactly what type of centrifuge will be most useful.

The good PM knows that there are resource trade-offs that need to be taken into consideration. A skilled machinist can make do with unsophisticated machinery to fabricate needed parts, but a beginning machinist cannot. Subcontracting can make up for an inadequate number of computer programmers, but subcontractors will have to be carefully instructed on the needs of the contractor, which is costly and may cause delays. Crises occur that require special resources not usually provided to the PM.

All these problems produce glitches in the otherwise smooth progress of the project. To deal with these glitches, the PM must scramble, elicit aid, work late, wheedle, threaten, or do whatever seems necessary to keep the project on schedule. On occasion, the additional required resources simply alter the project's cost–benefit ratio to the point that the project is no longer cost-effective. Obviously, the PM attempts to avoid these situations, but some of what happens is beyond the PM's control.

The problems of time and budget are aggravated in the presence of a phenomenon that has been long suspected but only proved in the mid-1980s (Gagnon et al., 1987). The individual who has the responsibility for performing and completing a task sometimes overestimates the time and cost required. That individual's immediate supervisor often discounts the worker's pessimism but, in so doing, may underestimate the time and cost. Moving up the management hierarchy, each successive level frequently lowers the time and cost estimates again, becoming more optimistic about the ability of those working for them to do with less—or, perhaps, more forgetful about what things were like when they worked at such jobs. The authors have informally observed—and listened to complaints about—such doings in a variety of organizations. We suspect that they reflect the superior's natural tendency to provide challenging work for subordinates and the desire to have it completed efficiently. The mere recognition of this phenomenon does not prevent it. Complaints to upper-level managers are usually met with a hearty laugh, a pat on the back, and a verbal comment such as "I know you can do it. You're my best project manager, and you can. . . . " We will consider the doubtful ethics in over/understating resource requirements and project schedules along with other ethical problems in Section 3.3.

Another issue may complicate the problem of resource acquisition for the PM. Project and functional managers alike perceive the availability of resources to be strictly limited and thus a strict "win–lose" proposition. Under these conditions, the "winners" may be those managers who have solid political connections with top management. Often, there are times in the life of any project when success or survival may depend on the PM's "friendship" with a champion or "sponsor" high in the parent organization (Pinto et al., 1989). For example (PMI, 2005), in 1994, a Chicago-based Commemoration Committee was formed to build a four-story, $1 million monument memorializing the 150th anniversary of the Irish potato famine. However, the PM selected depended on a church sponsor to support the project, but in 1999, the church sponsor who championed the project had moved on to another city, and the church thus stopped supporting the project. This illustrates the difficulty of a long, multiyear effort when the sponsor leaves.

Acquiring and Motivating Personnel

A major problem for the PM is the fact that most of the people needed for a project must be "borrowed" from elsewhere in the organization conducting the project. With few exceptions, they are borrowed from the functional departments. The PM must negotiate with the functional department managers for the desired personnel and then, if successful, negotiate with the people themselves to convince them to take on these challenging temporary project assignments.

Most functional managers cooperate when the PM comes seeking good people for the project, but the cooperative spirit has its limits. The PM will be asking for the services of the two types of people most needed and prized by the functional manager: first, individuals with scarce but necessary skills and second, top producers. Both the PM and the functional manager are fully aware that the PM does not want a "has-been," a "never-was," or a "never-will-be." Perceptions about the capabilities of individuals may differ, but the PM is usually trying to borrow precisely those people the functional manager would most like to keep.

A second issue may reduce the willingness of the functional manager to cooperate with the PM's quest for quality people. At times, the functional manager may perceive the project as more glamorous than his or her function and hence a potent source of managerial glory. The functional manager may thus be a bit jealous or suspicious of the PM, a person who may have little interest in the routine work of the functional area even if it is the bread and butter of the organization.

Project Management in Practice

A Surprise "Director of Storm Logistics" for Katrina

One day, Melvin Wilson was simply a marketing manager for small 1,250-employee Mississippi Power in Gulfport, Mississippi. But the next day, after Hurricane Katrina hit New Orleans and Gulfport, he was suddenly the firm's "Director of Storm Logistics," responsible for restoring power to 195,000 customers within 12 days. Although Mississippi Power's primary storm center at headquarters was knocked out, they had a backup storm center 5 miles inland. However, when Wilson got there, the cars were floating in the parking lot, so he moved his small group in charge to a third location, an old service office without electricity or running water. In spite of the phone lines being down, the group managed to get word of their needs to the outside world, and within days, 11,000 repairmen from 24 states and Canada came to help. To support the 11,000 workers, the group needed housing, beds, food, clean water, showers, laundry, bulldozers, 5,000 trucks, 140,000 gallons of fuel each day, 8,000 tetanus shots, and hundreds of other such items. Directing such a massive project as the restoration of power was far beyond the experience of little Mississippi Power's group, but they succeeded, and the power was restored to every customer who could handle it within 12 days.

Questions

1. Why do you think Wilson was appointed Director?
2. What would have been the first set of tasks Wilson would have considered after requesting help?

Source: D. Cauchon, "The Little Company That Could," *USA Today*, 2005.

On its surface, the task of motivating good people to join the project does not appear to be difficult, because the kind of people who are most desired as members of a project team are those naturally attracted by the challenge and variety inherent in project work. The subordinate who is being seduced to leave the steady life of the functional area for the glamour of a project can be gently reminded that the functional manager retains control of personnel evaluation, salary, and promotion for those people lent out to projects. (A few exceptions to these general rules will be discussed in Chapter 5.) There may even be comments about how easy it is to lose favor or be forgotten when one is "out of sight."

Unless the PM can hire outsiders with proven ability, it is not easy to gather competent people; but having gathered them, they must be motivated to work. Because the functional manager controls pay and promotion, the PM cannot promise much beyond the challenge of the work itself. Fortunately, that is often sufficient (Pinto et al., 1989) since many of the project personnel are professionals and experts in their respective specialties.

A story has it that when asked "How do you motivate astronauts?" a representative of NASA responded, "We don't motivate them, but, boy, are we careful about whom we select." The issue of motivating people to join and work creatively for a project is closely related to the kind of people who are invited to join. The most effective team members have some common characteristics. A list of the most important of these follows, but only the first is typically considered during the usual selection process.

1. **High-quality technical skills**   Team members should be able to solve most of the technical problems of a project without recourse to outside assistance. Even if the relevant functional department has furnished technical specialists to the project, the exact way technology is applied usually requires adaptation by the project team.

2. **Political, and general, sensitivity**   It is obvious that the PM requires political skills of a high order. Though it is less obvious, project team members also need to be sensitive to organizational politics and similar matters outside their realm of normal interaction. Project success is dependent on support from senior management in the parent organization. This support depends on the preservation of a delicate balance of power between projects and functional units and between the projects themselves. The balance can be upset by individuals who demand their own way or are otherwise insensitive to political and organization needs and constraints external to the project.

3. **Strong problem orientation**   Hughes (1998) has shown that the chances for successful completion of a multidisciplinary project are greatly increased if project team members are *problem-oriented* rather than *discipline-oriented*, as noted earlier. Problem-oriented people tend to learn and adopt whatever problem-solving techniques appear helpful, but discipline-oriented individuals tend to view the problem through the eyes of their discipline, ignoring aspects of the problem that do not lie within the narrow confines of their educational expertise.

4. **Strong goal orientation**   Projects do not provide a comfortable work environment for individuals whose focus is on activity rather than on results. Work flow is rarely even, and for professionals, a 60-hour week is common, as are periods when there seems to be little to do. "Clock watchers" will not be successful team members.

5. **High self-esteem**   As we noted earlier, a prime law for projects (and one that applies equally well to the entire organization) is: *Never let the boss be surprised*. Projects can rapidly get into deep trouble if team members hide their failures, or even a significant risk of failure, from the PM. Of course, the PM must be aware that "shooting the messenger who brings bad news" will immediately stop the flow of any negative information. Individuals on the team should have sufficiently high levels of self-esteem that they are not threatened by acknowledgment of their own errors or by pointing out possible problems caused by the work of others.

The PM should expect conflict with the creation of a new project team where the individual team members do not know one another. To help navigate the conflict, it is helpful if the PM understands the way teams tend to develop. One of the more popular classic models of team development is one referred to as the "Tuckman ladder" (Tuckman, 1965), which suggests that teams progress through the following four development phases:

- **Forming**   Team members come together for the first time and begin learning about their roles and responsibilities.
- **Storming**   Work on the project begins, but initially the team members tend to work independently, which often leads to conflict.
- **Norming**   In this phase, the team members begin to establish team norms and team cohesiveness develops. Individual team members reconcile their behaviors to support the overall team, and trust develops.
- **Performing**   With norms and trust established, teams function as a cohesive unit focused on accomplishing the goals of the project.

In addition to these four phases, a fifth phase, "**adjourning**," has been proposed. In the adjourning phase, the work of the project is completed and the team members return to their functional departments or move on to another project. While teams tend to progress through these phases in the listed order, it is also important to point out that they can get stuck in one or more of the phases, backtrack to an earlier phase, and never make it to the later phases. Similarly, if the team members have worked together previously, it is possible that one or more phases may be skipped.

Dealing with Obstacles

"What I need is a list of specific unknown problems that we will encounter."[2]
Anonymous manager

One characteristic of any project is its uniqueness, and this characteristic means that the PM will have to face and overcome a series of crises. These crises affect not only the project but the PM as well, and his or her ability to make trade-offs to keep the project on track, a topic discussed further in the following text. From the beginning of the project to its closure, crises appear without warning. The better the planning, the fewer the crises, but no amount of planning can take account of the myriad changes that can and do occur in the project's environment.

One of the most serious crises is a change in the required project scope (better known as "scope creep"), typically initiated by the client. As Brox (2012) notes, saying "no" directly is not the best tactic. Rather, the PM needs to frame responses to such requests in terms of the trade-offs required to achieve the change so clients can see for themselves what the trade-offs are. The PM can then make recommendations on alternatives. But as an ethical professional, the PM cannot ignore the ramifications of the scope change without informing the stakeholders of its impacts.

The successful PM is a firefighter by avocation. At the inception of the project, the "fires" tend to be associated with resources. The technical plans to accomplish the project have been translated into a budget and schedule and forwarded up the managerial hierarchy

---

[2] The authors received this and several other "Management Quotes" in an e-mail communication. They were reported to be entries in a magazine contest and supposedly came from "real-life managers." They have been set in a distinctive box so they will be easy to recognize. We list other such quotes in similar boxes, but without credit and without repeating this footnote.

or sent to the client for approval. In an earlier section, we noted that some of the budget and schedule are pared away at each successive step up the hierarchy. Each time this happens, the budget and schedule cuts must be translated into changes in the technical plans. Test procedures may be shortened, and suppliers' lead times may be cut. The required cost and schedule adjustments are made, a nip here and a tuck there. To the people affected, these may well be crises. As we will note in Chapter 7, an obvious cure for these crises is to "pad" the budget when it is originally submitted. This is unethical, a bad idea, and generally creates more serious problems than it solves.

To be useful, experience must be generalized and organized. Managing a project is much like managing a business. Business firms often develop special routines for dealing with various types of fires. Human resource departments help put out "people fires" just as engineering helps deal with "mechanical fires." Firefighting, to be optimally effective, should be organized so that fires are detected and recognized as early as possible. What clearly differentiates successful PMs from their counterparts is their *problem-finding* ability. This allows the fires to be assigned to project team members who specialize in dealing with specific types of fires. Although this procedure does not eliminate crises, it does reduce the pain of dealing with them.

This emphasis on the need for firefighting raises another issue worth a brief comment. Some individuals thrive on dealing with crises. They have been referred to as "adrenalin junkies." If a PM finds such people fighting fires in her or his project, the PM should be aware that she or he may have found an arsonist. The wise PM will keep a careful eye on those who appear to be addicted to the excitement of crises.

Some projects are highly complex, and this poses obstacles all by itself. As Burba (2013) notes, however, there are sometimes clues to help the PM prepare. Two of these relate to people: multiple stakeholders and the number of project team members. Although stakeholders can put up innumerable obstacles to a project if they are dead set against it, the project team members inherently bring obstacles that external stakeholders usually do not, such as their personal vices, competitions, jealousies, and problems. Another clue is an ambiguity of project features, resources, or phases, so that various aspects of the project depend on a multiplicity of uncontrollable elements.

Burba describes three approaches that are paramount for handling complex projects. The first is communicating effectively with all stakeholder groups (discussed in more detail in Chapter 4) and always keeping an open line to external stakeholders and internal sponsors who actively support the project. Second, be sure to learn as much about the client as possible and especially the problems and solutions in dealing with them in the past. Third, leadership is a critical skill for handling complex projects. This means always being on the lookout for even weak signals of trouble and being ready to respond. The ability to revise plans and rectify conflicting interests is crucial.

As the project nears completion, obstacles tend to be clustered around two issues: first, last-minute schedule and technical changes and second, a series of problems that have as their source the uncertainty surrounding what happens to members of the project team when the project is completed. These two types of problems are very different from one another, as well as from the problems that faced the PM earlier in the life cycle of the project.

The way to deal with last-minute schedule and technical changes is "the best you can." In some cases where the project team proactively engages in significant upfront planning, potential disruptions to the project are anticipated and contingency plans are developed upfront. More typically, however, the PM simply accepts that such disruptions and changes will occur to the project, believing there is little that can be done except to be prepared to "scramble."

Coping with the uncertainty surrounding what happens at the end of a project is a different matter. The issue will be covered at greater length in Chapter 13, but it deserves mention here because it is certainly an obstacle that the PM must overcome. The key to solving such problems is communication. The PM should make open communications between the PM and team members first priority. The notion of "open communications" requires that emotions, feelings, worries, and anxieties be communicated, as well as factual messages.

Making Project Goal Trade-Offs

As noted previously, one of the PM's primary roles is making trade-offs between the project goals of cost, time, and scope and, of course, risk and the ancillary goals. The PM must also make trade-offs between project progress and process—that is, between the technical and managerial functions. The first set of trade-offs is required by the need to preserve some balance between the project time, cost, and scope goals. Conventional wisdom had it that the precise nature of the trade-offs varied depending on the stage of the project life cycle. At the beginning of the life cycle, when the project is being planned, scope was felt to be the most important of the goals, with cost and schedule sacrificed to the technical requirements of the project. Following the design phase, the project builds momentum, grows, and operates at peak levels. Because it accumulates costs at the maximum rate during this period, cost was felt to take precedence over scope and schedule. Finally, as the project nears completion, schedule becomes the high-priority goal, and cost (and perhaps scope) suffers. Research (Kalu 1993) has shown that these assumptions, sensible as they seem, are not true.

During the design or formation stage of the project life cycle, there is no significant difference in the importance PMs place on the three goals. It appears that the logic of this finding is based on the assumption that the project should be designed to meet all the client-set goals. If compromises must be made, each of the objectives is vulnerable.

Schedule is the dominant goal during the buildup stage, being significantly more important than scope, which is in turn significantly more important than cost. Kloppenborg et al. (1990, p. 127) conjectures that this is so because scheduling commitments are made during the buildup stage. Scheduling and scope are approximately tied for primacy during the main stage of the life cycle when both are significantly more important than cost. During the final stage, phaseout, scope is significantly more important than schedule, which is significantly more important than cost. Table 3.1 shows the relative importance of each objective for each stage of the project life cycle.

The second set of trade-offs concerns sacrificing smoothness of running the project team for technical progress. Near the end of the project, it may be necessary to insist that various team members work on aspects of the project for which they are not well trained or which they do not enjoy, such as copying or collating the final report. The PM can get a fairly good reading on team morale by paying attention to the response to such requests.

TABLE 3.1	Relative Importance of Project Objectives during Different Stages of the Project Life Cycle		
Life Cycle Stage	**Cost**	**Schedule**	**Scope**
Formation	1	1	1
Buildup	3	1	2
Main	3	1	1
Phaseout	3	2	1

Note: 1 = high importance.
Source: Kloppenborg et al. (1990, p. 78).

The PM also has responsibility for other types of trade-offs, ones rarely discussed in the literature of project management. If the PM directs more than one project, he or she must make trade-offs between the several projects. As noted earlier, it is critical to avoid the appearance of favoritism in such cases. Thus, we strongly recommend that when a PM is directing two or more projects, care should be taken to ensure that the life cycles of the projects are sufficiently different that the projects will not demand the same constrained resources at the same time, thereby avoiding forced choices between projects.

In addition to the trade-offs between the goals of a project, and in addition to trade-offs between projects, the PM will also be involved in making choices that require balancing the goals of the project with the goals of the firm. In fact, while the previous discussion descriptively describes the way PMs often make trade-offs among the project goals, prescriptively the PM should make these trade-offs in a way that best supports the organization's mission and strategy. For example, a nonprofit charity with extremely limited resources would likely not have the option of increasing a project's budget in order to enhance the scope of the project or complete the project sooner. On the other hand, a technology firm that competes on the basis of being first to the market would be justified in going over budget to ensure that the project was finished on time.

Suffice it to say, such choices are common. Indeed, the necessity for such choices is inherent in the nature of project management. However, be warned: the PM's enthusiasm about a project—a prime requirement for successful project management—can easily lead him or her to consider some unethical actions such as: (1) overstating the benefits of a project, (2) understating the probable costs of project completion, (3) ignoring technical difficulties in achieving the required level of performance, and (4) making trade-off decisions that are clearly biased in favor of the project but antithetical to the goals of the parent organization. Similarly, this enthusiasm can lead the PM to take risks not justified by the likely outcomes.

Finally, the PM must make trade-off decisions between the project, the firm, and his or her own career goals. Depending on the PM's attitudes toward risk, career considerations might lead the PM to take inappropriate risks or avoid appropriate ones.

Project Management in Practice

Shanghai Unlucky with Passengers

Photo by Ji Yueming/Color China Photos/ZUMA Press. (©) Copyright 2006 by Color China Photos

To speed passengers to Shanghai's new international airport, China built a magnetic levitation (maglev) train that runs every 10 minutes from Shanghai's business center to the Pudong International Airport. Reaching speeds over 300 miles an hour, it whisks people to the airport 20 miles away in less than 8 minutes. However, according to the vice director of the train company, "We are not lucky with ticket sales," since the trains are virtually empty. The reason is in order to meet the project's time deadline and budget, the train station was located 6 miles outside the city center, requiring lengthy public transportation to get there. So in spite of the technical, budget, and timing success of the project, it failed to meet the needs of the passengers. China is currently investigating on extending the line to the downtown area, but that will be a much more expensive and time-consuming project.

Questions

1. **Was Shanghai "unlucky," or was something else the problem?**
2. **Who was the client for this project? Why didn't the client complain?**
3. **Did this project seem to follow the objectives life cycle of Table 3.1?**
4. **What ancillary goals were traded off in this project?**

Source: Project Management Institute. "A Derailed Vision," *PM Network*, Vol. 18.

Maintaining a Balanced Outlook

Sometimes it is difficult to distinguish whether a project is heading for failure or success. Indeed, what appears to be a failure at one point in the life of a project may look like success at another. The reality is that projects often run into technical problems or snags. The psychic consequences of such technical snags can be more serious than the snags themselves. The occurrence and solution of technical problems tend to cause waves of pessimism and optimism to sweep over the project staff.

There is little doubt that these mood swings can have a destructive effect on performance. The PM must cope with these alternating periods of elation and despair, and the task is not simple. Performance will be the strongest when project team members are "turned on," but not so much that they blandly assume that "everything will turn out all right in the end," no matter what. Despair is even worse because the project is permeated with an attitude that says, "Why try when we are destined to fail?"

Maintaining a balanced, positive outlook among team members is a delicate job. Setting budgets and schedules with sufficient slack to allow for Murphy's law, but not sufficient to arouse suspicion in cost and time-conscious senior management, is also a delicate balance.

Breadth of Communication

Communication is the seventh specific knowledge area in **PMBOK**. The topic will be discussed further in the later sections of this chapter as well as in Chapter 4. As pointed out clearly in the Reading section at the end of this chapter, communication skills, especially listening and persuading, are the most important skills in successfully managing projects.

Chapter 10

As is the case with any manager, most of the PM's time is spent communicating with the many stakeholders interested in the project. Running a project requires constant selling, reselling, and explaining the project to outsiders, top management, functional departments, clients, and a number of other such stakeholders to the project, as well as to members of the project team itself. The PM is the project's liaison with the outside world, but the manager must also be available for problem solving in the lab, for crises in the field, for threatening or cajoling subcontractors, and for reducing interpersonal conflict between project team members. And all these demands may occur within the span of 1 day—a typical day, cynics would say.

To some extent, every manager must deal with these special demands; but for a PM, such demands are far more frequent and critical. As if this were not enough, there are also certain fundamental issues that the manager must understand and deal with so that the demands noted can be handled successfully. First, the PM must know *why* the project exists; that is, the PM must fully understand the project's intent. The PM must have a clear definition of how *success* or *failure* is to be determined. When making trade-offs, it is easy to get off the track and strive to meet goals that were really never intended by top management.

Second, any PM with extensive experience has managed projects that failed. As is true in every area of business we know, competent managers are rarely ruined by a single failure, but repeated failure is usually interpreted as a sign of incompetence. On occasion, a PM is asked to take over an ongoing project that appears to be heading for failure. Whether or not the PM will be able to decline such a doubtful honor depends on factors unique to each situation: the PM's relationship with the program manager, the degree of organizational desperation about the project, the PM's seniority and track record in dealing with projects such as the one in question, and other matters, not excluding the PM's being engaged elsewhere when the "opportunity" arises. Managing successful projects is difficult enough that the PM is, in general, well advised not to volunteer for undertakings with a high probability of failure.

Third, it is critical to have the support of top management (Pinto et al., 1989). If support is weak, the future of the project is clouded with uncertainty, and if it is an R&D project, it is more likely to be closed (Green, 1995). Suppose, for example, that the marketing vice president is not fully in support of the basic project concept. Even after all the engineering and manufacturing work has been completed, sales may not go all out to push the product. In such a case, only the chief executive officer (CEO) can force the issue, and it is very risky for a PM to seek the CEO's assistance to override a lukewarm vice president. If the VP acquiesces and the product fails (and what are the chances for success in such a case?), the PM looks like a fool. If the CEO does not force the issue, then the VP has won and the PM may be out of a job. As noted earlier, political sensitivity and acumen are mandatory attributes for the PM. The job description for a PM should include the "construction and maintenance of alliances with the leaders of functional areas."

Project Management in Practice

The Wreckmaster at a New York Subway Accident

At 12:16 A.M., in late August, a 10-car subway train on the Lexington Line beneath New York City jumped the track and crashed in the subway tunnel. Damage was massive—five cars were derailed, one was cut in half, another bent in two, possibly 150 persons injured, four dead. The train ripped out the steel-girder support columns used to hold up the tunnel ceiling, as well as the street above which immediately sunk a half inch. Two tracks and a third rail had been ripped out, and two signal sets, two switches, and an air compressor room destroyed.

When such an emergency occurs, the New York City Transit Authority (NYCTA) immediately appoints a project master, called a "Wreckmaster," to oversee the handling of the disaster rescue and repair activities and make sure that operations are returned to a safe condition as soon as possible. In this case, the goal was to have the subway back to normal operation by Tuesday morning rush hour, September 3, after the 3-day holiday weekend. Such disasters are handled in eight phases:

Phase 1: Respond to injury—Get people out of danger, provide needed medical care, remove bodies, and ensure that no victims remain in the debris.

Phase 2: Secure the area—Simultaneously with phase 1, eliminate other threats to life and property by disconnecting power, providing emergency lighting and ventilation, stopping other trains from entering the area, and keeping nonrelevant pedestrian and vehicular traffic out.

Phase 3: Initiate command facilities—Concurrent with phases 1 and 2, set up and activate command and coordination structure for all emergency activities.

Phase 4: Remove debris—Collect and remove the elements and debris of the accident which would hinder rescue, cleanup, or repair.

Phase 5: Remove damaged equipment—Use cranes, cutting torches, and other equipment to remove the large, major equipment.

Phase 6: Facility repair—Repair the facilities as quickly as possible for continuing and normal use.

Emile Wamsteker / AP Photo

A worker looks at the wreckage of a subway car following a derailment.

Phase 7: Test—Make certain that all facilities are fully operational and safe by testing under the watchful eye of engineering, operations, and safety.

Phase 8: Cleanup—Clean the premises to the best possible state to permit normal operations.

The crash was heard at NYCTA's Union Square District 4, and about 40 transit police officers ran to assist passengers at the smoke-filled scene. Soon, officers from District 2, the Fire Department, and the Office of Emergency Management joined them. The Fire Department brought fans to help clear the smoke and steel cable to rope the wreckage to the support pillars so they could reach people still in the train cars without the roof caving in on them. Buses were dispatched to transport people to hospitals, and the Red Cross provided food and drink for the injured. Some rescuers fainted from heat exhaustion as the temperature climbed to over 110 °F in the tunnel, and two dozen police and fire workers were treated for injuries and smoke inhalation. Transit police officer Emanuel Bowser was riding the train when it crashed but helped people get off for more than 4 hours after the crash even though he had a broken arm and fingers himself.

After learning about the crash, NYCTA appointed Larry Gamache, general superintendent of track operations, as Wreckmaster. Larry set up team captains to coordinate activities throughout each phase of the disaster operations.

A command center was established at a nearby subway station to direct and coordinate the operations. Gamache formulated a mental flow chart of how work needed to proceed. Each task had to be analyzed to determine what tasks had to precede it and what tasks could be conducted concurrently with it. Gamache also initiated regular meetings for all involved stakeholders. This kept everyone informed of what progress had been made and provided them with estimates of future progress so activities could be coordinated and sequenced.

The plan was to remove the wreckage as quickly as possible from one track to allow work trains to reach the disaster site, bringing needed materials to the site, and removing debris. Since work had to continue throughout the Labor Day weekend on 12-hour shifts, facilities for the workers—food, drink, toilets—also had to be provided. Diesel trains pulled out the five cars that didn't derail, but getting out the other five was a special problem. A new Hoersh hydraulic jacking system was brought in from another district that could lift a 44-ton car, move it sideways, and set it back down on the tracks. Using these jacks reduced by half the labor required to rerail the cars, thereby significantly expediting the recovery. As work progressed through the long weekend, it became apparent that the disaster recovery plan would meet its Tuesday morning completion goal, and in fact, trains began running again by late evening on Monday.

Lawrence Gamache, Wreckmaster

Larry Gamache started at NYCTA 24 years ago as a trackworker and progressed through many managerial positions on his way to general superintendent, track operations. His experience over those years clearly qualified him for the responsibility of this assignment, particularly his involvement as field supervisor of several earlier derailments.

He was also highly involved in a 3-year subway reconstruction project that required extensive coordination and negotiation with other city agencies, communities, and political leaders, all the while battling inclement weather and difficult conditions—yet, the project was completed ahead of time and well under budget. This experience, too, was valuable in coordinating the activities of the many groups involved in the disaster recovery.

Questions

1. **In what phase of the disaster plan does providing for alternate services probably occur? In what phase does bringing new equipment and supplies occur?**

2. **How much preplanning could be done for wrecks such as these in terms of disaster teams, command center locations, task sequencing, and so on?**

3. **What experience credentials does NYCTA look for in appointing wreckmasters?**

Source: S. Nacco, "PM in Crisis Management at NYCTA: Recovering from a Major Subway Accident," *PM Network*, Vol. 6.

Fourth, the PM should build and maintain a solid information network. It is critical to know what is happening both inside and outside the project in order to head off potential problems, a major skill of successful PMs, as noted earlier. The PM must be aware of customer complaints and department head criticism, who is favorably inclined toward the project, when vendors are planning to change prices, or if a strike is looming in a supplier industry. Inadequate information can blind the PM to an incipient crisis just as excessive information can desensitize the PM to early warnings of trouble.

Finally, the PM must be flexible in as many ways, with as many people, and about as many activities as possible throughout the entire life of the project. The PM's primary mode of operation is to trade off resources and criteria accomplishment against one another. Every decision the PM makes limits the scope of future decisions, but failure to decide can stop the project in its tracks.

Negotiation

In order to meet the demands of the job of a PM—acquiring adequate resources, acquiring and motivating personnel, dealing with obstacles, making project goal trade-offs, maintaining a balanced outlook, and establishing a broad network of communication—the PM must be a highly skilled negotiator. There is almost no aspect of the PM's job that does not depend directly on this skill. We have noted the need for negotiation at several points in the previous pages, and we will note the need again and again in the pages that follow. The subject is so important, and Chapter 4 is devoted to a discussion of the matter.

3.3 | Attributes of Effective Project Managers

The selection of a PM is one of the two or three most important decisions concerning the project. In this section, we note a few of the many skills the PM should possess in order to have a reasonable chance of success.

The following is a list of some of the most popular attributes, skills, and qualities that have been sought when selecting PMs:

- A strong technical background
- A hard-nosed manager
- A mature individual
- Someone who is currently available
- Someone on good terms with senior executives
- A person who can keep the project team happy
- One who has worked in several different departments
- A person who can walk on (or part) the waters

These reasons for choosing a PM are not so much wrong as they are "not right." They miss the key criterion. Above all, the best PM is *the one who can get the job done*! As any senior manager knows, hard workers are easy to find. What is rare is the individual whose focus is on the completion of a difficult job, a "closer." Of all the characteristics desirable in a PM, this *drive to complete the task* is the most important.

If we consider the earlier sections of this chapter, we can conclude that there are four major categories of skills that are required of the PM and serve as the key criteria for selection, given that the candidate has a powerful bias toward task completion. Moreover, it is not sufficient for the PM simply to possess these skills; they must also be perceived by others. Both the fact and the perception are important.

Credibility

The PM needs two kinds of credibility. First is *technical credibility*. The PM must be perceived by the client, senior executives, the functional departments, and the project team as possessing sufficient technical knowledge to direct the project. A PM with reasonable technical competence seems to be associated with project success and is seen by project team members to be a "positive" leadership characteristic (Zimmerer et al., 1998). (We remind the reader that "technical credibility" includes technical knowledge in such arcane fields as accounting, law, psychology, anthropology, religion, history, playwriting, Greek, and a host of other nonhard sciences.) The PM does not need to have a high level of expertise, know more than any individual team members (or all of them), or be able to stand toe-to-toe and intellectually slug it out with experts in the various functional areas. Quite simply, the PM has to have a reasonable understanding of the base technologies on which the project rests, must be able to explain project technology to senior management, and must be able to interpret the technical needs and wants of the client (and senior management) to the project team. Similarly, the PM must be able to hear the problems of the project team and understand them sufficiently to address them, possibly by communicating them to upper management.

Second, the PM must be *administratively credible*. The PM has several key administrative responsibilities that must be performed with apparently effortless skill. It goes without saying that effective time management and organizational skills are critical (the online Appendix to this chapter provides a primer on time management). One of the administrative responsibilities is to the client and senior management—to keep the project on schedule and within cost and to make sure that project reports are accurate and timely. This can place the PM in an ethically awkward situation sometimes. Another responsibility is to the project team—to make sure that material, equipment, and labor are available when and where needed. Still another responsibility is to represent the interests of all stakeholders (team, management, functional departments, community, and client) to one another. The PM is truly the "person in the middle." Finally, the PM is responsible for making the tough trade-off decisions for the project and must be perceived as a person who has the mature judgment and courage to do so consistently.

Sensitivity

The preceding pages contain many references to the PM's need for political sensitivity. There is no point in belaboring the issue further. In addition to a good, working set of political antennae, the PM needs to sense interpersonal conflict on the project team or between team members and outsiders. Successful PMs are not conflict avoiders. Quite the opposite, they sense conflict early, then confront and deal with it before the conflict escalates into interdepartmental and intradepartmental warfare.

The PM must keep project team members "cool." This is not easy. As with any group of humans, rivalries, jealousies, friendships, and hostilities are sure to exist. The PM must persuade people to cooperate irrespective of personal feelings, to set aside personal likes and dislikes, and to focus on achieving project goals.

Finally, the PM needs a sensitive set of technical sensors. It is common, unfortunately, for otherwise competent and honest team members to try to hide their failures. Individuals who cannot work under stress would be well advised to avoid project organizations. In the pressure-cooker life of the project, failure is particularly threatening. Remember that we staffed the team with people who are task-oriented. Team members with this orientation may not be able to tolerate their own failures (though they are rarely as intolerant of failure in others) and may hide failure rather than admit to it. The PM must be able to sense when things are being "swept under the rug" and are not progressing properly.

Leadership, Ethics, and Management Style

Leadership has been defined (Kruse, 2013) as "**. . . a process of social influence, which maximizes the efforts of others, towards the achievement of a goal.**" Much has been written about how interpersonal influence is generated and the impact of leadership characteristics on team performance—for examples, see Jiang et al. (1998); Scott et al. (1998); and others in the bibliography.

The skills needed for leadership will probably vary depending on who is being asked. For example, top management might well have different answers from the PMs themselves and certainly will be different from the project team members. Since *leadership* "maximizes the efforts of others," the Project Management Institute (2013) conducted a leadership survey by asking project *practitioners* (those whose efforts are to be maximized): What kinds of skills does a PM need to become a project "leader?" There were six primary skills identified: 29 percent said "communication," 26 percent "people," 16 percent "strategic," 12 percent "requirements gathering," 12 percent "leadership," and 5 percent "time management." Note that most of these are soft skills and are discussed in this chapter. Even a seemingly mechanical task such as requirements gathering has a crucial soft element to it, particularly in teasing out what the "real" success measures of a project are. Moreover, the topic of time management is addressed in the online Appendix to this chapter where the soft elements are also discussed.

The following discussion is based on Müller and Turner (2010). Many approaches have been postulated to develop a coherent leadership theory: the trait school, the behavioral school, and the contingency school, to mention only the first three of several. Recently, the competency school has combined parts of all earlier "schools" by defining various leadership qualities with three major areas of competence: intellectual (IQ), managerial (MQ), and emotional (EQ). The leadership competencies associated with the three areas are shown in Table 3.2.

It has been well established that for different types of projects to be successful, PMs need different types of skills. Müller and Turner (2010) showed that engineering (and construction) projects, IT projects, and organizational change projects all required different levels of the 15 competencies to be successful. Further, they showed that the competency levels required varied with the complexity of the project, the importance of the project, and the type of contract under which the project was carried out.

While we will return to the relationship between leadership competencies, level of complexity, and project success, including project type, in later chapters, at this point, it is worth elaborating a bit more on the emotional intelligence (EQ) competency. In fact, there is research that suggests that EQ is the single best predictor of job performance. For example, best-selling author Daniel Goleman cites research suggesting that EQ is a critical factor in explaining differences between the best leaders and mediocre leaders and that EQ accounted for approximately 90 percent of the success of leaders (Goleman, 1998). According to this research, the top leaders demonstrated strengths in the same emotional competencies we have described as critical for PMs including influence, team leadership, and political awareness. Similarly, Swanson (2012) reports that those PMs who use EQ outperform their peer PMs by 32 percent in leadership effectiveness and development.

So what exactly is EQ? Fundamentally, emotional intelligence governs a person's ability to effectively deal with and in fact harness their emotions to achieve positive outcomes. According to Swanson (2012), EQ is comprised of four foundational skills: self-awareness,

TABLE 3.2 **Three Aspects of Leadership and Fifteen Leadership Competencies**

Area of Competence	Competency
Intellectual (IQ)	1. Critical analysis and judgment 2. Vision and imagination 3. Strategic perspective
Managerial (MQ)	4. Engaging communication 5. Managing resources 6. Empowering 7. Developing 8. Achieving
Emotional (EQ)	9. Self-awareness 10. Emotional resilience 11. Motivation 12. Sensitivity 13. Influence 14. Intuitiveness 15. Conscientiousness

Source: Dulewicz et al. (2003).

self-management, social awareness, and relationship management. Some researchers consider self-awareness and self-management to be personal competencies and consider social awareness and relationship management as social competencies.

EQ begins with self-awareness or a person's ability to observe and recognize his or her own emotions. Becoming more self-aware of our emotions in turn positions us to better manage our emotions. Thus, self-management is associated with the ability to positively manage our thoughts, behaviors, and actions based on the understanding of our emotions gained through self-awareness. In effect then, self-management reflects our ability to manage our emotional reactions given the situation or circumstances in which we find ourselves.

While self-awareness focuses on understanding our own emotions, social awareness is focused on understanding the emotions of others. Understanding our own emotions is certainly important in helping us guide how we respond to a particular set of circumstances. By the same token, understanding the other person's emotions is also important in helping us choose how we respond. For example, it is likely that the most effective way to respond would be different when a team member is angry versus when the team member is hurt. Thus, social awareness is based on developing effective listening, empathy, and observational skills. The goal is to truly understand what the other person is feeling. Furthermore, when it comes to emotions, there is no right or wrong. Our job is to be an objective observer of these emotions so that we can choose effective courses of action given the emotions we and the people we are interacting with are currently feeling.

Practically speaking, developing your social awareness skills requires developing your listening and observational skills. Effective listening requires an ability to focus your attention on what the other person is saying and not thinking about what you are going to say in response. Effective listening also means letting the other person finish before you respond. It is also useful to give the speaker feedback to show that you are listening such as nodding or smiling while the person is speaking. Pay attention to the main points made by the speaker, the speakers' tone of voice, how quickly the person is speaking, and the person's body language. And very importantly, ask questions based on your sincere interest in understanding the other person's perspective, which will usually not be interpreted as being judgmental.

However, worthy goals, self-awareness, self-management, and social awareness are not our end goals. Rather, these are means to the overarching goal of building quality relationships. More specifically, relationship management is based on our ability to use both our awareness of our own emotions and the other person's emotions to positively manage our interactions and ultimately build quality relationships. Swanson (2012) notes that EQ will lead PMs to ask questions such as: How can we collaborate more effectively with one another on this project? Or, what reservations do you imagine the client will have, and how can we address them? Or, how has this project addressed the needs of all the stakeholders involved?

The good news about EQ is that there are proactive steps you can take to enhance your EQ. Travis Bradberry and Jean Greaves provide an EQ assessment and numerous practical strategies for enhancing EQ in their book *Emotional Intelligence 2.0* (Bradberry and Greaves, 2009). This book should be required reading for all PMs.

Beyond EQ, another aspect of leadership that is an important trait in a PM is a strong sense of ethics. There is a considerable amount of attention to this topic in the news media these days, both good and bad, such as Enron, Lehman Brothers's use of Repo 105 (to get debt off their balance sheet), and of course, Bernie Madoff. Though less clear, some situations raise serious ethical questions such as the following:

- BP's subcontracting and safety procedures before the Gulf oil spill
- Goldman Sachs betting both ways on the synthetic CDO (collateralized debt obligation) it created for John Paulson to bet against the housing market

- Protection payments made to terrorists by firms
- Mining companies' safety procedures

Nixon (1987) has identified some ethical missteps that are relatively common in business:

- "Wired" bids and contracts (the winner has been predetermined)
- "Buy-in" (bidding low with the intent of cutting corners or forcing subsequent contract changes)
- Kickbacks
- "Covering" for team members (group cohesiveness)
- Taking "shortcuts" (to meet deadlines or budgets)
- Using marginal (substandard) materials
- Compromising on safety
- Violating standards
- Consultant (e.g., auditors) loyalties (to employer or to client or to public)

A PM, particularly in the public sector, may easily become embroiled in the ethics concerning such issues as pollution, public safety, industrial plant locations, the use of public lands, and so on. A Code of Ethics for PMs was created at the PMI 1982 symposium on Project Management, updated and approved in 1989, again in 1995, and once more in 2006. The 2006 version of the Code resulted from extended discussions and is roughly eight times the length of earlier versions—including appendices. It is available to anyone at the PMI website, *www.PMI.org*. The issue is receiving an increasing amount of attention.

Anyone seriously considering a career in project management should study the new code. It focuses on behavior that will lead to a high trust level between the PM, project team members, senior management, the client, and other stakeholders. The section entitled "Honesty" should be read, reread, and read once again. We will revisit the subjects of honesty and trust in almost every chapter of this book.

An "ethics audit" has also been recommended for nonprofit organizations (Schaefer et al., 1998), and we would recommend a similar audit for any firm. The extent of this subject is far beyond what we can cover here, but, fortunately, there are a number of excellent books on the topic (Blanchard et al., 1988; Pastin, 1986). A concise bibliography on business ethics is included in Robb (1996).

While a great deal has been written about the leadership attributes required or desirable in a PM, comparatively little has been written about the proper management style for a PM. Shenhar (1998) classifies projects across two dimensions and concludes that management style should be adapted to certain differences in the type of project. His dimensions are: (1) the level of technological uncertainty and (2) the level of system complexity. As the uncertainty increases from "low tech" to "high tech," the appropriate management style progresses from "firm, rigid, and formal" to "highly flexible." As the system complexity increases from simple to highly complex, the style progresses from "in-house informal" to "remote and highly formal."

Ability to Handle Stress

Throughout this chapter and elsewhere in this book, we have noted that the life of the PM is rarely serene. The PM is surrounded by conflict, often caught in an irrational management structure (described further in Chapter 5), and trapped in a high-stress occupation.

Kent (2008) identifies six signs of excessive stress in the workplace: (1) inability to switch off work issues, (2) disturbed sleep, (3) lack of pleasure in nonwork-related leisure activities, (4) difficulty concentrating or making decisions, (5) tendency to anger quickly, and (6) lack of energy. There are ways to deal with excessive stress. It is best if the organization is attuned to the problem and monitors their PMs and employees for work overload. In addition, as we discussed earlier in the context of EQ, the PM should be self-aware and spot the danger signals early. Kent suggests several ways to control stress:

1. Keep a journal, taking time to reflect on the events of the day.
2. Prioritize all tasks facing you, eliminating tasks that do not really need to be done, transferring or delegating what you can, delaying low priority items, and minimizing the scope of any subtask that is not crucial to your overall task (the online Appendix to this chapter provides a primer on effective time management).
3. Give yourself time to unwind from high-stress meetings, perhaps by taking a short walk or doing 15 minutes of exercise or meditation. Avoid meditating on the high-stress meeting.
4. Engage in after-work physical activities that take your mind off the tasks.
5. Improve your physical surroundings so they are pleasant, enjoyable, and comfortable, helping you to relax.
6. Become aware of the control you do or do not have over events. One of the great laws of living is "Do not develop anxiety about things over which you have no control!"

One way PMs try to handle excess work is by "multitasking." But as Hunsberger (2008) points out, this does not work. In fact, multitasking is a misnomer. What you are doing is switching back and forth between tasks. You lose time whenever you do this. Her advice is to divide your tasks into small steps, prioritize them on a to-do list, be proactive by tackling and completing tasks as soon as possible, and then cross them off the list (see the online Appendix for additional ideas on effective time management). If you can't finish in one sitting, leave notes that trigger your memory about where you were when you were interrupted. We will have more to say about the pitfalls of multitasking when we discuss the concept of the Critical Chain in Chapter 9.

There are numerous factors in life that cause stress, and PMs are as subject to them as other humans. There do, however, appear to be four major causes of stress often associated with the management of projects. First, some PMs never develop a reasonably consistent set of procedures and techniques with which to manage their work. Second, many simply have "too much on their plates." Third, some have a high need to achieve that is consistently frustrated. Fourth, the parent organization is in the throes of major change.

This book is primarily devoted to helping the PM deal with the first cause of stress. As for the second cause, we would remind the PM to include himself/herself as a "resource" when planning a project. Almost all project management software packages will signal the planner when a project plan calls for a resource to be used beyond its capacity (see Chapters 9 and 10). Such signals, at least, provide PMs with some evidence with which to discuss the work load with the appropriate senior manager.

Concerning the third cause of stress, Slevin (1989) points out that stress results when the demands made on an individual are greater than the person's ability to cope with them, particularly when the person has a high need for achievement. It is axiomatic that senior managers give the toughest projects to their best PMs. It is the toughest projects that are most apt to be beset with unsolvable problems. The cure for such stress is obvious, except to the senior managers who continue the practice.

Finally, in this era of restructuring and downsizing, stress from worry about one's future is a common condition in modern organizations. Dealing with and reducing these stresses as well as the stress resulting from everyday life is beyond the scope of this book as well as the expertise of its authors. Fortunately, any bookstore will have entire sections devoted to the subject of stress and its relief.

Project Management in Practice

Growing Stress at Twitter

As Kathy Norlen, operations project manager at Twitter points out, the company is growing awfully fast. At the beginning of 2009, Twitter had 5 million registered users; 20 months later, it had 125 million. Every day, another 300,000 people sign up for a new account. In its first 3½ years, it sent out 10 billion tweets; in the last 5 months, it sent out another 10 billion tweets. Worse, the demand ebbs and flows with great volatility and without warning, ranging from an average of 750 tweets per second to over 3,000 when some exciting world event happens. The problem is to keep Twitter's site running smoothly with all this growth and volatility of demand.

Although responsible for routine applications management and hardware allocation projects, as well as leading high-profile 4-month projects such as establishing a custom-built data center near Salt Lake City, UT, when there is a database problem affecting service, Norlen says that its "all hands on deck." For these crisis situations, Twitter has established an "on-call" roster of top managers to take charge, and then, as Norlen puts it, you drop everything and get to work! It's a chaotic environment for leading projects with "no model to follow" and no processes in place, so Norlen has to be creative and invent them, but that's what makes being a project manager so appealing.

Questions

1. Which of Kent's six ways to keep stress under control do you think might work for a project manager at Twitter?
2. Would you like Norlen's job? Why (not)?
3. Is it possible in a fast-growth company to avoid stress?

Source: M. Wheatley, "Avoiding the Fail Whale," *PM Network*, Vol. 24.

3.4 | Problems of Cultural Differences

In this section, we raise a number of issues that plague certain projects. Sometimes these projects require cooperation by individuals and groups from different countries. Sometimes they require cooperation by individuals or groups in one country, but from different industries or even from different divisions of the same firm. It is not, however, the geographical or organizational differences that matter, it is the differences in *cultures*. Moreover, it is not merely the differences in culture that matter, it is also differences in the *environments* within which projects are conducted, as we mentioned at the start of this chapter, the economic, political, legal, and sociotechnical environments. While the impacts of these dissimilarities are greatest and most visible in the case of international projects, they exist to some extent any time different organizations (including different parts of one organization) are asked to work together on a project. Throughout this book, we emphasize that the PM must manage and reduce conflict between the stakeholders in a project: the project team, client, senior management, and the public. If the stakeholders represent different nations, industries, and firms, the conflicts and problems besetting the project are greater by an order of magnitude.

"Culture" refers to the entire way of life for a group of people. It encompasses every aspect of living and has four elements that are common to all cultures: technology, institutions, language, and arts (*The World Book*, 1997). The *technology* of a culture includes such things as the tools used by people, the material things they produce and use, the way they prepare food, their skills, and their attitudes toward work. It embraces all aspects of their material lives. The *institutions* of a culture make up the structure of the society: the organization of the government, the nature of the family, the way in which religion is organized, the division of labor, the kind of economic system adopted, the system of education, and the way in which voluntary associations are formed and maintained.

Language, another ingredient of all cultures, is always unique because it is developed in ways that meet the expressed needs of the culture. The translation of one culture's language into another's is rarely precise because words carry connotative meanings as well as denotative meanings. The English word "apple" may denote a fruit, but it also connotes health ("keeps the doctor away"), bribery ("for the teacher"), New York city, a color, a computer, a dance (late 1930s), favoritism ("of my eye"), as well as several other things. Finally, the *arts* or aesthetic values of a culture are as important to communication as the culture's language. Aesthetic values dictate what is found beautiful and satisfying. If a society can be said to have "style," it is from the culture's aesthetic values that style has its source.

Culture and the Project

A nation's culture affects projects in many ways. One of the most obvious ways is in how people of different cultures regard time. In the United States and several other Western industrialized nations, time is highly valued as a resource (Smith et al., 1993). We say, "Time is money." It isn't, of course, but the expression is one way of expressing impatience with delay and lateness. Latin Americans, on the other hand, hold quite different views of time. The pace of life differs from one culture to another, just as do the values that people place on family or success. The PM conducting a construction project in South America will learn that to be half-an-hour late to a project meeting is to be "on time." In Japan, lateness causes loss of face. In some cultures, the quality of the work is seen to be considerably more important than on-time delivery. The great value placed on time in the United States and the distaste for tardiness leads to a common perception that U.S. managers are "impatient."

The fundamental philosophy of staffing projects varies greatly in different cultures. In Latin America, for example, the *compadre* system leads a manager to give preference to relatives and friends when hiring.[3] U.S. managers feel that such practices are a major source of inefficiency in Latin American firms. In fact, there appears to be scant evidence that this is so. One private study of several firms in the U.S. and Latin American chemical industries indicates that the differences in management practices between U.S. and Latin American chemical firms were, in general, significantly less than the differences between the U.S. chemical firms and U.S. clothing manufacturers.

The United States is, by far, the most litigious society on this planet. This does not mean that there are fewer disagreements in other societies, but rather that there is less recourse to courts of law and, therefore, more recourse to trust and negotiation as a means of resolving conflict. Many authors have noted that trust plays an important role in business relationships (e.g., Gogal et al., 1988). The impact of trust on project management, with its dependence on the ability and willingness of others to meet commitments, is clear. The importance of trust is also demonstrated by the critical role played by the *compadre* system in Latin America. Use of a general agreement with the extended family, as trusted suppliers to a project, for example, is a substitute for the detailed and highly explicit contracts usually required for dealing with "arm's-length" suppliers in the United States.

Certain types of collaboration between competitors have grown rapidly, even in the United States. SEMATECH is a consortium of semiconductor manufacturers conducting joint research projects in the field, one example among many of collaborative efforts allowed by the National Cooperative Research Act of 1984. European nations have also backed research consortia and Japan has initiated more than 60 research consortia, some with more than 40 members (Lynn et al., 1988).

---

[3] We are quite aware that the *compadre* system is a system of networks of extended family members, and is far more complex than is implied in this simple example.

The move to collaborative projects has also been transnational. Airbus Industries, the British–French–German–Spanish venture, operating with financial support from their several governments, has achieved outstanding success in commercial aircraft development and production. Other examples are CFM International composed of GE (USA) and Snecma (France), and International Aero Engines composed of Pratt & Whitney (USA), Rolls Royce (UK), Japan Aero Engines, MTU (Germany), and Fiat (Italy).

A view almost uniformly held by other societies is that U.S. managers understand everything about technology and nothing about people (Smith et al., 1993). This view apparently originates in the desire to "get down to business," while many foreign cultures—certainly Asian, Middle Eastern, Latin American, and southern European—value "getting to know you" as a precursor to the trust required to have satisfying business relationships. In many cultures, the manager is expected to take a personal interest in his or her subordinates' lives, to pay calls on them, to take an interest in the successes of family members, and to hold a caring attitude. On the other hand, it is clear that U.S. PMs are being urged to value cultural diversity in ways that are often not shared by their foreign cohorts.

For at least three-quarters of the world's population, relationship comes above all else: above time, above budget, and above specification. The savvy PM knows this and knows that he or she will always be balancing, for instance, the needs of the Japanese for meeting deadlines against the Latin American tendency toward a more relaxed approach to dealing with others (Dodson, 1998). We will have much more to say about negotiation in the next chapter.

For some years, management theorists have been writing about "corporate culture." We call these "microcultures" to differentiate them from the broader national or regional cultures about which we have been writing. It is just as true, though less obvious, to observe that microcultures vary from industry to industry and from firm to firm just as cultures do from nation to nation. Sales techniques perfectly permissible in one industry, the wholesale automobile industry, for instance, would cause outrage and lawsuits in the business-machine industry. Promises have very different meanings in different areas of business. No one takes seriously the "promised" date of completion of a software application project, any more than a finish-date promise made by a home-remodeling contractor.

The impact of interindustry, interfirm, and intrafirm microcultural diversity on the PM is significant. Perhaps more than any other type of manager, the PM is dependent on commitments made by people, both inside and outside the parent organization, who owe little allegiance to the project, have little cause for loyalty to the PM, and over whom the PM has little or no *de jure* authority. Hence, the PM must know whose promises can be relied upon and whose cannot. In a major study of 50 transnational projects, Hauptman et al. (1996) found that with product development teams, the skill with which they handled two-way communication and cultural differences was critical to success. On the positive side, Levinson et al. (1995) spell out several steps that allow "interorganizational learning" for groups that form international alliances (see also Fedor et al., 1996).

Popular movies and television to the contrary, the intentions of foreign governments and their officials are rarely evil. Foreign governments are usually devoted to ensuring that local citizens are well-treated by invading companies, that national treasures are not disturbed, that employment for their nationals is maximized, that some profits are reinvested in the host country, that safety regulations are not violated, and that other unintended exploitations are prevented. At times, rules and regulations may result from ancient traditions—no consumption of alcoholic beverages in Islamic nations, no consumption of pork products in Israel.

The job description of any PM should include responsibility for acquiring a working knowledge of the culture of any country in which he or she is to conduct a project. As far

Project Management in Practice

Success at Energo by Integrating Two Diverse Cultures

A major project involving some hundreds of millions of dollars was stymied due to the cultural differences between the owner/client, a state-run Middle East developer, and the contractor, a state-run European international designer and builder of industrial and construction projects. As can be imagined, the difference in the cultures is extreme and includes religions, the role of women in society, the difference in power between managers and workers, and the style of management itself. These differences were exacerbated by the conditions surrounding the project: an isolated desert, poor communication, extremely harsh living/working conditions, and a highly unstable legal/political environment (taxes, regulations, restrictions, and even client reorganizations) that was changing daily.

The client and contractor came to realize that the two separate organizational systems created an interface, or boundary, between them that was almost impenetrable. They thus decided to try to integrate the two systems into one unified system (see Exhibit 1). This was done methodically,

with a plan being drawn up, environmental impacts recognized, restructuring of the overall organization, designing the integration, and then implementing the design.

As perhaps expected, neither side's personnel were able to give up their perspective to see the larger picture. The project managers kept working on this issue, however, watched for problems, did a lot of management-by-walking-around, and gradually, the integration began to occur, gathering speed as it went. At project closure, when all costs and engineering changes were hammered out for final payment by tough external bargaining agents (rather than by principled negotiation, typically), no agreement could be reached. Instead, the project managers were brought back and allowed to close the project in their own fashion. They simply continued the integration process they had used earlier and quietly phased out the successful project.

Questions

1. **What was the key to solving this dilemma?**
2. **How did the two PMs implement their strategy?**
3. **What actions in Exhibit 1 might have been key to making this project a success?**

	The Project Style Characteristics	Actions
Physical Appearance:	Counterparts working together (teamwork) Project-related pictures, charts, and schedules on office walls	Tour the site with counterpart project manager daily Make your office look like a "war room"
Myths and Stories:	We are one team with two sides Both cultures are interesting Both sides' interests should be satisfied We trust young managers Get the job done Separate yourself from the position and stick to the problem Both project managers are good, and committed to the project	Whenever possible, let the counterparts have a joint office Organize group visits to local historical sites
Ceremonies:	Gather ideas and information from all over the project organization Frequent meetings at all levels Frequent social gatherings and festivities	From time to time, attend lower-level joint project meetings Celebrate each key event completion
Management Style:	Plan, organize, and control with your counterparts Make decisions No finger pointing for wrong decisions, learn the lesson Quickly execute the decision If you need help, don't hesitate to refer to your boss	Ask counterparts for joint report on an issue Recognize high-performance managers monthly

Source: D. Z. Milosevic, "Case Study: Integrating the Owner's and the Contractor's Project Organization," *Project Management Journal*, Vol. 21.

EXHIBIT 1 Examples of Integrative Actions

as possible, the project should be conducted in such a way that host-country norms are honored. To do so, however, will often raise problems for management of the parent firm. An unwelcome truth is that the cultures of many countries will not offer a female PM the same level of respect shown a male PM. Thus, senior management is faced with the awkward choice of violating its own policy against sex discrimination or markedly increasing the risk of project failure. The same problem may also exist with the use of a Jewish PM in an Arab country, or an Armenian PM in Turkey.

In Chapter 5, we will discuss "virtual" projects, which are transfunctional and/or geographically dispersed. Multicultural projects are "virtual" by definition. In recent years, communication problems have been greatly eased for virtual projects through email, the Internet, conference calls, and videoconferencing (Dodson, 1998). While overused email may be a curse for project managers, it is also a blessing when frequent communication with other organizations is required. Of course, these technologies do not relieve the PM from the demands of cultural sensitivity. Though it is not electronic, the technology of negotiation is critical for the PM with a multicultural project. Dodson writes:

> *Project management is ultimately expectation management. Effective management of expectations requires negotiation skills that eclipse more quantitative, "metrical" skills. Projects are only as successful as the degree to which the project manager is an effective negotiator. . . .*

We have already noted the difference in the bottom-up flow of information in American projects and the top-down flow in countries where the management style is authoritarian. Grinbergs et al. (1993) compare the managerial characteristics of Swiss and American managers/engineers of the same general age, education, and salary levels, all of whom were working on software projects. The study revealed that Swiss managers were "much more formal" with each other than Americans. This demonstrates the interaction of interpersonal style and language. Because we emphasize planning so strongly in this book, we find the differences in the Swiss and American approaches to planning of special interest. "The U.S. respondents did not consider thorough planning and a long-term strategy as absolute prerequisites for beginning a project. . . . Though promptness is highly valued in both countries, long-term strategy is considered much more important in the Swiss company" (Grinbergs et al., 1993, p. 24).

In addition to these areas, the Swiss and Americans differed in a number of other ways of import to the PM. The Swiss showed a stronger work ethic, were more resistant to change, were more risk averse, more accepting of bureaucracy, and more focused on quality. The Americans were more collegial, more willing to experiment and innovate, had a shorter time horizon, and communicated more openly.

Dinsmore et al. (1993) list factors that they contend require special consideration by the PM heading a multicultural project. We have already noted some of these factors, and others are obvious: the importance of language and culture, the need to deal with the politics and politicians in the host nation, the fact that the PM may have to use indigenous staff members, the possibility of input supply and technology problems, and the need to obey local laws and customs. In addition, they note two other matters that may cause serious problems for the PM. First, there are additional risk factors such as kidnapping, disease, and faulty medical care. Of course, in many countries, project workers may face less risk from crime than in their home country as well as easier access to medical care. Second, the PM may have to provide for the physical and psychological needs of people who are transferred to the host nation and must live in a "strange land with different customs and way of life." They refer to this as the "expatriate way of life."

In the next chapter, we consider the task of negotiating for the resources to implement the project plan and work breakdown structure (WBS), which will then complete our treatment of Part I: Project Initiation.

Summary

This chapter addressed the subject of the PM. The PM's role in the organization and responsibilities to both the organization and the project team were discussed first. Common PM career paths were also described. Next, the unique demands typically placed on PMs were detailed, and the task of selecting the PM was addressed. Finally, the issue of culture and its effect on project communication and success was discussed.

The following specific points were made in the chapter.

- Two factors crucial to the success of the project are its support by top management and the existence of a problem orientation, rather than discipline orientation, within the team members.
- Compared to a functional manager, a PM is a generalist rather than a specialist, a synthesizer rather than an analyst, and a facilitator rather than a supervisor.
- The PM has responsibilities to the parent organization, the project itself, and the project team. The unique demands on a PM concern seven areas:
  - Acquiring adequate physical resources
  - Acquiring and motivating personnel
  - Dealing with obstacles
  - Making goal trade-offs
  - Maintaining a balanced outlook in the team
  - Communicating with all stakeholders
  - Negotiating
- The most common characteristics of effective project team members are as follows:

  - High-quality technical skills
  - Political sensitivity
  - Strong problem orientation
  - High self-esteem

- To handle the variety of project demands effectively, the PM must understand the basic goals of the project, have the support of top management, build and maintain a solid information network, and remain flexible about as many project aspects as possible.
- The best person to select as PM is the one who will get the job done.
- Valuable skills for the PM are technical and administrative credibility, political sensitivity, and an ability to get others to commit to the project, a skill otherwise known as leadership.
- Some important points concerning the impact of culture on project management are as follows:

  - Cultural elements refer to the way of life for any group of people and include technology, institutions, language, and art.
  - The project environment includes economic, political, legal, and sociotechnical aspects.
  - Examples of problematic cultural issues include the group's perception of time and the manner of staffing projects.
  - Language is a particularly critical aspect of culture for the project.

Glossary

Analytic Approach Breaking problems into their constituent parts to understand the parts better and thereby solve the problem

Benefit–Cost A ratio to evaluate a proposed course of action

Champion A person who spearheads an idea or action and "sells" it throughout the organization

Contingency Plan An alternative for action if the expected result fails to materialize

Culture The way of life of any group of people

Discipline An area of expertise

Environment Everything outside the system that delivers inputs or receives outputs from the system

Facilitator A person who helps people overcome problems, either with technical issues or with other people

Functional One of the standard organization disciplines such as finance, marketing, accounting, or operations

Microculture The "corporate culture" within the organization, or even project

Systems Approach A wide-ranging, synthesizing method for addressing problems that considers multiple and interacting relationships. Commonly contrasted with the analytic approach

Technological Having to do with the methods and techniques for doing something

Trade-Off Allowing one aspect to get worse in return for another aspect getting better

Questions

Material Review Questions

1. How does the project act as a stepping stone for the PM's career?

2. Name the categories of skills that should be considered in the selection of a PM.

3. Discuss the PM's responsibilities toward the project team members.

4. What are the major differences between functional managers and PMs?

5. What are some of the essential characteristics of effective project team members?

6. What is the most important selection characteristic of a PM?

7. What project goals are most important during the project life-cycle stages?

8. Why must project management team members have good technical skills?

9. Describe each of the four elements of culture.

10. Identify some important types of project environments.

11. Contrast culture, microculture, and multiculture.

12. In what ways is language crucial in project management?

13. Identify the five multicultural factors requiring special consideration.

Class Discussion Questions

14. Can you think of several ways to assure "breadth of communication" in a project? Do you think "socialization" off the job helps or hinders?

15. Contrast the prime law for projects, "Never surprise the boss," with the corporate adage "Bad news never travels up."

16. How does a PM, in some cases, work like a politician?

17. What are some of the conflicts that are bound to occur between stakeholders that have legitimate interests in the project?

18. PMs must be generalists rather than specialists. Yet, team members need to have more specialized, technical skills. Can a generalist manage a team of specialists effectively?

19. Why do you think cost drops in importance as an objective right after the formation stage?

20. Why is it more difficult to keep the project on its time and cost schedules the later the project gets in its life cycle?

21. Suppose that you have a talented scientist temporarily working for you on a client contract who is due to be transferred back to her regular job. Although you could do without her efforts at this point of the contract, you happen to know that she will be laid off for lack of work at her regular job and her personal financial situation is dire. You feel it is important that her talent be kept on the company payroll, although keeping her on the contract will increase expenses unnecessarily. Is the transfer decision a business decision or an ethical one? Why? If the decision were yours to make, what would you decide?

22. How is communication through art different than through language?

23. What should a firm do when an accepted practice in a foreign country is illegal in its own country?

24. Do you agree that the trend now is to become less of a generic PM and more of a specialist? If so, then how do you gain a wide range of experience for that next job opportunity?

Incidents for Discussion

Smithson Company

Keith Smithson is the CEO of the Smithson Company, a privately owned, medium-size computer services company. The company is 20 years old and, until recently, had experienced rapid growth. Mr. Smithson believes that the company's recent problems are closely related to the depressed Asian economy.

Brianna Smatters was hired as the director of corporate planning at Smithson 6 months ago. After reviewing the performance and financial statements of Smithson for the last few years, Ms. Smatters has come to the conclusion that the economic conditions are not the real problem, but rather exacerbate the real problems. She believes that in this Internet era, Smithson Company's services are becoming obsolete but the department heads have not been able to cooperate effectively in reacting to information technology threats and opportunities. She believes that the strong functional organization impedes the kinds of action required to remedy the situation. Accordingly, she has recommended that Mr. Smithson create a new position, manager of special operations, to promote and use project management techniques. The new manager would handle several critical projects in the role of PM.

Mr. Smithson is cool to the idea. He believes that his functional departments are managed by capable professional people. Why can't these high-level managers work together more efficiently? Perhaps a good approach would be for him to give the group some direction (what to do, when to do it, who should do it) and then put the functional manager most closely related to the problems in charge of the group. He assumes that the little push from him (Smithson) as just described would be enough to "get the project rolling."

Questions

After this explanation Ms. Smatters is more convinced than ever that a separate, nonfunctional PM is required. Is she right? If you were Smatters, how would you sell Mr. Smithson on the idea? If a new position is created, what other changes should be made?

Newcastle Nursing and Rehabilitation Residence

The Newcastle Nursing and Rehabilitation Residence (NNRR) is a 135-bed skilled nursing home. NNRR is considering converting a 36-bed wing of their main building for use by patients who require ventilator-assisted breathing.

The rooms will be slightly smaller than optimum for ventilator patients, but just exceed the recommended minimum square footage. Enlarging the rooms is not an economic option. In the main, the conversion will require the addition of electrical wiring to power oxygen-concentrators that extract 95 percent pure oxygen from room air, portable ventilators that supply the oxygen under pressure to assist breathing, and small, motor-driven suction devices to remove excess mucus from a patient's airway. These rooms must also be connected to an emergency generator that automatically starts and supplies electrical current if the main electrical supply fails. Finally, pressure sensors must be connected from each ventilator unit to a sound device located in the hallway of the ventilator wing. These units sound a strident signal and cause a hallway light to flash if there is a sharp drop in the airway pressure of a ventilator patient. In addition to these power needs associated with ventilator patients, power outlets are needed for several machines that dispense tube feedings of medicines and nutrition, and for IVs, radios, and similar entertainment devices. Each bed itself needs a power outlet as does the air mattress pump. Because all rooms are double occupancy, each room needs two full sets of the outlets.

The equipment noted earlier is normally plugged in at all times when the patient is in his or her room. Otherwise well patients, however, are moved daily into a "day room" equipped with a large screen TV and chairs and tables. Most patients must be moved with their portable ventilators and concentrators or bottled oxygen. Patients who are well enough eat their meals in the day room and socialize with each other and with visitors. (The socialization is a quiet process because a large majority of the patients breathe through a tube inserted in their trachea and are unable to speak aloud.)

The Senior Administrator, Steve Murphy, has decided to set up the conversion process as a project. Mr. Murphy is considering the choice of a PM. He is trained in business, not hospital design. He feels a Registered Nurse or Licensed Practical Nurse might be an appropriate PM. He also feels that a Respiratory Therapist (RT) might be a good choice because RTs are responsible for using the major electrical equipment. Finally, he thinks that the installation and placing of all the outlets might be better handled by a representative of the electrical contractor who must carry out the major part of the room conversion.

Questions

Who should Mr. Murphy choose? Defend your choice.

International Microcircuits, Inc.

Megan Bedding, vice president of sales for International Microcircuits, Inc. (IM), was delighted when IM was one of the few firms invited to enter a bid to supply a large industrial customer with their major product in a small foreign country. However, her top salesperson for that region had just called and informed her of certain "expectations" of doing business in the country:

1. Local materials representing at least 50 percent of the product's value must be purchased in reciprocity.

2. The local politicians will expect continual significant donations to their party.

3. Industrial customers normally receive a 40 percent "rebate" (kickback) when they purchase goods from suppliers such as IM. (IM's profit margin is only 20 percent.)

With this new information, Megan was unsure about changing or proceeding with the bid. If it was withdrawn, a lot of effort would be wasted as well as a chance to get a foothold in the international market. But if she proceeded, how could these expectations be met in a legal and ethical way?

Questions

Devise a solution that addresses Megan's concerns.

Continuing Integrative Class Project

The task for the class now is to select a PM. But heed the advice given in the chapter that the best PM is the one "who can get the job done," not the one who is just "available." This is a particularly dangerous pitfall for a class project where everyone is busy and no one had expected to be called upon to lead a major project. Moreover, resist the temptation of naming two people as co-PMs—that rarely works unless these people have a history of working well together in previous projects. With two PMs, no one knows who is responsible for what and tasks may fall through the cracks. In theory, the work of the PM should be no more, and possibly less, than the other members of the class, especially if the project is well organized and well run. The main responsibilities of the PM (and perhaps in concert with subteam heads) are to organize the project, schedule the tasks, and stay on top of progress. However, if problems, or maybe personality feuds, crop up, the PM may find that these are taking a lot more time than was expected. When a PM is finally selected, it is important for the class, and especially any subteam heads, if such exist, to give full allegiance to the PM in getting the work done and upholding the workload they agreed to handle. Bear in

mind also that there will probably be one or more people in the class who will need to do more than their fair share of the work because of unexpected problems that crop up during the term. The historian should record the process of selecting the PM: What criteria were used to select the PM? Were any important criteria discussed in the book overlooked? Were criteria used that were not mentioned in the book? Was the process dominated by one or more team members?

Bibliography

Blanchard, K., and N. V. Peale. *The Power of Ethical Management*. New York: Morrow, 1988.

Bradberry, T., and J. Greaves. *Emotional Intelligence 2.0*. San Diego: TalentSmart, 2009.

Brox, D. "Say No." *PM Network*, May 2012.

Burba, D. "The Complexity Equation." *PM Network*, November 2013.

Dinsmore, P. C., and M. M. B. Codas. "Challenges in Managing International Projects." In P. C. Dinsmore, ed., *The AMA Handbook of Project Management*. New York: AMACOM, 1993.

Dodson, W. R. "Virtually International." *PM Network*, April 1998.

Dulewicz, V., and M. J. Higgs. "Design of a new instrument to assess leadership dimensions & styles." In *Henley Working Paper HWP 0311*, Henley Management College, Henley-on-Thames, UK, 2003.

Fedor, K. J., and W. B. Werther, Jr. "The Fourth Dimension: Creating Culturally Responsive International Alliances." *IEEE Engineering Management Review*, Fall 1997, as reprinted from *Organizational Dynamics*, Autumn 1996.

Foti, R. "Today's Project Manager." *PM Network*, April 2003.

Gogal, H. C., and L. R. Ireland. "Project Management: Meeting China's Challenge." *Project Management Journal*. February 1988.

Gagnon, R. J., and S. J. Mantel, Jr. "Strategies and Performance Improvement for Computer-Assisted Design." *IEEE Transactions on Engineering Management*, November 1987.

Goleman, D. *Working with Emotional Intelligence*. New York: Bantam Books, 1998.

Green, S. G. "Top Management Support of R&D Projects: A Strategic Leadership Perspective." *IEEE Transactions on Engineering Management*, August 1995.

Grinbergs, A., and A. H. Rubenstein. "Software Engineering Management: A Comparison of Methods in Switzerland and the United States." *IEEE Transactions on Engineering Management*, February 1993.

Hauptman, O., and K. K. Hirji. "The Influence of Process Concurrency on Project Outcomes in Product Development: An Empirical Study of Cross-Functional Teams." *IEEE Transactions on Engineering Management*, May 1996.

Hughes, T. P. *Rescuing Prometheus*. New York, Pantheon, 1998.

Hunsberger, K. "Juggling Act." *PM Network*, September 2008.

Ireland, L. R., W. J. Pike, and J. L. Schrock. "Ethics for Project Managers." *Proceedings of the 1982 PMI Seminar/Symposium on Project Management*, Toronto, Ontario, Canada.

Jiang, J. J., G. Klein, and S. Margulis. "Important Behavioral Skills for IS Project Managers: The Judgments of Experienced IS Professionals." *Project Management Journal*, March 1998.

Kalu, T. C. U. "A Framework for the Management of Projects in Complex Organizations." *IEEE Transactions on Engineering Management*, May 1993.

Kent, S. "Stretched Thin." *PM Network*, April 2008.

Kloppenborg, T J., and S. J. Mantel, Jr. "Trade-offs on Projects: They May Not Be What You Think." *Project Management Journal*, March 1990.

Kotter, J. P. "What Effective General Managers Really Do." *Harvard Business Review*, November–December 1982.

Kruse, K. *What Is Leadership?* http://www.forbes.com/sites/kevinkruse/2013/04/09/what-is-leadership/.

Levinson, N. S., and M. Asahi. "Cross-National Alliances and Interorganizational Learning." *IEEE Engineering Management Review*, Fall 1997, as reprinted from *Organizational Dynamics*, Autumn 1995.

Lynn, L. H., and T. J. McKeown. *Organizing Business: Trade Associations in America and Japan*. Washington, D.C.: American Enterprise Institute for Public Policy Research, 1988.

Matson, E. "Congratulations, You're Promoted" and "Project: You." *Fast Company*, as reprinted in *Engineering Management Review*, Winter 1998.

Medcof, J. W., J. Hauschildt, and G. Keim. "Realistic Criteria for Project Manager Selection and Development." *Project Management Journal*, September 2000.

Müller, R., and R. Turner. "Leadership Competency Profiles of Successful Project Managers." *International Journal of Project Management*, Vol. 28, 2010.

Nixon, M. A. "Legal Lights: Business Ethics." *Project Management Journal*, September 1987.

Norrie, J., and D. H. T. Walker. "A Balanced Scorecard Approach to Project Management Leadership." *Project Management Journal*, December 2004.

Pastin, M. *The Hard Problems of Management*. San Francisco: Jossey-Bass, 1986.

Pinto, J. K., and D. P. Slevin. "The Project Champion: Key to Implementation Success." *Project Management Journal*, December 1989.

Project Management Institute. "Leadership Survey." *PM Network*, December 2013, p. 7.

Project Management Institute. "Slow Motion." *PM Network*, April 2005, p. 1.

Robb, D. J. "Ethics in Project Management: Issues, Practice, and Motive." *PM Network*, December 1996.

Sahlin, J. P. "How Much Technical Training Does a Project Manager Need?" *PM Network*, May 1998.

Schaefer, A. G., and A. J. Zaller. "The Ethics Audit for Non-profit Organizations." *PM Network*, March 1998.

Scott, S. G., and R. A. Bruce. "Following the Leader in R&D: The Joint Effect of Subordinate Problem-Solving Style and Leader-Member Relations on Innovative Behavior." *IEEE Transactions on Engineering Management*, February 1998.

Shenhar, A. J. "From Theory to Practice: Toward a Typology of Project-Management Styles." *IEEE Transactions on Engineering Management*, February 1998.

Slevin, D. P. *The Whole Manager*. New York: AMACOM, 1989.

Smith, L. A., and J. Haar. "Managing International Projects." In P. C. Dinsmore, ed., *The AMA Handbook of Project Management*. New York: AMACOM, 1993.

Starke, S. "Going Against the Grain." *PM Network*, July 2012.

Swanson, S. A. "Measuring the Intangibles." *PM Network*, July 2012.

The World Book. Chicago: Field Enterprises, 1997.

Tuckman, B., "Developmental Sequence in Small Groups." *Psychological Bulletin* 63(6), 384–399, 1965.

Whitten, N. "Attributes of the Successful Project Leader." *PM Network*, June 1996.

Zimmerer, T. W., and M. M. Yasin. "A Leadership Profile of American Project Managers." *Project Management Journal*, March 1998.

Zupek, R. "Sun Sets on Silicon Valley?" *PM Network*, May 2010.

The following case involves a PM who stumbles into a public project somewhat by accident. The project starts out as one thing and evolves into something else. Acquiring sufficient resources for the project is a major difficulty, and competition may be troublesome as well. A consultant is hired who conducts two surveys to gather more information and makes recommendations based on the survey evidence and experience. The case illustrates the varied skills necessary to be a successful PM and the myriad opportunities/difficulties some projects entail.

Case

The National Jazz Hall of Fame[4]   Cornelis A. de Kluyver, J. Giuliano, J. Milford, and B. Cauthen

Mr. Robert Rutland, founder of the National Jazz Hall of Fame, poured himself another drink as he listened to some old jazz recordings and thought about the decisions facing him. Established about 1 year ago, the National Jazz Hall of Fame (NJHF) had achieved moderate success locally but had not yet attracted national recognition. Mr. Rutland wondered how much support existed nationally, what services the NJHF should provide and for whom, and what the NJHF should charge for those services. He also thought about other jazz halls of fame and their implications for the NHJF. Although he had engaged an independent consultant to find some answers, the questions still lingered.

Jazz

The word "jazz," according to Dr. David Pharies, a linguistics scholar at the University of Florida, originally meant copulation, but later identified a certain type of music. Amid the march of funeral bands, jazz music began in New Orleans in the

early 1900s by combining Black spirituals, African rhythms, and Cajun music; Dixieland jazz became the sound of New Orleans. Jazz traveled from New Orleans, a major trade center, on river boats and ships and reached St. Louis, Kansas City, Memphis, Chicago, and New York. Musicians in these cities developed local styles of jazz, all of which remained highly improvisational, personal, and rhythmically complex. Over the years, different sounds emerged—swing, big band, be-bop, fusion, and others—indicating the fluidity and diversity of jazz. Jazz artists developed their own styles and competed with one another for recognition of their musical ability and compositions. Such diversity denied jazz a simple definition, and opinions still differed sharply on what exactly jazz was. It was difficult, however, to dispute Louis Armstrong's statement that "if you have to ask what jazz is, you'll never know."

Origins of the National Jazz Hall of Fame

Mr. Rutland, a history professor at the University of Virginia, which is in Charlottesville, discovered that renovation plans for the city's historic district excluded the Paramount Theater, a local landmark. The Paramount was constructed in the 1930s and used as a performance center and later as a movie theater. It was closed in the 1970s and now was in danger of becoming dilapidated. Alarmed by the apparent lack of interest in saving

---

[4]Reprinted with permission. Copyright the Darden Graduate Business School Foundation, Charlottesville, VA.

the Paramount, Mr. Rutland began to look for opportunities to restore and eventually use the theater. The most attractive option to him was to establish a jazz hall of fame that would use the theater as a museum and performance center; this would capitalize on the theater's name, because the Paramount Theater in New York City was a prominent jazz hall during the 1930s and 1940s. Mr. Rutland mentioned his idea—saving the theater by establishing a jazz hall of fame—to several friends in Charlottesville. They shared his enthusiasm, and together they incorporated the National Jazz Hall of Fame and formed the board of directors in early 1983. A few prominent jazz musicians, such as Benny Goodman and Chick Corea, joined the NJHF National Advisory Board. The purpose of the NJHF was to establish and maintain a museum, archives, and concert center in Charlottesville to sponsor jazz festivals, workshops, and scholarships and to promote other activities remembering great jazz artists, serving jazz enthusiasts, and educating the public on the importance of jazz in American culture and history.

The First Year's Efforts

Immediately after incorporation, the directors began their search for funds to save the Paramount and to establish the NJHF and soon encountered two difficulties. Philanthropic organizations refused to make grants because no one on the board of directors had experience in a project such as the NJHF. In addition, government agencies such as the National Endowment for the Arts and the National Endowment for the Humanities considered only organizations in operation for at least 2 years. However, some small contributions came from jazz enthusiasts who had read stories about the NJHF in *Billboard*, a music industry magazine, and in the Charlottesville and Richmond newspapers.

By mid-1983, the board of directors discovered that to save the Paramount, at least $600,000 would be needed, a sum too large for them to consider. They decided, however, that out of their love for jazz they would continue to work to establish the NJHF in Charlottesville.

Despite these setbacks, Mr. Rutland and the other directors believed that the first year's activities showed promise. The NJHF sponsored three concerts at local high schools. The concerts featured such jazz greats as Maxine Sullivan, Buddy Rich, and Jon Hendricks and Company, and each concert attracted more than 500 people. Although the NJHF lost some money on each concert, the directors thought that the concerts succeeded in publicizing and promoting the NJHF. In addition, a fundraiser at a Charlottesville country club brought $2,000 to the NJHF, and Mr. Rutland started the NJHF newsletter. The collection of objects for the museum was enlarged, and Louis Armstrong and Duke Ellington were posthumously inducted into the NJHF. At the end of the first year, enthusiasm among board members was still high, and they believed that the NJHF could survive indefinitely, albeit on a small scale.

But a Hall of Fame in Charlottesville . . .

Mr. Rutland believed that a hall of fame could succeed in Charlottesville, though other cities might at first seem more appropriate. More than 500,000 tourists annually were attracted to

Charlottesville (1980 population: 40,000) to visit Thomas Jefferson's home at Monticello, James Monroe's home at Ash Lawn, and the Rotunda and the Lawn of the University of Virginia, where total enrollment was 16,000. Mr. Jefferson designed the Rotunda and the buildings on the Lawn and supervised their construction. The Virginia Office of Tourism promoted these national landmarks as well as the city's two convention centers. In addition, 13 million people lived within a 3-hour drive of Charlottesville. If Charlottesville seemed illogical for a hall of fame, Mr. Rutland reasoned, so did Cooperstown, New York, home of the Baseball Hall of Fame and Canton, Ohio, location of the Professional Football Hall of Fame. He thought that successful jazz festivals in such different places as Newport, Rhode Island, and French Lick, Indiana, showed that location was relatively unimportant for jazz. Moreover, a Charlottesville radio station recently switched to a music format called "Memory Lane," which featured classics by Frank Sinatra, Patti Page, the Mills Brothers, the Glenn Miller Orchestra, and numerous others. The station played much jazz, and won the loyalty of many jazz enthusiasts in the Charlottesville area. The success of "Memory Lane" indicated to Mr. Rutland that the Charlottesville community could provide the NJHF with a base of interest and loyalty. Most important, Mr. Rutland believed that he and his friends possessed the commitment necessary to make a jazz hall of fame succeed.

And Halls of Fame in Other Cities?

Although no national organization operated successfully, several local groups claimed to be *the* Jazz Hall of Fame, as Billboard magazine reported.

BILLBOARD 4/28/84

Hall of Fame in Harlem

by Sam Sutherland and Peter Keepnews

CBS Records and the Harlem YMCA have joined forces to establish a Jazz Hall of Fame. The first induction ceremony will take place on May 14 at Avery Fisher Hall, combined with a concert featuring such artists as Ramsey Lewis, Hubert Laws, Ron Carter, and an all-star Latin Jazz ensemble. Proceeds from the concert will benefit the Harlem YMCA.

Who will the initial inductees be, and how will they be chosen? What's being described in the official literature as "a prestigious group of jazz editorialists, critics, producers, and respected connoisseurs" (and, also, incidentally, musicians—among those on the panel are Miles Davis, Dizzy Gillespie, Cab Calloway, Max Roach, and the ubiquitous Dr. Billy Taylor) will do the actual selecting, but nominations are being solicited from the general public. Jazz lovers are invited to submit the names of six artists, three living and three dead, to: The Harlem YMCA Jazz Hall of Fame, New York, NY 10030. Deadline for nominations is May 1.

BILLBOARD, 5/19/84

One, Two, Many Halls of Fame?

by Sam Sutherland and Peter Keepnews

Monday night marks the official launch of the Harlem YMCA Jazz Hall of Fame (Billboard, April 28), a project in which CBS Records is closely involved. The Hall's first inductees are being unveiled at an Avery Fisher Hall concert that also includes performances by, among others, Sarah Vaughan and Branford Marsalis.

The project is being touted as the first jazz hall of fame, a statement that discounts a number of similar projects in the past that never quite reached fruition. But first or not, the good people of CBS and the Harlem YMCA are apparently in for some competition.

According to a new publication known as JAMA, the Jazz Listeners/Musicians Newsletter, Dizzy Gillespie—who also is a member of the Harlem YMCA Jazz Hall of Fame committee—"promised in Kansas City, Mo. to ask musicians for help in establishing an International Jazz Hall of Fame" in that city. The newsletter quotes Gillespie, whom it describes as "honorary chairman of the proposed hall," as vowing to ask "those musicians who were inspired by jazz"—among them Stevie Wonder, Quincy Jones, and Paul McCartney (?)—to contribute financially to the Kansas City project, which, as envisioned by the great trumpeter, would also include a jazz museum, classrooms, and performance areas.

Is there room for two Jazz Halls of Fame? Do the people involved in the New York city project know about the Kansas City project, and vice versa? (Obviously Gillespie does, but does anyone else?) Remember the New York Jazz Museum? Remember the plaques in the sidewalk on 52nd Street (another CBS Records brainchild)?

The notion of commemorating the contributions of the great jazz musicians is a noble one. It would be a shame to see the energies of the jazz community get diverted into too many different endeavors for accomplishing the same admirable goal—which, unfortunately, is what has tended to happen in the past.

BILLBOARD, 5/26/84

Also noted: the first inductees in the Harlem YMCA Jazz Hall of Fame (Billboard, May 19) have been announced. The posthumous inductees are, to nobody's great surprise, Louis Armstrong, Duke Ellington, Count Basie, Charlie Parker, and—a slight surprise, perhaps—Mary Lou Williams. The living honorees are Roy Eldridge, Dizzy Gillespie, Miles Davis, Ella Fitzgerald, and Art Blakey.

The New York Jazz museum (which the 5/19/84 article referred to) was established in the early 1970s but quickly ran out of money and was closed a few years later. In the early 1960s, a jazz museum was established in New Orleans, and because of insufficient funds, all that remained was the Louis Armstrong Memorial Park, the site of an outdoor jazz festival each summer. Tulane and Rutgers universities each possessed extensive archives containing thousands of phonograph records, tape recordings, posters, books, magazines, journals, and other historic pieces and memorabilia. Neither university, however, considered its archives a hall of fame.

Other Halls of Fame

The more prominent halls of fame in the United States were the Baseball, the Professional Football, the College Football, and the Country Music Hall of Fame. These and many other halls of fame were primarily concerned with preserving history by collecting and displaying memorabilia, compiling records, and inducting new members annually.

Mr. Rutland visited most of the other halls of fame and learned that they were usually established by a significant contribution from an enthusiast. In the case of the Country Music Hall of Fame, some country music stars agreed to make a special recording of country hits and to donate the royalties to the organization.

Mr. Rutland was especially interested in The Country Music Hall of Fame because of similarities between country music and jazz. Country music, similarly to jazz, had a rich cultural history in America, and neither type of music was the most popular in the United States.

The Country Music Hall of Fame (CMHF) was established in 1967 in Nashville after a cooperative fundraising effort involving the city, artists, and sponsors. By 1976, the CMHF included a museum, an archives, a library, and a gift shop. More than one-half million people visited the CMHF in 1983, partly because of the nearby Grand Ole Opry, the premier concert hall for country music where the Grand Ole Opry cable radio broadcasts originated. Of the CMHF's $2.1 million annual budget, 85 percent came from admissions, 10 percent from sales at the gift shop and by mail, and 5 percent from donations. In the past 2 years, the CMHF had formed the Friends of Country Music, now more than 2,000 people who donated $25 each per year and who received a country music newsletter every 3 months and discounts on CMHF merchandise.

The National Association of Jazz Educators

Mr. Rutland was uncertain how much and what type of support he could get from the National Association of Jazz Educators. This organization, with 5,000 members, primarily coordinated and promoted jazz education programs.

Performance programs were normally offered through music departments. Most high schools and colleges had bands that played a variety of jazz arrangements as part of their repertoire. Band conductors usually had a music degree from a major university and belonged to the National Association of Jazz Educators.

Most of the jazz appreciation courses offered in schools throughout the United States treated jazz as a popular art form, as a barometer of society, rather than as a subject of interest in itself. Some educators believed that jazz greats such as Louis Armstrong and Duke-Ellington should be honored not as jazz musicians, but as composers such as George Gershwin and Richard Rogers. Indeed, a prominent jazz historian told Mr. Rutland that jazz might benefit more from breaking down this distinction between jazz artists and composers than from reinforcing it.

The National Survey

To get some of the answers to his many questions, Mr. Rutland engaged an independent consultant who conducted two surveys; the first was a national survey and the second a tourist survey. For the national survey, the consultant designed a questionnaire to gauge the respondent's level of interest in both jazz and the concept of a National Jazz Hall of Fame and to determine the respondent's demographics. A sample size of 1,300 was used, and the mailing covered the entire continental United States. The mailing list, obtained from the Smithsonian Institution in Washington, D.C., contained names and addresses of people who had purchased the "Classic Jazz Record Collection," as advertised in *Smithsonian* magazine. Of the 1,300 questionnaires, 440 were sent to Virginia residents and 860 to residents of other states in order to provide both statewide and national data. Of the questionnaires that went to other states, the majority was targeted toward major cities and apportioned according to the interest level for jazz in each city as indicated by the circulation statistics of *Downbeat*, a jazz magazine. Of the 860 questionnaires sent to the other states, 88 were sent to residents of Chicago, 88 to Detroit, 83 to New York City, 60 to San Francisco, 56 to Philadelphia, 56 to Washington, DC, 52 to Los Angeles,

46 to Charlotte, 46 to Miami, 45 to Dallas, 42 to Atlanta, 42 to Houston, 30 to Denver, 28 to Kansas City, 28 to New Orleans, 28 to St. Louis, 27 to Boston, and 15 to Seattle. Of the 1,300 questionnaires, 165, or 12.7 percent, were returned.

As shown in Exhibit 1, 79 percent of the respondents were 35 years of age or older, 73 percent were male, and the majority were well-educated, professionals, and had an annual income of more than $50,000. Of interest also was that 75 percent of the respondents contributed $200 or more per year to different nonprofit organizations. Since the sample included a large number of record buyers of age 50 or older, the consultant weighted the survey results with age data obtained from the Recording Industry Association of America to make the survey results representative of all jazz-record buyers.

The survey also showed in Exhibit 2 that swing was the most popular form of jazz, followed by Dixieland, and then more traditional forms of jazz, from which the consultant concluded that a nostalgic emphasis should gather support from jazz enthusiasts of all ages and that later, the National Jazz Hall of Fame could promote more contemporary forms of jazz.

As for services, the survey suggested in Exhibit 3 that respondents most wanted a performance center or concert hall. A museum and seminars were also popular choices. The consultant was surprised by the strong interest in information about jazz recordings because the average respondent did not buy many records. A newsletter was rated relatively unimportant by most respondents. Most gratifying for Mr. Rutland was that respondents on average were willing to contribute between $20.00 and $30.00 per year to the National Jazz Hall of Fame, with a weighted average contribution of $23.40.

The Tourist Survey

In addition to conducting the National Survey, the consultant developed a questionnaire and interviewed approximately 100 tourists to the Charlottesville area at the Western Virginia

Demographics	Percentage of Respondents	Percentage of All Record Buyers*	Census Data**
Age—35	79	37	43
Sex—Male	73	82	49
Education—Grad+	54	24***	31
Job—Professional	57	26	22
Income—$50,000+	50	23	7
Non-profit Contr. $200/year+	75		

*Source: Consumer Purchasing of Records and Pre-recorded Tapes in the United States, 1970–1983, Recording Industry Association of America.
**Source: U.S. Department of Commerce, Bureau of the Census, 1982.
***Source: Simmons Market Research Bureau, 1982.

EXHIBIT 1 Survey Results: Demographics of Respondents

Type of Interest	Percentage of Respondents Answering with a 4 or 5 Rating	Weighted Percentage of Respondents Answering with a 4 or 5 Rating
General Interest in Music	62	71
Dixieland	62	70
Swing	87	81
Traditional	63	66
Improvisational	41	48
Jazz Rock	25	47
Fusion	15	9
Pop Jazz	27	53
Classical	68	73

EXHIBIT 2 Survey Results: Preferences for Different Styles of Jazz

Service	Percentage of Respondents Answering with a 4 or 5 Rating	Weighted Percentage of Respondents Answering with a 4 or 5 Rating
Performance Center	70	83
Concert Hall	66	79
Artist Seminars	50	62
Nightclub	52	57
Museum	57	57
Tourist Center	42	48
Audio-Visual Exhibitions	57	55
Shrine	55	52
Educational Programs	48	51
Record Information	71	69
History Seminars	38	54
Member Workshops	25	34
Lounge	37	45
Financial Support		
at $10.00/year	17	13
at $20.00/year	30	26
at $30.00/year		
Number of Contributors	62	64

EXHIBIT 3 Survey Results: Preferences for Services Offered

Visitors Center near Monticello. About 140,000 tourists stopped at the center annually to collect information on attractions nearby and throughout the state. The respondents came from all areas of the country, and most were traveling for more than one day. Almost 70 percent said they like jazz, mostly Dixieland and big band, and more than 60 percent indicated they would visit a Jazz Hall of Fame. The average admission they suggested was $3.50 per person.

The Consultant's Recommendations

The consultant limited his recommendations to the results of the two surveys. As a result, the question of whether the efforts in other cities to establish a National Jazz Hall of Fame would make the Charlottesville project infeasible was still unresolved. In a private discussion, however, the consultant intimated that "if the other efforts are as clumsily undertaken as many of the previous attempts, you will have nothing to worry about." He thought it was time that a professional approach was taken toward this project. Specifically, he made three recommendations:

1. Launch a direct mail campaign to the 100,000 people on the Smithsonian jazz mailing list. The focus of the mailing should be an appeal by a jazz great such as Benny Goodman to become a Founding Sponsor of the National Jazz Hall of Fame. He estimated that the cost of the campaign would range between $25,000 and $30,000; however, with an average contribution of $25.00 per respondent, a response rate of only 2 percent would allow the National Jazz Hall of Fame to break even.

2. Appoint a full-time executive director with any funds exceeding the cost of the mailing. The principal responsibilities of the executive director would be to organize and coordinate fundraising activities, to establish a performance center and museum, and to coordinate the collection of memorabilia and other artifacts.

3. Promote the National Jazz Hall of Fame at strategic locations around Charlottesville to attract tourists and other visitors. The Western Virginia Visitors Center was a prime prospect in his view for this activity. He calculated that 50,000 tourists annually at $3.00 each would provide sufficient funds to operate and maintain the National Jazz Hall of Fame.

The consultant also identified what he considered the critical elements for his plan's success. First, the National Jazz Hall of Fame should be professional in all of its services and communications to jazz enthusiasts. Second, the executive director should have prior experience in both fundraising and direct mail; he should have a commitment to and love for jazz, as well as administrative skill and creativity. Third, the National Jazz Hall of Fame should communicate frequently with Founding Sponsors to keep their interest and excitement alive. Finally, to ensure the enthusiastic cooperation of city officials, local merchants, and the Charlottesville community, he thought that more local prominence for the National Jazz Hall of Fame would prove indispensable.

The National Jazz Hall of Fame—Dream or Reality

As he paged through the consultant's report, Mr. Rutland wondered what to make of the recommendations. While he was encouraged by a national base of support for his idea, he was unsure how the Board of Directors would react to the consultant's proposals. With less than $2,500 in the bank, how would they get the necessary funds to implement the plan? Yet he knew he had to make some tough decisions, and quickly, if he wanted to make his dream a reality.

Questions

1. What is the project Mr. Rutland is trying to manage? Has it stayed the same?
2. Identify the various stakeholders in the project, including the competition.
3. Of the skills mentioned in the chapter that a project manager needs, which are most important here? Why?
4. What credibility does Mr. Rutland have? Is he a leader?
5. What cultures are relevant to this project? Describe the project environment.
6. What should Mr. Rutland do? Include the following issues:
   - Budget: acquiring adequate resources
     o philanthropic organizations
     o governmental agencies
     o donations
     o memberships
     o visitors
   - Budget: expenditures (consider Paramount theatre)
   - Performance: services/activities to offer
   - Competition
   - Schedule: deadlines, windows, milestones

The following reading integrates two views about the requirements for good PMs. One view concerns the personal and managerial characteristics of PMs and their ability to lead a team, regardless of the project. The other view considers the critical problems in the project in question and the PM's talents relative to these problems. A survey is first described, and then the critical problems that projects face are identified from the survey responses. Next, the skills required of PMs, as indicated by the survey respondents, are detailed. Finally, the skills are related back to the critical project problems for an integrated view of the requirements for a successful PM.

Reading

Juggling Act[5]   A. G. Richardson

Few PMs have the luxury of devoting 100 percent of their time to one project. Instead, many find themselves responsible for multiple ongoing projects at once. This balancing act is laden with challenges: scheduling and resource conflicts, long hours that can lead to burnout, and the constant struggle to keep a dizzying number of milestones on track.

But knowing how to juggle the personal project portfolio is necessary for professional success, says Linky van der Merwe, PMP, senior PM, Microsoft Consulting Services, Cape Town, South Africa.

In theory, it's simple.

"Make sure that you know yourself well enough to know your limits and how much pressure you can handle," she says. "Never take on more projects than you can handle or you risk jeopardizing your professionalism and your integrity."

In practice, though, juggling projects can easily overload even seasoned project professionals. Here are four areas rife with potential pitfalls and tips on how to avoid them.

Balancing Stakeholder Demands

Annette M. Suh, PMI-RMP, PMP, recently juggled one project with more than 50 stakeholders, along with four other projects of similar size. To keep the schedules and demands straight, Ms. Suh, a senior PM at data security firm Cloudmark Incorporated, San Francisco, California, USA, didn't even consider trying to store all the information in her head.

"What gets you through this successfully is that you write it down," she says. "Block off time on your calendar to check in on every project you have. I like to color-code projects, so I can see at a glance what relates to each project. I also keep meeting minutes with attendance, so I know who was present when decisions or commitments were made. With a large group, it's impossible to keep track any other way."

When reviewing project notes, pay special attention to the most powerful and influential stakeholders, says Ms. van der Merwe. Using key stakeholders' management and communication plans can make it easier to track specific demands and prioritize between projects.

Checking in, even briefly, with all stakeholders creates the opportunity to evaluate the project's alignment with organizational goals before prioritizing, according to Arindam Das, PMP, principal, business services at Bangalore, India-based Infosys Ltd., a PMI Global Executive Council member.

"Take a long-term perspective, and see that everyone's objectives are taken care of in a balanced manner," Mr. Das says. "Continuous communication and dialogue with all stakeholders, including occasional joint meetings, will reduce conflict."

When the strategic imperatives and business benefits of different projects are not articulated, project professionals may face unnecessary confusion and conflict, he says.

Managing Shared Resources

With a shared resource pool, working closely with other PMs is a must, says Ms. van der Merwe. "Determine priorities during milestone weeks to ensure the resources are available."

Guy Grindborg also suggests building "think" time into project plans to reflect on the best approaches to manage resources. "We're getting so caught up in doing, and we're running all the time, that we don't stop to think about the 'why,'" says Mr. Grindborg, PMP, vice president and senior consultant at Dallas, Texas, USA-based International Institute for Learning, a PMI Global Executive Council member. "Stop and think."

Further mitigate resourcing risks by creating a detailed staffing plan in advance, says Mr. Das. If a resource-pool manager is available, include him or her in personnel plans. "See that there are operational-level agreements on meeting staffing requirements," he says. "Getting required resources late is a sure-fire path to project failure."

Mr. Das encourages project professionals to learn the needs and abilities of team members. Knowing their strengths and weaknesses can ensure that the right people are in the right roles on the right projects.

"You need to see that they are given necessary training and assigned the right kind of work, so that they operate at their optimum level of performance and feel satisfied about their contribution," he says.

Finding Work/Life Balance

With multiple projects in various stages of execution, project professionals not only face time constraints at work but may also feel the stress of work bleeding into their personal time.

To maximize what gets done during work hours, Mr. Das applies a time-boxing technique. "It forces you to accept less-than-perfect solutions in certain situations, but at the end of the day, you are in a balanced state, and you achieve more," he says. "Other techniques, like using a four-quadrant, urgent-important chart, help you achieve more in less time."

PMs with multiple projects may not always be able to avoid 80-hour weeks, but to minimize this possibility, Mr. Das suggests staggering project schedules whenever possible. This creates breathing room between start and end dates, milestones, and peak periods—and gives the PM time for a personal life, he says.

A high-level outline for each project can be a lifesaver for time-crunched PMs. "Project managers need to make sure they understand how they are going to use their week and their days, and what types of activities they will do each day," advises Mr. Grindborg.

Staying on Schedule

Multiple projects mean multiple teams. If team members overlap on related projects, consider having one status meeting to avoid running from meeting to meeting, says Ms. van der Merwe.

"Resource and scheduling conflicts are better taken care of, because the joint meetings provide visibility of what is going on with other projects," she says. "I've used a spreadsheet-type of status reporting template before, giving feedback about multiple related projects with details about project goals, start and end dates, summary of progress, risks, and issues."

To prevent drowning in different schedules, Mr. Das suggests PMs use an umbrella approach. "Developing an integrated plan helps in managing all the projects better," he says. "This gives a single view of timeline, milestones and critical paths, and provides much better clarity."

Technology and tools can automate mundane operational activities, freeing up more time across the portfolio for the critical tasks on each project. The time Mr. Das used to spend monitoring myriad data points and generating management reports is now spent paying more attention to core issues and faster decision-making.

"You may not need to develop jazzy dashboards, but do ensure that you have some mechanisms to seamlessly convert raw data from different sources into information and insight that helps in managing your projects," he says.

Successfully juggling the schedules for numerous projects takes not only project management skills, but also knowledge of one's own capabilities.

"Have a clear set of goals and set limits," says Ms. Suh. "Be honest about what will happen if your own balance is out of sorts."

Too Many Balls in the Air

If project managers find stress levels spiraling out of control or the quality of their work slipping, they may need to say "enough" to their current workloads.

Annette M. Suh, PMI-RMP, PMP, Cloudmark Incorporated, San Francisco, California, USA, suggests meeting with a supervisor to discuss exactly what is going on and develop a plan to prioritize or redistribute the workload.

"Outline what will happen if things continue this way," she says. "Realize when you've taken on too much. And know your strengths and weaknesses."

Arrive at this meeting with hard evidence, such as plans and schedules, to illustrate the workload, its hours and its problems, says Guy Grindborg, PMP, International Institute for Learning, Dallas, Texas, USA.

"Show me you can't do this, and I'll help you," he says. "When I hear 'I can't do this or that because of work,' I know there is a problem."

Turning down additional projects and saying "no" should be part of a project manager's skill set—especially if that's the only way to maintain professional standards on each project, adds Linky van der Merwe, PMP, Microsoft Consulting Services, Cape Town, South Africa.

Always running late, over budget, and with less-than-ideal quality are clear warning signs that project managers have too many projects, she says.

Questions

1. How many project managers do you think are actually managing more than one project at a time?
2. The article keeps giving advice for handling the pressure of multiple projects. How much do you think the pressure increases relative to the number of projects being handled (most of which will typically share many of the same resources)?
3. Given the four areas in the article that seem to cause problems with multiple projects, which relate to project management issues and which to other issues, and what are they?

CHAPTER 4

Managing Conflict and the Art of Negotiation

Conflict has been mentioned many times thus far in this book. This chapter is about conflict. It is also about negotiation—the skill required to resolve most conflicts. As was discussed in Chapter 1, satisfying stakeholder needs should not be viewed as a zero-sum game where satisfying one stakeholder must come at the expense of another. Ideally, the Project Manager (PM) should seek to identify opportunities that satisfy all stakeholder needs simultaneously by aligning the goals of all stakeholders with the purpose of the project.

Unfortunately, this ideal is often in stark contrast to the reality of projects that are characterized by considerable conflict. The question thus arises: Why is there so much conflict on projects? One of several causes is that conflict arises when people working on the same project have somewhat different ideas about how to achieve project objectives. But why should such a disagreement occur? Is there not "one best way?" There may be one best way, but exactly which way is the "one best" is a matter surrounded by uncertainty. For example, the client of the project's outputs often has a substantially different point of view than those at the input end of the project, such as suppliers, or functional managers. And other stakeholders may have even different points of view, such as the project's top management, the local community, or the project firm's lawyers. Most conflicts have their roots in uncertainty, and negotiation is a way of managing the resultant risk. Therefore, this chapter is also about risk management, about dealing with conflicts that often arise from uncertainty.

As we will see in Chapter 6, the process of planning a project usually requires inputs from many people. Even when the project is relatively small and simple, planning may involve the interaction of almost every functional and staff operation in the organization. It is virtually impossible for these interactions to take place without conflict, and when a conflict arises, it is helpful if there are acceptable methods to reduce or resolve it. And, of course, we should mention that some people are more receptive to negotiation and compromise than others, who may be more insistent on having their own way, or see the world as trying to frustrate their every desire. Personalities vary tremendously and always need to be considered in evaluating ways to reduce conflicts within projects.

Conflict has sometimes been defined as the process that begins when one party perceives that the other has frustrated, or is about to frustrate, some concern of his or hers. While conflict can arise over issues of belief or feelings or behavior, our concern in this chapter is focused for the most part on goal conflicts that occur when an individual or group pursues goals different from those of other individuals or groups. A party to the conflict will be satisfied when the level of frustration has been lowered to the point where no action, present or future, against the other party is contemplated. When all parties to the conflict are satisfied at this point, the conflict is said to be resolved.

There are, of course, many ways to resolve conflict, as described in detail in the reading "Methods of Resolving Interpersonal Conflict" at the end of this chapter, such as withdrawal, smoothing, compromise, forcing, and confrontation/problem-solving. As noted there, confrontation/problem-solving (i.e., facing the issue directly, such as by nego-tiation) is the most effective method while forcing, or brute force, is the most ineffective. Brute force is, of course, a time-honored method, as is the absolute rule of the monarch, but the rule of law is the method of choice for modern societies if negotiation or arbitration has not already succeeded—in spite of occasional lapses. Conflict resolution is the ultimate purpose of law.

Organizations establish elaborate and complex sets of rules and regulations to settle disputes between the organization itself and the individuals and groups with whom it inter-acts. Contracts between a firm and its suppliers, its trade unions, and its customers are written to govern the settlement of potential conflicts. But the various stakeholders do not always agree about the meaning of a law or a provision in a contract. It is also important to recognize that contracts are simply legal documents that may provide legal protection after problems arise, but they do not ensure a smoothly running project. Instead, building trust and good relationships among stakeholder groups is the best approach for ensuring a smooth-running project. Furthermore, no agreement, however detailed, can cover all the circumstances that might arise in the extensive relationships between the buyer and the seller of complicated industrial equipment, between the user and the supplier of engi-neering consulting services, between the producer and user of computer programs—the list of potential conflicts is endless. Our overcrowded courts are witness to the extent and variety of conflict. According to the web page of the New York State Bar Association, there are approximately 850,000 lawyers in the United States. The great majority of this group that numbers between 25 and 35 percent of the world's supply of lawyers are employed in helping conflicting parties to adjudicate or settle their differences.

In this chapter we examine the nature of negotiation as a means of reducing or resolving the kinds of conflict that typically occur within projects. But before we begin the discussion, it must be made quite clear that *this chapter is not a primer on how to nego-tiate*; a course in negotiation is beyond the scope of this book (for such information, see the "Bibliography" section). Rather, this chapter focuses on the roles and applications of negotiation in the management of projects. Note also that we have given minimal attention to negotiations between the organization and outside vendors. In our experience, this type of negotiation is conducted sometimes by the PM, sometimes by the project engineer, but most often by members of the organization's purchasing department.

Debate over the proper technical approach to a problem often generates a collabo-rative solution that is superior to any solution originally proposed. Conflict often edu-cates individuals and groups about the goals/objectives of other individuals and groups in the organization, thereby satisfying a precondition for valuable win–win negotiations (see Section 4.3). Indeed, the act of engaging in win–win negotiations serves as an example of the positive outcomes that can result from such an approach to conflict resolution.

In Chapter 3 we noted that negotiation was a critical skill required of the PM. No PM should attempt to practice his or her trade without explicit training in negotiation. In this chapter we describe typical areas of project management where this skill is mandatory. In addition, we will cover some appropriate and inappropriate approaches to negotiation, as well as a few characteristics of successful negotiation suggested by experts in the field or indicated by our experience. We will also note some ethical issues regarding negotiation. There are probably more opportunities for ethical missteps in handling conflicts and nego-tiations than in any other aspect of project management. Unlike other chapters, we will use comparatively few illustrative examples. Successful negotiation tends to be idiosyncratic to the actual situation, and most brief examples do little to help transform theory into practice. We have, however, included a vignette at the end of the chapter. This vignette was adapted from "real life"; the names were changed to protect innocent and guilty alike.

Project Management in Practice

© Xinhua/ZUMAPress.com

Quickly Building a Kindergarten through Negotiation

The idea to build a school for orphans and poor children in an African slum in 30 days was suggested as fodder for a Norwegian television "reality" show. Only 1 of the 10 Scandinavian team members recruited had any construction experience and only one, Ms. Lange, a PMP, had any project management experience. As might be expected, the challenges of climate, food, language, and especially culture shock were nearly overwhelming to the small team. The heat was sweltering to the northern Europeans and the food was tasteless—Lange had to negotiate with the hotel's kitchen staff in order to add more spices in the food. But the cultural change was the most challenging, particularly regarding time since African time was much more casual than Scandinavian time and the team was on a limited-time schedule. For example, to help secure local buy-in, Lange engaged a local carpenter to build the desks and tables for the school. When she checked back a few days before the furniture was due, she was shocked to find that he hadn't even started the work: "Time is unpredictable; I will call you," he said.

Lange found that negotiation seemed to be required for everything. "Negotiation skills definitely were the most valuable of all the project management training that I have taken." She found that she constantly needed to count to 10 in her interactions, reflect on where these people were coming from, and figure out how to create a win–win situation that would satisfy both parties. The townsfolk began to refer to her as "The Diplomat." Impressed with the foreigners who were trying to help them, the local villagers pitched in to help on the project. Lange found that, rather than going through official channels, she made better progress personally talking with many of the women who were doing the work, which solved a lot of the problems the team encountered.

However, as the end of their time began to arrive, success appeared unlikely. As the team considered how disappointed the children and villagers would be to not have the school completed, they decided to work in shifts throughout the night. The increased commitment paid off, and the school was done by the time the "reality show" was over.

Questions

1. **Is time unpredictable? What did the carpenter mean?**

2. **Did Ms. Lange use any of the principles of negotiation in this project?**

3. **At some point do you think the team had to think about the goals of the reality show compared to the needs of the orphan and poor African children?**

Source: B. G. Yovovich, "Worlds Apart," *PM Network*, Vol. 24.

4.1   Identifying and Analyzing Stakeholders

As emphasized previously, the best approach for managing conflict is to proactively take steps to align the goals of the various stakeholders with the purpose of the project. To facilitate this, several techniques for identifying and analyzing stakeholders are discussed in this section.

Before the goals of the stakeholders can be aligned with the purpose of the project, they must be identified. Most commonly the expert judgment of the PM and project team are employed to identify the stakeholders. After identifying the stakeholders, a stakeholder register should be created to maintain key information about them, including contact information, their requirements and expectations, and what stage in the project they have the most interest in. In addition, separate from the stakeholder register, a stakeholder issue log should be maintained to catalog issues that arise and how they were resolved.

Once the stakeholders have been identified, a number of tools can be used to analyze them to gain insight about how to manage the relationship with them. And as additional information is learned about a stakeholder, the stakeholder register should be updated.

For the purpose of illustrating a couple of representative stakeholder analysis tools, we will use the example of a process improvement project that is about to be launched at a hospital with the goal of reducing the turnaround times for patients' stress tests. The turnaround time for a stress test is measured as the elapsed time from when the stress test was ordered by a cardiologist until the results are signed off by a radiologist. Delays in receiving the results from stress tests impact the timeliness of treating patients, which in turn impacts the patients' length of stay at the hospital. For the purpose of this example, we further assume that during an early project team meeting, the PM and process improvement team identified the following stakeholder groups: radiologists, cardiologists, hospital administration, the stress test technicians, and the patients/families.

One tool that is useful for analyzing stakeholders is the Power-Interest Grid. As its name suggests, this tool analyzes stakeholders on two dimensions: (1) their interest in the project and (2) their relative power in the organization. Based on these two dimensions, the model suggests the appropriate relationship between the PM and the stakeholder group from *monitoring* to *keeping informed*, to *keeping satisfied*, to *closely managing*. Figure 4.1 provides an illustrative Power-Interest Grid for the stress test process improvement project.

Referring to Figure 4.1, we observe that the PM should closely manage the cardiologists and hospital administrators given their high interest in the project and their power in the organization. Likewise, the radiologists should be kept satisfied. Finally, the patients/families should be monitored and the test technicians kept informed on the status of the project.

In addition to thoughtfully considering the type of relationship the PM and project team should have with stakeholders, it is also important to assess how much engagement and commitment is needed from various stakeholder groups in order for the project to succeed. A useful tool for accessing the level of commitment needed from stakeholders is the Commitment Assessment Matrix. In this matrix, both the current level of commitment and the desired level of commitment are assessed for each stakeholder group.

Figure 4.2 provides an example Commitment Assessment Matrix for the stress test process improvement project. In comparing the current and desired levels of commitment to the process improvement project, we observe that the cardiologists are more committed than desired, perhaps indicating the risk that they will interfere in unproductive ways with the project. On the other hand, for the project to succeed, greater commitment is needed from the test technicians and especially the radiologists. Thus, the PM and project team need to develop an appropriate communication plan to reduce the cardiologists' commitment to the project and to substantially increase the commitment of the test technicians and radiologists.

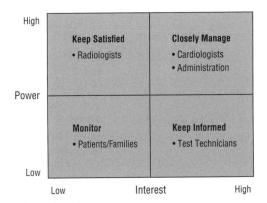

FIGURE 4.1   Illustrative Power-Interest Grid for stress test process improvement project.

Level of Commitment	Stakeholder Groups				
	Cardiologists	Test Technicians	Administration	Patients/ Families	Radiologists
Strongly Support	X ↓	O ↑			O ↑
Support	O		X O	X O	
Neutral		X			
Opposed					X
Strongly Opposed					

X = current level of commitment
O = desired level of commitment

FIGURE 4.2   Illustrative Commitment Assessment Matrix for stress test process improvement project.

Section 13.3

Managing stakeholder engagement is an important process, and because of this was added as a new knowledge area in the most recent update to the **PMBOK**. According to Section 13.3 in the PMBOK, managing stakeholder engagement involves the following activities:

- Obtaining and confirming stakeholders' commitment to the project's success at the appropriate stages in the project
- Communicating with stakeholders to manage their expectations
- Proactively addressing stakeholder concerns before they become major issues
- Resolving issues in a timely fashion once they have been identified

4.2   Conflict and the Project Life Cycle

In this section, following a brief discussion of the project life cycle, we will categorize the types of conflicts that frequently occur in the project environment and then amplify the nature of these conflicts. Finally, we will link the project life cycle with the fundamental conflict categories and discover that certain patterns of conflict are associated with the different periods in the life of a project. With this knowledge, the PM can do a faster and more accurate job of diagnosing the nature of the conflicts he or she is facing, thereby reducing the likelihood of escalating the conflict by dealing with it ineffectually.

More on the Project Life Cycle

Various authors have defined the stages of the project life cycle (see Figures 1.3, 1.4, and 1.5) in different ways. A typical definition consisting of four stages is that of Adams et al. (1983): conceptualization, planning, execution, and termination. During the first stage, senior management tentatively, sometimes unofficially, approves preliminary planning for a project. Often, this management recognition is preceded by some strictly unofficial "bootleg" work to test the feasibility of an idea. Initial planning is undertaken, basic objectives are often adopted, and the project may be "scoped out." The second stage is typified by detailed planning, budgeting, scheduling, and the aggregation of resources. In the third stage, the lion's share of the actual work on the project is accomplished. During the final stage of the life cycle, work is completed and products are turned over to the client or user. This stage also includes disposition of the project's assets and personnel. It may even include preparation for the initial stage of another related project to follow.

Project Management in Practice

Stakeholder Involvement at Nemours Children's Hospital

Unfortunately, the burden of having a child that requires hospitalization is often compounded by excessive paperwork and the need for the patients and families to physically navigate a maze of administrative, testing, and treatment areas. In an effort to remedy this, the scope for a $397 million project to create the new Nemours Children's Hospital in Orlando, Florida, was to deliver a user-friendly experience by developing a more integrated approach for providing care for its patients. In particular, the vision was to have most, if not all, of the support and treatment activities available on the patient's floor. The project team also understood that without stakeholder buy-in this vision could not be achieved.

One key stakeholder group was the patients and their families. To get input from this user-group, an advisory council of patients and families was created and their input solicited for alternative designs that were mocked up at an off-site preview center. For example, parents could step into inpatient and outpatient rooms, while children could try out alternative mattresses. The advisory council provided valuable input such as the child who noticed a scary shadow on the ceiling when lying on the bed. In reflecting on the project, the team felt that allowing the advisory council to provide input on specific options as opposed to asking them to help redesign the rooms helped ensure the project did not fall behind its schedule. Constructing the center also served another stakeholder group, the general public, where almost 4,000 people toured the preview center prior to the hospital's opening.

Staffing a new hospital was another major project challenge. For example, in the year before the hospital was to open, 700 physicians and nurses were screened. But an important difference between healthcare employees and employees in other professions is that healthcare workers have to be licensed. Thus, another important stakeholder group was the Florida licensing board. In particular, it was important that the board not be overwhelmed with hundreds of healthcare workers all seeking their licenses at once. To address this, three Nemours employees were dedicated to helping with licensing issues. One of these employees worked fulltime on building relationships with the state agencies.

One complication that plagues most projects related to constructing a brand new facility is that input from the employees, another critical stakeholder group, is not available because most of them have not been hired yet. This was the case at Nemours where staff would not be hired until a few months before the hospital was to open. Not having employee input early in the project creates an almost certain guarantee that changes will need to be made later in the project, which in turn can have important implications for the project's scope. To address this, Nemours created an oversight committee with expertise on healthcare regulations to review the change requests originating from the newly hired employees. Suggested changes that were needed to meet regulations were approved. Approvals of other change requests were evaluated on the basis of their impact on patient care and cost-effectiveness.

In the end, the project was an overwhelming success. With 137 beds and 630,000 square feet, the hospital opened on time and was completed on budget. The project was also a finalist for the 2013 PMI Project of the Year Award.

Questions

1. **How did stakeholder involvement contribute to the success of the project?**

2. **Were there any risks to involving stakeholders in the construction of the new children's hospital? What steps did the project team take, or what could they have taken to mitigate these risks?**

Source: L. La Plante, and P. Mack, "It Takes a Village," *PM Network*, Vol. 27.

Categories of Conflict

All stages of the project life cycle appear to be typified by conflict. In early research, Thamhain et al. (1975a, 1975b) did extensive research on conflicts in projects. These conflicts centered on matters such as schedules, priorities, staff and labor requirements, technical factors, administrative procedures, cost estimates, and, of course, personalities (Afzalur, 1992). Thamhain et al. collected data on the frequency and magnitude of conflicts of each type during each stage of the project life cycle. Multiplying conflict frequency by a measure of conflict magnitude and adjusting for the proportion of PMs who reported each specific type of conflict, they derived an estimate of the "intensity" of the conflicts.

On examination of the data, it appears that the conflicts fall into three fundamentally different categories:

1. Groups working on the project may have different goals and expectations.
2. There is significant uncertainty about who has the authority to make decisions.
3. There are interpersonal conflicts between the stakeholders in the project.

Some conflicts reflect the fact that the day-to-day work on projects is usually carried out by many different units of the organization, units that often differ in their objectives and technical judgments. The result is that these units have different expectations about the project, its costs and rewards, its relative importance, and its timing. Conflicts about schedules, intra- and interproject priorities, cost estimates, and staff time tend to fall into this category. At base, they arise because the PM and the functional managers have very different goals. The PM's concern is the project. The primary interest of the functional manager is the daily operation of the functional department.

Other conflicts reflect the fact that both technical and administrative procedures are important aspects of project management. Uncertainty about who has the authority to make decisions on resource allocation, on administrative procedures, on communication, on technological choices, and on all the other matters affecting the project produces conflict between the PM and the other stakeholders. It is simple enough (and correct) to state that the functional manager controls who works on the project and makes technical decisions, while the PM controls the schedule and flow of work. In practice, in the commonly hectic environment of the project, amid the day's countless little crises faced by project and functional manager alike, the distinction is rarely clear.

Finally, some conflicts reflect the fact that human beings are an integral part of all projects. In an environment that depends on the cooperation of many persons, it seems inevitable that some personalities will clash. Also, in conflicts between the project and the client, or between senior management and the project, it is the PM who personifies the project and thus is generally a party to the conflict.

We can categorize these conflicts as conflict over differing goals, over uncertainty about the locus of authority, and between personalities. For the entire array of conflict types and stakeholders, see Table 4.1.

The three types of conflict seem to involve the stakeholders to the project in identifiable ways. The different goals and objectives of the PM, senior management, and functional managers are a major and constant source of conflict. For example, senior management (at times, arbitrarily) is apt to fix all three parameters of the project—time,

TABLE 4.1 Project Conflicts by Category and Stakeholder

Stakeholder	Categories of Conflict		
	Goals	Authority	Interpersonal
Project team	Schedules	Technical	Personality
	Priorities		
Client	Schedules	Technical	
	Priorities		
Functional and senior management	Schedules	Technical	Personality
	Priorities	Administrative	
	Labor cost		

cost, and scope—and then to assume that the PM will be able to achieve all the preset targets. Underestimation of cost and time is a natural consequence of this practice, and it leads directly to conflict between the PM, as a representative of the project team, and senior management. A second consequence is that the PM tries to pass the stringent cost and time estimates along to functional managers whose units are expected to perform certain work on the project. More conflict arises when the functional managers complain that they cannot meet the time and cost restrictions. All this tends to build failure into the job of managing a project, another source of conflict between the PM and senior management.

Functional managers also may not see eye-to-eye with the PM on issues such as the project's priority or the desirability of assigning a specifically named individual to work on the project, or even the applicability of a given technical approach to the project. In addition, the client's priorities and schedule, whether an inside or outside client, may differ radically from those of senior management and the project team. Finally, the project team has its own ideas about the appropriateness of the schedule or level of project staffing. The Thamhain et al. (1975a) data show that these goal-type conflicts occur in all stages of the project's life cycle, though they are particularly serious in the early stages. Regardless of the timing, in many cases it is not certain just whose priorities are ruling.

There are, of course, a number of methods for settling conflicts about priorities between projects, as well as intraproject conflicts. Often, the project selection model used to approve projects for funding will generate a set of projects ranked by some measure of value. It is also common for senior management to determine interproject priorities. The relative importance of the various tasks in an individual project is set by the PM, who allocates scarce resources depending on the requirements of schedule, task difficulty, resource availability, and similar considerations. The existence of these methods for resolving priority conflicts is all too often irrelevant, because there is a powerful tendency for both project and functional managers to optimize their individual interests, with little regard for the total organization.

Locus-of-authority conflicts are endemic to projects. The project team and the client tend to focus on the technical procedures, debating the proper approach to the project, or perhaps how to solve individual problems that can occur at any stage. Senior management has other fish to fry. Not only do they insist that the PM adopt and maintain a set of administrative procedures that conform to organizational and legal standards, but they also are quite concerned with who reports to whom and whose permission is required to take what action. The astute reader will note that such concerns are not entirely appropriate for projects. Our discussions with senior managers lead us to the obvious conclusion that it is common for senior management to want the efficiency and other advantages of projects but simultaneously to attempt to maintain the managerial comforts of traditional hierarchical structures—a sure source of conflict.

The conflict-resolution potential of partnering and project charters should be quite clear. Neither technique will stop conflicts from arising, but they will sharply lower the intensity of the conflicts as well as provide a framework for resolving conflict. They will even allow an environment in which the PM and functional managers can take positions that support the total organization rather than suboptimizing the project or the function.

Project managers will often find themselves arguing for scheduling or resource priorities from functional managers who outrank them by several levels. Neither the functional nor the project managers are quite sure about their levels and boundaries of authority. A constant complaint of project managers is "I have to take the responsibility, but I have no authority at all."

People problems arise, for the most part, within the project team, though functional managers may clash with PMs—the former accusing the latter of being "pushy," and the latter accusing the former of "foot dragging." In our experience, most personality clashes on the project team result from differences in technical approach or philosophy of problem solving, and in the methods used to implement the project results. Of course, it is quite possible that a personality conflict causes a technical conflict. It is also possible that any type of conflict will appear, at first blush, to be a personality clash.

Next we put these conflicts into the chronological perspective of the project life cycle.

Project Formation

In the initial stage of the project life cycle, most of the conflict centers around the inherent confusion of setting up a project in the environment of matrix management. Almost nothing about the project or its governance has been decided. Even the project's technical objectives, not clearly defined or established, are apt to be understood only in the most general sense. Moving from this state of semi-chaos to the relatively ordered world of the buildup stage is difficult. To make this transition, four fundamental issues must be handled, although not necessarily in the order presented here.

First, the technical objectives of the project must be specified to a degree that will allow the detailed planning of the buildup stage to be accomplished. Second, commitment of resources to the project must be forthcoming from senior management and from functional managers. Third, the priority of the project, relative to the priorities of the parent organization's other projects, must be set and communicated. We feel the project's priority must be set as early as possible in the life of the project. (While it will probably not save the project from delay in the event of a mandate, it stands as an important political signal to functional managers about which projects take precedence in case of resource conflicts.) Fourth, the organizational structure of the project must be established to an extent sufficient for the WBS and RACI matrix to be prepared during the next stage.

These conditions are not sufficient, but they are most certainly necessary if the conflicts typical of the formation stage are to be resolved—at least at a reasonable level—and not simply carried forward to the buildup stage in an exacerbated state.

The PM who practices conflict avoidance in this stage is inviting disaster in the next. The four fundamental issues above underlie critical but down-to-earth matters such as these: *Which* of the functional areas will be needed to accomplish project tasks? *What* will be the required level of involvement of each of the functional areas? How will conflicts over resources/facility usage between this and other projects be settled? What about those resource/facility conflicts between the project and the routine work of the functions? *Who* has the authority to decide the technical, scheduling, personnel, and cost questions that will arise? Most important, *how* will changes in the parent organization's priorities be communicated to everyone involved?

Note that three of the four fundamental issues—delimiting the technical objectives, getting management commitment, and setting the project's relative priority—must be resolved irrespective of what organizational form is selected for the project. It should also be noted that the organizational structure selected will have a major impact on the ways in which the conflicts are handled. The more independent and standalone the project, the more authoritative the role played by the PM. The weaker the project and the more functional ties, the more authority is embedded in the functional managers. Lack of clarity about the relative power/influence/authority of the PM and the functional managers is a major component of all conflicts involving technical decisions, resource allocation, and scheduling.

Project Buildup

Thamhain et al. (1975a, p. 39) note that conflict occurring in the buildup stage "over project priorities, schedules, and administrative procedures … appears as an extension from the previous program phase." This is the period during which the project moves (or should move) from a general concept to a highly detailed set of plans. If the project is independent and standalone, the PM seeks a commitment of *people* from the functional departments. If the project is functionally tied down, the PM seeks a commitment of *work* from the functional departments. In either case, the PM seeks commitment from functional managers who are under pressure to deliver support to other projects, in addition to the routine, everyday demands made on their departments.

As the project's plans become detailed, conflicts over technical issues build—again, conflicts between the PM and the functional areas tend to predominate. Usually, the functional departments can claim more technical expertise than the PM, who is a "generalist." On occasion, however, the PM is also a specialist. In such situations, discussions between the functional manager and the PM about the best technical approach often result in conflict. The total level of conflict is at its highest in this transition period.

Main Program

Schedules are still a major source of conflict in the main program phase of the project life cycle, though the proximate cause of schedule-related conflict is usually different than in the earlier stages. Project plans have been developed and approved by everyone involved (although, perhaps, grudgingly), and the actual work is under way. Let us make an assumption that is certain to be correct; let us assume that some activity runs into difficulty and is late in being completed. Every task that is dependent on this late activity will also be delayed. Some of these subsequent activities will, if sufficiently late and if the late work is not made up, delay the entire project.

In order to prevent this consequence, the PM must try to get the schedule back on track. But catching up is considerably more difficult than falling behind. Catching up requires extra resources that the functional groups who are doing the "catching up" will demand, but which the PM may not have.

The more complex the project, the more difficult it is to trace and estimate the impact of all the delays, and the more resources that must be consumed to get things back on schedule. Throughout this book we have referred to the PM's job of managing time/cost/scope trade-offs. Maintaining the project schedule is precisely an exercise in managing trade-offs, but adding to the project's cost or scaling down the project's technical capabilities in order to save time are trade-offs the PM will not take if there is any viable alternative. The PM's ability to make trade-offs is often constrained by contract, company policy, and ethical considerations. In reality, trade-off decisions are quite difficult.

Like schedule conflicts, technical conflicts are frequent and serious during the main program stage. Also like schedule conflicts, the source of technical conflict is somewhat different than in earlier stages. Just as a computer and a printer must be correctly linked together in order to perform properly, so must the many parts of a project. These linkages are known as *interfaces*. The number of interfaces increases rapidly as the project gets larger, which is to say that the system gets more complex. As the number of interfaces increases, so does the probability that problems will arise at the interfaces. The need to manage these interfaces and to correct incompatibilities is the key to the technical conflicts in the main program phase.

Project Phase-out

As in the main program stage, schedule is the major source of conflict during project phase-out. If schedule slippage has occurred in the main program stage (and it probably has), the consequences will surely be felt in this final stage. During phase-out, projects with firm deadlines develop an environment best described as hectic. The PM, project team, and functional groups often band together to do what is necessary to complete the project on time and to specification. Cost overruns, if not outrageously high, are tolerated—though they may not be forgiven and they will certainly be remembered.

Technical problems are comparatively rare during phase-out because most have been solved or bypassed earlier. Similarly, working interfaces have been developed and put in place. If the project involves implementing a technology in an outside client's system, technical conflicts will probably arise, but they are usually less intense.

Thamhain et al. (1975b, p. 41) note that personality conflicts are the second-ranked source of conflict during phase-out. They ascribe these conflicts to interpersonal stress caused by the pressure to complete the project, and to individuals' natural anxiety about leaving the project either to be assigned to another or to be returned to a functional unit. In addition, we have observed conflict, sometimes quite bitter, focused on the distribution of the project's capital equipment and supplies when the project is completed. Conflict also arises between projects phasing out and those just starting, particularly if the latter need resources or personnel with scarce talents being used by the former.

The way in which Thamhain et al. have defined conflict as having its source in differences about goals/expectations, uncertainty about authority, and interpersonal problems precludes identifying conflict as occurring between discipline-oriented and problem-oriented team members. We do not argue that Thamhain et al. are in error, but merely that their classification does not specifically include a type of conflict we feel is both frequent and important. Much of the conflict identified during our discussion of planning in Chapter 6, it seems to us, is due to discipline/problem-orientation differences. A clear example comes from an interview recorded during Pelled et al.'s (1994, p. 23) research on conflict in multifunctional design teams. One team member speaking of another said, "He will do whatever he thinks is right to get his [own] job done, whether or not it's good for [the company] or anyone else." In context, it is clear that this conflict was between a problem-oriented individual and one who was discipline oriented.

Project Management in Practice

A Consensus Feasibility Study for Montreal's Archipel Dam

To assess the desirability of a feasibility study evaluating the costs and benefits of constructing a dam within the St. Lawrence river basin, Quebec initiated an interdepartmental evaluation. The evaluation concluded that a feasibility study that considered the hydroelectric power generated, the flood control possible, and the shoreline restoration for recreation was justified. It was recommended that a central authority act as PM for the study.

Thus, a new body called "Secretariat Archipel" was created to directly supervise the feasibility study. However, they chose to use a democratic "consensus" approach between all 10 governmental departments rather than a central authority approach. It was believed that this consensus approach would lead to a solution acceptable to all, while protecting the jurisdictional responsibilities of all departments.

Although this approach apparently avoided difficult conflicts, a poststudy evaluation of the process concluded that it was neither effective nor efficient. By discarding the recommendation for a central authority body, a leadership gap arose in the decision framework and veto rights were abused by many of the participants.

In terms of effectiveness, the recommendations of the study are questionable: that the dam be postponed. Considering efficiency, the study appeared to take 1–2 longer than necessary, with a correspondingly higher cost.

In retrospect, the consensus approach appeared to have been selected to protect the fields of jurisdiction of each governmental department rather than for defining the best project for the community. Although consensus is a highly desirable goal for public studies, leadership cannot be abandoned in the process. Attempting to avoid conflict through mandated consensus simply defeats the purpose of any study in the first place, except a study to determine what everyone commonly agrees upon.

Questions

1. Given the results of the study, did the consensus approach indeed lead to a solution acceptable to all? Why wasn't everyone happy with this outcome?

2. Based on this case situation, does the consensus approach lead to what is best for the overall community? Why (not)?

3. What approach should have been adopted to determine what was best for the overall community?

Source: R. Desbiens, R. Houde, and P. Normandeau, "Archipel Feasibility Study: A Questionable Consensus Approach," *Project Management Journal*, Vol. 20.

The upshot is simple. As we noted in Chapter 1, conflict is an inherent characteristic of projects, and the PM is constantly beset by conflict. The ability to reduce and resolve conflict in ways that support achievement of the project's goals is a prime requisite for success as a PM. The primary tool to accomplish conflict resolution and reduction is negotiation, and the method of handling conflict established in the project formation stage will set the pattern for the entire project. Therefore, the style of negotiation adopted by the PM is critical.

4.3 | Dealing with Conflict

With a better understanding of the relationship between the project life cycle and conflict, we now turn our attention to the strategies employed to deal with conflict. Following this, we discuss in greater detail the preferred technique for resolving conflict, namely, negotiation.

When we think of the ways people deal with conflict, it is helpful to consider how they approach the situation along two dimensions. On the one hand, we can consider how assertive the parties are, which can range from being unassertive to assertive. On the other hand, we can evaluate how cooperative the parties are, ranging from uncooperative to cooperative. Based on these two dimensions, researchers Kenneth Thomas and Ralph Kilmann (1975) identified five strategies people use to deal with conflict, as illustrated in Figure 4.3.

Referring to Figure 4.3, approaching a situation assertively and being unwilling to cooperate is referred to as a "competing" strategy. When a competing strategy is employed, the person is viewing the situation as though someone *must* lose in order for the other to win, or, in this case, I win and you lose (win–lose). This competing strategy may be appropriate in situations where the decision must be made quickly.

Alternatively, when the position is not asserted aggressively but the person is still unwilling to cooperate, we have a conflict "avoiding" strategy. This is a lose–lose strategy because you are not cooperating with the other person to help them achieve their goals nor are you actively pursuing your own goals. An avoiding strategy might be applied when the issue is not that important to you or you deem the detrimental effects from the conflict outweigh the benefits of resolving the issue in a desirable way.

When you assertively state your position but do so in a spirit of cooperation, you are employing a "collaborating" strategy. Here your focus is on achieving your goals but with the recognition that the best solution is one that benefits both parties. Thus, the collaborating strategy can be considered a win–win strategy. This is the preferred strategy in most situations and particularly in situations where the needs of both parties are important.

In situations where you do not assert your position and focus more on cooperating with the other party, you are employing an "accommodating" strategy. In this case, the focus is on resolving the issue from the other person's point of view. Here the situation can be described as I lose, you win, or lose–win. It would be appropriate to employ the accommodating strategy when you were wrong or the issue is much more important to the other person.

Finally, when you take a middle ground position on both dimensions you are "compromising." In these cases, nobody wins and nobody loses. Thus, you have likely arrived at a solution that you and the other party can live with but are not particularly happy

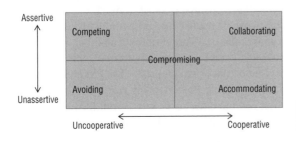

FIGURE 4.3 Conflict resolution strategies.

about. You might employ a compromising strategy when the potential benefits of trying to develop a win–win solution are exceeded by the costs.

The value of this framework is it helps us to recognize that there are alternative strategies that can be utilized to resolve conflicts. Successful project management requires that when conflict arises, the situation is carefully evaluated and the approach for managing the conflict is proactively chosen in a way that best enhances the quality of the relationship between the parties.

4.4 The Nature of Negotiation

As just noted, while there are a variety of approaches for dealing with conflict, generally speaking the favored technique for resolving conflict is *negotiation*. What is negotiation? Herb Cohen's *You Can Negotiate Anything* says in his outstanding classic (1980, p. 15) that "Negotiation is a field of knowledge and endeavor that focuses on gaining the favor of people from whom we want things." Other authors define negotiation differently, but do not appreciably extend Cohen's definition. Even if no single definition neatly fits all the activities we label "negotiation," we do recognize that such terms as "mediate," "conciliate," "make peace," "bring to agreement," "settle differences," "moderate," "arbitrate," "adjust differences," "compromise," "bargain," "dicker," and "haggle" (*Roget's International Thesaurus*, 1993) are synonyms for "negotiate" in some instances.

Most of the conflicts that involve the organization and outsiders have to do with property rights and contractual obligations. In these cases, the parties to negotiation see themselves as opponents. Conflicts arising inside the organization may also appear to involve property rights and obligations, but they typically differ from conflicts with outsiders in one important way: As far as the firm is concerned, they are conflicts between allies, not opponents. Wall (1985, pp. 149–150) makes this point neatly:

> *Organizations, like groups, consist of interdependent parts that have their own values, interests, perceptions, and goals. Each unit seeks to fulfill its particular goal . . . and the effectiveness of the organization depends on the success of each unit's fulfillment of its specialized task. Just as important as the fulfillment of the separate tasks is the integration of the unit activities such that each unit's activities aid or at least do not conflict with those of the others.*

One of the ways in which organizations facilitate this integration is to establish "*lateral relations* [which] allow decisions to be made horizontally across lines of authority" (Wall, 1985, p. 150). Because each unit will have its own goals, integrating the activities of two or more units is certain to produce the conflicts that Wall says should not take place. The conflicts may, however, be resolved by negotiating a solution, if one exists, that produces gains (or minimizes losses) for all parties. Raiffa (1982, p. 139) defines a Pareto-optimal solution to the two-party conflict and discusses the nature of the bargaining process required to reach optimality, a difficult and time-consuming process. While it is not likely that the conflicting parties will know and understand the complex trade-offs in a real world, project management, many-persons/many-issues conflict, the general objective is to find a solution such that no party can be made better off without making another party worse off by the same amount or more, that is, a Pareto-optimal solution.

The concept of a Pareto-optimal solution is important. Approaching intraproject conflicts with a desire to win a victory over other parties is inappropriate. The PM must remember that he or she will be negotiating with project stakeholders many times in the future. If he or she conducts a win–lose negotiation and the other party loses, from then on he or she will face a determined adversary who seeks to defeat him or her. This is not helpful. The proper outcome of this type of negotiation should be to optimize the outcome in terms of overall organizational goals. Although it is not always obvious how to do this, negotiation is clearly the correct approach.

During the negotiation process, an ethical situation often arises that is worth noting. Consider the situation where a firm requests an outside contractor to develop a software package to achieve some function. When the firm asks for a specific objective to be accomplished, it frequently does not know if that is a major job or a trivial task because it lacks technical competence in that area. Thus, the contractor has the opportunity to misrepresent the task to its customer, either inflating the cost for a trivial task or minimizing the impact of a significant task in order to acquire the contract and then boosting the cost later. The ethics of the situation require that each party in the negotiation be honest with the other, even in situations where it is clear that there will not be further work between the two.

4.5 Partnering, Chartering, and Scope Change

Projects provide ample opportunity for the PM to utilize her or his skills at negotiation. There are, however, three situations commonly arising during projects that call for the highest level of negotiating skill the PM can muster: the use of subcontractors, the use of input from two or more functional units to design and develop the project's mission, and the management of changes ordered in the project's deliverables and/or priorities after the project is underway (Hughes, 1998). The former probably accounts for more litigation than all other aspects of the project combined. The last two are, in the authors' experience, by far the most common and most troublesome issues project managers report facing.

Partnering

In recent years there has been a steady growth in the frequency of outsourcing parts of projects (Smith, 1998). External suppliers, increasingly, are delivering parts of projects, including tangible products and services as well as intangible knowledge and skills. There are many reasons beyond avoidance of litigation that firms enter partnering arrangements with each other, for example, diversification of technical risk, avoidance of capital investment, reducing political risk on multinational projects, shortening the duration of the project, and pooling of complementary knowledge, among others (Beecham et al., 1998, p. 192).

Traditionally, relations between the organization carrying out a project and a subcontractor working on the project are best characterized as adversarial. The parent organization's objective is to get the deliverable at the lowest possible cost, as soon as possible. The subcontractor's objective is to produce the deliverable at the highest possible profit with the least effort. These conflicting interests tend to lead both parties to work in an atmosphere of mutual suspicion and antagonism. Indeed, it is almost axiomatic that the two parties will have significantly different ideas about the exact nature of the deliverable itself. The concept of "partnering" has been developed to replace this atmosphere with one of cooperation and mutual helpfulness, but the basically adversarial relationship makes cooperation difficult in the best of cases (Larson et al., 1997).

Cowen et al. (1992, p. 5) define partnering as follows:

Project partnering is a method of transforming contractual relationships into a cohesive, cooperative project team with a single set of goals and established procedures for resolving disputes in a timely and effective manner.

They present a multistep process for building partnered projects. First, the parent firm must make a commitment to partnering, select subcontractors who will also make such a commitment, engage in joint team-building exercises, and develop a "charter" for the project (see the next subsection for a description of such a charter). Second, both parties must implement the partnering process with a four-part agreement on: (1) "joint evaluation" of the project's progress; (2) a method for resolving any problems or disagreements; (3) acceptance of a goal for continuous improvement (also known as "total quality management," or TQM) for the joint project; and (4) continuous support for the process of partnering from senior management of both parties. Finally, the parties commit to a joint review of "project execution" when the project is completed. Beecham et al. (1998, p. 194ff) note several things that can "doom" partnering agreements, and they develop several "propositions" that lead to success. Partnering is an attempt to mitigate the risks associated with subcontracting. Consider the nature of the steps listed above. Clearly, there are specific risks that must be managed in each of them.

Each step in this process must be accompanied by negotiation, and the negotiations must be nonadversarial. The entire concept is firmly rooted in the assumption of mutual trust between the partners, and this assumption, too, requires nonadversarial negotiation. Finally, these articles focus on partnering when the partners are members of different organizations. We think the issue is no less relevant when the partners are from different divisions or departments of the same parent organization. Identical assumptions hold, identical steps must be taken, and interparty agreements must be reached for partnering to succeed.

The concept of partnering, however, goes far beyond two-party agreements between buyer and seller or interdepartmental cooperation on a project. The use of multiparty consortia to pursue technological research objectives is common. As noted in Chapter 3, SEMATECH is a consortium of semiconductor manufacturers for the purpose of conducting joint research projects in the field. The consortium was exempted from prosecution under the U.S. antitrust laws when the National Cooperative Research Act of 1984 was passed expressly to allow such cooperation among competitors.

There are a great many such groups of competitors engaged in cooperative research and other cooperative activities (not, one hopes, in price-setting or other illegal activities). They exist worldwide and are often multinational in their membership; for example, Airbus Industry (originally British, French, Spanish, and German) and International Aero Engines (originally the United States, Japan, Germany, Italy, and the United Kingdom), as mentioned in Chapter 3.

Airbus Industry is not only a consortium of private firms from four different nations, but each of the four governments subsidized their respective private firms. This venture, apparently undertaken in order to foster a European competitor to the United States' Boeing Aircraft, resulted in a successful competitor in the market for commercial aircraft.

Partnering, however, is not without its problems. There can be no doubt that those who have not had much experience with partnering underrate its difficulty. Partnering requires strong support from senior management of all participants, and it requires continuous support of project objectives and partnering agreements (Moore et al., 1995). Above all, and most difficult of all, it requires open and honest communication between the partners. With all of its problems, however, partnering yields benefits great enough to be worth the efforts required to make it work correctly (Baker, 1996; Larson et al., 1997).

Chartering

The agreements between groups partnering on large endeavors are often referred to as *charters*. A project (program, etc.) charter is a detailed written agreement between the stakeholders in the project, that is, the client or sponsor, the PM, senior management, the functional managers who are committing resources and/or people to a specific project (program, etc.), and even possibly others such as community groups or environmental entities. Bear in mind, the charter may take many different forms. Typically, it gives an overview of the project and details the expected deliverables, including schedules, personnel, resource commitments, risks, and evaluation methods (see Chapter 6). It attests to the fact that all the stakeholders are "on the same page," agreeing about what is to be done, when, and at what cost. Note that if there is such an agreement, there is also an implication that none of the parties will change the agreement unilaterally, or, at least, without prior consultation with the other stakeholders. Many projects do not have charters, which is one reason that many projects do not meet their scope, are not completed on time, and/or are not completed on budget.

In Chapter 6, we also describe an iterative process for developing the *project plan*, a detailed listing of all the work and procedures involved in executing the project. We note that it is not uncommon for the individuals or groups who make commitments during the process of developing the project plan to sign off on their commitments.

An informal project charter appears in Cowen et al. (1992, Figure 2, p. 8), in which the various members of the partnering team sign a commitment to

- Meet design intent
- Complete contract without need for litigation
- Finish project on schedule:
    - Timely resolution of issues
    - Manage joint schedule
- Keep cost growth to less than 2 percent …

Of course, to meet the underlying purpose of a charter, even these less-specific terms assume an agreement on the "design intent," the schedule, and costs.

Scope Change

The problem of changing the scope expected of a project is a major issue in project management and constitutes part of the second **PMBOK** knowledge area. No matter how carefully a project is planned, it is almost certain to be changed before completion. No matter how carefully defined at the start, the scope of most projects is subject to considerable uncertainty. There are three basic causes for change in projects. Some changes result because planners erred in their initial assessment about how to achieve a given end or erred in their choice of the proper goal for the project. Technological uncertainty is the fundamental causal factor for either error. The foundation for a building must be changed because a preliminary geological study did not reveal a weakness in the structure of the ground on which the building will stand. An R&D project must be altered because metallurgical test results indicate another approach should be adopted. The project team becomes aware of a recent innovation that allows a faster, cheaper solution to the conformation of a new computer.

PMBOK

Chapter 5

Other changes result because the client/user or project team learns more about the nature of the project deliverable or about the setting in which it is to be used. An increase in user or team knowledge or sophistication is the primary factor leading to change. A computer program must be extended or rewritten because the user thinks of new uses for the software. Physicians request that intensive care units in a hospital be equipped with laminar air-flow control in order to accommodate patients highly subject to infection who might otherwise not be admissible in an ICU. The fledgling audio-addict upgrades the specifications for a system to include very high frequencies so that his dog can enjoy the music, too.

A third source of change is the mandate. This is a change in the environment in which the project is being conducted. As such, it cannot be controlled by the PM. A new law is passed. A government regulatory unit articulates a new policy. A trade association sets a new standard. The parent organization of the user applies a new criterion for its purchases. In other words, the rules of conduct for the project are altered. A state-approved pollution control system must be adopted for each chemical refinery project. The state government requires all new insurance policies to conform to a revised law specifying that certain information must be given to potential purchasers. At times, mandates affect only priorities. The mandate in question might move a very important customer to the "head of the line" for some scarce resource or service.

To some extent, risk management techniques can be applied to scope change. Technological uncertainty can be mitigated by careful analysis of the technologies involved, including the use of technological forecasting. Risk of scope change caused by increased user knowledge can only be managed by improving the up-front communication with the client and then establishing a formal process to handle change (see Chapter 11 for more about this). Finally, mandates are, for the most part, unpredictable. These can be "managed" only by having some flexibility built into the budget and schedule of the project. Ways of doing this sensibly will be discussed in the following two chapters.

As Greek philosopher Heraclitus said, "Nothing endures but change." It is thus with projects, but whatever the nature of the change, specifications of the deliverables must be altered, and the schedule and budget recalculated. Obviously, negotiation will be required to develop new agreements between the stakeholders to the project. These negotiations are difficult because most of the stakeholders will have a strong interest in maintaining the status quo. If the proposed change benefits the client and increases the cost of the project, the producer will try to sequester some of the user's potential benefit in the form of added charges to offset the added cost. The client will, of course, resist. All parties must, once again, seek a Pareto-optimal solution—always a difficult task.

Change by mandate raises an additional problem. Not only are the project's deliverables, budget, and schedule usually changed, the *priorities* of other projects are typically changed too, if only temporarily while the mandate receives the system's full attention. Suddenly, a PM loses access to key resources because they are urgently required elsewhere. Key contributors to a project miss meetings or are unable to keep promised task-delivery dates. All too often, the PM's response to this state of affairs is anger and/or discouragement. Neither is appropriate.

> *This project is so important, we can't let things that are more important interfere with it.*
> *Anonymous*

After discussing priorities with both PMs and senior managers, it has become clear to us that most firms actually have only three levels of priority (no matter how ornate the procedure for setting project priorities might seem to be). First, there are the high-priority projects, that is, the "set" of projects currently being supported. When resource conflicts arise within this high-priority set, precedence is typically given to those projects with the earliest due date (more about this is in Chapter 9). Second, there are the lower-priority projects, the projects "we would like to do when we have the time and money." Third, occasionally, there are urgent projects—mandates—that must be done immediately. "Customer A's project must be finished by the end of the month." "The state's mandate must be met by June 30." Everything else is delayed to ensure that mandates are met. As noted earlier, we will have more to say on this subject in Chapter 11.

While project charters and partnerships would certainly help the PM deal with conflicts that naturally arise during a project, the use of charters and partnering is growing slowly—though outsourcing is growing rapidly. It is understandably difficult to convince senior managers to make the firm commitments implied in a project charter in the face of a highly uncertain future. Functional managers are loath to make firm commitments for precisely the same reason. So, too, the client, aware of her or his own ignorance about the degree to which the project output will meet his or her needs, is cautious about commitment—even when a procedure for negotiating change exists.

Partnering is a recently developed concept, and in our litigious society any system for conflict resolution that asks parties to forego lawsuits is viewed with considerable suspicion. Indeed, we find that a great many organizations preach "team building," "TQM," and "employee involvement," but many fail to practice what they preach. For each participative manager you find, we can show you a dozen micromanagers. For each team player ready to share responsibility, we can show you a dozen "blame placers." The era of project charters and partnering is approaching, but it is not yet here.

4.6 | Some Requirements and Principles of Negotiation

The word "negotiation" evokes many images: the United States President and Congress on the annual federal budget, the "Uruguay Round" of the GATT talks, a player's agent and the owner of an NFL team, the buyer and seller of an apartment complex, attorneys for husband and wife in a divorce settlement, union and management working out a collective bargaining agreement, tourist and peddler haggling over a rug in an Ankara market. But as we noted in the introduction to this chapter, none of these images is strictly appropriate for the PM who must resolve the sorts of conflicts we have considered in the previous section.

The key to understanding the nature of negotiation as it applies to project management is the realization that few of the conflicts arising in projects have to do with *whether* or not a task will be undertaken or a deliverable produced. Instead, they have to do with the precise *design* of the deliverable and/or *how* the design will be achieved, by *whom*, *when*, and at *what cost*. The implication is clear: *The work of the project will be done*. If conflicts between any of the stakeholders in the project escalate to the point where negotiations break down and work comes to a halt, everyone loses. *One requirement* for the conflict reduction/resolution methods used by the PM is that *they must allow the conflict to be settled without irreparable harm to the project's objectives*.

A closer consideration of the attorneys negotiating the divorce settlement makes clear a second requirement for the PM negotiating conflicts between stakeholders to the project. While the husband and wife (or the rug peddler and tourist) may employ unethical tactics during the negotiation process and, if not found out, profit from them at the expense of the other party, it is much less likely for the attorneys representing the husband and wife to do so—particularly if they practice law in the same community. The lawyers know that they will have to negotiate on other matters in the future. Any behavior that breeds mistrust will make future negotiations extremely difficult, perhaps impossible. The rug peddler assumes no further contact with the tourist, so conscience is the sole governor of his or her ethics. A *second requirement* for the conflict resolution/reduction methods used by the PM is that *they allow (and foster) honesty between the negotiators*.

The conflicting stakeholders to a project are not enemies or competitors, but rather allies—members of an alliance with strong common interests. It is a *requirement of all conflicting parties to seek solutions to the conflict that not only satisfy their own individual needs but also satisfy the needs of other parties to the conflict, as well as the needs of the parent organization*. In the language of negotiation, this is called a "win–win" solution. Negotiating to a win–win solution is the key to conflict resolution in project management.

Fisher et al. (1983, p. 11) have developed a negotiation technique that tends to maintain these three requirements. They call it "principled negotiation," that is, win–win. The method is straightforward; it is defined by four points.

1. **Separate the people from the problem** The conflicting parties are often highly emotional. They perceive things differently and feel strongly about the differences. Emotions and objective fact get confused to the point where it is not clear which is which. Conflicting parties tend to attack one another rather than the problem. To minimize the likelihood that the conflict will become strictly interpersonal, the substantive problem should be carefully defined. Then everyone can work on it rather than each other.

2. **Focus on interests, not positions** Positional bargaining occurs when the PM says to a functional manager: "I need this subassembly by November 15." The functional manager responds: "My group can't possibly start on it this year. We might be able to deliver it by February 1." These are the opening lines in a dialogue that sounds suspiciously like the haggling of the tourist and the rug peddler. A simple "Let's talk about the schedule for this subassembly" would be sufficient to open the discussion. Otherwise, each party develops a high level of ego involvement in his or her position and the negotiation never focuses on the real interests and concerns of the conflicting parties—the central issues of the conflict. The exchange deteriorates into a series of positional compromises that do not satisfy either party and leave both feeling that they have lost something important.

   In positional negotiation, the "positions" are statements of immediate wants and assume that the environment is static. Consider these positional statements: "I won't pay more than $250,000 for that property." Or, as above, "We might be able to deliver it by February 1." The first position assumes that the bidder's estimates of future property values are accurate, and the second assumes that the group's current workload (or a shortage of required materials) will not change. When negotiation focuses on interests, the negotiator must determine the underlying concern of the other party. The real concerns or interests of the individuals stating the positions quoted above might be to earn a certain return on the investment in a property, or to not commit to delivery of work if delivery on the due date cannot be guaranteed. Knowledge of the other party's interests allows a negotiator to suggest solutions that satisfy the other party's interests without agreeing with the other's position.

3. **Before trying to reach agreement, invent options for mutual gain** The parties-in-conflict usually enter negotiations knowing the outcome they would like. As a result, they are blind to other outcomes and are not particularly creative. Nonetheless, as soon as the substantive problems are spelled out, some effort should be devoted to finding a wide variety of possible solutions—or elements thereof—that advance the mutual interests of the conflicting parties. Success at finding options that produce mutual gain positively reinforces win–win negotiations. Cohen (1980) reports on a conflict between a couple in which "he" wanted to go to the mountains and "she" wanted to go to the shore. A creative win–win solution sent them both to Lake Tahoe.

4. **Insist on using objective criteria** Rather than bargaining on positions, attention should be given to finding standards (e.g., market value, expert opinion, law, company policy) that can be used to determine the quality of an outcome. Doing this tends to make the negotiation less a contest of wills or exercise in stubbornness. If a functional manager wants to use an expensive process to test a part, it is acceptable for the PM to ask if such a process is required to ensure that the parts meet specified quality standards.

Fisher et al. (1983) have had some success with their approach in the Harvard (Graduate School of Business) Negotiation Project. Use of their methods increases the chance of finding win–win solutions.

There are many books on negotiation, some of which are listed in the bibliography of this chapter. Most of these works are oriented toward negotiation between opponents, not an appropriate mindset for the PM, but all of them contain useful, tactical advice for the PM. Wall's book (1985) is an excellent academic treatment of the subject. Fisher et al. (1983) is a clear presentation of principled negotiation and contains much that is relevant to the PM. In addition, Cohen (1980) is a superb guide to win–win negotiation. The importance of negotiation is beginning to be recognized by the project management profession (Grossman, 1995; Long, 1997; Robinson, 1997), but the subject has not yet found its way into the **PMBOK** in discussions about conflict.

9.3, 9.4

Among the tactical issues covered by most books on negotiation are things the PM, as a beginning negotiator, needs to know. For example, what should a negotiator who wishes to develop a win–win solution do if the other party to the conflict adopts a win–lose approach? What do you do if the other party tries to put you under psychological pressure by seating you so that a bright light shines in your eyes? What do you do if the other party refuses to negotiate in order to put you under extreme time pressure to accept whatever solution he or she offers? How do you settle what you perceive to be purely technical disputes? How should you handle threats? What should be your course of action if a functional manager, with whom you are trying to reach agreement about the timing and technology of a task, goes over your head and attempts to enlist the aid of your boss to get you to accept a solution you feel is less than satisfactory? How can you deal with a person you suspect dislikes you?

Almost every writer on negotiation emphasizes the importance of understanding the interests of the person with whom you are negotiating. As we noted above, the positions taken by negotiators are not truly understandable without first understanding the interests and concerns that prompt those positions. The statement that a test requested for May 15 cannot be run until June 2 may simply mean that the necessary test supplies will not be delivered until the latter date. If the PM can get the supplies from another source in time for the May 15 deadline, the test can be run on schedule. But the ability to do this depends on knowing *why* the test was to be delayed. If the negotiation remains a debate on positions, the PM will never find out that the test could have been run on time. *The key to finding a negotiator's interests and concerns is to ask "Why?" when he or she states a position.*

In the next chapter, we move to the first task of the PM, organizing the project. We deal there not only with various organizational forms, such as functional, project, and matrix, but also with the organization of the project office. This task includes setting up the project team and managing the human element of the project.

Summary

This chapter addressed the need for negotiation as a tool to resolve project conflicts. We discussed the nature of negotiation and its purpose in the organization. We also described various categories of conflict and related them to the project life cycle. We followed this by identifying a number of requirements and principles of negotiation. Finally, we presented a short vignette illustrating an actual negotiation situation.

Specific points made in the chapter were these:

- Negotiation within the firm should be directed at obtaining the best outcome for the organization, not winning.

- There are three traditional categories of conflict: goal oriented, authority based, and interpersonal.

- There are also three traditional sources of conflict. They are the project team itself, the client, and functional and senior management. We added the problem/discipline orientation of people working on the project.

- Critical issues to handle in the project formation stages are delimiting technical objectives, getting management commitment, setting the project's relative priority, and selecting the project organizational structure.

- The total level of conflict is highest during the project buildup stage.
- Scheduling and technical conflicts are most frequent and serious in the project buildup and main program stages, and scheduling conflicts in particular during the phase-out stage.

- Project negotiation requirements are that conflicts must be settled without permanent damage, the methodology must foster honesty, and the solution must satisfy both individuals' and the organization's needs.
- One promising approach to meeting the requirements of project negotiation is called "principled negotiation."

Glossary

Interfaces The boundaries between departments or functions.

Lateral Relations Communications across lines of equivalent authority.

Pareto-Optimal Solution A solution such that no party can be made better off without making another party worse off by the same amount or more.

Positional Negotiation Stating immediate wants on the assumption that the environment is static.

Principled Negotiation A process of negotiation that aims to achieve a win–win result.

Stakeholders Individuals or groups with a special interest in a project, usually the project team, client, senior management, and specific public interest groups that impact or are impacted by the project.

Win–win When both parties are better off in the outcome.

Questions

Material Review Questions

1. Review and justify the placement of the seven types of conflicts into the nine cells of Table 4.1.

2. Discuss each of the four fundamental issues for potential conflict during the project formation stage.

3. Identify the types of likely conflicts during the project buildup, main program, and phase-out stages.

4. What are the three main requirements of project negotiation?

5. Describe the four points of principled negotiation.

6. What is the objective of negotiation?

7. What are the four categories of conflict?

8. What is "principled negotiation"?

Class Discussion Questions

9. Summarize the vignette in the chapter in terms of the negotiation skill used. Comment on the appropriateness and ethical aspects related to "burying" the cost.

10. What will be the likely result of a win–win style manager negotiating with a win–lose style manager? What if they are both win–lose styled?

11. Reallocate the placement of the seven types of conflicts into the nine cells of Table 4.1 according to your own logic.

12. How does the type of project organization affect each of the types of conflicts that occur over the project life cycle?

13. Project managers are primarily concerned with project interfaces. At what rate do these interfaces increase with increasing project size?

14. The critical term in the concept of principled negotiation is "position." Elaborate on the multiple meanings of this term relative to negotiation. Can you think of a better term?

15. Give an example of a Pareto-optimal solution in a conflict.

16. Given that many conflicts are the result of different stakeholders having different interests, is it possible to achieve a win–win situation?

17. The chairman of Cadbury Schweppes PLC, G.A.H. Cadbury suggests (1987) the following test for an ethical action: Would you be embarrassed to have it described in the newspaper? Is this a sufficient test for ethics? Can you think of any others?

Incidents for Discussion

Pritchard Soap Co.

Samantha (Sam) Calderon is manager of a project that will completely alter the method of adding perfume to Pritchard Soap's "Queen Elizabeth" gift soap line. The new process will greatly extend the number of available scents and should result in a significant increase in sales. The project had been proceeding reasonably well, but fell several weeks behind when the perfume supplier, the Stephen Marcus Parfumissary, was unable to meet its delivery deadline because of a wildcat strike.

Under normal circumstances this would not have caused problems, but the project had been subject to a particularly long evaluation study and now was in danger of not being ready for the holiday season. The major scheduling problem concerned Pritchard's toxicity lab. Kyle Lee, lab manager, had been most cooperative in scheduling the Queen Elizabeth perfumes for toxicity testing. He had gone out of his way to rearrange his own schedule to accommodate Sam's project. Because of the strike at Marcus, however, Sam cannot have the perfumes ready for test as scheduled, and the new test date Lee has given Sam will not allow her to make the new line available by the holidays. Sam suspects that the project might not have been approved if senior management had known that they would miss this year's holiday season.

Questions

1. What was the source of change in this project and how will it affect the project's priority? What are Sam's alternatives? What should she do?

Sutton Electronics

Eric Frank was still basking in the glory of his promotion to marketing PM for Sutton Electronics Corporation, manufacturer of electronic fire alarm systems for motels, offices, and other commercial installations. Eric's first project involved the development of a marketing plan for Sutton's revolutionary new alarm system based on sophisticated circuitry that would detect and identify a large number of dangerous gases as well as smoke and very high temperatures. The device was the brainchild of Ira Magee, vice-president of research and the technical wizard responsible for many of Sutton's most successful products.

It was unusual for so young and relatively inexperienced an employee as Eric to be given control of such a potentially important project, but he had shown skill in handling several complex, though routine, marketing assignments. In addition, he had the necessary scientific background to allow him to understand the benefits of Magee's proposed gas detection system.

Four weeks into the project, Eric was getting quite worried. He had tried to set up an organizational and planning meeting several times. No matter when he scheduled the meeting, the manager of the manufacturing department, Jaki Benken, was unable to attend. Finally, Eric agreed that manufacturing could be represented by young Bill Powell, a Benken protégé who had just graduated from college and joined Sutton Electronics. However, Eric was doubtful that Powell could contribute much to the project.

Eric's worry increased when Powell missed the first planning meeting completely and did not appear at the second meeting until it was almost over. Powell seemed apologetic and indicated that plant floor crises had kept him away from both meetings. The project was now 5 weeks old, and Eric was almost 3 weeks late with the marketing master plan. He was thinking about asking Ira Magee for help.

Questions

1. Do you think that Eric should involve Magee at this point? If so, what outcome would you expect? If not, what should he do?

Continuing Integrative Class Project

The topic of negotiation will come up in two guises during the class project: When the PM is trying to assign tasks to the team members and they are resisting, and also possibly when the PM or class is negotiating for resources with the Instructor, the Dean, or others. The topic of conflict can arise at any time and over any issue, obviously. In all these circumstances, the individuals would be well advised to recall the principles of negotiation (or quickly refer back to this chapter). The class historian should also be noting when conflicts and bargaining occurred during the project, as well as its nature, how effectively it was addressed, and if and how it was ultimately resolved.

Bibliography

Adams, J. R., and S. E. Barndt. "Behavioral Implications of the Project Life Cycle." In D. I. Cleland and W. R. King, eds., *Project Management Handbook.* New York: Van Nostrand Reinhold, 1983.

Afzalur, R. M. *Managing Conflict in Organizations.* Westport, CT: Praeger, 1992.

Baker, K. R. "Measuring the Benefits of Partnering." *PM Network*, June 1996.

Beecham, M. A., and M. Cordey-Hayes. "Partnering and Knowledge Transfer in the U.K. Motor Industry." *Technovation*, March 1998.

Cadbury, G. A. H. "Ethical Managers Make Their Own Rules." *Harvard Business Review*, September–October 1987.

Cohen, H. *You Can Negotiate Anything.* Secaucus, New York: Lyle Stuart Inc., 1980.

Cowen, C., C. Gray, and E. W. Larson. "Project Partnering." *Project Management Journal*, December 1992.

Fisher, R., and W. Ury. *Getting to Yes.* Harmondsworth, Middlesex, G.B.: Penguin Books, 1983.

Grossman, J. "Resolve Conflicts so Everybody Wins." *PM Network*, September 1995.

Hughes, T. P. *Rescuing Prometheus*, New York: Pantheon, 1998.

Larson, E. W., and J. A. Drexler, Jr. "Barriers to Project Partnering: Reports from the Firing Line." *Project Management Journal*, March 1997.

Long, A. "Negotiating the Right Decision." *PM Network*, December 1997.

Moore, C. C., J. D. Maes, and R. A. Shearer. "Recognizing and Responding to the Vulnerabilities of Partnering." *PM Network*, September 1995.

Pelled, L. H., and P. S. Adler. "Antecedents of Intergroup Conflict in Multifunctional Product Development Teams: A Conceptual Model." *IEEE Transactions on Engineering Management*, February 1994.

Raiffa, H. *The Art and Science of Negotiation.* Cambridge: Belknap/Harvard Press, 1982.

Robinson, T. "When Talking Makes Things Worse!" *PM Network*, March 1997.

Roget's International Thesaurus. New York: Thomas Y. Crowell, 1993.

Smith, M. B. "Financial Constraints on Service and Outsourcing Projects." *PM Network*, October 1998.

Thamhain, H. J., and D. L. Wilemon. "Conflict Management in Project Life Cycles." *Sloan Management Review*, Summer 1975a.

Thamhain, H. J., and D. L. Wilemon. "Diagnosing Conflict Determinants in Project Management." *IEEE Transactions on Engineering Management*, February 1975b.

Thomas, K., and R. Kilmann. *The Handbook of Industrial and Organizational Psychology*, edited by Marvin Dunnette, Chicago: Rand McNally, 1975.

Wall, J. A., Jr. *Negotiation: Theory and Practice.* Glenview, IL: Scott, Foresman, 1985.

The following case is based on an actual event that demonstrates a nonpositional negotiating style. The case provides students with the opportunity to consider the types of conflict that occur within a project and how various negotiation techniques can be used to address these conflicts.

Case

Negotiation in Action—The Quad Sensor Project   S. J. Mantel, Jr. Consulting Project

Dave Dogers, an experienced PM, was assigned the project of designing and setting up a production system for an industrial instrument. The instrument would undoubtedly be quite delicate, so the design and fabrication methods for the shipping container were included in the project. Production of containers capable of meeting the specifications in this case were outside the experience of the firm, but one engineer in the container group had worked with this type of package in a previous job. This engineer,

Jeff Gamm, was widely recognized as the top design engineer in the container group.

During the initial meetings on the project, which was organized as a weak matrix, Dogers asked Tab Baturi, manager of the Container Group, to assign Gamm to the project because of his unique background. Baturi said he thought they could work it out and estimated that the design, fabrication of prototypes, and testing would require about 4 weeks. The package design could not start until several shape parameters of the instrument had been set and allowable shock loadings for the internal mechanisms had been determined.

The R&D group responsible for instrument design thought it would require about 9 months of work before they could complete specifications for the container. In addition to the actual design, construction, and test work, Gamm would have to meet periodically with the instrument design team to keep track of the project and to consult on design options from the container viewpoint. It was estimated that the entire project would require about 18 months.

Seven months into the project, at a meeting with Dave Dogers, the senior instrument design engineer, Richard Money, casually remarked: "Say, Dave, I thought Jeff Gamm was going to do the package for the Quad Sensor."

"He is, why?" Dogers replied.

"Well," said the engineer, "Gamm hasn't been coming to the design team meetings. He did come a couple of times at the start of the project, but then young McCutcheon showed up saying that he would substitute for Gamm and would keep him informed. I don't know if that will work. That package is going to be pretty tricky to make."

Dogers was somewhat worried by the news the engineer had given him. He went to Gamm's office, as if by chance, and asked, "How are things coming along?"

"I'm up to my neck, Dave," Gamm responded. "We've had half a dozen major changes ordered from Baker's office (V.P. Marketing) and Tab has given me the three toughest ones. I'm behind, getting behinder, and Baker is yelling for the new container designs. I can't possibly do the Quad Sensor package unless I get some help—quick. It's an interesting problem and I'd like to tackle it, but I just can't. I asked Tab to put McCutcheon on it. He hasn't much experience, but he seems bright."

"I see," said Dogers. "Well, the Quad Sensor package may be a bit much for a new man. Do you mind if I talk to Tab? Maybe I can get you out from under some of the pressure."

"Be my guest!" said Gamm.

The next day Dogers met with Tab Baturi to discuss the problem. Baturi seemed depressed. "I don't know what we're supposed to do. No sooner do I get a package design set and tested than I get a call changing things. On the Evans order, we even had production schedules set, had ordered the material, and had all the setups figured out. I'm amazed they didn't wait till we had completed the run to tell us to change everything."

Baturi continued with several more examples of changed priorities and assignments. He complained that he had lost two designers and was falling further and further behind. He concluded: "Dave, I know I said you could use Gamm for the Quad Sensor job, but I simply can't cut him loose. He's my most productive person, and if anyone can get us out from under this mess, he can. I know McCutcheon is just out of school, but he's bright. He's the only person I can spare, and I can only spare him because I haven't got the time to train him on how we operate around here—if you can call this 'operating.'"

The two men talked briefly about the poor communications and the inability of senior management to make up its collective mind. Then Dogers suggested, "Look, Tab, Quad Sensor is no more screwed up than usual for this stage of the project. How about this? I can let you borrow Charlotte Setter for 3–4 weeks. She's an excellent designer and she's working on a low-priority job that's not critical at the moment. Say, I'll bet I can talk Anderson into letting you borrow Levy, too, maybe half time for a month. Anderson owes me a favor."

"Great, Dave, that will help a lot, and I appreciate the aid. I know you understand my problem and you know that I understand yours." Baturi paused and then added, "You realize that this won't take much pressure off Jeff Gamm. If you can get him the designing help he needs he can get more done, but I can't release him for the amount of time you've got allocated for the Quad Sensor."

They sat quietly for a while, then Dogers said, "Hey, I've got an idea. Container design is the hard problem. The production setup and test design isn't all that tough. Let me have Gamm for the container design. I'll use McCutcheon for the rest of the project and get him trained for you. I can get Carol Mattson to show him how to set up the shock tests and he can get the word on the production setup from my senior engineer, Dick Money."

Baturi thought a moment. "Yeah, that ought to work," he said. "But Gamm will have to meet with your people to get back up to speed on the project. I think he will clean up Baker's biggest job by Wednesday. Could he meet with your people on Thursday?"

"Sure, I can arrange that," Dogers said.

Baturi continued. "This will mean putting two people on the package design. McCutcheon will have to work with Gamm if he is to learn anything. Can your budget stand it?"

"I'm not sure," Dogers said, "I don't really have any slack in that account, but . . ."

"Never mind," interrupted Baturi, "I can bury the added charge somewhere. I think I'll add it to Baker's charges. He deserves it. After all, he caused our problem."

Questions

1. What categories of conflict occurred in this project?
2. At what stage was the project?
3. What negotiation techniques were used here?
4. How successful were they?

The following article discusses six tips for negotiating in a project setting. The author identifies effective (have a strategy, listen) and ineffective (don't argue) methods and points out that these techniques can be learned just like any skill.

Reading

Power of Persuasion* D. Brox

The question isn't, "Do you negotiate?" It's "How *well* do you negotiate?"

From requesting more resources to changing a stakeholder requirement, project professionals must negotiate every day.

Some people seem to have an innate ability to persuade others, but even the most timid project manager can hone his or her negotiation skills.

"The skills of a negotiator are just like any other technical skills you can learn," says David Freedman, sales director at Huthwaite International, a negotiation skills consultancy in Wentworth, South Yorkshire, England. "Very seldom are these skills inherent in people's DNA."

Project managers may lack the authority to make big decisions, but they can still influence factors such as budget, scope, timelines, and resources.

Before heading into your next negotiation, remember the following tips.

Think Positive

You might not have authority, but that's no reason to take a defeatist attitude, says Aarathi Villivallam, PMI-RMP, PMP, a program manager at Unisys, a global IT consultancy in Bengaluru, India.

"Often, project managers are not keen to negotiate, thinking that negotiating for something reflects poorly on their capabilities," she says. "Also, they interpret requests as orders and agree to them meekly. Get over these misapprehensions fast."

Remain flexible when requests for changes arise—and don't launch immediately into negotiation mode.

"Don't say no to something that might seem like an unreasonable request at first," says Tres Roeder, PMP, president of Roeder Consulting, a project management training, consulting, and coaching firm in Cleveland, Ohio, USA. "Instead, say, 'I can do that, but there are going to be tradeoffs.'"

Develop the Necessary Traits

Mr. Roeder explains that there are six core traits important in negotiating:

- Awareness: Assess whom you're dealing with and that person's style.
- Whole-body decisions: Use your head, heart, and gut to be fully informed.
- Clear communication: Meet face-to-face if possible and explicitly spell out why you're making a request.
- Adaptability: Know when to hold your ground and when to back down.
- Diplomacy: Be sensitive and understanding.
- Persistence: Don't give up, but also be careful not to push too hard.

Practice these skills every day, starting in small ways, such as listening to how people respond when you describe project setbacks and propose solutions, suggests Karen Brown, PhD, professor of project management leadership at the Thunderbird School of Global Management in Glendale, Arizona, USA, and coauthor of *Managing Projects: A Team-based Approach* [McGraw-Hill, 2010].

Problems constantly arise during projects: A key team member falls ill and can't work for two weeks; essential equipment breaks down and requires repair time not allotted in the initial schedule; or materials are not available at the assumed price.

"Many project managers tend to hide this information from sponsors and other decision makers because they think they can correct the problem on their own," Dr. Brown says. "The result is that many project managers don't step forward to negotiate a new schedule or budget until it's woefully too late."

Instead of concealing these issues, keep the sponsor, customer, and other high-level stakeholders informed of setbacks so they are mentally prepared when it comes time to negotiate.

"The project manager who surprises the sponsor by attempting to negotiate a three-month extension just weeks before the project deadline will not have much credibility," she says.

Negotiation in Action

Project: Construction of the London Olympics infrastructure.

Problem: Lack of resources. You've got a limited supply of the equipment necessary for cycling and weightlifting.

Don't: Say, "Clearly we've only got a finite amount of resources. As far as we can see, the obvious solution is *x.*" You haven't explained your side and your language doesn't leave room for negotiation, says David Freedman, Huthwaite International, Wentworth, South Yorkshire, England.

Do: Ask questions such as, "How many people are you expecting for the weightlifting event? What sort of TV audience are you anticipating?" Then ask similar questions about cycling to ascertain which event is most important to the sponsor.

Negotiation: Propose, "Cycling seems to be our priority— even if it means cutting some corners on weightlifting. Have I got you right there?" Wait for the sponsor's confirmation.

Result: You've established that you understand your stakeholders' priorities, and your proposal is more likely to succeed.

---

*Reprinted from *PM Network*, Vol. 25, with permission. Copyright Project Management Institute.

Do Your Homework—and Recruit Powerful Allies

"There's an alarmingly high percentage of people who enter a negotiation without a strategy—and don't even know the importance of one," says Keld Jensen, chairman of the Centre for Negotiation at the Copenhagen Business School and CEO of the MarketWatch Centre for Negotiation, a consultancy in Copenhagen, Denmark. "Project managers should use their time before the negotiation wisely to make the actual process go smoothly. They should always know their starting point, targets, overall objectives, and threshold of pain going into the negotiation meeting."

"It never pays to be spontaneous in negotiations," Ms. Villivallam says. "It's necessary to have all the facts and a good understanding of the other side's objectives."

Do some research. Know the original scope, timelines, budget, goals, and how your proposed changes will positively impact the project.

"If you are getting squeezed on deadlines, it can be a good opportunity to ask and obtain approval to procure higher-skilled resources," Ms. Villivallam says.

A good project negotiator should also target key players, especially those in a position to make final decisions. You want some of these people on your side—the sooner the better. Keep them involved throughout the project life cycle in various ways, such as weekly status reports and updated financial forecasts. You can also invite them to sit in on at least one project status call with the customer or key end-users. This way, if things go poorly during negotiations, these decision see p. 165 makers are more likely to help.

"By engaging stakeholders this way, you've kept your project in front of them, and they remember both you and the project," says Brad Egeland, an independent IT project manager in Las Vegas, Nevada, USA. "You've become the squeaky wheel that gets the grease without ever having to be the annoying squeaky wheel. When the time comes that you need help negotiating something with the end-user, they're already familiar with the project and with you, and feel some unwritten responsibility to assist."

Ask Questions

"The more you can find out about the other party's position, the more likely you'll be able to frame your offer in a way that takes account of it," Mr. Freedman says. "You can only do that if you ask a lot of questions."

For instance, Mr. Egeland managed a team that was developing a website for his client to log in and check on the status of repairs to jet and aircraft parts. To deal with scope creep that impacted the original timeline, he needed to determine which functionalities were critical. He accomplished this by asking the client which phase of implementation was most urgent.

"I negotiated the timeline and provided them with a phased implementation on the new requirements, meaning the most important functionality was provided as quickly as possible, and the remaining functionality was implemented with the next scheduled phase of the project," Mr. Egeland says.

Huthwaite International's research has shown that skilled negotiators ask significantly more questions than average negotiators do.

By asking questions to gain insight on expectations, project managers can vastly improve their ability to communicate and obtain buy-in from the other party, Mr. Jensen says.

Listen

A project manager must discern the other side's true priorities, says Daisy Ruiz Diaz Lovera, PMP, service manager at Pixeon, a diagnostic imaging company in Florianopolis, Santa Catarina, Brazil. Know what they value so you can use that information to move negotiations forward. Is staying on budget more important to the sponsor than meeting deadlines? If you need more time to implement the project, knowing that the client values budget more may be your bargaining chip to win the additional time.

"It is difficult to negotiate without having established good communication," Ms. Ruiz Diaz Lovera says. "Especially in a long-term project, it is important to invest in the relationship. Even in virtual projects the ideal is to have some face-to-face meetings with the team to be able to build the basis of a relationship and future negotiations. It is more difficult to establish trust from a distance."

When meeting with the project sponsor, talk less and listen more to learn as much as possible about the project goals, she adds.

Once you're familiar with what the other party deems important, you can rank the tasks and start to plan your negotiation strategy.

> **TIP**
> **Don't argue,** *says Keld Jensen, MarketWatch Centre for Negotiation, Copenhagen, Denmark. "Most negotiators are confused about negotiation and think it's an argumentation game. On the contrary: The more information you argue, the less information you gain from the counterpart. Information is king."*

Explain Your Dilemma

The other side needs to understand where you're coming from, and one of the best ways to accomplish this is to state exactly what the consequences of denying your request would be.

"The biggest mistake project managers make is not selling the problem before they make a request," Dr. Brown says.

For example, if you need to purchase a material to develop a new product, don't just tell your project sponsor, "I need this material."

Instead, provide details about the situation. Something along the lines of, "We've encountered some problems in our preliminary tests. It looks like the material we initially chose isn't going to work. The project is going to fail unless we find an alternative material."

This approach should leave stakeholders eager to hear a potential solution.

Follow these tips and you will find yourself in a better position to receive the help you need. After all, the project and your reputation are on the line.

Questions

1. What two core traits of the six would you pick as the most important?

2. Select some negotiation situation and then describe what background information you would need to develop a negotiation strategy.

3. Why is keeping the key stakeholders aware of details and progress on the project important?

4. Describe three reasons that asking questions is helpful in negotiating.

5. Why is explaining your dilemma a powerful way to negotiate?

The Project in the Organizational Structure

A firm, if successful, tends to grow, adding resources and people, developing an organizational structure. Commonly, the focus of the structure is specialization of the human elements of the group. As long as its organizational structure is sufficient to the tasks imposed on it, the structure tends to persist. When the structure begins to inhibit the work of the firm, pressures arise to reorganize along some other line. The underlying principle will still be specialization, but the specific nature of the specialization will be changed.

Any elementary management textbook covers the common bases of specialization. In addition to the ever-popular functional division, firms organize by product line, by geographic location, by production process, by business process, by type of customer, by subsidiary organization, by time, and by the elements of vertical or horizontal integration. Indeed, large firms frequently organize by several of these methods at different levels. For example, a firm may organize by major subsidiaries at the top level; the subsidiaries organize by product groups; and the product groups organize into customer divisions. These, in turn, may be split into functional departments that are further broken down into production process sections, which are set up as three-shift operating units.

In the past decade or so, a new kind of organization structure has appeared in growing numbers—the project organization, a.k.a. "enterprise project management" (Dinsmore, 1998; Levine, 1998; Williams, 1997), also known as "managing organizations by projects," the "project-oriented firm," and other names. Such organizations have been described as applying "project management practices and tools across an enterprise" (Levine, 1998). The software industry is a heavy user of the enterprise project management concept since it has long made a practice of developing major software application programs by decomposing them into a series of comparatively small software projects, generally known as a "program" (but not a software computer program). Once the projects are completed, they are integrated into the whole application system. And beyond just internal programs consisting of multiple projects, there are also multiorganizational projects where many external organizations are involved in the projects. And even bigger yet are the megaprojects involving great sums of money, tremendous complexity, multiple organizations and contractors, and years-long schedules, e.g., the Manhattan Project, the Heathrow T5 terminal, Boston's Big Dig, Project Apollo, and others.

A great many firms, both software and nonsoftware firms alike, have now adopted a system whereby their traditional business is carried out in the traditional way, but anything that represents a change is carried out as a project. One hospital, for example, operates the usual departments in what, for them, are the usual ways. At the same time, the hospital supports several dozen projects oriented toward developing new health care products, or changing various aspects of standard medical and administrative methods.

In some cases a project-oriented structure is a natural fit to an organization's traditional business. For example, consulting firms assign staff to specific client engagements, and as the engagements are completed the employees are reassigned to new client engagements. Likewise, firms that construct large office buildings assign their equipment and human resources to specific projects.

There are many reasons for the rapid growth of project-oriented organizations, but most of them can be subsumed in four general areas. First, speed and market responsiveness have become absolute requirements for successful competition. It is no longer competitively acceptable to develop a new product or service using traditional methods in which the potential new product is passed from functional area to functional area until it is deemed suitable for production and distribution. *First-to-market* is a powerful competitive advantage. Further, in many industries it is common (and necessary) to tailor products specifically for individual clients. Suppliers of hair care products or cosmetics, for example, may supply individual stores in a drug chain with different mixes of products depending on the purchase patterns, ethnic mix of customers, and local style preferences for each store.

Second, the development of new products, processes, or services regularly requires inputs from diverse areas of specialized knowledge. Unfortunately, the exact mix of specialties appropriate for the design and development of one product or service is rarely suitable for another product or service. Teams of specialists that are created to accomplish their ad hoc purpose and disband typify the entire process.

Third, the rapid expansion of technological possibilities in almost every area of enterprise tends to destabilize the structure of organizations. Consider communications, entertainment, banks, consumer product manufacturing and sales, the automotive industry, aircraft manufacture, heavy electrical equipment, machine tools, and so forth without end. Mergers, downsizing, reorganizations, spin-offs, new marketing channels, and other similar major disturbances all require system-wide responsiveness from the total organization. Again, no traditional mechanism exists to handle change on such a large scale satisfactorily—but project organization can.

Finally, TV, movies, novels, and other mythology to the contrary, a large majority of senior managers we know rarely feel much confidence in their understanding of and control over a great many of the activities going on in their organizations. The hospital mentioned above became a project-oriented organization because its new CEO strongly felt that she had no way of understanding, measuring, or controlling anything going on in the hospital except for the most routine, traditional activities. Transforming nonroutine activities into projects allowed her to ensure that accountability was established, projects were properly planned, integrated with other related activities, and reported routinely on their progress.

Moving from a nonproject environment to one in which projects are organized and used to accomplish special tasks to a full-fledged project-oriented organization presents senior management of a firm with an extraordinarily difficult transition. A full treatment of this subject is beyond the scope of this book, but several observations are in order. First, the process is time consuming. Even when the required resources are available and senior management is fully committed to the transition, it is still an arduous process. Our experience indicates that when all goes well, the transition rarely requires less than 3 years. In an excellent article on the process of leading fundamental change in a complex organization, Kotter (1997) lists eight steps that must be successfully completed if the change is to be accomplished. Most of these are dependent on active leadership from top management.

It is important to point out that there is no universally best organizational structure. For industries such as management consulting, the nature of the work naturally lends itself to a project-oriented organization. In other industries, the nature of the work, the firm's competitive strategy, the regulatory environment, and so on may suggest other organizational structures such as organizing the work by discipline, by geography, or by business process.

Regardless of whether the organization is conducting a few occasional projects or is fully project oriented and carrying on scores of projects, any time a project is initiated, three organizational issues immediately arise. First, a decision must be made about how to tie the project to the parent firm. Second, a decision must be made about how to organize the project itself. Third, a decision must be made about how to organize activities that are common to other projects.

In Chapter 3 we discussed the selection of the project manager (PM) and described the difficulties and responsibilities inherent in the PM's role. This chapter focuses on the interface between the project and its parent organization (i.e., how the project is organized as a part of its host). In the latter part of this chapter, we begin a discussion of how the project itself is organized, a discussion that will be continued in the next chapter.

First we look at the three major organizational forms commonly used to house projects and see just how each of them fits into the parent organization. (These three forms are also emphasized in **PMBOK**.) We examine the advantages and disadvantages of each form and discuss some of the critical factors that might lead us to choose one form over the others. We then consider some combinations of the fundamental forms and briefly examine the implications of using combination structures. Finally, we discuss some of the details of organizing the project team, describing the various roles of the project staff. We then turn to the formation and operation of a *project management office* (PMO) whose charge is usually to increase the "maturity" of project management (Aubry, 2015) throughout the organization and can thus provide critically important services for all projects. The skill with which the PMO organizes, administers, and carries out its responsibilities will have a major impact on the ability of projects to meet their objectives. We also describe some of the behavioral problems that face any project team. Finally, we discuss the impact that various ways of structuring projects may have on intraproject conflict in project-oriented firms.

2.1.3

To our knowledge, it is rare for a PM to have much influence over the interface between the organization and the project, the choice of such interfaces usually being made by senior management. The PM's work, however, is strongly affected by the project's position in the organizational structure, and the PM should understand its workings. Experienced PMs do seem to mold the project's organization to fit their notions of what is best. One project team member of our acquaintance remarked at length about how different life was on two projects run by different PMs. Study of the subtle impacts of the PM on the project structure deserves more attention from researchers in the behavioral sciences.

5.1 | Projects in a Functional Organization

As one alternative for giving the project a "home" in a functionally structured organization, we can make it a part of one of the functional divisions of the firm, usually the function that has the most interest in ensuring its success or can be most helpful in implementing it. We commonly think of the functions of an organization as being those of Finance, Marketing, Operations (or Manufacturing), Human Resources, and so on. However, to consider a slightly different type of organization, Figure 5.1 is the organizational chart for the University of Cincinnati, a functionally organized institution. If U.C. (the "funder") undertook the development of a Master of Science program in Project Management (or perhaps an MPM), the project would probably be placed under the *general supervision* of the senior vice president and provost (the "sponsor"), under the *specific supervision* of the dean of the College of Business (the "project owner"), and might be managed by a senior faculty member (the PM) with a specialty in operations management. It might

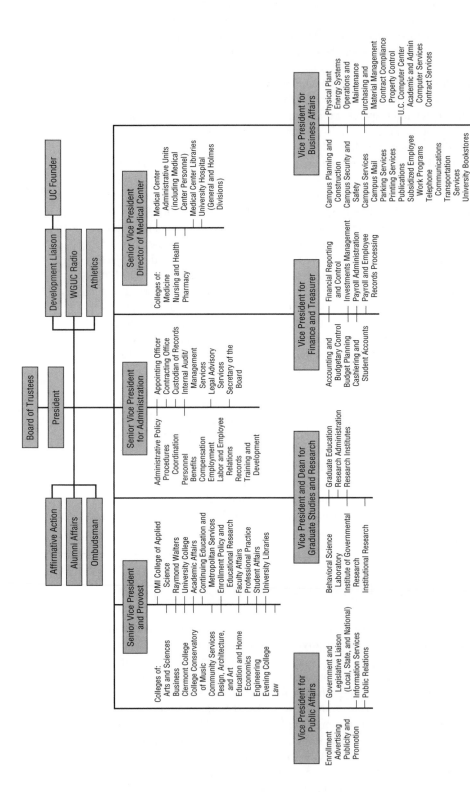

FIGURE 5.1   University of Cincinnati organization chart.

also be placed under the general supervision of the V.P. and dean for Graduate Studies and Research. Note that more than one choice of supervision may exist, and if the project needs resources from some of the other functional areas, they are expected to help support the project. For example, if the project is housed in the business school under the direct supervision of the dean of the business school, input from the engineering school may be needed.

Another way a project may be organized in a functional organization is to assign the work to all the relevant functional divisions with either top management overseeing the effort or else someone assigned to coordinate their efforts, perhaps as a project manager or possibly as just a facilitator. A project to increase the percentage of women in senior administration might thus involve all the university's functions and might be coordinated through the President's office, the Affirmative Action office, or possibly using someone from Personnel in the Administration function.

There are advantages and disadvantages of using a functional placement for a project, assuming that the organization is functionally organized. The major advantages are as follows:

1. There is maximum flexibility in the use of staff. If the proper functional division has been chosen as the project's home, the division will be the primary administrative base for individuals with technical expertise in the fields relevant to the project. Experts can be temporarily assigned to the project, make the required contributions, and immediately be reassigned to their normal work.

2. Individual experts can be utilized by many different projects. With the broad base of technical personnel available in the functional divisions, people can be switched back and forth between the different projects with relative ease.

3. Specialists in the division can be grouped to share knowledge and experience. Therefore, the project team has access to whatever technical knowledge resides in the functional group. This depth of knowledge is a potential source of creative, synergistic solutions to technical problems.

4. The functional division also serves as a base of technological continuity when individuals choose to leave the project, and even the parent firm. Perhaps just as important as technological continuity is the procedural, administrative, and overall policy continuity that results when the project is maintained in a specific functional division of the parent firm.

5. Finally, and not the least important, the functional division contains the normal path of advancement for individuals whose expertise is in the functional area. The project may be a source of glory for those who participate in its successful completion, but the functional field is their professional home and the focus of their professional growth and advancement.

Just as there are advantages to using a functional placement, there are also disadvantages:

1. A primary disadvantage of this arrangement is that the client is not the focus of activity and concern. The functional unit has its own work to do, which usually takes precedence over the work of the project, and hence over the interests of the client.

2. The functional division tends to be oriented toward the activities particular to its function. It is not usually problem oriented in the sense that a project should be to be successful.

3. Occasionally in functionally organized projects, no individual is given full responsibility for the project. This failure to pinpoint responsibility usually means that the PM is made accountable for some parts of the project, but another person is made

accountable for one or more other parts. Little imagination is required to forecast the lack of coordination and chaos that results.

4. The same reasons that lead to lack of coordinated effort tend to make response to client needs slow and arduous. There are often several layers of management between the project and the client.

5. There is a tendency to suboptimize the project. Suboptimization occurs when one part of the organization is optimized to the detriment of the overall organization. Project issues that are directly within the interest area of the functional home may be dealt with carefully, but those outside normal interest areas may be given short shrift, if not totally ignored.

6. The motivation of people assigned to the project tends to be weak. The project is not in the mainstream of activity and interest, and some project team members may view service on the project as a professional detour.

7. Such an organizational arrangement does not facilitate a holistic approach to the project. Complex technical projects such as the development of a jet aircraft or an emergency room in a hospital simply cannot be well designed unless they are designed as a totality. No matter how good the intentions, no functional division can avoid focusing on its unique areas of interest. Cross-divisional communication and sharing of knowledge is slow and difficult at best.

Project Management in Practice

Reorganizing for Project Management at Prevost Car

At Prevost Car in Quebec City, Canada, the vice-president (VP) of production was told that he would have to expand production capacity 31 percent in the next 5 months. In the past, such a task would start with a bulldozer the next day and the work would be under way, but no one knew at what cost, what timetable, or what value to the firm. Realizing that he needed some fresh ideas, a structured approach, and that there was no allowance for a mistake, the VP contacted a project management consulting firm to help him.

The consulting firm set up a 5-day meeting between their project managers, a value engineering expert, and the seven foremen from Prevost's main factory to scope out the project. The group produced a report for senior management outlining a $10 million project to expand the main factory by 60,000 square feet, and a follow-on potential to make a further expansion of 20 percent more. The detail of the plan came as a revelation to top management who approved it after only 2 days of study. After it was completed on time and on budget, the firm also committed to the additional 20 percent expansion, which also came in as planned.

The success of this project resulted in "infecting" Prevost Car with the project management "bug." The next major task, an initiative to reduce workplace injuries, was thus organized as a project and was also highly successful. Soon, all types of activities were being handled as projects

at Prevost. The use of project management in manufacturing firms is highly appropriate given their need to adapt quickly to ferocious international competition, accelerating technological change, and rapidly changing market conditions. In addition, Prevost has found that project management encourages productive cooperation between departments, fresh thinking and innovation, team approaches to problems, and the highly valued use of outside experts to bring in new ideas, thereby breaking current short-sighted habits and thinking. As Prevost's VP states: "Right now it's a question of finding what couldn't be better managed by project."

Questions

1. Surely this was not the first time Prevost needed to make a significant change in their firm. Why do you think this was the first time the VP called upon a project management consulting firm?

2. Do you expect there was some concern among top management that no bulldozer was working the next day?

3. This example well illustrates the trend to using project management to do everything in organizations that used to be done in other ways. Can everything be better executed using project management? If not, what are the characteristics of those tasks that cannot?

Source: M. Gagne, "Prevost Car—The Power of Project Management," *PM Network*, Vol. 11.

5.2 | Projects in a Projectized Organization

At the other end of the organizational spectrum (in terms of project structure) is the projectized organization. Here the firm's administrative support groups (HR, Legal, Finance, Controller, etc.) report to the President or CEO as staff units. The line units are the various standalone projects being undertaken in the organization. Each project has a full complement of the functions needed for its operation, though some members may serve on two or more projects. Each standalone project is a self-contained unit with its own technical team, its own staff, and so on. Some parent organizations prescribe administrative, financial, personnel, and control procedures in detail. Others allow the project almost total freedom within the limits of final accountability. There are examples of almost every possible intermediate position. Figure 5.2 illustrates the projectized organization and its standalone projects.

As with the functional organization, standalone projects have unique advantages and disadvantages. The former are as follows:

1. The project manager has full line authority over the project. Though the PM must report to a senior executive in the parent organization, there is a complete work force devoted to the project. The PM is like the CEO of a firm that is dedicated to carrying out the project.

2. All members of the project work force are directly responsible to the PM. There are no functional division heads whose permission must be sought or whose advice must be heeded before making technological decisions. The PM is truly the project director.

3. When the project is removed from the functional division, the lines of communication are shortened. The entire functional structure is bypassed, and the PM communicates directly with senior corporate management. The shortened communication lines result in faster communications with fewer communication failures.

4. When there are several successive projects of a similar kind, the projectized organization can maintain a more or less permanent cadre of experts who develop considerable skill in specific technologies. Indeed, the existence of such skill pools can attract customers to the parent firm. Lockheed's famous "Skunk Works" was such a team of experts who took great pride in their ability to solve difficult engineering problems. The group's name, taken from the Li'l Abner comic strip, reflects the group's pride, irreverent attitude, and strong sense of identity.

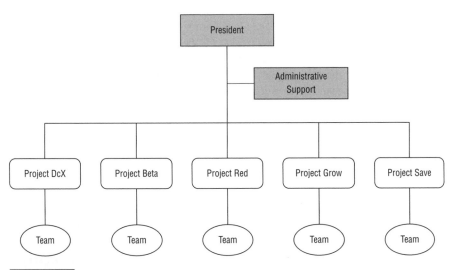

FIGURE 5.2   The projectized organization.

5. The project team that has a strong and separate identity of its own tends to develop a high level of commitment from its members. Motivation is high and acts to foster the task orientation discussed in Chapter 3.

6. Because authority is centralized, the ability to make swift decisions is greatly enhanced. The entire project organization can react more rapidly to the requirements of the client and the needs of senior management.

7. Unity of command exists. While it is easy to overestimate the value of this particular organizational principle, there is little doubt that the quality of life for subordinates is enhanced when each subordinate has one, and only one, boss.

8. Projectized organizations are structurally simple and flexible, which makes them relatively easy to understand and to implement.

9. The organizational structure tends to support a holistic approach to the project. A brief explanation of the systems approach was given in Chapter 3, and an example of the problems arising when the systems approach is not used appears in Section 5.3 of this chapter. The dangers of suboptimization or focusing on and optimizing the project's subsystems rather than the total project are often a major cause of technical failure in projects.

While the advantages of the projectized organization make a powerful argument favoring this structure, its disadvantages are also serious:

1. When the parent organization takes on several projects, it is common for each one to be fully staffed. This can lead to considerable duplication of effort in every area from clerical staff to the most sophisticated (and expensive) technological support units. If a project does not require a full-time personnel manager, for example, it must have one nonetheless because personnel managers come in integers, not fractions, and staff is usually not shared across projects.

2. In fact, the need to ensure access to technological knowledge and skills results in an attempt by the PM to stockpile equipment and technical assistance in order to be certain that it will be available when needed. Thus, people with critical technical skills may be hired by the project when they are available rather than when they are needed. Similarly, they tend to be maintained on the project longer than needed, "just in case." Disadvantages 1 and 2 combine to make this way of organizing projects very expensive.

3. Removing the project from technical control by a functional department has its advantages, but it also has a serious disadvantage if the project is characterized as "high technology." Though individuals engaged with projects develop considerable depth in the technology of the project, they tend to fall behind in other areas of their technical expertise. The functional division is a repository of technical lore and is well positioned to advance the state-of-the-art in the discipline, but it is not readily accessible to members of the standalone project team.

4. Projectized project teams seem to foster inconsistency in the way in which policies and procedures are carried out. In the relatively sheltered environment of the project, administrative corner-cutting is common and easily justified as a response to the client or to technical exigency. "They don't understand our problems" becomes an easy excuse for ignoring dicta from headquarters.

5. In projectized organizations, the project takes on a life of its own. Team members form strong attachments to the project and to each other. A disease known as *projectitis* develops. A strong "we–they" divisiveness grows, distorting the relationships between project team members and their counterparts in the parent organization. Friendly rivalry may become bitter competition, and political infighting between projects is common.

6. Another symptom of projectitis is the worry about "life after the project ends." Typically, there is considerable uncertainty about what will happen when the project is completed. Will team members be laid off? Will they be assigned to low-prestige work? Will their technical skills be too rusty to be successfully integrated into other projects? Will our team ("that old gang of mine") be broken up?

5.3 | Projects in a Matrixed Organization

In an attempt to couple some of the advantages of the standalone project in the projectized organization with some of the desirable features of the functional project, and to avoid some of the disadvantages of each, the matrixed project organization was developed. In effect, the functional and the projectized organizations represent extremes. The matrixed project organization is a combination or *hybrid* of the two. It is a standalone project organization overlaid on the functional divisions of the parent firm.

Being a combination of standalone projectized and functional organization structures, a matrix organization can take on a wide variety of specific forms, depending on which of the two extremes (functional or standalone) it most resembles. The "projectized" or "strong" matrix most resembles the projectized organization. The "functional" or "weak" matrix most resembles the functional form of organization. Finally, the "balanced" matrix lies in between the other two. In practice, there is an almost infinite variety of organizational forms between the extremes, and the primary difference between these forms has to do with the relative power/decision authority of the project manager and the functional manager.

Because it is simpler to explain, let us first consider a strong matrix, one that is similar to a standalone project. Rather than being a standalone organization, like the standalone project, the matrix project is not separated from the parent organization. Consider Figure 5.3. Although not always the case, here the project manager of Project 1, PM_1, reports to a program manager who also exercises supervision over two other projects having to do with the same program. Project 1 has assigned to it three people from the manufacturing division, one and one-half people from marketing, one-half of a person each from finance and personnel, four individuals from R & D, and perhaps others not shown. These individuals come from their respective functional divisions and are assigned to the project full-time or part-time, depending on the project's needs. It should be emphasized that *the PM controls when and what these people will do, while the functional managers control who will be assigned to the project and how the work will be done, including the technology used.*

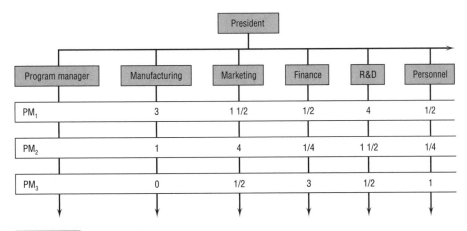

FIGURE 5.3 The matrix organization.

With heavy representation from manufacturing and R&D, Project 1 might involve the design and installation of a new type of manufacturing process for a new product Alpha. Project 2 could involve marketing for the new product. Project 3 might concern the installation of a new financial control system for the new product. All the while, the functional divisions continue on with their routine activities.

There is no single executive to whom PMs generally report. If a project is merely one of several in a specific program, the PM typically reports to a program manager, if there is one. It is not uncommon, however, for the PM to report to the manager of the functional area that has a particular interest in the project. If several projects on mathematics are being conducted for the Office of Naval Research (ONR), for instance, it would be normal for the PMs to report to the ONR section head for Mathematical Sciences. In smaller firms with only a few projects, it is common for the PM to report directly to a senior executive.

At the other end of the spectrum of matrix organizations is the functional or weak matrix. A project might, for example, have only one full-time person, the PM. Rather than having an individual functional worker actually assigned to the project, the functional departments devote *capacity* to the project, and the primary task of the PM is to coordinate the project activities carried out by the functional departments. For example, the PM of a project set up to create a new database for personnel might request that the basic design be done by the information technology (IT) group in the administrative division. The personnel job would then be added to the normal workload of the IT group. The priority given to the design might be assigned by senior management or might be the result of negotiations between the PM and the head of the IT group. In some cases, the IT group's charges for the job might also be subject to negotiation. The task could even be subcontracted to an outside vendor.

Between these extremes is the balanced matrix, which is typically anything but balanced. There are many different mixtures of project and functional responsibilities. When a functional group's work is frequently required by projects, it is common to operate the group as a functional unit rather than to transfer its people to the project. For instance, a toxicology unit in a cosmetic business, a quality assurance group in a multiproduct manufacturing firm, or a computer graphics group in a publishing firm might all be functionally organized and take on project work much like outside contractors. While the PM's control over the work is diminished by this arrangement, the project does have immediate access to any expertise in the group, and the group can maintain its technological integrity.

We have previously discussed the difference between discipline-oriented individuals and those who are problem-oriented, indicating that the latter are highly desirable as members of project teams. Both de Laat (1994) and Kalu (1993) stand as adequate testimony to the fact that discipline-oriented team members tend to become ardent supporters of their functional areas, sometimes to the detriment of the project as a whole. The resultant power struggles may stress the PM's skills in conflict reduction.

The matrixed project approach has its own unique advantages and disadvantages. Its strong points are as follows:

1. The project is the point of emphasis. One individual, the PM, takes responsibility for managing the project, for bringing it in on time, within cost, and to specification (scope). The matrix organization shares this virtue with the standalone project organization.

2. Because the project organization is overlaid on the functional divisions, temporarily drawing labor and talent from them, the project has reasonable access to the entire reservoir of technology in all functional divisions. When there are several projects, the talents of the functional divisions are available to all projects, thus sharply reducing the duplication required by the standalone project structure.

3. There is less anxiety about what happens when the project is completed than is typical of the standalone project organization. Even though team members tend to develop a strong attachment for the project, they also feel close to their functional "home."

4. Response to client needs is as rapid as in the standalone project case, and the matrix organization is just as flexible. Similarly, the matrix organization responds flexibly and rapidly to the demands made by those inside the parent organization. A project nested within an operating firm must adapt to the needs of the parent firm or the project will not survive.

5. With matrix management, the project will have—or have access to—representatives from the administrative units of the parent firm. As a result, consistency with the policies, practices, and procedures of the parent firm tends to be preserved. If nothing else, this consistency with parent firm procedures tends to foster project credibility in the administration of the parent organization, a condition that is commonly undervalued.

6. Where there are several projects simultaneously under way, matrix organization allows a better companywide balance of resources to achieve the several different time/cost/scope targets of the individual projects. This holistic approach to the total organization's needs allows projects to be staffed and scheduled in order to optimize total system performance rather than to achieve the goals of one project at the expense of others.

7. While standalone projects and functionally organized projects represent extremes of the organizational spectrum, matrix organizations cover a wide range in between. We have differentiated between strong and weak matrices in terms of whether the functional units supplied individuals or capacity to projects. Obviously, some functional units might furnish people and others only supply capacity. There is, therefore, a great deal of flexibility in precisely how the project is organized—all within the basic matrix structure—so that it can be adapted to a wide variety of projects and is always subject to the needs, abilities, and desires of the parent organization.

The advantages accruing to the matrix structure are potent, but the disadvantages are also serious. All of the following disadvantages involve conflict—between the functional and project managers for the most part.

1. In the case of functionally organized projects, there is no doubt that the functional division is the focus of decision-making power. In the standalone project case, it is clear that the PM is the power center of the project. With matrix organizations, the power is more balanced. Often, the balance is fairly delicate. When doubt exists about who is in charge, the work of the project suffers. If the project is successful and highly visible, doubt about who is in charge can foster political infighting for the credit and glory. If the project is a failure, political infighting will be even more brutal to avoid blame.

2. While the ability to balance time, cost, and scope between several projects is an advantage of matrix organizations, that ability has its dark side. The set of projects must be carefully monitored as a set, a tough job. Further, the movement of resources from project to project in order to satisfy the several schedules may foster political infighting among the several PMs, all of whom tend to be more interested in ensuring success for their individual projects than in helping the total system optimize organization-wide goals.

3. For strong matrices, problems associated with shutting down a project are almost as severe as those in standalone project organizations. The projects, having individual identities, resist death. Even in matrix organizations, projectitis is still a serious disease.

4. In matrix-organized projects, the PM controls administrative decisions and the functional heads control technological decisions. The distinction is simple enough when writing about project management, but for the operating PM the division of authority and responsibility inherent in matrix management is complex. The ability of the PM to negotiate

TABLE 5.1   **Project Characteristics and Project Home**

Project Characteristics	Project Home				
	Functional Organization	Matrixed Organization			Projectized
		Weak	Balanced	Strong	
Authority of PM	Little to None	Low	Low to Moderate	Moderate to High	High to Complete
Availability of Resources	Little to None	Low	Low to Moderate	Moderate to High	High to Complete
Ownership of Project Budget	Functional Manager	Functional Manager	Shared	PM	PM
Role of PM	Part-time	Part-time	Full-time	Full-time	Full-time
Project Administrative Staff	Part-time	Part-time	Part-time	Full-time	Full-time

(Adapted from Table 2-1, PMI **PMBOK** 5th Edition, p. 22.)

anything from resources to technical assistance to delivery dates is a key contributor to project success. Success is doubtful for a PM without strong negotiating skills.

5. Matrix management violates the management principle of unity of command. Project workers have at least two bosses, their functional heads and the PM. There is no way around the split loyalties and confusion that result. Anyone who has worked under such an arrangement understands the difficulties. Those who have not done so cannot appreciate the discomforts it causes. To paraphrase Plato's comment on democracy, matrix management "is a charming form of management, full of variety and disorder."

Modern matrix management today strives to achieve many more goals than when it was adopted decades ago. For example, IBM is organized as a multidimensional matrix (Grant, 2008). There is a "business" organization (structured around hardware, software, and services), a "geographical" orientation (regions/countries), a "functional" home, "customer" groupings, "distribution channel" specialties, and "new business development" thrusts. If the old form of matrix management was confusing, the new form can be overwhelming. But modern organizations find that they have many more goals to achieve and must be multidexterous, achieving a more complex organizational integration but without hampering their flexibility, responsiveness, and performance. The solution many organizations have come up with has been to be more formal and controlling for the operational activities such as business and distribution channel goals (more centralized) while more informal (dotted-line relationships) for the functional, geographic, and customer activities, and even less formal, even voluntary or self-organizing, for knowledge management activities such as new business development.

Table 5.1 contrasts and summarizes key characteristics of projects in functional, projectized, and matrixed organizations.

Virtual Projects

Virtual projects are those in which work on the project team crosses time, space, organizational, or cultural boundaries. Thus, a virtual team may work in different time zones, be geographically dispersed, work in different organizations, or work in different cultures. In all cases, the rise of virtual projects has been facilitated by the use of the Internet and other communication technologies. In many of these cases, the project team is often organized in some matrix type of structure rather than a functional or standalone project form. Kalu (1993, p. 175) further defines *virtual positions* as "task processes, the performance of which requires composite membership" in both project and functional organizations. When complex organizations conduct projects, virtual positions are typical because projects usually require input from several functional departments. This creates overlapping and shared responsibility for the work with functional managers and PMs sharing responsibility for execution of the project.

Gratton (2007) also offers some rules for success when organizations find they must use geographically dispersed virtual teams for some of their projects.

- Only use virtual teams for projects that are challenging and interesting. But also be sure the project is meaningful to the company as well as the team.

- Solicit volunteers as much as possible—they'll be more enthusiastic and dedicated to the success of the project.

- Include a few members in the team who already know each other, and make sure one in every six or seven are "boundary spanners" with lots of outside contacts.

- Create an online resource for team members to learn about each other (especially how they prefer to work), collaborate, brainstorm, and draw inspiration.

- Encourage frequent communication, but not social gatherings (which will occur at more natural times anyway).

- Divide the project work into geographically independent modules as much as possible so progress in one location isn't hampered by delays in other locations.

Project Management in Practice

Software Firm Yunio Avoids Complex Technologies

Chris Mathews, cofounder and CEO of China-based start-up software maker Yunio, avoids cumbersome gadgetry and complex interfaces to manage his global project teams. He prefers techniques and technologies that seem natural and comfortable for the virtual teams. His focus is clear communication, regardless of the technology used. And when a message can be sent by example, he prefers that to other, less-effective forms of communication. For instance, when working with his Chinese teams he found that it wasn't the norm for team members to let their colleagues know when they would be absent, or how to reach them. To set an example, he started e-mailing team members whenever he would be unable to attend a meeting. For individual teams or groups, he creates separate, distinct mailing lists. As his example was adopted by the teams, it became part of Yunio's culture whereby new employees automatically adopted it too.

Although Mathews uses e-mail for important matters where a written record is desirable, he finds other technologies can be more appropriate for other uses. To keep communication as simple and seamless as possible, he only uses wiki for teams larger than 15 people because it's a large investment requiring input from an online community of users to create content. Wikis become increasingly efficient, particularly for knowledge management, as the team grows. For less than 15 people, he prefers group chats but supplemented by chat logs. Instant messages don't require instant responses so they allow team members to drop a quick note to someone without requiring a response. Since his workers use instant messaging anyway, it's a natural communication tool for chats. Mathews believes that the use of tech products don't define how to manage virtual teams but rather are just part of the toolkit; smart management is about picking the most appropriate tool to communicate clearly.

Questions

1. **Does managing virtual teams require more attention to communication technology?**

2. **Would communicating by example work for nonvirtual project managers?**

3. **What are the trade-offs project managers should consider when trying to select the most effective communication medium?**

Source: M. S. Zoninsein, "Less Is More," *PM Network*, Vol. 24.

5.4 Projects in Composite Organizational Structures

The complexities of the real world rarely lead firms to organize their projects in any of the previous "pure" forms, so what we tend to see in practice is some combination of two or three or more different forms. In a functional organization, there may be project divisions along with marketing and finance, or in a matrix division there may be a staff project reporting to the CEO (or treasurer, or . . .), and so on. We call these "composite" structures.

As an example, organization by territory is especially attractive to national organizations whose activities are physically or geographically spread, and where the products have some geographical uniqueness, such as ladies' garments. So we may have projects such as spring fashion designs being run within each territory. But suppose each territory also sells to different kinds of customers, like retailers, wholesalers, and consumers; or perhaps civilians and military. Project organization within customer divisions is typically found when the projects reflect a paramount interest in the needs of different types of customers. Then we might also have matrixed projects that cross the various territories and focus on customer preferences, or projectized if it is a single project, such as installing a customer relationship management (CRM) software database for all the territories.

If both functional and projectized divisions coexist in a firm, this would result in the composite form shown in Figure 5.4. This form is rarely observed for a long duration. What is done, instead, is to spin off the large, successful, long-run projects as subsidiaries or independent operations. Many firms nurture young, unstable, smaller projects under the wing of an existing division, then wean them to standalone projects with their own identity, as in Figure 5.4, and finally allow the formation of a *venture team*—or, for a larger project, *venture firm*—within the parent company. For example, Texas Instruments did this with the Speak and Spell® toy that was developed by one of its employees, and 3M did this with their Post-It® Notes.

The composite form leads to flexibility. It enables the firm to meet special problems by appropriate adaptation of its organizational structure. There are, however, distinct dangers involved in using the composite structure. Dissimilar groupings within the same accountability center tend to encourage overlap, duplication, and friction because of incompatibility of interests. Again, we have the conditions that tend to result in conflict between functional and project managers.

Figure 5.5 illustrates another common solution to the problem of how to organize a project. The firm sets up what appears to be a standard form of functional organization, but it adds a staff office to administer all the projects. This frees the functional groups of administrative problems while it uses their technical talents. In a large specialty chemical firm, this organizational form worked so well that the staff office became the nucleus of a full-scale division of the firm whose sole purpose was to administer projects. Much has been written about the use of a "project management office," which, as noted in earlier chapters and shown in Figure 5.5, is an equivalent structure; more will be said about the PMO in Section 5.6.

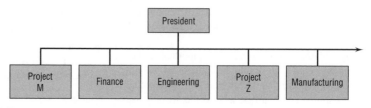

FIGURE 5.4 A functional/projectized composite organization.

For single projects, this is basically the functional organization described earlier, but if used for multiple projects, and particularly if a PMO is used, this organization is similar to the matrix form. The main difference is that this form would typically be used for small, short-term projects where the formation of a full-fledged matrix system is not justified. This mixed form shares several advantages and disadvantages of the matrix structure, but the project life is usually so short that the disease of projectitis is rarely contracted. If the number or size of the projects being staffed in this way grows, a shift to a formal matrix organization naturally evolves.

Though the ways of interfacing project and parent organization are many and varied, most firms eventually adopt the matrix form as the basic method of housing their growing number of projects. To this base, occasional standalone, functional, and composite projects may be added if these possess special advantages; otherwise, they will be added to the matrix due to the relatively low cost of managing them and their enhanced ability to get access to broad technical support.

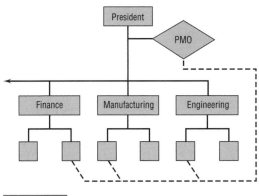

FIGURE 5.5 A functional/staff organization.

5.5 Selecting a Project Form

The choice of how to organize a project is not addressed to PMs or aspiring PMs. It is addressed to senior management. Very rarely does the PM have a choice about the way the project interfaces with the parent organization. Indeed, the PM is rarely asked for input to the interface choice. Even experienced practitioners find it difficult to explain how one should proceed when trying to choose. The choice is determined by the situation, but even so is partly intuitive. There are few accepted principles of design and no step-by-step procedures that give detailed instructions for determining what kind of structure is needed and how it can be built. All we can do is consider the nature of the potential project, the characteristics of the various organizational options, the advantages and disadvantages of each, the cultural preferences of the parent organization, and make the best compromise we can.

In general, the functional form is apt to be the organizational form of choice for projects where the major focus must be on the in-depth application of a technology. Also, the functional form is preferred for projects that will require large capital investments in equipment or buildings of a type normally used by the function.

If the firm engages in a large number of similar projects (e.g., construction projects), the projectized form of organization is preferred. The same form would generally be used for one-time, highly specific, unique tasks that require careful control and are not appropriate for a single functional area—the development of a new product line, for instance. One problem projectized organizations typically face is how to resolve the tensions between flexibility and control. Research on projectized firms (Gann et al., 2012) indicates that these firms tend to develop suborganizational "baronies" of three types: dominions, tight federations, or loose federations. Each of these offers significant competencies for the firm but also present special management and leadership challenges.

When the project requires the integration of inputs from several functional areas and involves reasonably sophisticated technology, but does not require all the technical specialists to work for the project on a full-time basis, the matrix organization is the only satisfactory solution. This is particularly true when several such projects must share technical experts. Another special case is when projects are created to change the way the parent organization is organized or communicates internally. Such projects typically require representation of all major parts of the parent to be successful. Matrix organizations are complex and present a difficult challenge for the PM, but are sometimes necessary.

If choice of project structure exists, the first problem is to determine the kind of work that must be accomplished. To do this requires an initial, tentative project plan (a topic covered in detail in Section 6.1). First, identify the primary deliverable(s) of the project. Next, list the major tasks associated with each deliverable. For each task, determine the functional unit that will probably be responsible for carrying out the task. These are the elements that must be involved in order to carry out the project. The problem is how best to bring them together—or, how best to integrate their work. Additional matters to be considered are the individuals (or small groups) who will do the work, their personalities, the technology to be employed, the client(s) to be served, the political relationships of the functional units involved, and the culture of the parent organization. Environmental factors inside and outside the parent organization must also be taken into account. By understanding the various structures, their advantages and disadvantages, a firm can select the organizational structure that seems to offer the most effective and efficient choice. Recent research (Lechler et al., 2010) indicates that the forms of project organizing do impact project success and that the more authority and responsibility the PM has, the more likely the project will be a success; hence, using functional managers as PMs will increase the chances of success.

We illustrate the process with an example in the Trinatronic, Inc. box using the following procedure.

1. Define the project with a statement of the objective(s) that identifies the major outcomes desired.

2. Determine the key tasks associated with each objective and locate the units in the parent organization that serve as functional "homes" for these types of tasks.

3. Arrange the key tasks by sequence and decompose them into work packages.

4. Determine which organizational units are required to carry out the work packages and which units will work particularly closely with which others.

5. List any special characteristics or assumptions associated with the project—for example, level of technology needed, probable length and size of the project, any potential problems with the individuals who may be assigned to the work, possible political problems between different functions involved, and anything else that seems relevant, including the parent firm's previous experiences with different ways of organizing projects.

6. In light of the above, and with full cognizance of the pros and cons associated with each structural form, choose a structure.

5.6 | The Project Management Office

Thus far in this chapter it has been tacitly assumed that however the project has been organized, it has, or has access to, sufficient skill, knowledge, and resources to accomplish any activities that may be required. As we shall see, this assumption is not always true. A primary task of the PM is to acquire the resources, technical skills, knowledge, and whatever is needed by the project. While this may be difficult, acquisition of the project's technical resources is mainly dependent on the PM's skill in negotiation as described in Chapter 4 and relationship with the project sponsor.

Even if the PM has all the resources needed, two problems remain. First, in the entire history of projects from the beginning of time until the day after tomorrow, no project has ever been completed precisely as it was planned. Uncertainty is a way of life for PMs and their projects. Second, the successful execution of a project is a complex managerial task and requires the use of planning, budgeting, scheduling, and control tools with

Project Management in Practice

Trinatronic, Inc.

Project objective: To design, build, and market a laptop computer that uses open standards where possible, and is capable of running all current engineering design and office productivity software packages. To satisfy security and confidentiality considerations, the computer should be able to maintain multiple versions of its operating information without needing to use offline storage.

In addition, the computer must be able to support video and audio conferencing capabilities, and must be compatible with European Common Market and U. S. "Green" standards for energy usage. The desired price point for this computer should be 10 percent below what we suspect competitors could offer.

Key Tasks	Organizational Units
A. Write specifications.	Mktg. Div. and R & D
B. Design hardware, do initial tests.	R & D
C. Engineer hardware for production.	Eng. Dept., Mfg. Div.
D. Set up production line.	Eng. Dept., Mfg. Div.
E. Manufacture small run, conduct quality and reliability tests.	Mfg. Div. and Q.A. Dept., Exec. V.P. staff
F. Write (or adopt) operating systems.	Software Prod. Div.
G. Test operating systems.	Q.A. Dept., Exec. V.P. staff
H. Write (or adopt) applications software.	Software Prod. Div.
I. Test applications software.	Q.A. Dept., Exec. V.P. staff
J. Prepare full documentation, repair and user manuals.	Tech. Writing Section (Eng. Div.) and Tech. Writing Section (Software Prod. Div.)
K. Set up service system with manuals and spare parts	Tech. Writing Section (Eng. Div.) and Tech.
L. Prepare marketing program.	Mktg. Div.
M. Prepare marketing demonstrations.	Mktg. Div.

Without attempting to generate a specific sequence for these tasks, we note that they seem to belong to seven categories of work.

1. Develop and prioritize requirements.
2. Design, build, and test hardware.
3. Design, write, and test software.
4. Set up production and service/repair systems with spares and manuals.
5. Prepare and implement a make-or-buy analysis.
6. Develop release plan.
7. Design marketing effort, with demonstrations, brochures, and manuals.

Based on this analysis, it would appear that the project will need the following elements:

- Groups to design the hardware and software.
- Groups to test the hardware and write and test the software.

- A group to engineer the production system for the hardware.
- A group to design the marketing program.
- A group to prepare all appropriate documents and manuals.
- And, lest we forget, a group to administer all the above groups.

These subsystems represent at least three major divisions and perhaps a half-dozen departments in the parent organization. The groups designing the hardware and the multiple operating systems will have to work closely together. The test groups may work quite independently of the hardware and software designers, but results improve when they cooperate.

Trinatronics has people capable of carrying out the project. The design of the hardware and operating systems is possible in the current state of the art, but to design such systems at a cost of 10% below potential competitors will require an advance in the state of the art. The project is estimated to take between 18 and 24 months, and to be the most expensive project yet undertaken by Trinatronics.

Based on the sketchy information above, it seems clear that a functional project organization would not be appropriate. Too much interaction between major divisions is required to make a single function into a comfortable organizational home for everyone. Either a standalone project or matrix structure is feasible, and given the choice, it seems sensible to choose the simpler standalone project organization if the cost of additional personnel is not too high. Note that if the project had required only part-time participation by the highly qualified scientific professionals, the matrix organization might have been preferable. Also, a matrix structure would probably have been chosen if this project were only one of several such projects drawing on a common staff base.

Questions

1. **Consider the applicability of a "weak" matrix structure for this project. What would be the pros and cons of this approach?**
2. **Consider the applicability of a "strong" matrix or "balanced" structure. What would be the pros and cons here?**

Source: S. J. Mantel, III. Consulting project.

---

which the neophyte PM may not be completely familiar. In addition, there are contractual, administrative, and reporting duties that must be performed in accord with the law, the wishes of the funder or project owner, and the rules of the organizational home of the project.

Dealing with uncertainties has come to be known as *risk management*, and in addition to managing trade-offs is one the PM's primary roles. We introduced the subject in Chapter 2 when the uncertainties of project selection were discussed. To deal with uncertainty, the parent organization must create some mechanism to manage it, a topic treated in detail in Chapter 6. In order to deal with the managerial and administrative issues of all its projects, and in a way that meets the parent organization's rules, many firms have created a *PMO* (Project Management Office). Liu et al. (2007) have shown that PMOs have a significantly positive impact on projects operating with high task uncertainty. In a recent PMI (2011) survey, it was found that three out of five respondents' organizations have PMOs. The PMO and its responsibilities are detailed in the introductory chapter of **PMBOK**®.

1.4.4

With the increasing role of projects in today's organizations and the move toward "management by projects," the need has arisen for an organizational entity to help manage these fast-multiplying forms of getting work done. This is the role of the PMO. According to Greengard (2013), nearly 7 out of 10 organizations have a PMO, although they go by different names. The most popular is the (Organization Unit) PMO; the next most common at slightly less than half is the Project Support Office; next is the Enterprise PMO; then at just over a third is the Center of Excellence; then the Project-Specific PMO; and last at about one out of six is the Change Management Office.

How does an organization know if it needs a PMO? Greengard states that if the organization is projectized, it needs a PMO. Otherwise, how do they know who's driving the delivery of their projects, who's establishing their methodology, who's managing the resources efficiently? Any organization that does more than a handful of projects should have a PMO. Some cues are: a lack of project transparency, significant discrepancies in project results, poor funder satisfaction rates, the inability to cost projects accurately, a high percentage of delayed or canceled projects, the existence of projects without clear ownership, a lack of visibility into how projects are performing, and high project failure rates. Also, a project management maturity assessment can be conducted to compare internal metrics and key performance indicators to industry averages.

There are also a variety of forms of PMOs to serve a variety of needs. Some of these are at a low level in the organization and others report to the highest levels. The best PMOs (Baker, 2007) have some common characteristics, however, including the traits of being run like the best businesses (a business plan, focused, emphasis on results), enjoying strong executive support, being future-oriented learning organizations, and offering the best project leadership in the organization.

Recent results from a Research Working Session of the Project Management Institute (2013a) also found that other common characteristics of contemporary PMOs is that they are centers of excellence that add value by facilitating decision making and change management; establishing best practice processes, standards, and procedures; and aligning projects to organizational strategy. Moreover, in contrast to the specificity of project management, PMOs should be open-ended and tailored to the needs of the specific organization based on its culture and strategy, whether it embraces project management or not, and its degree of executive support for a PMO.

PMI (2013b) also launched a Thought Leadership Series to address the issues of demonstrating the value of PMOs, how they are viewed in the business world, what a PMO entails, what different kinds of PMOs exist, and what they do. The result was five reports: "Why Good Strategies Fail: Lessons for the C-Suite," "Strategic PMOs Play a Vital Role in Driving Business Outcomes," "The Impact of PMOs on Strategy Implementation," "PMO Frameworks," and "Strategic Initiative Management: The PMO Imperative."

Purposes of the Project Management Office

Before discussing the purpose and services offered by PMOs, consider the following statistics reported by Block et al. (2001). When asked the reasons for initiating a PMO, almost two-thirds of the respondents indicated a need for establishing consistent project management standards and methods and that the PMO was initiated by senior management direction. About half the respondents also indicated a need to eliminate project delays and correct poor project planning. A bit less than 40 percent wanted to improve project performance and eliminate cost overruns. Last, about a quarter of the respondents indicated they wished to reduce customer dissatisfaction. The 2011 PMI survey mentioned earlier found that having a PMO was a key practice in improving project performance, and their roles now commonly include portfolio management, program management, monitoring project success metrics, and managing project resource allocation.

A major contribution of PMOs is to establish project administration procedures for selecting, planning, budgeting, and scheduling projects as well as to serve as a repository for reports on the performance of the planning, budgeting, scheduling, and resource allocation processes. PMO files also often contain reports on risk management, project audits, evaluations, and histories. As reflected by the reasons for initiating the PMOs in the first place, 78 percent of the respondents to Block et al. (2001) indicated that their PMO established and maintained standard project processes (practices and procedures), 64 percent offered consulting help on projects, and 58 percent offered training and mentoring services. About half performed project tracking and slightly fewer conducted portfolio management. Only 28 percent maintained a stable of project managers for future project needs.

Although specific goals may be articulated for the PMO, a major purpose (Block, 1998; Bolles, 1998) is to instill good project management practices throughout the organization, what is known as its "supportive" role. Another major purpose, known as its "controlling" role, is ensuring that the firm's portfolio of projects supports the organization's overall goals and strategy, as described in Chapter 2. In this case, the PMO is the critical tie between strategic management and the project managers. In cases where the PMO has taken on responsibility for projects across the organization, the PMO is often renamed the Enterprise Project Management Office (EPMO), or given a similar name. Mihalic (2013) states that executives these days are looking to EPMOs to merge strategic integration with tactical execution to deliver greater project success. The goal is to provide the leadership and services that allow for the successful selection, execution, and management of programs and projects to achieve the objectives in the organization's strategic plan.

Project Management in Practice

A Project Management Office Success for the Transportation Security Administration

The Transportation Security Administration (TSA) had only 3 months and $20 million to build a 13,500-square-foot coordination center, involving the coordination of up to 300 tradespeople working simultaneously on various aspects of the center. A strong PMO was crucial to making the effort a success. The PMO accelerated the procurement and approval process, cutting times in half in some cases. They engaged a team leader, a master scheduler, a master financial manager, a procurement specialist, a civil engineer, and other specialists to manage the multiple facets of the construction

project, finishing the entire project in 97 days and on budget, receiving an award from the National Assn. of Industrial and Office Properties for the quality of its project management and overall facility.

Questions

1. **What is surprising about the success of this non-profit agency?**

2. **Is the role of the PMO in this case unusual?**

Source: Project Management Institute. "PMO Speeds Success for Transportation Facility," *PM Network*, Vol. 18.

In a recent study of PMOs following the financial crisis and Great Recession of 2008–9 (Gale 2010), it was found that more than half the PMOs now report to the highest levels of management and work on high-value strategic tasks such as managing the governance process (72 percent of those reporting), advising executives (64 percent), and participating in strategic planning (62 percent). In terms of payoffs, they reduced the number of failed projects by 31 percent, delivered 30 percent of projects under budget, and saved U.S. companies an average of $567,000 per project. PMOs show the greatest value when their project portfolio performance matches the strategic objectives of the organization. If they have no vision or mission and no measures of success, they risk getting labeled as administrative overhead and cut in tough times.

In one case, a PMO was initiated when management wanted more insight into what was happening in their projects. The PMO reorganized projects to ensure they were all in sync with the firm's goals, and had a clear business case that aligned with the organizational strategy. The PMO then not only tracked the projects but also issued monthly management reports with at-a-glance information about every project. The reports also show how each completed project helps the firm meet its objectives. To provide management with forward-looking information about potential issues that might jeopardize each project's ability to deliver on its strategic goals, all projects maintain risk registers that are consolidated into a risk report at the end of each month.

It is important to understand that the role of the PMO is that of an *enabler/facilitator* of projects, not the *doer* of projects. Top management cannot allow the EPMO or the PMO to usurp the technical aspects—scheduling, budgeting, etc.—of running the project. Those are the project manager's responsibility. Although the PMO may, on occasion, become involved in some project management tasks, it should be for the purpose of facilitating liaison with top management, not to do the work of the project team.

Forms of Project Management Offices

There are various levels of competence, sophistication, and responsibility of PMOs. That is, some organizations may only want a limited PMO that represents an information center, reporting on project progress and assessing the organization's project maturity. At the next level, the PMO may establish project management procedures and practices, promulgate lessons learned from prior projects, create a database for risk analysis, help project managers with administrative and managerial matters, and possibly even offer basic training in project management. At the upper level, the PMO may establish a resource database and monitor interproject dependencies, manage the project portfolio to ensure attainment of the organization's goals, audit and prioritize individual projects, and generally establish an enterprise project management system. Aubry (2015) studied 184 PMO changes and found that increasing the PMO's supportive role improved project performance, business performance, and project management maturity, but increasing its controlling role had no effect on project performance.

Another way of organizing the PMO has to do with the reporting level of the office. If they place it in a functional department such as Information Technology or Engineering, the main responsibility of the PMO will be to help the department's project managers with their individual projects. If the PMO is established at the business level, it may take on more responsibility for good project management practices and possibly offer basic training. At higher organizational levels, the PMO's responsibilities will broaden and become less tactical and more strategic.

In recent years, several large organizations conducting scores or more (sometimes hundreds) of projects have created multiple PMOs, each overseeing and aiding projects in their individual unit of the organization. An EPMO is occasionally also created to oversee the multiple PMOs and ensure that they follow organizational standards for managing projects. While a PMO is typically only division-wide in a large organization, the EPMO is system-wide and responsible for policy making and organizational change. The 2011 PMI survey also found that EPMOs tend to focus on the strategic aspects of project management. In such cases, PMO contact with senior management is conducted through the EPMO, typically used to manage the project selection process as well as to communicate relevant organizational policy to the PMOs, direct risk management activities, establish processes for audits and reviews, and act as the organizational repository for project records.

Tasks of the Project Management Office

To achieve its goals, PMOs and EPMOs commonly perform many of the following tasks (Block, 1999):

- Establish and enforce good project management processes such as procedures for bidding, risk analysis, project selection, progress reports, executing contracts, and selecting software
- Assess and improve the organization's project management maturity
- Develop and improve an enterprise project management system
- Offer training in project management and help project managers become certified
- Identify, develop, and mentor project managers and maintain a stable of competent candidates
- Offer consulting services to the organization's project managers
- Help project managers with administrative details such as status reports
- Establish a process for estimation and evaluation of risk
- Determine if a new project is a good "fit" for the changing organization
- Identify downstream changes (market, organization) and their impacts on current projects: Are the projects still relevant? Is there a need to change any project's scope? Are there any cost effects on the projects?
- Review and manage the organization's project risk portfolio, including limiting the number of active projects at any given time and identifying and reining in runaway projects as well as managing potential disasters

4. **Establish credibility throughout the organization** The support of one or two stakeholders is insufficient. Generate reports demonstrating the successes of the PMO in the language of executives. Use simple, clear measures that show the impact of the PMO on the business. Confine each report to one page of text and graphics that tells a story at a glance—keep it short and simple.

5. **Get the best people for the PMO** Great methods and practices can never compensate for not having quality staff and PMs.

Another way to initiate the project is through a pilot program in one of the areas that falls under the responsibility of the PMO project sponsor. Following its completion, the pilot project can be assessed, any mistakes corrected, and the benefits publicized to the rest of the organization. As the PMO expands and interacts with more and more projects, its benefits to the organization will increase progressively with its reach.

Unfortunately, not all PMOs are successful. Greengard (2013) reports that about one-third fail to accomplish their desired results, and Gale (2011) further notes that half of all PMOs fail the first time they are tried. According to Tennant (2001), one of the primary problems of PMOs is that the executives who establish PMOs often do not understand project management practices themselves. Thus, they have unrealistic expectations of the PMO, such as providing temporary help for a project in trouble, or to obtain cost reductions from ongoing projects. The PMO is not a quick fix for saving projects that are failing; its primary objective is to improve project management processes over the long run.

PMOs cannot be expected to correct upper management failures such as inappropriate project goals, insufficient project support, and inadequate resource availability. Interestingly, a recent trend in project organizations is the outsourcing of the PMO functions themselves. One has to wonder if this is a sign of impending trouble or a wise recognition of the limitations of upper management knowledge. In that vein, some of the warning signs of it being time to shut down or outsource a PMO are as follows (Greengard, 2013): when senior-level support is waning, when the organization no longer has the institutional expertise for the PMO, when the PMO doesn't seem to be paying its way, and when the PMO has met its objectives.

A key to successfully implementing a PMO is getting the right staff on board. As Gale (2013) points out, this task is composed of two parts: getting the right leader for the PMO and then getting the correctly skilled and proper number of the staff. For PMOs tasked with implementing high-priority strategic initiatives, only 41 percent received adequately skilled personnel and only 31 percent received sufficient staff to carry out projects, so this is apparently a major problem in implementing PMOs.

Gale notes that the leader of the PMO should be someone not only with the proper tool sets for that organization but also someone who will be responsible for the career development of the project managers the PMO is working with. For the staff, it is crucial to have people with a wide range of skills and experience, especially if the staff numbers will be limited. Thus, it isn't wise to simply pick from people who are "available" but to select those with the proper management training, diverse project management experience, and certification in project management. As part of their experience, every staff member should have experience with a project that failed, and be able to reflect on why it failed and what they learned from it. A diverse variety of staff are also useful; the junior staffer with competence collecting and analyzing data serves a very different need in the PMO than the senior, experienced staffer who might be tasked with questioning processes and improving them.

The PMO also needs staffers who are honest about risks and problems and can sift through data and information to arrive at solutions that will solve the core problem. Communication skills are especially important for PMO staff, in terms of brutal honesty but also fluency in speaking at both the strategic, executive level and the tactical, technical level. This includes building presentations that quickly and effectively communicate their message to every audience. Last, they should be good at influencing others to follow their advice.

5.7 | The Project Team

Teamwork is a lot of people doing what I say.   *Anonymous Boss*

In this section we consider the makeup of the project team, bearing in mind that different projects have vastly different staffing needs. The role of the project team takes up most of Chapter 9 in **PMBOK®**. Then we take up some problems associated with staffing the team. Last, we deal with a few of the behavioral issues in managing this team.

9.2–9.4

To be concrete during our discussion of project teams, let us use the example of a software engineering project to determine how to form a project team. Assume that the size of our hypothetical project is fairly large. In addition to the PM, the following key team members might be needed, plus an appropriate number of systems architects, engineers, testers, clerks, and the like. This example can be applied to a construction project, a medical research project, or any of a wide variety of other types of projects. The titles of the individuals would change, but the roles played would be similar.

- **Systems Architect**   The systems architect is in charge of the basic product design and development and is responsible for functional analysis, specifications, drawings, cost estimates, and documentation.

- **Development Engineer**   This engineer's task is the efficient production of the product or process the project engineer has designed, including responsibility for manufacturing engineering, design and production of code, unit testing, production scheduling, and other production tasks.

- **Test Engineer**   This person is responsible for the installation, testing, and support of the product (process) once its engineering is complete.

- **Contract Administrator**   The administrator is in charge of all official paperwork, keeping track of standards compliance (including quality/reliability), funder (engineering) changes, billings, questions, complaints, legal aspects, costs, and negotiation of other matters related to the contract authorizing the project. Not uncommonly, the contract administrator also serves as project historian and archivist.

- **Project Controller**   The controller keeps daily account of budgets, cost variances, labor charges, project supplies, capital equipment status, etc. The controller also makes regular reports and keeps in close touch with both the PM and the company controller. If the administrator does not serve as historian, the controller can do so.

- **Support Services Manager**   This person is in charge of product support, subcontractors, data processing, purchasing, contract negotiation, and general management support functions.

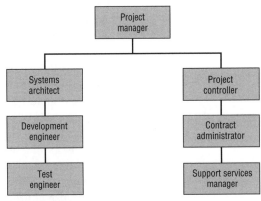

Of these top project people, it is most important that the systems architect and the project controller report directly to the PM (see Figure 5.6). This facilitates control over two of the main goals

FIGURE 5.6 Typical organization for software projects.

of the project: technical performance and budget. (The PM is usually in personal control of the schedule.) For a large project, all six project officials could work out of the project office and report directly to the PM.

To staff the project, the PM works from a forecast of personnel needs over the life cycle of the project. This is done with the aid of some special charts. First, a *work breakdown structure* (WBS) is prepared to determine the exact nature of the tasks required to complete the project. (The WBS is described in detail and illustrated in Chapter 6.) The skill requirements for these tasks are assessed and like skills are aggregated to determine work force needs. Be warned that development of the WBS may involve consultations with external experts. The PM needs to understand, plan for, and closely monitor the effects on current projects of these consultations. It is common for these experts to be pulled away from their own work in order to deal with planning needs arising elsewhere in a WBS. From this base, the functional departments are contacted to locate individuals who can meet these needs.

On occasion, certain tasks may be subcontracted. This option may be adopted because the appropriately skilled personnel are unavailable or cannot be located, or subcontractors can deliver for lower cost, or even because some special equipment required for the project is not available in-house. The need to subcontract is growing as firms "downsize." If the proper people (and equipment) are found within the organization, however, the PM usually must obtain their services from their home departments. Many firms insist on using "local" resources when they are available, in order to maintain better control over resource usage and quality. Typically, the PM will have to negotiate with both the functional department head and the employee, trying to "sell" the employee on the challenge and excitement of working on the project and trying to convince the department head that lending the employee to the project is in the department head's best interest.

There are other people, not necessarily technical, who are also critical to the project's success and should report directly to the PM or to the PM's deputy (often the systems architect):

- Senior project team members who will be having a long-term relationship with the project
- Those with whom the PM will require continuous or close communication
- Those with rare skills necessary to project success.

Remember that the PM must depend on reason when trying to convince a department head to lend their valuable people to the project. The functional department head, who sees the project as a more or less glamorous source of prestige in which the department cannot share, has little natural motivation to be cooperative. Once again, project success depends on the political and negotiating skill of the PM as much as on the technical skill of the team.

Thus far, we have tacitly assumed a fairly strong matrix or projectized organization for the project in our example. In recent years, the use of weaker matrices has become more and more frequent. In many firms, when PMs are asked for the number of people who report directly to them, the answer "None!" is not uncommon. Most common of all, it seems to us, is the matrix organization with a project manager, one or two key skilled contributors who may be full-time members of the project, and a wide variety of services or capacity supplied to the project by functional groups in the parent organization. Such structures are often found in R&D projects that are part of larger programs being carried out by a parent firm. In a pharmaceutical project, for example, one or two senior scientists and laboratory technicians may be assigned to the project, but the work involved in toxicity testing, efficacy testing, and writing the product insert is supplied to the project in the form of deliverables from functional units rather than people assigned directly to the project to carry out the work.

Although the PM has to bargain for fewer individuals in these weaker matrix structures than in the case of stronger matrices, the PM's negotiating skills are just as critical. It is typical for the success of weak-matrix projects to be dependent on the skills of the few technical specialists who are assigned directly to the project. The ability of the PM to negotiate for skilled technicians as well as for the *timely* delivery of services from functional departments is a key determinant of success.

5.8 Human Factors and the Project Team

With a reminder of the need for the PM to possess a high level of political sensitivity, we can discuss some other factors in managing project teams, all the while remembering that the principles and practices of good, general management also apply to the management of projects. We discuss them from the viewpoint of the PM as an individual who must cope with the personal as well as the technical victories and frustrations of life on a project. The issues of managing the project team are mainly included in the Human Resource Management knowledge area of **PMBOK®**.

 PMBOK

Chapter 9

Meeting schedule and cost goals without compromising performance appears to be a technical problem for the PM. Actually, it is only partly technical because it is also a human problem—more accurately, a technical problem with a human dimension. Project professionals tend to be perfectionists. It is difficult enough to meet project goals under normal conditions, but when, out of pride of workmanship, the professionals want to keep improving (and thus changing) the product, the task becomes almost impossible. Changes cause delays. Throughout the project, the manager must continue to stress the importance of meeting due dates. It also helps if the PM establishes, at the beginning of the project, a technical change procedure to ensure control over the incidence and frequency of change. (It would not, however, be wise for the PM to assume that everyone will automatically follow such a procedure.)

Another problem is motivating project team members to accomplish the work of the project. Unfortunately, the PM often has little control over the economic rewards and promotions of the people working on the project. This is especially true when the matrix is weak. This does not, however, mean that the PM cannot motivate members of the project team. In a famous classic study of what motivates technical employees such as engineers, scientists, and professionals on a project team, they found that recognition, achievement, the work itself, responsibility, advancement, and the chance to learn new skills are strong motivators (see Herzberg, 1968). It is the PM's responsibility to make sure that project work is structured in such a way as to emphasize these motivational factors. We have also found that the judicious use of "thank you" notes from the PM to those functional managers who have supplied the project with capable and committed individuals and/or effective and efficient capacity is a potent motivator—copies to the relevant individuals and to the functional manager's boss, of course. (It is also important not to write such notes if the performance was mediocre or poor.)

The use of participative management is also a way of motivating people. This is not a new theory. The concept suggests that the individual worker (or team) should play a significant role in deciding what means should be employed in meeting desired ends, and in finding better ways of accomplishing things. Recent participative programs such as Six Sigma, Total Quality Management (TQM), continuous improvement teams (CIT), self-directed work teams (SDWT), and more recently, agile project management teams may have slightly different structures and vary somewhat in the amount of decision-making authority and autonomy exercised by the team, but they are all aimed at improving worker performance as well as improving production methods and product quality. We will discuss agile project management further in Chapter 6.

The adoption of such methods *empowers* the team (as well as its individual members) to take responsibility and to be accountable for delivering project objectives. Some advantages of empowerment for project teams are given as follows:

1. It harnesses the ability of the team members to manipulate tasks so that project objectives are met. The team is encouraged to find better ways to do things.

2. Professionals do not like being micromanaged. Participative management does not tell them how to work but, given a goal, allows them to design their own methods (usually within some constraints on their authority).

3. The team members know they are responsible and accountable for achieving the project deliverables.

4. There is a good chance that synergistic solutions will result from team interaction.

5. Team members get timely feedback on their performance.

6. The PM is provided a tool for evaluating the team's performance.

Project Management in Practice

South African Repair Success through Teamwork

When a fire broke out in the carbonate regeneration column in a major facility of Sasol, a leading South African coal, chemical, and crude-oil company, it was crucial to get it fixed immediately. It was determined that the damaged portion of the 19-foot-wide, 231-foot-long column would have to be cut out and replaced before the facility could operate again. Time was of the essence, and only 40 days were allowed for the repair project.

To achieve this unheard-of schedule, a number of special ground rules were established:

- The project is to be schedule-driven, not cost-driven.
- There is no float anywhere on the project.
- Always plan to reduce scheduled times, not meet them.
- Resources are not to be considered as a limitation.
- Communication will be continuous across all levels.
- Safety will not be compromised.
- Quality will not be compromised.

In addition, special effort was directed toward making the project team strive to reduce time on the project. First, it was made clear that a higher premium would be placed on team performance than on individual performance. The "soft" aspects of management were always taken into consideration: making sure transport was available, accommodations were acceptable, food was available, excessive overtime was avoided, communication forms matched each member's preferences (verbal, phone, written, etc.), and so on. A communication board was installed and updated twice daily to communicate project progress, and especially time saved on the schedule with the person's name who achieved it. There were both twice-daily shift change meetings, where each shift communicated with the previous shift about progress and problems, and twice-daily planning meetings, where the work activities of the next 2 days were planned in minute detail.

The response to this level of project team attention was overwhelming. People raised ideas for saving even 5 minutes on the schedule. Enthusiasm for the project, and saving project time, became the dominant culture. As a result, the project was completed in only 25 days, 15 days early, with a corresponding cost savings of over $21 million out of an $85 million budget.

Questions

1. Of the special ground rules, which ones do you think really gave impetus to the speed of the project?

2. What do you think was the primary factor that changed the culture for this project?

3. Given that this project cut about 40 percent off the schedule and 25 percent off the cost, what is the message about the importance of teamwork?

Source: I. Boggon, "The Benfield Column Repair Project," *PM Network*, Vol. 10.

All of these items serve to increase motivation among members of the project team. Informal discussions with many project team leaders lead us to the same conclusions, but the success of SDWTs (and all other teams) is ultimately dependent on a clear statement of what the team is expected to accomplish. Senior management must "make the effort to clearly delineate project goals, responsibilities, and authority" in order to reap the advantages of project teams (Nelson, 1998, p. 43). Finally, it is important to remember that giving a project to a team does not supersede the need for competent project management skills.

In Chapter 6, we cover the process of planning projects in detail, and we emphasize the use of the WBS to organize the activities of the project. It is a detailed planning and scheduling technique directed toward achievement of the objectives of the project. The PM (and sometimes the client) works with members of the project team and a comprehensive set of written plans is generated by this process. The resulting document is not only a plan but also a control mechanism. Because the system of developing the plan is participative and makes team members accountable for their specific parts of the overall plan, it motivates them, and also clearly denotes the degree to which team members are mutually dependent. The importance of this latter outcome of the planning process is not well recognized in the literature on team building.

However, bringing people together, even when they belong to the same organization and contribute their efforts to the same objectives, does not necessarily mean that they will behave like a team. Organizing the team's work in such a way that team members are mutually dependent, and recognize it, will produce a strong impetus for the group to form a real team. Project success will be associated with teamwork, and project failure will surely result if the group does not work as a team.[1] If many or most of the team members are also "problem oriented," the likelihood of the group forming an effective team is further increased.

In an extensive research study on the matter, Tippet et al. (1995) conclude that overall results show that companies are generally doing a poor job of team building. Lack of effective rewards, inadequate individual and team performance feedback mechanisms, and inadequate individual and team goal-setting are all weak areas (Tippet, 1995, p. 35). Regarding one particular detrimental team behavior, He (2012) investigated the effect of "free-riding" in teams and found that a combination of enhancing team morale and controlling team size counteracts this undesirable behavior. Finally, Lencioni (2002) has written a wonderful little book on team building that he describes as "a leadership fable." If one can read only one work on teams, this would be our first choice.

---

[1]Though team formation is not even mentioned, a reading of A. S. Carlisle's (1976) article, "MacGregor," is instructive. The article is a classic on the power of delegation and was clearly the inspiration for Blanchard and Johnson's *The One Minute Manager*. The Carlisle paper reports on a plant manager who delegates most operating decisions to his subordinates and insists that they help in solving one another's problems. As a result, they form a team that would be the envy of any project manager.

The use of matrix project organizations raises an additional problem. Team members come and go. The constant turnover of team members makes it difficult to build and maintain a team (Bushe, 2010). When a new member of the team arrives, he or she must be brought up to date on the project. Almost always, this job is left to experienced team members, who are often beset with the pressure of their own work and resent the interruption. Some things can be done to help, if not totally solve the problem. The PM should identify some team members who are personally outgoing and knowledgeable. These individuals can be asked to meet with new members and help them engage the technical aspects of the project. The PM must, of course, make sure that this additional work can be accommodated in the schedules of the old hands. Interpersonal contact is often made easier for all parties through the use of software (Underwood, 2008). Also, increased specialization can reduce the amount of information that must be passed along and can result in an emphasis on the fact that all team members are dependent on other team members for success. A sense of mutual dependency will also tend to raise the level of cohesiveness and commitment to all members of the project.

Another behavioral problem for the PM is interpersonal conflict. The problem is so pervasive that conflict between project team members and between team members and outsiders (including the client) seems to be the natural state of existence for projects. It is our strong feeling that the PM who cannot manage conflict is doomed to failure. Negotiation, as we have indicated before, is the PM's primary tool for resolving conflict, but we caution the reader once again that conflict can also be a highly creative force in a project team, particularly when it is controlled by an astute PM.

In 1975, Thamhain et al. (1975) published the classic work on the focus and nature of conflict in projects. In spite of its age, this information still holds true today and we include it here. We have found their insights just as relevant today as they were in 1975. Table 5.2, based on Thamhain et al., relates the most likely focus of conflict to specific stages of the project life cycle. The table also suggests some solutions. When the project is first organized, priorities, procedures, and schedules all have roughly equal potential as a focus of conflict. During the buildup phase, priorities become significantly more important than any other conflict factor; procedures are almost entirely established by this time. In the main program phase, priorities are finally established and schedules are the most important cause of trouble within the project, followed by technical disagreements. Getting adequate support for the project is also a point of concern. At project finish, meeting the schedule is the critical issue, but interpersonal tensions that were easily ignored early in the project can suddenly erupt into conflict during the last hectic weeks of the life cycle. Worry about reassignment exacerbates the situation. Both Tables 5.2 and 5.3 show conflict as a function of stage in the project life cycle as well as by source of the conflict, but Table 5.3 also shows the *frequency* of conflict by source and stage of the life cycle.

It seems clear to us that most of the conflict on project teams is the result of individuals focusing on the project through the eyes of their individual discipline or department (de Laat, 1994). Such people are not problem oriented and thus are rarely effective members of project teams. Dewhurst (1998, p. 34) defines a group of individuals working independently as a "Name-Only-Team" or a "NOT." If teamwork is vital to success, then for a NOT, the "work group math (is) $2 + 2 = 3$ or less." The infighting that results when discipline-oriented individuals introduce conflict to a project team is perceived by most team members to be "political." If the PM allows project decisions to be dictated by the infighting, the project is apt to fail (Pinto, 1997, p. 31).

Conflict can be handled in several ways, as described in Chapter 4, but one thing is certain: Conflict avoiders do not make successful project managers. On occasion, compromise appears to be helpful, but most often, gently confronting the conflict is the method of choice. Much has been written about conflict resolution and there is no need to summarize

TABLE 5.2   Major Sources of Conflict during Various Stages of the Project Life Cycle

Lift Cycle Phase	Major Conflict Source and Recommendations for Minimising Dysfunctional Consequences	
	Conflict Source	**Recommendations**
Project formation	Priorities	Clearly defined plans. Joint decision making and/or consultation with affected parties. Stress importance of project to organization goals.
	Procedures	Develop detailed administrative operating procedures to be followed in conduct of project.
		Secure approval from key administrators.
		Develop statement of understanding or charter.
	Schedules	Develop schedule commitments in advance of actual project commencement.
		Forecast other departmental priorities and possible impact on project.
Buildup phase	Priorities	Provide effective feedback to support areas on forecasted project plans and needs via status review sessions.
	Schedules	Schedule work breakdown packages (project subunits) in cooperation with functional groups.
	Procedures	Contingency planning on key administrative issues.
Main program	Schedules	Continually monitor work in progress.
		Communicate results to affected parties.
		Forecast problems and consider alternatives.
		Identify potential trouble spots needing closer surveillance.
	Technical	Early resolution of technical problems.
		Communication of schedule and budget restraints to technical personnel.
		Emphasize adequate, early technical testing.
		Facilitate early agreement on final designs.
	Labor	Forecast and communicate staffing requirements early.
		Establish staffing requirements and priorities with functional and staff groups.
Phaseout	Schedules	Close schedule monitoring in project life cycle.
		Consider reallocation of available staff to critical project areas prone to schedule slippages.
		Attain prompt resolution of technical issues that may affect schedules.
	Personality and labor	Develop plans for reallocation of people upon project completion.
		Maintain harmonious working relationships with project team and support groups. Try to loosen up high-stress environment.

Source: Thamhain et al., 1975.

TABLE 5.3	Number of Conflicts during a Sample Project			
Phase of Project				
Start	**Early**	**Main**	**Late**	**Sources of Conflict**
27	35	24	16	Project priorities
26	27	15	09	Admin. procedures
18	26	31	11	Technical trade-offs
21	25	25	17	Staffing
20	13	15	11	Support cost estimates
25	29	36	30	Schedules
16	19	15	17	Personalities
153	**174**	**161**	**111**	**Total**

Source: Thamhain et al., 1975.

that literature here beyond noting that the key to conflict resolution rests on the manager's ability to transform a win–lose situation into win–win.

In the next chapter, we move from organizational issues to project planning tasks. We address the topics of coordination, interface management, and risk management. We also present some major project management concepts and tools such as the WBS and RACI matrix.

Summary

This chapter described the various organizational and governance structures that can be used for projects, and detailed their advantages. An appropriate procedure for choosing the best form was described and two examples were given. The chapter then moved into a discussion of the role of the PMO and project management maturity. Following this, discussion turned to the project team itself, describing the organization of the project office staff and the human issues, such as motivation and conflict, the project manager will face. Specific points made in the chapter were these:

If the project is to be included in a functional organization, it should be placed in that unit with the greatest interest in its success or the unit that can provide the most help. Though there are advantages in this mode of organizing, the disadvantages are greater.

The projectized form of organizing has its advantages and disadvantages. Though the disadvantages are not as severe as with the functional form, they are nevertheless significant.

The matrix organization combines the functional and projectized forms in an attempt to reap the advantages of each. While this approach has been fairly successful, it also has its own unique disadvantages. There are many variants of the pure forms of organization, and various staff and "mixed" structures are commonly used to handle special projects. The best form for

a particular case requires consideration of the characteristics of the project compared with the various advantages and disadvantages of each form.

A useful procedure for selecting an organizational form for a project is:

1. Identify the specific outcomes desired.
2. Determine the key tasks to attain these outcomes and identify the units within the parent organization where these tasks would normally be assigned.
3. Sequence the key tasks and group them into logical work steps.
4. Determine which project subsystems will be assigned which steps, and which subsystems must closely cooperate.
5. Identify any special firm or project characteristics, constraints, or problems that may affect how the project should be organized.
6. Consider all of the above relative to the pros and cons of each organizational form as a final decision is made.

Every project should have a project office, even if it must be shared with another project.

Larger, more complex multiorganizational or mega-projects may include, in addition to the PM, a project engineer, manufacturing engineer, field manager, contract administrator, project controller, and support service manager. If an organization engages in multiple projects, a PMO (or EPMO) may also be warranted.

Those on the project team who should report directly to the PM are the project engineer and project controller as well as:

1. Senior team members who will have a long-term relationship with the project.

2. Those with whom the PM will be continuously or closely communicating.

3. Those with rare skills needed for project success.

Perfectionism, motivation, and conflict are often the major behavioral problems facing the PM. Participative management programs can be a useful tool for addressing the first two, while gentle confrontation usually works best for the latter.

Sources of project conflict are often priorities and policies at first, schedule and technical problems during the main phase, and schedule and personal issues near termination.

Glossary

Functional Management The standard departments of the organization that represent individual disciplines such as engineering, marketing, purchasing, and so on.

Holistic The whole viewed at one time rather than each piece individually.

Matrix Organization A method of organizing that maintains both functional supervisors and project supervisors. A strong matrix operates closer to a projectized organization, while a weak matrix operates more like a functional organization.

Maturity The sophistication and experience of an organization in managing multiple projects.

Mega-projects These are huge, highly complex projects costing enormous amounts, consisting of multiple contractors and subcontractors, and taking years to complete.

Mixed Organization This approach includes both functions (disciplines) and projects in its hierarchy.

Multi-organizational Projects These are typically very large projects that involve many organizations.

Parent Organization The firm or organization within which the project is being conducted.

Program Manager This person is typically responsible for a number of related projects, each with its own project manager.

Projectized Organization This form of organizing is characterized by projects being the main subdivisions of the organization, and general administrative functions common to all projects being a staff office reporting to the President or CEO.

Project Management Office An office to deal with multiple projects and charged with improving the project management maturity and expertise of the organization, as well as increasing the success rate of projects.

Projectitis A social phenomenon, inappropriately intense attachment to the project.

Subcontract Subletting tasks out to smaller contractors.

Suboptimization The optimization of a subelement of a system, perhaps to the detriment of the overall system.

Work Breakdown Structure (WBS) The WBS shows the work elements of a project hierarchically, moving from tasks to subtasks, to work packages, and so on. The WBS can be thought of as the basis of the project plan where each level in the WBS breaks down the work activities into greater detail (see Chapter 6).

Questions

Material Review Questions

1. What is a program manager? How does this job differ from that of a project manager?

2. Identify the advantages and disadvantages of the matrix form of organization.

3. Name the four basic types of project organization and list at least one characteristic, advantage, and disadvantage of each.

4. Give some major guidelines for choosing an organizational form for a project.

5. Why is the PMO so important?

6. Identify three ways of dealing with a conflict associated with projects.

7. What are some advantages and disadvantages of housing a project in a functional form?

8. What are the systems architect's duties?

9. What are the major sources of conflict throughout the life cycle?

10. What are the major tasks of a PMO?

11. What does the term "project management maturity" mean?

12. Where do most firms fall on the maturity scale?

Class Discussion Questions

13. Discuss some of the differences between managing professionals and managing other workers or team members.

14. Human and political factors loom large in the success of projects. Given the general lack of coverage of this subject in engineering and science education, how might a PM gain the ability to deal with these issues?

15. A disadvantage of the projectized organization has to do with the tendency of project professionals to fall behind in areas of technical expertise not used on the project. Name several ways that a project manager might avoid this problem.

16. Discuss the effects of the various organizational forms on coordination and interaction, both within the project team and between the team and the rest of the firm.

17. Describe, from Table 5.3, the probable reasons for the changing number of conflicts over the course of the project in the following areas:

    a. Priorities

    b. Administrative procedures

    c. Technical trade-offs

    d. Schedules

18. How would you organize a project to develop a complex new product such as a new color fax–copy–scanner–printer machine? How would you organize if the product was simpler, such as a new flash drive?

19. What do you think may be the purpose of a WBS? How might it aid the PM in organizing the project?

20. Why do you think the average total conflict increases during the "early program phase" (Table 5.3)?

21. What should be the role of the project manager in conflict management?

22. Is it ethical to employ participative management solely as a way to motivate employees?

23. What are the pros and cons of the head of a PMO reporting to senior management? To departmental management?

24. Is project management maturity focused on doing better on multiple projects or single projects?

25. Which of the many purposes of project portfolio management are most important to a firm with a low project management maturity? Which to a firm with high maturity?

Incidents For Discussion

Shaw's Strategy

Colin Shaw has been tapped to be an accounting project manager for the second time this year. Although he enjoys the challenges and opportunity for personal development afforded to him as a project manager, he dreads the interpersonal problems associated with the position. Sometimes he feels like a glorified baby-sitter handing out assignments, checking on progress, and making sure everyone is doing his or her fair share. Recently Colin read an article that recommended a very different approach for the project manager in supervising and controlling team members. Colin thought this was a useful idea and decided to try it on his next project.

The project in question involved making a decision on whether to implement an activity-based costing (ABC) system throughout the organization. Colin had once been the manager in charge of implementing a process costing system in this same division, so he felt very comfortable about his ability to lead the team and resolve this question. He defined the objective of the project and detailed all the major tasks involved, as well as most of the subtasks. By the time the first meeting of the project team took place, Colin felt more secure about the control and direction of the project than he had at the beginning of any of his previous projects. He had specifically defined objectives and tasks

for each team member and had assigned completion dates for each task. He had even made up individual "contracts" for each team member to sign as an indication of their commitment to completion of the assigned tasks per schedule dates. The meeting went very smoothly, with almost no comments from team members. Everyone picked up a copy of his or her "contract" and went off to work on the project. Colin was ecstatic about the success of this new approach.

Questions

Do you think he will feel the same way 6 weeks from now? Compare this approach with his previous approach.

Hydrobuck

Hydrobuck is a medium-sized producer of gasoline-powered outboard motors. In the past it has successfully manufactured and marketed motors in the 3- to 40-horsepower range. Executives at Hydrobuck are now interested in larger motors and would eventually like to produce motors in the 50- to 150-horsepower range.

The internal workings of the large motors are quite similar to those of the smaller motors. However, large, high-performance outboard motors require power trim. Power trim is simply a hydraulic system that serves to tilt the outboard motor up or down on the boat transom. Hydrobuck cannot successfully market the larger outboard motors without designing a power trim system to complement the motor.

The company is financially secure and is the leading producer of small outboard motors. Management has decided that the following objectives need to be met within the next 2 years:

1. Design a quality power trim system.
2. Design and build the equipment to produce such a system efficiently.
3. Develop the operations needed to install the system on the outboard motor.

The technology, facilities, and marketing skills necessary to produce and sell the large motors already exist within the company.

Questions

What alternative types of project organization would suit the development of the power trim system? Which would be best, if Hydrobuck's project management maturity is high? If it is low? Discuss your reasons for selecting these types of organizations.

Continuing Integrative Class Project

The job of organizing the project for speedy, competent execution on budget is a major factor in the success of every project. We are not concerned here with where the project resides in the college and who it reports to—it reports to the Instructor—but rather the internal organization of the project. It can be handled as a set of tasks where everyone in the class has some given responsibilities and a specified time to deliver the results, or through a set of teams responsible for different sets of project tasks. If the class is small, the former may be adequate, but for a larger class, it may be more efficient and practical to set up subteams (though probably NOT a third layer of sub-sub teams). For a class of say 35, five or six subteams may be optimal. This gives a uniform set of about five to seven direct reports for each

manager, including the PM. Of course, some subteams may need fewer workers and others more, but they should be close to the right size. Again, recall that one constraint on the organization is that the subteams cannot all be completely independent. There are two reasons for this. One is that doing some of the work across all the chapters will be more valuable to an individual student (e.g., answering all the Review Questions) than doing all the work for just one chapter and then being ignorant of all the other topics. The second is that in real projects there is typically considerable interaction, even conflict. If the project could be divided into a set of tasks that can all be done by different departments without interacting with each other, there is no need to set up a project to do the work!

Bibliography

Aubry, M. "Project Management Office Transformations: Direct and Moderating Effects that Enhance Performance and Maturity." *Project Management Journal*, November, 2015.

Baker, B. "In Common." *Project Management Journal*, September 2007.

Block, T. R. "The Project Office Phenomenon." *PM Network*, March 1998.

Block, T. R. "The Seven Secrets of a Successful Project Office." *PM Network*, April 1999.

Block, T. R., and J. D. Frame. "Today's Project Office: Gauging Attitudes." *PM Network*, August 2001.

Bolles, D. "The Project Support Office." *PM Network*, March 1998.

Bushe, G. R., "When People Come and Go." *The Wall Street Journal*, August 23, 2010.

Carlisle, A. S. "MacGregor." *Organizational Dynamics*. New York: AMACOM, Summer 1976.

Cicmil, S., and D. Hodgson. "New Possibilities for Project Management Theory: A Critical Judgement." *Project Management Journal,* December 2006.

Cleland, D. I. *Strategic Management of Teams*. New York: Wiley, 1996.

de Laat, P. B. "Matrix Management of Projects and Power Struggles: A Case Study of an R&D Laboratory." *IEEE Engineering Management Review*, Winter 1995. Reprinted from *Human Relations*, Vol. 47, No. 9, 1994.

Dewhurst, H. D. "Project Teams: What Have We Learned?" *PM Network*, April 1998.

Dinsmore, P. C., "How Grown-Up Is Your Organization?" *PM Network*, June 1998.

Dinsmore, P. C. "Converging on Enterprise Project Management." *PM Network*, October 1998.

Gale, S. F. "The PMO Survival Guide." *PM Network*, November 2010.

Gale, S. F. "The PMO: Something of Value." *PM Network*, August 2011.

Gale, S. F. "The Right Crew Wanted." *PM Network*, December 2013.

Gann, D., S. Salter, M. Dodgson, and N. Phillips. "Inside the World of the Project Baron." *MIT Sloan Management Review*, Spring 2012.

Grant, R. M. "The Future of Management: Where Is Gary Hamel Leading Us?" *Long Range Planning*, 2008, pp. 469–482.

Gratton, L. "Working Together . . . When Apart." *Wall Street Journal*, June 16–17, 2007.

Greengard, S. "No PMO? How to Know When You Need One." *PM Network*, December 2013.

He, J. "Counteracting Free-Riding with Team Morale—An Experimental Study." *Project Management Journal*, June 2012.

Herzberg, F. H. "One More Time: How Do You Motivate Employees?" *Harvard Business Review*, January–February 1968.

Ibbs, C. W., and Y. H. Kwak. "Assessing Project Management Maturity." *Project Management Journal*, March 2000.

Kalu, T. Ch. U. "A Framework for the Management of Projects in Complex Organizations." *IEEE Transactions on Engineering Management*, May 1993.

Kotter, J. P. "Leading Change: Why Transformation Efforts Fail." *Harvard Business Review*, March/April 1995. Reprinted in *IEEE Engineering Management Review*, Spring 1997.

KPMG, "Global IT Project Management." <http://www.kpmg.com/>, 2005.

Lechler, G. and D. Dvir. "An Alternative Taxonomy of Project Management Structures: Linking Project Management Structures and Project Success." *IEEE Engineering Management Review*, Vol. 57, No. 2, 2010.

Lencioni, P. *The Five Dysfunctions of a Team*. San Francisco, CA: Jossey-Bass, 2002.

Levine, H. A. "Enterprise Project Management: What Do Users Need? What Can They Have?" *PM Network*, July 1998.

Liu, L., and P. Yetton. "The Contingent Effects on Project Performance of Conducting Project Reviews and Deploying Project Management Offices." *IEEE Transactions on Engineering Management*, November 2007.

Lubianiker, S. "Opening the Book on the Open Maturity Model." *PM Network*, March 2000.

Mihalic, J. "From the Board: Leading the Way with Thought Leadership." *PMI Today*, September 2013.

Nelson, B. "Energized Teams: Real World Examples." *PM Network*, July 1998.

Pennypacker, J. S., and K. P. Grant. "Project Management Maturity: An Industry Benchmark." *Project Management Journal*, March 2003.

Pinto, J. K. "Twelve Ways to Get the Least from Yourself and Your Project." *PM Network*, May 1997.

Project Management Institute. "Survey Reveals How Organizations Succeed." *PMI Today*, February 2011.

Project Management Institute. "Research Working Session: Transforming and Transformed: The Life Cycle, Role Assignment and Future of the PMO." *PMI Today*, January 2013a.

Project Management Institute. "Thought Leadership Series: PMO—Essential for Managing Strategic Initiatives." *PMI Today*, December 2013b.

Tennant, D. "PMO Failure: An Observation," *PM Network*, October 2001.

Thamhain, H. J., and D. L. Wilemon. "Conflict Management in Project Life Cycles." *Sloan Management Review*, Summer 1975.

Tippet, D. D., and J. F. Peters. "Team Building and Project Management: How Are We Doing?" *Project Management Journal*, December 1995.

Underwood, R., "OK, Everybody, Let's Do This! Managing Projects and Collaborating with Co-Workers." *Inc. Magazine*, July 2008.

Williams, G. "Implementing an Enterprise Project Management Solution." *PM Network*, October 1997.

The following case describes a firm struggling with its organizational structure as it expands its successful commercial business into the governmental contracts arena. This new source of business, however, requires extensive competence in project management, which is new to the firm. As the governmental business grows, the firm has continued to alter its organizational structure, but its performance and incentive systems also need to be changed now, and the impact of those changes on the commercial business is unclear.

Case

Acorn Industries[2]   Harold R. Kerzner, PhD

Acorn Industries, prior to July of 1996, was a relatively small Midwestern corporation dealing with a single product line. The

company dealt solely with commercial contracts and rarely, if ever, considered submitting proposals for government contracts. The corporation at that time functioned under a traditional form of organizational structure, although it did possess a somewhat decentralized managerial philosophy within each division. In 1993, upper management decided that the direction of the

[2]Reprinted with permission. Copyright John Wiley & Sons, 2013.

company must change. To compete with other manufacturers, the company initiated a strong acquisition program whereby smaller firms were bought out and brought into the organization. The company believed that an intensive acquisition program would solidify future growth and development. Furthermore, due to their reputation for possessing a superior technical product and strong marketing department, the acquisition of other companies would allow them to diversify into other fields, especially within the area of government contracts. However, the company did acknowledge one shortcoming that possibly could hurt their efforts—it had never fully adopted, nor implemented, any form of project management.

In July of 1996, the company was awarded a major defense contract after four years of research and development and intensive competition from a major defense organization. The company once again relied on their superior technological capabilities, combined with strong marketing efforts, to obtain the contract. According to Chris Banks, the current marketing manager at Acorn Industries, the successful proposal for the government contract was submitted solely through the efforts of the marketing division. Acorn's successful marketing strategy relied on three factors when submitting a proposal:

1. Know exactly what the funder wants.
2. Know exactly what the market will bear.
3. Know exactly what the competition is doing and where they are going.

The contract awarded in July 1996 led to subsequent government contracts and, in fact, eight more were awarded amounting to $80 million each. These contracts were to last anywhere from seven to ten years, taking the company into early 2009 before expiration would occur. Due to their extensive growth, especially with the area of government contracts as they pertained to weapon systems, the company was forced in 1997 to change general managers. The company brought in an individual who had an extensive background in program management and who previously had been heavily involved in research and development.

Problems Facing the General Manager

The problems facing the new general manager were numerous. Prior to his arrival, the company was virtually a decentralized manufacturing organization. Each division within the company was somewhat autonomous, and the functional managers operated under a Key Management Incentive Program (KMIP). The prior general manager had left it up to each division manager to do what was required. Performance had been measured against attainment of goals. If the annual objective was met under the KMIP program, each division manager could expect to receive a year-end bonus. These bonuses were computed on a percentage of the manager's base pay, and were directly correlated to the ability to exceed the annual objective. Accordingly, future planning within each division was somewhat stagnant, and most managers did not concern themselves with any aspect of organizational growth other than what was required by the annual objective.

Because the company had previously dealt with a single product line and interacted solely with commercial contractors, little, if any, production planning had occurred. Interactions between research and development and the production engineering departments were virtually nonexistent. Research and Development was either way behind or way ahead of the other departments at any particular time. Due to the effects of the KMIP program, this aspect was likely to continue.

Change within the Organizational Structure

To compound the aforementioned problems, the general manager faced the unique task of changing corporate philosophy. Previously, corporate management was concerned with a single product with a short-term production cycle. Now, however, the corporation was faced with long-term governmental contracts, long cycles, and diversified products. Add to this the fact that the company was almost devoid of any individuals who had operated under any aspect of program management, and the tasks appeared insurmountable.

The prime motivating factor for the new general manager during the period from 1997 to 1999 was to retain profitability and maximize return on investment. In order to do this, the general manager decided to maintain the company's commercial product line, operating it at full capacity. This decision was made because the company was based in solid financial management and the commercial product line had been extremely profitable. According to the general manager, Ken Hawks,

> *The concept of keeping both commercial and government contracts separate was a necessity. The commercial product line was highly competitive and maintained a good market share. If the adventure into weaponry failed, the company could always fall back on the commercial products. At any rate, the company at this time could not solely rely on the success of government contracts, which were due to expire.*

In 1996, Acorn reorganized its organizational structure and created a program management office under the direct auspices of the general manager (see Exhibit I).

Expansion and Growth

In late 1996, Acorn initiated a major expansion and reorganization within its various divisions. In fact, during the period between 1996 and 1997, the government contracts resulted in the acquiring of three new companies and possibly the acquisition of a fourth. As before, the expertise of the marketing department was heavily relied upon. Growth objectives for each division were set by corporate headquarters with the advice and feedback of the division managers. Up to 1996, Acorn's divisions had not had a program director. The program management functions for all divisions were performed by one program manager whose expertise was entirely within the commercial field. This particular program manager was concerned only with profitability and did not closely interact with the various funders. According to Chris Banks,

> *The program manager's philosophy was to meet the minimum level of performance required by the contract. To attain this, he required only adequate performance. As Acorn began to become more involved with government contracts, the position remained that given a choice between high technology with low reliability, and vice-versa, the company would always select an acquisition with low technology and high reliability. If we remain somewhere in between, future government contracts should be assured.*

At the same time, Acorn established a Chicago office headed by a group executive. The office was mainly for monitoring for government contracts. Concurrently, an office was established in Washington to monitor the trends within the Department of Defense and to further act as a lobbyist for government contracts. A position of director of marketing was established to interact with the program office on contract proposals. Prior to 1997, the marketing division had always been responsible for contract proposals. Acorn believed that marketing would always, as in the past, set the tone for the company. However, in 1997, and then again in 1998 (see Exhibits II and III), Acorn underwent further organizational changes. A full-time director of program management was appointed with further subdivisions of project managers responsible for the various government contracts. It was at this time that Acorn realized the necessity of involving the program manager more extensively in contract proposals. One faction within corporate management wanted to keep marketing responsible for contract proposals. Another decided that a combination between the marketing input and the expertise of the program director must be utilized. According to Chris Banks,

> *We began to realize that marketing no longer could exclude other factors within the organization when preparing contract proposals. As project management became a reality, we realized that the program manager must be included in all phases of contract proposals.*

Prior to 1996, the marketing department controlled most aspects of contract proposals. With the establishment of the

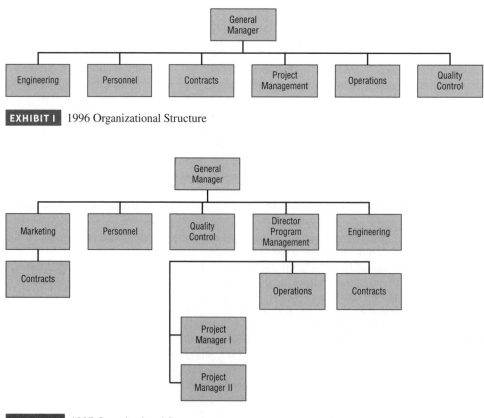

EXHIBIT I 1996 Organizational Structure

EXHIBIT II 1997 Organizational Structure

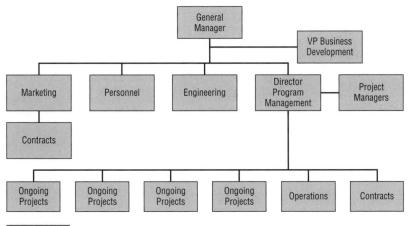

1998 Organizational Structure (10/1/1998)

program office, interface between the marketing department and the program office began to increase.

Responsibilities of the Project Manager

In 1997, Acorn, for the first time, identified a director of program management. This individual reported directly to the general manager and had under his control:

1. The project managers
2. The operations group
3. The contracts group

Under this reorganization, the director of program management, along with the project managers, possessed greater responsibility relative to contract proposals. These new responsibilities included:

1. Research and development
2. Preparation of contract proposals
3. Interaction with marketing on submittal of proposals
4. Responsibility for all government contracts
   a. Trade-off analysis
   b. Cost analysis
5. Interface with engineering department to insure satisfaction of funder's desires

Due to the expansion of government contracts, Acorn was now faced with the problem of bringing in new talent to direct ongoing projects. The previous program manager had had considerable power over operations and maintained a singular philosophy. Under his tenure, many bright individuals left Acorn because future growth and career patterns were questionable. Now that the company is diversifying into other product lines, the need for young talent is crucial. Project management is still in the infancy stage.

Acorn's approach to selecting a project manager was dependent upon the size of the contract. If the particular contract was between $2 and $3 billion, the company would go with

the most experienced individual. Smaller contracts would be assigned to whoever was available.

Interaction with Functional Departments

Due to the relative newness of project management, little data was available to the company to fully assess whether operations were successful. The project managers were required to negotiate with the functional departments for talent. This aspect has presented some problems due to the long-term cycle of most government contracts. Young talent within the organization saw involvement with projects as an opportunity to move up within the organization. Functional managers, on the other hand, apparently did not want to let go of young talent and were extremely reluctant to lose any form of autonomy.

Performance of individuals assigned to projects was mutually discussed between the project manager and the functional manager. Problems arose, however, due to the length of projects. In some instances, if an individual had been assigned longer to the project manager than to the functional manager, the final evaluation of performance was submitted. In some instances, adequate performance was rated high in order to maintain an individual within the project scheme. According to some project managers, this aspect was a reality that must be faced, due to the shortage of abundant talent.

Current Status

In early 1998, Acorn began to realize that an orders shortage relative to government contracts would possibly occur in late 2001 or early 2003. Acorn initiated a three-pronged attach to fill the apparent void:

1. Do what you do best.
2. Look for similar product lines.
3. Look for products that do not require extensive R&D.

To facilitate these objectives, each division within the corporation established its own separate marketing department. The prime objective was to seek more federal funds through successful contract proposals and utilize these funds to increase investment into R&D. The company had finally realized that the success of the corporation was primarily attributed to the selection of the proper general manager. However, this had been accomplished at the exclusion of proper control over R&D efforts. A more lasting problem still existed, however. Program management was still less developed than in most other corporations.

Questions

1. How should Acorn organize now, considering both their commercial business and their growing government business?

2. How can Acorn quickly increase its project management maturity?

3. What should Acorn do about the KMIP incentive program?

4. Should the functional or project managers be responsible for performance evaluations? How should Acorn handle the positive evaluation bias by PMs?

5. As Acorn continues to grow, should it consider adopting a matrix structure?

6. How should Ken Hawks proceed now? What should he do first, and then what should follow?

The following reading responds to the current trend in organizations to institute PMOs for any of a variety of reasons. Without careful planning and clear direction, the viability of every PMO can be in jeopardy, and, once having failed, will probably never be reconsidered. Although the insights are presented in a chronological order, all four of the recommendations should be followed constantly, whether a new PMO or one with a long history of successes.

Reading

Four Steps To A Stronger PMO[3]   S. F. Gale

Project management offices (PMOs) completed an average of US$100 million worth of projects in 2012 and delivered roughly US$71 million in value in increased revenue and cost reductions. Yet only one-third of PMOs say they've realized their full potential in contributing business value to their organization, according to PMI's *Pulse of the Profession™ In-Depth Report: The Impact of PMOs on Strategy Implementation.*

Time may be one factor in a PMO's power: Established PMOs deliver projects with higher quality and greater business success, according to a PwC survey. The longer these PMOs are around, the stronger they become—and the more successful the projects under their umbrellas. PMOs in place for six years or more report that 62 percent of projects achieve the intended business benefit and 74 percent of projects are deemed high-quality, the PwC survey says.

Yet tapping a PMO's full potential takes far more than simply throwing open the doors and waiting.

"A successful PMO needs to deliver business value, not only to be respected but also to show its worth," says Claudio Barbosa Rodrigues, PMP, PMO manager for SAP implementation at mining company Vale, Rio de Janeiro, Brazil. To demonstrate that value, consider this step-by-step guide to strengthening the power of a PMO.

1. Hone the Mission

It sounds so easy, yet it's easy to overlook: A PMO without purpose is more likely to flounder than flourish. "The main purpose of a PMO isn't just to provide reports. The main goal is to be the strategic driver of company goals, to deliver business value," says Mr. Barbosa Rodrigues.

Whether building or revamping a PMO, "first, do an audit of everything going on," says Tara McLaren, head of the PMO for markets and international banking at the Royal Bank of Scotland, a PMO Global Executive Council member, London, England. In the Pulse in-depth report, 51 percent of respondents agreed that aligning projects with strategic objectives has the greatest potential for adding value to organizational activities.

To assess that alignment, the PMO staff should start with a detailed audit of everything going on. Review the current portfolio, also taking an inventory of each project's progress, earned value, obstacles and the anticipated ROI.

Armed with this inventory, the PMO leaders should meet with members of the executive team to report the findings and discuss how the organization's goals should shape the PMO's purpose moving forward. If the strategic goals are to increase revenues or cut division costs, for instance, any revisions to the PMO charter will be very different than if the organization is focused on consolidating systems, expanding into new markets or improving quality outcomes, says Ms. McLaren

"Once you know what the business wants to achieve next, you can show the executive team how the PMO can help do it."

Last June, the executive team at the Royal Bank of Scotland set a goal of cutting the IT budget in half while still delivering the same number of quality projects. Ms. McLaren responded by creating a project business case for moving all of the globally dispersed non-customer-facing IT team members to the bank's IT center in India. She showed the executive team different project scenarios, identified near-term opportunities to cut costs over the next six months and made a long-term plan for hitting the new budget targets.

---

[3]Reprinted from PM Network with permission. Copyright Project Management Institute Inc.

"A good PMO is a problem solver," she says. "If you can come up with ways to help your company resolve issues and save money, you'll get the support and authority you want."

Marrying the PMO's purpose to the organization's strategy means executive leaders are more likely to seek out the PMO for upfront guidance, says Jonathan Price, PMP, account PMO start-up lead for HP Enterprise Services, a PMO Global Executive Council member in London, England. "When a PMO is 100 percent aligned with the organization's goals, its leaders can indicate which are the most valuable programs and projects in terms of company ROI and resource capacity," he says. "This helps the organization avoid waste by not focusing on non-priority programs and projects.

2. Set the Standards

Standardized practices, tools, training, and governance reduce risk, while key performance indicators (KPIs) measure project outcomes and increase the resulting earned value. Those processes are all a vital part of the PMO's value proposition. "The PMO's ROI comes from the fact that they establish consistent project metrics, align projects with strategic goals and use a shared project management resource pool effectively," says Jayant Patil, PMP, global head of program management group for Quinnox Consultancy Services, Mumbai, India. "But it's not enough to go off the guidelines and templates – PMOs have to demonstrate how they connect to business value to be respected."

In some ways, that's easiest to prove on troubled projects, says Mr. Price, as standardized processes make it easy to flag and course-correct a project in peril. "That's the benefit to sell—the ability to intervene early and have processes move struggling projects from amber to green instead of red," he says.

Setting and assessing standards doesn't stop once the project's over. More than 60 percent of high-performing PMOs—ones that complete 80 percent or more of projects on time, on budget and within the original business goal—assess project quality and collect feedback from the project owner, compared with only 33 percent of lower-performing PMOs.

3. Cultivate Support

The most effective PMOs have powerful supporters at the executive level, championing the value of project management and imbuing the PMO with both responsibility and authority.

In the best-case scenario, these executives are the ones who initiated the PMO's creation. But PMO leaders who aren't lucky enough to inherit strong executive support have to woo the executive team to their way of thinking, says Dennis Schwabe, PMP, corporate PMO manager for chemical products manufacturer Fritz Industries, Mesquite, Texas, USA. "You have to make sure leaders understand what project management is about."

In PMI's in-depth PMO report, 43 percent of respondents said that a better understanding of project management throughout the organization would make the PMO more effective. More than one-third of survey respondents said increased engagement with senior leaders would make the difference.

If executives haven't had the experience of understanding and working with a strong project management methodology,

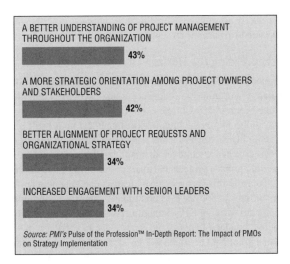

Source: PMI's Pulse of the Profession™ In-Depth Report: The Impact of PMOs on Strategy Implementation

Respondents Agreeing That PMOs Helped

they can't be criticized for not understanding its value to the business. But they can be educated, Mr. Schwabe says. "A strategic project management course for executives would help them understand how governance, training, metrics, and the right project management skill set will add strategic value to the organization in meeting their corporate objectives."

Even a brief presentation with a few key statistics on the cost savings and time savings the PMO could deliver can make a powerful impact on reluctant executives. During the presentation, PMO leaders should leverage examples of past projects with cost overruns or missed schedules that could have been prevented with a PMO, suggests Mr. Price. "Build support by selling the PMO's plan to stakeholders who have the influence to support you," he says. "If you can show them how spending 100,000 pounds can abate 2 million pounds, that is a powerful benefit proposal."

And don't let the conversation stop once the PMO is off the ground. It is not enough to copy the executive stakeholders on status reports or give them a dashboard of project progress. "PMO leaders have to speak to executives in their language," says Ms. McLaren. "Use a concise and non-technical manner."

Depending on the reporting level, she limits executive communiques to the following:

- High-level status reports on all projects
- Additional information about any project that's troubled, including potent mitigation strategies
- Key achievements to date
- Resource updates and forecasts
- Milestones that have been achieved or are on the 30-day radar, including review of the business benefits linked to those milestones.

"Only communicate very high-level business deliverables, rather than long and drawn-out minor details," she says. Executive stakeholders will appreciate the focused approach and are more likely to engage with the information—exactly what a PMO needs to strengthen support.

4. Keep Eyeing the Horizon

If projects are consistently on time and within budget, funders are happy and milestones are met, some executives may doubt the need for a PMO. Combine that doubt with a directive to cut costs, and suddenly the high-performing PMO finds itself on the chopping block. Mr. Price has witnessed several occasions over his career when executives dismantled PMOs for budget reasons, only to have projects fall apart in the wake of that decision.

To avoid this scenario, PMO leaders can't become complacent, he says. "You have to continually monitor your impact." That means tracking KPIs, including project outcome, added efficiencies, financial benefits and quality results. "KPIs will show whether the PMO is effective," he says. "If you are measuring and reporting those KPIs, the value should be obvious."

Seventy-seven percent of high-performing PMOs are routinely involved in results monitoring and assessment, according to PMI's Pulse in-depth report.

And if the KPIs aren't showing results, the PMO needs to make changes. Mr. Schwabe encourages PMO leaders to reevaluate business objectives annually to ensure the office is meeting the charter goals and that the goals are still relevant to the business. "You want to be sure you are still aligned with corporate strategy," he says. Because if things have changed—a new CEO or a shift in business priorities—the PMO needs to change along with them, he says. "Corporate strategy must drive the PMO, so the PMO can drive success."

Questions

1. Which of the four steps is the most important to maintaining the viability of the PMO?

2. What educational mission does the PMO have to undertake to be effective?

3. How can regular PMO success potentially lead to termination of the PMO?

4. Why might a new CEO pose a threat to the existence of a PMO?

CHAPTER 6

Activity Planning: Traditional and Agile

This chapter initiates our discussions of *Scope and Time Management*, critical **PMBOK** knowledge areas. Time management is an extensive topic which is further discussed in Chapters 8–11. Similarly, risk will be discussed in Chapter 7.

 PMBOK

Chapters 5, 6, 11

In the *Reader's Digest* (March 1998, p. 49), Peter Drucker is quoted on planning: "Plans are only good intentions unless they immediately degenerate into hard work." To make such a transformation possible is no easy task. Inadequate planning is a cliché in project management. Occasionally, articles appear in project management periodicals attesting to the value of good planning. Indeed, Brian Tracy, author of *Eat that Frog!* (2007), argues that every minute allocated to planning saves as much as 10 minutes in execution. Of course, effective planning requires avoiding the opposite pitfall of killing the plan with over-analysis. This leads to the well-known "paralysis by analysis." In an excellent article, Langley (1995) finds a path in-between the two extremes.

Thus far, we have dealt with initiating a project. Now we are ready to begin the process of planning the work of the project in such a way that it may be translated into the "hard work" that actually leads to the successful completion of the project. There are several reasons why we must use considerable care when planning projects. The primary purpose of planning, of course, is to establish a set of directions in sufficient detail to tell the project team exactly what must be done, when it must be done, what resources will be required to produce the deliverables of the project successfully, and when each resource will be needed. The entire planning process is, of course, dependent on gathering the correct requirements from the client or project owner in the first place. **PMBOK** lists a number of tools and techniques to help in doing this, including interviews, focus groups, facilitated workshops, group creativity techniques (described in the online Appendix B for this book), questionnaires, and surveys.

PMBOK

5.2.2

The plan must be designed by the PM, overseen by the project owner and sponsor, in such a way that the project outcome also meets the objectives, both direct and ancillary, of the parent organization, as reflected by the project portfolio, business case, or other strategic selection process used to approve the project. Because the plan is only an estimate of what and when things must be done to achieve the scope or objectives of the project, it is always carried out in an environment of uncertainty. Therefore, the plan must include allowances for risk and features that allow it to be *adaptive*, that is, to be responsive to things that might, and often do, disrupt it while it is being carried out. One frequent such disruption— "scope creep," or the tendency of project objectives to be changed by the client through the project owner, senior management such as the sponsor, or individual project workers with little or no discussion with the other stakeholders actively interested or engaged in the work of the project—is particularly common in software projects. In addition, the plan must also contain methods to ensure its integrity, which is to say it must include means of controlling (see Chapter 11) the work it prescribes.

Finally, and quite apart from the deliverables required by the project itself, the plan must include any constraints on activities and input materials proscribed by law and society, a group of very important stakeholders. Among the many sources of outside constraints are the Food and Drug Administration, the Occupational Health and Safety Administration, other federal and state laws and regulations, various engineering societies, labor unions, and the "Standard Practices" of many different industries. Such constraints are meant to protect us all from unsafe or harmful structures, machines, equipment, services, and practices.

There is an extensive literature on project planning. Some of it is concerned with the strategic aspects of planning, being focused on the choice of projects that are consistent with the organization's goals. Another group of works is aimed at the process of planning individual projects, given that they have been chosen as strategically acceptable. Most fields have their own accepted set of project planning processes. Except for the names given to the individual processes, however, they are all similar, as we shall soon see.

The purpose of planning is to facilitate later accomplishment. The world is full of plans that never become deeds. The planning techniques covered here are intended to smooth the path from idea to accomplishment. It is a complicated process to manage a project, and plans act as a map of this process. The map must have sufficient detail to determine what must be done next but be simple enough that workers are not lost in a welter of minutiae.

In the pages that follow, we discuss a somewhat formal method for the development of a project charter (similar to a proposal, or preliminary plan) and final project plan. Almost all project planning techniques differ only in the ways they approach the process of planning. Most organizations, irrespective of the industry, use essentially the same processes for planning and managing projects, but they often call these processes by different names. What some call "setting objectives," others call "defining the scope" of the project, or "identifying requirements." What some call "evaluation," others call "test and validation." No matter whether the project is carried out for an inside or outside client, the project's "deliverables" must be "integrated" into the client's processes.

Project Management in Practice

Beagle 2 Mars Probe a Planning Failure

As the Beagle 2 Mars probe designed jointly by the European Space Agency and British National Space Center headed to Mars in December of 2003, contact was lost and it was never heard from again. In retrospect, it appears that inadequate project planning (and replanning) was to blame. Excessive pressure on time, cost, and weight compromised the mission right from the start. With insufficient public funding, the design team had to spend much of their time raising private funds instead of addressing difficult technical issues. In addition, late changes forced the team to reduce the Beagle's weight from 238 pounds to 132 pounds! And when the three airbags failed to work properly in testing, a parachute design was substituted but inadequately tested due to lack of time.

A review commission recommended that in the future:

- Requisite financing be available at the outset of a project

- Formal project reviews be conducted on a regular basis

- Phase-gates be established where all stakeholders reconsider the project

- Expectations of potential failure be included in the funding consideration

- Robust safety margins be included and funded for uncertainties

Questions

1. **What should the PM have done about the challenges facing this project?**

2. **Are the recommendations complete? Would you add anything else?**

Source: Project Management Institute. "Mars or Bust," *PM Network*, Vol. 18.

We have adopted an approach that we think makes the planning process straightforward and fairly systematic, but it is never as systematic and straightforward as planning theorists would like. At its best, planning is tortuous. It is an iterative process yielding better plans from not-so-good plans, and the iterative process of improvement seems to take place in fits and starts. The process may be described formally, but it does not occur formally. Bits and pieces of plans are developed by individuals, by informal group meetings, or by formalized planning teams, and then improved by other individuals, groups, or teams, and improved again, and again. Both the plans themselves and the process of planning should start simple with the *project charter* which is then further elaborated and eventually becomes the *project plan*. In this chapter, we focus on designing the physical aspects of the project, defining what the project is supposed to accomplish, and who will have to do what for the project's desired output to be achieved. Here we describe the actual process of project planning. Organizing the work of the project, acquiring a PM, and forming a project team are parts of project initiation. The project's budget and schedule are major parts of the project plan, but we delay discussion of them until Chapters 7 and 8. Indeed, what must be done to test and approve project outputs at both interim and final stages, and what records must be kept are both parts of the project plan and these are covered in later chapters, as is the part of the plan that covers closing out the project. There is nothing sacrosanct about this sequence. It is simply in the order that these parts of the project plan tend to develop naturally.

6.1 | Traditional Project Activity Planning

It is crucial that the project's objectives be clearly tied to the overall mission, goals, and strategy of the organization, such as might be reflected in the project portfolio process. In the project charter, senior management should delineate the firm's intent in undertaking the project, outline the scope of the project, and describe how the project's desired results reinforce the organization's goals. Without a clear beginning, project planning (and later progress) can easily go astray. It is also vital that a senior manager call and be present at the *project chartering workshop or "launch" meeting*, an initial coordinating meeting, as a visible symbol of top management's commitment to the project. As Brox (2012) points out, the sponsor and other key stakeholders should participate in this meeting for the purpose of establishing the project, agreeing on the top deliverables, discussing resourcing, establishing schedule and budget tolerances (so the PM knows when to check in with the sponsor), and defining the high-level risks. Having these key stakeholders involved early on creates buy-in and fosters early communication on potential issues and risks.

The individual leading the launch meeting is first to define the scope of the project as detailed in the charter. The success of the project launch meeting is absolutely dependent on the existence of a well-defined set of objectives. Unless all parties to the planning process have a clear understanding of precisely what it is the project is expected to deliver, planning is sure to be inadequate or misguided. At the launch meeting, the project is discussed in sufficient detail that potential contributors develop a general understanding of what is needed. If the project is one of many similar projects, the meeting will be short and routine, a sort of "touching base" with other interested units. If the project is unique in most of its aspects, extensive discussion may be required.

It is useful to also review the major risks facing the project during the launch meeting. The known risks will be those identified during the project selection process. These are apt to focus largely on the market reaction to a new process/product, the technical feasibility of an innovation, and like matters. The risk management plan for the project must be started at the launch meeting so that later risk identification can be extended to include the technology of the process/product, the project's schedule, resource base, and a myriad of other risks facing the project but not really identifiable until the final project plan has begun to take form. In addition to the matters discussed below, one of the outcomes of the project planning process will be the formulation of the project's risk management group and the initial risk management plan that the group develops during the process of planning the project.

While various authors have somewhat different expectations for the project launch meeting (e.g., see Knutson, 1995; Martin et al., 1998), we feel it is important not to allow plans, schedules, and budgets to go beyond the most aggregated level, especially if the project deliverables are fairly simple and do not require much interdepartmental coordination. To fix plans in more detail at this initial meeting tends to prevent team members from integrating the new project into their ongoing activities and from developing creative ways of coordinating activities that involve two or more organizational units. Worse still, departmental representatives will later be asked to make "a ballpark estimate of the budget and time required" to carry out this first-blush plan. Everyone who has ever worked on a project is aware of the extraordinary propensity of preliminary estimates to metamorphose instantaneously into firm budgets and schedules. Remember that this is only one of a series of meetings that will be required to plan projects of more than minimal complexity.

It is critical to the future success of the project to take the time required to do a technically and politically careful job of planning. This may mean many meetings and participatory decision making, but it is well worth the effort. In confirmation of this view, a survey of 236 PMs across a wide variety of projects (White et al., 2002) found that there were five criteria used to judge project success: on time, on budget, to scope, fit between the project and the organization, and the impact of the project on the performance of the organization. But the four top-ranking factors critical to project success were as follows: a realistic schedule, adequate resources, clear scope, and support from senior management, all products of careful planning with a solid charter.

Whatever the process, the outcome must be that (1) technical scope is established (though perhaps not "cast in concrete"); (2) basic areas of performance responsibility are accepted by the participants; (3) any tentative delivery dates or budgets and their tolerances set by the parent organization are clearly noted; and (4) a risk management group is created. Each individual/unit accepting responsibility for a portion of the project should agree to deliver, by the next project meeting, a preliminary but detailed plan about how that responsibility will be accomplished. Such plans should contain descriptions of the required tasks, and estimates of the budgets (labor and resources) and schedules.

Simultaneous with these planning activities, the risk management group develops a risk management plan that includes proposed methodologies for managing risk, the group's budget, schedule, criteria for dealing with risk, and required reports. Further, necessary inputs to the risk data base are described and various roles and responsibilities for group members are spelled out, as noted in **PMBOK** (Project Management Institute, 2013). It must be emphasized that the process of managing risk is not a static process. Rather, it is ongoing, with constant updating as more risks are identified, as some risks vanish, as others are mitigated—in other words as reality replaces conjecture—and new conjecture replaces old conjecture.

Chapter 11

The various parts of the project charter, including the risk management plan, are then scrutinized by the group and combined into a composite project plan. The composite plan, still not completely firm, is approved by each participating group, by the PM, and then by senior organizational management. Each subsequent approval hardens the plan somewhat, and when senior management has endorsed it, any further changes in the project's scope must be made by processing a formal *change order*. If the project is not large or complex, informal written memoranda can substitute for the change order. The main point is that no *significant* changes in the project are made, without written notice, following top management's approval. The definition of "significant" depends on the specific situation and the people involved. A useful tool for facilitating the management of changes to a project's scope is the Requirements Traceability Matrix. With this matrix, a table is created that links the source of each project requirement to the project objectives, WBS deliverables, etc. intended to satisfy it. A variety of fields (columns) can be incorporated in the Requirements Traceability Matrix depending on the intended use of the matrix. A quick search of the Web will yield a variety of templates that are application-ready for use. An example is shown in **PMBOK**, p. 119.

5.2.3.2

The PM generally takes responsibility for gathering the necessary approvals and *assuring* that any changes incorporated into the plan at higher levels are communicated to, and approved by, the units that have already signed off on the plan. Nothing is as sure to enrage functional unit managers as to find that they have been committed by someone else to alterations in their carefully considered plans without being informed. Violation of this procedure is considered a betrayal of trust. Several incidents of this kind occurred in a firm during a project to design a line of children's clothing. The anger at this *change without communication* was so great that two chief designers resigned and took jobs with a competitor.

Because senior managers are almost certain to exercise their prerogative to change the plan, the PM should always return to the contributing units for consideration and reapproval of the plan as modified. The final, approved result of this procedure is the project plan. When the planning phase of the project is completed, it is valuable to hold one additional meeting, a postplanning review. This meeting should be chaired by an experienced PM who is not connected with the project (Antonioni, 1997). The major purpose of the postplanning review is to make sure that all necessary elements of the project plan have been properly developed and communicated.

Outside Clients

When the project is to deliver a product/service to an outside client, the fundamental planning process described above is unchanged except for the fact that the project's scope cannot be altered without the *client's* permission. A common "planning" problem in these cases is that marketing has promised deliverables that engineering may not know how to produce on a schedule that manufacturing may be unable to meet. This sort of problem usually results when the various functional areas are not involved in the planning process at the time the original proposal is made to the potential client. We cannot overstate the importance of a carefully determined set of *deliverables*, accepted by both project team and client (Martin et al., 1998).

Two objections to such early participation by engineering and manufacturing are likely to be raised by marketing. First, the sales arm of the organization is trained to sell and is expected to be fully conversant with all technical aspects of the firm's products/services. Further, salespeople are expected to be knowledgeable about design and manufacturing lead times and schedules. On the other hand, it is widely assumed by marketing (with some justice on occasion) that manufacturing and design engineers do not understand sales techniques, will be argumentative and/or pessimistic about client needs in the presence of the client, and are generally not "housebroken" when customers are nearby. Second, it is expensive to involve so much technical talent so early in the sales process—typically, prior to issuing a bid or proposal. It can easily cost a firm more than $10,000 to send five technical specialists on a short trip to consider a potential client's needs, not including a charge for the time lost by the specialists. The willingness to accept higher sales costs puts even more emphasis on the selection process.

The rejoinder to such objections is simple. It is almost always cheaper, faster, and easier to do things right the first time than to redo them. When the product/service is a complex system that must be installed in a larger, more complex system, it is appropriate to treat the sale like a project, which deserves the same kind of planning. A great many firms that consistently operate in an atmosphere typified by design and manufacturing crises have created their own panics. (Software producers and computer system salespeople take note!) In fairness, it is appropriate to urge that anyone meeting customers face to face should receive some training in the tactics of selling.

Project Charter Elements

As noted earlier, the initial project planning task is the development of the project charter. The project charter is a high-level document that helps to define the scope of the project and is typically submitted to get project approval to move on to develop a project plan. Given a project charter, approvals really amount to a series of authorizations. The PM is authorized to direct activities, spend monies (usually within preset limits), request resources and personnel, and start the project on its way. Senior management's approval not only signals its willingness to fund and support the project but also notifies subunits in the organization that they may commit resources to the project.

The process of developing the project charter varies from organization to organization, but should contain the following elements as described in **PMBOK®**:

4.1

- **Purpose**   This is a short summary directed to top management and those unfamiliar with the project. It contains a statement of the general goals of the project and a brief explanation of their relationship to the firm's objectives (i.e., the "Business Case," where we see how profits are gained). The Business Case includes not only market opportunities and profit potentials but also the needs of the organization, any customer requests for proposals, technological advancement opportunities, and regulatory, environmental, and social considerations. A properly crafted Business Case should succinctly provide the financial and strategic justification for the project.

- **Objectives**   This contains a more detailed statement of the general and ancillary goals of the project and their priorities, what constitutes success, and how the project will be closed out. The statement should include measurable objectives such as profit and competitive aims from the Business Case as well as technical goals.

- **Overview**   This section provides a high-level description of the project and its requirements. Both the managerial and the technical approaches to the work are also described. The technical discussion describes the relationship of the project to available technologies. For example, it might note that this project is an extension of work done by the company for an earlier project. The subsection on the managerial approach takes note of any deviation from routine procedure—for instance, the use of subcontractors for some parts of the work. Also included here is a description of the assumptions the project is based on and contingency plans if the assumptions don't prove to be correct, and the procedures for changes in the project, including scope, budget, and schedule.

- **Schedules**   This section outlines the various schedules and lists all *milestone* events and/or phase-gates. Each summary (major) task is listed, with the estimated time obtained from those who will do the work. The projected baseline schedule is constructed from these inputs. The responsible person or department head should sign off on the final, agreed-on schedule.

- **Resources**   There are three primary aspects to this section. The first is the budget. Both capital and expense requirements are detailed by task, which makes this a *project budget*, with one-time costs separated from recurring project costs. Second is a complete list and description of all contractual items such as customer-supplied resources, liaison arrangements, project review and cancellation procedures, proprietary requirements, purchasing/procurement contracts (knowledge area 9 in **PMBOK**), any specific management agreements (e.g., use of subcontractors), as well as the technical deliverables and their specifications, delivery schedules, and a specific procedure for changing any of the above. Third is the set of cost monitoring and control procedures. In addition to the usual routine elements, the monitoring and control procedures must also include any special resource requirements for the project such as special machines, test equipment, laboratory usage or construction, logistics, field facilities, and special materials. Finally, any constraints on the above should also be noted here.

Chapter 12

- **Stakeholders**   This section lists the key stakeholders. The topic of identifying and analyzing stakeholders was discussed in Chapters 2–5. Key insights from this analysis should be included here. Besides the client, community, and other external stakeholders, the section also lists the expected personnel requirements of the project, especially the PM, project owner, and project sponsor. In addition, any special skill requirements, training needed, possible recruiting problems, legal or policy restrictions on work force composition, and security clearances should be noted here. It is helpful to time-phase personnel needs to the project schedule, if possible. This makes clear when the various types of contributors are needed and in what numbers. These projections are an important element of the budget, so the personnel, schedule, and resources sections can be cross-checked with one another to ensure consistency.

- **Risk Management Plans**   At a high-level, this covers potential problems as well as potential lucky breaks that could affect the project. One or more issues such as subcontractor default, unexpected technical breakthroughs, strikes, hurricanes, new markets for the technology, and sudden moves by a competitor are certain to occur—the only uncertainties are which, when, and their impact. In fact, the timing of these disasters and benefits is not random since there are definite times in every project when progress depends on subcontractors, the weather, or timely technical successes. Plans to deal with favorable or unfavorable contingencies should be developed early in the project's life. No amount of planning can definitively solve a potential crisis, but preplanning may avert or mitigate some. As Zwikael et al. (2007) report, in high-risk projects better project planning improved success on four measures: schedule overrun, cost overrun, technical performance, and customer satisfaction. They conclude that improving the project plan is a more effective risk management approach than using the usual risk management tools.

- **Evaluation Methods**   Every project should be evaluated against standards and by methods established at the project's inception, allowing for both the direct and ancillary goals of the project, as described in Chapter 1. This section contains a brief description of the procedures to be followed in monitoring, collecting, storing, auditing, and evaluating the project, as well as in the postproject ("lessons learned") evaluation following project termination.

These are the elements that constitute the project charter and are the basis for more detailed planning of the budgets, schedules, work plan, and general management of the project. Once this project charter is fully developed and approved, it is disseminated to all interested parties. It is also important to point out that creating the project charter is not a one-time event where it is completed and then filed away never again to see the light of day. Rather, the project charter should be a living document that is continuously updated as conditions change.

Once the project charter is completed and the project approved, a more detailed project plan can be developed. According to **PMBOK**, a proper project plan addresses the following issues:

4.2.3

- The process for managing change
- A plan for communicating with and managing stakeholders

- Specifying the process for setting key characteristics of the project deliverable (technically referred to as configuration management)
- Establishing the cost baseline for the project and developing a plan to manage project costs
- Developing a plan for managing the human resources assigned to the project
- Developing a plan for continuously monitoring and improving project work processes
- Developing guidelines for procuring project materials and resources
- Defining the project's scope and establishing practices to manage the project's scope
- Developing the Work Breakdown Structure
- Developing practices to manage the quality of the project deliverables
- Defining how project requirements will be managed
- Establishing practices for managing risk
- Establishing the schedule baseline and developing a plan to manage the project's schedule

Before proceeding, we should reiterate that this formal planning process just described is required for relatively large projects that cannot be classified as "routine" for the organization. The time, effort, and cost of the planning process is not justified for routine projects such as most plant maintenance projects. Admittedly, no two routine maintenance projects are identical, but they do tend to be quite similar. It is useful to have a generic plan for such projects, but it is meant to serve as a template that can easily be modified to fit the specific routine project at hand.

A Whole-Brain Approach to Project Planning

In today's fiercely competitive environment, project teams are facing increasing pressure to achieve project performance goals while at the same time completing their projects on time and on schedule. Typically, PMs and project team members rely on the "left" side or the analytical part of the brain to address these challenges. Indeed, if you are a business or

---

Project Management in Practice

Child Support Software a Victim of Scope Creep

In March 2003, the United Kingdom's Child Support Agency (CSA) started using their new £456 million ($860 million) software system for receiving and disbursing child support payments. However, by the end of 2004 only about 12 percent of all applications had received payments, and even those took about three times longer than normal to process. CSA thus threatened to scrap the entire system and withhold £1 million ($2 million) per month in service payments to the software vendor. The problem was thought to be due to both scope creep and the lack of a risk management strategy. The vendor claimed that the project was disrupted constantly by CSA's 2500 change requests, while CSA maintained

there were only 50, but the contract did not include a scope management plan to help define what constituted a scope change request. And the lack of a risk management strategy resulted in no contingency or fallback plans in case of trouble, so when project delays surfaced and inadequate training became apparent, there was no way to recover.

Questions

1. What was the source of the problem here?
2. How might a project charter as described above have helped avoid these shortcomings?
3. What would you suggest to recover the project?

Source: Project Management Institute. "Lack of Support," *PM Network*, Vol. 19.

engineering student, the vast majority of techniques that you have been exposed to in your studies rely on the logical and analytical left side of your brain. On the other hand, art students and design students tend to be exposed to techniques that rely more on imagination and images, which utilize the creative "right" side of the brain. Importantly, many activities associated with project management can be greatly facilitated through the use of a more balanced whole-brain approach (Brown et al., 2002).

One whole-brain approach that is particularly applicable to project management in general, and project planning in particular, is "mind mapping." Mind mapping is essentially a visual approach that closely mirrors how the human brain records and stores information. In addition to its visual nature, another key advantage associated with mind mapping is that it helps to tap the creative potential of the entire project team, which, in turn, helps increase both the quantity and quality of ideas generated. Because project team members tend to find mind mapping enjoyable, it also helps generate enthusiasm, helps obtain buy-in from team members, and often gets quieter team members more involved in the planning process.

To illustrate the creation of a mind map to identify the work that must be done to complete a project, consider a project launched at a business school to reimagine its full-time MBA program. The mind mapping planning session is initiated by taping a large sheet of paper (e.g., 6 ft × 3 ft) on a wall. (One good source of such paper is a roll of butcher's wrapping paper. Several sheets can be taped together to create a larger area if needed. Alternatively, sheets of flip chart can be taped together.) It is recommended that the paper be oriented in landscape mode to help stimulate the team's creativity as people are used to working in portrait mode. In addition, team members should stand during the mind mapping exercise.

The process begins by writing the project goal at the center of the page. As is illustrated in Figure 6.1a, the full-time MBA project team defined the goal for the project as "Develop Game Changing MBA Program." In particular, notice the inspirational language used in defining the project goal, which helps further to motivate team members and stimulate their creativity.

Once the project goal is defined, team members can brainstorm to identify the major tasks that must be done to accomplish this goal. In developing the mind map for the MBA project, the project team initially identified three major tasks: (1) identify important trends in business and higher education; (2) gain an understanding of student needs and interests; and (3) predict competencies that MBA graduates will need to be successful in their careers. As illustrated in Figure 6.1b, these major tasks branch off from the project goal.

Developing the mind map proceeds in this fashion whereby activities in the mind map are sequentially broken down into greater detail. For example, Figure 6.1c illustrates how

> **Develop Game Changing MBA Program**

FIGURE 6.1a   Begin mind mapping with statement of project's objective.

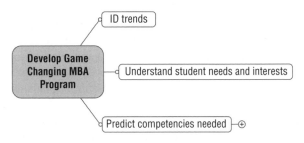

FIGURE 6.1b   Major tasks branch off from project goal.

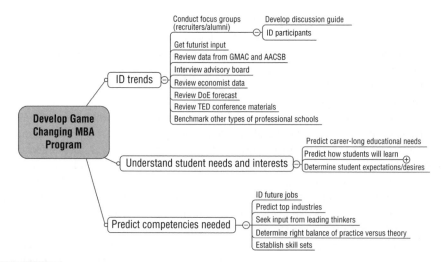

FIGURE 6.1c Major tasks are further broken down into more detailed tasks.

the three initial activities were subsequently broken down into greater detail. Figure 6.2 provides the final mind map for the full-time MBA project.

A few comments regarding the process of mind mapping are in order. First, when initially developing the mind map, color, word size, word shape, and pictures should all be used to add emphasis. In fact, team members should be encouraged to use pictures and images in the mind map to represent activities instead of using words. The reason for this is because the brain processes and responds to symbols and pictures differently than it does to words. When using words, key words as opposed to full sentences should be used. Also, it should be noted that it is OK to be messy when developing the original mind map. Indeed, one should not expect the original mind map to resemble something as polished as the mind map shown in Figure 6.2. Rather, the mind map will typically need to go through several iterations of polishing and refining. It should also be noted that the polishing and refining can be greatly facilitated with the use of a computer graphics program (the software package Mindjet MindManager was used to create Figures 6.1 and 6.2). Typically, one person on the project team will take ownership for cleaning up the original mind map and distributing it to the other team members for additional input.

In addition, when the initial mind map is being created, multiple team members should contribute to the mind map simultaneously as ideas occur to them. In fact, a best practice is to designate one team member as the facilitator to ensure that all team members are involved and contributing, and to ensure that team members are focusing on identifying the work that must be done—not goals for the project. Finally, at the most detailed level, seek to express tasks using a verb and a noun (e.g., develop guidelines, identify participants).

Unfortunately, it is all too common for projects to go over budget and/or be completed late. In many cases, insufficient upfront planning is the major culprit. With inadequate upfront planning, important tasks are overlooked, which in turn results in underestimating the project budget and duration. Mind mapping is a fast and effective tool that can greatly facilitate comprehensively identifying the work that needs to be completed, which in turn helps minimize problems that result from inadequate upfront planning and overlooking important work elements.

Finally, it is worth noting that a polished and refined mind map facilitates a number of other project-related activities. For example, the mind map can be easily converted into the traditional WBS (discussed shortly). Furthermore, the mind map can be used to facilitate

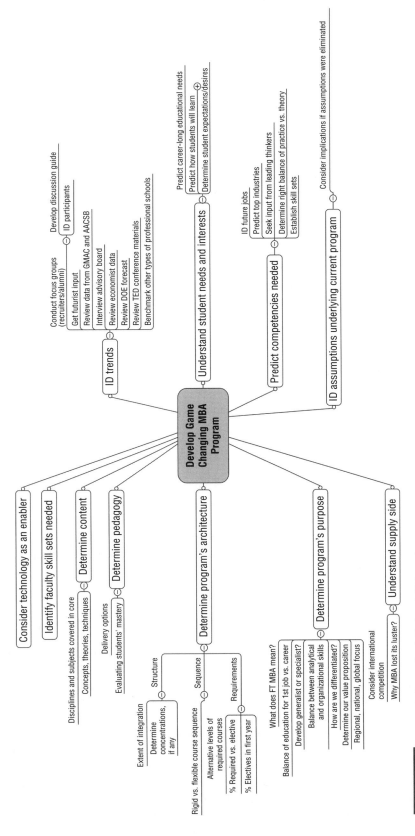

FIGURE 6.2   Final mind map for full-time MBA project.

risk analysis, setting project team meeting agendas, allocating resources to project activities, and developing the project schedule (see Brown et al., 2002, for additional details on the use of mind mapping for project management).

Project Planning in Action

Once the project activities are identified via the creation of a mind map or some other approach, project planning continues by considering the sequence of these activities required to carry the project from start to completion. Not only is this a natural way to think about a project; it also helps the planner decide the necessary sequence of things—a necessary consideration for determining the project schedule and duration. In a fascinating paper, Aaron and his colleagues (1993) described the planning process used at a telecommunications firm.

Using a planning process oriented around the life-cycle events common for software and hardware product developers, they divide the project into nine segments:

- Concept evaluation
- Requirements identification
- Design
- Implementation
- Test
- Integration
- Validation
- Customer test and evaluation
- Operations and maintenance

Each segment is made up of activities and milestones (significant event points). As the project passes through each segment, it is typically subjected to a series of "stage-gates" (also known as "phase-gates," "toll-gates," "quality-gates," etc.) that must be successfully passed before proceeding to the next segment. Note that the planning process must pass through the stage gates as well as the physical output of the project itself. For example, the requirements identification segment must meet the appropriate quality standards before the design segment can be started, just as design must be approved before implementation can begin.

The WBS: A Key Element of the Project Plan

4.2

In this and the following sections of this chapter, and in Chapters 7 and 8 on budgeting and scheduling, we move into the details of (and some tools for) developing the project plan, essentially an elaboration of the elements of the project charter. As **PMBOK®** points out, the project charter is one of the major inputs to the project plan. We need to know exactly what is to be done, by whom, and when. All activities required to complete the project must be precisely delineated and coordinated. The necessary resources must be available when and where they are needed and in the correct amounts. Some activities must be done sequentially, but some may be done simultaneously. If a large project is to come in on time and within cost, a great many things must happen when and how they are supposed to happen. Yet, each of these details is uncertain and thus each must be subjected to risk management. In this section, we propose a conceptually simple method to assist in sorting out and planning all this detail. It is a *hierarchical planning system*—a method of constructing a work breakdown structure (WBS).

To accomplish any specific project, a number of major activities must be undertaken and completed. Make a list of these activities in the general order in which they would occur. This is Level 1. A reasonable number of activities at this level might be anywhere between 2 and 20. (There is nothing sacred about these limits. Two is the minimum possible breakdown, and 20 is about the largest number of interrelated items that can be comfortably sorted and scheduled at a given level of aggregation.) Now break each of these Level 1 items into 2 to 20 tasks. This is Level 2. In the same way, break each Level 2 task into 2 to 20 subtasks. This is Level 3. Proceed in this way until the detailed tasks at a level are so well understood that there is no reason to continue with the work breakdown; this will usually be at the individual worker level. As a rule of thumb, the lowest level tasks should have a duration of a few hours to a few days. The more familiar the team is with the work, the longer the durations can be of the lowest level tasks.

It is important to be sure that all items in the list are at roughly the same level of task generality. In writing a book, for example, the various chapters tend to be at the same level of generality, but individual chapters are divided into finer detail. Indeed, subdivisions of a chapter may be divided into finer detail still. It is difficult to overstate the significance of this simple dictum. It is central to the preparation of most of the planning documents that will be described in this chapter and those that follow.

The logic behind this simple rule is persuasive. We have observed both students and professionals in the process of planning. We noted that people who lack experience in planning tend to write down what they perceive to be the first activity in a sequence of activities, begin to break it down into components, take the first of these, break it further, until they have reached a level of detail they feel is sufficient. They then take the second step and proceed similarly. If they have a good understanding of a basic activity, the breakdown into detail is handled well. If they are not expert, the breakdown lacks detail and tends to be inadequate. Further, we noted that integration of the various basic activities was poor. An artist of our acquaintance explained: When creating a drawing, the artist sketches in the main lines of a scene, and then builds up the detail little by little over the entire drawing. In this way, the drawing has a "unity." One cannot achieve this unity by drawing one part of the scene in high detail, then moving to another part of the scene and detailing it. The artist asked a young student to make a pen-and-ink sketch of a fellow student. The progress at three successive stages of his or her drawing is shown in Figure 6.3.

This illustrates the "hierarchical planning process." The PM will probably generate the most basic level (Level 1) and possibly the next level as well. Unless the project is quite small, the generation of additional levels will be delegated to the individuals or groups who have responsibility for doing the work. Maintaining the "hierarchical planning" discipline will help keep the plan focused on the project's deliverables rather than on the work at a subsystem level. It is also worth pointing out that the WBS should reflect all the work that is needed to be done in order to complete the project, including the work of managing the project. At each level the work listed should roll up to the next level such that no extra work is required. This condition is referred to as the 100 percent rule.

Some project deliverables may be time sensitive in that they may be subject to alteration at a later date when certain information becomes available. A political campaign is an example of such a project. A speech may be rewritten in whole or in part to deal with recently released data about the national economy, for instance. This describes a planning process that must be reactive to information or demands that change over time. This type of process is sometimes called "rolling wave planning." Nevertheless, the overall structure of the reactive planning process still should be hierarchical.

FIGURE 6.3 Hierarchical planning.

Sometimes a problem arises because some managers tend to think of outcomes when planning and others think of specific tasks (activities). Many mix the two. The problem is to develop a list of both activities and outcomes that represents an exhaustive, nonredundant set of results to be accomplished (outcomes) and the work to be done (activities) in order to complete the project.

In this hierarchical planning system, the objectives are taken from the project charter. This aids the planner in identifying the set of required activities for the objectives to be met, a critical part of the project plan. Each activity has an outcome (event) associated with it, and these activities and events are decomposed into subactivities and subevents, which, in turn, are subdivided again.

Assume, for example, that we have a project whose purpose is to acquire and install a large copy machine in a hospital records department. In the hierarchy of work to be accomplished for the installation part of the project, we might find tasks such as "Develop a plan for preparation of the floor site" and "Develop a plan to maintain records during the installation and test period." These tasks are two of a larger set of jobs to be done. The task "... preparation of the floor site" is subdivided into its elemental parts, including items such as "Get specifics on copy machine mounting points," "Check construction specifications on plant floor," and "Present final plan for floor preparation for approval." A form that may help to organize this information is shown in Figure 6.4. (Additional information about each element of the project will be added to the form later when budgeting and scheduling are discussed.)

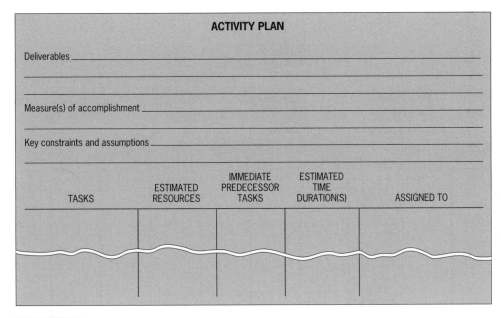

ACTIVITY PLAN

Deliverables _____
_____
_____

Measure(s) of accomplishment _____
_____

Key constraints and assumptions _____
_____

TASKS	ESTIMATED RESOURCES	IMMEDIATE PREDECESSOR TASKS	ESTIMATED TIME DURATION(S)	ASSIGNED TO

FIGURE 6.4   A form to assist hierarchical planning.

The Work Breakdown Structure

Using this hierarchical planning process results in a work breakdown structure known as a WBS. The WBS is the main tool for managing the project scope as described in **PMBOK®**. The WBS is not one thing. It can take a wide variety of forms that, in turn, serve a wide variety of purposes. In many ways, the WBS is a simplified form of the project plan focused on the actual tasks of the project. It often shows the organizational elements associated with a project subdivided into hierarchical units of tasks, subtasks, work packages, etc. Figure 6.5 is such a WBS for a conference. The Food group in the Facilities staff has responsibility for meals and drinks, including coffee breaks and water pitchers in the conference rooms. Five different food functions are shown, each presumably broken down into more detailed tasks. In this case, the account numbers for each task are shown so that proper charges can be assigned for each piece of work done on the project.

5.4

Professor Andrew Vazsonyi has called this type of diagram a *Gozinto chart*, after the famous Italian mathematician Prof. Zepartzat Gozinto (of Vazsonyi's invention). Readers will recognize the parallel to the basic organizational chart depicting the formal structure of an organization, or the Bill of Materials in a Materials Requirements Planning (MRP) system. Another form of the WBS is an outline with the top organizational (Level 1) tasks on the left and successive levels appropriately indented. Most current project management software will generate a WBS on command. Microsoft's Project®, for example, links the indented activity levels with a Gantt chart that visually shows the activity durations at any level.

In general, the WBS is an important document and can be tailored for use in a number of different ways. It may illustrate how each piece of the project contributes to the whole in terms of performance, responsibility, budget, and schedule. It may, if the PM wishes, list the vendors or subcontractors associated with specific tasks. It may be used to document that all parties have signed off on their various commitments to the project. It may note detailed specifications for any work package, establish account numbers, specify hardware/software to be used, and identify resource needs. It may serve as the basis for making cost estimates or estimates of task duration. Largely, the WBS is a planning tool, but it may also be used as an aid in monitoring and controlling projects. Again, it is important to remember

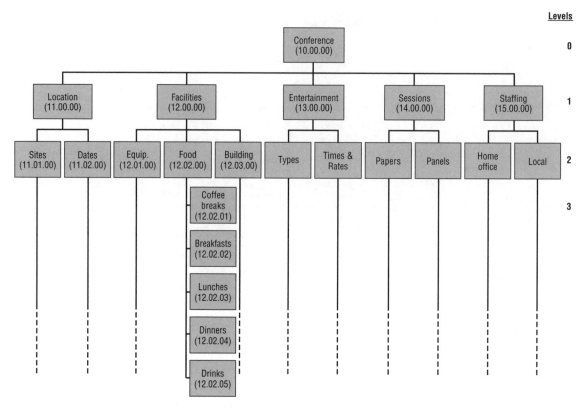

FIGURE 6.5 Work breakdown structure (account numbers shown).

that no single WBS contains all of the elements described and any given WBS should be designed with specific uses in mind. Its uses are limited only by the needs of the project and the imagination of the PM. No one version of the WBS will suit all needs, so the WBS is not *a* document, but any given WBS is simply one of many possible documents.

However, in constructing the WBS, all work package information should be reviewed with the individuals or organizations who have responsibility for doing or supporting the work in order to verify the WBS's accuracy. Resource requirements, schedules, and subtask relationships can now be aggregated to form the next higher level of the WBS, continuing on to each succeeding level of the hierarchy. At the uppermost level, we have a summary of the project, its budget, and an estimate of the duration of each work element. For the moment, we are ignoring uncertainty in estimating the budget and duration of work elements.

As we noted, the actual form the WBS takes is not sacrosanct. Figure 6.6 shows a partial WBS for a college "Career Day," which includes the activities, who is responsible, the time each task is expected to take, which tasks must precede each task, and any external resources needed for that task. However, not all elements of the WBS shown in Figure 6.6 may be needed in other cases. In some cases, for example, the amounts of specific resources required may not be relevant. In others, "due dates" may be substituted for activity durations. The appearance of a WBS will probably differ in different organizations. In some plans, numbers may be used to identify activities; in others, letters. In still others, combinations of letters and numbers may be used. An example of a WBS to acquire a subsidiary is illustrated in Figures 6.7a and 6.7b. A verbal "WBS" was written in the form of a memorandum, Figure 6.7a, and was followed by the more common, tabular plan shown in Figure 6.7b. Only one page of a five-page plan is shown. The individuals and groups mentioned developed similar plans at a greater level of detail. (Names have been changed at the request of the firm.)

WBS

Steps	Responsibility	Time (weeks)	Prec.	Resources
Career Day				
1. Contact Organizations				
a. Print forms	Secretary	6	–	Print shop
b. Contact organizations	Program manager	15	1.a	Word processing
c. Collect display information	Office manager	4	1.b	
d. Gather college particulars	Secretary	4	1.b	
e. Print programs	Secretary	6	1.d	Print shop
f. Print participants' certificates	Graduate assistant	8	–	Print shop
2. Banquet and Refreshments				
a. Select guest speaker	Program manager	14	–	
b. Organize food	Program manager	3	1.b	Caterer
c. Organize liquor	Director	10	1.b	Dept. of Liquor Control
d. Organize refreshments	Graduate assistant	7	1.b	Purchasing
3. Publicity and Promotion				
a. Send invitations	Graduate assistant	2	–	Word processing
b. Organize gift certificates	Graduate assistant	5.5	–	
c. Arrange banner	Graduate assistant	5	1.d	Print shop
d. Contact faculty	Program manager	1.5	1.d	Word processing
e. Advertise in college paper	Secretary	5	1.d	Newspaper
f. Class announcements	Graduate assistant	1	3.d	Registrar's office
g. Organize posters	Secretary	4.5	1.d	Print shop
4. Facilities				
a. Arrange facility for event	Program manager	2.5	1.c	
b. Transport materials	Office manager	.5	4.a	Movers

FIGURE 6.6 Partial WBS for college "Career Day."

Occasionally, planners attempt to plan by using "Gantt charts," a network device commonly used to display project schedules (see Figure 6.8). The Gantt chart was invented as a scheduling aid. In essence, the project's activities are shown on a horizontal bar chart with the horizontal bar lengths proportional to the activity durations. The activity bars are connected to predecessor and successor activities with arrows. The project schedule integrates the many different schedules relevant to the various parts of the project. It is comprehensive and may include contractual commitments, key interfaces and sequencing, milestone events, and progress reports. In addition, a time contingency reserve for

---

MEMO

To allow Ajax to operate like a department of Instat, we must do the following by the dates indicated.

September 24

Ajax Management to be advised of coming under Instat operation. The Instat sales department will begin selling Ajax Consumer Division production effective Jan. 1, 1996. There will be two sales groups: (1) Instat, (2) Ajax Builder Group.

October 15

Instat Regional Managers advised—Instat sales department to assume sales responsibility for Ajax products to distribution channels, Jan. 1, 1996.

October 15

Ajax regional managers advised of sales changes effective Jan. 1, 1996.

October 15

Instat Management, Bob Carl, Van Baker, and Val Walters visit Ajax management and plant. Discuss how operations will merge into Instat.

October 22

Ajax regional managers advise Ajax sales personnel and agents of change effective Jan. 1, 1996.

October 24

Brent Sharp and Ken Roadway visit Instat to coordinate changeover.

October 29

Instat regional managers begin interviewing Ajax sales personnel for possible positions in Instat's sales organization.

November 5

Instat regional managers at Ajax for sales training session.

November 26

Walters visits Ajax to obtain more information.

November 30

Data Processing (Morrie Reddish) and Mfg. Engineering (Sam Newfield): Request DP tapes from Bob Cawley, Ajax, for conversion of Ajax to Instat eng. records: master inventory file, structure file, bill of materials file, where-used file, cross-reference Instat to Ajax part numbers, etc. Allow maximum two weeks until December 14, 1995, for tapes to be at Instat.

December 3

ADMINISTRATIVE (Val Walters): Offer Norwood warehouse for sublease.

December 3

SALES (Abbott and Crutchfield): Week of sales meeting . . . Instruction of salespeople in Ajax line . . . including procedure in writing Ajax orders on separate forms from Instat orders . . . temporarily, adding weight and shipping information, and procedure below: Crutchfield to write procedure regarding transmission of orders to Instat, credit check, and transmission of order information to shipping point, whether Norwood, San Francisco, or, later, Instat Cincinnati.

FIGURE 6.7a Partial WBS for merger of Ajax Hardware into Instat Corp (page 1 of 5).

unforeseeable delays might be included. While it is a useful device for displaying project progress, it is somewhat awkward for project planning. Nevertheless, the two most common tools used to manage projects, as reported in the survey by White et al. (2002), were project management software and Gantt charts. As reported by a working professional student in an MBA class, the Gantt chart integrated all the pieces of her project so she could see the entire project and how the pieces fit together. This phenomenon of major PM reliance on the Gantt chart has been reported in many studies.

At this point, it might be helpful to sum up with a description of how the planning process actually works in many organizations. Assume that you, the PM, have been given responsibility for developing the computer software required to transmit medical X-rays from one location to another over the Internet. There are several problems that must be solved to accomplish this task. First, the X-ray image must be digitized. Second, the digitized image must be transmitted and received. Third, the image must be displayed (or printed) in a way that makes it intelligible to the person who must interpret it. You have a team of four programmers and a couple of assistant programmers assigned to you. You also have a specialist in radiology assigned part-time as a medical advisor.

WBS

Objective: Merger of Ajax Hardware into Instat Corp.			
Steps	**Due Date**	**Responsibility**	**Precedent**
1. Ajax management advised of changes	September 24	Bob Carl, Van Baker	–
2. Begin preparing Instat sales dept. to sell Ajax Consumer Division products effective 1/1/96	September 24	Bob Carl	1
3. Prepare to create two sales groups: (1) Instat, (2) Ajax Builder Group effective 1/1/96	September 24	Bob Carl	1
4. Advise Instat regional managers of sales division changes	October 15	Bob Carl	2,3
5. Advise Ajax regional managers of sales division changes	October 15	Van Baker	2,3
6. Visit Ajax management and plan to discuss merger of operations	October 15	Bob Carl, Van Baker, Val Walters	4,5
7. Advise Ajax sales personnel and agents	October 22	Van Baker	6
8. Visit Instat to coordinate changeover	October 24	Brent Sharp, Ken Roadway	6
9. Interview Ajax sales personnel for possible position	October 29	Instat regional managers	7
10. Sales training sessions for Ajax products	November 5	Instat regional managers	9
11. Visit Ajax again	November 26	Val Walters	8,10
12. Request DP tapes from Bob Cawley for conversion	November 30	Morrie Reddish, Sam Newman	6
13. Offer Norwood warehouse for sublease	December 3	Val Walters	11
14. Write order procedures	December 3	Doug Crutchfield	10
15. Sales meeting (instruction—product line and procedures)	December 3	Fred Abbott, Doug Crutchfield	14
16. DP tapes due for master inventory file, bill of materials, structure file	December 14	Bob Cawley	12
. . .			
. . .			
. . .			

FIGURE 6.7b Tabular partial WBS for Ajax-Instat merger based on Figure 6.7a.

Your first action is to meet with the programmers and medical advisor in order to arrive at the technical requirements for the project. From these requirements, the project mission statement and detailed specifications will be derived. (Note that the original statement of your "responsibility" is too vague to act as an acceptable mission statement.) The basic actions needed to achieve the technical requirements for the project are then developed by the team. For example, one technical requirement would be to develop a method of measuring the density of the image at every point on the X-ray and to represent this measurement as a numerical input for the computer. This is the first level of the project's WBS.

Responsibility for accomplishing the first-level tasks is delegated to the project team members who are asked to develop their own WBS for each of the first level tasks. These are the second-level WBS. The individual tasks listed in the second-level plans are then divided further into third-level WBS detailing how each second-level task will be

Subproject		Task	Responsible Dept.	Dependent Dept.	2011												2012											
					J	F	M	A	M	J	J	A	S	O	N	D	J	F	M	A	M	J	J	A	S	O	N	D
Determine need	A1	Find operations that benefit most	Industrial				△ ▲																						
	A2	Approx. size and type needed	Project Eng.	I.E.						- -	- -	△ ▲																	
Solicit quotations	B1	Contact vendors & review quotes	P.E.	Fin., I.E., Purch.								○	●	△ ○	▲	⊡												
Write appropriation request	C1	Determine tooling costs	Tool Design	I.E.									○		●	△												
	C2	Determine labor savings	I.E.	I.E.											▲	△												
	C3	Actual writing	P.E.	Tool Dsgn., Fin., I.E.														△ ○										
Purchase machine tooling, and gauges	D1	Order	Purchasing	P.E.															△									
	D2	Design and order or manufacture tooling	Tool Design	Purch., Tooling																				△				
	D3	Specify needed gauges and order or mfg.	Q.C.	Tool Dsgn., Purch.																				△ ○				
Installation and startup	E1	Install	Plant Layout	Mill- wrights																					△			
	E2	Train employees	Personnel	P.E. Mfg.																					△			
	E3	Runoff	Mfg.	Q.C.																								△ ⊡

Legend:
* Project completion □ Contractual commitment △ Planned completion ▲ Actual completion
∧ Status date ○ Milestone planned ● Milestone achieved --- Planned progress — Actual progress

Note: As of Jan. 31, 2012, the project is one month behind schedule. This is due mainly to the delay in task C1, which was caused by the late completion of A2.

FIGURE 6.8 Project schedule displayed as a Gantt chart.

accomplished. The process continues until the lowest level tasks are perceived as "units" or "packages" of work appropriate to a single individual.

Early in this section, we advised the planner to keep all items in a WBS at the same level of "generality" or detail. One reason for this is now evident. The tasks at any level of the WBS are usually monitored and controlled by the level just above. If senior managers attempt to monitor and control the highly detailed work packages several levels down, we have a classic case of micromanagement. Another reason for keeping all items in a given level of the WBS at the same level of detail is that planners have an unfortunate tendency to plan in great detail all activities they understand well, and to be dreadfully vague in planning activities they do not understand well. The result is that the detailed parts of the plan are apt to be carried out and the vague parts of the plan are apt to be given short shrift.

In practice, this process is iterative. Members of the project team who are assigned responsibility for working out a second-, third-, or lower-level WBS generate a tentative list of tasks, resource requirements, task durations, predecessors, etc., and bring it to the delegator for discussion, amendment, and approval. This may require several amendments and take several meetings before agreement is reached. The result is that delegator and delegatee both have the same idea about what is to be done, when, and at what cost. Not uncommonly, the individuals and groups that make commitments during the process of developing the WBS actually *sign-off* on their commitments. The whole process involves negotiation and, of course, like any managers, delegators can micromanage their delegatees, but micromanagement will not be mistaken for negotiation—especially by the delegatees.

Human Resources: The RACI Matrix and Agile Projects

To identify the personnel needed for the project, it may be useful to create a table that shows the staff, workers, and others needed to execute each of the WBS tasks. One such approach, called an *Organizational Breakdown Structure* (OBS), displays the organizational units responsible for each of the various work elements in the WBS, or who must approve or be notified of progress or changes in its scope, since the WBS and OBS may well not be identical. That is, some major section of the WBS may be the responsibility of two or more departments, while for other sections of the WBS, two or more, say, may all be the responsibility of one department. Such a document can be useful for department managers to see their total responsibilities for a particular project.

Another approach to identifying the human resources needed for the project is to use the *RACI* (Responsible, Accountable, Consult, Inform) *matrix*. This approach is recommended by **PMBOK®** in its Human Resources Management chapter. This type of chart is also known as a *responsibility matrix*, a *linear responsibility chart*, an *assignment matrix*, a *responsibility assignment matrix*, and similar such names. Sometimes Approval is used instead of Accountable if the organization is carefully monitoring the project. The PM is typically accountable for the activities of the project, but individual department heads or service departments such as Purchasing or Human Resources may be accountable for some specific tasks.

The matrix shows critical interfaces between units that may require special managerial coordination. With it, the PM can keep track of who must approve what, who must be notified, and other such relationships. Such a chart is illustrated in Figure 6.9. If the project is not too complex, the responsibility chart can be elaborated with additional roles (see Figure 6.10).

9.1.2

Activity	Task	Responsibility					
		Project Office				Field Oper.	
		Project Manager	Contract Admin.	Project Eng.	Industrial Eng.	Field Manager	
Determine need	A1	A		C	R		
	A2	I	A	R	C		
Solicit quotations	B1	A	I	R		C	
Write approp. request	C1	I	R	A	C		
	C2		C	A	R		
	C3	C	I	R		I	
"	"						
"	"						
"	"						

Legend:
R   Responsible
C   Consult
I   Inform
A   Accountable

FIGURE 6.9 RACI matrix.

	Vice-president	General manager	Project manager	Manager engineering	Manager software	Manager manufacturing	Manager marketing	Subprogram manager manufacturing	Subprogram manager software	Subprogram manager hardware	Subprogram manager services
Establish project plan	6	2	1	3	3	3	3	4	4	4	4
Define WBS		5	1	3	3	3	3	3	3	3	3
Establish hardware specs		2	3	1	4	4	4				
Establish software specs		2	3	4	1		4				
Establish interface specs		2	3	1	4	4	4				
Establish manufacturing specs		2	3	4	4	1	4				
Define documentation		2	1	4	4	4	4				
Establish market plan	5	3	5	4	4	4	1				
Prepare labor estimate			3	1	1	1		4	4	4	4
Prepare equipment cost estimate		3	1	1	1			4	4	4	4
Prepare material costs			3	1	1	1		4	4	4	4
Make program assignments			3	1	1	1		4	4	4	4
Establish time schedules		5	3	1	1	1	3	4	4	4	4

1 Actual responsibility   4 May be consulted
2 General supervision   5 Must be notified
3 Must be consulted   6 Final approval

FIGURE 6.10 Simplified responsibility chart.

6.2 | Agile Project Planning

Thus far, with the exception of using mind maps, we have been discussing the traditional method for planning projects, commonly known as the "waterfall" approach. Traditional approaches have proven to work well for many projects. There are, however, projects for which the traditional methods do not suffice, mainly because they assume that the scope of the project can be well determined and the technology of developing the scope is well understood. This is not always the case. Since change is a constant, Agile Project Management (APM) was developed to embrace change rather than resisting it the way waterfall project management does. Indeed, a key characteristic of APM is that it incorporates adaptive planning such that the project plan is updated as circumstances change. Employing adaptive planning is particularly valuable for projects characterized by uncertainty, requirements that vary, and have short deadlines.

From time to time we have mentioned the fact that software and IT projects have had a very high failure rate—over budget, over schedule, and delivering less than the desired output. When compared to construction projects, for example, software projects are characterized by a much higher degree of uncertainty about the exact nature of the desired output, and often by a client (funder) who does not understand the complexity of the projects and lacks the knowledge to communicate fully with the project team. The result, understandably, has a high probability of client dissatisfaction with the completed project. (Much of the following description is based on Burba, 2013; Chi-Cheng, 2009; Fewell, 2010 and 2011; Hass, 2007; Hildebrand, 2010; Holt, 2015; Hunsberger, 2011; Jackson, 2012; Layton, 2012; and O'Brien, 2015.)

The major source of the problem appears to be the complexity of modern business organizations. They are involved in complex relationships with each other, with customers, with suppliers, and operate in an environment of rapid technological change and intense global competition. Their need for complex information systems is a result of the complexity in which they operate.

In an effort to lower costs, improve project outcomes, and reduce project completion times, a group of 17 software developers in 2001 leveraged lean management principles and other continuous improvement methodologies to develop a new approach to project management. This new approach was spelled out in the Manifesto for Agile Software Development (agilemanifesto.org, March 2017):

> *"We are uncovering better ways of developing software by doing it and helping others do it. Through this work we have come to value:*
> - *Individuals and interactions over processes and tools*
> - *Working software over comprehensive documentation*
> - *Customer collaboration over contract negotiation*
> - *Responding to change over following a plan*
>
> *That is, while there is value in the items on the right, we value the items on the left more."*

From this Agile Manifesto, the following set of 12 Agile Principles were developed to guide the implementation of APM (agilemanifesto.org/principles.html, March 2017):

1. Our highest priority is to satisfy the customer through early and continuous delivery of valuable software.
2. Welcome changing requirements, even late in development. Agile processes harness change for the customer's competitive advantage.
3. Deliver working software frequently, from a couple of weeks to a couple of months, with a preference to the shorter timescale.
4. Business people and developers must work together daily throughout the project.
5. Build projects around motivated individuals. Give them the environment and support they need, and trust them to get the job done.
6. The most efficient and effective method of conveying information to and within a development team is face-to-face conversation.
7. Working software is the primary measure of progress.
8. Agile processes promote sustainable development. The sponsors, developers, and users should be able to maintain a constant pace indefinitely.
9. Continuous attention to technical excellence and good design enhances agility.
10. Simplicity—the art of maximizing the amount of work not done—is essential.
11. The best architectures, requirements, and designs emerge from self-organizing teams.
12. At regular intervals, the team reflects on how to become more effective, then tunes and adjusts its behavior accordingly.

With APM, a project is completed in stages that last from 1 to 4 weeks. These stages are commonly referred to as iterations, sprints, or milestones. During each stage, project team members are given detailed instructions on the work that is to be completed during the stage. Furthermore, a key element of APM is that the quality of the work for a given stage must be approved before the next stage can be started. Verifying that the quality standards are met at the end of each stage well positions the project team to identify the causes of problems and make rapid adjustments. In more traditional approaches to project management, long gaps between the creation and identification of problems can impede correcting the problems.

Thus, in contrast to the traditional waterfall approach to project management where progress flows from one stage to another, APM utilizes fixed-length stages or iterations. Also, based on lean principles, APM emphasizes maximizing the value of the project as defined by the customer. Table 6.1 further contrasts APM from the traditional waterfall approach.

While the waterfall method is commonly viewed as a "batch" process, APM is viewed as a flow process, where deliverables are produced in a "flow" manner. An analogy often used is that of a cake, which is built in horizontal layers, but consumed in vertical slices. Waterfall project management attempts to deliver the entire cake, while APM delivers a small layer at a time. That is, the work is divided up so that smaller segments can be completed rapidly, that is, via sprints, and presented for review, feedback, and hopefully

TABLE 6.1 Comparison of Agile Project Management with Traditional Waterfall Approach

Dimension	Agile Project Management	Traditional Waterfall Approach
Planning	Short-term plans that are adjusted as project progresses	Attempts to stick to long-term plans made in advance
Client involvement	Throughout the project	Beginning and end of project
Project execution	Broken down into incremental stages called iterations or sprints	Work completed based on comprehensive and highly structured plan
Communication	Open, frequent (daily) communication among stakeholders encouraged	Mainly for project control
Feedback on results	At the end of each iteration	At the end of the project
Work structure	Integrated cross-functional team	Team members tend to work independently and rely on project manager to coordinate tasks
Project leadership	Self-managed teams with project manager as facilitator of process	Project manager allocates work to team members and controls process
Team member feedback	Open communication encouraged by all team members	Feedback typically provided confidentially by project manager
Process ownership	Team	Project manager
Experimentation	Encouraged to identify ways to best meet customer requirements	Discouraged in order to meet project deadline and stay on budget
Scope	Flexible	Rigid
Change	Welcome and expected part of project	Resisted and often requires formal change order request
Priorities	Customer is top priority followed by team and then scope	Schedule is top priority followed by scope and then team
Measures of success	Agile Triangle: value (extrinsic quality), quality (intrinsic quality), constraints (cost, schedule, and scope)	Iron Triangle: cost, schedule, and scope

Project Management in Practice

Agile Project to Create Website Following Earthquake

In February of 2010, Chile was rocked by a devastating earthquake measuring 8.8 on the Richter scale. The earthquake killed 700 people and displaced another 1.5 million people. With such chaos, there was an extremely urgent need to create a location that could serve as a single source of information.

Within hours of the earthquake, a software developer tweeted to solicit the help of information technology (IT) volunteers to create a website. By the end of that day, 60 IT professionals gathered in a small office in Mapocho Valley to launch a project to develop the website. Critical features of the website were to help citizens locate family and friends and to provide a mechanism for people to donate money to the relief efforts. To accomplish this, an interface would need to be created for the website, the website would need to be integrated with Google's Person Finder app, and a Facebook app would need to be created to help people search for missing family members.

To achieve the goal of creating a single source of information as fast as possible, the project team adopted several aspects of APM including the following:

- Using self-organizing teams consisting of people from multiple disciplines to complete project deliverables
- Sprints of 24 hours to deliver rapid iterations of project deliverables
- Stand-up meetings every 8 hours to report on progress and prioritize goals for the next 8 hours
- The creation of Workflow Boards so that teams could choose tasks without having to wait for task assignments

By all accounts the project was an overwhelming success. The first version of the website went live by the end of the first day and the fully functional website was completed in less than 1 week.

Questions

1. **Do you think this project could have achieved the same success using the traditional waterfall approach?**
2. **In general, do crisis situations naturally lend themselves to APM?**

Source: S. F. Gale, "Agile to the Rescue," *PM Network*, January 2012.

offering value for the client. During the duration of each sprint, the client has agreed to "freeze" the scope, so that the tasks can be considered fixed, or concrete. This feedforward of results from the project team to the client and the feedback from the client to the team allows for a collaborative project environment, which strongly enhances the likelihood of project success.

APM is distinguished by this close and continuing contact between clients and the project team, and an iterative and adaptive planning process. Project requirements are a result of client/team interaction, and the requirements change as the interaction leads to a better understanding on both sides of the project requirements, priorities, and limitations. Another difference from the waterfall approach with its emphasis on schedule first, then the scope, and lastly the team is that in APM the emphasis is on the customer first, the team second, and the scope third.

Project team membership will, of course, vary with the nature of the project and its deliverables. Agile IT project teams, for example, are typically small, located at a single site, and composed of a PM, the client/end user, an IT architect, two code writers, and a business analyst in the client's industry. As noted above, the group develops the project requirements and priorities. One requirement is selected, usually the highest value or priority or most complex item, and the team tackles that item. The resulting output is tested by a test case developed during the requirements development phase. The entire team collaborates in dealing with the requirements. The PM's role is to "facilitate" rather than to "control" the process.

Given several requirements, the team deals with them one at a time. Not uncommonly, the solution to a second or third requirement may depend on altering the solution to the first requirement. One consultant notes that if the client changes the requirements, "we just deliver the new requirements" and ignore the previous ones. If the client wants more, they simply expand the engagement. Note, however, that within each sprint, agile has to still meet schedule, budget, and scope expectations. Although agile provides flexibility, the trade-off is a loss of efficiency. This iterative process is not only collaborative, it must also be adaptive.

It is also obvious that problem-oriented team members who have the interpersonal skills needed for collaboration are a necessity. The willingness of team members to share knowledge is an essential condition for agile projects. Not incidentally, the willingness to share knowledge is also a key to success in traditionally organized projects. A PM who attempts to control an agile project as he or she might control a traditional project is most certainly the wrong person for the job.

Project Management in Practice

Using Agile to Integrate Two Gas Pipeline Systems

Lowell Georgia/Science Source Images

When TransCanada acquired American Natural Resources Co. of the U.S.A., they were faced with the problem of integrating 21,000 miles of American's natural gas pipelines with their own Canadian system within a 2-year time frame. Different pipeline regulatory procedures between the two countries meant establishing new processes and governance procedures to certify the integrity of the complete network. The project team consisted of 14 engineers and one software manager, each with their own sub-teams to integrate the pipelines. The project started with a big Gantt chart for task scheduling, but since the team wasn't fully dedicated to this project and still had their normal responsibilities, task due dates often were not met. In addition, as the team acquired more data, the project parameters and scope kept changing. To respond to these constant changes, the project team moved toward a more agile management process.

Although they didn't adopt all the tools of agile, they did make use of some that were especially needed for this project. For example, there were daily 15-minute sub-team

"stand-ups" (less talking when no chairs), and weekly meetings with the entire project team. This gave the workers the latest information on changes, problems, manpower availability, priorities, and other information to identify and solve roadblocks. The meetings promoted the needed inter-communication to keep the project moving while adapting to the constant changes.

To track actual progress, the project manager created a high-level list of the project's tasks and, because he could trust the skill of the senior engineering sub-task managers, then regularly updated the amount of hours left to *complete* each of the tasks (note: *not* hours put in). Such daily reporting helped the sub-teams keep their focus on the results while aware of the daily changes that might affect them. This constant updating of information came in handy when the project was thrown off schedule by a vendor delay, but the ability of the project manager to alert the project's stakeholders far in advance was positively received. Even though the project ran late, management was nevertheless pleased to know about the problem far ahead of time and why it occurred.

The project manager here pointed out that agile is simply a way to deal with projects that are in constant flux by shortening the feedback loops and keeping everyone apprised of changes so they can coordinate their efforts. Thus, it is best for organizations working in dynamic, turbulent environments. It isn't particularly useful on projects with standard processes for completing them (like building a *new* pipeline), or with a project team that has workers who are inexperienced, unskilled, or unfamiliar with each other. The team needs to be able to trust the judgment of each of its members, and be able to collaborate and coordinate with them.

Questions

1. In an Agile project, the client or a representative of the client is a member of the team. Why was that not done here?

2. What aspects of agile (APM) were and were not used here?

3. What might be some problems with using agile for a standard project, or one with standard processes?

Source: C. Hildebrand, "The Sweet Spot," PM Network, Vol. 24.

While APM was originally developed for software development, it has been applied to other areas including product development and engineering. Any project that involves a high-risk technology, varying requirements, unusual complexity, great volatility, high uncertainty, a short delivery time, a rapidly changing business environment, or is especially innovative or experimental is a candidate for APM, but success requires personnel who are qualified by personality, knowledge, and a desire for the APM experience.

A number of benefits are commonly attributed to APM including the following:

- Better project outcomes as a result of issues being identified earlier.
- Increased customer satisfaction as a result of receiving customer input and feedback throughout the project.
- Improved morale of project team members resulting from the use of self-managed teams and having greater autonomy. Furthermore, the short iterations help mitigate employee burnout.
- Increased collaboration and project visibility resulting from daily sprint reviews.

With all the attention that APM is receiving, it is important to point out that many of its tenants can be easily incorporated in more traditional project management approaches. For example, there is nothing that prevents increasing customer involvement in the traditional waterfall approach. Likewise, there is nothing inherent to traditional project management that prohibits greater experimentation. The point being that rather than viewing APM as an all or nothing approach to project management, there is nothing that precludes a project manager from adopting a subset of APM best practices. The Reading at the end of this chapter refers to this as "agile hybrid." Finally, it is worth noting that related to the popularity of APM, the Project Management Institute offers a certification in APM—the Agile Certified Practitioner (PMI-ACP).

Project Management in Practice

The Current State of Agile Project Management

VersionOne, an enterprise software development company with products to support agile project teams, has conducted an annual survey for the last 10 years to better understand usage and trends of APM in software development. For its tenth annual *State of Agile* survey, data was collected between July and November 2015 and included 3880 completed surveys. Because of the diversity of respondents including industries represented, size of the organizations, and experience with agile, the survey provides many useful insights into the state of APM. For example, 44 percent of the respondents worked at organizations with less than 1000 people, while 25 percent of the respondents worked at organizations with more than 20,000 employees. Respondents also represented a variety of industries including software (26 percent of respondents), financial services (14 percent), and professional services (11 percent).

A number of other industries were also represented including healthcare, government, insurance, telecom, retail, manufacturing, media, Internet services, transportation, consumer products, and utilities. Likewise, the respondents represented a diverse group in terms of their experience with APM with 19 percent indicating they had less than a year of experience, while 25 percent had more than 5 years of experience. Finally, it is worth pointing out that the percent of respondents coming from outside North America has been steadily increasing. In the tenth annual survey, 56 percent of the respondents were from North America, while 26 percent were from Europe and 11 percent were from Asia.

A key insight from the survey relates to why organizations are adopting APM. For the last 3 years, the top two reasons for adopting APM were to accelerate product delivery (62 percent of respondents) and to enhance the ability to manage changing priorities (56 percent). The respondents also cited numerous additional reasons for adopting APM including to increase productivity (55 percent), enhance software quality (47 percent), and enhance delivery predictability (44 percent).

Furthermore, the results of the survey suggest that APM is helping organizations achieve these goals. The top three benefits respondents cited stemming from their APM initiatives have been constant over the last five surveys: ability to manage changing priorities (87 percent), increased team productivity (85 percent), and improved product visibility (84 percent). Other key benefits cited by the respondents included increased team morale, better delivery predictability, faster time to market, enhanced software quality, and reduced project risk.

Related to the reasons why organizations adopt APM and the benefits of deploying it, the survey also provides insights into how success with APM is accessed. According to the survey, for the last several years, the top three ways organizations accessed the success of their APM initiatives were on-time delivery (58 percent), product quality (48 percent), and customer satisfaction (46 percent).

Of course, APM is not a panacea for all that is deficient in traditional project management approaches and there are ample examples of agile projects that have failed (although in the survey only 1 percent of respondents stated that overall their organization's APM implementation was not successful). Some of the leading reasons cited by survey respondents for agile project failures included company culture not aligned with agile values (46 percent), lack of experience with APM (41 percent), and lack of management support (38 percent). In addition to providing insight into the leading causes of agile project failures, the respondents provided insights into the key barriers for expanding APM adoption. The key barriers cited by the respondents included organizational culture (55 percent), general resistance to change (42 percent), and the existence of more rigid project

management frameworks (40 percent). To help ensure APM initiatives are successful, the respondents suggest the following:

- Implement consistent processes and practices (43 percent)
- Utilize a common tool across teams (40 percent)
- Utilize the services of agile consultants and trainers (40 percent)
- Obtain executive sponsorship (37 percent)

Finally, while specific agile tools and methodologies are beyond our scope, it is interesting to observe which agile techniques were most commonly employed by the survey respondents. The top three agile techniques the respondents reported using included daily stand-up meetings (83 percent), prioritized backlogs (82 percent), and short iterations (79 percent). The most common tools used to support agile projects included taskboards (82 percent), bug tracker (80 percent), and spreadsheets (74 percent).

Questions

1. **What do the results of the survey suggest about the applicability of APM beyond software development?**

2. **What is your reaction to the tips offered to help ensure APM initiatives are successful?**

Source: The 10th Annual State of Agile Report, VersionOne, 2016, http://www.agile247.pl/wp-content/uploads/2016/04/VersionOne-10th-Annual-State-of-Agile-Report.pdf

6.3 | Coordination Through Integration Management

PMBOK

Chapters 4, 11

This section covers the **PMBOK**® knowledge area 1 concerning *Project Integration Management*. The most difficult aspect of implementing the plan for a complex project is the coordination and integration of the various elements of the project so that they meet their joint goals of scope, schedule, and budget in such a way that the total project meets its goals.

As projects become more complex, drawing on knowledge and skills from more areas of expertise—and, thus, more subunits of the parent organization as well as more outsiders—the problem of coordinating multidisciplinary teams (MTs) becomes more troublesome. At the same time, and as a result, uncertainty is increased. As the project proceeds from its initiation through the planning and into the actual process of trying to generate the project's deliverables, still more problems arise. One hears, "We tried to tell you that this would happen, but you didn't pay any attention." This, as well as less-printable remarks, are what one hears when the members of an MT do not work and play well together—in other words, when the various individuals and groups working on the project are not well integrated. Rather than operating as a team, they work as separate and distinct parts, each of which has its own tasks and is not much interested in the other parts.

The intricate process of coordinating the work and timing of the different groups is called *integration management*. The RACI matrix discussed earlier is a useful aid to the PM in carrying out this task. It displays the many ways the members of the project team (which, as usual, includes all of the actors involved, not forgetting the client and outside vendors) must interact and what the rights, duties, and responsibilities of each will be.

Recent work on managing the interfaces focuses on the use of MTs to plan the project as well as design the products/services the project is intended to produce. There is general

Project Management in Practice

Trying to Install a Wind Farm in the Middle of the North Sea

Eugene Suslo / Shutterstock

Denmark's objective of supplying half its national power needs through wind energy by 2025 counted heavily on DONG (Dansk Olie og Naturgas) Energy's "Horns Rev 2" 209-megawatt offshore wind farm, the largest in the world, to be located 30 kilometers (19 miles) off the western Jutland, Denmark coast in the North Sea. Over 600 people and 7 suppliers, all led by 7 PMs plus a quality control manager and a commissioning manager, constituted the multidisciplinary project team for this effort. The project consisted of installing 91 turbines over a 35-square-kilometer (14 square mile) area. The 50+ meter-long blades that catch the wind and turn the turbines are mounted on shafts 115 meters (377 feet) above the surface of the water. The electricity generated by the wind farm at capacity could supply 200,000 homes.

Even though the point was to locate the farm where there was a strong, constant wind, this created the major problem facing the team—the difficulty of working in these 36 kilometer winds and icy, 3-meter-high (10-foot) waves out in the rough sea. Traveling to the site could take up to 3 hours, and labor and supplies had to be unloaded and unpacked in the harsh weather. The difficult conditions limited the time the teams could work, and increased the risk and complexity of every decision. In addition, safety issues became top priority because the work was under such extreme conditions, and far from medical care. As a result, it was critical to eliminate errors and risks because once offshore, the team was coping with weather, logistics, and time, which increased the scale of any problems tenfold!

Hence, massive attention was paid to quality planning on-shore, before heading out to sea. There was a quality plan for every key event to ensure equipment and tasks would meet requirements. Every part that was delivered was rigorously inspected and anything that was missing or wrong had to be corrected before being sent out to sea. And when any troubles were encountered, they were addressed immediately. In one case, a problem arose that was going to take the supplier 2 months to repair; through creative troubleshooting, the team came up with a plan that would combine two tasks and in the process reduce the time to 2 weeks. The focus on creative problem solving among the MTs rather than placing blame allowed the project to be completed successfully. Ancillary benefits included bringing new knowledge and working practices to the company, plus enabling many members of the team to move into higher-ranking positions, including two engineers who are becoming PMs themselves.

Questions

1. Contrast the difficulties and risks of this project with those of NASA in the "Ignoring Risk . . ." PMIP sidebar in Section 6.5.

2. How important was it to have just the right competencies and dependabilities on the multidisciplinary teams?

3. Relate the detail of their "quality plan for each key event" to what you might expect their WBS looked like.

Source: S. F. Gale, "A Closer Look," *PM Network*, Vol. 24.

agreement that MT has a favorable impact on product/service design and delivery. Work by Hauptman et al. (1996, p. 161) shows that MTs have had a "favorable impact . . . on attainment of project budget goals, but achieves this without any adverse impact on quality, cost or schedule." The process also was associated with higher levels of team job satisfaction.

The use of MTs in product development and planning is not without its difficulties. Successfully involving cross-functional teams in project planning requires that some structure be imposed on the planning process. The most common structure is simply to define the task of the group as having the responsibility to generate a plan to accomplish whatever is defined as the project scope. There is considerable evidence that this is not sufficient for complex projects. Using MT creates what might well be considered a "virtual" project. In Chapter 4, we noted the high level of conflict in many virtual projects. It follows that MT

Project Management in Practice

An Acquisition Failure Questions Recommended Practice

Keith Brofsky/Media Bakery

When the Belgian bank Fortis joined with the Royal Bank of Scotland and the Spanish Banco Santander to acquire the Dutch bank ABN Amro, the integration project involved over 6000 people and was expected to take 3 to 4 years to complete. The objective was to evaluate what each side brought to the table and select the best technologies through extensive communication and brainstorming. The first 9 months were spent evaluating every system and project that would be affected by the merger, resulting in a portfolio of 1000 projects that needed to be accomplished. A third of the projects were IT system choices, which were to be based on multiple criteria such as functionality, cost, maintainability, etc. The plan was to make the choices based on facts instead of emotions, relying on ABN Amro's data and including them in the decision making.

The biggest set of system projects involved mapping and integrating the IT systems. But ABN Amro had thousands of applications and resisted sharing their information, which led to constant conflicts, delays, and artificial obstacles. The result was that Fortis spent thousands of hours to complete even the simplest projects. The years-long project duration also hindered progress since the longer a project takes, the more conflicts, especially cultural (that can't be solved simply with additional resources), will arise. Eventually, the problems and delays depleted Fortis' capital, and, exacerbated by the global credit crisis, they went bankrupt.

Fortis was then sold to the French bank BNP Paribas. In contrast to Fortis' approach, BNP set up an 18-month project to phase out all of Fortis' systems and move Fortis' accounts and data into their own system. They integrated the Fortis team into their own organizational structure and put their own people into the key roles—there was no discussion, just work to do. It was a top-down approach that was easier, faster, and more efficient, though it didn't sit well with the Fortis employees. After the integration was complete, BNP refocused on rebuilding any lost morale. For example, most of the Fortis people kept their jobs, and BNP opened four global centers in Brussels (called BNP Paribas Fortis) to show their interest in strengthening the bank's national and global presence.

Questions

1. Do long project durations in other industries also lead to conflicts and project problems?

2. Was the difficulty in this situation due to the upset ABN Amro employees, or were there more serious project planning problems?

3. Do you agree with the "solution" exemplified by BNP? Might there be some compromise plan?

Source: S. F. Gale, "A Closer Look," *PM Network*, Vol. 24.

tends to involve conflict. Conflict raises uncertainty and thus requires risk management. Obviously, many of the risks associated with MT involve intergroup political issues. The PM's negotiating skill will be tested in dealing with intergroup problems, but the outcomes of MT seem to be worth the risks. At times, the risks arise when dealing with an outside group. For an interesting discussion of such issues and their impact on project scope, see Seigle (2001).

Managing Projects by Phases and Phase-Gates

In addition to mapping the interfaces (a necessary but not sufficient condition for MT peace), the process of using MTs on complex projects must be subject to some more specific kinds of control. One of the ways to control any process is to break the overall objectives of the process into shorter-term phases (frequently using natural milestones) and to focus the MT on achieving the milestones, as is done in APM. If this is done, and if multidisciplinary cooperation and coordination can be established, the level of conflict will likely fall. At least there is evidence that if team members work cooperatively and accomplish their short-term goals, the project will manage to meet its long-term objectives; moreover, the outcome of any conflict that does arise will be creative work on the project.

The project life cycle serves as a readily available way of breaking a project up into component phases, each of which has a unique, identifiable output. Careful reviews should be conducted at the end of each "phase" of the life cycle, with feedback given to the entire project team each time a project review was conducted.

Another attack on the same problem was tied to project quality, again, via the life cycle (Aaron et al., 1993). They created 10 phase-gates associated with milestones for a software project. To move between phases, the project had to pass a review. (They even noted that in the early stages of the project when there is no "inspectable product," that ". . . *managing quality on a project means managing the quality of the subprocesses* that produce the delivered product." Emphasis in the original.) While feedback is not emphasized in this system, reports on the finding of project reviews are circulated. The quality-gate process here did not allow one phase to begin until the previous phase had been successfully completed, but many of the phase-gate systems allow sequential phases to overlap in an attempt to make sure that the output of one phase is satisfactory as an input to the next. Another approach that also overlaps phases is called "fast tracking," and here the phases are run in parallel as much as possible to reduce the completion time of the project; of course, this also increases the project risk as well. (The use of the phase-gate process for project control is demonstrated in Chapter 11, Section 11.2.)

There are many such interface control systems, but the ones that appear to work have two elements in common. First, they focus on relatively specific, short-term, interim outputs of a project with the reviews including the different disciplines involved with the project. Second, feedback (and feedforward) between these disciplines is emphasized. No matter what they are called, it must be made clear to all involved that cooperation between the multiple disciplines is required for success, and that all parties to the project are mutually dependent on one another.

Finally, it should be stressed that phase-gate management systems were not meant as substitutes for the standard time, cost, and scope controls usually used for project management. Instead, phase-gate and similar systems are intended to create a process by which to measure project progress, to keep projects on track and aligned with the current strategy, and to keep senior management informed about the current state of projects being carried out.

This topic completes our discussion of project activity planning. Next, we address the subject of budgeting and look at various budgeting methods. The chapter also addresses the issues of cost estimation and its difficulty, and simulation to handle budgetary risk of both costs and revenues.

Summary

In this chapter we initiated planning for the project in terms of identifying and addressing the tasks required for project completion. We emphasized the importance of initial coordination of all parties involved and the smooth integration of the various systems required to achieve the project objectives. Then we described some tools such as the WBS, the RACI matrix, and the Gozinto chart to aid in the planning process. We then described the APM approach and pointed out that it is now being used in a wide variety of industries. We also briefly investigated several methods for controlling and reducing conflict in complex projects that use multidisciplinary teams.

Specific points made in the chapter are these:

- The preliminary work plans are important because they serve as the basis for personnel selection, budgeting, scheduling, and control.

- Top management should be represented by the project owner in the initial coordinating meeting where technical objectives are established, participant responsibility is accepted, and preliminary budgets and schedules are defined.

- The approval and change processes are complex and should be handled jointly by the PM and project owner.

- Common elements of the project charter are the overview, statement of objectives/scope, general approach, contractual requirements, schedules, resources, stakeholders, personnel, risk management plans, and evaluation procedures.

- Mind mapping can greatly facilitate the project planning process.

- The hierarchical approach to project planning is most appropriate and can be aided by a tree diagram of project subsets, called a Gozinto chart, and a WBS. The WBS relates the details of each subtask to its task and provides the final basis for the project budget, schedule, personnel, and control.

- A RACI matrix is often helpful to illustrate the relationship of personnel to project tasks and to identify where coordination is necessary.

- When multifunctional teams are used to plan complex projects, their task interfaces must be integrated and coordinated. The use of milestones and phase-gates throughout the project's schedule can help with this integration process.

The APM approach was developed specifically for project situations where complexity, frequent changes, short deadlines, and varying requirements are typical.

Whereas the traditional waterfall approach can be viewed as a batch process, moving from one phase-gate to another, the Agile approach is more of a flow process using short sprints to deliver one requirement at a time.

Glossary

Agile Project Planning An approach developed for software projects but now applied in many other kinds of projects that interfaces with the customer on a short-cycle, iterative basis for constant replanning.

Bill of Materials The set of physical elements required to build a product.

Effectiveness Achieving the objectives set beforehand; to be distinguished from efficiency, which is measured by the output realized for the input used.

Engineering Change Orders Product improvements that engineering has designed after the initial product design was released.

Gozinto Chart A pictorial representation of a product that shows how the elements required to build a product fit together.

Hierarchical Planning A planning approach that breaks the planning task down into the activities that must be done at each managerial level. Typically, the upper level sets the objectives for the next lower level.

Integration Management Managing the problems that tend to occur between departments and disciplines, rather than within individual departments.

Materials Requirements Planning (MRP) A planning and material ordering approach based on the known or forecast final demand requirements, lead times for each fabricated or purchased item, and existing inventories of all items.

Milestones Natural subproject ending points where payments may occur, evaluations may be made, or progress may be reassessed.

Mind Mapping A process for pictorially representing ideas from a group so they can build upon each of the presented ideas and further elaborate them.

Phase-Gates Preplanned points during the project where progress is assessed and the project cannot resume until re-authorization has been approved.

Project Charter A proposal for a project that summarizes at a high level the main aspects of the project for approval.

Project Plan The nominal plan for the entire project to which deviations will be compared.

RACI Matrix A table showing, for each project task, who is responsible, accountable, who should be consulted, and who needs to be informed. (Also known as a responsibility or assignment chart.)

Sprint A short stage lasting 1 to 4 weeks in an agile project.

Work Breakdown Structure (WBS) A description of all the tasks to complete a project, organized by some consistent

perspective and containing a variety of information needed for that perspective.

Work Statement A description of a task that defines all the work required to accomplish it, including inputs and desired outputs.

Questions

Material Review Questions

1. Describe the approach of APM and how it differs from the normal approach.

2. Any successful project charter must contain nine key elements. List these items and briefly describe the composition of each.

3. What are the general steps for managing each work package within a specific project?

4. Describe the "hierarchical planning process" and explain why it is helpful.

5. What is shown on a RACI matrix? How is it useful to a PM?

6. What should be accomplished at the initial coordination meeting?

7. Why is it important for the functional areas to be involved in the project from the time of the original proposal?

8. What are the basic steps to design and use the WBS?

9. What is the objective of interface management?

10. Contrast the Project Plan, the Project Charter, and the WBS.

11. Contrast milestones with phase-gates.

12. How can a mind map be used to facilitate project planning?

13. How can Agile cope with the constant change in requirements that drives most traditional project managers crazy?

14. Why has Agile been adopted outside the software programming industry where it was developed?

Class Discussion Questions

15. What percentage of the total project effort do you think should be devoted to planning? Why?

16. Why do you suppose that the coordination of the various elements of the project is considered the most difficult aspect of project implementation?

17. What kinds of risk categories might be included in the project charter?

18. In what ways may the WBS be used as a key document to monitor and control a project?

19. Describe the process of subdivision of activities and events that composes the tree diagram known as the WBS or Gozinto chart. Why is the input of responsible managers and workers so important an aspect of this process?

20. Why is project planning so important?

21. What are the pros and cons concerning the early participation of the various functional areas in the project plan?

22. Task 5-C is the critical, pacing task of a rush project. Fred always nitpicks anything that comes his way, slowing it down, driving up its costs, and irritating everyone concerned. Normally, Fred would be listed as "Notify" for task 5-C on the responsibility matrix, but the PM is considering "forgetting" to make that notation on the chart. Is this unethical, political, or just smart management?

23. How might we plan for risks that we cannot identify in the risk management section of the project charter?

24. Might milestones and phase-gates both occur at the same point of a project? Will the same activities be happening?

25. Why was APM developed? Do you think this might be the way of the future for project management?

26. What are the advantages of using mind mapping to facilitate project planning?

27. How could deep experience managing projects using the traditional waterfall method hinder someone's ability to manage a project using Agile?

28. Would Agile work in situations involving known and unchanging requirements, low complexity, and long deadlines such as with many construction projects?

29. Might traditional and Agile be simply two end points on a spectrum of approaches that combine the elements of each?

30. In addition to your regular responsibilities, your supervisor has just assigned you to be in charge of your organization's annual golf tournament. It is expected that 100 to 150 employees will enter the tournament. In addition to organizing the event, you are also responsible for promoting it. Your budget for the event is $25,000. Develop a mind map to identify the tasks that need to be completed for the golf tournament project.

Incidents for Discussion

Ringold's Pool and Patio Supply

John Ringold, Jr., just graduated from a local university with a degree in industrial management and joined his father's company as executive vice president of operations. Dad wants to break John in slowly and has decided to see how he can do on a project that John Sr. has never had time to investigate. Twenty percent of the company's sales are derived from the sale of above-ground swimming pool kits. Ringold's does not install the pools. John Sr. has asked John Jr. to determine whether or not they should get into that business. John Jr. has decided that the easiest way to impress Dad and get the project done is personally to estimate the cost to the company of setting up a pool and then call some competitors and see how much they charge. That will show whether or not it is profitable.

John Jr. remembered a method called the work breakdown structure (WBS) that he thought might serve as a useful tool to estimate costs. Also, the use of such a tool could be passed along to the site supervisor to help evaluate the performance of work crews. John Jr.'s WBS is shown in Table A. The total cost John Jr. calculated was $185.00, based on 12.33 labor-hours at $15.00/labor-hour. John Jr. found that, on average, Ringold's

TABLE A Pool Installation WBS

Works Tasks	Labor-Hours (estimated)
Prepare ground surface	2.67
Clear	1
Rake	$\frac{1}{3}$
Level	1
Sand bottom	$\frac{1}{3}$
Lay out pool frame	2.50
Bottom ring	
Side panels	$\frac{1}{2}$
Top ring	1
Add plastic liner	0.50
Assemble pool	1.66
Build wooden support	3.00
Layout	1
Assemble	2
Fill and test	2.00
Total	12.33

competitors charged $229.00 to install a similar pool. John Jr. thought he had a winner. He called his father and made an appointment to present his findings the next morning. Since he had never assembled a pool himself, he decided to increase the budget by 10 percent, "just in case."

Questions

Is John Jr.'s WBS projection reasonable? What aspects of the decision will John Sr. consider?

Stacee Laboratories

Stacee Labs, the research subsidiary of Stacee Pharmaceuticals, Inc., has a long history of successful research and development of medical drugs. The work is conducted by standalone project teams of scientists that operate with little in the way of schedules, budgets, and precisely predefined objectives. The parent company's management felt that scientific research teams should not be encumbered with bureaucratic record-keeping chores, and their work should go where their inspiration takes them.

A Special Committee of Stacee Pharm's Board of Directors has completed a study of Stacee Labs and has found that its projects required a significantly longer time to complete than the industry average and, as a result, were significantly more expensive. These projects often lasted 10 to 15 years before the drug could be released to the market. At the same time, Stacee Labs projects had a very high success rate.

The board called in a management consultant, Ms. Millie Tasha, and asked her to investigate the research organization briefly and report to the board on ways in which the projects could be completed sooner and at lower expense. The board emphasized that it was not seeking nit-picking, cost-cutting, or time-saving recommendations that might lower the quality of Stacee Labs's results.

Ms. Tasha returned after several weeks of interviews with the lab's researchers as well as with senior representatives of the parent firm's Marketing, Finance, Government Relations, and Drug Efficacy Test Divisions, as well as the Toxicity Test Department. Her report to the Board began with the observation that lab scientists avoided contact with Marketing and Governmental Relations until they had accomplished most of their work on a specific drug family. When asked why they waited so long to involve marketing, they responded that they did not know what specific products they would recommend for sale until they had completed and tested the results of their work. They added that marketing was always trying to interfere with drug design and wanted them to make exaggerated claims or to design drugs based on sales potential rather than on good science.

Ms. Tasha also noted that lab scientists did not contact the toxicity or efficacy testing groups until scientific work was completed and they had a drug to test. This resulted in long delays because the testing groups were usually occupied with other matters and could not handle the tests promptly. It usually took many months to organize and begin both toxicity and efficacy testing.

In Ms. Tasha's opinion, the only way to make significant cuts in the time and cost required for drug research projects was to form an integrated team composed of representatives of all the groups who had a major role to play in each drug project and to have them involved from the beginning of the project. All parties could then follow progress with drug development and be prepared to make timely contributions to the projects. If this were done, long delays and their associated costs would be significantly reduced.

Questions

Do you think Millie Tasha is right? If so, how should new drug projects be planned and organized? If Stacee Pharmaceutical goes ahead with a reorganization of lab projects, what are the potential problems? How would you deal with them? Could scope creep become more of a problem with the new integrated teams? If so, how should it be controlled?

Continuing Integrative Class Project

It is now time to plan the project tasks and make assignments. First, schedule a team meeting and identify the work that must be done by creating a mind map. Once the initial mind map is created, have one team member clean it up and enter it into a software program (e.g., Word, PowerPoint, Visio, Mindjet MindManager). Distribute the cleaned up mind map until ideas are exhausted and the team believes it has a comprehensive list of the project activities. Identify any milestones and phase-gates. Make sure everyone is aware of their role in the project, their specific deadlines, and the available resources.

Historian, observe the work processes and note areas where the team did well and areas for improvement. For example, was the PM effective at including everyone in the planning process or did he or she allow a subset of the team to dominate the process? During the mind mapping, did the team focus on identifying the work that needed to be done or did they drift to discussing tangential topics such as the goals for the project. Based on your observations, what practices would you continue in future projects? What would you recommend doing differently?

Bibliography

Aaron, J. M., C. P. Bratta, and D. P. Smith. "Achieving Total Project Control Using the Quality Gate Method." *Proceedings of the Annual Symposium of the Project Management Institute*, San Diego, October 4, 1993.

Antonioni, D. "Post-Planning Review Prevents Poor Project Performance." *PM Network*, October 1997.

Bigelow, D. "Planning Is Important—Why Don't We Do More of It?" *PM Network*, July 1998.

Brown, K. A., and N. L. Hyer. "Whole-Brain Thinking for *Project Management*." *Business Horizons*, May–June 2003.

Brox, D. "Say No." *PM Network*, May 2012.

Burba, D. "Policing the Agile Expressway." *PM Network*, November 2013.

Chi-Cheng, H. "Knowledge Sharing and Group Cohesiveness on Performance: An Empirical Study of Technology R&D Teams in Taiwan." *Technovation*, November 2009.

Fewell, J. "Led Astray." *PM Network*, October 2010.

Fewell, J. "Are You Agile?" *PM Network*, December 2011.

Hass, K. B. "The Blending of Traditional and Agile Project Management." *PM World Today*, May 2007.

Hauptman, O., and K. K. Hirji. "The Influence of Process Concurrency on Project Outcomes in Product Development: An Empirical Study of Cross-Functional Teams." *IEEE Transactions on Engineering Management*, May 1996.

Hildebrand, C. "Agile." *PM Network*, August 2010.

Holt, C. J., *Agile Project Management*. Blue Fox Publishing, 2015.

Hunsberger, K. "Change Is Good." *PM Network*, February 2011.

Jackson, M. B. "Agile: A Decade In." *PM Network*, April 2012.

Knutson, J. "How to Manage a Project Launch Meeting." *PM Network*, July 1995.

Layton, M. C., *Agile Project Management for Dummies*. Hoboken, NJ: John Wily and Sons, 2012.

Martin, P. K., and K. Tate. "Kick Off the Smart Way." *PM Network*. October 1998.

O'Brien, H., *Agile Project Management*. CreateSpace Independent Publishing Platform, 2015.

Project Management Institute. *A Guide to the Project Management Body of Knowledge (PMBOK® Guide)*, 5th ed., Newtown Square, PA: Project Management Institute, 2013.

Seigle, G. "Government Projects: Expect the Unexpected." *PM Network*, November 2001.

choice to achieve the "lightning rod" effect whereby any negative concern was directed to an outsider. Also, the consultant—as an outsider—could criticize and comment in ways that should not be done by the engineering department managers who will have long-term working relationships among each other. It was agreed in advance that a consensus would be sought to the greatest possible extent, avoiding any votes on how to handle particular issues which leaves the "nay" votes feeling that their interests have been overridden by the majority. If consensus could not be achieved, then the issue would be sidestepped to be deferred for later consideration; if sufficiently important, then a joint solution could be developed outside the session without the pressure of a fixed closing time.

Phase III. Project plan development

The output of Phase II (the set of consensus conclusions) represented both guidelines and specific conclusions concerning the nature of a PM&C system. Recognizing that the PM&C program will be viewed as a model project and that it should be used as such, serving as an example of what is desired, the program manager prepared a project plan for the PM&C program. The remainder of this paper is primarily concerned with the discussion of this plan, both as an example of how to introduce a PM&C system and how to make a project plan. The plan discussed in this paper and illustrated in Figures 3 to 11 is the type of plan that is now required before any capital project may be submitted to the approval process at Heublein.

Phase IV. Implementation

With the plan developed in Phase III approved, it was possible to move ahead with implementation. Implementation was in accordance with the plan discussed in the balance of this paper. Evaluation of the results was considered a part of this implementation.

Project Plan

A feature of the guidelines developed by the engineering managers in Phase II was that a "menu" of component parts of

a project plan was to be established in the corporate PM&C system, and that elements of this menu were to be chosen to fit the situational or corporate tracking requirements. The menu is:

1. Introduction
2. Project Objectives
3. Project/Program Structure
4. Project/Program Costs
5. Network
6. Schedule
7. Resource Allocation
8. Organization and Accountability
9. Control System
10. Milestones or Project Subdivisions

In major or critical projects, the minimal set of choices from the menu is specified by corporate staff (the definition of a "major" or "critical" project is a part of the PM&C procedure). For "routine" projects, the choice from the menu is left to the project manager.

In the PM&C plan, items 6 and 7, Schedule and Resource Allocation, were combined into one section for reasons which will be described as part of the detailed discussions of the individual sections which follow.

Introduction

In this PM&C system, the Introduction is an executive summary, with emphasis on the justification of the project. This can be seen from the PM&C Program Introduction shown in Figure 3. It is to the advantage of everyone concerned with a project to be fully aware of the reasons for its existence. It is as important to the technicians as it is to the engineers or the corporate financial department. When the project staff clearly comprehends the reason for the project's existence, it is much easier to enlist and maintain their support and wholehearted efforts. In the Heublein PM&C system, it is expected that the introduction section of a project plan will include answers to these questions: What

---

External and internal factors make it urgent to ensure most efficient use of capital funds. Implementation of a project management and control ("PM&C") system has been chosen as one way to improve the use of capital funds. The Corporate Management Committee defined this need.

Subsequently, Corporate Facilities and Manufacturing Planning performed a feasibility study on this subject. A major conclusion of the study was to develop the system internally rather than use a "canned" system. An internally developed system can be tailored to the individual Groups, giving flexibility which is felt to be essential to success. Another conclusion of the study was to involve Group engineering managers in the design and implementation of the system for better understanding and acceptance.

This is the detailed plan for the design and implementation of a corporate-wide PM&C System. The short-term target of the system is major capital projects; the long-term target is other types of projects, such as new product development and R&D projects. The schedule and cost are:

Completion Date: 1 year from approval.

Cost: $200,000, of which $60,000 is out of pocket.

FIGURE 3 Introduction to PM&C program project plan.

type of project is involved? What is the cost-benefit relationship? What are the contingency plans? Why is it being done this way (that is, why were alternatives rejected)? Figure 3 not only illustrates this approach, but is the executive summary for the Heublein PM&C system.

Objectives

Goals for a project at Heublein must be stated in terms of deliverable items. To so state a project objective forces the definition of a clear, comprehensible, measurable, and tangible objective. Often, deliverable items resulting from a project are documents. In constructing a residence, is the deliverable item "the house" or is it "the certificate of occupancy"? In the planning stages of a project (which can occur during the project as well as at the beginning), asking this question is as important as getting the answer. Also, defining the project in terms of the deliverables tends to reduce the number of items which are forgotten. Thus, the Heublein PM&C concept of objectives can be seen to be similar to a "statement of work" and is not meant to encompass specifications (detailed descriptions of the attributes of a deliverable item) which can be included as appendices to the objectives of the project.

Figure 4 shows the objectives stated for the Heublein PM&C program. It illustrates one of the principles set for objective statement: that they be hierarchically structured, starting with general statements and moving to increasingly more detailed particular statements. When both particular and general objectives are defined, it is imperative that there be a logical connection; the particular must be in support of the general.

Project Structure

Having a definition of deliverables, the project manager needs explicit structuring of the project to:

- Relate the specific objectives to the general.
- Define the elements which comprise the deliverables.
- Define the activities which yield the elements and deliverables as their output.
- Show the hierarchical relationship among objectives, elements, and activities.

The work breakdown structure (WBS) is the tool used to meet these needs. While the WBS may be represented in either indented (textual) or tree (graphical) formats, the graphic tree format has the advantage of easy comprehension at all levels. The tree version of the WBS also has the considerable advantage that entries may be made in the nodes ("boxes") to indicate charge account numbers, accountable staff, etc.

Figure 5 is a portion of the indented WBS for the PM&C Program, showing the nature of the WBS in general and the structure of the PM&C Program project in particular. At this point we can identify the component elements and the activities necessary to achieve them. A hierarchical numbering system was applied to the elements of the WBS, which is always a convenience. The 22 Design Phase Reports (2100 series in Figure 5) speak for themselves, but it is important to note that this WBS is the original WBS: All of these reports, analyses, and determinations were defined prior to starting the program and there were no requirements for additional items.

General Objectives

1. Enable better communication between Group and Corporate management with regard to the progress of major projects.
2. Enable Group management to more closely monitor the progress of major projects.
3. Provide the capability for Group personnel to better manage and control major projects.

Specific Objectives[a]

1. Reporting and Control System
   - For communication of project activity with Group and between Group and Corporate.
   - Initially for high-cost capital projects, then for "critical," then all others.
2. Procedures Manual
   - Document procedures and policies.
   - Preliminary manual available for use in general educational seminars.
3. Computer Support Systems
   - Survey with recommendations to establish need for and value of computer support.
4. General Educational Package
   - Provide basic project planning and control skills to personnel directly involved in project management, to be conducted by academic authority in field.
   - Technical seminars in construction, engineering, contract administration, and financial aspects of project management.

[a]Defined at the PM&C Workshop, attended by representatives of Operating Groups.

FIGURE 4   Objectives of PM&C program.

Activity	PM&C Mgr	Consultant	Mgrs. of Eng.				Dir F&MP
			FS/F	GPG	Wines	Spirits	
Program Plan	I	P					A
Design-Phase Reports	I	P	P	P	P	P	
Procedures Manual	I						A
Reporting & Control System	I	P	P	P	P	P	
Computer Support Survey	I	P					P
Project Planning & Control Seminar	A	I					P
Technical Seminars	I		P	P	P	P	A
Legend: I: Initiate/Responsibility							
A: Approve							
P: Provide input							

FIGURE 8 Accountability matrix for PM&C program.

name to be mapped to the task or element of the WBS, and it is good practice to place the name of the responsible entity or person in the appropriate node on the WBS.

However, accountability may have multiple levels below the top level of complete responsibility. Some individuals or functions may have approval power, veto power without approval power, others may be needed for information or advice, etc. Often, such multilevel accountability crosses functional and/or geographical boundaries and hence communication becomes of great importance.

A tool which has proved of considerable value to Heublein where multilevel accountability and geographical dispersion of project staff is common is the "accountability matrix," which is shown in Figure 8.

The accountability matrix reflects considerable thought about the strategy of the program. In fact, one of its great advantages is that it forces the originator (usually the project manager) to think through the process of implementation. Some individuals must be involved because their input is essential. For example, all engineering managers were essential inputs to establish the exact nature of their needs. On the other hand, some individuals or departments are formally involved to enlist their support, even though a satisfactory program could be defined without them.

Control System

The basic loop of feedback for control is shown in Figure 9. This rationale underlies all approaches to controlling projects. Given that a plan (or budget) exists, we then must know what is performance (or actual); a comparison of the two may give a variance. If a variance exists, then the cause of the variance must be sought. Note that any variance is a call for review; as experienced project managers are well aware, underspending or early completions may be as unsatisfactory as overspending and late completions.

The PM&C program did not involve large purchases, or for that matter, many purchases. Nor were large numbers of people

working on different tasks to be kept track of and coordinated. Thus, it was possible to control the PM&C Program through the use of Gantt conventions, using schedule bars to show plan and filling them in to show performance. Progress was tracked on a periodic basis, once a week.

Figure 10 shows the timing of the periodic reviews for control purpose and defines the nature of the reports used.

Milestones and Schedule Subdivisions

Milestones and Schedule Subdivisions are a part of the control system. Of the set of events which can be, milestones form a limited subset of events, in practice rarely exceeding 20 at any given level. The milestones are predetermined times (or performance states) at which the feedback loop of control described above (Figure 9) should be exercised. Other subdivisions of the project are possible, milestones simply being a subdivision by events. Periodic time subdivisions may be made, or division into phases, one of the most common. Figure 11 shows the milestones for the PM&C Program.

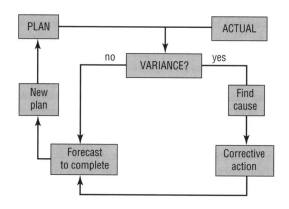

FIGURE 9 The basic feedback loop of control.

1. Periodic status checking will be performed monthly.
2. Labor costs will be collected manually and estimated where necessary from discussion with Group engineering management.
3. Out-of-pocket costs will be collected through commitments and/or invoice payment records.
4. Monthly status reports will be issued by the PM&C Program project manager including:
   a. Cost to date summaries.
   b. Cost variances.
   c. Schedule performance relative to schedule in Gantt format.
   d. Changes in scope or other modifications to plan.
5. Informal control will be exercised through milestone anticipation by the PM&C Program project manager.

FIGURE 10 Control system.

Summary

The Heublein PM&C Program met the conditions for a successful project in the sense that it was completed on time and within the budgeted funds. As is so often the case, the existence of a formal plan and continuing reference to it made it possible to deal with changes of scope. Initial reaction to the educational package was so favorable that the population of attendees was increased by Group executives and engineering managers.

To deliver on time and within budget, but to deliver a product which does not serve the client's needs, is also unsatisfactory. Did this PM&C Program achieve the "General Objectives" of Figure 4? As is so often the case in managerial systems and educational programs, we are forced to rely on the perceptions of the clients. In this PM&C Program, the clients are Corporate Management, Group Management, and most importantly, the Managers of Engineering and their staffs. In the short run, the latter two operational clients are primary. In addition to informal feedback from them, formal feedback was obtained in the form of Impact Statements (item number 4000 in the WBS of Figure 5). The Impact Statements concerned the impact of the PM&C Program on the concerned organization ("How many labor-hours are expected to be devoted to the PM&C System?") and response to the PM&C Program ("Has this been of value to you in doing your job better?").

Clearly, the response of perceived value from the operating personnel was positive. Can we measure the improvement which we believe to be taking place in the implementation of capital and other projects? It may be years before the impact (positive or negative) can be evaluated, and even then there may be such confounding with internal and external variables that no unequivocal, quantified response can be defined.

At this point we base our belief in the value of the PM&C Program on the continuing flow—starting with Impact Statements—of positive perceptions. The following is an example of such a response, occurring one year after the exposure of the respondent:

> . . . find attached an R&D Project Tracking Diagram developed as a direct result of the [PM&C] seminar . . . last year. [In the seminar we called it] a Network Analysis Diagram. The Product Development Group has been using this exclusively to track projects. Its value has been immeasurable. Since its inception, fifteen new products have gone through the sequence. . . .

Date	Description
Feb 5	Program plan approved by both Corporate & Groups
Feb 26	Reporting and control system approved by Corporate and Groups
Mar 5	Organizational impact analysis report issued
Apr 7	Basic project planning and control seminars completed
Aug 24	Final procedures manual approved Technical Seminars completed Computer support systems survey completed
Nov 30	Final impact assessment report issued

FIGURE 11 Milestones.

Questions

1. Which of the project planning aids described in the chapter was used in the case?
2. How did their project plan differ from the project charter described in the chapter?
3. How did their WBS differ from that described in the chapter? How did their accountability matrix differ?
4. What was wrong with the previous focus on cost-benefit? Does the PM&C system still include a cost-benefit analysis?
5. Why did lagging depreciation legislation increase the importance of using capital funds optimally?
6. What do you think of developing a system that accommodates the unique needs of each group versus developing a more standardized system? What are the advantages and disadvantages of each approach?

The following reading updates the practical applications of Agile in terms of adjusting and combining it with other approaches including the traditional waterfall method taught in most textbooks. It also emphasizes the changes that are needed in project transitioning to Agile, not only within the team but also within the organization as well as outside stakeholders. Last, it illustrates the application of Agile to other applications beyond the original software programming area.

Reading

The Evolution of Agile[2]   S. F. Gale

Agile has inexorably changed the project management landscape. That's largely due to its adaptability: Iterative development allows teams to deliver functional pieces of a project quickly and adjust on the fly.

Now project managers are taking adaptability to the next level, blending methodologies to make new agile hybrids.

"I don't believe that agile or Scrum is always the right choice," says Børge Haugset, research scientist at SINTEF ICT, a research organization in Trondheim, Norway. "Quite the opposite: When highly skilled teams can pick and choose the tools and rules that work for them, they can hit gold."

To break out of the typical agile framework, teams can use workflow boards from lean manufacturing process, Kanban, or task backlogs borrowed from Scrum. And more often than not, that combination includes traditional practices such as those in *A Guide to the Project Management Body of Knowledge* (*PMBOK® Guide*), says Mike Cottmeyer, founder and president of LeadingAgile, an agile consultancy in Atlanta, Georgia, USA.

Hybrid Toolbox

Agile: Short iterations of work are delivered with little up-front documentation of specs or requirements. Frequent delivery aims to ensure visibility of progress, creating opportunities for real-time feedback and changes in scope throughout the life cycle.

Kanban: Tasks are placed on a physical board to create a workflow that shows team members what needs to be accomplished and in what order. The idea is to encourage small, continuous changes and consensus-based decision-making without the constant oversight of a leader.

Scrum: Project leaders create a prioritized backlog of tasks which teams deliver in sprints, implementing groups of tasks from the top down. Each sprint has a defined time-line, after which working iterations are shared with the customer, who then offers feedback. Daily meetings, or scrums, are used to keep tabs on progress.

Rapid Application Development: Software development teams quickly produce prototypes, followed by writing small pieces of code with less planning.

Waterfall: Projects proceed sequentially through a series of phases beginning with written specs or system requirements, and moving through design, implementation, testing and release. Phases can last for weeks or months.

Even though an agile hybrid model may not have the fine-grained project plans of a traditional waterfall environment, teams still need to meet schedule, budget and ROI expectations.

"That's where the *PMBOK® Guide* comes in," Mr. Cottmeyer says, drawing parallels between rolling-wave planning and project roadmaps. "You don't know what you need until you need it. But the further out you plan, the more abstract you have to be. It's thinking about traditional project portfolio management in smaller increments."

Raya, an IT company in Cairo, Egypt, is a hybrid convert. The company realized its waterfall approach wasn't allowing its teams to consistently deliver projects with the expected quality and timeliness. So it implemented agile, and the transition went well—at first, says Ali Zewail, general manager of software development and technology services at Raya. His team launched two major software development projects as agile pilots. Both met budget goals, one came in ahead of the deadline, and customers were pleased with the results.

But the next projects didn't deliver the same stellar results, and the novelty of the new approach started to wear off.

"There was a real learning curve that we had to accept," Mr. Zewail admits. "We had to change our mindset and our corporate culture if we were going to really be agile for the long term."

Project leaders opted for a hybrid approach, applying strategies from the *PMBOK® Guide* to the company's agile formula. Teams began using audits and lessons learned, and established measures of project success to create accountability and ensure that teams were adopting the same techniques across the enterprise.

No Longer Buried in Paperwork

One of agile's basic tenets is to require less documentation and fewer defined specifications at the front end of the project, instead of relying upon constant tweaking throughout the life cycle. The goal is to free project team members from the need to document everything so they can focus on quickly producing high-quality deliverables.

"Too much focus on documentation can be difficult to maintain, especially if documentation is seen as an 'extra chore' by many agile developers," Mr. Haugset says. "On the other hand, too little documentation makes the project more difficult to understand, especially if key components are undocumented."

Adopting an agile hybrid lets teams adapt the documentation processes as the project progresses. At the outset, when ideas are broadly defined and changes anticipated, less documentation is required. But as iterations are completed and reviewed with the client, the scope narrows and the need for documentation is more evident.

Mr. Haugset uses traditional quality-assurance tests to help shape the documentation process to ensure problems don't go unnoticed and that the project remains strategically aligned to organizational goals. These tests are conducted during reviews to evaluate the inputs, functionality and expected outputs of each iteration.

---

[2] Reprinted from PM Network with permission. Copyright Project Management Institute Inc.

Transition Tips

My project team is in the planning stages of transitioning to an agile environment from a more traditional, waterfall-style environment. Recognizing that becoming agile is more of a paradigm shift than a simple implementation of a collection of processes, we are developing a strategy document that lays out the progression from current state to desired future state.

Accordingly, I'm curious as to whether anyone has experience driving the transformation to agile, and if any light can be shed on the timing and sequence of applicable implementation activities. Additionally, any insight into change management frameworks that have helped to facilitate this change would be very much appreciated!

—Matt Lee

I'D SUGGEST taking an agile approach to the transition. You should expect your desired future state definition to change as you gain experience and use retrospectives to figure out what works for your workplace. Keep your strategy document simple, with a focus on what you want to achieve by transitioning to agile.

Our reason to experiment with agile was to resolve ongoing issues with our projects. After the first pilot projects, it was easy to say that an agile approach was addressing these issues and therefore providing real value. When the value is visible and tangible, it is easy to get buy-in to continue the rollout.

For timing, I suggest getting just enough training to get a pilot project team going as soon as you can. That team will give you feedback as to how to proceed.

We've always treated our waterfall-ish project framework with a "do what makes sense for your project" attitude. We are doing the same with agile. I'm on our agile core team. We developed and present our in-house agile training and are assigned as agile coaches as needed. We facilitate sharing knowledge, experience and lessons learned across the project teams. The practice of frequent feedback through retrospectives is a valuable benefit of agile. Use it to tune your processes.

—Rebecca Jahelka

"The tests act as mediators to enhance communication between the client and the team, and to help us jointly define when something is done, meaning the team has made something that runs in a way that the customer understands and agrees upon."

Every time the team completes a sprint, a test is conducted, and the results are added to a database. "It acts as a safety harness to ensure the code is correct," Mr. Haugset says.

Winning Minds

Whatever combination of techniques a project team uses, one constant remains when any element of agile is introduced: Team members must be self-directed, focused, strong communicators and able to make quick decisions.

"The core of the agile philosophy is that people need to talk to each other and work together," Mr. Haugset says. "That requires a lot of trust among the team and an unbelievable amount of customer cooperation."

It also requires more talent and experience than might be necessary in a waterfall environment, where higher-level designers can leave the actual coding to those with less experience. "If you have a detailed spec with clear requirements defined at the beginning of a project, it is simple for any developer to create," he says. "But when you incorporate agile techniques, you shift a lot more responsibility to the team members, so you need them to be able to make the right choices. To do that, they need to be skilled."

Adopting agile in any form also often takes a radical change in attitude—and not just among team members.

"Sometimes the biggest hurdles are political," warns Richard Banfield, CEO of Fresh Tilled Soil, a user experience and interface design firm in Boston, Massachusetts, USA.

Project leaders must devote time to change management, including educating stakeholders. If they don't understand the rapid pace of iterative deliverables, and when and how they will be required to deliver feedback, stakeholders can logjam the process.

Pivot Points

Organizations should always be looking for trouble—and shift their project management approach accordingly.

If a project team is experiencing unexpected bottlenecks, for example, it could implement a Kanban workflow board so everyone involved can see, at a glance, how the project is progressing. Team members can then choose tasks that best align with their skill set and the project's need in real time—rather than waiting for a team leader to assign them.

Or, on smaller projects when the need for a deliverable model is more urgent, team members can apply rapid application development techniques and construct prototypes to flesh out user requirements in a "feature-light" version that serves as a proof of concept.

"The key is being able to recognize that when something doesn't work, try something else," says Richard Banfield, Fresh Tilled Soil, Boston, Massachusetts, USA.

Mr. Banfield's team learned that lesson last year when it started to rebuild the foundation application for Communispace, a social marketing and research platform, using a purely agile process.

The project team delivered frequent iterations that required a steady stream of stakeholder feedback. But the client required more time to respond because of the number of stakeholders.

The project team adapted, slowing its sprints from 2 to 4 weeks to get the client's leadership team accustomed to the process.

"As they got more comfortable, we were able to speed things back up," Mr. Banfield says.

To avoid such delays, he now begins many projects with an educational phase for leadership teams. "We have to be sensitive to the client structure and customer satisfaction," Mr. Banfield says.

It takes time to adapt—and a hybrid approach can work as a stepping stone.

"Project managers and developers need to understand that agile isn't a set of unbreakable laws," Mr. Banfield says. "It's about using what works and recognizing that there will always be exceptions."

Because in the end, being able to adapt is the essence of any agile process.

Agile Branches Out

Agile project management is the brainchild of the software development world, but that doesn't mean it's not applicable in other fields. These days, agile is used on projects spanning an array of sectors, from construction to event planning.

"Agile can help any organization improve its delivery capacity," says Karen White, PMP, PMI Fellow, Weare, New Hampshire, USA-based author of Agile Project Management: A Mandate for the 21st Century. *"Smaller companies that don't have the capacity for traditional project management can apply the concepts of agile project management techniques to better manage their projects."*

Daily stand-up meetings—a cornerstone of agile—help companies "identify the day's priorities and discuss concerns without wasting a lot of time," says Ms. White, principal of Applied Agility, an agile project management consulting company supporting not-for-profit and small businesses.

Agile enables teams to focus on near-term tasks, even when the project is a wine tasting event months away, as was recently the case with Ms. White. Instead of spending valuable resource time on ticket sales (which wouldn't occur for another several weeks), she led the planning committee through a series of sprints focused on near-term objectives such as finding volunteers, choosing the venue and planning logistics.

"It's about approaching the project in little chunks, looking at what you can get done today and worrying about the other stuff later," she says.

Questions

1. Contrast Agile with Scrum in terms of structure and frequency of delivery.
2. Can project teams switch from traditional Waterfall to Agile by themselves? What will happen if they try?
3. Is there a danger in abandoning plans and documentation with Agile?
4. The "Agile branches out" sidebar points out that Agile is even used in construction. What types of construction would probably not?

Budgeting and Risk Management

In Chapter 6, we reviewed the planning process and gave some guidelines for designing the project plan. We now begin our discussion of **PMBOK** knowledge area 4: *Project Cost Management*. We treat the subject here in terms of planning (or budgeting) for the costs of project resources, but we will reconsider the issue in Chapter 9 when we discuss the allocation of resources to project tasks.

Chapter 7

First priority is, of course, obtaining resources with which to do the work. Here, the Project Manager (PM) needs to work with the project owner and the project sponsor to develop a budget that will be acceptable to the funder and/or the project steering committee representing senior management. Senior management approval of the project budget does exactly that. A budget is a plan for allocating resources. Thus, the act of budgeting is the allocation of scarce resources to the various endeavors of an organization. The outcomes of the allocation process often do not satisfy managers of the organization who must live and work under budget constraints. It is, however, precisely the pattern of constraints in a budget that embodies organizational policy. The degree to which the different activities of an organization are fully supported by an allocation of resources is one measure of the importance placed on the outcome of the activity. Most of the senior managers we know try hard to be evenhanded in the budgetary process, funding each planned activity at the "right" level—neither overfunding, which produces waste and encourages slack management, nor underfunding, which inhibits accomplishment and frustrates the committed.

The budget is not simply one facet of a plan, nor is it merely an expression of organizational policy; it is also a monitoring and control mechanism. The budget serves as a standard for comparison, a baseline from which to measure the difference between the actual and planned uses of resources. As the manager directs the deployment of resources to accomplish some desired objective, resource usage should be monitored carefully. This allows deviations from planned usage to be checked against the progress of the project, and exception reports can be generated if resource expenditures are not consistent with accomplishments. Indeed, the pattern of deviations (variances) can be examined to see if it is possible, or reasonable, to forecast significant departures from the budget. We illustrate this process in Chapter 10 when we discuss the use of "earned value" (costs derived from the project budget) to monitor and control the project and forecast the project completion time and costs. With sufficient warning, it is sometimes possible to implement corrective actions. In any event, such forecasting helps to decrease the number of undesirable surprises for senior management.

But be warned! The budget expended (resource usage) does not measure the actual level of work completed on the project. The budget alone, therefore, is not a sufficient measure of a project's progress. Budgets play an important role in the entire process of management. It is clear that budgeting procedures must associate resource use with the achievement of organizational goals, or the planning/control process becomes useless. If budgets are not tied to achievement, management may ignore situations where funds are being spent far in advance of accomplishment but are within budget when viewed by time period. Similarly, management may misinterpret the true state of affairs when the budget is overspent for a given time period, but outlays are appropriate for the level of task completion. Data must be collected and reported in a timely manner, or the value of the budget in identifying and reporting current problems or anticipating upcoming problems will be lost. The reporting process must be carefully designed and controlled. It is of no value if the data are sent to the wrong person or the reports take an inordinately long time to be processed through the system. For example, one manager of a now defunct, large computer company complained that, based on third-quarter reports, he was instructed to act so as to alter the fourth-quarter results. However, he did not receive the instructions until the first quarter of the following year.

In Chapter 6, we described a planning process that integrated the planning done at different levels of the project in the work breakdown structure (WBS). If we cost the WBS, step by step, we develop a project budget. Viewed in this way, *the budget is a reflection of the WBS in another form.*

Let us now consider some of the various budgeting methods used in organizations. These are described in general first, then with respect to projects. We also address some problems of cost estimation, with attention to the details and pitfalls. We consider some of the special demands and concerns with budgeting for projects. Next, we present some techniques for improving one's skills at budget and cost estimation or estimating and forecasting of any kind. Printouts of project budgets from project management software packages will be shown in Chapter 10, where we cover project management information systems. Finally, we address the issue of risk in budgeting through the use of simulation.

7.1 | Estimating Project Budgets

In order to develop a budget, we must forecast what resources the project will require, the required quantity of each, when they will be needed, and how much they will cost, including the effects of potential price inflation. Uncertainty is involved in any forecast, though some forecasts have less uncertainty than others. An experienced cost estimator can forecast the number of bricks that will be used to construct a brick wall of known dimensions within 1 to 2 percent. The errors, however, are apt to be much larger for an estimate of the number of programmer hours or lines of code that will be required to produce a specific piece of software. While the field of software science makes such estimates possible, the level of uncertainty is considerably higher, and the typical error size is much larger.

In many fields, cost-estimating methods are well codified. For example, in fields such as construction, costs can often be estimated by *scaling* the various cost elements appropriately. For example, building 1 mile of a four-lane road can be estimated from the individual cost elements of previously constructed two-lane roads—for example, the asphalt cost may be double while the cost of the road's shoulders may be the same. Similarly, *parametric estimating* relies on well-known statistical correlations between various factors such as the total cost of a house relative to the square feet of living area. The databases of purchasing departments include multitudes of information devoted to the techniques of estimating the quantities of materials and labor required to accomplish specific jobs. In addition, on the Internet are links detailing what materials, services, and machines are available and from whom. Every business has its own rules of thumb for cost estimating. These usually distill the collective experience gained by many estimators over many years. An experienced producer of books, for example, can leaf through a manuscript and, after asking a few questions about the number and type of illustrations and the quality of paper to be used, can make a fairly accurate estimate of what it will cost to produce a book.

Project Management in Practice

Pathfinder Mission to Mars—on a Shoestring

In 1976, NASA's two Viking Mars-lander missions took 6 years and $3 billion (in 1992 dollars) to develop. Twenty-one years later, Mars Pathfinder and Sojourner Rover landed on Mars once again, but at a development cost of only $175 million, representing a whopping 94 percent cost reduction over the earlier mission. This amazing cost reduction was achieved through a variety of means, but the most important was perhaps the philosophical one that this was a design-to-cost project rather than a design-to-performance project. Given this philosophy, the scope of the mission was intentionally limited and "scope-creep" was never an issue:

- to achieve a successful landing
- return of engineering telemetry
- acquisition and transmission of a *single*, partial panoramic image
- successful rover deployment and 7 sol (Martian day) operation on the surface
- completion of a 30 sol lander mission meeting all engineering, science, and technology objectives
- one successful alpha proton X-ray spectrometer measurement of a Martian rock and soil sample.

The means of limiting the cost of the mission were multiple and creative:

- development was cost-capped, with no opportunity for more funds

The Pathfinder Rover explores Martian terrain.
NASA/JPL

- identifying a set of "de-scope" options, which could be implemented in case the cost grew beyond the fixed budget
- mission, flight, and ground systems designs were driven by existing hardware and system capability
- a project cash reserve of 27 percent of the total budget was held back and carefully planned for time-phased release throughout the duration of the project
- mission designers/builders transitioned into the testers/operators to save documentation, time, labor cost, and chance of error
- existing NASA mission infrastructure was used rather than designing new systems
- instituting time-phased "what if" and lien lists for real or potential current and anticipated items of cost growth during the project
- choosing to use a "single-string" but higher risk design and offsetting the risk by using more-reliable parts
- 70 percent of major procurements contracts were fixed-price rather than cost-plus
- creative procurement, such as existing equipment spares, and accounting, such as lower burden rate personnel

On July 5, the Mars Sojourner Rover rolled down its deployment ramp, and the resulting pictures made the headlines on newspapers around the world. The mission continued for almost 3 months and returned 2.6 gigabites of scientific and engineering data, 16,000 lander camera images, 550 rover camera images, 8.5 million environmental measurements, and the results of 16 chemical rock/soil experiments and 10 technology rover experiments.

Questions

1. How did a change in philosophy make such a drastic difference in project cost?
2. Why was the mission scope so limited? Why even spend the money to go to Mars with such limited objectives?
3. Describe their "de-scope," "lien list," and "cash reserve" approaches.
4. Recent design-to-cost interplanetary projects have also had some spectacular failures. Is this the natural result of this new philosophy?

Source: C. Sholes and N. Chalfin, "Mars Pathfinder Mission," *PM Network*, Vol. 13.

We will have more to say about gathering budget data shortly. Before doing so, however, it is helpful to understand that developing project budgets is much more difficult than developing budgets for more permanent organizational activities. The influence of history is strong in the budget of an ongoing activity. Many entries are simply "last year's figure plus X percent," where X is any number the budgeter feels "can be lived with" and is probably acceptable to the person or group who approves the budgets.

While the project budgeter cannot always depend on tradition as a basis for estimating the current project budget, it is not uncommon for the budgeter to have budgets and audit reports for similar past projects to serve as guides. Although we maintain that all projects are unique, many are not very different from their predecessors and can serve as reasonable guides when forecasting current project budgets. In these cases, analogous estimating may be helpful where historical data from past similar projects is used to estimate aspects of the current project such as the duration of activities or the cost of key resources.

Tradition also aids the estimation process in another way. In the special case of R&D projects, it has been found that project budgets are stable over time when measured as a percent of the total allocation to R&D from the parent firm, though within the project, the budget may be reallocated among activities. There is no reason to believe that the situation is different for other kinds of projects, and we have some evidence that shows stability similar to that of R&D projects.

This notion has been formalized in the practice of "life cycle costing." The life cycles of past projects are studied as models for the way costs accrue over the life cycles of similar projects. Given information about costs during the early life of a project, the model can be used to forecast the total cost over the project's life cycle.[1]

A more interesting estimation technique that also depends on actual costs early in the life of a project is based on earned value analysis (Zwikael et al., 2000). (For a description of earned value analysis, see Chapter 10.) Early actual costs on a project are compared to their estimates, and the remaining costs are adjusted by assuming a constant actual-to-estimate cost ratio. The assumption of a constant ratio gives the lowest average estimation error (11 percent) of the five different predictors tested.

For multiyear projects, another problem is raised. The plans and schedules for such projects are set at the beginning of project life, but over the years, the forecast resource usage may be altered by the availability of alternate or new materials, machinery, or personnel—available at different costs than were estimated, giving rise to both the risk of inflation and technological risk. The longer the project life, the less the project manager (PM) can trust that traditional methods and costs will be relevant.

Tradition has still another impact on project budgeting. Every organization has its idiosyncrasies. One firm charges the project's R&D budget with the cost of training sales representatives on the technical aspects of a new product. Another adopts special property accounting practices for contracts with the government. Unless the PM understands the organizational accounting system, there is no way to exercise budgetary control over the project. The methods for project budgeting described next are intended to avoid these problems as much as possible, but complete avoidance is out of the question. The PM simply must be familiar with the organization's accounting system!

One aspect of cost estimation and budgeting that is not often discussed has to do with the *actual* use of resources as opposed to the accounting department's assumptions about how and when the resources will be used. For instance, suppose that you have estimated that $5,000 of a given resource will be used in accomplishing a task that is expected to

---

[1]We do not demonstrate it here, but Crystal Ball® can fit distributions to historical data. This is done by selecting the *F*it button in CB's Distribution Gallery window. Then specify the location of the data. CB considers a wide variety of probability distributions and offers the user optional goodness-of-fit tests—see the Crystal Ball® *User Manual*.

require 5 weeks. The actual use of the resource may be none in the first week, $3,000 worth in the second week, none in the third week, $1,500 in the fourth week, and the remaining $500 in the last week. Unless this pattern of expenditure is detailed in the plan, the accounting department, which takes a linear view of the world, will spread the expenditure equally over the 5-week period. This may not affect the project's budget, but it most certainly affects the project's cash flow, a matter of major interest to the firm's comptroller. In the reading "Three Perceptions of Project Cost" at the end of this chapter, these three different views of costs and the problems they often cause are described in detail. The PM must be aware of not only the resource requirements and the specific time pattern of resource usage, but also how the expenses will affect their firm's cash flows. This subject will be revisited in Chapter 9.

Another aspect of preparing budgets is especially important for project budgeting. Every expenditure (or receipt) must be identified with a specific project task (and with its associated milestone, as we will see in the next chapter). Each element in the WBS has a unique account number to which charges are accrued as work is done. These identifiers are needed for the PM to exercise budgetary control.

With these things in mind, the issue of how to gather input data for the budget becomes a matter of some concern. There are two fundamentally different strategies for data gathering, top-down and bottom-up.

Top-Down Budgeting

This strategy is based on collecting the judgments and experiences of top and middle managers, and available past data concerning similar activities. These managers estimate overall project cost as well as the costs of the major subprojects that comprise it. These cost estimates are then given to lower-level managers, who are expected to continue the breakdown into budget estimates for the specific tasks and work packages that comprise the subprojects. This process continues to the lowest level.

The process parallels the hierarchical planning process described in the previous chapter. The budget, similarly to the project, is broken down into successively finer detail, starting from the top, or most aggregated level following the WBS. It is presumed that lower-level managers will argue for more funds if the budget allocation they have been granted is, in their judgment, insufficient for the tasks assigned. This presumption is, however, often incorrect. Instead of reasoned debate, argument sometimes ensues, or simply sullen silence. When senior managers insist on maintaining their budgetary positions—based on "considerable past experience"—junior managers feel forced to accept what they perceive to be insufficient allocations to achieve the objectives to which they must commit.

Discussions between the authors and a large number of managers support the contention that lower-level managers often treat the entire budgeting process as if it were a "zero-sum game," a game in which any individual's gain is another individual's loss. Competition among junior managers is often quite intense.

The advantage of this top-down process is that aggregate budgets can often be developed quite accurately, though a few individual elements may be significantly in error. Not only are budget categories stable as a percent of the total budget, the statistical distribution of each category (e.g., 5 percent for R&D) is also stable, making for high predictability. Another advantage of the top-down process is that small yet costly tasks need not be individually identified, nor need it be feared that some small but important aspect has been overlooked. The experience and judgment of the executive are presumed automatically to factor all such elements into the overall estimate. Questions put to subordinates, however, indicate that senior management has a strong bias toward underestimating costs.

Project Management in Practice

Convention Security: Project Success through Budget Recovery

For the Democratic National Convention (DNC) in Denver, Colorado, the 1010-person Colorado State Patrol (CSP) was charged with providing security for an expected 80,000 people, plus 32 governors, many members of Congress, and the presidential entourage. Specific security assignments were state buildings and adjacent areas; dignitary protection for members of Congress, governors, and candidates' families; and assisting with traffic and crowd control including closing of roads and freeways during rush hour, all in addition to their regular statutory patrol duties throughout the state. Yet, the budget was tight and resources carefully rationed. In addition, they had to work with a mass of other agencies, including the Secret Service, FBI, Federal Emergency Management Agency, and of course, the Denver Police Department. Moreover, CSP was not in control of the project and had to meld its plans and activities with the other agencies.

Fortunately, CSP had recently established a Project Management Office (PMO), which jumped into action when the charge came through. The PMO checked with other cities about how they had done their planning and executed their responsibilities. Using this information, they set up subcommittees to plan activities and evaluate the risks regarding staffing, budget, scheduling, crowd control, communications, etc. which resulted in a 600+ page plan regarding 72 different risk factors and 61 stakeholders. Since CSP was not the primary decision-maker, they had to develop multiple plans with alternate contingencies. In their planning process, they found that sometimes it was going to be necessary to agree to disagree and that somebody—not always the same person—was going to have to make the difficult calls.

As each day of the convention arrived, all the agencies coordinated on changes in strategies and plans. For example, CSP had planned on using 200 troopers for the convention, but found they needed over 500! This required a major rebalancing act, changing plans and duties of the CSP members to execute their charge while also providing adequate patrol services across the state. Project management tools played a major role in this rebalancing by handling procurement costs, equipment management such as the logistics for food and weapons for the troopers, identifying where resources could be borrowed from other agencies, and then tracking their use for proper return, etc. These same project tools allowed CSP to afterward track documents and costs and records such as timesheets and reports so they could accurately pay invoices, reimbursements, and overtime charges. As it turned out, CSP successfully met all its task duties while meeting its cost goal of staying within 10 percent of initial cost projections!

Questions

1. **How is a project for an event such as a multi-day convention different from a project such as building a house?**

2. **Does 72 different risk factors seem like a lot to plan for? How important was CSP's contingency planning for this project?**

3. **How does not being in control of decisions and plans affect the PM?**

4. **Does being off by 150 percent in the estimate for human resources required for a project surprise you? What do you think happened? How do you think they managed to accommodate this change without exceeding the budget?**

Source: S. Greengard, "Unconventional Thinking," *PM Network*, Vol. 24.

Bottom-Up Budgeting

In this method, elemental tasks, their schedules, and their individual budgets are constructed, again following the WBS. The people doing the work are consulted regarding times and budgets for the tasks to ensure the best level of accuracy. Initially, estimates are made in terms of resources, such as labor hours and materials. These are later converted to dollar equivalents. Standard analytic tools such as learning curve analysis and work sampling are employed where appropriate to improve the estimates. Differences of opinion are resolved by the usual discussions between senior and junior managers. If necessary, the PM and the functional manager(s) may enter the discussion in order to ensure the accuracy of the estimates. The resulting task budgets are aggregated to give the total direct costs of the project. The PM adds such indirect costs as general and administrative (G&A), possibly a project *reserve* for contingencies, and then a profit figure to arrive at the final project budget.

7.2.2.6

As described in **PMBOK**, a *reserve analysis* is typically done for the risks in a project that might escalate the costs. The reserve is included within the baseline budget and is known as a *contingency* reserve. It is for the "known unknowns" in the project where the defined responses to the risks are detailed, but their amounts are not yet precisely known. The contingency amounts can be for individual activities, either a percentage or fixed amount, which would then be aggregated for the entire project and added to the baseline budget, or could just be a percentage of the entire baseline budget, such as 7 percent, or both.

There is also a *management* reserve, which is not part of the baseline budget and is intended for the "unknown unknowns." In either case, the reserves are checked as the project progresses and may need to be increased (permission must be requested) if new risks are discovered, or decreased and released for other projects, if the risks are avoided. Finally, there are also *time* reserves that work exactly like the cost reserves. These are described in **PMBOK** as well. It is more common with time reserves to have both activity buffers *and* a project buffer.

6.5.2.6

Bottom-up budgets should be, and usually are, more accurate in the detailed tasks, but it is critical that all elements be included. It is far more difficult to develop a complete list of tasks when constructing that list from the bottom up than from the top down. Just as the top-down method may lead to budgetary game playing, the bottom-up process has its unique managerial budget games. For example, individuals overstate their resource needs because they suspect that higher management will probably cut all budgets. Their suspicion is, of course, quite justified, as Gagnon (1987) and others have shown. Managers who are particularly persuasive sometimes win, but those who are consistently honest and have high credibility win more often.

The advantages of the bottom-up process are those generally associated with participative management. Individuals closer to the work are apt to have a more accurate idea of resource requirements than their superiors or others not personally involved. In addition, the direct involvement of low-level managers in budget preparation increases the likelihood that they will accept the result with a minimum of grumbling. Involvement also is a good managerial training technique, giving junior managers valuable experience in budget preparation as well as the knowledge of the operations required to generate a budget.

While top-down budgeting is common, true bottom-up budgets are rare. Senior managers see the bottom-up process as risky. They tend not to be particularly trusting of ambitious subordinates who may overstate resource requirements in an attempt to ensure success and build empires. Besides, as senior managers note with some justification, the budget is the most important tool for control of the organization. They are understandably reluctant to hand over that control to subordinates whose experience and motives are questionable. This attitude is carried to an extreme in one large corporation that conducts several dozen projects simultaneously, each of which may last 5 to 8 years and cost millions of dollars. PMs do not participate in the budgeting process in this company, nor did they, until recently, have access to project budgets during their tenure as PMs. Reconciling top-down with bottom-up budgets is obviously an area where the earlier principles of negotiation and conflict management, as described in Chapter 4, would be useful.

Work Element Costing

The actual process of building a project budget—either top-down or bottom-up or, as we will suggest, a combination of both—tends to be a straightforward but tedious process. While the budget may include revenues (e.g., milestone payments by the client), the major task in creating the budget is estimating the costs for each of the project's work elements. Basically, each work element in the WBS is evaluated for its resource requirements, and the cost of each resource is estimated. We discuss this in more detail next and then give some suggestions for ways to improve the cost-estimating process in Section 7.2.

Suppose that a work element is estimated to require 25 hours of labor by a technician. The specific technician assigned to this job is paid $17.50/hr. Overhead charges to the project are 84 percent of direct labor charges. The appropriate cost appears to be

$$25 \text{ hr} \times \$17.50 \times 1.84 = \$805.00$$

but the accuracy of this calculation depends on the precise assumptions behind the 25-hour estimate. Industrial engineers have noted that during a normal 8-hour day, no one actually works for all 8 hours. Even on an assembly line, workers need breaks called "personal time." This covers such activities as visiting the water cooler, the restroom, making a call home, blowing one's nose, and all the other time-consuming activities engaged in by normal people in a normal workplace. A typical allowance for personal time is 12 percent of total work time. If personal time was not included in the 25-hour estimate made earlier, then the cost calculation becomes

$$1.12 \times 25 \text{ hr} \times \$17.50 \times 1.84 = \$901.60 \text{ [2]}$$

The uncertainty in labor cost estimating lies in the estimate of hours to be expended. Not including personal time ensures an underestimate.

Direct costs for resources and machinery are charged directly to the project and are not usually subject to overhead charges. If a specific machine is needed by the project and is the property of a functional department, the project may "pay" for it by transferring funds from the project budget to the functional department's budget. The charge for such machines will be an operating cost ($/hr or $/operating cycle), plus a depreciation charge based on either time or number of operating cycles. Use of general office equipment, for example, copy machines, drafting equipment, and coffeemakers, is often included in the general overhead charge.

In addition to these charges, there is the *General and Administrative (G&A)* charge. This is composed of the cost of senior management, the various staff functions, and any other expenses not included in overhead. G&A charges are a fixed percent of either the direct costs or the total of all direct and indirect costs.

Project Management in Practice

Managing Costs at Massachusetts' Neighborhood Health Plan

In just a 2-year period, Medicaid reduced its rate of reimbursement by 20 percent while the State of Massachusetts imposed higher eligibility requirements for health subscribers, thereby significantly reducing Neighborhood Health Plan's (NHP) revenues and threatening its viability. In the past, NHP had controlled costs by controlling hospital bed utilization and increasing preventive medicine. However, no matter how low hospital utilization is, if hospital contract rates are expensive, the cost to NHP will be high. Thus, NHP chartered a project team to help it manage costs through better selection and management of hospital contracts. More specifically, the team's charter was to develop a method to examine hospital contracts to assure that proposed rates were financially viable to NHP but high-quality care would be available when needed.

The team first selected the top 10 to 20 hospitals based on total annual payments from NHP for analysis. From these, they determined that to control costs effectively, NHP's contracting philosophy would have to change from the current 95 percent of all line items per episode to a fixed cost per episode

or per day per type of stay. The team then constructed a spreadsheet that allowed cost comparisons to be made across hospitals, which allowed management to bargain for lower rates or, if hospitals were inflexible, suggest to health centers what alternative hospitals to refer patients to. This and later developments by the team significantly enhanced management's ability to contain their costs while guaranteeing that quality care would be available when needed. It also allowed management to examine and respond to contracts and proposed contract changes in a timely and informed manner.

Questions

1. **Wouldn't higher eligibility requirements for subscribers cut NHP's health-care costs? Why did this exacerbate NHP's situation?**

2. **Explain the trade-off between hospital utilization and contract rates.**

3. **How did changing from a line item pay plan to an episode plan allow comparisons and save costs?**

Source: J. H. Hertenstein and K. A. Vallancourt, "Contract Management = Cost Management," *PM Network*, Vol. 11.

---

[2]In a weak matrix project, the Technical Assistance Group representing the technician would submit a lump-sum charge to the project, calculated in much the same way. The charge would, of course, include the costs noted in the rest of this section.

Thus, a fully costed work element would include direct costs (labor, resources, and special machinery) plus overhead and G&A charges. We advise the PM to prepare two budgets: one with overheads and G&A charges, and one without. The full cost budget is used by the accounting group to estimate the profit earned by the project. The budget that contains only direct costs gives the PM the information required to manage the project without being confounded with costs over which the PM has no control. Let us now consider a combination of top-down and bottom-up budgeting.

An Iterative Budgeting Process—Negotiation-in-Action

In Chapter 6, we recommended an iterative planning process with subordinates[3] developing WBS plans for the tasks for which they were responsible. Superiors review these plans, perhaps suggesting amendments. The strength of this planning technique is that primary responsibility for the design of a task is delegated to the individual accountable for its completion, and thus, it utilizes participative management (or "employee involvement"). If done correctly, estimated resource usage and schedules are a normal part of the planning process at all planning levels. Therefore, the superior constructing a WBS at the highest level would estimate resource requirements and durations for each of the steps in the WBS. Let us refer to the superior's estimate of resource requirements for a particular task as R. Similarly, the subordinate responsible for that task estimates the resource requirements as r.

In a perfect world, R would equal r. We do not, however, live in a perfect world. As a matter of fact, the probable relationship between the original estimates made at the different levels is $R \ll r$. This is true for several reasons, three of which are practically universal. First, the farther one moves up the organizational chart away from immediate responsibility for doing the work, the easier, faster, and cheaper the job looks to the superior than to the one who has to do it. This is because the superior either does not know the details of the task or has conveniently forgotten the details, as well as how long the job takes and how many problems can arise. Second, wishful thinking leads the superior to underestimate cost (and time), because the superior has a stake in representing the project to senior management as a profitable venture. Third, the subordinate is led to build in some level of protection against failure by adding an allowance for "Murphy's Law" onto a budget that already may have a healthy contingency allowance.

Assuming that the superior and subordinate are reasonably honest with one another (any other assumption leads to a failure in win-win negotiations), the two parties meet and review the subordinate's WBS. Usually, the initial step toward reducing the difference in cost estimates is made by the superior who is "educated" by the subordinate in the realities of the job. The result is that the superior's estimate rises. The next step is typically made by the subordinate. Encouraged by the boss's positive response to reason, the subordinate surrenders some of the protection provided for by the budgetary "slop," and the subordinate's estimate falls. The subordinate's cost estimate is still greater than the superior's, but the difference is considerably decreased.

The pair now turn their attention to the technology of the task at hand. They carefully inspect the subordinate's work plan, trying to find a more efficient way to accomplish the desired end. It may be that a major change can be made that allows a lower resource commitment than either originally imagined. It may be that little or no further improvement is possible. Let us assume that moderate improvement is made but that the subordinate's estimate is still somewhat greater than the superior's, although both have been altered by

---

[3]We use the terms "superior" and "subordinate" here for the sole purpose of identifying individuals working on different relative levels of a project's WBS. We recognize that in a matrix organization, it is not uncommon for PMs ("superiors") to delegate work to individuals ("subordinates") who do not report to the PM and who may even be senior to the PM on the parent firm's organizational chart.

the negotiations thus far. What should the superior do, accept the subordinate's estimate or insist that the subordinate make do with the superior's estimate?

In order to answer this question, we must digress and reconsider the concept of the project life cycle. In Chapter 1, we presented the usual view of the project life cycle in Figure 1.3, shown here as Figure 7.1 for convenience. This view of the life cycle shows decreasing returns to inputs as the project nears completion. Figure 1.5 is also shown here as Figure 7.2 for convenience. In this case, the project shows increasing returns to inputs as the project nears completion. In order to decide whether to adopt the subordinate's resource estimate or the superior's, we need to know which picture of the life cycle represents the task under consideration. Note that we are treating the subordinate's task as if it were a project, which is perfectly all right because it has the characteristics of a project that were described in Chapter 1. In addition, note that we do not need to know the shape of the life cycle with any precision, merely if it is a stretched-S or stretched-J shape.

Remember that the superior's and subordinate's resource estimates are not very far apart as a result of the negotiations preceding this decision. If the life cycle curve is a stretched-S (as in Figure 7.1), showing diminishing marginal returns, we opt for the superior's estimate because of the small impact on completion that results from withholding a small amount of resources. The superior might say to the subordinate, "Jeremy, what can you get me for R? We will have to live with that." If, on the other hand, the life cycle curve is a stretched-J, showing increasing marginal returns as in Figure 7.2, the subordinate's estimate should be chosen because of the potentially drastic effect a resource shortage would have on project completion. In this event, the superior might say, "OK, Brandon, we have got to be sure of this job. We'll go with your numbers." If the disagreement had concerned schedule (duration) instead of resources, the negotiation process and underlying logic would be unaltered.

This is a time-consuming process. At the same time, the PM is negotiating with the several subordinates responsible for the pieces of the PM's WBS, each of the subordinates is negotiating with their subordinates, and so on. This multilevel process is messy and not particularly efficient, but it allows a free flow of ideas up and down the system at all levels. This iterative process tends to reduce the uncertainty in budget estimations. The debate

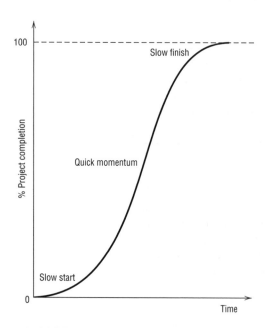

FIGURE 7.1 The standard stretched–S project life cycle. (Figure 1.3 reproduced.)

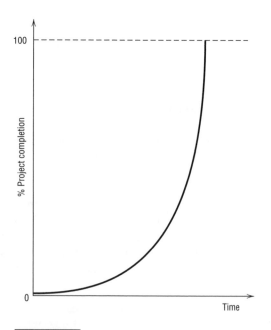

FIGURE 7.2 Another possible project life cycle—the stretched–J. (Figure 1.5 reproduced.)

over processes and their associated costs means that the uncertainty in budget estimates is very likely to be reduced.

It is worth emphasizing that ethics is just as important in negotiations within an organization as in negotiations between an organization and an outside party. In this case, the superior and subordinate have the responsibility to be honest with each other. For one thing, they must continue to work together in the future under the conditions of mutual trust. Second, it is ethically necessary to be honest in such negotiations.

Comments on the Budget Request Process

The budget process often begins with an invitation from top management for each division to submit a *budget request* for the coming year. Division heads pass the invitation along to departments, sections, and subsections, each of which presumably collects requests from below, aggregates them, and passes the results back up the organizational ladder.

This sounds like bottom-up budgeting, but there is an important difference between this procedure and a true bottom-up system. Along with the formal invitation for submission of a budget request, in the iterative system, another message is passed down—a much less formal message that carries the following kinds of information: the percent by which the wage bill of the organization may be increased or must be decreased, organizational policy on adding to or cutting the work force, the general attitude toward capital expenditures, knowledge about which projects and activities are considered to be high priority and which are not, and a number of other matters that, in effect, prescribe a set of limits on lower-level managers. As the budget requests are passed back up the organization, they are carefully inspected for conformity to guidelines. If they do not conform, they are "adjusted," often with little or no consultation with the originating units. Senior management tends to adopt an autocratic stance on budget making for many reasons, but two are very common: the need to feel in control of the budget, and the feeling that a tight budget will somehow motivate subordinates to perform more efficiently. We know of no particular evidence to support such views, but they are quite common. Moreover, they lead to budgetary game playing and increase the uncertainty surrounding the budgetary process.

The less autocratic the organization (and the less pressured it is by current financial exigencies), the greater the probability that this process will allow dialog and some compromise between managerial levels. Even the most *participative* firms, however, will not long tolerate lower-level managers who are not sensitive to messages relating to budget limitations. It makes little difference whether budget policy is passed down the system by means of formal, written policy statements or as a haphazard set of oral comments informally transmitted by some senior managers and practically neglected by others; the PM's budget request is expected to conform to policy. Ignorance of the policy is no excuse. Repeated failure to conform will be rewarded with a ticket to "corporate Siberia." It is the budget originator's responsibility to find out about budget policy. Again we see the importance of political sensitivity. The PM's channels of communication must be sensitive enough to receive policy signals even in the event that a noncommunicative superior blocks those signals.

One final comment about budgets concerns the impact of changes on the budget. Projects are known for having innumerable changes, sometimes due to scope changes by the customer, sometimes due to problems concerning the project itself such as delays, cost overruns, resource price increases, and other such matters. Obviously, for such changes, the budget will always need to be reconsidered and perhaps re-estimated (and reapproved). For cases where some project tasks might exceed the budget, PMs often keep a "reserve" (e.g., 5 percent) from the project budget (taken from each of the task budgets proportionally) to handle unexpected task overages. Another alternative particularly useful for projects with many highly uncertain tasks is to design the project with an upfront "de-scope" strategy so that if the costs are running too high, some of the less important scope requirements can be scaled back or eliminated during the project, thereby saving cost. Regardless of the alternative used, it is always wise to consider the probability that costs will exceed the budget and what might be done ahead of time to avoid that problem.

Cost Category Budgeting vs. Project/Activity Budgeting

Another facet of budgeting has to do with the degree to which a budget is category-oriented or project/activity-oriented, a distinction we have mentioned before. The traditional organizational budget is category-oriented often based upon historical data accumulated through

Project Management in Practice

Habitat for Humanity Wins a Big One

Loudoun Habitat for Humanity (LHH) of Sterling, VA, had everything going its way in its proposal to the Loudoun County Housing Trust Committee for $876,000 to help purchase, build, and redevelop 21 local properties for low-income families:

- The county had a $3 million housing fund available specifically to develop housing for low- and moderate-income families.

- The $876,000 would enable LHH to apply for federal stimulus funding earmarked for projects such as this, which, together with private donations, would bring in another $2,630,000 for a total of $3.5 million.

- There was no other competing group in the area building homes for low-income families.

- LHH had good construction, project management, and financial expertise to successfully execute this project within the schedule and budget.

© Jim West/ZUMAPress.com

Still, LHH had to make a successful 2-hour presentation to the Committee, convincing them of their qualifications and the attractive business case the proposal offered. But, despite prodding and frequent calls, LHH didn't hear back from the Committee, and the deadline for federal stimulus funds was approaching quickly. So LHH developed a strategy of writing letters, calling, and using any contacts available to explain the urgency of the timeline. Finally, they heard from the committee, which denied their application; apparently there had been at least one committee member who would rather use the funds to invest in high-density rentals. But this made no sense to LHH since then the county stimulus money for affordable housing would be denied, the county's political inclination didn't support high-density subsidized rentals so the zoning application would probably be rejected, and the recent U.S. fiscal crisis has reduced the value of the low-income tax credits needed to make such a project viable.

However, the Committee's recommendation had to be approved by the County Board of Supervisors, and LHH was able to make a presentation there, outlining the advantages of their proposal and the disadvantages of the high-density rentals proposal. But again, they didn't hear anything. With time running out, they made an effort to contact each of the nine supervisors, catching three in person and delivering letters to the others. The odds were stacked against them because to accept LHH's proposal meant overturning the Committee's recommendation. The Board decided in LHH's favor, but only approved $500,000 for a major portion of their proposal. But it came just in time for LHH to win federal stimulus funds to leverage that money and allow them to proceed with the major portion of their plan.

Questions

1. Did LHH seem to have a "de-scope" plan?

2. Did LHH seem to understand the County Committee's budget allocation process?

3. How did the concept of partnering (Chapter 4) apply in this example? Why do you think the Committee was insensitive to this opportunity?

Source: S. F. Gale, "A Closer Look," *PM Network*, Vol. 24.

a traditional, category-based, cost accounting system (Coburn, 1997). Individual expenses are classified and assigned to basic budget *lines* such as phone, materials, personnel-clerical, utilities, direct labor, etc., or to production centers or processes. These expense lines are gathered into more inclusive categories and are reported by organizational unit—for example, by section, department, and division. In other words, the budget can be overlaid on the organizational chart. Table 7.1 shows one page of a typical, category-oriented monthly budget report for a real-estate project.

TABLE 7.1   Typical Monthly Category Budget for a Real-Estate Project (page 1 of 6)

	Current			
	Actual	**Budget**	**Variance**	**Pct.**
Corporate—Income Statement				
Revenue				
8430 Management fees				
8491 Prtnsp reimb—property mgmt	7,410.00	6,222.00	1,188.00	119.0
8492 Prtnsp reimb—owner acquisition	.00	3,750.00	3,750.00–	.0
8493 Prtnsp reimb—rehab	.00	.00	.00	.0
8494 Other income	.00	.00	.00	.0
8495 Reimbursements—others	.00	.00	.00	.0
Total revenue	7,410.00	9,972.00	2,562.00–	74.3
Operating expenses				
Payroll & P/R benefits				
8511 Salaries	29,425.75	34,583.00	5,157.25	85.0
8512 Payroll taxes	1,789.88	3,458.00	1,668.12	51.7
8513 Group ins & med reimb	1,407.45	1,040.00	387.45–	135.3
8515 Workmen's compensation	43.04	43.00	.04–	100.0
8516 Staff apartments	.00	.00	.00	.0
8517 Bonus	.00	.00	.00	.0
Total payroll & P/R benefits	32,668.12	39,124.00	6,457.88	83.5
Travel & entertainment expenses				
8512 Travel	456.65	300.00	156.65–	152.2
8522 Promotion, entertainment & gift	69.52	500.00	430.48	13.9
8523 Auto	1,295.90	1,729.00	433.10	75.0
Total travel & entertainment exp	1,822.07	2,529.00	706.93	72.1
Professional fees				
8531 Legal fees	419.00	50.00	369.00–	838.0
8532 Accounting fees	289.00	.00	289.00–	.0
8534 Temporary help	234.58	200.00	34.58–	117.2

TABLE 7.2 Project Budget by Task and Month

Task	Estimate	Monthly Budget 1	2	3	4	5	6
a	2,000	1,300	700				
b	5,000		1,600	3,400			
c	7,000		1,300	4,500	1,200		
d	5,800		2,500	3,300			
e	4,000			2,300	1,000	700	
f	3,000				1,000	1,000	1,000
g	1,000					100	900
	27,800	1,300	6,100	13,500	3,200	1,800	1,900

With the advent of project organization, it became necessary to organize the budget in ways that conformed more closely to the actual pattern of fiscal responsibility. Under traditional budgeting methods, the budget for a project could be split up among many different organizational units, which diffused control so widely that it was frequently nonexistent. It was often almost impossible to determine the actual size of major expenditure activities in a project's budget. In light of this problem, ways were sought to alter the budgeting process so that budgets could be associated directly with the projects that used them. This need gave rise to project budgeting. Table 7.2 shows a project-oriented budget divided by task/ activity and expected time of expenditure.

If a program consists of a set of separate projects, the use of project budgeting for each project allows those project budgets to be aggregated for the program as a whole by time periods. Moreover, the program can also have its own monthly category budget (as shown in Table 7.1, with the categories down the left side), but this may require dividing up the revenues (if any) and expenses for each of the projects' activities (tasks) into the appropriate categories. In addition, each organizational unit can present its projects' revenues and expenses by adding additional columns to Table 7.1, with one column for "regular operations" and the other columns for each project (or program). Again, however, this may take extra effort to break out the tasks by organizational unit as well as activity if the tasks involve more than one organizational unit.

The estimation of capital costs raises special problems. Accounting systems in different industries handle capital costs differently. Further, estimation requires highly specialized knowledge because the prices of some durable goods, for example, machine tools, rise and fall in response to much different forces than affect the prices of other equipment, for example, computer systems or aircraft. In an interesting two-part article, Sigurdsen (1996a, 1996b) notes that capital costs are variant with quantity of output and compares two methods of making capital cost estimates.

7.2 Better Cost Estimating and Bidding

The cooperation of several people is required to prepare cost estimates for a project. If the firm is in a business that routinely requires bids to be submitted to its funders, it will have "professional" (experienced) cost estimators on its staff. The major responsibility of the professional estimators is to reduce the level of uncertainty in cost estimates so that the firm's bids can be made in the light of expert information about its potential costs. In these cases, it is the job of the PM to generate a description of the work to be done on the project in sufficient detail that the estimator can know what cost data must be collected. Frequently, the project will be too complex for the PM to generate such a description without considerable help from experts in the functional areas.

Even with the finest of experts working to estimate resource usage, the one thing that is certain is that things will not go precisely as planned. There are two fundamentally different ways to manage the risks associated with the chance events that occur on every project. The simpler and far more common way is to make an allowance for contingencies—usually 5 or 10 percent of the estimated cost. Just why these numbers are chosen in preference to 6 or 9, for instance, we do not know. We strongly prefer another method in which the forecaster selects "most likely, optimistic, and pessimistic" estimates. We illustrate this method in the next section when we apply simulation to the discounted cash flow problem in the Ceramic Sciences example from Chapter 2.

Turning now to the problem of estimating direct costs,[4] PMs often find it helpful to collect direct cost estimates on a form that not only lists the estimated level of resource needs but also indicates when each resource will be needed and notes if it is available (or will be available at the appropriate time). Figure 7.3 shows such a form. It also has a column for identifying the person to contact in order to get specific resources. This table can be used for collating the resource requirements for each task element in a project or for aggregating the information from a series of tasks onto a single form.

Note that Figure 7.3 contains no information on overhead costs. The matter of what overhead costs are to be added and in what amounts is unique to the firm, beyond the PM's control, and generally a source of annoyance and frustration to one and all. The allocation of overhead is arbitrary by its nature, and when the addition of overhead cost causes an otherwise attractive project to fail to meet the organization's economic objectives, the project's supporters are apt to complain bitterly about the "unfairness" of overhead cost allocation.

At times, firms support projects that show a significant incremental profit over direct costs but are not profitable when fully costed. Such decisions can be justified for a number of reasons, such as the following:

- To develop knowledge of a technology
- To get the organization's "foot in the door"
- To obtain the parts or service portion of the work
- To be in a good position for a follow-on contract
- To improve a competitive position
- To broaden a product line or a line of business

All of these are adequate reasons to fund projects that, in the short term, may lose money but provide the organization with the real option for future growth and profitability. It is up to senior management to decide if such reasons are worth it.

---

[4]Our emphasis on estimating direct costs and on focusing on resources that are "direct costed" in the WBS is based on our belief that the PM should be concerned with only those items over which he or she has some control—which certainly excludes overheads. The PM, however, may wish to add some nonchargeable items (e.g., photocopying) to the resource column of the WBS simply to "reserve" that item for use at a specific time.

Project Name_____

Date_____

Task Number _____

RESOURCES NEEDED

Resources	Person to Contact	How Many/ Much Needed	When Needed	Check (✔) if Available
People: Managers, Supervisors				
Professional & Technical				
Nontechnical				
Money				
Materials: Facilities				
Equipment				
Tools				
Power				
Space				
Special Services: Research & Test				
Typing/clerical				
Reproduction				
Others				

FIGURE 7.3 Form for gathering data on project resource needs.

Project Bids and RFPs

PMBOK

Chapter 12

The topic of bidding on requests for proposals is highly relevant to the **PMBOK** knowledge area (9) of *Procurement*. Many types of procurement involve soliciting bids on a project through a request for proposals (RFP). Hence, it is important to determine what documentation is needed to evaluate a project that is being considered. We have spoken about costs, benefits, risks, profits, timing, and other such matters in general terms, but now we are looking at the specifics that need to be documented in response to a requested bid. The set of documents submitted for evaluation is called the *project proposal*, whether it is brief (a page or two) or extensive, and regardless of the formality with which it is presented. Several issues face firms preparing bid proposals, particularly firms in the aerospace, construction, defense, and consulting industries. These are as follows:

1. Which projects should be bid on?
2. How should the proposal-preparation process be organized and staffed?
3. How much should be spent on preparing proposals for bids?
4. How should the bid prices be set? What is the bidding strategy? Is it ethical?

Generally, these decisions are made on the basis of their overall expected values, perhaps as reflected in a scoring model. In-house proposals submitted by a firm's personnel to that firm's top management do not usually require the extensive treatment given to proposals submitted to outside clients or agencies such as the Department of Defense. For the Department of Defense, a proposal must be precisely structured to meet the requirements contained in the official RFP or Request for Quotation (RFQ)—more specifically, in the Technical Proposal Requirements (TPR) that is part of the RFP or RFQ.

The details of the construction and preparation of a proposal to be submitted to the government or other outside funder are beyond the scope of this book. Fortunately, the subject has been well treated by Knutson (1996a, 1996b, and 1996c), but it should be noted that customs, practices, rules, and laws concerning proposals vary from nation to nation (e.g., see Jergeas et al., 1997). We comment only on the general approach next.

All bid proposals should begin with a short summary statement (an "Executive Summary") covering the fundamental nature of the proposal in *minimally technical language*, as well as the general benefits that are expected. All proposals should be accompanied by a "cover letter." The cover letter is a key marketing document and is worthy of careful attention. In addition to the Executive Summary and the cover letter, every proposal should deal with four distinct issues: (1) the nature of the technical problem and how it is to be approached; (2) the plan for implementing the project once it has been accepted; (3) the plan for logistic support and administration of the project; and (4) a description of the group proposing to do the work, plus its past experience in similar work.

The precise way in which the contents of a proposal are organized usually follows the directions found in the TPR or RFP, the stated requirements of a specific potential funder, the traditional form used by the organization issuing the proposal, or, occasionally, the whim of the writer. As is the case with most products, the highest probability of acceptance will occur when the proposal meets the expectations of the "buyer," as to form and content. At times, there is a tendency to feel that "nontechnical" projects (which usually means projects not concerned with the physical sciences or a physical product) are somehow exempt from the need to describe how the problem will be approached and how the project will be implemented—including details such as milestones, stage gates, schedules, and budgets. To deal with nontechnical projects casually is folly and casts considerable doubt on the proposer's ability to deliver on promises. (It is all too common for projects concerned with the development of art, music, drama, and computer software, among other "nontechnical" areas, to be quite vague as to deliverables, deadlines, and costs.) On the other hand, when the proposal is aimed at another division or department of the same parent organization, the technical requirements of the proposal may be greatly relaxed, but the technical approach and implementation plan are still required—even if presented in an informal manner.

The Technical Approach
The proposal begins with a general description of the problem to be addressed or project to be undertaken. If the problem is complex, the major subsystems of the problem or project are noted, together with the organization's approach to each. The presentation is in sufficient detail that a knowledgeable reader can understand what the proposer intends to do. The general method of resolving critical problems is outlined. If there are several subsystems, the proposed methods for interfacing them are covered.

In addition, any special client requirements are listed along with proposed ways of meeting them. All test and inspection procedures to assure performance, quality, reliability, and compliance with specifications are noted.

The Implementation Plan

The implementation plan for the project contains estimates of the time required, the cost, and the materials used. Each major subsystem of the project is listed along with estimates of its cost. These costs are aggregated for the whole project, and totals are shown for each cost category. Hours of work and quantities of material used are shown (along with the wage rates and unit material costs). A list of all equipment costs is added, as is a list of all overhead and administrative costs.

Depending on the wishes of the parent organization and the needs of the project, project task schedules (e.g., time charts, network diagrams, Gantt charts) are given for each subsystem and for the system as a whole. (See Chapter 8 for more about time charts, network diagrams, and Gantt charts.) Personnel, equipment, and resource usages are estimated on a period-by-period basis in order to ensure that resource constraints are not violated. Major milestones are indicated on the time charts. Contingency plans are specifically noted. For any facility that might be critical, load charts are prepared to make sure that the facility will be available when needed.

The Plan for Logistic Support and Administration

The proposal includes a description of the ability of the proposer to supply the routine facilities, equipment, and skills needed during any project. Having the means to furnish artist's renderings, special signs, meeting rooms, stenographic assistance, reproduction of oversized documents, computer graphics, word processing, video teleconferencing, and many other occasionally required capabilities provides a "touch of class." Indeed, their unavailability can be irritating. Attention to detail in all aspects of project planning increases the probability of success for the project—and impresses the potential funder.

It is important that the proposal contain a section explaining how the project will be administered. Of particular interest will be an explanation of how control over subcontractors will be administered, including an explanation of how proper subcontractor performance is to be ensured and evaluated. The nature and timing of all progress reports, budgetary reports, audits, and evaluations are covered, together with a description of the final documentation to be prepared for users of the proposed deliverables. Termination procedures are described, clearly indicating the disposition of project personnel, materials, and equipment at project end.

A critical issue, often overlooked, that should be addressed in the administrative section of the proposal is a reasonably detailed description of how *change orders* will be handled and how their costs will be estimated. Change orders are a significant source of friction (and lawsuits) between the organization doing the project and the client. The client rarely understands the chaos that can be created in a project by the introduction of a seemingly simple change. To make matters worse, the group proposing the project seems to have a penchant for misleading the potential client about the ease with which "minor" changes can be adopted during the process of implementing the project. Control of change orders is covered in Chapter 11.

Past Experience

All proposals are strengthened by including a section that describes the past experience of the proposing group. It contains a list of key project personnel together with their titles and qualifications. For outside clients, a full résumé for each principal should be attached to the proposal. When preparing this and the other sections of a proposal, the proposing group should remember that the basic purpose of the document is to convince a potential funder that the group and the project are worthy of support. The proposal should be written accordingly.

Learning Curves   If the project being costed is one of many similar projects, the estimate of each cost element is fairly routine. If the project involves work in which the firm has little experience, cost estimating is more difficult, particularly for direct labor costs. For example, consider a project that requires 25 units of a complex electronic device to be assembled. The firm is experienced in building electronic equipment but has never before made this specific device, which differs significantly from the items routinely assembled.

Experience might indicate that if the firm were to build many such devices, it would use about 70 hours of direct labor per unit. If labor is paid a wage of $12 per hour, and if benefits equal 28 percent of the wage rate, the estimated labor cost for the 25 units is

$$(1.28)(\$12/\text{hr})(25 \text{ units})(70 \text{ hr/unit}) = \$26,880$$

In fact, this would be an underestimate of the actual labor cost because more time per unit output is used early in the production process. Studies have shown that human performance usually improves when a task is repeated. In general, performance improves by a fixed percent each time production doubles. More specifically, *each time the output doubles, the worker hours per unit decrease to a fixed percentage of their previous value.* That percentage is called the *learning rate*. If an individual requires 10 minutes to accomplish a certain task the first time it is attempted and only 8 minutes the second time, that person is said to have an 80 percent learning rate. If output is doubled again from two to four, we would expect the fourth item to be produced in

$$8(0.8) = 6.4 \text{ min}$$

Similarly, the eighth unit of output should require

$$6.4(0.8) = 5.12 \text{ min}$$

and so on. The time required to produce a unit of output follows a well-known formula:

$$T_n = T_1 n^r$$

where

T_n = the time required for the nth unit of output,
T_1 = the time required for the initial unit of output,
n = the number of units to be produced, and
r = log decimal learning rate/log 2.

The total time required for all units of a production run of size N is

$$\text{total time} = T_1 \sum_{n=1}^{N} n^r$$

Tables are widely available or easily created with spreadsheets   for both unit and cumulative times.

In the example of the electronic device just given, assume that after producing the twentieth unit, there is no significant further improvement (i.e., assembly time has reached a steady state at 70 hours). Further assume that previous study established that the usual learning rate for assemblers in this plant is about 85 percent. We can estimate the time required for the first unit by letting $T_n = 70$ hours by the unit $n = 20$. Then

$$r = \ln 0.85/\ln 2$$
$$= -0.1626/0.693$$
$$= -0.235$$

and

$$70 = T_1(20)^r$$
$$T_1 = 141.3 \text{ hr}$$

Now we know the time for the initial unit. We can create a spreadsheet as shown in Table 7.3 that uses the time for the first unit to calculate the unit times for unit n and cumulative times for units 1 to n. From Table 7.3, we see that the time to complete the first 20 units is 1,752.44 hours.

The last five units are produced in the steady-state time of 70 hours each. Thus, the total assembly time is

$$1752.44 + 5(70 \text{ hr}) = 2102.44 \text{ hr}$$

We can now refigure the direct labor cost.

$$2102.44(\$12)(1.28) = \$32{,}293.48$$

Our first estimate, which ignored learning effects, understated the cost by

$$\$32{,}293.48 - \$26{,}880 = \$5{,}413.48$$

or about 17 percent. Figure 7.4 illustrates this source of the error.

In recent years, learning curves have received increasing interest from PMs, particularly in the construction industry. Methods have been developed (Amor et al., 1998) for approximating composite learning curves for entire projects and for approximating total cost from the unit learning curve. Badiru (1995) has included learning curve effects in his concept of "critical resource diagramming" (discussed further in Chapter 8).

	A	B	C	D	E	F	G
1	t_1	141.3					
2	Learning Rate:	85.0%					
3							
4	n	Unit Time	Cumulative Time		=B$1*A6^(LN(B$2)/LN(2))		
5	1	141.30	141.30				
6	2	120.11	261.41				
7	3	109.21	370.62		=C5+B6		
8	4	102.09	472.71				
9	5	96.89	569.59				
10	6	92.83	662.42				
11	7	89.54	751.96				
12	8	86.78	838.73				
13	9	84.41	923.15				
14	10	82.35	1005.50				
15	11	80.53	1086.03				
16	12	78.91	1164.94				
17	13	77.44	1242.38				
18	14	76.11	1318.48				
19	15	74.88	1393.37				
20	16	73.76	1467.13				
21	17	72.72	1539.85				
22	18	71.75	1611.60				
23	19	70.85	1682.44				
24	20	70.00	1752.44				

TABLE 7.3 Using a spreadsheet to calculate unit and cumulative times.

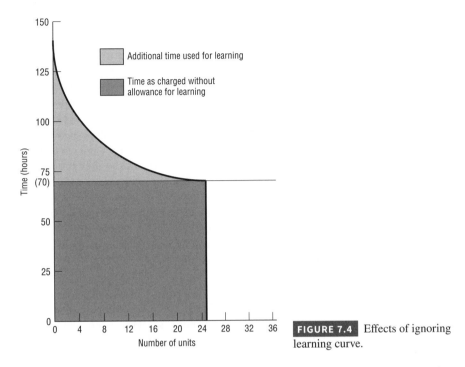

FIGURE 7.4 Effects of ignoring learning curve.

Remember that we are attempting to reduce the risk inherent in estimating costs. Therefore, for any task where labor is a significant cost factor and the production run is reasonably short, the PM should take the learning curve into account when estimating costs.

The implications of this conclusion should not be overlooked. We do not often think of projects as "production," but they are. While the construction, electronics, and aircraft assembly industries have used learning curves for many years, other industrial areas have been slow to follow. For example, research (Gagnon et al., 1987) has shown that the learning curve effect is important to decisions about the role of engineering consultants on computer-assisted design (CAD) projects. The same is assuredly true for the design of advertising campaigns or charity drives. The failure to consider performance improvement is a significant cause of errors in project cost estimation.

A Special Case of Learning—Technological Shock

If the parent organization is not experienced in the type of project being considered for selection, performance measures such as time to installation, time to achieve 80 percent efficiency, cost to install, and the like are quite uncertain and often will be seriously underestimated. It is interesting to observe that an almost certain, immediate result of installing a new, cost-saving technology is that costs rise. Sometimes we blame the cost increases on resistance to change, but a more sensible explanation is that when we alter a system, we disturb it, and it reacts in unpredictable ways. A steelmaker recalling the installation of the then new technology for manufacturing tinplate by electrolysis remarked, "We discovered and installed the world's first electrolytic method for making scrap. It took a year before we had that line running the way it was designed." Of course, if the organization is experienced, underestimation is not likely to be a serious problem. The Reliance Electric Company undertook several "18-month" plant construction projects that they predicted, accurately, would require 36 months to build from decision to the point when the plant was capable of operating at or above three-fourths capacity. (Note the potential for ethical problems here.) To the extent possible, past knowledge of system actions and reactions should be built into estimates of future project performance.

Other Factors

Depending on the reference, anywhere from about three-fifths to five-sixths of projects fail to meet their time, cost, and/or scope (specification) objectives (see, for example, Frame, 1998). The record of Information Technology (IT) projects is particularly poor, according to article after article in the journals of the Project Management Institute. Possibly, the problem is that Dilbert's pointy-haired boss sets arbitrary and impossible goals. Possibly, scope-creep impacts all projects [though cost overruns are not necessarily associated with changing scope (Christensen et al., 1998)]. Possibly, PMs use wildly optimistic estimates in order to influence the project selection process. Or maybe they are simply unaware of good cost (or time) estimating practices. For example, there are at least 45 estimating models available for IT projects, but few IT PMs use any of them. Some IT workers flatly refuse to estimate time and cost for IT projects on the grounds that there is too much uncertainty—and, we suspect, in an attempt to avoid responsibility. Possibly, all of these things, and even others, act together. Possibly, adoption of agile project management (as discussed in the previous chapter) will help reduce the failure rate.

While the number of things that can increase risk by producing errors in cost estimates is almost without limit, some problems occur with particularly high frequency. Changes in resource prices are one of these. The most commonly used solution to this problem is to increase all cost estimates by some fixed percentage. A more useful approach is to identify each input that accounts for a significant portion of project cost and estimate the direction and rate of price change for each.

The determination of which inputs account for a "significant" portion of project cost is not difficult, although it may be somewhat arbitrary. Suppose, for example, that our initial, rough cost estimate (with no provision for future price changes) for a project with an objective of setting up a small storefront accounting office is $1 million and is to be spent over a 3-year period in approximately equal amounts per year. If we think personnel costs will comprise about 60 percent of that total, also spread equally over time, the wage/salary bill will be about $600,000. Split into three equal amounts, we have expenditures of $200,000 per year. If we estimate that wage/salary rates will increase by 6 percent per year, our expenses for the second year rise to $212,000 (an increase of $12,000), and to $224,720 in the third year (a further increase of $12,720). Failure to account for wage/salary inflation would result in an underestimate of project cost of $36,720. This is an error of slightly more than 4 percent of the estimated personnel cost and almost 2.5 percent of the total project budget.

Further improvements can be made by taking into account the fact that the prices of different inputs often change at very different rates and sometimes in different directions. A quick examination of the Bureau of Labor Statistics (BLS) wage and price indices, which cover a very large number of specific commodities and wage rates, will reveal that even in periods of stable prices, the prices of some things rise while others fall and still others do not change appreciably. Thus, the PM may wish to use different *inflators/deflators* for each of several different classes of labor or types of commodities. While most PMs are concerned only with price increases, any industry submitting competitive bids on projects must remember that failure to be aware of falling prices will lead to cost overestimates and uncompetitive bids.

Other elements that need to be factored into the estimated project cost include an allowance for waste and spoilage. No sane builder would order "just enough" lumber to build a house. In addition, personnel costs can be significantly increased by the loss and subsequent replacement of project professionals. For example, new people go through a learning period, which, as we have seen, will have a negative effect on production. Thus, it may well cost more to replace a person who leaves the project with a newcomer who has approximately the same level of experience.

We have already mentioned the inclination PMs and project sponsors have toward understating the costs of a project in order to make it appear more profitable to senior managers, as well as the proclivity of lower-level project workers to overestimate costs in order to protect themselves. If the project is in its initial planning stage as a response to a RFP from an outside organization, over- and underestimates of cost can have a serious impact on the probability of winning the contract—or on the level of profit, if a win occurs.

Serious ethical problems may arise during the process of estimating costs and submission of bids in response to an RFP. If the job is to be paid on a cost-plus basis, or even if it is a fixed-fee project, with fee increases allowed for special circumstances, some bidders may "low ball" a contract (submit underestimated costs). By doing this, they hope to win the bid, counting on the opportunity to increase costs or to plead special circumstances once the job is underway. At times, clients have been known to give favored bidders a "last look" at supposedly sealed bids so that the favored bidder can submit a winning bid, often with an unwritten agreement to allow some cost escalation at a later date. There is considerable opportunity for unethical behavior during cost estimating and bidding. Further, estimating and bidding practices vary widely from industry to industry.

Finally, there is plain bad luck. Delays occur for reasons that cannot be predicted. Machinery with the reliability of a railroad spike suddenly breaks down. That which has never failed fails. Every project needs an "allowance for contingencies."

Project Management in Practice

The Emanon Aircraft Corporation

Emanon Aircraft is a major manufacturer of aircraft parts, specializing in landing gear parts and assemblies. They are located in a highly industrialized midwestern state. The local area suffers from somewhat higher than average unemployment, partly because Emanon has experienced a downturn in business. In the past 3 years, they have lost out on a number of landing gear contracts, being underbid by competitors from other areas of the country. Senior management studied the problem but has come to no conclusion about what can be done. They have hired a consulting team from a nearby university to study the situation and make a recommendation.

Business in the aircraft industry is not significantly different than in many other industries specializing in the building of complex machines. Aircraft builders are primarily assembly operations. They build planes from subassemblies and parts manufactured by themselves or by subcontractors. When an order is received to build some number of a given type of plane, the builder (prime contractor) requests bids for the proper number of a certain part or subassembly from appropriate subcontractors.

The university consulting team studied three aspects of Emanon's landing gear operation: the manufacturing process, the cost structure, and the bidding behavior and profit structure on landing gear bids.

First, they determined that the manufacturing process was reasonably efficient and not significantly different from Emanon's competitors. Second, they found that all competitors were using approximately the same level of markup when determining their cost-plus price. When examining the cost structure, however, they noted that in the past 3 years, the firm consistently ran negative cost variances in material accounts. That is, the amount of material actually used in the construction of landing gears was approximately 10 percent less than that the plan indicated. The team was unsure of this finding because there were only a few winning contracts for landing gears during the past 3 years.

Third, an investigation was conducted on the estimating and purchase of materials for this department. It exposed the following facts. Three-and-a-half years ago, Emanon was late making a delivery of landing gear parts. The firm paid a large penalty and was threatened with loss of further business with the prime contractor. The late delivery resulted when Emanon ordered an insufficient quantity of a special steel alloy used in landing gear struts and was unable to purchase any on the open market. The steel company required a manufacturing lead time of more than 90 days, so Emanon's delivery was late.

As a result, the purchasing official who had responsibility for this contract was demoted. The new purchasing official handled the problem in a straightforward manner by regularly inflating the material estimates by 10 percent. The cost of material is about half of the total cost of landing gear production, which resulted in bids that were approximately 5 percent above the competition.

Questions

1. **How did inflating the material costs solve purchasing's "lateness" problem?**

2. **What alternatives were available to Emanon besides demoting the purchasing manager?**

3. **What should Emanon do now?**

Source: S. J. Mantel, Jr. Consulting project.

Some writers and instructors differentiate four bases for estimating costs: experience, quantitative (statistical) methods, constraints, and worksheets. They discuss the advantages and disadvantages of each and then, typically, decide that one or another gives the best results. We feel strongly that all four are useful and that no single approach to cost estimating should be accepted as the best or rejected out of hand. The best estimators seem to employ an eclectic approach that uses, as one said, "anything that works." The wise PM takes into account as many known influences on the project budget as can be predicted. What cannot be predicted must then, by experience, simply be "allowed for." There are two other factors, particularly common to projects involving intangible outputs such as software programming, that need to be mentioned relating to cost estimation and the schedule. These two factors have been identified in a classic and highly readable work—*The Mythical Man-Month*—by Brooks (1975).

First, most projects involve a tangible medium that tends not to be under our control— the wood splits, the paint smears—and thus, we blame implementation problems of our "good" ideas on these physical elements. So, when we are working with a purely intellectual medium that has no physical elements, such as computer code, we are highly optimistic and foolishly assume that all will go well. However, when any project consisting of a series of components can only be successful if all of the components are successful, and each component has a small probability of failing, the chances of the overall project being successful may be very poor. Consider, for example, a software program consisting of 1000 lines of code, each of which is 0.999 reliable. The chance of the program itself working is only about 36 percent!

The second factor is what Brooks calls "the mythical man-month" and relates to our tendency to assume that workers and time are interchangeable. Thus, when a schedule slips, the traditional response is to add labor, which is like trying to douse a fire with gasoline. Our assumption that workers and time are interchangeable is correct only when a task can be partitioned such that there is no communication needed between the workers. Most projects, however, especially computer programming, are not set up that way and the more workers that are added require even more workers to train, as well as lines of communication to coordinate their efforts. Thus, three workers require three times as much pairwise intercommunication as two, and four require six times as much, etc. This result is captured in Brooks' law: *Adding manpower to a late software project makes it later.*

7.3 | Project Risk Management

There has been a great leap of interest in risk management in the last few years to the point that 71 percent of organizations now practice risk management, according to Brox (2012b). Marcelino-Sadaba et al. (2014) designed and tested a simple but thorough project risk management methodology/guide for small- to medium-sized enterprises that considered a variety of project types in both manufacturing and service organizations. They found that the time required to use the guide averaged 3.77 percent of the total project time for their test projects, which consumed about one person per year of a 40-hour per week effort (or two people for 6 months, four people for 3 months, etc.). They also found that this percentage dropped with larger projects, since setup time tended to take the same amount of time regardless of project size. In addition, the guide was easily understood and used by experienced managers, even if they had no experience in project management. The most difficult task the managers faced was identifying metrics for project success that included nonfinancial aspects such as customer satisfaction, meeting requirements and objectives, and project value. The main problem encountered was applying the guide to outsourced tasks of the project. Secondary problems related to communicating with external stakeholders and finding the right definition of the project objectives.

Although there are many processes that can be used to control risk, the human factor is still probably the major element in risk management. As described in **PMBOK**, the risk attitudes of both organizations and individual stakeholders can be influenced by their risk appetite (what level of risk they are willing to assume), tolerance (the amount of risk they can withstand), and threshold (the amount of risk they are willing to take on to achieve a specific reward). Their risk attitude can be influenced by their perceptions, biases, and tolerances.

Kaplan et al. (2012) point out that individuals have many other characteristics that can also influence their risk attitudes, such as overestimating their ability to influence chance events and being overconfident in their own forecasts. And a recent danger for organizations is the tendency to handle risks by compartmentalizing them, labeling the compartments, and thereby dismissing the risks as having been dealt with. Another organizational problem regarding risk is failing to separate the function for strategy from the function for handling risk—these two areas require almost opposite personalities and cannot be handled by the same set of people. Even at that, risk managers often fall into the trap of "going native" and failing to see the risks in an exciting new endeavor.

Brox (2012b) also points out that communications regarding risk should be tailored to the stakeholder audience being addressed, since they each will have very different concerns about project risks. Specifically, senior managers will want a summarized version of the risk issues such as their severity and likelihood and what trade-offs are available. On the other hand, team members are best informed through regular team meetings and will want to know the details about how the risks will affect their work, how priorities were decided, and how the risks will be mitigated. The business managers are more interested in the big picture and whether the project will be finished on time and budget, that is, the potential impact on the relationship with the client. If multiple issues exist, it is best to group them by some commonality such as root cause, consequences, or mitigation method. Finally, external stakeholders must be handled delicately and in separate groups depending on their interests in the project. It is best to avoid jargon and give full and detailed explanations, all while emphasizing the benefits of the project to their interests. Some recent books on project risks and ways of handling them are: Hillson et al. (2012), Jordan (2013), Royer (2000), Salkeid (2013), and Ward et al. (2012).

This section covers the **PMBOK®** knowledge area 8, concerning *Project Risk Management*. The Project Management Institute's (PMI) publication *A Guide to the Project Management Body of Knowledge (PMBOK® Guide) 5th Edition, 2013*, states that "project risk[5] management includes the processes of conducting risk management planning, identification, analysis, response planning, and controlling," and as we shall see next, another subprocess needs to be added.

PMBOK

11.0

PMBOK

Chapter 11

1. **Risk Management Planning**—deciding how to approach and plan the risk management activities for a project.

2. **Risk Identification**—determining which risks might affect the project and documenting their characteristics.

3. **Qualitative Risk Analysis**—performing a qualitative analysis of risks and conditions to prioritize their impacts on project objectives.

4. **Quantitative Risk Analysis**—estimating the probability and consequences of risks and hence the implications for project objectives.

5. **Risk Response Planning**—developing procedures and techniques to *enhance opportunities* and *reduce threats* to the project's objectives.

---

[5]It is important for the reader to recall that the word "risk" has two meanings. One relates to the probability that an event will occur. The other is associated with danger or threat. The proper meaning of the word is determined by the context in which it is used.

6. **Risk Monitoring and Control**—monitoring residual risks, identifying new risks, executing risk reduction plans, and evaluating their effectiveness throughout the project life cycle.

We add here a seventh subprocess, based on the discussion concerning the identification of risks in **PMBOK®**.

11.2.3

7. **The Risk Management Register**—creating a permanent register of identified risks, methods used to mitigate or resolve them, and the results of all risk management activities.

We treat each subprocess in turn, including useful tools and techniques where appropriate.

1. Risk Management Planning

It is never too early in the life of a project to begin managing risk. A sensible project selection decision cannot be made without knowledge of the risks associated with the project. Therefore, the risk management plan and initial risk identification must be carried out before the project can be formally selected for support. The risk management group must, therefore, start work as soon as a potential project is identified. Gale (2011) reviewed some strategic lessons learned from a series of major catastrophes various companies experienced. One of these was to consolidate the risk management tasks for all projects at the portfolio level rather than the project level, just like insurance companies do. This reduces the cost of each project having to incorporate risk costs into their project bids, while saving the firm money on events that usually don't happen. However, another lesson learned was that some low-cost contingency planning at the project level was extremely valuable when such events do in fact occur, rather than just throwing money at the problem.

At first, project risks are loosely defined—focusing for the most part on externalities such as the state of technology in the fields that are important to the project, business conditions in the relevant industries, and so forth. The response to external risks is usually to track the pertinent environments and estimate the chance that the project can survive various conditions. Not until the project is in the planning stage will such risks as those associated with project technology, schedule, budget, and resource allocation begin to take shape.

Project Management in Practice

Risk Analysis vs. Budget/Schedule Requirements in Australia

Sydney, Australia's M5 East Tunnel was constructed under strict budgetary and schedule requirements, but given the massive traffic delays now hampering commuters, the requirements may have been excessive. Due to an inexpensive computer system with a high failure rate, the tunnel's security cameras frequently fail, requiring the operators to close the tunnel due to inability to react to an accident, fire, or excessive pollution inside the tunnel. The tunnel was built to handle 70,000 vehicles a day, but it now carries 100,000, so any glitch can cause immediate traffic snarls. A managerial risk analysis, including the risk of overuse, might have anticipated these problems and mandated a more reliable set of computers once the costs of failure had been included.

Questions

1. When the project was finished, do you think it was considered a success or a failure? Why?

2. Which risk management subprocess might have identified the danger in using a cheap computer system?

3. What type of risk analysis approach would have been most appropriate in this situation?

4. How does a PM guard against the danger of a short-term success but longer-term failure?

Source: Project Management Institute. "Polluted Progress," *PM Network*, Vol. 19.

Kaplan et al. (2012) have concluded that managing risks depends on which of three types of risks are being faced. First, there are *preventable* risks from within the organization and are thus controllable through active preventive measures such as mission or value guidelines, strict boundary limits conveyed through the organization's culture and code of conduct, senior role models, strong internal control systems, and the audit function. Another lesson learned that Gale (2011) reports is that senior managers need to create a culture of safety in their organizations because injuries and deaths during a catastrophic event take on much greater importance and attention. The investment in safety, as it turns out, saves considerable money for the firm in the long run as well—a profitable investment.

Second are *strategy* risks from the risks the organization takes to conduct profitable or viable activities. Here risks can be controlled through a risk management system to reduce, contain, or control the risks by means such as independent outside experts who challenge management thinking, embedded internal experts, or a risk management group that collects information and evaluates and prioritizes the risks. With all these approaches, the result is not necessarily to decrease the risks but perhaps to even increase the risks, if that looks feasible to achieve higher rewards.

And third are *external* risks—economic, legal, natural, political, competitive—that are beyond the organization's control or influence. Here a risk system is needed that will identify these risks and find ways to mitigate their impact. In addition to the approaches used for strategy risks, other techniques have included stress tests, scenario planning, and war-gaming. A final lesson reported by Gale (2011) was how important it was to coach the C-suite managers in how to publicly respond to a catastrophe, rather than the ad hoc response such as CEO Tony Hayward offered when the BP oil spill occurred, saying "I'd like my life back," and then going on a yacht race during the spill.

Because risk management often involves analytic techniques not well understood by PMs not trained in the area, some organizations put risk specialists in a project office, and these specialists staff the project's risk management activities. For a spectacularly successful use of risk management on a major project, see Christensen et al. (2001), a story of risk management in a Danish bridge construction project.

Ward (1999) describes a straightforward method for conducting **PMBOK®**'s six subprocesses that includes a written report on risk management, if not the creation of a risk register. Two major problems in the way that risk management is carried out by the typical organization are that (1) risk identification activities routinely fail to consider risks associated with the project's external environment; and (2) they focus on misfortune, overlooking the risk of positive things happening.

11.2.3

2. Risk Identification

The risks faced by a project are dependent on the technological nature of the project, as well as on the many environments (economic, cultural, etc.) in which the project exists. Indeed, the manner in which the process of risk management is conducted depends on how one or more environments impact the project. The corporate culture is one such environment. So consider, for instance, the impact of a strong corporate "cost-cutting" emphasis on how risk managers identify project risks—they will probably focus on the project's cost elements, such as personnel and resource allocation. (Note that this culture will carry over to the *process* of risk management as well—carrying out the six or seven subprocesses—not merely to the identification of risks.)

 The need to consider the many environments of almost any project is clear when one examines the recent articles on risk management (e.g., Champion, 2009; Taleb, 2009). It is typical to consider only the internal environment of the project, for example, the technical and interpersonal risks, and occasionally, negative market risks for the project. Articles on risks in IT and software projects rarely go beyond such matters—Jiang et al. (2001) is an example. This is a thoughtful development of a model for generating numerical measures for IT project risks. The specific user of the IT and the institutional setting of the project are considered, but competitors, the IT market, user industries, the legal environment, and several other relevant environments are ignored.

In Chapter 2, we described the use of the Delphi method for finding numeric weights and criteria scores for the important factors in selecting projects for funding. The Delphi method is also useful when identifying project risks and opportunities for risk analysis models. Indeed, one of the first applications was forecasting the time period in which some specific technological capability would become available. The Delphi method is commonly used when a group must develop a consensus concerning such items as the importance of a technological risk, an estimate of cash flows, a forecast of some economic variable, and similar uncertain future conditions or events. Other such methods are "brainstorming," "nominal group" techniques, checklists, attribute listing, and other such creativity and idea generation methods (see the website of this book for descriptions).

Cause–effect ("fishbone") diagrams (see Figure 7.5), flow charts, influence diagrams, SWOT analysis, and other operations management techniques (Meredith et al., 2013) may also be useful in identifying risk factors. The flexibility of cause–effect diagrams makes them a useful tool in many situations. For example, the outcome of "failure" of the project can be the outcome on the right side of the fishbone and then the major factors that could cause that—bad economy, performance weakness, high pricing, competing products, etc.—can be the stems that feed into this failure, and the reasons for these various factor failures can be added to the stems. Similarly, we could put the failure factor "performance weakness" as the outcome on the right and list the factors that might cause that: weak engineering, poor materials, etc. Alternatively, we might look at the "risk" that the project might be a great success, much better than we had expected, and the factors that might cause that to occur: beat competing products to the market, booming economy, exceptionally low price, and other such positive reasons.

Another approach to identifying risks is to watch for early warning signs (EWS) as the project begins and progresses through to completion. Williams et al. (2012) did a study on EWS and responses to them and found that PMs were not good at detecting or acting on EWS because of an optimism bias, excessive faith in more experienced managers, interpersonal effects, group thinking, political pressure, the organizational culture, and limited time for problem-searching. All this was especially true when the project was complex, had high

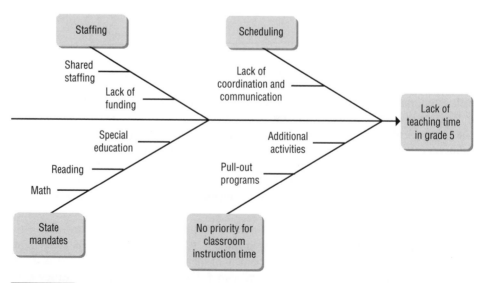

FIGURE 7.5   Fishbone diagram to identify potential factors.

uncertainties, was considered to be unique, and even when a strict stage gate procedure was in place that clearly stated what exactly was to be reviewed—and in these cases required more insight/gut feel to identify risks. Better communication, knowledge, and experience also helped in these situations. In any event, it was found that the risk assessment process *itself* was much more important in identifying risks than the measures employed.

Williams et al. also found that the EWS changed over the course of the project and were able to identify three project stages with the most common EWS. The first was during the *setup* of the project, and here the primary EWS were unclear goals, tenuous assumptions, and confusion about how the project work fit with the goals and expected benefits of the project. In the *early* stage, the EWS related more to the stakeholders in the project and included confusion over who was responsible for what, team overreliance on outside consultants, and vague answers to questions and criticisms. Then in the execution stage, the EWS were lack of documentation, a constant churn of people, continually unfulfilled promises, people greatly over or under-working, frequently changing decisions, and excessive subcontractor claims and requests for time extensions. Overall EWS for the entire project were of two types: measures/assessments, and gut feel. EWS of the former included missing numbers or information, incomplete or missing documents, late/unclear reports, and missed milestones. EWS of the latter were generally poor communication, a strained atmosphere, lack of trust, arguments, and changes in position on issues over time.

3. Qualitative Risk Analysis

The purpose of qualitative risk analysis is to prioritize the risks identified in the previous step so attention can be directed to the most important ones. The qualitative nature of this process makes it quite flexible, useful, and quick to apply; in addition, it can be used for both threats and opportunities. A subjective (or if available, objective) estimate of the probability of the risk occurring is needed, perhaps from a Delphi approach used with a group of experts in the risk area. The probability values need not be precise and, for that matter, could just be a rank on a 1 to 5 scale, or even simply "low," "medium," or "high."

A sense of the impact of the threat or opportunity is also needed, and should consider all important objectives of the project, including cost, timing, scope, and ancillary objectives. To attain an overall measure of the impact, each objective should be scaled and weighted in importance. Then the impact of the threat on each objective can be found in a manner similar to the "Gettin' Workin'" scoring model described in Chapter 2 with the result being a percentage of 100, a number from 1 to 5, or again just "low, medium, or high."

Once the probability and impact levels are found, a Risk Matrix can be constructed as in Figure 7.6. Here we just show the simplest version with nine cells corresponding to "low, medium, and high" categories, but a 1 to 5 range would have 25 cells to consider, and a percentage of 100 could be divided into as many cells as would be useful. As we see in Figure 7.6, for example, we have identified as "critical" those threats with a high value on one measure and a medium or high value on the other measure: in this case, high probability–medium impact, high on each, and medium probability–high impact. The other cells can be categorized in a similar manner, and here we used just three categories in a symmetrical manner: "critical," "monitor," and "ignore." However, for some threats, it may be appropriate to use four, or perhaps just two, categories, and the cells may be categorized differently for each threat. Conversely, if the Risk Matrix cell categories seem appropriate for all threats, then one matrix can be used to illustrate the distribution of all threats, as we have done in Figure 7.6 by listing the five threats (for example) in their corresponding cells.

Finally, the same approach can be used for opportunities, considering the possibility of positive impacts. In this case, the matrix shows which risk opportunities are most important to focus attention on and try to bring about and which to ignore. The responses to both critical threats and critical opportunities will be discussed in Step 5.

6. Risk Monitoring and Control

11.6.2

Bowles (2011) suggests four risk-oriented measures that organizations should track: (1) How often a risk assessment is conducted/updated; (2) How often a risk assessment is reviewed; (3) The number of risks initially rated as low that later became high; and (4) The percentage of actual risks that developed that had been identified beforehand. The **PMBOK** lists risk reassessments as a major risk control tool for risk management and also risk audits that examine and document the effectiveness of various risk responses, as well as the risk management process in general. The topic of monitoring will be covered in detail in Chapter 10 and control in Chapter 11, so we defer our remaining discussion of risk monitoring and control until we reach those chapters.

7. The Risk Register

If the risk management system has no memory, the task of risk identification will be horrendous. But the system can have a memory—at least the individuals in the system can remember. Relying on the recollections of individuals, however, is itself "risky." To ensure against this particular risk, the risk management system should maintain an up-to-date risk register that includes, but is not restricted to, the following:

- identification of all environments that may impact on the project
- identification of all assumptions made in the preliminary project plan that may be a source of risk for the project
- a list of all risks identified by the risk management group, complete with their estimated impacts on the project and estimates of their probability of occurring
- a complete list of all "categories" and "key words" used to categorize risks, assumptions, and environments so that all risk management groups can access past work done on risk management
- the details of all qualitative and quantitative estimates made on risks, on states of the project's environment, or on project assumptions, complete with a brief description of the methods used to make such estimates
- minutes of all group meetings including all actions the group developed to deal with or mitigate each specific risk, including the decision to ignore a risk
- the actual outcomes of identified risks and, if a risk came to occur, the results of actions taken to mitigate or transfer the risk or invoke the contingency plan

If all this work on data collection is going to be of value to the parent organization beyond its use on the project at hand, the risk register must be available to anyone proposing to perform risk management on a project for the organization. Almost everything a risk management group does for any project should be retained in the risk register. Second, all risks must be categorized, the environments in which projects are conducted must be identified, and the methods used to deal with or mitigate them must be described.

The use of multiple key words and categories is critical because risk information must be available to managers of widely varied disciplines and backgrounds. Organizations may be conducting a great many projects at any given time. If each risk management team has to start from scratch, without reference to what has been learned by previous groups, the management of risk will be extremely expensive, take a great deal of time, and will not be particularly effective. Rest assured that even with all the experience of the past readily available, mistakes will occur. If past experience is not available, the mistakes of the past will be added to those of the future.

Alderton (2012) reported on two risk registers, one more extensive that included many of the items in the aforementioned bulleted list and the other more direct that included just the vulnerability (schedule, budget, specific benefit, security); the level of risk (low, medium, high); a brief description of the threat; and the recommended risk response. Each risk was then plotted on a risk map (matrix) as in Figure 7.6, and those risks of most concern in the upper right portion of the matrix were then carefully monitored. In summary, Alderton suggested: (1) that the risk register begin immediately at the project charter stage because the earlier the response to a developing risk, the less disruption incurred; (2) engaging diverse stakeholders in the risk management process because they can often see very different or unexpected risks; (3) re-evaluate the risks regularly; and (4) the best way to minimize scope risk is to engage the most competent people to work on the project.

The **PMBOK** adds another important factor for the risk register—the risk attitudes of the various stakeholders. The risk management context is in reality a combination of not just the strategic risk exposure but also the risk attitudes of the stakeholders. Hence, it is the combination of these two elements, as captured on a strategic risk scoring sheet that identifies the true risks to a project.

11.1.2.1

A final question remains. How well does risk management contribute to project success? Research by Krane et al. (2012) tried to discern how risk focus by the project team and risk focus by the client might differ and thus have an effect on project "success." The thinking was that the team would be focused on short-term operational survival until turnover to the client, whereas the client would be focused on strategic benefits, both short-term client benefits and long-term societal benefits and sustainability. The results indicated that

Project Management in Practice

Facebook Risks Interruption to Move a Terabyte

Working on the bleeding edge of innovation is standard procedure for Facebook. To do so, however, speed is critical to their operation, and the combination of speed and innovation brings with it high risk. But Facebook is accustomed to handling risk. For example, a recent project involved a multimillion dollar effort to move a *terabyte* of data from a near-capacity data center to a new, higher-capacity data warehouse by the end of the year, only 100 days away, at the time. A terabyte (that is, a trillion bytes, or a million megabytes) is equivalent to 250 billion "Likes" on Facebook—a lot of data!

The project involved two phases: building and outfitting the new warehouse and then transferring the data. The new data warehouse was designed so the servers could handle four times as much data as the current ones, and the processors and software were upgraded as well, with the result that the new data warehouse could hold eight times more data and move and manage it more efficiently, all of which represented a savings of millions of dollars in energy costs. Given the short timeline and the importance of the hardware and software working together without a hitch, the project team took many steps to reduce the risks. First, they set clear expectations with both the vendors and internal stakeholders up front so everyone could fit their objectives into those of Facebook's. In additions, they conducted round-the-clock testing of the hardware, the software, and the ability of both to work together to deliver the speed, volume, and accuracy Facebook was depending on.

To transfer the data to the new warehouse, they had a choice between loading the data onto the equipment before physically moving it to the warehouse (but risking lost or damaged equipment in the move) and moving and checking the equipment first, and then flowing the data directly to the new site (but risking a network outage or a site crash disrupting their entire website). They took the risk of the latter, but planned multiple risk avoidance steps. First, they had to calculate how long it would take to flow the terabyte of data, assuming no network failures or power outages—3 weeks! But there was still a risk that the data flow would use too much network capacity and affect the website. To avoid this, the team built a customer application to throttle the data by limiting and monitoring the bandwidth throughout the entire 3-week data flow. They also performed constant error-checking and data-level corrections to keep the flow synchronized and alert the team if problems arose. Their up-front detailed planning, constant monitoring, and risk avoidance measures paid off in a successful data move to the new warehouse, on time with no delays or downtime.

Questions

1. Would you consider the completion of the first hardware phase a milestone or a phase-gate review?

2. What type of risk responses did Facebook use?

3. What other approaches might Facebook have used to handle the risks? (Hint: consider the seven risk subprocesses.)

Source: S. F. Gale, "A Closer Look," *PM Network*, Vol. 24.

the major focus of both was on operational risks, but the client also focused somewhat on the short-term benefits. The fact that the owner only focused on the "top-10" of all the risks presented by the team probably led to this result.

However, recent research by de Bakker et al. (2011) in the IS/IT industry has revealed that stakeholders deliberately use risk management to influence others to alter their behavior regarding their awareness of the project context and their responsibilities for the success of the project. Risk management activities seem to increase positive feelings and trust, and synchronize the perceptions of stakeholders, which stimulates action and increases its effectiveness, making for more predictable situations and reduced uncertainty, which leads to increased project success. As noted earlier, it isn't the measures or procedures of risk management that is the key, but the group awareness of threats to the project that seems to improve the chances of success.

One final warning is appropriate to users of quantitative risk analysis methods. To quantify risk via simulation or any other scientific method is a reasonable picture of reality only to the extent that the assumptions made about the input data are accurate. Even if they are, such a picture of the future is not the same as managing it. As we have said elsewhere, models do not make decisions, people do. Risks should be understood, and once understood, people must decide what to do about them. Without this last step, risk identification and analysis are useless.

7.4 | Quantitative Risk Assessment Methodologies

Failure Mode and Effect Analysis (FMEA)

FMEA (Stamatis, 2003) is the application of a scoring model such as those used for project selection in Chapter 2. It is straightforward and extensively used, particularly in engineering, and is easily applied to risk by using six steps.

1. List the possible ways a project might fail.

2. Evaluate the severity (S) of the impact of each type of failure on a 10-point scale where "1" is "no effect" and "10" is "very severe."

3. For each cause of failure, estimate the likelihood (L) of its occurrence on a 10-point scale where "1" is "remote" and 10 is "almost certain."

4. Estimate the inability to detect (D) a failure associated with each cause. Using a 10-point scale, "1" means detectability is almost certain using normal monitoring/control systems and "10" means it is practically certain that failure will not be detected in time to avoid or mitigate it.

5. Find the *Risk Priority Number* (**RPN**) where $RPN = S \times L \times D$.

6. Consider ways to reduce the S, L, and D for each cause of failure with a significantly high **RPN**. (We discuss this in Step 5: Risk Response Planning.)

Table 7.4 illustrates the use of FMEA for the same five threats we considered in Step 4 previously, but here we use more precise data. As we see from the RPN numbers, the biggest threats are: Can't acquire tech knowledge (2), and Client changes scope (3). Threat 2 has a great severity, should it occur, and threat 3 is quite likely, though the severity is much less damaging. The cost threat (4) and the recession threat (5) can probably be ignored for now since their likelihoods are so low. The tight schedule (1) will have some repercussions and is also quite likely, but we will see it coming early and can probably take steps to avoid or mitigate it. Some extensions of FMEA use additional scoring categories such as Ability to Mitigate (even if the threat cannot be detected).

TABLE 7.4   A FMEA example

Threat	Severity, S	Likelihood, L	Ability to Detect, D	RPN
1. Tight schedule	6	7.5	2	90
2. Can't acquire tech knowledge	8.5	5	4	170
3. Client changes scope	4	8	5	160
4. Costs escalate	3	2	6	36
5. Recession	4	2.5	7	70

Decision Tree Analysis

This tool (Meredith et al., 2002) is simple in concept and especially useful for situations where sequential events happen over time. For example, it would be appropriate for calculating the probability of getting one head and one tail in two tosses of a fair coin, or perhaps the probability of getting a head on the first toss and a tail on the second toss (which would have a different probability), or just the probability of getting a tail on the second toss. If we are only interested in probabilities, we call the tree a probability tree. But if there are some actions we are considering anywhere along the tree—before the first probability event, say, or between events—and we want to evaluate which action(s) would be best, then it is called a decision tree. Figure 7.7 illustrates such a tree (a solved one, here), but a very simple one with only one set of actions to choose from and one set of events; however, it could be extended to multiple actions and/or events, if desired, quite easily.

A decision tree is created from the left (but solved from the right, at the end), with either a decision node (a square) or a probability node (a circle) occurring first. In the example shown, an automobile manufacturer is considering whether a new car model development project should consider only a gas model, only a hybrid model, or both gas

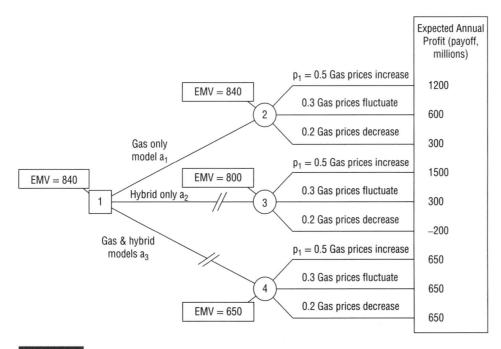

FIGURE 7.7   Decision tree based on expected monetary value (EMV).

and hybrid models. In this example, there are three options being considered, so there are three alternatives emanating from the decision node, each one posing some risk and opportunity depending on what happens to the price of fuel over the coming years. Thus, there is an event that affects the returns the auto manufacturer gets; in this case, we have simplified the possible event outcomes into three categories of "gas prices increase," "gas prices fluctuate up and down," or "gas prices decrease." (Note that the probabilities of each outcome are identical for each decision choice because the decision the auto manufacturer makes does not affect the price of gas.) Under each possible outcome of the event (whose probabilities we need to be able to estimate), the auto manufacturer's decision choice will result in a different payoff, shown on the far right. Note, for example, that if the auto manufacturer chooses to develop only a hybrid model and gas prices decrease, the firm would expect to lose $200 million dollars. To evaluate each of these outcomes and make a decision, the auto manufacturer needs a decision rule. If our rule was to "never pursue any alternative that might lose money," then this two-outcome policy would rule out the hybrid-only decision alternative. Another rule, if the decision-makers at the auto manufacturer were optimists, might be to pursue whichever alternative provides the greatest opportunity for maximizing the payoff, in which case the auto manufacturer would choose the hybrid-only option with a maximum payoff of $1,500 million from "gas prices increase."

However, we normally use a different rule, called Expected Monetary Value (abbreviated EMV) because this maximizes our return over the indefinite future, that is, the long-run average. The process of "solving" the decision tree is to work from the right, with the outcomes (profits, in this case), and multiply each outcome times the probability of the event resulting in that outcome, called the expected value of that outcome, and then adding up all the expected values for that event node–decision choice combination. For example, the EMV for event node 2 would be $(0.5 \times 1200) + (0.3 \times 600) + (0.2 \times 300) = 840$, which we write on the tree next to its event node. When we have done this with all of the event nodes for that decision, we compare them, double strike the lesser valued decision choices, and can then choose the best alternative choice for that decision node, in this case, developing a "gas-only model."

The use of decision trees for risk analysis easily handles both threats and opportunities, as seen in the example. The tool is attractive because it visually lays out everything that may happen in the future (that is, all risks and all decision choices). The tree can be used for individual risks, if they are independent, or joint risks on the same tree. For example, in our earlier use of FMEA, we might have interdependencies between risk 2 (can't acquire tech knowledge) and risk 3 (client changes scope).

General Simulation Analysis

Simulation combined with sensitivity analysis (see Chapter 6) is also useful for evaluating projects while they are still in the conceptual stage. Using the net present value approach, for example, we would support a project if the net present value of the cash flows (including the initial cash investment) is positive and represents the best available alternative use of the funds. When these flows are estimated for purposes of analysis, it is well to avoid the *full-cost* philosophy that is usually adopted. The full-cost approach to estimating cash flows necessitates the inclusion of arbitrarily determined overheads in the calculation—some of which are not affected by changes in product or process and thus are not relevant to the decision. The only relevant costs are those that will be changed by the implementation of the new process or product.

The determination of such costs is not simple. If the concept being considered involves a new process, it is necessary to go to the detailed *route sheet*, or *operations sequence sheet*, describing the operation in which the new process would be used. Proceeding systematically through the operating sequence step by step, one asks whether the present time and cost required for this step are likely to be altered if the new process concept is installed.

Project Management in Practice

Ignoring Risk Contrasted with Recognizing Risk in Two Industries

© U.S. Coast Guard/ZUMAPress.com

Everyone is familiar with the U.S. oil well disaster when BP's Deepwater Horizon oil platform blew up and sank, releasing a massive oil spill into the Gulf of Mexico. BP immediately faced public and governmental questioning about whether the accident could have been prevented, whether corners had been cut, how much oil was leaking into the Gulf, what risk management procedures were followed, and many others. Unfortunately, BP didn't respond well and the oil disaster became a public relations disaster as well.

Oil and disaster experts point out that since the *Exxon Valdez* oil spill in Alaska 21 years ago, there has been no improvement in pollution cleanup technology. The same booms and skimmers are being used now as they were used then. Yet, it was clear that sooner or later, there would be another big spill; yet, the oil industry was completely unprepared for this certainty. Amazingly, these firms do not seem to consider even the most basic risk management techniques, such as Murphy's Law: "What *can* go wrong, *will* go wrong."

Surely, it would have been wise to use some common sense such as employing redundant valves, testing the casings and well equipment as they went, such as the blowout preventer.

Huffington Post tech blogger Philip Neches makes some interesting contrasts by describing how NASA handles such risks when they design their extremely complex spacecraft and missions. How might it fail? How likely is it to fail in this way? How serious is the failure if it does fail; is there little impact, or is it "mission critical?" A billion dollar effort plus the lives of any astronauts are at risk here. In contrast, BP's mission of drilling a well 5,000 feet below the surface of the sea, clearly a challenge, is still much simpler. But any oil company should know that if they choose to engage in such risky projects, they will also need a plan to recover if a spill occurs and then handle the massive negative public relations and media attention. In the long run, it's much easier to evaluate the risks up front, make the right decisions, and monitor and test as you go.

Questions

1. **What do you think are the reasons BP took such a relaxed attitude toward the Gulf well compared to NASA?**

2. **Why hasn't the oil industry funded research and technology for oil spill cleanup efforts, do you think?**

3. **Why didn't a billion dollar firm have a public relations department prepared for the contingency of a massive oil spill?**

4. **Compare NASA's approach with risk analysis as described in the chapter. Then with FMEA. What's the same? What's different?**

Source: S. F. Gale, "Crude Awakening," *PM Network*, Vol. 24.

If, and only if, the answer is yes, three estimates (optimistic, most likely, and pessimistic) are made of the size of the expected change. These individual estimated changes in production cost and time, together with upstream or downstream time and cost changes that might also result (e.g., a production method change on a part might also alter the cost of inspecting the final product), are used to generate the required cash flow information—presuming that the time savings have been properly costed. This estimation process will be explained in detail in Chapter 8.

The preceding analysis gives a picture of the proposed change in terms of the costs and times that will be affected. The uncertainty associated with each individual element of the process is included. Simulation runs will then indicate the likelihood of achieving various levels of costs and benefits. Note also that investigation of the simulation model will expose the major sources of uncertainty in the final cost and benefit distributions.

Those without considerable experience in simulation should use this tool with caution. Simulation software is indifferent to assumptions, contrary-to-fact, and cares not a wit that the experimenter specifies a statistical distribution that implies a universe that never was nor ever will be. In such cases, the results of the simulation—often taken by the unwary as an estimate of reality—are apt to mislead.

The duration of project activities, the amounts of various resources that will be required to complete a project, the estimates made of the value of accomplishing a project, all these and many other aspects of a project are uncertain. While a PM may be able to reduce uncertainty, it cannot be eliminated. Decisions must be made in the face of the ambiguity that results from uncertain information. Risk estimation and analysis does not remove the ambiguity; it simply describes the uncertainties in a way that provides the decision-maker with a useful insight into their nature.

To apply risk analysis, one must make assumptions about the probability distributions that characterize key parameters and variables associated with a decision and then use these to estimate the *risk profiles* or probability distributions of the outcomes of the decision. This can be done analytically or by *Monte Carlo simulation* (Meredith et al., 2002), an easy-to-use

Project Management in Practice

Simulating the Failure of California's Levees

California's 2600-mile long system of levees east of San Francisco is arguably the most worrisome infrastructure risk in America—called a "ticking time bomb" by some—whose failure would top the economic cost of Katrina. The berms supporting the levees protect half a million people, 4 million acres of farmland, and the drinking water supply for most of southern California. To help decide where to invest to protect these levees, a gigantic threat-assessment simulation software program is being used. It was constructed after Hurricane Katrina by 300 top scientists and engineers to see how waves and flood waters from 152 computer-simulated storms might swamp New Orleans. The software is being modified for California, where the greater threat is earthquakes, but California has seven times the length of levees as New Orleans, and they're in worse condition.

Questions

1. What would be involved in changing the simulation threat from hurricanes to earthquakes?

2. What process do you think would be used to analyze the simulation results?

Source: A. Aston and M. Arndt. "If the Levees Fail in California," *Business Week*, 2007.

© Sacramento Bee/ZumaPress.com

technique that is well adapted to evaluating the risk in certain situations. When the decisions involve several input variables or parameters, simulation is highly preferable to the tedious calculations required by analytic methods such as decision or probability trees. The simulation software (in our case, Crystal Ball®, an Excel® Add-In) allows the decision to be represented by a mathematical model and then selects samples from the assumed distributions for each input variable or parameter. The software then plugs these inputs into the model and finds the outcome(s) of the decision. This process is repeated many times, and the statistical distribution of the outcomes is then displayed. The object of this process is to show the decision-maker the distribution of the outcomes. This risk profile can then be used to assess the risk associated with the situation as uncertainty increases, and the distribution of outcomes becomes more spread out. Of course, in addition to risk, other factors might be relevant, such as strategic concerns, socio/political factors, and impact on market share.

David Matheson, CEO of SmartOrg Inc. in California (Gale, 2007), says that "Vague terms lead to bad decisions. You need to define success in quantifiable terms so that everyone is on the same page … you need robust ways to discuss uncertainties quantified in the language of probability." By estimating the range and distribution for costs and revenues and using these to calculate the projected profitabilities, PMs have a way to make project selection decisions. Simulation is the perfect tool to do this!

Following a few comments about the nature of the input data and assumptions, we illustrate the use of Crystal Ball® (CB) to aid in the risk analysis of a potential investment. We show another application of CB simulation again in Chapter 8 to determine the likelihood of project completion by various times.

Monte Carlo Simulation

Similarly to decision trees, simulation (see Meredith et al., 2002) can also handle both threats and opportunities and sequential events as well. We start with a model; for example, "Estimated Revenues minus Estimated Costs equals Expected Profits." The advantage of simulation is that we don't need to divide probabilistic events into a limited number of categories. Instead, we estimate optimistic, typical, and pessimistic values for each probabilistic input and use standard distributions for these events. We then randomly select inputs from these distributions a thousand or more times to generate a frequency distribution of outcomes. The frequency distributions thereby give us the probabilities of losing more than a certain amount of money, or making at least a certain amount, or taking longer, or shorter, than a certain amount of time to complete the project, and other such important information. We include two examples of this approach. In this chapter, we simulate project cash flows and inflation rates that are uncertain and thus subject the project to monetary risk. Then in Chapter 8, we simulate the task times of project activities to determine the effect on the overall project completion time and the risk probability of being late.

Ceramic Sciences Revisited   There is great value in performing risk analysis in order to confront the uncertainties in project selection. Reconsider the Ceramic Sciences example we solved in Chapter 2, Section 2.2, devoted to finding the discounted cash flows associated with a project. Setting this problem up in Excel® is straightforward, and the earlier solution is shown here in Table 7.5 for convenience. We found that the project cleared the barrier of a 13 percent hurdle rate for acceptance. The net cash flow over the project's life is just under $400,000, and discounted at the hurdle rate plus 2 percent annual inflation, the net present value of the cash flow is about $18,000.

Now let us assume that the expenditures in this example are fixed by contract with an outside vendor. Thus, there is no uncertainty about the outflows, but there is, of course, uncertainty about the inflows. Assume that the estimated inflows are as shown in Table 7.6 and include a most likely estimate, a minimum (pessimistic) estimate, and a maximum (optimistic) estimate. (In Chapter 8, "Scheduling," we will deal in more detail with the methods and meaning of making such estimates.) Both the beta and the triangular statistical distributions are well suited for modeling variables with these three parameters. In earlier versions of Crystal Ball® (CB), the beta distribution was complicated and not particularly intuitive to use, so the triangular distribution was adopted as a reasonably good approximation of the beta. Use of a new beta distribution, labeled "BetaPERT" by CB in its Distribution Gallery, has been simplified in CB 11.1.2.2. We will use it in this example and in the simulations used elsewhere in this book.[6]

The hurdle rate of return is fixed by the firm, so the only remaining variable is the rate of inflation that is included in finding the discount factor. We have assumed a 2 percent rate with a normal distribution, plus or minus 1 percent (i.e., 1 percent represents three standard deviations).

It is important to remember that other approaches in which only the most likely estimate of each variable is used are equivalent to an assumption of certainty. The major benefit of simulation is that it allows all possible values for each variable to be considered. Just as the distribution of possible values for a variable is a better reflection of reality (as the estimator sees reality) than a single "most likely" value, the distribution of outcomes developed by simulation is a better forecast of uncertain future reality than a forecast of any single outcome can be. As any security analyst knows, a forecast of corporate quarterly earnings of $0.50–0.58 per share is far more likely to be accurate than a forecast of $0.54 per share. In general, precise forecasts will be precisely wrong.

TABLE 7.5 Single-Point Estimate of the Cash Flows for Ceramic Sciences, Inc.

1	Hurdle Rate	13.0%		
2	Inflation Rate	2.0%		
3	A	B	C	D
4	Year	Inflow	Outflow	Net Flow
5	20X0*	$0	$125,000	−$125,000
6	20X0	$0	$100,000	−$100,000
7	20X1	$0	$90,000	−$90,000
8	20X2	$50,000	$0	$50,000
9	20X3	$120,000	$15,000	$105,000
10	20X4	$115,000	$0	$115,000
11	20X5	$105,000	$15,000	$90,000
12	20X6	$97,000	$0	$97,000
13	20X7	$90,000	$15,000	$75,000
14	20X8	$82,000	$0	$82,000
15	20X9	$100,000	$0	$100,000
16	Total	$759,000	$360,000	$399,000
17	NPV			$17,997
18	*t = 0 at the beginning of 20X0			

= B5 − C5 [Copy to D6:D15]

= $65,000 cost savings + $35,000 salvage value

= D5 + NPV(B1 + B2,D6:D15)

[6]The instructions for its use are the same for either the beta or the triangular distribution, so the reader (or the instructor) may select either.

	A	B	C	D
TABLE 7.6		**Pessimistic, Most Likely, and Optimistic Estimates of the Cash Flows for Ceramic Sciences, Inc.**		
1		**Minimum**	**Most Likely**	**Maximum**
2	**Year**	**Inflow**	**Inflow**	**Inflow**
3	20X2	$35,000	$50,000	$60,000
4	20X3	95,000	120,000	136,000
5	20X4	100,000	115,000	125,000
6	20X5	88,000	105,000	116,000
7	20X6	80,000	97,000	108,000
8	20X7	75,000	90,000	100,000
9	20X8	67,000	82,000	91,000
10	20X9	81,000	100,000	111,000
11				
12	**Total**	$621,000	$759,000	$847,000

Using CB to run a Monte Carlo simulation requires us to define two types of cells in the Excel® spreadsheet. The cells that contain uncertain variables or parameters are defined as *assumption cells*. For the Ceramic Sciences case, these are the cells in Table 7.5, cells B8:B15 for the inflows and cell B2 for the rate of inflation.[7] The cells that contain outcomes of interest in the model are called *forecast cells*, cell D14 in Table 7.5. Each forecast cell typically contains a formula that is dependent on one or more of the assumption cells. Simulations may have many assumption and forecast cells, but they must have at least one of each. Before proceeding, open Crystal Ball and make a copy of Table 7.5.

To illustrate the process of defining an assumption cell, consider cell B5, the cash inflow estimate for 20X2. We can see from Table 7.6 that the minimum expected cash inflow is $35,000, the most likely cash flow is $50,000, and the maximum is $60,000. Also remember that we decided to model all these flows with the BetaPERT (or triangular, if you wish) distribution.

Once one has entered the original information in Table 7.5, the process of defining the assumption cells and entering the pessimistic and optimistic data is straightforward and involves six steps:[8]

1. Click on cell B5 to select it as the relevant assumption cell.
2. Select the Crystal Ball tab in Excel and from the Crystal Ball ribbon, select "**Define Assumptions**" at the very-left of the Crystal Ball ribbon. CB's **Distribution Gallery** is now displayed as shown in Figure 7.8.

---

[7]Note that while it would be more accurate to generate a separate inflation rate for each year, we have chosen to randomly generate an average inflation rate for the entire planning period. The model could be extended to generate individual inflation rates for each year, but doing so would require calculating the discount factor for each year separately and would preclude the use of Excel's NPV function.

[8]It is generally helpful for the reader to work the problem as we explain it. If Crystal Ball® Add-In has been installed on your computer but is not running, select **File/Options/Add-Ins**. Next, at the bottom of the displayed dialog box, click on the **"Go"** button after "**Manage/Excel Add-Ins**." In the next dialog box, click on the **CB** checkbox and select **OK**. If the CB Add-In has not been installed on your computer, download a CB trial copy using the instructions that accompany this book to install it.

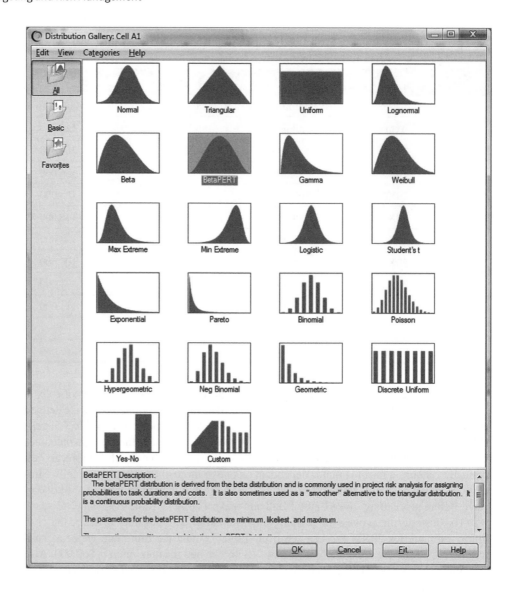

FIGURE 7.8 Crystal Ball®'s Distribution Gallery.

3. CB allows you to choose from a wide variety of probability distributions. Click on the **BetaPERT** (or Triangular) box and then click the "**OK**" button to select it.

4. CB's BetaPERT distribution dialog box is displayed as in Figure 7.9. It may have numbers in the boxes, but ignore them. If it does not otherwise appear exactly as in Figure 7.9, click "**Parameters**" in the menu at the top of the BetaPERT distribution box, and then select "**Minimum, Most Likely, Maximum**" at the top of the drop-down menu.

5. In the "**Name:**" textbox at the top of the dialog box, enter a descriptive label, for example, *Cash Inflow 20X2*. Then enter the pessimistic, most likely, and optimistic estimates from Table 7.6 in the appropriate cells below the distribution.

6. Click on the "**Enter**" button and then the "**OK**" button.

Now repeat steps 1 through 6 for the remaining cash flow assumption cells (cells B6:B12). Remember that the proper information to be entered is found in Table 7.6.

When finished with the cash inflow cells, the assumption cell for inflation can be defined. For cell B5, specify the normal distribution. We decided earlier to use a 2 percent

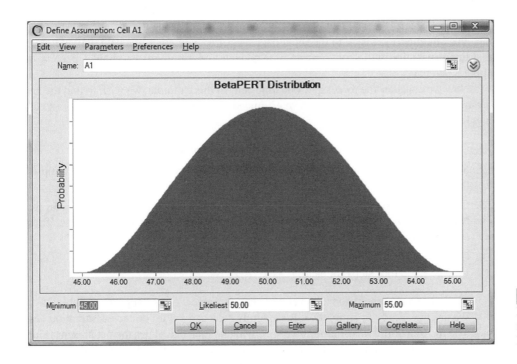

FIGURE 7.9 Crystal Ball® dialog box for model inputs assuming the BetaPERT distribution.

inflation rate, plus or minus 1 percent. Recall that the normal distribution is "bell-shaped" and that the mean of the distribution is its center point. Also recall that the mean, plus or minus three standard deviations, includes 99+ percent of the data. The normal distribution dialog box, Figure 7.10, calls for the distribution's mean and its standard deviation. The mean will be 0.02 (2 percent) for cell B5. The standard deviation will be .0033 (one third of the ±1 percent range). (Note that Figure 7.10 displays only the first two decimal places of the standard deviation although the actual standard deviation of .0033 is used by the program. If you wish to see the .0033, you may click on "Preferences" at the top of the box,

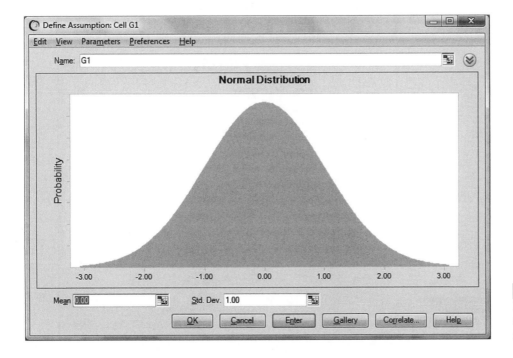

FIGURE 7.10 Crystal Ball® dialog box for model inputs assuming the normal distribution.

then select "Chart," "Axis," "Cell format," "Number," and change the "2" to "4." Then use the "OK" button to get back to the input data sheet.) As you enter this data, you will note that the distribution will show a mean of 2 percent and a range from about 1 percent to about 3 percent.

Now we consider the forecast or outcome cell. In this example, we wish to find the net present value of the cash flows we have estimated. The process of defining a forecast cell involves four steps.

1. Click on the cell **D14** to identify it as containing an outcome that interests us.
2. Select the menu option **Define Forecast** from the Crystal Ball ribbon at the top of the screen.
3. CB's **Define Forecast** dialog box is now displayed as shown in Figure 7.11. In the **Name:** textbox, enter a descriptive name such as *Net Present Value of Project*. Then enter a descriptive label such as *Dollars* in the **Units:** textbox.
4. Click **OK**. There is only one Forecast cell in this example, but there may be several. Use the same four steps for each.

When you have completed all entries, what was Table 7.5 now appears as Table 7.7.

We are now ready to simulate. CB randomly selects a value for each assumption cell based on the probability distributions we specified and then calculates the net present value of the project. By repeating this process many times, we can get a sense of the distribution of possible outcomes or, in this case, possible values of the project's NPV.

Approximately in the center of the CB ribbon, you will see the command **Run Preferences.** Below it is the **"Trials"** box. This box specifies how many times the model will be replicated. For this example, set it to 1,000. To run the simulation, click on the green Start Arrow in the CB ribbon.

The distribution of NPVs resulting from simulating this project 1,000 times is displayed in Figure 7.12. Statistical information on the distribution is shown in Figure 7.13. The NPVs had a mean of $11,086 and a standard deviation of $8,115. We can use this information to make probabilistic inferences about the NPV of the project such as the probability that the project will have a positive NPV, the probability that the project's NPV will exceed $10,000, or the probability that the project's NPV will be between $5,000 and $10,000.

FIGURE 7.11 Crystal Ball® dialog box for the model forecast or outcome.

TABLE 7.7	Three-Point Estimates of Cash Flows and Inflation Rate for Ceramic Sciences, Inc. All Assumptions and Forecast Cells Defined.			
1	**Hurdle Rate**	13.0%		
2	**Inflation Rate**	2.0%		
3	A	B	C	D
4	**Year**	**Inflow**	**Outflow**	**Net Flow**
5	20X0*	$0	$125,000	−$125,000
6	20X0	$0	$100,000	−$100,000
7	20X1	$0	$90,000	−$90,000
8	20X2	$50,000	$0	$50,000
9	20X3	$120,000	$15,000	$105,000
10	20X4	$115,000	$0	$115,000
11	20X5	$105,000	$15,000	$90,000
12	20X6	$97,000	$0	$97,000
13	20X7	$90,000	$15,000	$75,000
14	20X8	$82,000	$0	$82,000
15	20X9	$100,000	$0	$100,000
16	**Total**	**$759,000**	**$360,000**	**$399,000**
17	**NPV**			**$17,997**
18	*t = 0 at the beginning of 20X0*			

Assumption Cells for Inflation

Assumption Cell for Inflows

Forecast Cell for NPV

CB provides considerable information about the forecast cell in addition to the frequency chart including percentile information, summary statistics, a cumulative chart, and a reverse cumulative chart. For example, to see the summary statistics for a forecast cell, click on the Extract Data button in the CB ribbon and check Statistics in the dialog box that is displayed. The Statistics view for the frequency chart (Figure 7.12) is illustrated in Figure 7.13.

Figure 7.13 contains some interesting information. There are, however, several questions that are more easily answered by using Figure 7.12, the distribution of the simulation's outcomes. For example, what is the likelihood that this project will achieve an NPV at least $10,000 above the hurdle rate including inflation? It is easy to answer this question. Note that there are black triangles at either end of the baseline of the distribution in Figure 7.12. By placing the cursor on the triangle on the left end of the simulation distribution baseline and sliding it to the $10,000 mark, the probability of a $10,000 or greater outcome can be read in the "Certainty" box. One can also find the same answer by deleting the "–Infinity" in the box in the lower left corner of the Frequency View and entering $10,000 in it, almost .74 in this simulation.

Even in this simple example, the power of including uncertainty in project budgets should be obvious. Because a manager is always uncertain about the amount of uncertainty, it is also possible to examine various levels of uncertainty quite easily using CB. We could, for instance, alter the degree to which the inflow estimates are uncertain by expanding or contracting the degree to which optimistic and pessimistic estimates vary around the most likely estimate. We could increase or decrease the level of inflation. Simulation runs made

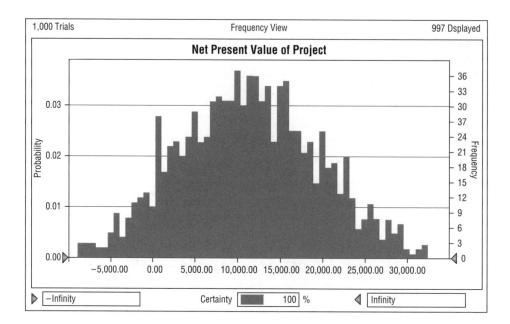

FIGURE 7.12 Frequency chart of the simulation output for net present value of Ceramic Sciences project.

with these changes provide us with the ability to examine just how sensitive the outcomes (forecasts) are to possible errors in the input data. This allows us to focus on the important risks and to ignore those that have little effect on our decisions.

Sensitivity Analysis

Sensitivity analysis, or what-if analysis, can be used for both quantitative models, its most common use, but also with qualitative models. The process is to go back into the model and change one of the parameters or variables and see what the impact is on the final result. In

FIGURE 7.13 Summary statistics of the simulation output for net present value of Ceramic Sciences project.

Statistics	Net Present Value of Project
Trials	1,000
Mean	11,086.17
Median	11,017.84
Mode	—
Standard Deviation	8,114.60
Variance	65,846,681.91
Skewness	0.1293
Kurtosis	2.69
Coeff. of Variability	0.7320
Minimum	−8,897.91
Maximum	37,689.89
Range Width	46,587.79
Mean Std. Error	256.61

this way, we can see what will have a major effect on the result, and thus our decision about what to do, and what won't affect it, or will have a trivial effect on the results so we don't need to worry about it. For example, with FMEA, we might see what a change in the severity of a threat might do, or in a decision tree, how the change in an outcome will change the result, or in simulation what changing a distribution might do to our profits. We can also consider what adding a new threat might do to our analysis, or adding a new branch in the decision tree, or inflation in our simulation. One weakness of sensitivity analysis is that a single change in the environment doesn't usually happen, and instead, many variables or parameters commonly change at the same time, which is harder to check and determine how it might affect our decision.

There is also a form of scenario sensitivity analysis, where the impact of alternative developments or scenarios in the completion of the project are predicted. For example, what would be the impact on the success of the project if the PM left the organization? If a major contractor suffered a strike by a labor union? If an important new technology did not perform as expected? If a competitor beat us to market? Once alternative scenarios are identified, they can be analyzed with the tools discussed earlier, including FMEA, decision trees, and Monte Carlo simulation. Contingency plans should be developed for scenarios where the predicted impact is particularly severe.

Dealing with Project Disasters

Thus far, we have focused mainly on risks that might be considered normal for any firm undertaking projects. We have dealt with these risks by using an "expected value" approach, as in the Ceramic Sciences example in Chapter 2; that is, the estimated loss (or gain) associated with a risky output times the probability that the loss (or gain) will occur. We might also compare the expected loss associated with a risk to the associated expected cost of *mitigating or preventing the loss associated with the risk*. If the reduction in expected loss due to risk mitigation or prevention is greater than its cost, we would invest in the risk mitigation/prevention.

But what about the case when the loss is catastrophic, even potentially ruinous, though it may have a very low probability of occurring; for example, a run on a bank; a strike at a critical supplier's plant; a flood that shuts down a construction project; an attack by a terrorist group on a building; or the discovery that a substance in a complex drug might cause toxic side effects? In many such cases, the cost of the risk may be massive, but the likelihood that it will occur is so small that the expected cost of the disaster is much less than many smaller, more common risks with far higher probabilities of occurring. This is typical of situations for which we purchase insurance, but what if such insurance is unavailable (usually because the pool of purchasers interested in such insurance is too small)? In Mallak et al. (1997), the authors suggest four approaches for project disaster planning: risk analysis, contingency planning, developing logic charts, and tabletop exercises.

An excellent book, *The Resilient Enterprise* (Sheffi, 2005), deals with risk management concerning many different types of disasters. The book details the methods that creative businesses have used to cope with catastrophes that struck their facilities, supply chains, customer bases, and threatened their survival. The subject is more complex than we can deal with here, but we strongly recommend the book.

In the next chapter, we address the subject of task scheduling, a topic of major importance in project management. More research and investigation have probably been conducted on the subject of scheduling than any other element of project management.

Summary

This chapter initiated the subject of project implementation by focusing on the project budget, which authorizes the PM to obtain the resources needed to begin work. Different methods of budgeting were described along with their impacts on project management. Then, a number of issues concerning cost estimation were discussed, particularly the effect of learning on the cost of repetitive tasks and how to use the concept of the learning curve.

Specific points made in the chapter were these:

- The intent of a budget is to communicate organizational policy concerning the organization's goals and priorities.
- There are a number of common budgeting methods: top-down, bottom-up, cost category, project/activity, and others not mentioned here.
- A form identifying the level of resource need, when it will be needed, who the contact is, and its availability is especially helpful in estimating costs.
- It is common for organizations to fund projects whose returns cover direct but not full costs in order to achieve long-run strategic goals of the organization.

- If projects include repetitive tasks with significant human input, the learning phenomenon should be taken into consideration when preparing cost estimates.
- The learning curve is based on the observation that the amount of time required to produce one unit decreases a constant percentage every time the cumulative output doubles.
- Other major factors, in addition to learning, that should be considered when making project cost estimates are inflation, differential changes in the cost factors, waste and spoilage, personnel replacement costs, and contingencies for unexpected difficulties.
- For handling uncertainty, risk analysis and simulation with sensitivity analysis are helpful.
- Risk management for both threats and opportunities has become increasingly important as projects become more complex and ill-defined. The seven subprocesses involved in managing the risks include helpful tools such as cause-effect diagrams, the risk matrix, FMEA, decision trees, simulation, a risk register, and a set of standard risk responses.

Glossary

Bottom-Up Budgeting A budgeting method that begins with those who will be doing the tasks estimating the resources needed. The advantage is more accurate estimates.

Cause–Effect (Fishbone) Diagram A chart showing all the factors and subfactors that can lead to a particular threat or opportunity.

Direct (or Variable) Cost These costs vary with output; e.g., labor costs, material costs, and sometimes the cost of capital equipment such as machinery that performs a specific function on each unit of output.

General & Administrative Cost (G&A) The cost of administration; e.g., Accounting, Human Resources, and Legal not charged as an Indirect Cost and not included in Overhead Cost. Sometimes the G&A is not reported as a separate item but is included in overhead cost. G&A is usually charged as a fixed percent of a direct cost such as labor.

Indirect (or Fixed) Cost These costs are associated with output, but do not vary with each unit of output; e.g., the cost of capital equipment not charged per piece of output, advertising, distribution, or sales. Costs are charged as a lump sum or as a fixed percent of some direct cost such as labor.

Overhead Costs Costs incurred by the firm, but not associated with any specific product or class of products; e.g., cost of building and ground maintenance, utilities, cost of plant security, cost of health insurance and pension plans. Typically charged as a fixed percent of some direct cost such as labor.

Failure Mode and Effect Analysis (FMEA) A risk assessment process that multiplies the levels of probability, impact, and inability to detect the risk to arrive at an overall risk priority number.

Learning Rate The percentage of the previous worker hours per unit required for doubling the output.

Monte Carlo Simulation A procedure that imitates real life by running thousands of values of distribution parameters to obtain an overall distribution of the outcomes of interest.

Project Budgeting Budgeting by project task/activity and then aggregating income and expenditures by project or program, often in addition to aggregation by organizational unit or category.

Risk Analysis A procedure that uses a distribution of input factors and probabilities and returns a range of outcomes and their probabilities.

Risk Matrix A chart showing probability on one side and impact on the other where threats and opportunities can be segmented into critical, monitor, or ignore cells.

Risk Register A database of risk information created by and available to PMs for their projects.

Sensitivity Analysis Investigation of the effect on the outcome of changing some parameters or data in the procedure or model.

Simulation A process where the structure of a situation is programmed and the probability distributions of the events are selected to give a probability distribution for the variable of interest, such as time or cost.

Top-Down Budgeting A budgeting method that begins with top managers' estimates of the resources needed for a project. Its primary advantage is that the aggregate budget is typically quite accurate because no element has been left out. Individual elements, however, may be quite inaccurate.

Variances The pattern of deviations in costs and usage used for exception reporting to management.

Questions

Material Review Questions

1. What are the advantages of top-down budgeting? Of bottom-up budgeting? What is the most important task for top management to do in bottom-up budgeting?

2. In preparing a budget, what indirect costs should be considered?

3. Describe the top-down budgeting process.

4. What is a variance?

5. Describe the learning curve phenomenon.

6. What is "program budgeting"?

7. What is the difference between project- and category-oriented budgets?

8. How does a risk analysis operate? How does a manager interpret the results?

9. What are the four parts of a technical proposal?

10. Describe how a risk matrix is constructed.

11. How would a decision tree be useful for a project manager?

12. Is the FMEA table more valuable than the risk matrix? Why (not)?

13. How far should the cause–effect diagram be broken down into subfactors?

14. Contrast the risk responses for threats and for opportunities.

Class Discussion Questions

15. Discuss ways in which to keep budget planning from becoming a game.

16. List some of the pitfalls in cost estimating. What steps can a manager take to correct cost overruns?

17. Why do consulting firms frequently subsidize some projects? Is this ethical?

18. What steps can be taken to make controlling costs easier? Can these steps also be used to control other project parameters, such as scope?

19. Which budgeting method is likely to be used with which type of organizational structure?

20. What are some potential problems with the top-down and bottom-up budgeting processes? What are some ways of dealing with these potential problems?

21. How is the budget planning process like a game?

22. Would any of the conflict resolution methods described in the previous chapter be useful in the budget planning process? Which?

23. How does the fact that capital costs vary with different factors complicate the budgeting process?

24. Why is learning curve analysis important to project management?

25. Why is it "ethically necessary to be honest" in negotiations between a superior and subordinate?

26. The chapter describes the problems of budgeting for S-shaped and J-shaped life-cycle projects. What might be the budgeting characteristics of a project with a straight line life cycle?

27. Interpret the columns of data in Figure 7.13. Does the $11,086 value mean that the project is expected to return only this amount of discounted money?

28. How would you find the probability in Figure 7.12 of an NPV of over $25,000?

29. Does the spread of the data in Table 7.4 appear realistic? Reconsider Table 7.4 to explain why the simulated outcome in Figure 7.13 is so much less than the value originally obtained in Table 7.3.

30. Identify some of the ethical issues that can arise in a bid response to an RFP.

31. Compare the advantages of risk matrices vs. FEMA tables for project management use.

32. Contrast decision trees and probability trees. How might each be used by PMs? Which would be the more valuable?

33. Could a cause–effect chart be used for two different risks at the same time? Would the end "problem" be the result of one risk or both concurrently?

34. Are the risk responses for threats or opportunities more important for PMs? Why?

Exercises

1. Top administrators in a university hospital have approved a project to improve the efficiency of the pharmaceutical services department by the end of the fiscal year to satisfy new state regulations for the coming year. However, they are concerned about four potential threats: (1) The cost to implement the changes may be excessive, (2) the pharmacists may resist the changes, (3) the project may run much longer than expected and not be ready for the coming fiscal year, and (4) the changes might reduce the quality of drug care in the hospital. The likelihood and negative impact of each threat have been solicited from the managers by a three-round Delphi process and are as follows, based on a seven-point scale where seven is the most likely and most negative impact:

Threat	Probability	Impact
1	5	3
2	6	5
3	3	4
4	4	7

Construct a risk matrix and identify what you would consider to be the "critical," "monitor," and "ignore" threats. Explain your reasoning. Recommend and justify a risk response for each threat.

2. The PM for the project in Exercise 1 has estimated the probabilities of not detecting the risks in time to react to them as follows, again on a seven-point scale: Threat 1:4, Threat 2:1, Threat 3:3, Threat 4:6. Construct a FMEA table to determine which risks are now the "critical," "monitor," and "ignore" threats. How have they changed from Exercise 1? Why? Does this new ranking seem more realistic?

3. You might not have realized it, but getting a college degree is a project. Assume that you are in a degree program in college and are concerned about getting your degree. Create a fishbone (cause–effect) diagram, with "failure to get degree" as the problem outcome. Identify at least four possible threat risks for this problem to occur. Then for each threat list at least three reasons/factors for how that threat could conceivably come to pass. Finally, review your diagram to estimate probabilities and impacts of each threat to getting your degree. Based on this analysis, what threats and factors should you direct your attention to, as the PM of your project to get your degree.

4. The yearly demand for a seasonal, profitable item follows the distribution:

Demand (units)	Probability
1,000	.20
2,000	.30
3,000	.40
4,000	.10

A manufacturer is considering launching a project to produce this item and could produce it by one of three methods:
a. Use existing tools at a cost of $6 per unit.
b. Buy cheap, special equipment for $1,000. The value of the equipment at the end of the year (salvage value) is zero. The cost would be reduced to $3 per unit.
c. Buy high-quality, special equipment for $10,000 that can be depreciated over four years (one fourth of the cost each year). The cost with this equipment would be only $2 per unit.

Set up this project as a decision tree to find whether the manufacturer should approve this project, and if so, which method of production to use to maximize profit. *Hint:* Compare total annual costs. Assume that production must meet all demand; each unit demanded and sold means more profit.

5. Given the following decision tree for a two-stage (decision) project to enter a joint venture, find the best alternatives (among $a_1–a_6$ in the figure) and their expected values. The outcomes shown are *revenues* and the investment expenses are in parentheses. Node 4 represents the situation where alternative a_1 was chosen, and then the top outcome with a 70 percent probability occurred; note that there is no choice of alternative if the 30 percent probability outcome occurred. Similarly with Node 5.

6. Medidata Inc. has identified three risk opportunities for their new medical database project. One is an opportunity to extend the database to include doctors as well as hospitals. This has a probability of a 3 and an impact on their profitability of a 3 on a 1–5 scale, where higher numbers are greater values of probability and profitability. Another is the opportunity to extend the database to other countries, particularly in Europe. For this, the probability is ranked only a 2 but the profitability impact is considered to be 4 due to the higher social interest by European governments. Finally, they might be able to interest nonusers such as pharmaceutical firms in using, or perhaps buying, their data. Here the probability is more certain, a 4, but the profitability would be only a 2. Construct an opportunity risk matrix, identify the "critical," "monitor," and "ignore" opportunities, and recommend risk responses for each opportunity.

7. Conduct a discounted cash flow calculation to determine the NPV of the following project, assuming a required rate of return of 0.2. The project will cost $75,000 but will result in cash inflows of $20,000, $25,000, $30,000, and $50,000 in each of the next 4 years.

8. In Exercise 7, assume that the inflows are uncertain but normally distributed with standard deviations of $1,000, $1,500, $2,000, and $3,500, respectively. Find the mean

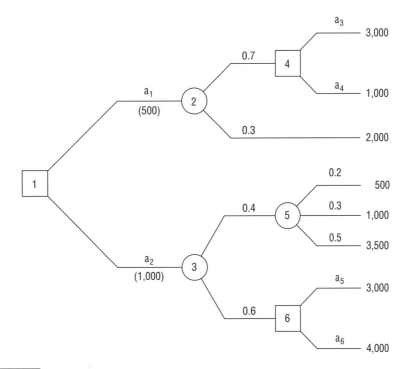

EXERCISE 5 Decision Tree.

forecast NPV using Crystal Ball®. What is the probability the actual NPV will be positive?

9. A production lot of 25 units required 103.6 hours of effort. Accounting records show that the first unit took 7 hours. What was the learning rate?

10. If unit 1 requires 200 hours to produce and the labor records for an Air Force contract of 50 units indicates an average labor content of 63.1 hours per unit, what was the learning rate? What total additional number of labor-hours would be required for a follow-on Air Force contract of 50 units? What would be the average labor content of this second contract? Of both contracts combined? If labor costs the vendor $10/hour on this second contract and the price to the Air Force is fixed at $550 each, what can you say about the profitability of the first and second contracts, and hence the bidding process in general?

11. Your firm designs PowerPoint slides for computer training classes, and you have just received a request to bid on a contract to produce the slides for an eight-session class. From previous experience, you know that your firm follows an 85 percent learning rate. For this contract, it appears the effort will be substantial, running 50 hours for the first session. Your firm bills at the rate of $100/hour and the overhead is expected to run a fixed $600 per session. The funder will pay you a flat fixed rate per session. If your nominal profit margin is 20 percent, what will be the total bid price, the per session price, and at what session will you break even?

12. A light manufacturing firm has set up a project for developing a new machine for one of its production lines. The most likely estimated cost of the project itself is $1,000,000, but the most optimistic estimate is $900,000 while the pessimists predict a project cost of $1,200,000. The real problem is that even if the project costs are within those limits, if the project itself plus its implementation costs exceed $1,425,000, the project will not meet the firm's NPV hurdle. There are four cost categories involved in adding the prospective new machine to the production line: (1) engineering labor cost, (2) nonengineering labor cost, (3) assorted material cost, and (4) production line downtime cost.

The engineering labor requirement has been estimated to be 600 hours, plus or minus 15 percent at a cost of $80 per hour. The nonengineering labor requirement is estimated to be 1,500 hours, but could be as low as 1,200 hours or as high as 2,200 hours at a cost of $35 per hour. Assorted material may run as high as $155,000 or as low as $100,000, but is most likely to be about $135,000. The best guess of time lost on the production line is 110 hours, possibly as low as 105 hours, and as high as 120 hours. The line contributes about $500 per hour to the firm's profit and overhead. What is the probability that the new machine project will meet the firm's NPV hurdle?

13. A 4-year financial project has estimates of net cash flows shown in the following table. It will cost $65,000 to implement the project, all of which must be invested at the beginning of the project. After the fourth year, the project will have no residual value. Assume that the cash flow

estimates for each year are best represented by a triangular distribution and that the hurdle rate is 20 percent.

a. Use Crystal Ball® to find the expected NPV of the project.

b. What is the probability that the project will yield a return greater than the 20 percent hurdle rate?

Year	Pessimistic	Most Likely	Optimistic
1	$14,000	$20,000	$22,000
2	19,000	25,000	30,000
3	27,000	30,000	36,000
4	32,000	35,000	39,000

14. If an inflation rate of 2 percent, normally distributed with a standard deviation of .333 percent, is assumed, what is the expected NPV of the project in Exercise 13, and what is the probability that it will qualify?

15. A cloud storage startup has decided to upgrade its server computers. It is also contemplating a shift from its Unix-based platform to a Windows-based platform. Three major cost items will be affected whichever platform they choose: hardware costs, software conversion costs, and employee training costs. The firm's technical group has studied the matter and has made the following estimates for the cost changes in $000s.

Using Crystal Ball® and assuming that the costs may all be represented by BetaPERT distributions, simulate the problem 1000 times. Given the information resulting from the simulation, discuss the decision problem.

	Windows			Unix		
	Low	Likeliest	High	Low	Likeliest	High
Hardware	100	125	200	80	110	210
Software	275	300	500	250	300	525
Training	9	10	15	8	10	17.5

Incidents For Discussion

Preferred Sensor Company

Sean Cole has been appointed PM of the Preferred Sensor Company's new sensor manufacturing process project. Sensors are extremely price-sensitive, and Preferred has done a great deal of quantitative work so it can accurately forecast changes in sales volume relative to changes in pricing.

The company president, "Dude" Sensor, has considerable faith in the firm's sensitivity model and insists that all projects that affect the manufacturing cost of sensors be run against the sensitivity model in order to generate data to calculate the return on investment. The net result is that PMs, like Sean, are under a great deal of pressure to submit realistic budgets so go/no-go project decisions can be made quickly. Dude has canceled several projects that appeared marginal during their feasibility stages and recently fired a PM for overestimating project costs on a new model sensor. The project was killed very early in the design stage, and 6 months later, a competitor introduced a similar sensor that proved to be highly successful.

Sean's dilemma is how to go about constructing a budget that accurately reflects the cost of the proposed new manufacturing process. Sean is an experienced executive and feels comfortable with his ability to come close to estimating the cost of the project. However, the recent firing of his colleague has made him a bit gun-shy. Only one stage out of the traditional four-stage sensor manufacturing process is being changed, so he has detailed cost information about a good percentage of the process. Unfortunately, the tasks involved in the process stage being modified are unclear at this point. Sean also believes that the new modification will cause someminor changes in the other three stages, but these changes have not been clearly identified. The stage being addressed by the project represents almost 50 percent of the manufacturing cost.

Question

Under these circumstances, would Sean be wise to pursue a top-down or a bottom-up budgeting approach? Why? What factors are most relevant here?

General Ship Company

General Ship Company has been building nuclear destroyers for the Navy for the last 20 years. It has recently completed the design of a new class of nuclear destroyer and will be preparing a detailed budget to be followed during construction of the first destroyer.

The total budget for this first destroyer is $290 million. The controller feels the initial project cost estimate prepared by the planning department was too low because the waste and spoilage allowance was underestimated. Thus, she is concerned that there may be a large cost overrun on the project and wants to work closely with the PM to control the costs.

Question

How would you monitor the costs of this project?

Continuing Integrative Class Project

Create a budget for your project using both top-down and bottom-up budgeting. Reconcile any differences by discussion between the PM, subgroup leaders, and the student(s) responsible for the task. For the purpose of developing the budget, determine appropriate labor rates for each team member, taking into account their administrative level.

Bibliography

Alderton, M. "Don't Leave Home Without It." *PM Network*, November 2012.

Amor, J. P., and C. J. Teplitz. "An Efficient Approximation for Project Composite Learning Curves." *Project Management Journal*, September 1998.

Badiru, A. B. "Incorporating Learning Curve Effects into Critical Resource Diagramming." *Project Management Journal*, June 1995.

Bowles, M. "Keeping Score." *PM Network*, May 2011.

Brooks, F. P. *The Mythical Man-Month*. Reading, MA: Addison-Wesley, 1975.

Brox, D. "Risk Talking Points." *PM Network*, June 2012b.

Champion, D. "Managing Risk in the New World." *Harvard Business Review*, October 2009.

Christensen, D. S., and J. A. Gordon. "Does a Rubber Baseline Guarantee Cost Overruns on Defense Acquisition Contracts?" *Project Management Journal*, September 1998.

Christensen, P. J., and J. Rydberg. "Overcoming Obstacles." *PM Network*, November 2001.

Coburn, S. "How Activity Based Costing Was Used in Capital Budgeting." *Management Accounting*, May 1997.

de Bakker, K., A. Boonstra, and H. Wortmann. "Risk Management Affecting Information Systems/Information Technology Project Success Through Communicative Action." *Project Management Journal*, April 2011.

Frame, J. D. "Risk Assessment Groups: Key Component of Project Offices." *PM Network*, March 1998.

Gagnon, R. J., and S. J. Mantel, Jr. "Strategies and Performance Improvement for Computer-Assisted Design." *IEEE Transactions on Engineering Management*, November 1987.

Gale, S. F. "A Series of Unfortunate Events." *PM Network*, January 2011.

Gale, S. F. "The Bottom Line," *PM Network*, August 2007.

Hillson, D., and P. Simon., *Practical Project Risk Management: The ATOM Method*, 2nd ed. Tyson's Corner, VA: Management Concepts Press, 2012.

Jergeas, G. F., and V. G. Cooke. "Law of Tender Applied to Request for Proposal Process." *Project Management Journal*, December 1997.

Jiang, J. J., and G. Klein. "Software Project Risks and Development Focus." *Project Management Journal*, March 2001.

Jordan, A. *Risk Management for Project Driven Organizations*. Plantation, FL: J. Ross Publishers, 2013.

Kaplan, R. S., and A. Mikes. "Managing Risks: A New Framework." *Harvard Business Review*, June 2012.

Knutson, J. "Proposal Management: Analyzing Business Opportunities." *PM Network*, January 1996a.

Knutson, J. "Proposal Management: Generating Winning Proposals, Part 1." *PM Network*, February 1996b.

Knutson, J. "Proposal Management: Generating Winning Proposals, Part 2." *PM Network*, March 1996c.

Krane, H. P., N. O. E. Olsson, and A. Rolstadas. "How Project Manager—Project Owner Interaction Can Work Within and Influence Project Risk Management." *Project Management Journal*, April 2012.

Langley, A. "Between 'Paralysis by Analysis' and 'Extinction by Instinct.'" *IEEE Engineering Management Review*, Fall 1995, reprinted from *Sloan Management Review*, Spring 1995.

Mallak, L. M., H. A. Kurstedt, Jr., and G. A. Patzak. "Planning for Crises in Project Management." *Project Management Journal*, June 1997.

Marcelino-Sadaba, S., A. Perez-Ezcurdia, A. M. Echeverria Lazcano, and P. Villanueva., "Project Risk Management Methodology for Small Firms." *International Journal of Project Management*, 32/2, 2014.

Meredith, J. R., S. M. Shafer, and E. Turban. *Quantitative Business Modeling*. Cincinnati, OH: Southwestern, 2002.

Meredith, J. R., and S. M. Shafer. *Operations Management for MBAs*, 5th ed. Hoboken, NJ: Wiley, 2013.

Royer, P. S. "Risk Management: The Undiscovered Dimension of Project Management." *PM Network*, September 2000. An extended version of this article appears in *Project Management Journal*, March 2000.

Salkeid, D. *Project Risk Analysis*. Burlington, VT: Ashgate Publishing Co., 2013.

Sheffi, Y. *The Resilient Enterprise*. Cambridge, MA: MIT Press, 2005.

Sigurdsen, A. "Principal Errors in Capital Cost Estimating Work, Part 1: Appreciate the Relevance of the Quantity-Dependent Estimating Norms." *Project Management Journal*, September 1996a.

Sigurdsen, A. "Principal Errors in Capital Cost Estimating, Part 2: Appreciate the Relevance of the Objective Cost Risk Analysis Method." *Project Management Journal*, December 1996b.

Stamatis, D. H. *Failure Mode and Effect Analysis: FMEA from Theory to Execution*, 2nd ed. ASQ Quality Press, 2003.

Taleb, N. N., D. G. Goldstein, and M. W. Spitznagel. "The Six Mistakes Executives Make in Risk Management." *Harvard Business Review*, October 2009.

Ward, S., and C. Chapman. *How to Manage Project Opportunities and Risks*, 3rd ed. Hoboken, NJ: Wiley, 2012.

Ward, S. "Requirements for an Effective Project Risk Management Process." *Project Management Journal*, September 1999.

Williams, T., O. J. Klekegg, D. H. T. Walker, B. Andersen, and O. M. Magnussen. "Identifying and Acting on Early Warning signs in Complex Projects." *Project Management Journal*, April 2012.

Zwikael, O., and A. Sadeh. "Planning Effort as an Effective Risk Management Tool," *Journal of Operations Management*, Vol. 25, pp. 755–767, 2007.

Zwikael, O., S. Globerson, and T. Raz. "Evaluation of Models for Forecasting the Final Cost of a Project." *Project Management Journal*, March 2000.

The following case describes a project where a franchisee of Fuddruckers has been selected to be the sole food vendor for the Crystal Coast Music Festival. Over the next couple of days, decisions regarding the menu items, order quantities, and prices need to be finalized. Complicating these decisions are a number of uncertainties including the weather, attendance, and the amount of food each attendee will consume.

Case

Fuddruckers and the Crystal Coast Music Festival   Scott M. Shafer and Shaunta McCracken, Wake Forest University

As Kathrayn Regan, director of marketing, gazed out the window of her Greensboro, North Carolina, office, her attention immediately shifted from the picture perfect day before her to wondering what the weather was like in Peletier, North Carolina. Of course, today's weather in Peletier was largely irrelevant. What really mattered was what the weather would be like a week from this coming Saturday, the date of the Crystal Coast Music Festival.

As director of marketing for CRC Management Company, a franchisee of Fuddruckers, Kathrayn was responsible for coordinating all aspects of being the sole food vendor for the music festival. As such, she needed to finalize the menu, determine the food prices, and determine the quantities of food to order. Complicating her decision were a number of uncertainties, including the weather and its impact on attendance, and how much food each attendee would consume. Kathrayn commented:

> One of my chief concerns is having enough product to meet customer demand. In the restaurant business, one bad experience can easily cancel out 10 good ones.

Steve Regan, president, summarized his feelings regarding his company's participation in the event:

> I am comfortable doing the event because there is essentially little upfront cost to us, but there is potential to make a reasonable profit and get some free advertising along the way. If this works out well for us, we might consider investing in a trailer and participating in more outdoor events in the future.

Kathrayn added, "Although the concert and advertising may also help us increase sales in our Jacksonville locations, my gut tells me we can clear a profit of over $25,000 if we plan this event right!"

The Crystal Coast Music Festival

The Crystal Coast Music Festival was to be held on June 2, at the Carteret County Speedway in Peletier, North Carolina. The event included some of the region's best beach music bands as well as top 40 and country music groups. This year's lineup included Diamond Rio, Marshall Tucker, Tim Rushlow, Clarence Carter, and Land of Oz. The festival was scheduled to run from noon until 7:00 P.M. Ten thousand tickets were printed for the festival; tickets cost $25 if purchased in advance and $35 at the gate.

The promoter of the event had a media budget of $125,000, which was spent on both print and radio advertisements. Although CRC Management Co., the owner of the local Fuddruckers, did not contribute to the media budget, the Fuddruckers name was mentioned in all advertisements. Kathrayn noted that "the advertisements will promote Fuddruckers as having the best burger on the east coast." The majority of the radio advertisements appeared on five radio stations in eastern North Carolina including 93.3 (alternative), 98.7 (oldies), 95.1 (country), 92.0 (rock), and 105.1 (rock).

Considering the likelihood of different weather conditions, Kathrayn felt there was about a 70 percent chance that 4001 to 8,000 people would attend the event. Likewise, she felt that there was about a 20 percent chance that between 2,000 and 4,000 people would attend the event, and a 10 percent chance that 8001 to 10,000 people would attend. In all cases, Kathrayn felt that any outcome within a given range was as likely as any other outcome. She explained:

> In my conversations with the promoter, he stated that in past years attendance was never less than 4,000.

The authors gratefully acknowledge the valuable suggestions of three anonymous reviewers. This case was prepared as the basis for class discussion rather than to demonstrate effective or ineffective management practices. Names have been disguised.

Of course, I asked to see his data, but he always seemed to evade my request. As I reflect on it now, I doubt he has any hard data to actually share with me. I also know that attendance will not exceed 10,000 because this is the total number of tickets printed for the event. Given the current weather forecast, I don't expect the event to be a sellout. The better the weather, the more likely it is that people will show up. On the other hand, there are 100,000 marines just 7 miles away at Camp Lejeune who generally have some time to kill on Saturdays. This and the radio advertising that hit a diverse crowd is what I used to develop my attendance projections.

Currently, the 1-week-ahead forecast predicted clear skies the day of the Crystal Coast Musical Festival. However, in monitoring the weather Kathrayn noticed that frequently the forecast changed abruptly from one day to the next. She further estimated that if the weather on the day of the event turned out to be sunny the likelihood of 4001 to 8,000 people attending would decrease to 50 percent while the likelihood of 8001 to 10,000 people attending would increase to 30 percent. Similarly, if it rained on the day of the event, Kathrayn estimated that there would be an 80 percent chance that 2,000 to 4,000 people would attend the event and a 20 percent chance that 4,001 to 8,000 people would attend.

Kathrayn further estimated that there was a 50 percent chance that the average event attendee would consume between 0.55 to 0.75 meals at the concert. Optimistically, she speculated that there was a 35 percent chance that attendees would consume 1 to 2 meals; pessimistically, she felt there was a 15 percent chance that people attending the event would consume 0.15 to 0.30 meals. Kathrayn explained:

Based on the time of the event, some people would eat once, some would eat twice, and some would probably just drink. Also, because it is an outside event, the weather would certainly affect the attendees' eating habits. When the weather is sunny with some clouds, people eat more; when it is hot and sunny with no clouds or rainy, they eat less.

Food Service Planning

Initially, Kathrayn needed to determine exactly what items would be offered at the musical festival. Once this decision was made, the amount to charge for each menu item and the quantities to order could then be considered. Kathrayn noted, "Because of the location of the concert, one complication with planning this event was having to deal with a supplier we have not dealt with previously. I worry that they won't have the food in stock."

In terms of the menu offerings, Kathrayn developed a limited menu option and a broad menu option. The limited menu option included ⅓-pound burgers, ¼-pound hot dogs, and potato chips. The broad menu option included the same menu options as the limited menu plus chicken sandwiches. A complication associated with the broad menu option was that the chicken had to be ordered almost 1 week prior to the event when the weather outlook was much less certain; the hamburger meat, hot dogs, and potato chips could all be ordered three days prior to the event (Exhibit 1).

At another outdoor concert event CRC participated in, the breakdown in unit demand (not sales dollars) for hamburgers, hot dogs, and chicken was 20 percent, 75 percent, and 5 percent, respectively. This event was a pop rock concert held in Winston-Salem, North Carolina. However, according to Kathrayn, it differed from the Crystal Coast Musical Festival in a number of significant ways. First, it was held consecutively over a Friday and Saturday night from 5 P.M. to 11 P.M. each night. Second, simultaneous performances were held on three stages spread out over several blocks. Finally, a younger audience was targeted.

Regarding the Crystal Coast Musical Festival, Kathrayn estimated that hamburgers would account for 50 percent of the demand, hot dogs for 30 percent, and chicken for 20 percent. She explained:

The marines that will be attending the Crystal Coast Musical Festival are more typical of our regular restaurant customers. Therefore, I adjusted the product mix based on our regular store sales. Also, the event held in Winston-Salem was more of a street festival where people stood and ate their food. I expect the people at the Crystal Coast Musical Festival will have lawn chairs and blankets to sit on when they eat their food.

	Monday	Tuesday	Wednesday	Thursday	Friday	Saturday
Chicken	Order		Arrives	Unwrap and Thaw	Marinate	Musical Festival
Hamburger/Hot Dogs			Order		Arrives and Grind	
Buns					Mix, Bake, and Cut	
Produce Caps*					Prepare	

* Produce caps consist of lettuce, tomato, pickle, and onion.

EXHIBIT 1 Planning Activities.

Menu Item	Cost	Anticipated Price[a]
⅓-pound hamburger patty	$1.01	$5.00
¼-pound hot dog	$0.55	$4.00
Chicken	$1.10	$5.25
Hamburger, Hot Dog, and Chicken Buns	$0.20	
Potato Chips	$0.40	
Produce (chicken and hamburgers)	$0.45	
Condiment Packs	$0.04	
Plate	$0.15	
Sales Tax for Prepared Food	1%	

[a]Hamburgers, hot dogs, and chicken sandwiches all served with potato chips. Price includes sales tax.

EXHIBIT 2   Cost and Pricing Data.

Kathrayn summarized cost data and the anticipated price for these menu items (Exhibit 2). Because of the perishable nature of the food and the distance of the event from CRC's other restaurants, any unused food would need to be discarded or perhaps donated to local food shelters. Furthermore, given the special nature of the event, Kathrayn did not anticipate significant shortage costs beyond the lost profits should they run out of one or more menu items. Another vendor was responsible for providing drink services.

In staffing the musical festival event, CRC would incur a number of other expenses. First, it was anticipated that the booth would be staffed with four salaried members from headquarters and two hourly workers who earn $7 per hour. In addition a tent would need to be rented for 3 days at a cost of $15, and a gas grill would need to be rented for 1 day at a cost of $15. Cooler space was to be provided by the event promoter.

Finally, in consideration for being the event's sole food vendor, CRC was required to supply a VIP tent for the musicians with food at no cost. Based on the number of acts, Kathrayn estimated that the musicians and their entourages would consume in the neighborhood of 150 to 250 hamburgers, with all quantities in this range equally likely.

The Decision

It was Friday afternoon, May 26. Kathrayn had just checked the Accuweather Web site (www.accuweather.com) for the fifth time today. The weather forecast was for clear the day of the event with thunderstorms the following two days. If Kathrayn decided to go with the broad menu option, she would need to place the order for the chicken Monday morning.

On Wednesday of next week, Kathrayn had scheduled a meeting with the event promoter. The purpose of the meeting was to get a count on the number of tickets sold to date. Based on this information and a more current weather forecast, Kathrayn would then need to quickly place the order for the hamburger meat, hot dogs, and potato chips late Wednesday afternoon.

The most pressing issue was whether to go with the limited or broad menu. If the broad menu was selected, how much chicken should be ordered Monday morning? Once these decisions were made, Kathrayn wanted to further analyze the situation regarding the quantities of hamburgers, hot dogs, and potato chips to order based on possible weather-attendance-consumption patterns. She thought that by undertaking such an analysis now she could develop guidelines for placing the order on Wednesday afternoon. The one thing she did know for certain was that there would be little time for this analysis Wednesday afternoon once she received the updated ticket sales information and weather forecast.

Questions

1. Does serving as the food vendor for the Crystal Coast Music Festival qualify as a project? Why or why not?

2. What are the sources of uncertainty facing Kathrayn Regan? Can anything be done to help mitigate the uncertainty?

3. Would you recommend Kathrayn go with the limited or broad menu? How much of each food item would you recommend Kathrayn order? (Hint: you might consider simulating alternative scenarios and comparing the results of the simulation runs.)

4. Based on your projected order quantities, develop a budget for the project.

This article clearly describes the dangers of our faster, more volatile, and more global markets for organizations that have trouble changing their structures and responses. Change involves more risk, but lack of change guarantees falling behind faster and faster. Resilience—the ability of a system to cope with change—is the solution. Being more agile, flexible, and executing faster and more efficiently are all components of resilience, but these must be ingrained in the organization, which takes time and conscious effort.

Reading

Building Resiliency[9]   D. Burba

In the 21st century, competitive disruption is business as usual. Just look at the airline industry: In less than 15 years, four upstart "super-connector" airlines—Emirates, Qatar, Etihad and Turkish—have surpassed the reach of formerly dominant carriers based in Europe. And they're beginning to move into the traditional turf of U.S.-based airlines.

How to respond to aggressive competitors and navigate volatile markets quickly and successfully is the crux of organizational agility. No longer a buzz-word, agility is a must-have for project success in rapidly evolving sectors—which these days is most.

"To be prepared for the future, you need both a culture and an organizational structure that provide the flexibility needed in a changeable environment," says Jorge Alberto Pérez Torres, PMP, organization deputy director at insurance firm Allianz, Mexico City, Mexico. "The word 'resilience'—the ability of a system to cope with change—fits very well in this case."

PMI's 2015 *Pulse of the Profession*®: *Capturing the Value of Project Management Through Organizational Agility* in-depth report found that 75 percent of organizations with a highly developed culture of agility are able to quickly respond to market conditions, compared to 12 percent of organizations with an underdeveloped culture of agility.

The contrast was similar with customer satisfaction ratings (85 percent compared to 23 percent).

Yet cultivating organizational agility isn't easy. Organizations aren't monoliths; they're made up of people, and getting people to change their habits of mind and behavior takes time and effort. When organizations create a culture of agility that enables projects and programs—their most strategic initiatives—to be completed faster and more efficiently than ever before, they are better positioned to thrive in uncertain economic conditions. According to the *Pulse* report, organizations can accomplish this by establishing a five-part, self-reinforcing framework consisting of supportive culture, strategic flexibility, collective leadership, capable people and adaptive process.

But the real challenge for organizations looking to increase their agility is figuring out how to ingrain these capabilities so deeply in the project culture that they become second nature. There's no getting around the time and conscious effort this requires.

Prepared for the Storm

The difference between managing projects, programs and portfolios now compared to 10 years ago is the speed at which change and risk management capabilities have to be used, says Herb Payan, PMP, senior vice president, digital strategies, Sony Music, Fort Lauderdale, Florida, USA.

"In the past, project management was all about efficiency and optimizing each process," he says. "Today, it's more about flexibility and agility, because market trends change during project cycles." Under such circumstances, change management at the portfolio level is critical. "I can look across the portfolio, and there's a lot more outside influence on it than there used to be," Mr. Payan says. "If you don't have good change management in the portfolio, you're going to spend a lot of time managing chaos."

The *Pulse* report bears his point out: Organizations with a highly developed culture of agility are more effective at organizational change. Sixty-seven percent are effective at anticipating changes in the external environment, compared to just 10 percent of organizations with an underdeveloped culture of agility. And 61 percent of them can effectively implement responsive or adaptive strategies to the changing environment, compared to 6 percent of organizations with an underdeveloped culture of agility.

Mastering both change and risk management boils down to three capabilities: the ability to monitor and respond to the external environment, the ability to standardize change and risk management practices throughout the organization, and the ability to translate knowledge gained through these practices into a better project portfolio.

Preventing Peril

How all this drives increased agility is simple: It prepares project and portfolio managers to make the right decisions in rapidly changing environments. In a tightly regulated industry such as banking, work on a deliverable often has to be done before the exact nature of upcoming regulations are known, says Marc Burlereaux, PMI-ACP, PMI-RMP, PMP, PgMP, business implementation manager, HSBC Private Bank, Geneva, Switzerland. Complicating matters, the project team often has to take into account regulations by both local and pan-European authorities.

Even when the pressure comes from within—decreasing time to market, for example—the importance of risk management remains. "In all these contexts, risk management is crucial to ensure delivery without putting the company at risk," says Mr. Burlereaux. "With too much pressure from management, there is a strong tendency to minimize risk impact. We then need a strong operational risk manager who is able to be vocal."

Organizational agility also requires all project teams to work from the same playbook. The 2015 *Pulse* report found that organizations with highly developed cultures of agility focus on project management training and development far more than those with low agility (66 percent compared to 13 percent of organizations with underdeveloped cultures of agility). The new 2015 study notes that organizations with highly developed cultures of agility succeed by embedding foundational practices across the business, including aligning business capabilities to strategy and integrating the voice of the customer into projects.

For Mr. Burlereaux, having standardized practices such as fully documenting projects has proven the key to managing

290 CHAPTER 7 Budgeting and Risk Management

initiatives in an industry—banking—that hasn't exactly lacked volatility and uncertainty in recent years.

"The main advantage of having a well-documented portfolio of projects was to be able to keep, shorten or stop initiatives, depending on simple criteria like cost to complete, benefits awaited versus benefits realized, or 'do or die' projects," he says. "An updated projects portfolio database is essential to make on-the-spot decisions to either maximize the benefits or make sure we keep the bare minimum in the portfolio in case of a stormy environment."

Structural Evolution

Whether there's a market meltdown or surging competitor, the ability to sail through the storm successfully requires everyone from the executive suite on down to be on board. If only a few superstars at an organization excel in change or risk management, for example, opportunities will be missed.

For example, Mr. Torres notes that organizations that rigorously follow a yearly budget struggle with agility, because they are shackled to a fixed amount of money that doesn't change as the project advances.

"Having the intention to be agile is not enough if the way we are organized is not profoundly changed in terms of policies, procedures, team structures, empowerment and trust," he says.

At Sony Music, that has meant flattening the organization so that everyone's voice is equal. That allows ideas, rather than titles, to drive the organization's culture.

"The people with the everyday workload, they know where the problems are. We have to listen to them," says Mr. Payan. "We have to go from, 'If my title is X, then I should have the answers,' to 'My job is to make sure the right solutions are implemented.'"

The organization also has embraced an ethos of "fail and fail fast." Rather than investing a great deal of time and effort in developing a prototype, they put out an imperfect model, get feedback and adjust. Identifying mistakes, he says, should be both accepted and rewarded, an attitude that he acknowledges requires a shift in mindset by typically risk-averse senior managers. The idea is that by giving teams the freedom to take more agile project approaches, the organization is growing its overall agility: It can get products to market faster and adjust them on the fly, avoiding long, costly development cycles. In a dynamic market, this can make the difference between beating a competitor and being left behind.

But the road to agility can be bumpy. "Many managers don't want to deal with agility because [they think] it is less governable and implies more freedom, and thus risk, for their teams," Mr. Torres says. Only by trusting team members to deliver using

essential checks and balances can project and program managers make their organizations more agile, he says.

But the onus is also on project managers to create an environment that fosters the ability to quickly make changes while taking the big picture into account. To implement organizational agility, "the number one most important thing is communication," says Becky Walker, PMP, government analyst at the Florida Department of Revenue, Tampa, Florida, USA. "In order for us to be our most efficient, we have to be aligned with the organizational strategy and have the resources to quickly respond to external changes."

That means project managers have to work hard to build their knowledge—both of their own organization's goals and capabilities, and also of industry trends and market dynamics. And when the time comes, they need to be able to blend strategy, goals and reality to make the right decision quickly.

The ability to adjust on a day-to-day basis to new market challenges while keeping an organization's strategic goals in mind is crucial, says Ms. Walker. "When challenges emerge, you have to ask yourself, 'What's the problem, and how can I solve it while still meeting my own performance measures and strategic goals?'"

Finally, she notes that assessing and calibrating strategic goals quarterly or annually isn't frequent enough in the current business environment. Organizations must have the ability make changes whenever challenges emerge. That requires everyone in the organization, particularly at the top, to acknowledge that hewing to the status quo in a dynamic environment won't work.

When they do, they'll see the benefits where they matter most—on the bottom line. The *Pulse* study found that increased organizational agility resulted in faster responses to changing market conditions, better organizational efficiency, improved customer satisfaction and greater business results. At a time when many organizations are treading water, those are powerful reasons to start thinking—and acting—differently.

Questions

1. Why do managers perceive organizational change, and the agility to change quickly and easily, as increasing risks?

2. The article emphasizes that increasing the organization's agility, although difficult, isn't the most challenging task. What is?

3. The first two of the three capabilities for mastering change and risk management seem sufficient. Why the third?

4. What's the problem with pressure from management to minimize risk impacts—shouldn't they be worried about risks too?

CHAPTER 8

Scheduling

In this and the following three chapters, we continue with the implementation of the project plans we made in Chapter 6. In this chapter, we examine some scheduling techniques that have been found to be useful in project management. We cover the Program Evaluation and Review Technique (PERT), the Critical Path Method (CPM), Gantt charts and briefly discuss Precedence Diagramming and report-based methods. Risk analysis and management will be considered as an inherent feature of all scheduling methods, and a simulation of a project schedule will be demonstrated.

While the topic of scheduling and particularly the mechanics of project scheduling tend to be more tactical in nature, it is important for the reader to keep in mind that there are important strategic implications associated with project scheduling. For example, in many projects such as the release of a new version of a software product, the construction of an office building, or the upgrade of the latest smartphone, nothing is more visible to senior management and customers than a project that misses its published deadline. In addition to increasing the cost of the project, missed deadlines can seriously damage an organization's brand and reputation. And with greatly shorter product lifecycles, missed deadlines can have serious consequences in terms of the ability of the organization to gain market share and may significantly limit the amount of time the organization has to recoup its investment in the project. Therefore, while our discussion of the mechanics of scheduling in this chapter takes a more tactical approach, it is important to not to lose sight of the strategic implications associated with project scheduling.

> *As of tomorrow, employees will only be able to access the building using individual security cards. Pictures will be taken next Wednesday, and employees will receive their cards in 2 weeks.*

In Chapter 9, we continue our discussion of scheduling and consider the special problems of scheduling when resource limitations force conflicts between concurrent projects or even between two or more tasks in a single project. We also look at Goldratt's "critical chain" (1997) and ways of expediting activities by adding resources.

8.1 Background

A schedule is the conversion of a project work breakdown structure (WBS) into an operating timetable. As such, it serves as the basis for monitoring and controlling project activity and, taken together with the plan and budget, is probably the major tool for the management of projects. In a project environment, the scheduling function is more important than it would be in an ongoing operation because projects lack the continuity of day-to-day operations and often present much more complex problems of coordination. Indeed, project scheduling is so important that a detailed schedule is sometimes a funder-specified requirement.

A properly designed, detailed schedule can also serve as a key input in establishing the monitoring and control systems for the project. In general, the schedule is developed down to the work package level, but in very large projects, the schedule for the project manager (PM) may only be two or three levels deep, with supplemental schedules for each major subproject.

The basic approach of all scheduling techniques is to form a network of activity and event relationships that graphically portrays the sequential relations between the tasks in a project. Tasks that must precede or follow other tasks are then clearly identified, in time as well as in function. Such a network is a powerful tool for planning and controlling a project and has the following benefits:

- It is a consistent framework for planning, scheduling, monitoring, and controlling the project.
- It illustrates the interdependence of all tasks, work packages, and work elements.
- It denotes the times when specific individuals and resources must be available for work on a given task.
- It aids in ensuring that the proper communications take place between departments and functions.
- It determines an expected project completion date.
- It identifies so-called critical activities that, if delayed, will also delay the project completion time.
- It also identifies activities with slack that can be delayed for specified periods without penalty or from which resources may be temporarily borrowed without harm.
- It determines the dates on which tasks may be started—or must be started if the project is to stay on schedule.
- It illustrates which tasks must be coordinated to avoid resource or timing conflicts.
- It also illustrates which tasks may be run, or must be run, in parallel to achieve the predetermined project completion date.
- It relieves some interpersonal conflict by clearly showing task dependencies.
- It may, depending on the information used, allow an estimate of the probability of project completion by various dates, or the date corresponding to a particular a priori probability.

Project Management in Practice

Massachusetts' Instant Bridges

The River Street Bridge replacement in Boston would normally have taken 2 years of road closures and detours for citizens but due to Boston's "accelerated approach," only required 2 days on one weekend in April. Workers prefabricated the bridge on an adjacent lot, then tore down the old span on a Friday night and slid the new bridge onto the old abutments, finished the fastening and testing, and opened it up to traffic on Monday. According to the head of the U.S. Federal Highway Administration, this accelerated approach will be the "new normal" in the future.

Questions

1. Given the pressure to speed up the completion of a project by compressing its schedule, what's the message here?

2. Do you expect this new way of replacing transportation infrastructure will be more or less expensive?

3. Why do you think this approach wasn't used sooner?

Source: "Instant Bridges," *PM Network*, Vol. 26.

8.2 | Network Techniques: PERT and CPM

With the exception of Gantt charts, to be discussed next, the most common approach to project scheduling is the use of network techniques such as PERT and CPM. The PERT was developed by the U.S. Navy in cooperation with Booz Allen Hamilton and the Lockheed Corporation for the Polaris missile/submarine project in 1958. The CPM was developed by DuPont, Inc., during the same time period.

In application, PERT has primarily been used for R&D projects, the type of projects for which it was developed, though its use is more common on the "development" side of R&D than it is on the "research" side. CPM was designed for construction projects and has been generally embraced by the construction industry. (There are many exceptions to these generalities. The Eli Lilly Company, for example, uses CPM for its research projects.)

The use of PERT has decreased sharply in recent years because a large majority of project management software generates CPM networks. The two methods are quite similar and are often combined for educational presentation.

Originally, PERT was strictly oriented to the time element of projects and used probabilistic activity time estimates to aid in determining the probability that a project could be completed by some given date. CPM, on the other hand, used deterministic activity time estimates and was designed to control both the time and cost aspects of a project, in particular, time/cost trade-offs. In CPM, activities can be "crashed" (expedited) at extra cost to speed up the completion time. Both techniques identified a project critical path with activities that could not be delayed and also indicated activities with slack (or float) that could be somewhat delayed without lengthening the project completion time. Some writers insist on a strict differentiation between PERT and CPM. This strikes us as unnecessary. One can estimate probabilistic CPM times and can "crash" PERT networks.

We might note in passing that the critical activities in real-world projects typically constitute less than 10 percent of the total activities. In our examples and simplified problems in this chapter, the critical activities constitute a much greater proportion of the total because we use smaller networks to illustrate the techniques.

Terminology

Let us now define some terms used in our discussion of networks.

Activity   A specific task or set of tasks that are required by the project, use up resources, and take time to complete.

Event The result of completing one or more activities. An identifiable end state that occurs at a particular time. Events use no resources.

Network The arrangement of all activities (and, in some cases, events) in a project arrayed in their logical sequence and represented by arcs and nodes. This arrangement (network) defines the project and the activity precedence relationships. Networks are usually drawn starting on the left and proceeding to the right. Arrowheads placed on the arcs are used to indicate the direction of flow—that is, to show the proper precedences. Before an event can be realized—that is, achieved—all activities that immediately precede it must be completed. These are called its predecessors. Thus, an event represents an instant in time when each and every predecessor activity has been finished.

Path The series of connected activities (or intermediate events) between any two events in a network.

Critical Activities, events, or paths that, if delayed, will delay the completion of the project. A project's critical path is understood to mean that sequence of critical activities (and critical events) that connects the project's start event to its finish event and which cannot be delayed without delaying the project.

To transform a project plan into a network, one must know what activities comprise the project and, for each activity, what its predecessors (or successors) are. An activity can be in any of these conditions: (1) it may have a successor(s) but no predecessor(s); (2) it may have a predecessor(s) but no successor(s); and (3) it may have both predecessor(s) and successor(s). The first of these is an activity that starts a network. The second ends a network. The third is in the middle. Figure 8.1 shows each of the three types of activities. Activities are represented here by rectangles (one form of what in a network are called "nodes") with arrows to show the precedence relationships. When there are multiple activities with no predecessors, it is usual to show them all emanating from a single node called "START,"[1] as in Figure 8.2. Similarly, when multiple activities have no successors, it is usual to show them connected to a node called "END."

The interconnections depend on the technological relationships described in the WBS. For example, when one paints a room, filling small holes and cracks in the wall and masking windows and woodwork are predecessors to painting the walls. Similarly, removing curtains and blinds, as well as pictures and picture hooks from the wall, is a predecessor to

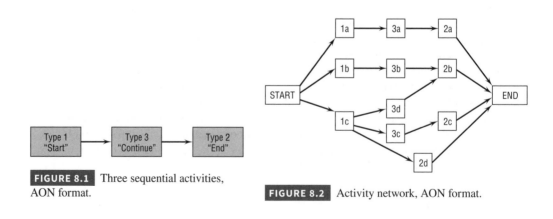

FIGURE 8.1 Three sequential activities, AON format.

FIGURE 8.2 Activity network, AON format.

Fig. 6.11

[1]It is traditional to use the word "START" to note the beginning of a network. The PMI used "START" in the first two editions of its Guide to the Project Management Body of Knowledge (**PMBOK**). However, in the third edition of **PMBOK**, they started denoting the first node in a network as "BEGIN." We will stay with "START."

spackling and masking. It is the nature of the work to be done that determines predecessor–successor relationships.

In the preceding examples, rectangles (nodes) represented the activities; hence, it was called an activity-on-node (AON) network. Another format for drawing networks is activity-on-arrow (AOA), as shown in Figure 8.3. Here, the activities are shown on the arrows, and the (circular) nodes represent events. If the project begins with multiple activities, they can all be drawn emanating from the initial node, and multiple activities can terminate in a single node at the end of the project.

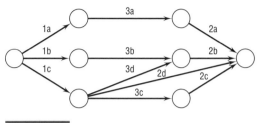

FIGURE 8.3   Activity network, AOA format.

Throughout most of this chapter, we adopt the AON format, but we will also demonstrate AOA network construction. This chapter is intended as an introduction to project scheduling at a level sufficient for the PM who wishes to use most commercial computerized project scheduling packages. For a deeper understanding of PERT and CPM, we refer the reader to Moder et al. (1983).

Recall the planning documents we developed in Chapter 6. In particular, the WBS contains the information we need. It is a list of all activities that must be undertaken in order to complete a specified task, the time each activity is expected to take, any nonroutine resources that will be used by the activity, and the predecessor activities for each activity. For example, we might have a WBS similar to that shown in Figure 8.4.

Constructing the Network, AON Version

We begin with the node called "START." Activities **a** and **b** have no predecessors, so we draw arrows out of START to each of them (Figure 8.5). As explained earlier, the arrowheads show the direction of precedence. Activity **c** follows **a**, activity **d** follows **b**, and activity **e** also follows **b**. Let's add these to our network in Figure 8.6a. Now, activity

WBS

Objective: To complete. . . . .

. . . .

Measures of Performance. . . . .

. . . .

Constraints . . . .

Tasks	*Precedence*	*Time*	*Cost*	*Who Does*
a	—	5 days	—	—
b	—	4 days	—	—
c	a	6 days	—	—
d	b	2 days	—	—
e	b	5 days	—	—
f	c,d	8 days	—	—

FIGURE 8.4   Sample WBS.

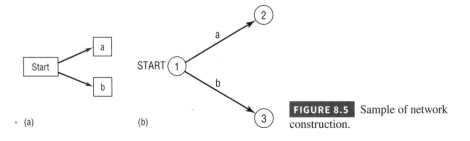

(a)   (b)

FIGURE 8.5   Sample of network construction.

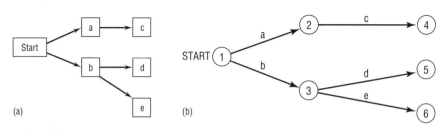

FIGURE 8.6 Sample of network construction.

f follows both **c** and **d**. The WBS does not indicate that any further activity is required to complete the task, so we have reached the end of this particular plan. We thus draw arrows from activities **e** and **f** to the node END, as shown in Figure 8.7a. Many of the project management software packages will generate these networks on request.

Constructing the Network, AOA Version

Again, we begin with a node (event) called "START." Referring to Figure 8.4, we observe that activities **a** and **b** have no predecessors, so we draw arrows labeled "a" and "b" from START and terminating in circle-shaped nodes numbered "2" and "3" for easy identification (Figure 8.5b). Activity **c** follows **a**, activity **d** follows **b**, and activity **e** also follows **b**. Let's add these arrows to our AOA network, labeling the arrows and nodes sequentially as we go (Figure 8.6b).

Note that activity **f** must follow both **c** and **d**, but any given activity must have its source in one and only one node. Therefore, **c** and **d** must terminate at the same node. Erase activity **d** and its node—it is now clear that hand-drawn networks should be drawn in pencil—and redraw **d** to end at the same node that terminates **c**. We now add activity **e** following **b**, and **f** following **c** and **d**. Because **e** and **f** have no successors, they will terminate at the END node (Figure 8.7b).

The choice between AOA and AON representation is largely a matter of personal preference. As we noted earlier, AON is typically used in the most popular PC-based commercially available computer software, and AON networks are easier to draw. AOA networks are slightly harder to draw because they sometimes require the use of *dummy* activities to aid in indicating a particular precedence, via a dashed arc. A dummy activity has no duration and uses no resources. Its sole purpose is to indicate a technological relationship. (AON networks do not require the use of dummy activities.) AOA networks clearly identify events in the network. These must be added as "zero-duration" activities in AON networks.

Figure 8.8 illustrates the proper way to use a dummy activity if two activities occur between the same *two* events. Figure 8.8 also shows why dummy activities may be needed for AOA networks. An activity is identified by its starting and ending nodes as well as its "name." For example, activities **a** and **b** both start from node 1 and end at node 2. Many computer programs that are widely used for finding the critical path and time for networks

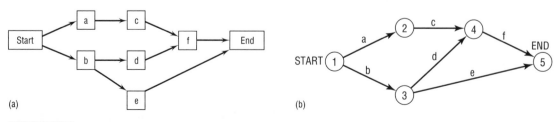

FIGURE 8.7 Sample of network construction.

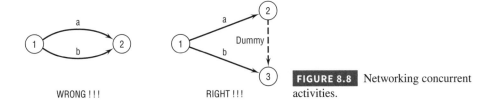

FIGURE 8.8 Networking concurrent activities.

require the nodes to identify which activity is which. In our example, **a** and **b** would appear to be the same, both starting at node 1 and ending at node 2. Figure 8.9 illustrates how to use a dummy activity in AOA format when activities **a**, **b**, and **c** must precede activity **d**, but only **a** and **b** must precede activity **e**. Finally, Figure 8.10 illustrates the use of dummy activities in a more complex setting. AON networks are widely used, but some firms favor AOA networks, so the PM should be familiar with both types.

Gantt (Bar) Charts and Microsoft Project® (MSP)

One of the oldest but still one of the most useful methods of presenting project schedule information is the Gantt chart, developed around 1917 by Henry L. Gantt, a pioneer in the field of scientific management. The Gantt chart shows planned and actual progress for a number of tasks displayed as bars against a horizontal timescale. It is a particularly effective and easy-to-read method of indicating the actual current status for each of a set of tasks compared to the planned progress for each item of the set. As a result, the Gantt chart can be helpful in expediting, sequencing, and reallocating resources among tasks, as well as in the valuable but mundane job of keeping track of how things are going. In addition, the charts usually contain a number of special symbols to designate or highlight items of special concern to the situation being charted. Although the Third Edition of **PMBOK** started calling these "bar charts," we will continue calling them Gantt charts here.

6.6.3

There are several advantages to the use of Gantt charts. First, even though they may contain a great deal of information, they are easily understood. While they do require frequent updating (as does any scheduling/control device), they are easy to maintain *as long as task requirements are not changed or major alterations of the schedule are not made*. Gantt charts provide a picture of the current state of a project. Gantt charts, however, have

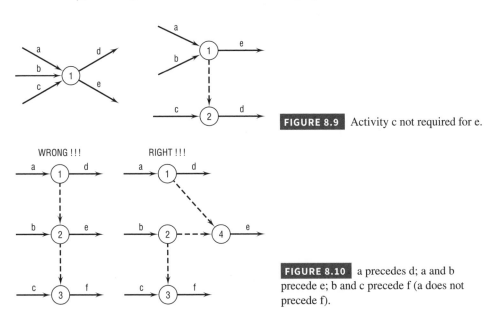

FIGURE 8.9 Activity c not required for e.

FIGURE 8.10 a precedes d; a and b precede e; b and c precede f (a does not precede f).

a serious weakness. If a project is complex with a large set of activities, it may be very difficult to follow multiple activity paths through the project. Gantt charts are powerful devices for communicating to senior management, but networks are usually more helpful in the hands-on task of managing the project.

Another significant feature of Gantt charts is that they are as easy to construct as a network. We use the example in the previous subsection to demonstrate how to construct such a chart.

As is true of many things, it is important for the student to be able to understand just what it is that networks and Gantt charts show (and what they do not show) before using Microsoft Project Management (MSP) or other software to draw complex networks and Gantt charts that the student will have to understand and use. Drawing networks and charts by hand is a quick way to develop that understanding. Once understanding is gained, however, software is easier, faster, and given a project of a size that reflects reality, far more cost-effective.

Consider the example in Figure 8.4 that was just used to illustrate how to draw a network. When we open MSP, the Gantt chart view is typically the default view displayed (at any time you can display the Gantt chart view by clicking on the Gantt chart button on the far left of the Task ribbon). The Gantt chart view contains two windows. On the left is a window that contains a form that is used to enter WBS data into the program. The Gantt chart is displayed in the right window. Entering the data is straightforward. We begin by entering an activity named "START." We assign it a duration of 0 days, which makes it a "milestone" rather than a true "activity." We now enter activity **a** with a duration of 5 days and then continue with the rest of the activities. At the end of the list, we add FINISH with 0-days duration, the project ending milestone.

The software automatically assigns a WBS ID number to each activity as you enter it. Be sure to use these ID numbers when you are specifying the precedence relationships between the tasks. You may delete or add columns if you wish. If you do not enter a specific start date, the MSP will default to the present date for its start date. As you enter data from the WBS, MSP will draw an AON network and a Gantt chart automatically. (The Gantt chart will be visible to the right of the form containing the WBS information. The Network Diagram will be visible by clicking the down arrow right below the Gantt chart button and selecting Network Diagram from the list of views displayed.) If the activity names and durations are entered without noting the appropriate predecessor information, all activities will be assumed to start on the same start date. As the predecessor information is entered, the proper relationships between the activities are shown (see Figures 8.11 and 8.12).

Our concern so far has simply been to show the technological dependencies in a network or Gantt chart. A glance at the AON network or the Gantt chart shows something interesting. If we sum up the activity times for all activities in the WBS, we see that there

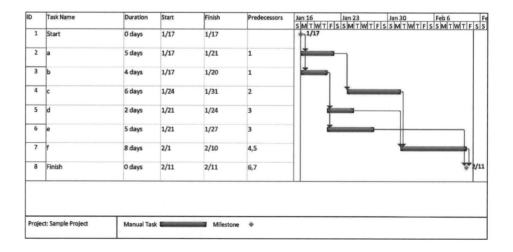

ID	Task Name	Duration	Start	Finish	Predecessors
1	Start	0 days	1/17	1/17	
2	a	5 days	1/17	1/21	1
3	b	4 days	1/17	1/20	1
4	c	6 days	1/24	1/31	2
5	d	2 days	1/21	1/24	3
6	e	5 days	1/21	1/27	3
7	f	8 days	2/1	2/10	4,5
8	Finish	0 days	2/11	2/11	6,7

Project: Sample Project   Manual Task ▬▬▬   Milestone ◆

FIGURE 8.11 MSP activity and Gantt chart for sample project in Figure 8.4.

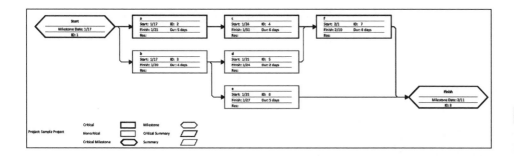

FIGURE 8.12 An MSP AON network for sample project in Figure 8.4.

are 30 days of work to schedule. But, as the network and chart show, the project is scheduled to start on January 17 and will be completed on February 11. That is 25 days, not 30. Further, MSP defaults to a work calendar with a 5-day week. If the calendar is adjusted to a 7-day week, the project will require only 19 days to be completed. It can be finished as early as February 5. Calculation by hand is not at all difficult, but MSP can do it faster and easier. It is important, however, to remember that software makes assumptions about such things as the number of days worked in a week, the number of hours per day that are worked, and several other matters that will be considered later. These assumptions may be changed if one wishes, but they must be considered every time the software is used to map a project.

This example illustrates both the strength and weakness of the Gantt chart. Its major strength is that it is easy to read. All popular project management software will prepare Gantt charts, and most have some options available for customization. On balance, ease of construction and ease of use have made the Gantt chart the most popular method for displaying a project schedule. Nonetheless, an AON network is still most useful for the PM to exercise control over the schedule, and the viewer may be misled if the Gantt chart is not read carefully or if it does not contain all appropriate information (Wilkens, 1997).

An Important Aside on Estimating Activity Times

Before solving the network to find the critical path and critical time of the entire network, we must note that *it is vital to good project management to be meticulously honest in estimating the time required to complete each of the various tasks included in the project.* Note that we did not say "meticulously accurate." This would not be possible in the uncertain world in which we all live. We said "honest," which means that time estimates should be unbiased, best guesses. It is unfortunate that this commandment is often disregarded.

Estimates of the time required to complete project activities should be estimated in the same way that required resources are estimated. As described in Chapter 7, both the PM and the people carrying out the activity should make estimates of the resources requirements. They should also make estimates of the activity duration. If duration estimates differ significantly between the two sources, the duration should be negotiated as in Chapter 7.

The tendency of too many managers is to set deadlines earlier than the project requires in order to "ensure" that the task will be completed in time. In an excellent, short article in the *Wall Street Journal*, Jared Sandberg (2007) points out that the false early deadline is common. A false deadline does not ensure that a task or project will be completed in time. Quite the opposite, it frequently results in tasks being completed late. The lie is easily discovered, and the result is that no one takes that manager's deadlines seriously thereafter. Some managers set deadlines on all tasks given to subordinates. They treat routine work and critically important work in the same way. This violates a primary rule of good time management, and the result is that "urgent" but unimportant tasks often squeeze out truly important activities, making them late (see Chapter 3 Appendix for more on effective time management practices).

Other sources of bias in time estimates result when project sponsors underestimate time and resource requirements in an attempt to ensure that their project will pass the

Project Management in Practice

Election Returns within Three Hours

© Xinhua/ZUMAPress.com

Panama's presidential election on May 3, 2009, was a tense drama, as most are, but in two and a half hours after the polls closed, the country heard the outcome. Given that many of the nation's citizens are located in small, remote villages, and others in dense jungles, miles from the nearest landlines, this was an impressive achievement. But it was no accident—it was the outcome of a major project to restore faith in the government of a country racked by the fraud of the 1983 Manuel Noriega dictatorship by providing quick feedback to the populace through compressed reporting schedules.

The essence of the project boiled down to two thrusts. The first was a decades-long continuing effort by Panama's Electoral Tribunal to establish a valid electoral database through mandatory birth and death records, plus biometric data (fingerprints, photo-recognition software, etc.) to capture key milestones in each citizen's life, so only eligible citizens could vote, only once and only for the candidates and issues relevant to their location. The second thrust was technological, involving the establishment and use of highly secure communication channels, including telephone lines, satellite phones, VHF radio links, and for this election, a new wireless application protocol (WAP) that was written from scratch, encrypted, authenticated, and extensively tested. To be sure it worked smoothly and securely, polling station attendants were trained in using the app and then the app was simulated for 12 extensive tests at polling stations. During the simulations, security experts and "ethical hackers" from the United States tested and probed the system's defenses, resulting in last-minute changes to both the software and the procedures for using it, such as password access.

In the press center for the election where voting details by province would be immediately posted, a giant 19- by 25-foot monitoring screen was installed to report the vote. This screen was surrounded by four smaller screens to provide more voting details such as number of valid, blank, and null votes, level of voting participation, local issues, interactive maps of the nation, and so on. Not surprisingly, the Electoral Tribunal responsible for elections is already preparing for the 2014 election and plans to extend the system to other elections, such as legislative and city mayoral and councilor elections.

Questions

1. This example consists of two projects: a long-term project to improve the election reporting cycle process and its validity, and the second to actually execute this new process in the 2009 national election. Which one do you think had the most pressure on its task schedule?

2. Which of Panama's two thrusts do you think was the more difficult? Why?

3. Which thrust do you suspect had the greatest pressure on its schedule?

Source: M. Wheatley, "Calling the Election," *PM Network*, Vol. 24.

barriers to project selection and when workers overestimate time and resource usage to ensure successful task completions and project delivery.

Given that schedules are based on honest best guesses, other major problems can cause serious errors in time estimates. In some projects, the client is directly engaged in evolving project deliverables, which means that deliverables, and thus activities, are likely to change before the project is completed. In many complex projects, not all activities are fully understood until the project has completed some earlier activities. These problems led to the development of agile project management that uses an iterative process for making time and resource estimates for these later, not well-understood activities. The same problem arises in a multiproject environment when one project "borrows" a critical resource from another project. Then, activities on the borrowed-from project may be delayed. This actual or potential lateness may not be discovered unless the PM conducts frequent, periodic, schedule-status reviews—a technique called "iterative scheduling," which allows appropriate rescheduling in conjunction with the client (Wheatly, 2010). Wheatly says that the following five clues can indicate when iterative scheduling is needed: late or vague progress reports, overdue deliverables, static progress indicators, longer work hours for team members, and a noticeable increase in minor "issues" affecting the project.

A final complication in estimating activity times is that for many if not most tasks, there are alternative ways for carrying out the work. For example, more experienced and productive employees may be allocated to do the work but at greater cost. Similarly, there may be alternative technologies that can be used, such as performing analysis manually versus investing in the development of an automated report generator. Furthermore, in some cases, the amount of resource capacity can be adjusted, for example, by increasing the staffing level, purchasing faster equipment, using overtime, or outsourcing portions of the work. In estimating activity times, it is important to perform what **PMBOK** refers to as an Alternative Analysis where alternative approaches for carrying out the work are identified and evaluated. With this short sermon, we return to solving the network we have created.

6.4.2.2

Solving the Network

Let us now consider a small project with 10 activities in order to illustrate the network technique. Table 8.1 lists the activities, their most likely completion times, and the activities that must precede them. Table 8.1 also includes optimistic and pessimistic estimates of completion time for each activity in the list. Actual activity time is expected rarely to be less than the optimistic time or more than the pessimistic time. (More on this matter shortly.)

Beginning with a node named START, connect the three activities with no predecessors (**a**, **b**, and **c**) to the Start node as in Figure 8.13.

TABLE 8.1   **Project Activity Times and Precedences**

Activity	Optimistic Time	Most Likely Time	Pessimistic Time	Immediate Predecessor Activities
a	10	22	22	—
b	20	20	20	—
c	4	10	16	—
d	2	14	32	a
e	8	8	20	b, c
f	8	14	20	b, c
g	4	4	4	b, c
h	2	12	16	c
i	6	16	38	g, h
j	2	8	14	d, e

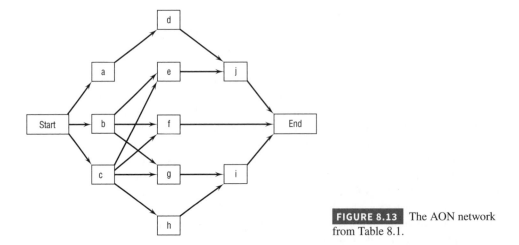

FIGURE 8.13 The AON network from Table 8.1.

Activity **d** has a predecessor of **a**, and thus, it follows **a**. Activities **e**, **f**, and **g** all must follow both **b** and **c** as predecessors. Activity **h** follows **c**. Activity **j** follows both **d** and **e**. Activity **i** follows **g** and **h**. Because there are no more activities, we must be at the end of the network. Add a node labeled "END" and connect any nodes without successor activities, in this case, **j**, **f**, and **i**, reading from top to bottom. As stated earlier, always show the direction of a connection with an arrowhead.

Calculating Activity Times

The next step is to calculate expected activity completion times from the data in Table 8.1. These expected completion times are found by using the three time estimates (optimistic, pessimistic, and most likely) in the table. Remember that these estimates are an expression of the risk associated with the time required for each activity. (The optimistic, pessimistic, and most likely estimates made for activity times are equally applicable to the estimates of resource usage made in Chapter 7, as are the calculations that follow.)

Once again, a short digression is helpful. Precisely what is meant by "optimistic," "pessimistic," and "most likely"? Assume that all possible times for some specific activity might be represented by a statistical distribution (e.g., the asymmetrical distribution in Figure 8.14). The "most likely" time, m, for the activity is the mode of this distribution. In theory, the "optimistic" and "pessimistic" times are selected in the following way. The PM, or whoever is attempting to estimate a and b, is asked to select a such that the actual time required by the activity will be a or greater about 99 percent of the time. Similarly, b is estimated such that about 99 percent of the time the activity will have a duration of b or less. (Some PMs or workers may be uncomfortable making estimates at this level of precision, but we will delay dealing with this problem for the moment.)

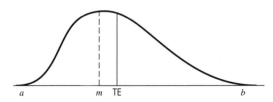

FIGURE 8.14 Distribution of all possible activity times for an activity.

The expected time, TE, is found by

$$TE = (a + 4m + b)/6$$

where

    a = optimistic time estimate
    b = pessimistic time estimate
    m = most likely time estimate, the mode

Note that in Table 8.1 some activity durations are known with certainty, which is to say that a, b, and m are the same (see activity **g**, for instance). Note further that the most likely time may be the same as the optimistic time ($a = m$) as in activity **e** or that the most likely time may be identical to the pessimistic time ($m = b$) as in activity **a**. The range about m may be symmetric where

$$m - a = b - m$$

as in activity **c**, or may be quite asymmetric ($m - a \neq b - m$), as in activities **h** and **i**.

The aforementioned formula for calculating expected times is based on the beta statistical distribution.[2] This distribution is used rather than the more common normal distribution because it is highly flexible in form and can take into account such extremes as where $a = m$ or $b = m$. It can also accurately model tasks with asymmetrical distributions (the normal distribution assumes a symmetrical distribution). This is particularly important in project management where there is often a greater probability of an activity taking longer than expected than being finished earlier than expected. For example, consider a status meeting that is scheduled to last 30 minutes. What is the likelihood that this meeting is finished 45 minutes early versus the likelihood that it runs 45 minutes over? Clearly, there is no chance that a 30-minute meeting can be finished 45 minutes early while those of you with experience with meetings will recognize the high probability of a 30-minute meeting running 45 minutes over! In this case, the distribution for the duration of the status meeting would be skewed to the right (as is illustrated by the distribution shown in Figure 8.14).

TE is an estimate of the mean of the distribution. It is a weighted average of a, m, and b with weights of 1-4-1, respectively. Again, we emphasize that this *same method can be applied to finding the expected level of resource usage given the appropriate estimates of the modal (i.e., most likely) resource level as well as optimistic and pessimistic estimates.*

This process of estimating activity times occasionally comes under criticism. In general, critics argue that when activity times are set, these come to be considered as targets. This argument maintains that PERT/CPM success is due to the *process* of estimating times rather than to the estimates themselves. That is, the estimates are said to become self-fulfilling prophecies. An additional argument (Williams, 1995) is that actual activity times are rarely less than the estimate of the mode, and are often greater, accounting for the right skew of the distribution. The cause is attributed to Parkinson's law: that work expands to fill the allotted time. If problems occur, the activity may require more time, but it will almost never require less. While no one, to the best of our knowledge, had proven this empirically, there is some anecdotal evidence that supports this notion. There is, however, also anecdotal evidence that supports the traditional assumption that three-time activity duration estimates are the "best guesses" of people who have experience in similar activities. In any

---

[2]We remind readers who would like a short refresher on elementary statistics and probability that one is available in Appendix A on this book's website.

event, our purpose here is to estimate the range of time required for each activity rather than argue with the underlying logic of the estimation process.

> *"Doing it right is no excuse for not meeting the schedule. No one will believe you solved this problem in one day! Now, go act busy for a few weeks and I'll let you know when it's time to tell them."*

The results of the expected value calculations are shown in Table 8.2 and are included in the activity nodes of Figure 8.15 as well. Also included in the table and in the nodes are measures of the uncertainty for the duration of each activity, the *variance*, σ^2, that is,

$$\sigma^2 = ((b-a)/6)^2$$

and the *standard deviation*, σ, which is given by

$$\sigma = \sqrt{\sigma^2}$$

This calculation of σ is based on the assumption that the standard deviation of a beta distribution is approximately one-sixth of its range, $(b-a)/6$.

Later in this chapter, we will argue for an amendment to the estimation procedure for the variance of activity times if the estimates of a and b are not made at the 99 percent level. Note that the format and calculations of Tables 8.1 and 8.2 lend themselves to the use of a spreadsheet program such as Excel,® as we did in Chapter 7 for cash flow. The equations for TE, σ^2, and σ can be entered once and copied to the rest of the rows.

Critical Path and Time

Consider again the project shown in Figure 8.15. Assume, for convenience, that the time units involved are days, that the first figure is the expected time, and that the second figure is the variance. How long will it take to complete the project? (For the moment, we will treat the expected times as if they were certain.) If we start the project on day 0, shown as ES (earliest start) at the upper left of each node in Figure 8.16, we can begin simultaneously

TABLE 8.2 Expected Activity Times (TE), Variances (σ^2), and Standard Deviations (σ)

Activity	Expected Time, TE	Variance, σ^2	Standard Deviation, σ
a	20	4	2
b	20	0	0
c	10	4	2
d	15	25	5
e	10	4	2
f	14	4	2
g	4	0	0
h	11	5.4	2.32
i	18	28.4	5.33
j	8	4	2

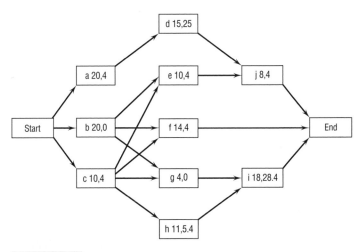

FIGURE 8.15 The AON network from Table 8.2, showing activity durations and variances.

working on activities **a**, **b**, and **c**, each of which has no predecessor activities. We will complete activity **a** in 20 days, activity **b** in 20 days, and activity **c** in 10 days, shown as EF (earliest finish) at the upper right of each of their respective nodes. These early finish times represent the earliest times that the following activities can begin.

Note that activity **e** not only requires the completion of activity **b** but also requires the completion of activity **c**, as shown by the two incoming arrows. Activity **e** cannot begin until all paths leading to it have been completed. Therefore, the ES for activity **e** is equal to the EF of the *latest* activity leading to it, 20 for activity **b**.

Proceeding similarly, we see that activity **j** has two predecessor activities, **d** and **e**. Activity **d** cannot start until day 20 (ES = 20), and it requires 15 days to complete. Thus, it will end (EF) a total of 35 days from the start of the project. Activity **e** may also start after 20 days, but it requires only 10 days, a total of 30 days from the project start. Because activity **j** requires the completion of both activities **d** and **e**, its ES is 35 days, the longest of the paths to it. Activity **i** has an ES of 24 days, the longest of the two paths leading to it, and END, the completion of the network, has a time of 43 days. The remaining ESs and EFs are shown in Figure 8.16.

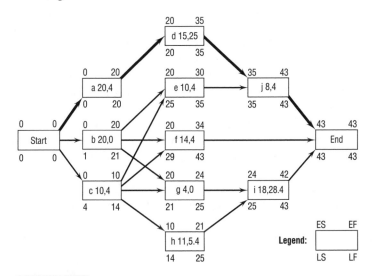

FIGURE 8.16 AON network showing earliest and latest start and finish times, and critical (bolded) path.

As can be seen, the longest of the paths through the network is **a-d-j** using 43 days, which means that 43 days is the shortest time in which the entire network can be completed. This is called the *critical time* of the network, and **a-d-j** is the *critical path*, usually shown as a bold line as in Figure 8.16.

In a simple network such as our example, it is easy to find and evaluate every path between start and finish to find the longest path. However, many real networks are considerably more complex, and finding all the paths can be taxing. Using the method illustrated earlier, there is no need to worry about the problem. Every node is characterized by the fact that one or more activities lead to it. Each of these activities has an expected duration and originates in an earlier node. As we proceed to calculate the ES and EF of each node, beginning at the start, we are *actually finding the critical path and time to each of the nodes* in the network. Note that activity **i** has an ES of 24 days, and its critical path is **b-g** rather than **c-h**, which requires 21 days, or **c-g**.

Although we will assume throughout this chapter that we always employ the "as-soon-as possible" approach to scheduling tasks ("early start"), there are situations where other approaches are sometimes used. One example is the simultaneous start, where all resources are launched at the beginning. Another is the simultaneous finish, where a facility such as a mobile X-ray unit trailer can be moved to its next location once all the tasks are finished. Of course, delay early on in a project runs the risk of delaying the overall project if some other activities inadvertently become delayed. One important reason for using an "as-late-as-possible" approach, described next, is that it delays the use of resources as much as possible, thereby optimizing the cash flow of the project, but again at some risk of delay.

Slack (aka, Float)

We will now focus on the latest possible starting times (LS) for the activities. As noted in the previous section, the ES for an activity is equal to the largest EF for its preceding activities. An important question for the PM is this: What is the latest time (LS) activity **i** could start without making the entire project late?

Refer again to Figure 8.16. The project has a critical time of 43 days. Activity **i** must therefore be finished by day 43, indicated by LF (latest finish time), placed at the bottom right of its node. In addition, activity **i** requires 18 days to be accomplished. Therefore, **i** *must* be started no later than day 25 (43 − 18 = 25) if the project is to be complete on day 43. The LS for activity **i** is thus 25, placed at the lower left corner of the node. Because **i** cannot begin until activities **g** and **h** have finished, the latest time (LF) for each of these is also day 25. The difference between the LS and the ES for an activity is called its *float* or *slack*. In the case of activity **i**, it must be started no later than day 25, but *could* be started as early as day 24, so it has one day of slack. It should be immediately obvious that all activities on the critical path have zero slack.[3] Zero slack activities cannot be delayed without making the project late.

For another example, consider activity **f**. Its ES is day 20, which is equal to the EF of its predecessor activity **b**. The LS for activity **f** is 43 − 14 = 29. If **f** is started later than day 29, it will delay the entire project. Activity **f** has slack of LS − ES = 29 − 20 = 9 days.

To find the slack for any activity, we make a backward pass (right to left) through the network just as we made a forward pass (left to right) to find the critical path and time and the ESs and EFs for successor activities. There is one simple convention we must adopt: *When there are two or more noncritical activities on a path, it is conventional to calculate the slack for each activity as if it were the only activity in the path.* Thus, when finding the

---

[3]"Float" and "slack" are synonyms. The PMI writes of "float." MSP uses the term "slack." We simply use the term "slack" out of habit.

TABLE 8.3   Times and Slacks for Network in Figure 8.16

Activity	LS	ES	Slack
a	0	0	0
b	1	0	1
c	4	0	4
d	20	20	0
e	25	20	5
f	29	20	9
g	21	20	1
h	14	10	4
i	25	24	1
j	35	35	0

slack for activity **i**, for example, we assume that none of **i**'s predecessors are delayed. Of course, if some activity, **x**, had 6 days of slack, and if an earlier activity was late, causing the event to be delayed say 2 days, then activity **x** would have only 4 days of slack, having lost 2 days to the earlier delay.

It is simple to calculate slack for activities that are immediate predecessors of the final node. As we move to earlier activities, it is just a bit more complicated. Consider activity **g**. Remembering our assumption that the other activities in the same path use none of the available slack, we see that activity **i** must follow **g** and that **g** follows activities **b** and **c**. Starting with activity **i**'s LS of 25, we subtract 4 days for **g** ($25 - 4 = 21$). Thus, **g** can begin no later than day 21 without delaying the network. The ES for **g** is day 20, so **g** has 1 day of slack.

As another example, consider activity **e**. Activity **e** must be completed by day 35, the LS of activity **j**. The LS for **e** is thus $35 - 10 = 25$. Its ES is day 20, so activity **e** has 5 days of slack. Table 8.3 shows the LS, ES, and slack for all activities.

On occasion, the PM may negotiate an acceptable completion date for a project, which allows for some slack in the entire network. If, in our example, an acceptable date was 50 working days after the project start, then the network would have a total of $50 - 43 = 7$ days of slack.

Some writers and MSP differentiate between "total" slack or float and "free" slack or float. Total slack is LF − EF or LS − ES as described earlier. Free slack is defined as the time an activity can be delayed without affecting the start time of *any* successor activity. Activity **h** could be delayed 3 days without affecting the start time of activity **i**. Activity **h** has 3 days of free slack and 4 days of total slack.

Precedence Diagramming

One shortcoming of the AOA network method is that it does not allow for leads and lags between two activities without greatly increasing the number of subactivities to account for this. In construction projects, in particular, it is quite common for the following restrictions to occur. (Node designations are shown in Figure 8.17.)

- **Finish to Start**   Activity 2 must not start before Activity 1 has been completed. This is the typical arrangement of an activity and its predecessor. Other finish–start

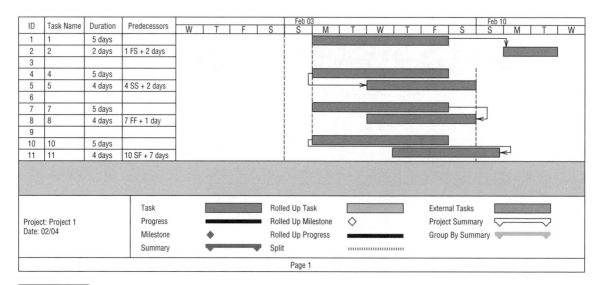

ID	Task Name	Duration	Predecessors
1	1	5 days	
2	2	2 days	1 FS + 2 days
3			
4	4	5 days	
5	5	4 days	4 SS + 2 days
6			
7	7	5 days	
8	8	4 days	7 FF + 1 day
9			
10	10	5 days	
11	11	4 days	10 SF + 7 days

FIGURE 8.17 Precedence diagramming conventions.

arrangements are also possible. If the predecessor information had been written "1FS + 2 days," Activity 2 would be scheduled to start at least 2 days after the completion of Activity 1, as shown in Figure 8.17. For instance, if Activity 1 was the pouring of a concrete sidewalk, Activity 2 might be any activity that used the sidewalk.

- **Start to Start**   Activity 5 cannot begin until Activity 4 has been underway for at least 2 days. Setting electrical wires in place cannot begin until 2 days after framing has begun.

- **Finish to Finish**   Activity 7 must be complete at least 1 day before Activity 8 is completed. If Activity 7 is priming the walls of a house, Activity 8 might be the activities involved in selecting, purchasing, and finally delivering the wallpaper. It is important not to hang the paper until the wall primer has dried for 24 hours.

- **Start to Finish**   Activity 11 cannot be completed before 7 days since the start of Activity 10. If Activities 10 and 11 are the two major cruising activities in a prepaid week-long ocean cruise, the total time cannot be less than the promised week. The S–F relationship is rare because there are usually simpler ways to map the required relationship.

Precedence diagramming is an AON network method that easily allows for these leads and lags within the network. MSP handles leads and lags without problems. Network node times are calculated in a manner similar to AON/AOA times. Because of the lead and lag restrictions, it is often helpful to lay out a Gantt chart to see what is actually happening. The richer set of precedence relationships allowed by AON is pertinent for a variety of projects, particularly construction projects. [For more details on this technique, see Moder et al. (1983).] Most current project management software will allow leads, lags, delays, and other constraints in the context of their standard AON network and Gantt chart programs.

Once Again, Microsoft Project®

Figures 8.18 and 8.19 depict the three-time Gantt chart and network diagram using the data in Table 8.4. The data to perform a PERT Analysis can be calculated by hand for small

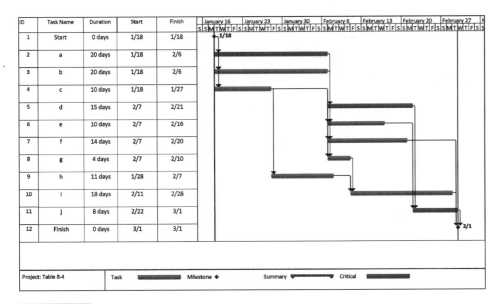

ID	Task Name	Duration	Start	Finish
1	Start	0 days	1/18	1/18
2	a	20 days	1/18	2/6
3	b	20 days	1/18	2/6
4	c	10 days	1/18	1/27
5	d	15 days	2/7	2/21
6	e	10 days	2/7	2/16
7	f	14 days	2/7	2/20
8	g	4 days	2/7	2/10
9	h	11 days	1/28	2/7
10	i	18 days	2/11	2/28
11	j	8 days	2/22	3/1
12	Finish	0 days	3/1	3/1

FIGURE 8.18   Gantt chart of Table 8.4.

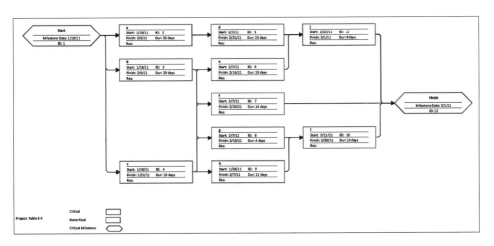

FIGURE 8.19   AON network of Table 8.4.

projects or by using Excel®. Notice in both figures that it is sometimes difficult to tell which activities precede activities **e**, **f**, **g**, and **h** (check Table 8.4).

In the next section, we show how to determine the probability that a project will be completed in a specified time. To do this, the standard deviation, σ, and variance, σ^2, for each activity duration are needed. MSP does not calculate these numbers. The variances and standard deviations for the activities in the project demonstrated here are shown in Table 8.2. Recall that

$$\sigma = (b-a)/6$$

and

$$\sigma^2 = ((b-a)/6)^2$$

TABLE 8.4   MSP Gantt Chart Version of Project Described in Table 8.1

ID	Task Name	Predecessors	Optimistic Duration	Most Likely Duration	Pessimistic Duration	Expected Duration
1	Start		0 days	0 days	0 days	0 days
2	a	1	10 days	22 days	22 days	20 days
3	b	1	20 days	20 days	20 days	20 days
4	c	1	4 days	10 days	16 days	10 days
5	d	2	2 days	14 days	32 days	15 days
6	e	3, 4	8 days	8 days	20 days	10 days
7	f	3, 4	8 days	14 days	20 days	14 days
8	g	3, 4	4 days	4 days	4 days	4 days
9	h	4	2 days	12 days	16 days	11 days
10	i	8, 9	6 days	16 days	38 days	18 days
11	j	5, 6	2 days	8 days	14 days	8 days
12	Finish	10, 11, 7	0 days	0 days	0 days	0 days

Exhibits Available from Software, a Bit More MSP

As we noted earlier and you have seen just now, project management software can illustrate the project as a Gantt chart and, in addition, show precedences, times, and other activity elements directly on the chart. Moreover, AOA and AON network diagrams, calendars, and other displays and reports can also be shown. For example, Figure 8.20 shows an MSP

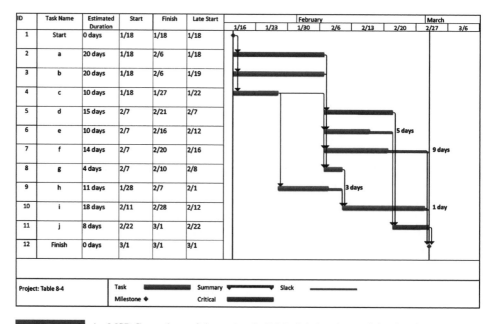

FIGURE 8.20   An MSP Gantt chart of the project in Table 8.4 showing activity durations and schedule, critical path, path connections, slack, and earliest and latest start and finish times.

Gantt chart for the project mentioned in Table 8.1 with the critical path, path connections, and LS and LF times depicted on the chart. It is simple to customize the information shown; for instance, early start and finish times, slack, special resource requirements, and several other items can be added to the nodes.

As another example, Figure 8.21 shows the basic Gantt chart for a video production project, including a summary task (ID 3) and two milestones. Figure 8.22 is the AON network diagram showing the critical path, path connections, task durations, milestones, resources, start and finish dates, and ID numbers. Figure 8.23 is the project calendar showing the calendar scheduling of the tasks on a monthly calendar with the critical path tasks highlighted. The calendar view depicted in Figure 8.23 is the default MSP view showing the tasks continuing over the weekends *even though no work may actually be conducted.* MSP's calendar default work schedule is 8 hours per day, 5 days

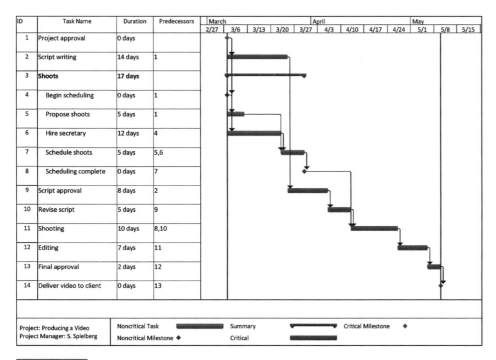

FIGURE 8.21 MSP Gantt chart for a video production project.

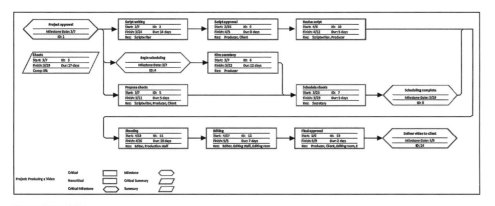

FIGURE 8.22 An MSP AON network for video project with critical path, durations, dates, milestones, and ID numbers.

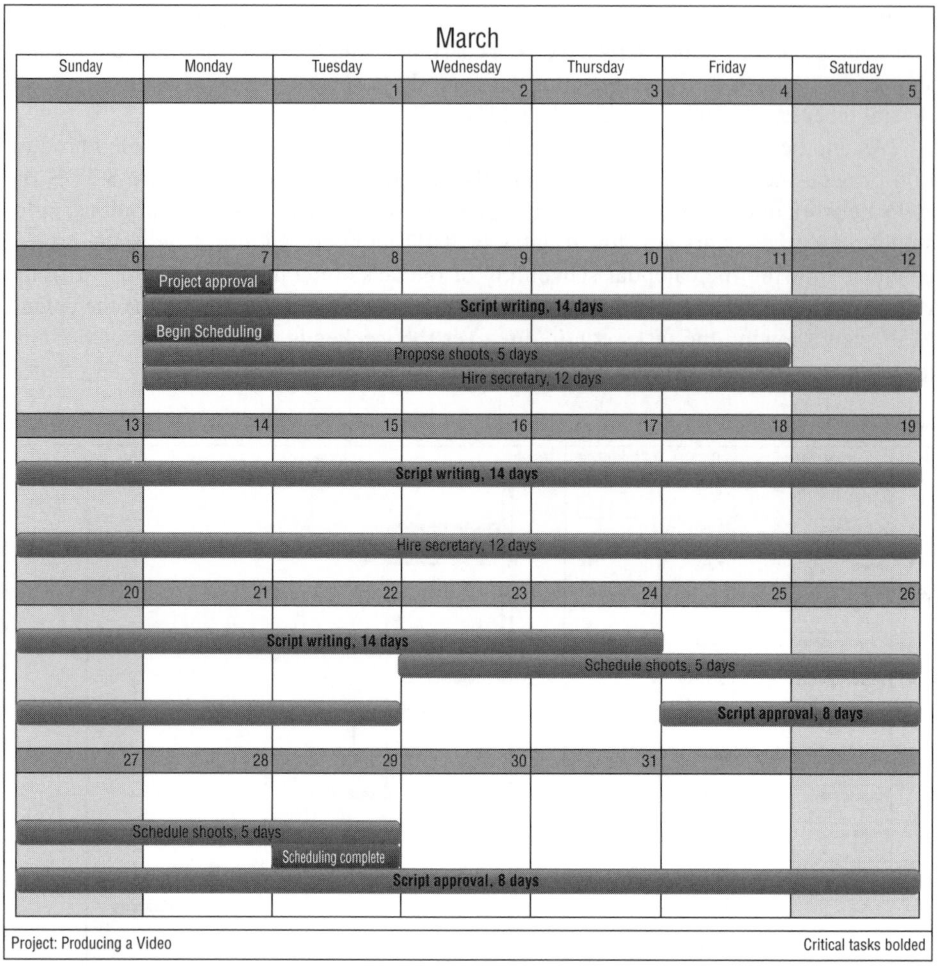

FIGURE 8.23 MSP calendar for video project; critical path is in bold print.

per week unless the user specifies a different workweek schedule, such as one that *does* work over the weekends.

Project progress should also be monitored and input to the software for updating the charts and reports. Such progress is indicated directly on the Gantt chart, such as that shown in Figure 8.24 for the video project. Note in the figure how the project completion milestone has been delayed to match actual completion dates of the updated project's tasks.

Uncertainty of Project Completion Time

When discussing project completion dates with senior management, the PM should try to determine the probability that a project will be completed by the suggested deadline—or find the completion time associated with a predetermined level of risk. With the information in Table 8.2, this is not difficult.

If we assume that the activities are statistically independent of each other, then the variance of a set of activities is equal to the sum of the variances of the individual activities comprising the set. From your study of statistics, recall that the variance of a population is a measure of the population's dispersion and is equal to the square of the population's

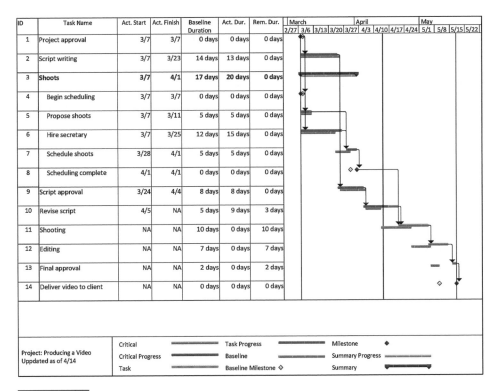

ID	Task Name	Act. Start	Act. Finish	Baseline Duration	Act. Dur.	Rem. Dur.
1	Project approval	3/7	3/7	0 days	0 days	0 days
2	Script writing	3/7	3/23	14 days	13 days	0 days
3	Shoots	3/7	4/1	17 days	20 days	0 days
4	Begin scheduling	3/7	3/7	0 days	0 days	0 days
5	Propose shoots	3/7	3/11	5 days	5 days	0 days
6	Hire secretary	3/7	3/25	12 days	15 days	0 days
7	Schedule shoots	3/28	4/1	5 days	5 days	0 days
8	Scheduling complete	4/1	4/1	0 days	0 days	0 days
9	Script approval	3/24	4/4	8 days	8 days	0 days
10	Revise script	4/5	NA	5 days	9 days	3 days
11	Shooting	NA	NA	10 days	0 days	10 days
12	Editing	NA	NA	7 days	0 days	7 days
13	Final approval	NA	NA	2 days	0 days	2 days
14	Deliver video to client	NA	NA	0 days	0 days	0 days

Project: Producing a Video
Uppdated as of 4/14

Critical — Task Progress — Milestone ◆
Critical Progress — Baseline — Summary Progress
Task — Baseline Milestone ◇ Summary

FIGURE 8.24 MSP Gantt chart for video project tracking progress to date.

standard deviation. The variances in which we are interested are the variances of the activities on the critical path and, as we will see shortly, of other paths that are close to being critical.

The critical path of our example includes activities **a**, **d**, and **j**. From Table 8.2, we find that the variances of these activities are 4, 25, and 4, respectively; and the variance for the critical path is the sum of these numbers, 33 days. Assume, as earlier, that the PM has promised to complete the project in 50 days. What are the chances of meeting that deadline? We find the answer by calculating Z, where

$$Z = (D - \mu) / \sqrt{\sigma_\mu^2}$$

and

D = the desired project completion time

μ = the critical time of the project, the sum of the TEs for activities on the critical path

σ_μ^2 = the variance of the critical path, the sum of the variances of activities on the critical path

Z = the number of standard deviations of a normal distribution (the standard normal deviate)

Z, as calculated earlier, can be used to find the probability of completing the project on time. Using the numbers in our example, $D = 50$, $\mu = 43$, and $\sigma_\mu^2 = 33$ (the square root of σ_μ^2 is 5.745), we have

$$Z = (50 - 43) / 5.745$$
$$= 1.22 \text{ standard deviations}$$

We turn now to Table 8.5, which shows the probabilities associated with various levels of Z. (Table 8.5 also appears on the last page facing the inside rear cover.) We go down the left column until we find $Z = 1.2$, and then across to column .02 to find $Z = 1.22$. The probability value of $Z = 1.22$ shown in the table is .8888, or almost 89 percent, which is the likelihood that we will complete the critical path of our sample project within 50 days of the time it is started. Figure 8.25 shows the resulting probability distribution of the project completion times.[4]

This same analysis can be greatly simplified by employing the built-in functions in Excel®. For example, Excel's Norm.Dist function can be used to find the probability of completing a path by a desired time. More specifically, the function is used as follows:

$$\text{Norm.Dist}(D, \mu, \sigma_\mu, \text{True})$$

where D is the desired completion time, μ is the expected time of the path, and σ_μ is the standard deviation of the path.

Plugging in these parameters yields:

$$\text{Norm.Dist}(50, 43, 5.745, \text{True}) = 0.888$$

We can work the problem backward as well. What deadline is consistent with a .95 probability of on-time completion? First, we go to Table 8.5 and look through the table until we find .95. The Z value associated with .95 is 1.645. (The values in the table are not strictly linear, so our interpolation is only approximate.) We know that   is 43 days and that $\sqrt{\sigma_\mu^2}$ is 5.745. Solving the equation for D, we have

$$D = \mu + 5.745 \ (1.6545)$$
$$= 43 + 9.45$$
$$= 52.45 \text{ days}$$

Again, Excel® provides a function that facilitates this calculation as follows:

$$\text{Norm.Inv}(\text{probability}, \mu, \sigma_\mu)$$

Plugging in for these parameters yields:

$$= \text{Norm.Inv}(0.95, 43, 5.745) = 52.45$$

Thus, we conclude that there is a 95 percent chance of finishing the project by 52.45 days. However, that is not quite true. There is a 95 percent chance of finishing path **a-d-j** in 52.45 days. Remember that this is a stochastic network. ("Stochastic"—sta kas' tik—is much nicer to say than "probabilistic" and means the same thing.) If the activities of the project are of uncertain duration, no one knows how long it will take to complete each of

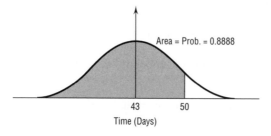

FIGURE 8.25 Probability distribution of project completion times.

[4]Our use of the normal distribution is allowed by the Central Limit theorem, which attests to the fact that the sum of independent activity times is normally distributed if the number of activities is large.

TABLE 8.5	Cumulative (Single Tail) Probabilities of the Normal Probability Distribution (Areas under the Normal Curve from $-\infty$ to Z)

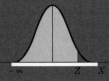

Example: The area to the left of Z = 1.34 is found by following the left Z column down to 1.3 and moving right to the .04 column. At the intersection read .9099. The area to the right of Z = 1.34 is 1 – .9099 = .0901. The area between the mean (center line) and Z = 1.34 is .9099 – .5 = .4099.

z	.00	.01	.02	.03	.04	.05	.06	.07	.08	.09
.0	.5000	.5040	.5080	.5120	.5160	.5199	.5239	.5279	.5319	.5359
.1	.5398	.5438	.5478	.5517	.5557	.5596	.5636	.5675	.5714	.5753
.2	.5793	.5832	.5871	.5910	.5948	.5987	.6026	.6064	.6103	.6141
.3	.6179	.6217	.6255	.6293	.6331	.6368	.6406	.6443	.6480	.6517
.4	.6554	.6591	.6628	.6664	.6700	.6736	.6772	.6808	.6844	.6879
.5	.6915	.6950	.6985	.7019	.7054	.7088	.7123	.7157	.7190	.7224
.6	.7257	.7291	.7324	.7357	.7389	.7422	.7454	.7486	.7517	.7549
.7	.7580	.7611	.7642	.7673	.7704	.7734	.7764	.7794	.7823	.7852
.8	.7881	.7910	.7939	.7967	.7995	.8023	.8051	.8078	.8106	.8133
.9	.8159	.8186	.8212	.8238	.8264	.8289	.8315	.8340	.8365	.8389
1.0	.8413	.8438	.8461	.8485	.8508	.8531	.8554	.8577	.8599	.8621
1.1	.8643	.8665	.8686	.8708	.8729	.8749	.8770	.8790	.8810	.8880
1.2	.8849	.8869	.8888	.8907	.8925	.8944	.8962	.8980	.8997	.9015
1.3	.9032	.9049	.9066	.9082	.9099	.9115	.9131	.9147	.9162	.9177
1.4	.9192	.9207	.9222	.9236	.9251	.9265	.9279	.9292	.9306	.9319
1.5	.9332	.9345	.9357	.9370	.9382	.9394	.9406	.9418	.9429	.9441
1.6	.9452	.9463	.9474	.9484	.9495	.9505	.9515	.9525	.9535	.9545
1.7	.9554	.9564	.9573	.9582	.9591	.9599	.9608	.9616	.9625	.9633
1.8	.9641	.9649	.9656	.9664	.9671	.9678	.9686	.9693	.9699	.9706
1.9	.9713	.9719	.9726	.9732	.9738	.9744	.9750	.9756	.9761	.9767
2.0	.9772	.9778	.9783	.9788	.9793	.9798	.9803	.9808	.9812	.9817
2.1	.9821	.9826	.9830	.9834	.9838	.9842	.9846	.9850	.9854	.9857
2.2	.9861	.9864	.9868	.9871	.9875	.9878	.9881	.9884	.9887	.9890
2.3	.9893	.9896	.9898	.9901	.9904	.9906	.9909	.9911	.9913	.9916
2.4	.9918	.9920	.9932	.9925	.9927	.9929	.9931	.9932	.9934	.9936
2.5	.9938	.9940	.9941	.9943	.9945	.9946	.9948	.9949	.9951	.9952
2.6	.9953	.9955	.9956	.9957	.9959	.9960	.9961	.9962	.9963	.9964
2.7	.9965	.9966	.9967	.9968	.9969	.9970	.9971	.9972	.9973	.9974
2.8	.9974	.9975	.9976	.9977	.9977	.9978	.9979	.9979	.9980	.9981
2.9	.9981	.9982	.9982	.9983	.9984	.9984	.9985	.9985	.9986	.9986
3.0	.9987	.9987	.9987	.9988	.9988	.9989	.9989	.9989	.9990	.9990
3.1	.9990	.9991	.9991	.9991	.9992	.9992	.9992	.9992	.9993	.9993
3.2	.9993	.9993	.9994	.9994	.9994	.9994	.9994	.9995	.9995	.9995
3.3	.9995	.9995	.9995	.9996	.9996	.9996	.9996	.9996	.9996	.9997
3.4	.9997	.9997	.9997	.9997	.9997	.9997	.9997	.9997	.9997	.9998

them. Therefore, no one knows how long any path through the network might take—except that it will undoubtedly be equal to or less than the sum of the pessimistic estimates of all activities in the path and will be equal to or greater than the sum of the optimistic estimates of all activities in the path—*assuming that the estimates are accurate.* When the project is initially analyzed, the path that originally appeared to be the critical path may or may not actually be critical. We will return to this issue several times before this chapter is complete.

Note that as D approaches μ, Z gets smaller, approaching zero. Table 8.5 shows that for $Z = 0$, the chance of on-time completion is 50–50. The managerial implications are all too clear. If the PM wants a reasonable chance of meeting a project deadline, there must be some slack in the project schedule. When preparing a project budget, it is quite proper to include some allowance for contingencies, referred to as reserve analysis. More specifically, one way to deal with the uncertainty associated with task durations is to add a time reserve or buffer to the estimated task durations. The amount of the time reserve can be based on adding some percent of the estimated duration (e.g., adding an additional 15 percent to each task duration), a fixed time (e.g., adding an extra day to all tasks), or based on insights gained on more sophistical analysis such as simulation analysis discussed later in this chapter. As the project progresses and more information is obtained, the time reserve may be allocated, reduced, increased, or perhaps eliminated. The same principle holds for preparing the overall project schedule. The allowance for contingencies in a schedule is *network slack,* and the wise PM will insist on some. The PM is also well advised to incorporate some reserve time for the activities related to *managing* the project.

Finally, to illustrate an interesting point, let's examine an apparently noncritical path, activities **b-g-i**. The variance of this path (from Figure 8.16) is $0 + 0 + 28.4 = 28.4$, which is slightly less than the variance of the critical path. The path time is 42 days. The numerator of the fraction $(D - \mu)/\sqrt{\sigma_\mu^2}$ is larger, and in this case, the denominator is smaller. Therefore, Z will be larger, and the probability of this path delaying project completion is less than for the apparently critical **a-d-j** path. But consider the noncritical path **c-h-i** with a time of $10 + 11 + 18 = 39$ days and a total variance of 37.8. (Remember, we are trying to find the probability that this noncritical path with its higher variance but shorter completion time will make us late, given that the critical path is 43 days.)

$$Z = (50 - 39)/6.15$$
$$Z = 1.79$$

The result is that we have a 96 percent chance for this noncritical path to allow the project to be on time. This can also be calculated using Excel:

$$= \text{Norm.Dist}(50, 39, 6.15, \text{True})$$

If the desired time for the network equaled the critical time, 43 days, we have seen that the critical path has a 50–50 chance of being late. What are the chances that the noncritical path **c-h-i** will make the project late? D is now 43 days, so we have

$$Z = (43 - 39)/6.15$$
$$= .65$$

$Z = .65$ is associated with a probability of .74 of being on time or $1 - .74 = .26$ of being late. This can also be calculated using Excel:

$$= 1 - \text{Norm.Dist}(43, 39, 6.15, \text{True})$$

Assuming that these two paths (**a-d-j** and **c-h-i**) are independent, the probability that *both* paths will be completed on time is the product of the individual probabilities, $(.50)(.74) = .37$, which is considerably less than the 50–50 we thought the chances were—hence, the probabilities computed using just the critical path are *always optimistic,* sometimes just a little but occasionally by a great deal! If the paths are not independent, the calculations become more complicated. We will describe an easier and more accurate way to determine project completion probabilities using *simulation* in the next section. Therefore, it is a good idea to always check noncritical paths that have activities with large variances and/or path times that are close to critical in duration (i.e., those with little slack).

This leads us to what is often referred to as *merge bias* (Hulett, 1996). Any time two or more paths of a network come together or merge, we have the case noted just now: the probability of both paths being on time is the product of the probabilities for the individual paths. If one of the paths is critical and the others have a reasonable amount of slack (and/or low path variance compared to the critical path), the problem of merge bias is rarely serious. If, however, a second path has low slack and significant path variance, we cannot ignore it and should use simulation.

Simulation is an obvious way to check the nature and impacts of interactions between probabilistic paths in a network. While this used to be difficult and time-consuming, software that simplifies matters greatly has now been developed. There are several excellent risk management and simulation software packages that link directly to one or more of the popular spreadsheet application packages. We prefer Crystal Ball®—a copy comes with this book—but Risk+® and @Risk® are also well regarded. All the aforementioned permit easy simulation of network interactions and yield data that show the probability of completing the networks by specific times (Levine, 1996). These simulations, of course, include the results of potential path mergers. As we have stated earlier, the methods noted here can also be applied to risk analysis for resources. If resource usage is related to the time required by an activity, then the uncertainty about time means that there is also uncertainty about resource use. If the relationship between activity time and resource use is known or can be assumed to be roughly linear over short periods of time, it is not difficult to estimate the resource equivalents of the simulation.

Toward Realistic Time Estimates

The calculations of expected network times and the uncertainty associated with those time estimates performed in the preceding sections are based, as we noted, on estimating optimistic and pessimistic times at the .99 level. That is, a is estimated such that the actual time required for an activity will be a or higher 99 percent of the time and will be b or lower 99 percent of the time. We then noted, parenthetically, that sometimes PMs are uncomfortable making estimates at that level of precision.

Solved Problem

Consider the following project (times given in days).

Activity	a	m	b	Predecessors
a	1	4	7	—
b	2	2	2	—
c	2	5	8	a
d	3	4	5	a
e	4	6	8	c, b
f	0	0	6	c, b
g	3	6	9	d, e

Find:

1. The network.

2. All expected activity times, variances, and slacks.

3. The critical path and expected completion time.

4. The probability the project will be done in 23 days.

5. The completion time corresponding to 95% probability.

Answer:

1.

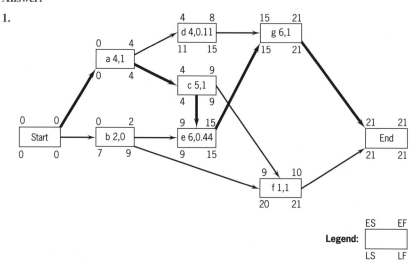

2.

Activity	TE	σ^2	Slack
a	4	1.00	0
b	2	0	7
c	5	1.00	0
d	4	0.11	7
e	6	0.44	0
f	1	1	11
g	6	1	0

3. Critical path (i.e., the path with the longest expected time) is **a-c-e-g** for a time of 21 days.

4. $Z = (23 - 21)/\sqrt{3.44} = 1.078$ for a probability of 85.9%. Alternatively using Excel we get: Norm. Dist(23, 21, 1.855, True) = 89.95%.

5. P = 0.95 corresponds to $Z = 1.65 = (T - 21)/1.855$, or T = 24.06 days. Using Excel we get: Norm.Inv(.95, 21, 1.855) = 24.05 days

Fortunately, in practice, it is not necessary to make estimates at the one-in-a-hundred level. Unless the underlying distribution is very asymmetric, no great error is introduced in finding TE if the pessimistic and optimistic estimates are made at the 95 percent or even

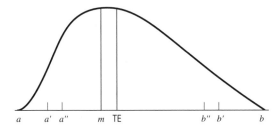

FIGURE 8.26   a, m, and b estimates at the 99, 95, and 90 percent levels.

at the 90 percent levels; that is to say, only once in 20 times (or 10 times for the 90 percent level) will the actual activity time be greater than or less than the pessimistic or optimistic estimates, respectively. *The formula for calculating the variance of an activity, however, must be modified.*

Recall that the calculation of variance is based on the assumption that the standard deviation of a beta distribution is approximately one-sixth of its range. Another way of putting this assumption is that a and b are estimated at the -3σ and $+3\sigma$ limits, respectively—roughly at the 99 + percent levels. Let the 95 percent estimates be represented by a' and b' and 90 percent estimates by a'' and b''. If we use a 95 or 90 percent estimation level, we are actually moving both a and b in from the distribution's tails so that the range will no longer represent $\pm 3\sigma$ (see Figure 8.26).

It is simple to correct the calculation of variance for this change. Consider the 95 percent estimates. Referring to Table 8.5, we can find the Z associated with .95 of the area under the curve from a' *to* ∞. For .95, Z is approximately -1.645. (Of course, this applies to the normal distribution rather than to the beta distribution, but this heuristic appears to work quite well in practice.) Similarly, $Z = 1.645$ for the area under the curve from $-\infty$ to b'.

The range between b' and a' represents $2(1.645)\sigma = 3.29\sigma$, rather than the 6σ used in the traditional estimate of the variance. Therefore, when estimating a' and b' at the 95 percent level, we should change the variance calculation formula to read

$$\sigma^2 = ((b' - a')/3.29)^2$$

For estimates at the 90 percent level (a'' and b'' in Figure 8.26), Z is approximately 1.28 and the variance calculation becomes

$$\sigma^2 = ((b'' - a'')/2.56)^2$$

In order to verify that this modification of the traditional estimator for the variance of a beta distribution gave good estimates of the true variance, we ran a series of trials using Statistical Analysis Systems' (SAS) PROC IML for beta distributions of different shapes and estimated a and b at the 95 and 90 percent levels. We then compared these estimates of a and b with the true variance of the distribution and found the differences to be quite small, consistently under 5 percent.

It is important to repeat that some managers do not have confidence in making estimates at the 99 percent level and prefer the 90 or 95 percent levels. If estimates are made at these levels, however, use of the traditional calculation for variance ($\{[b - a]/6\}2$) will result in a serious underestimation of path variances and introduce considerable error into estimates of the probabilities of completing projects by specific dates. But again, we caution readers that nothing will help the PM manage risk if the input data are biased or carelessly developed.

Project Management in Practice

Hosting the Annual Project Management Institute Symposium

Planning and implementing a national conference for a society that will draw about 1,000 attendees is a major project. The tasks involved in hosting such an event are considerable and involve selecting a program committee, choosing a theme, contacting exhibitors, making local arrangements, planning the program, and on and on.

Pittsburgh was selected as host city/chapter for the 1992 Project Management Institute's annual September seminar/symposium. The objectives for the event were three: (1) to deliver a high-quality, value-added program that would be useful and last for years to come, (2) to offer a social and guest program that would reflect well on the host city, and (3) to meet strict financial criteria. The first task after selecting the city and hotel facilities was to put together the project team and chairperson. This included managers in charge of each of the tracks, the social program, the local arrangements, and all the other details. The project team was organized using a functional approach. Pittsburgh PMI Chapter officers had most of the primary responsibilities, with members from nine other chapters assisting in other duties.

Next was the development of the WBS, shown in Figure A, and the Gantt chart of activity schedules, shown in Figure B. As seen in the Gantt chart, scheduling all the

Work Breakdown Structure and Tasks

S/S Project Management

- Recruit Project Team
- Establish Organizational Procedures
- Establish CAO Support Levels and Budget
- Issue Reports to VP-Tech and Board of Directors
- Develop S/S Goals and Objectives
- Assemble and Issue Post-S/S Report

Technical Program

- Develop S/S Theme
- Strategize Tracks and SIGs
- Recruit Technical Program Team
- Develop Selection Process Procedures
- Interface with Education Committee on Workshops
- Plan and Issue Call for Papers/Panel Discussion
- Recruit Invited Papers/Panel Discussions
- Recruit Moderators
- Develop and Issue Master Schedule for Presentations
- Select Printer
- Plan and Issue Abstract Books and Proceedings
- Organize Awards for Speakers' Breakfasts

- Identify Audio/Visual Requirements
- Develop and Issue Post-S/S Technical Report

Social Guest Program

- Establish Objectives
- Identify Available Activities
- Analyze Cost-Benefit
- Identify Recommendations
- Complete Contracts
- Recruit Staff

Speakers

- Identify Candidates and Related Benefits and Costs
- Make Recommendations and Obtain Approval
- Complete Contracts
- Maintain Periodic Contact
- Host Speakers

Publicity/Promotion

- Theme Establishment and Approval
- Logo Development and Approval
- Video Production
- Promotional Materials
- Identification and Approval
- Advertising: PMI, Public and Trade Media Releases
- Regional Newsletter Articles

Finance

- Initiate Code of Accounts
- Develop Procedures of Financial Operation
- Develop Independent Auditing Procedure
- Initiate Separate Banking Account
- Develop Cash Flow Estimates/Projections
- Develop and Issue Standard Reports
- Interact with CAO on Account Reconciliation
- Develop and Issue Post-S/S Financial Report

Corporate Sponsorship

- Establish Participation Philosophy
- Target Prime Corporations
- Solicit Participation
- Recognition

Facilities Vendor/CAO Support

- Contract with Host and Backup Hotels
- Staff Recruiting
- (Details to be Identified and Scheduled with PMI Executive Director and Events Manager)

FIGURE A The Work Breakdown Structure.

work for a major conference such as this is an overwhelming effort. In the WBS, the major task was the development of the technical program. For PMI'92, the technical program offered 22 workshops composed of 70 technical papers, special panel discussions, and case studies. The technical tracks included engineering and construction, pharmaceuticals, utilities, software, automotive, R&D, defense, education, and manufacturing. The workshops included sessions on preparing for the PMI certification examinations, learning about Taguchi concepts of statistical quality control, and future practice in project management. All of these also required careful scheduling.

The vendor program included exhibits by dozens of vendors and a large number of showcase sessions for in-depth demonstrations of their wares. The social program included a golf tournament, numerous social activities to meet with colleagues, tours of Pittsburgh's attractions, and a wide variety of entertainment opportunities.

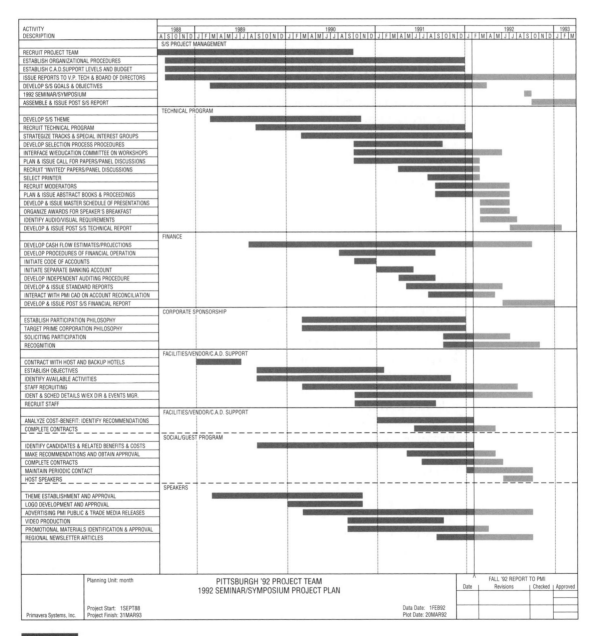

FIGURE B   Gantt chart.

All in all, a conference such as PMI's is as difficult a project as many firms face in their competitive markets.

Questions

1. Elaborate on the uniqueness of this WBS.

2. Based on the Gantt chart, when did the symposium actually occur?

3. Why are there activities scheduled after the symposium? When is the project finally done?

4. What is the total project length? What does this imply about PMI's planning for their annual symposia?

Source: PMI Staff, "Catch the Spirit . . . at Pittsburgh," *PM Network*, Vol. 6.

8.3 Risk Analysis Using Simulation with Crystal Ball®

As we have emphasized often in this book, life with projects is characterized by uncertainty. The time required to carry out an activity, the cost and availability of a resource, the success of a research experiment, the wishes of the client, and the actions of a competitor, as well as the vagaries of the weather, ups and downs of interest rates, and the random moods of a senior manager are typical of the things that can upset the most carefully planned and managed project. While it is possible through careful preplanning to reduce somewhat the degree of uncertainty surrounding any project, uncertainty can never be eliminated. We can, however, manage the uncertainty so as to reduce the impact of the ambiguities existing in our uncertain world.

As we noted previously, one method of managing the uncertainty is to perform risk analysis on the data involved in our managerial decisions. This requires us to make assumptions about the probability distributions of the variables and parameters affecting our decisions. These assumptions allow us to adopt Monte Carlo simulation models and evaluate the impact of given managerial decisions. The decision is modeled mathematically. Individual values for each variable in the model are selected at random from the probability distributions we specified, and the outcome of the model is calculated. This process is repeated many times, and the model's output for each repetition is used to construct a statistical distribution of all of the outcomes. This distribution shows the *risk profile* of the decision. The risk profile is considered along with the parent organization's strategies and policies, the wishes of the client, and many other factors when making the decision.

In Chapter 7, we used Crystal Ball® (CB) to simulate a decision process that measured whether or not a project was above an organization's hurdle rate of return. We have noted several times that the same kind of simulation might be used to manage the uncertainty involved in deciding at what level to budget a project. We can now examine its use in scheduling projects. Let us reconsider the data we have previously analyzed from Table 8.1. The analytical approach to finding the duration of the critical path of the network as well as path times for the network's other paths is based on our assumption that the probability distribution used for activity times was best described as a beta distribution. CB can thus use the beta distributions to generate random numbers for the simulation.

Figure 8.27 shows a model for simulating project completion times. It is surprisingly simple for what seems to be such a complex problem. Having entered CB, we label the columns, first one for each activity (columns A–J), and then one for each path through the network (columns K–R), and finally one for "completion time" (column S). The most difficult job one faces is identifying all of the paths to be evaluated. For small networks, this is not difficult, but for large networks, it may be. The MSP network of the problem can be a major help.

Recalling that it is easier to follow instructions if the software is running, entering the data into the spreadsheet that CB presents to you is simple.

1. After entering the appropriate column labels, click on cell **A3** and enter "20" from your earlier solution for the expected time of activity **a**.

2. Click on **Define Assumption** button in the Crystal Ball ribbon.

3. The gallery of distributions will appear, select the BetaPERT, and then click **OK**.

4. In the BetaPERT **Distribution** box, enter from Table 8.4 (Section 8.2) the pessimistic, most likely, and optimistic estimates for activity **a** and click on **OK**. Note that after assumption cells are defined in Crystal Ball, they are shaded green in the Excel worksheet.

   An anomaly worth mentioning concerns activity **b**. If you call up the BetaPERT distribution and attempt to enter 20-20-20, the three times given in the problem, CB will not allow it, because these numbers will not define a distribution. Do not define cell B3 as an assumption cell. Merely enter 20 in the cell and continue with the next entry. It will be treated by CB as a "constant," which, of course, it is. Activity **g** is also a cell listing a constant or deterministic time. Since these activities do not need to be defined with assumption cells, they will not be shaded in green.

5. Continue entering data until you have completed all activities.

6. If you counted carefully, you found eight paths through the network (cf. rows 8–15 in Figure 8.27). Enter the path identification for each in row 2 and then enter the formula for path duration for each of the paths in row 3. Note that these formulas simply sum the activity TEs for each path.

7. Now enter the formula that calculates the project duration in cell S3, labeled "Completion Time" (cf. row 16). After entering the formula in cell S3, select cell S3, and then click the **Define Forecast** button in the Crystal Ball ribbon. Type in "Project Completion Time," or whatever you choose for a title for the forecast cell, and then click **OK**. The formula will find the longest of the paths for each simulation. That will be the critical path for a given trial.

8. Now click on the "Start" green arrow in the Crystal Ball ribbon to begin the simulation model. You can watch the results being shown on your screen in the form of a statistical distribution.

The statistical distribution you see when running a simulation will be similar to Figure 8.28, the project completion time frequency chart. (If you wish to find out the likelihood of completing the project in 52 days, for example, simply enter the number 52, or number of your choice, in the box that reads "+ Infinity." Then press **Enter**. The probability you seek will appear in the **Certainty** cell, as in Figure 8.29.) Note that your results will vary from the results shown here due to the randomness inherent in simulation analysis.

If you click on the View menu option displayed at the top left in Figures 8.28 and 8.29, you can see other information, Figures 8.30 and 8.31. In Figure 8.30, View/Statistics was selected, which shows several interesting statistics about the distribution in Figure 8.28. The distribution of 1000 completion times had a mean of 47.8 days and a median of 47.6 days. Recall that the expected critical path completion time with the beta distribution was 43 days. The greater mean time found by simulation is due to the impact of path mergers. Selecting View/Percentiles displays **Percentiles** data in Figure 8.31 or the percent of the trials completed at or below the days shown. You can also use the View menu item to display the cumulative frequency distribution and the reverse cumulative frequency distribution. Finally, to return to the frequency distribution view shown in Figures 8.28 and 8.29, select View/Frequency.

	A	B	C	D	E	F	G	H	I	J	K	L	M	N	O	P	Q	R	S
1	Activity	Activity	Activity	Activity	Activity	Activity	Activity	Activity	Activity	Activity	Path	Path	Path	Path	Path	Path	Path	Path	Completion
2	a	b	c	d	e	f	g	h	i	j	a-d-j	b-e-j	b-f	b-g-i	c-e-j	c-f	c-g-i	c-h-i	Time
3	18	20	10	16	12	14	4	10	20	8	42	40	34	44	30	24	34	40	44
4																			
5																			
6	**Key**																		
7	*Formulas:*																		
8	Cell K3	=A3 + D3 + J3																	
9	Cell L3	=B3 + E3 + J3																	
10	Cell M3	=B3 + F3																	
11	Cell N3	=B3 + G3 + I3																	
12	Cell O3	=C3 + E3 + J3																	
13	Cell P3	=C3 + F3																	
14	Cell Q3	=C3 + G3 + I3																	
15	Cell R3	=C3 + H3 + I3																	
16	Cell S3	=MAX(K3:R3)																	

FIGURE 8.27 Crystal Ball® simulation-ready spreadsheet for project described in Table 8.1.

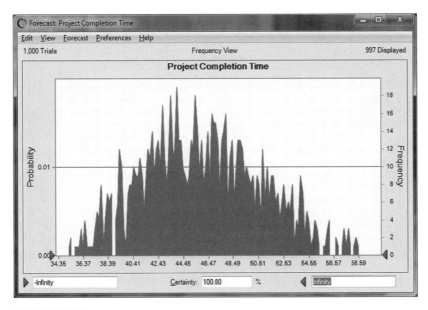

FIGURE 8.28   CB frequency chart for project completion time.

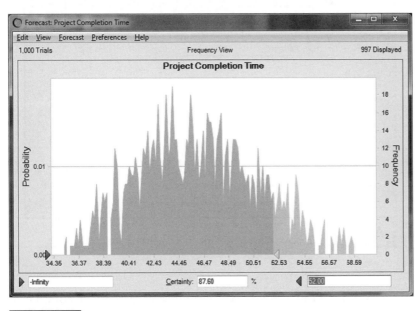

FIGURE 8.29   CB probability chart of project completion time in 52 days.

The value of simulation is well demonstrated by this simple example. The problem of gathering a large amount of information about path mergers, the probability of completion for a number of different times, and the impact of different assumptions about activity distributions by use of analytical methods are formidable even with spreadsheets to handle the calculations. Simulation handles these issues easily.

At times, PMs avoid the whole issue by suggesting that all they "really need to know" is the expected time of completion, the fastest time the project could be completed, and the latest possible time for completion. If one examines the optimistic and pessimistic times for each activity, we can readily find those times. The fastest time is

Forecast: Project Completion Time

Edit Preferences View Run Help

Cell S3 **Statistics**

Statistic	Value
Trials	1,000
Mean	47.78
Median	47.62
Mode	—
Standard Deviation	5.39
Variance	29.03
Skewness	0.18
Kurtosis	2.35
Coeff. of Variability	0.11
Range Minimum	33.82
Range Maximum	61.50
Range Width	27.68
Mean Std. Error	0.17

FIGURE 8.30 CB summary statistics for project completion time.

Forecast: Project Completion Time

Edit Preferences View Run Help

Cell S3 **Percentiles**

Percentile	Days
0%	33.82
10%	40.87
20%	42.85
30%	44.49
40%	45.91
50%	47.62
60%	48.90
70%	50.83
80%	52.77
90%	55.11
100%	61.50

FIGURE 8.31 CB percentile probabilities of completing project in n days.

30 days, and the critical path is **b-e-j**; the slowest time is 70 days with critical path **c-h-i**. The likelihood of either path occurring, that is, that activities **b**, **e**, and **j** all take minimum values at the same time (or that **c**, **h**, and **i** take on their maximum values) is so small as to be negligible. [If the estimates are made at the 3-sigma level, the probability that an activity would have a duration at or less than the optimistic estimate is $(1-.9987)=.0013$. The probability that all three activities would simultaneously be at or below their estimates is $.0013^3=.000000002$, and this ignores the more improbable condition that all other activities would simultaneously maintain the required small values.] The project could, of course, be delayed for far more than 70 days, but that would be caused by some external, catastrophic event not contemplated when generating the original time estimates. (The possibility that this type of event may occur is precisely why we will advise PMs to continue to update risk identification, assessment, and analysis as long as the project is underway.)

Incorporating Costs into the Simulation Analysis

In the previous chapter, we addressed the topic of budgeting. As you can likely imagine, the cost to complete a project is driven in a large part by the time required to complete the project. The longer it takes to complete a task, the more resources that are required, which in turn leads to greater costs. Furthermore, in a similar manner to activity durations being uncertain, the cost to complete an activity can be uncertain. For example, the cost to complete an activity may depend on which resources are assigned to it as well as how many resources are assigned to it. Therefore, it stands to reason that we can get a better understanding of the uncertainty surrounding the project's budget by incorporating both schedule and cost uncertainty into our analysis. This is perhaps best illustrated with an example.

For the purpose of our discussion, consider a project with the activity precedence relationships, estimated activity durations, and activity cost information shown in Table 8.6. As is shown in the table, optimistic, most likely or normal, and pessimistic activity durations and cost rates have been estimated for each activity. These cost rates are multiplied by the activity duration to determine the cost of the activity. For example, activity A's most likely duration is 10 days. At a normal cost rate then, we expect activity A to cost \$750 (10 days × \$75/day).

Previously, simulation was used to develop the distribution of project completion times. We now extend this analysis with a brief, new example by utilizing estimates for both the activity durations and activity costs to develop the distribution of the cost of completing the project. The AON diagram is illustrated in Figure 8.32, and from this, the enhanced simulation model is shown Table 8.7. The same steps discussed earlier were used to define Assumption Cells for the activity durations (cells A3:H3), the cost rates of each activity (A7:H7), and for the Forecast Cells for the total project duration (cell M3) and total project cost (cell I11). More specifically, Assumption Cells for the activity durations using the BetaPERT distribution with the three time estimates in Table 8.6 were created in cells A3:H3 of Table 8.7. The paths through the project were then determined, and formulas for the time to complete each path were entered in cells I3:L3.

Assumption cells for the cost rate of each activity were next created in cells A7:H7 based on the assumption that cost rates follow a triangular distribution. Formulas were added to calculate the cost of each activity in cells A11:H11. Again, the cost of completing

TABLE 8.6   **Sample Project with Uncertain Activity Durations and Cost Rates**

Activity	Pred.	Activity Durations			Cost Rates (\$/Day)		
		Opt.	Most Likely	Pess.	Opt.	Normal	Pess.
a	–	8	10	16	50	75	100
b	a	11	12	14	35	40	50
c	b	7	12	19	20	30	45
d	b	6	6	6	15	25	30
e	b	10	14	20	25	30	35
f	c, d	6	10	10	40	50	75
g	d	5	10	17	20	25	35
h	e, g	4	8	11	60	70	85

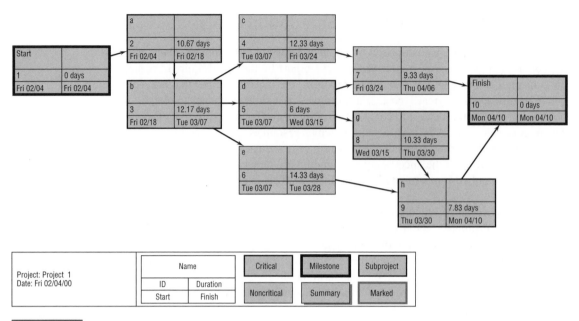

FIGURE 8.32 Sample project network solved with MSP.

an activity was computed by multiplying its duration in row 3 by its cost rate in row 7. Note that in this simulation model, we have two sources of uncertainty: the activity durations and cost rates for the activities (except for Activity D whose duration is known with certainty). To complete the simulation model, formulas that calculate the project completion time (cell M3) and the cost of the project (cell I11) were added and then these cells were defined as Forecast Cells.

The distribution of the total cost of the project based on simulating the project 1000 times is shown in Figure 8.33. Similarly, summary statistics for the total cost of the project are shown in Table 8.8. As can be observed from Table 8.8, the analysis suggests that project is expected cost $3,606.76 with a range of $2,646.95 to $4,338.51.

TABLE 8.7 Simulation Model to Analyze the Cost of Completing the Project with Both Uncertain Activity Cost Rates and Uncertain Activity Durations

	A	B	C	D	E	F	G	H	I	J	K	L	M	N
1	Activity	Activity	Activity	Activity	Activity	Activity	Activity	Activity	Path	Path	Path	Path	Completion	
2	a	b	c	d	e	f	g	h	a-b-c-f	a-b-d-f	a-b-d-g-h	a-b-e-h	Time	
3	10	12	12	6	14	10	10	8	44	38	46	44	46	
4														
5	Cost Rate	Cost Rate	Cost Rate	Cost Rate	Cost Rate	Cost Rate	Cost Rate	Cost Rate						
6	a	b	c	d	e	f	g	h						
7	75	40	30	25	30	50	25	70						
8														
9	Activity Cost	Activity Cost	Activity Cost	Activity Cost	Activity Cost	Activity Cost	Activity Cost	Activity Cost	Total					
10	a	b	c	d	e	f	g	h	Cost					
11	$750.00	$480.00	$360.00	$150.00	$420.00	$500.00	$250.00	$560.00	$3,470.00					
12														
13	New Formulae													
14	Cell A11	=A3*A7 copy to B11:H11												
15	Cell I11	=SUM(A11:H11)												

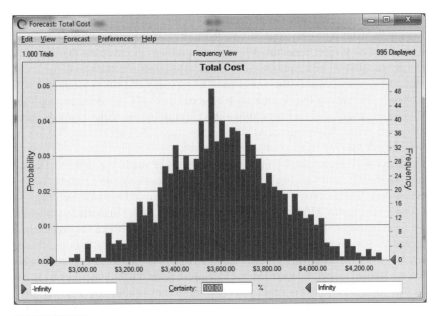

FIGURE 8.33 CB Frequency chart for project total cost.

TABLE 8.8	CB Summary Statistics for the Total Cost of the Project

Forecast: Total Cost

Edit View Forecast Preferences Help

1,000 Trials

Statistic	Forecast values
▶ Trials	1,000
Base Case	$3,470.00
Mean	$3,606.76
Median	$3,600.55
Mode	---
Standard Deviation	$245.54
Variance	$60,291.17
Skewness	0.0736
Kurtosis	3.06
Coeff. of Variability	0.0681
Minimum	$2,646.95
Maximum	$4,338.51
Mean Std. Error	$7.76

Traditional Statistics or Simulation?

The PM no longer has much choice about dealing with uncertainty. When the first edition of this book was written in 1985, three-time PERT/CPM was used by a few hardy souls, but uncertainty was more or less ignored by a large majority of those involved with projects. "Allowances for contingencies" were made as a sort of insurance against time and budget overruns, but little more attention was paid to risk. Times have changed. Formal risk management systems are now standard practice in many firms, and risk management is used by many others on specific types of projects that are considered "risky." The management of risk is not an issue. The only issue is how to do it.

The subject of project scheduling brings the problem of choosing the methods used to perform quantitative risk analysis into focus. The standard statistical methods were explained and demonstrated in the section on "Uncertainty of Project Completion Time," in this chapter. Following the section on traditional methods, we demonstrated and discussed simulation as a way of accomplishing essentially the same analysis, but more accurately and easily. We recommend simulation—*but only after the analyst has a good understanding of the traditional statistical approach.*

Both methods require that the three time estimates be made and that the TE be found for each activity. TE (and variance) is easily calculated on almost any commercially available spreadsheet. Using statistics, TE and variance must also be found for each path—again, easily done by computer. Most real projects, however, are larger than the hypothetical projects we used here to explain and illustrate the techniques of project management. When dealing with larger projects and their many paths, it is difficult merely to find those paths that may be critical or near critical. This must be done whether using statistics or simulation. But the statistical method requires one to analyze potential path mergers by hand. This increases the difficulty to extraordinary levels, not to mention adding a horrendous level of tedium. Of course, whichever method is chosen, it is rarely required to evaluate every path carefully. Paths that are significantly shorter than the critical path can usually be safely ignored. Unless their variance is extremely high, there is little chance that they will affect the project duration. As a rule of thumb, if the sum of a path's expected time plus 2.33 of its standard deviations is less than the specified time, the probability of this path taking longer than the specified time is less than 1 percent and the path can be safely ignored.

Irrespective of the method chosen, the PM will not know much about activity durations until the project gets underway. The actual critical path cannot be known until it becomes an historical fact. Even if we make three time estimates for activities and then calculate TE for each, the TEs can remain uncertain. As the project gets underway, it often seems like everything tends to disrupt the schedule: worker personalities, miscommunication, team characteristics, the PM's personality, the client, upper management, resources. And if we cannot determine which path through a project will turn out to be the critical path until after the fact, we also cannot determine how much slack any given path will have. As noted earlier, the wise PM will recalculate the network and critical path regularly and always with updated data.

Nonetheless, careful analysis, be it by traditional statistics or by simulation, is important. It provides much better insight into the risks associated with project duration than the PM can get in any other way—including a call to Miss Cleo. The result is that the PM cannot devote his or her managerial attention solely to the critical path. There is no way of knowing which path will turn out to be critical, and thus, attention must be given to all activities and paths. It is useful, every once in a while, for the PM to remember that if an activity has a great deal of slack, the people working on that activity have no sense of urgency about completing it. The activity is apt to lose its slack rapidly. Indeed, attempting to identify and manage the critical path at the beginning of the project can be rather detrimental to completing the project on time. More specifically, team members assigned to tasks that are not on the critical path may perceive that missing their deadlines will not impact the project since their work is not on the critical path. As these tasks fall behind schedule, the critical path changes and what was thought to be the critical path earlier in the project is no longer critical. Therefore, it is important that the PM carefully manage all paths and activities that may potentially impact the project's ability to be completed on time.

Crystal Ball® is an excellent piece of software and makes simulation a reasonably easy tool with which to simulate project durations. We prefer CB because it is user friendly, and also because it can display its results in a wide variety of formats. CB also allows the user to interact with the software by responding immediately to changes in the parameters of a simulation.

Project Management in Practice

Designing and Delivering a Rush Vehicle for War

As the focus of war in the Middle East shifted from Iraq to Afghanistan, the soldiers needed a new mode of off-road transport that was light but still IED and mine resistant. This was a rush project to design and deliver lifesaving war equipment. Firms bidding on the new M-ATV (mine-resistant, ambush-protected, all-terrain vehicle) had to submit proposals, produce test vehicles for the army, and start production within 7 months, a textbook case of how a defense firm's project management must now adapt to new conditions on the spur of moment.

Bidders had to submit their proposal, procedure plan, and a 1-foot-square armor vehicle panel for testing in 1 month. If the armor was approved, then the bidder had one more month to deliver two vehicles to the army for testing. Oshkosh Defense Division of Oshkosh Corp. in Wisconsin was one of the bidders and realized that the tight schedule meant they wouldn't have time to develop new components, they would have to use existing, proven components they were already familiar with such as the chassis, armor, and suspension system. In addition, they could see that the tight time frame would require them to start testing the vehicle parallel with production. Thus, the project team hit the road to Nevada where the vehicle could be tested in desert conditions like those in Afghanistan. Problems were immediately relayed back to Wisconsin, where the production team jumped into fixing them. To stay on schedule, the team met at 6 am every morning to go over that day's activities so they would meet project milestones.

When Oshkosh's vehicles passed the first round of army tests, they had only 5 days to produce three more vehicles for more extensive testing—they were delivered in 3 days! Two months later, Oshkosh was awarded a billion dollar contract for 2,244 M-ATVs. Another billion dollar order for 1,700 vehicles soon followed. Within 1 year after submitting their proposal, Oshkosh was producing over 1,000 M-ATVs per month, for a total of over 8,000. U.S. Secretary of Defense Robert Gates noted the best solution isn't always the most elaborate and that this type of ultraefficient schedule will be the model for similar military projects in the future.

Questions

1. **What price per vehicle did the army pay? Although not the hundreds of millions often paid for a new plane, why such a high price compared to, say, a car?**

2. **Given the long history of expensive and years-late military equipment projects, why wasn't this approach used sooner?**

3. **What might be the weaknesses of this new approach?**

Source: D. Burba, "Breaking the Mold," *PM Network*, Vol. 24.

© Stocktrek Images

8.4 | Using These Tools

The development of user-friendly software such as Microsoft Project®, Crystal Ball®, and Excel® that do similar jobs has made the use of tools we have described thus far available to anyone with a project to manage. We are aware that gathering the input data for the software is usually more difficult than entering and processing it, but it is doable. For example, refer to the Apartment Complex example (Figure 8.34). The information in this example was gathered and processed by people who had just been introduced to the subject.

Figure 8.34 is a portion of a 48-step WBS for the syndication of an apartment complex. Note that several of the steps are obvious composites of multistep tasks designed for a lower level (e.g., see steps 1–4). Figure 8.35 is an AON network of Figure 8.34. The firm also has a Gantt chart version of the network that is used for tracking each project. Figure 8.34 also contains three time estimates of the "calendar" time used for each step (in days) and of the "resource" time used for each step (in hours). The time estimate 2(10) is read "2 days, 10 labor-hours." The duplicate data are useful for scheduling workloads. The model served as a template for a complex problem and not only improved the process but shortened the time required to carry it out.

We are reluctant to give advice about which tools to use. If the PM indulges in a bit of experimentation with the major systems, their relative advantages and disadvantages in a given application will become evident.

In the next chapter, we investigate the scheduling problem further when multiple projects require a set of common resources to be shared. Again, a number of techniques are useful for resource allocation and activity expediting under such circumstances.

Task	*a* *days (hours)*	*m* *days (hours)*	*b* *days (hours)*
1. Product package received by Secy. in Real Estate (R.E.) Dept.	n/a	(.3)	(.4)
2. Secy. checks for duplicates, and forwards all packages in Atlanta region (but not addressed to R.E staff member) to Atl. via fast mail. Atl. office sends copy of submittal log to L.A. office on weekly basis.	n/a	(.2)	(.3)
3. Secy. dates, stamps, logs, checks for duplication, makes new file, checks for contact source, adds to card file all new packages. Sends criteria letter to new source. Sends duplication letter. Forwards package to Admin. Asst. (AA).	(.7)	(.7)	(.9)
4. AA reviews package, completes Property Summary Form, forwards to L.A. Reg. Acquisit. Director officer or to R.E. staff member to whom package is addressed (RAD).	(.5)	(.5)	(.7)
Total 1–4	1(1.7)	1(1.7)	3(2.3)
5. Person to whom package forwarded determines action. (May refer to other or retain for further review.) "Passes" sent to Secy. for files. "Possibles" retained by RAD for further review.	1(.5)	1(.5)	1(1)
•	•	•	•
•	•	•	•
•	•	•	•
48. Legal issues Post Closing Memorandum.	2(5)	5(8)	10(10)

FIGURE 8.34   WBS for syndication of an apartment complex.

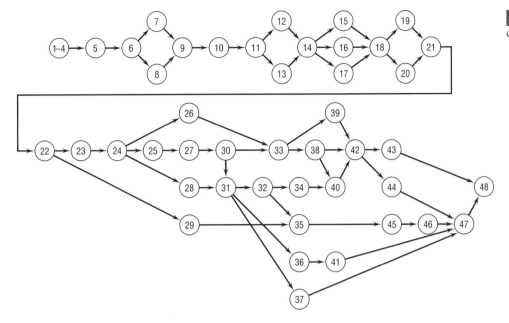

FIGURE 8.35 Apartment complex network.

Summary

In this chapter, the scheduling aspect of project implementation was addressed. Following a description of the benefits of using a network for planning and controlling a project, the AOA and AON approaches were described, as were Gantt charts.

Specific points covered in the chapter were these:

- Scheduling is particularly important to projects because of complex coordination problems.

- The network approach to scheduling offers a number of specific advantages of special value for projects.

- Critical project tasks typically constitute fewer than 10 percent of all the project tasks.

- Network techniques can adopt either an AON or activity-on-arc framework without significantly altering the analysis.

- Networks are usually constructed from left to right, indicating activity precedence and event times as the network is constructed. Through use of the network, critical activities and events are identified, early and late activity start times are found, available slacks for each activity are determined, and probabilities of project completion by various times are calculated.

- Gantt charts, a monitoring technique, are closely related to network diagrams but are more easily understood and provide a clearer picture of the current state of the project. However, while offering some advantages, they also have some drawbacks, such as not clearly indicating task precedence and dependencies.

Glossary

Activity A specific project task that requires resources and time to complete.

Activity-on-Arrow (Activity-on-Node) The two ways of illustrating a network: placing the activities on the arcs or on the nodes.

Arc The line connecting two nodes.

Crash In CPM, an activity can be conducted at a normal pace or at an expedited pace, known as crashing, at a greater cost.

Critical An activity or event that, if delayed, will delay project completion.

Event An end state for one or more activities that occurs at a specific point in time.

Gantt Chart A bar chart illustrating multiple, time-based activities on a horizontal timescale.

Milestone A clearly identifiable point in a project or set of activities that commonly denotes a reporting requirement or completion of a large or important set of activities.

Network A combination of interrelated activities and events depicted with arcs and nodes.

Node A point where one or more lines (arrows) begin or terminate, commonly used for depicting an event or activity.

Path A sequence of lines and nodes in a network.

Questions

Material Review Questions

1. Define *activity*, *event*, and *path* as used in network construction. What is a dummy activity?

2. What characteristic of the critical path times makes them critical?

3. What two factors are compared by Gantt charting? How does the Gantt chart differ in purpose from the WBS?

4. Contrast total slack and free slack.

5. When is each scheduling technique appropriate to use?

6. What is the difference between AON and AOA diagrams?

7. How does simulation determine the probabilities of various project completion times?

8. Briefly summarize how a network is drawn.

9. Define "late start time," "early start time," and "early finish time."

10. How is the critical path determined?

11. What is "slack," and why is it important?

Class Discussion Questions

12. How do you think the approach of developing three time estimates for a task's duration could be used to estimate costs for manufacturing?

13. What are some benefits of the network approach to project planning? What are some drawbacks?

14. What is your position on the statements in the Using These Tools section?

15. Why is AOA or AON of significant value to the PM?

16. How would you deal with project scheduling uncertainty?

17. How would you calculate free slack?

18. How are activity times estimated?

19. Should the critical path activities be managed differently from noncritical path activities? Explain.

20. Precedence diagramming extends the standard task relationship in a network to three additional situations. Can you think of any others?

Exercises

1. Given the following information, draw the AON diagram:

Activity	Immediate Predecessor
1	—
2	—
3	1, 4
4	2
5	2
6	3, 5

2. Convert the following AON diagram to an AOA diagram.

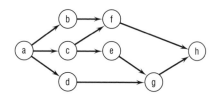

3. Find the three errors in the following diagram:

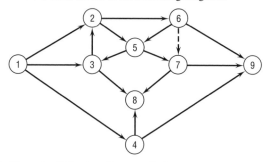

4. Given the following diagram, find:

   a. The critical path.

   b. How long it will take to complete the project.

   c. The ES, LS, EF, and LF for each activity.

   d. The slack for each activity.

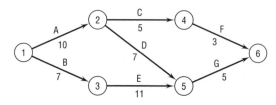

5. Convert the AOA diagram in Exercise 4 to an AON diagram. How would the AON diagram change if there had been a dummy from node 2 to node 3 in Exercise 4?

6. Convert each of the following AOA diagrams into AON diagrams.

a.

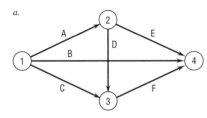

b.

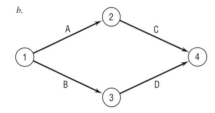

7. Given the following activities and precedences, draw an AOA or AON diagram:

Activity	Immediate Predecessor
A	—
B	—
C	A
D	A, B
E	A, B
F	C
G	D, F
H	E, G

8. Given the following network,

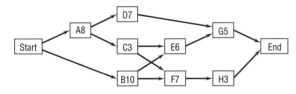

a. What is the critical path?

b. How long will it take to complete this project?

c. Can activity **B** be delayed without delaying the completion of the project? If so, how many days?

9. Given the estimated activity times below and the network in Exercise 8,

Activity	a	m	b
A	6.5	7.5	14.5
B	8.5	10.5	12.5
C	2.5	3.5	4.5
D	6.5	7.5	8.5
E	5.5	5.5	9.5
F	5.5	7.5	9.5
G	4.5	6.5	8.5
H	2.5	3.5	3.5

what is the probability that the project will be completed within (based on the path with the longest expected time):

a. 21 days?

b. 22 days?

c. 25 days?

10.

Activity[5]	a	m	b
AB	3	6	9
AC	1	4	7
CB	0	3	6
CD	3	3	3
CE	2	2	8
BD	0	0	6
BE	2	5	8
DF	4	4	10
DE	1	1	1
EF	1	4	7

Find

a. The AOA network and the path with the longest expected duration.

b. All event slacks.

c. Critical path to event D.

d. The probability of completing the path with the longest expected duration in 14 days.

e. The effect if CD slips to 6 days; to 7 days; to 8 days.

....

[5]The nomenclature AB means the activity *between* nodes A and B.

11.

Activity[6]	TE
AB	1
AC	2
AD	3
DC	4
CB	3
DE	8
CF	2
BF	4
IJ	2
CE	6
EF	5
FG	10
FH	11
EH	1
GH	9
EJ	3
GI	8
HJ	6

a. Draw the AOA diagram.

b. Find the critical path.

c. Find the expected project completion time.

12. The Denver Iron & Steel Company is expanding its operations to include a new drive-in weigh station. The weigh station will be a heated/air-conditioned building with a large floor and small office. The large room will have the scales, a 15-foot counter, and several display cases for its equipment.

Before erection of the building, the PM evaluated the project using AON analysis. The activities with their corresponding times were recorded in Table A.

Using AON analysis, find the path with the longest expected duration, the slack times, and the expected completion time.

13. Miracle Marketing has received a contract from a large pharmaceutical firm to design a nationwide advertising campaign for their recently approved cancer drug. The drug is easily taken, compared with current intravenous drugs, and can be administered from home. Miracle Marketing has assigned to the task a PM who, in turn, has delegated minor subprojects to subordinate managers.

The project was evaluated using AOA analysis. Due to the extensive length of the project, many activities were combined: The following is the result.

Activity[7]	Time (months)
AB: Obtain patient lists	3
BC: Select interviewees	6
BD: Engage interviewers	2
BF: Train interviewers	5
BE: Interview patients	4
CD: Collate results	9
DG: Summarize data	20
FG: Analyze results	6
EH: Identify main advantages	11
EI: Select advantages for ads	19

(Continued)

TABLE A

#	Activity	Times			Preceding Tasks
		Optimistic	Most Likely	Pessimistic	
1	Lay foundation	8	10	13	—
2	Dig hole for scale	5	6	8	—
3	Insert scale bases	13	15	21	2
4	Erect frame	10	12	14	1, 3
5	Complete building	11	20	30	4
6	Insert scales	4	5	8	5
7	Insert display cases	2	3	4	5
8	Put in office equipment	4	6	10	7
9	Finishing touches	2	3	4	8, 6

---

[6]See nomenclature note in Problem 10.

[7]See nomenclature note in Problem 10.

Activity[7]	Time (months)
GJ: Determine media mix	1
HK: Compare to ad budget	3
IL: Revise mix for budget	9
LM: Select ad style	12
KN: Choose ad type	7
TO: Design ad campaign	4
MN: Check with sponsor	15
NP: Revise ad campaign	13
OP: Present for approval	10

Find the critical path and expected completion time.

14. The following chart was prepared at the beginning of a HRM (Human Resource Management) crash hiring project. The project begins with two activities: Assemble interview team (A) and Budget resources (B).

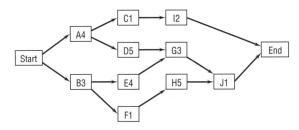

The duration, in days, follows the letter of each activity. What is the critical path? Which activities should be monitored most closely?

At the end of the first week, it was noted that activity **A** was completed in 2.5 days, but activity **B** required 4.5 days. What impact does this have on the project? Are the same activities critical?

15. Given the following financing project being considered by a venture firm, find the probability of completing the path with the longest expected duration by 17 weeks; by 24 weeks. By what date is management 90 percent sure that this path will be completed?

	Time (weeks)		
Activity[8]	Optimistic	Most Likely	Pessimistic
1-2: Collect firm data	5	11	11
1-3: Analyze data	10	10	10

	Time (weeks)		
Activity[8]	Optimistic	Most Likely	Pessimistic
1-4: Determine need	2	5	8
2-6: Determine profitability	1	7	13
3-6: Evaluate risk	4	4	10
3-7: Interview owners	4	7	10
3-5: Check references	2	2	2
4-5: Evaluate industry	0	6	6
5-7: Evaluate economy	2	8	14
6-7: Decide funding	1	4	7

If the venture firm can complete the project for the funder within 18 weeks, it will receive a bonus of $10,000. But if the project delays beyond 22 weeks, it must pay a penalty of $5,000 due to lost opportunity. If the firm can choose whether or not to bid on this project, what should its decision be if the project is only a breakeven one normally?

16. Given an auditing project with the following activities,

Activity	Standard Deviation	Critical?	Duration
a, add	2	yes	2
b, balance	1		3
c, count	0	yes	4
d, deduct	3		2
e, edit	1	yes	1
f, finance	2		6
g, group	2	yes	4
h, hold	0	yes	2

Find:

a. The probability of completing the critical path in 12 weeks (or less), as the client desires.

b. The probability of completing the critical path in 13 weeks (or less).

c. The probability of completing the critical path in 16 weeks (or less), the client's drop-dead date.

d. The number of weeks required to assure a 92.5 percent chance of completing the critical path, as guaranteed by the auditing firm.

[7] See nomenclature note in Problem 10.

[8] See nomenclature note in Problem 10.

17. The following network is a compressed representation of the prospectus of a start-up firm that plans to develop a new, bioelectronic computer chip.

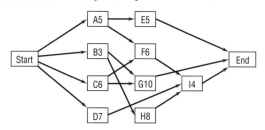

Note that four activities, the biological elements, can start immediately.
Find:
a. The critical path.
b. The earliest time to complete the project.
c. The slack on activities **E**, **F**, and **H**.

18. The events of the project below are designated as 1, 2, and so on.
a. Draw the network.
b. Find the critical path.
c. Find the slacks on all the activities.

Activity	Prec. Evt.	Suc. Evt.	TE (weeks)	Prec. Activ.
a	1	2	3	none
b	1	3	6	none
c	1	4	8	none
d	2	5	7	a
e	3	5	5	b
f	4	5	10	c
g	4	6	4	c
h	5	7	5	d, e, f
i	6	7	6	g

19. Given the following network (times are in weeks), determine:
a. The ES, LS, EF, and LF for each activity.
b. The slacks on all activities.
c. The critical activities and path.

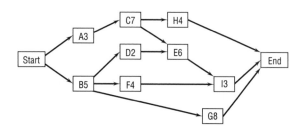

20. Given the schedule in Table B for a liability work package done as part of an accounting audit in a corporation, find:
a. The critical path.
b. The slack time on "process confirmations."
c. The slack time on "test pension plan."
d. The slack time on "verify debt restriction compliance."

TABLE B

Activity	Duration (days)	Preceding Activities
a. Obtain schedule of liabilities	3	none
b. Mail confirmation	15	a
c. Test pension plan	5	a
d. Vouch selected liabilities	60	a
e. Test accruals and amortization	6	d
f. Process confirmations	40	b
g. Reconcile interest expense to debt	10	c, e
h. Verify debt restriction compliance	7	f
i. Investigate debit balances	6	g
j. Review subsequent payments	12	h, i

21. In the website development project network shown in the following figure, the number alongside each activity designates the activity duration (TE) in weeks.

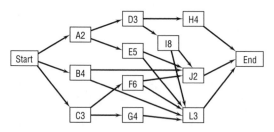

Determine:
a. The ES and LS for each activity.
b. The earliest time that the website can be completed.
c. The slack on all activities.
d. The critical activities.
e. The critical path.

22. Given the following information regarding a project concerning an initial public offering (IPO),

Activity	TE (weeks)	Preceding Activities
a: Check feasibility	3	none
b: Determine funding	1	none
c: Find possible banks	3	a
d: Select two possibles	4	a
e: Interview two banks	4	b
f: Analyze funding costs	5	b
g: What chance of success?	2	c, e
h: Sign contract	3	f

  a. Draw the network.

  b. What is the critical path?

  c. When will the offering be available (completion of the project)?

  d. What is the effect on the project if activity **e** (approvals) takes an extra week? Two extra weeks? Three extra weeks?

23. Construct a network for the aerospace launch project below and find its critical path.

Activity	TE (weeks)	Preceding Activities
a: Check controls	3	none
b: Check propellants	5	a
c: Check personnel	3	a
d: Assemble items	1	c
e: Move to launch pad	3	h
f: Run system tests	4	b, d
g: Check astronauts	2	c
h: Ground stations go?	3	g, f
i: Countdown	1	e, h

24. Construct a network for the following training and development project.

Activity	TE (weeks)	Preceding Activities
a: Select personnel	3	none
b: Invite personnel	5	none
c: Budget ok?	14	a
d: Prepare materials	5	a

Activity	TE (weeks)	Preceding Activities
e: Engage instructor	4	b
f: Select date	7	b
g: Remind personnel	8	d, e
h: Start project	5	g, f

  a. Draw the network.

  b. Find the critical path.

  c. Assume activity **a** (hire trainers) took 5 weeks. Replan the project.

  d. From where would you suggest transferring resources, and to what activities, so that the original target training date may be maintained?

25. Resolve part (d) of Exercise 10 assuming the values of a and b are given at the 95 percent level. Repeat, assuming the values are given at the 90 percent level.

26. Using the information below, draw an AOA network. Find the path with the longest expected duration, and use it to compute the number of days you would be 95 percent sure the project would be completed. Calculate the slack, earliest start, and latest start times for each activity and show in table form. Does any path come close to causing a problem in determining the probability of project completion based on just using the path with the longest expected duration?

Activity	Time (days) a	Time (days) m	Time (days) b
1–2	6	8	10
1–3	5	6	7
1–4	6	6	6
2–6	0	0	0
2–7	10	11	12
3–6	12	14	16
4–5	5	8	11
4–9	7	9	11
5–6	8	10	12
5–9	0	0	0
6–7	14	15	16
6–8	10	12	14
7–10	9	12	15
8–10	0	4	14
9–11	5	5	5
10–11	7	8	9

27. Given the following activities required for staging a community play on Independence Day,

   a. Construct an AON diagram.

   b. Determine the earliest expected completion time for the play.

   c. Based on the path with the longest expected duration, what completion date are you 80 percent confident of achieving? 40 percent confident?

   d. Will a 1-day delay in this project be serious?

		Time (days)		
Activity	**Predecessor**	**a**	**m**	**b**
1	—	2	4	6
2	—	5	5	5
3	2	3	5	7
4	1	7	10	13
5	1	11	12	13
6	2,4	5	6	7
7	3	9	10	11
8	3,6	5	7	9
9	4	7	9	11
10	5	3	3	3
11	7	15	17	19
12	8	6	8	10
13	9, 10	7	8	15
14	7	12	14	16
15	12, 13	16	17	18

28. Draw an AON network using the following data and find the probability of completing the path with the longest expected duration in 44 days, the official opening date.

		Time (days)		
Activity	**Predecessor**	**a**	**m**	**b**
1	—	6	10	14
2	1	0	1	2
3	1	16	20	30
4	2	3	5	7
5	4	2	3	4
6	3	7	10	13
7	4	1	2	3
8	7	0	2	4

		Time (days)		
Activity	**Predecessor**	**a**	**m**	**b**
9	3, 7	2	2	2
10	9	2	3	4
11	8	0	1	2
12	10, 11	1	2	3

29. Simulate Exercise 27 to find the probabilities of project completion. Use a triangular distribution for defining activity time distributions. After a 1,000-trial simulation, examine the statistical information generated and compare the output of the simulation with your findings in Exercise 27. Briefly explain the significant similarities and differences. (Optional: Modify your simulation model and determine the probability that the path with the longest expected duration actually is the critical path. What are the managerial implications associated with your results?)

30. Simulate Exercise 28 to find the probabilities of project completion. Use a BetaPERT distribution for defining activity time distributions. After a 1,000-trial simulation, examine the statistical information generated and compare the output of the simulation with your findings in Exercise 28. Briefly explain the significant similarities and differences. (Optional: Modify your simulation model and determine the probability that the path with the longest expected duration actually is the critical path. What are the managerial implications associated with your results?)

31. Tasks, duration in weeks, and predecessors are listed in the following table:

Task	**Predecessors**	**Duration**
a	—	2
b	—	2
c	a, b	4
d	c	3
e	a, b, c	1
f	d, e	2
g	f	3
h	g	1

   a. Construct a Gantt chart using MSP.

   b. Assuming the default 5-day workweek, calculate the critical path of the project.

   c. Calculate the project duration.

32. In the following table, project activities in days are listed with three time estimates for duration in days and predecessors for the activities.

Activity	Optimistic Time	Most Likely Time	Pessimistic Time	Predecessors
a	5	7	12	—
b	8	8	8	—
c	2	6	10	a
d	12	14	19	a, b
e	6	6	12	c, d
f	3	12	18	b, e
g	6	8	10	f

a. Calculate the expected time of each activity using MSP.

b. Construct a Gantt chart using MSP.

c. Use MSP to draw a network diagram.

d. Assuming a 5-day workweek, calculate the critical path of the project.

e. Calculate the slack for the activities.

Incidents for Discussion

Yankee Chair Company

The Yankee Chair Company was anxious to get a new model rocking chair onto the market. Past efforts to introduce new models had resulted in frustrating failures. Bret Ricks, President of Yankee Chair, was determined that it would not happen again with the newest model. He had no confidence in his current management team, so he hired Jan Dymore, a local consultant, to organize and manage this project. He assigned a Yankee Chair manager, Tom Gort, to work with Dymore to start developing some talent for project management within the company. Dymore decided to set up a PERT network and guided Gort through the process of listing activities, assigning precedence, and estimating completion times. She also explained the critical path concept to Gort, who by this time had a reasonable grasp of the project direction. At the first review session with Mr. Ricks, the PERT approach was accepted enthusiastically, but toward the end of the review, Dymore made some critical remarks about the product design and was subsequently released from the project.

Ricks then asked Gort if he could carry on the PERT approach by himself. Gort jumped at the chance, but later in his office, he began to question whether or not he really could use the PERT network effectively. Dymore had made a guess at what the critical path would be and how long the project would take, but she had also told Gort that several other calculations had to be made in order to calculate the exact time estimates for each activity and the variances of those activity times. Gort really did not understand the mathematics involved and certainly did not want to look bad in Ricks' eyes, so he decided to take Dymore's guess at the critical path and get the best possible estimates of those activity times. By concentrating his attention on the critical path activities and ignoring the variance issues, he figured he could bring the project in on time.

Questions

Will Gort's approach work? How much more of a gamble is Gort taking than any PM normally takes? What should Gort watch out for?

Cincinnati Software

Cincinnati Software, which currently specializes in the installation of manufacturing resource planning (MRP II) systems in small firms, is planning a major expansion into installing the new enterprise resource planning (ERP) systems. This major expansion into the hottest software area will be organized as an in-house project of strategic importance. The company has selected a PM and team to follow the project through to completion. The project team is very interested in selecting an appropriate scheduling technique for the project. The PM has thus set the following guidelines for the selection process: simple; able to show durations of events, the flow of work, and the relative sequence of events; able to indicate planning and actual flow, which items may proceed at the same time, and how far they are from completion. The assistant PM favors the Gantt chart, the finance representative likes PERT, and the information technology department head prefers CPM.

Questions

If you were the PM, which method would you use, and why?

Continuing Integrative Class Project

It is now time to construct the project schedule. You may do this by hand or using a software package for project management as mentioned in Chapter 1. Begin with your WBS and determine the precedence relationships among the activities at the most detailed level of your project's WBS. Next, develop the three time estimates for each activity. Based on the precedence relationships and time estimates, create a network diagram for your project. Develop a simulation model for your project and determine the distribution of project completion times for your project. Finally, analyze your project and determine what deadlines will provide you and your team a 75 percent and 90 percent chance of completing the project on time.

Bibliography

Badiru, A. B. "Activity-Resource Assignments Using Critical Resource Diagramming." *Project Management Journal*, September 1993.

Evans, J. R., and D. L. Olson, *Introduction to Simulation and Risk Analysis*, Upper Saddle River, NJ: Prentice-Hall, 1998.

Goldratt, E. M. *Critical Chain*. Great Barrington, MA: North River, 1997.

Hulett, D. T. "Schedule Risk Analysis Simplified." *PM Network*, July 1996.

Levine, H. A. "Risk Management for Dummies, Part 2." *PM Network*, April 1996.

Moder, J. J., C. R. Phillips, and E. W. Davis. *Project Management with CPM, PERT, and Precedence Diagramming*, 3rd ed. New York: Van Nostrand Reinhold, 1983.

Project Management Institute. *A Guide to the Project Management Body of Knowledge*, 5th ed. Newtown Square, PA: Project Management Institute, 2013.

Sandberg, J. "Rise of False Deadline Means Truly Urgent Often Gets Done Late." *Wall Street Journal*, January 28 2007.

Wheatly, M. "Up for Adaptation." *PM Network*, July 2010.

Wilkens, T. T. "Are You Being Misled by Your Progress Gantt Chart?" *PM Network*, August 1997.

Williams, T. M. "What Are PERT Estimates?" *Journal of the Operational Research Society*, Vol. 44, No. 12, 1995.

The following case presents a real project (in aggregate form) that allows the student to compare the critical path solution approach for both completion time and cost as well as a simulated solution for time variability and then also for both time and cost variability. The student should better understand the risk of projects running late and overbudget after this exercise.

Case

NutriStar Energy, Inc.[9] S. Shafer

Wesley James had recently arrived in Boston from Manchester, UK for a position as Project Owner at NutriStar Energy, Inc. He was now meeting with Ava Smith, President of NutriStar, to discuss his upcoming duties and responsibilities associated with their latest product, the Nutri-Sports Energy Bar.

As Ava explained: "NutriStar produces a line of vitamins and nutritional supplements. We recently introduced our Nutri-Sports Energy Bar, which is based on new scientific findings about the proper balance of macronutrients in the body. Fortunately, the energy bar has quickly become popular among elite athletes and others who focus on eating an optimal balance of macronutrients. One distinguishing feature of the Nutri-Sports Energy Bar is that each bar contains 50 milligrams of eicosapentaenoic acid (EPA), a substance strongly linked to reducing the risk of cancer but found in only a few foods, such as salmon. We were able to include EPA in our sports bars because we had previously developed and patented a process to refine EPA for our line of fish-oil capsules."

"Because of the success of the Nutri-Sports Energy Bar in the United States, we are considering offering it in Latin America. With our domestic facility currently operating at capacity, we have decided to investigate the option of adding approximately 10,000 square feet of production space to our facility in Latin America, at a cost of $5.1 million."

"This is where you come in, Wesley. The project to expand the Latin American facility involves four major phases: (1) concept development, (2) definition of the plan, (3) design and construction, and (4) start-up and turnover. During the concept development phase, a project owner, that will be you, is chosen to oversee all four phases of the project and given a budget to develop a plan. The outcome of the concept development phase consists of just a rough plan, feasibility estimates for the project, and a rough schedule. Also, a justification for the project and a budget for the next phase will be needed."

"In the plan definition phase, the project owner selects and works with a project manager to oversee the activities associated with this phase. Plan definition consists of four major activities that are completed more or less concurrently: (1) defining the project scope, (2) developing a broad schedule of activities, (3) developing detailed cost estimates, and (4) developing a plan for staffing. The outputs of this phase are combined into a detailed plan and proposal for management specifying how much the project will cost, how long it will take, and what the deliverables are."

"If the project gets management's approval and provides the appropriations, the project progresses to the third phase, design and construction. This phase consists of four major activities: (1) detailed engineering, (2) mobilization of the construction employees, (3) procurement of production equipment, and (4) construction of the facility. Typically, the detailed engineering and the mobilization of the construction employees are done concurrently. Once these activities are completed, construction of the facility and procurement of the production equipment are done concurrently. The outcome of this phase is the physical construction of the facility."

"The final phase, start-up and turnover, consists of four major activities: pre-start-up inspection of the facility, recruiting and training the workforce, solving start-up problems, and determining optimal operating parameters (called *centerlining*). Once the pre-start-up inspection is completed, the workforce is recruited and trained at the same time that start-up problems are solved. Centerlining is initiated upon the completion of these activities. The desired outcome of this phase is a facility operating at design requirements."

"The cost to complete an activity depends on both the amount of time required to complete the task and the cost rate of performing the activity. I have compiled two tables here for you. Table A provides optimistic, most likely, and pessimistic time estimates for the major activities. Table B provides similar estimates for the cost rates to complete the activities. Like time estimates, the cost rate to complete the facility expansion project can vary for a number of reasons such as using more or less expensive resources, price changes in labor and materials, the need to outsource work that was expected to be performed in-house, and so on. According to the data in Tables A and B, Concept Development is expected to cost $24,000, 12 months at $2,000/month."

TABLE A   Three Time Estimates for NutriStar Production Facility Expansion Project

Activity	Optimistic Time (months)	Most Likely Time (months)	Pessimistic Time (months)
A: Concept Development	3	12	24
Plan Definition			
B: Define project scope	1	2	12
C: Develop broad schedule	0.25	0.5	1
D: Detailed cost estimates	0.2	0.3	0.5
E: Develop staffing plan	0.2	0.3	0.6
Design and Construction			
F: Detailed engineering	2	3	6
G: Facility construction	8	12	24
H: Mobilization of employees	0.5	2	4
I: Procurement of equipment	1	3	12
Start-up and Turnover			
J: Pre-start-up inspection	0.25	0.5	1
K: Recruiting and training	0.25	0.5	1
L: Solving start-up problems	0	1	2
M: Centerlining	0	1	4

TABLE B Three Cost Rate Estimates for NutriStar Production Facility Expansion Project

Activity	Optimistic Cost Rate ($/Month)	Most Likely Cost Rate ($/Month)	Pessimistic Cost Rate ($/Month)
A: Concept Development	1,900	2,000	2,300
Plan Definition			
B: Define project scope	23,750	25,000	28,750
C: Develop broad schedule	15,200	16,000	18,400
D: Detailed cost estimates	28,500	30,000	34,500
E: Develop staffing plan	27,000	30,000	33,000
Design and Construction			
F: Detailed engineering	360,000	400,000	440,000
G: Facility construction	112,500	125,000	156,250
H: Mobilization of employees	270,000	300,000	330,000
I: Procurement of equipment	360,000	400,000	440,000
Start-up and Turnover			
J: Pre-start-up inspection	90,000	100,000	110,000
K: Recruiting and training	540,000	600,000	660,000
L: Solving start-up problems	90,000	100,000	110,000
M: Centerlining	45,000	50,000	55,000

"Well, that's it Wesley! We're glad to have you on board and look forward to working with you. Do you have any questions?"

Questions

1. Draw a network diagram for this project. Identify which path you expect to be the critical path and its expected completion time. Which paths are most likely to threaten this path in terms of becoming critical?

2. Simulate the completion of this project 1,000 times assuming that activity times follow a triangular distribution and that the cost rates are known with certainty and equal to the most likely cost rate. Estimate the mean and standard deviation of the project completion time and the project cost. How does the time compare to your previous answer based solely on the critical path?

3. Develop histograms for both the project completion time and the cost to complete the project. What do these histograms tell you?

4. Using the results of your simulation analysis, calculate the probability that the project can be completed within 30 months. What is the probability that the project will take longer than 40 months? What is the probability that the project will take between 30 and 40 months? What is the probability the project will cost $5.1 million or less to complete? The probability the project will cost between $5 and $6 million to complete?

5. Modify your simulation model to determine the probability that the path you expected to be the critical path actually was the critical path? What are the managerial implications of this?

6. Simulate the completion of this project 1,000 times assuming that the activity times follow a triangular distribution and that the cost rates are also triangularly distributed. Estimate the mean and standard deviation of the project completion time and project cost. How do these results compare to the results you obtained in Question 2?

7. Would you expect there to be a relationship between the duration of an activity and the cost *rate* to complete the activity? If so, how could your simulation model be modified to reflect this relationship?

This brief reading illustrates the kinds of things that can go wrong in a project and delay it, but also the kinds of remedies PMs can come up with to keep the project on schedule. The types of creative remedies available to PMs are then summarized.

Reading

Without Further Delay[10]   M. Bowles

A resourcing delay is hard enough to handle at sea level. High in the Andes mountains, it can potentially doom a project.

On a recent mining project in that South American range, procurement of the main equipment wasn't going to happen on time. Because it was an activity in the critical path, the entire schedule would be compromised.

Almost every project professional has been there. It's how you handle such a crisis that makes the difference between success and failure.

In this case, Edwin Monzón, PMI-RMP, PMI-SP, PMP, project scheduler for Antamina, a mining company in San Marcos, Peru, identified the holdup as quickly as possible.

This was accomplished by analyzing the variation between baseline dates and forecast dates from purchase status reports and expediting status reports for every purchase order. The project control group created a "traffic light" tool that identified the variances by color.

"This let us identify, quickly and easily, the procurement delays in a project with a lot of purchase orders," Mr. Monzón says.

The project risk management plan had a cost contingency for change in the method of transportation for delayed purchase orders.

"In my project, it was better to pay for air transportation than pay for a contractor claim for stopped resources—both people and equipment," he adds.

By switching the method of transporting the supplies from sea to air, his project team was able to make up the time.

But just as that scheduling conflict was under control, another cropped up.

"As soon as the equipment began to arrive at the mine, we had a strike led by the local community, which delayed the equipment installation," Mr. Monzón says.

There are seemingly endless glitches that can throw off a project's schedule—stakeholder issues, poor planning and lack of resources, to name a few. So it's no wonder many projects fail to deliver on time.

While some scheduling challenges can't always be avoided, project managers can regain lost time and get their projects back on track without sacrificing quality or team morale.

In Mr. Monzón's case, he built a time contingency into the schedule to account for possible risks.

"According to our project risk-management plan, we had assigned schedule contingency to the equipment installation activity that helped the project be completed on time," he says.

Danger: Scheduling Pitfalls Ahead

There may not be a single reason why a project gets thrown off-kilter. There are, however, plenty of mistakes that practically

ensure a project will fall behind schedule—poor initial planning being a prime culprit.

"We usually say, 'If you failed to plan, you planned to fail,'" says Lofty Sabry, CAPM, PMI-RMP, PMI-SP, PMP, PgMP, owner of the project management consultancy EMP (Experts Project Management) in Dubai, United Arab Emirates.

In many cases, project sponsors or company executives push to start the project quickly rather than dedicate time to good planning, according to Don Wessels, PMP, senior consultant and instructor on the project and program management business unit of Management Concepts, a training firm in Vienna, Virginia, USA.

Scheduling problems can quickly result from several issues, Mr. Monzón says, including:

- Deficient scope definition
- Poor stakeholder identification
- Lack of a resource usage plan
- No risk-management plan
- Poor constraint identification

Some sort of project planning must take place at the start, Mr. Wessels says. Bring together key stakeholders, team members and a facilitator to discuss requirements and scope.

"The project launch or rapid project planning process doesn't have to take a long time, but it's a crucial step," he says. "It's important to get everyone on board at the start. If you don't have full participation from stakeholders and team members, you won't have full buy-in. This could cause serious problems and might not be reconciled until much later in the project."

Another common scheduling pitfall: lack of clear executive mission. Without it, project priorities are established based on individual politics or agendas rather than the organization's goals, says Harold "Mike" Mosley Jr., PMP, program director of the nuclear construction division of Zachry, a project management, engineering, procurement and construction contractor in San Antonio, Texas, USA. He is also the committee chair for PMI's *Practice Standard for Scheduling – Second Edition*.

Mr. Mosley was part of a project with an engineering team in Boston, Massachusetts, USA that worked for several years before construction work began on the project. The project sponsor refused to bring together the two remote teams. As a result, they never developed a good working relationship, he says.

"The executive's priorities were on short-term cost savings rather than the long-term benefit," Mr. Mosley adds. "The project and cost and schedule suffered as a result."

Instead, Mr. Wessels says, a clear executive mission should be communicated at the start of the project and reinforced throughout.

[10]Reprinted from *PM Network* with permission. Copyright Project Management Institute Inc.

Prevention Is the Best Medicine

Avoid scheduling delays in the first place by incorporating these five strategies:

1. **Create the project plan well in advance.**

    "If you don't start planning the project until you're ready to go, you'll always be in recovery," says Harold "Mike" Mosley Jr., PMP, Zachry, San Antonio, Texas, USA.

2. **Get a good grasp of stakeholders' requirements.**

    Gather six to eight key stakeholders to not only discuss their requirements but also to better understand the rationale behind them. "Ask, 'What will you gain? How does that tie back to the organizational mission?'" says Don Wessels, PMP, Management Concepts, Vienna, Virginia, USA.

3. **Involve more than just the key stakeholders in the planning.**

    "A lot of times, one group or person will do it and expect everyone to follow it," Mr. Mosley says. But even the lowest-ranked team member can offer valuable insight. "You don't have to be an expert on the topic to give a possible solution or idea. Sometimes a fresh set of eyes can be the solution," he says.

4. **Conduct a schedule risk analysis as part of the planning.**

    Create a contingency plan based on the specific project risks, says Edwin Monzón, PMP, PMI-RMP, PMI-SP, Antamina, San Marcos, Peru. "For example, in a mining project in South America, the time contingency plan should be aligned with risks like community strikes, complex procurement in remote locations and low performance for work in high altitudes," he says.

5. **Establish a team operating agreement.**

    In it, include how team members will work together, how they will handle issues and, if an issue can't be resolved, who will handle it, Mr. Wessels says.

"At the end of each major piece of work, a control gate review of deliverables should be conducted to ensure the project is performing as planned and is still aligned with the mission of the organization and delivering the value for which the project was started," he says. "It's a periodic opportunity to stress the mission and determine if the mission has changed."

Poor resourcing can also be detrimental to a project's schedule.

"When there aren't enough resources, the project team is forced into overtime, and morale drops dramatically," Mr. Wessels says.

Improperly skilled resources can be just as problematic.

"'Availability' is not a skill set. You can't just use the next available body," he says. "In addition to quality and inefficiency issues, team morale will suffer because they know they aren't doing well."

The immediate reaction to the first sign of a schedule delay is often to have teams work harder, longer, faster. But that's not always the best answer.

For one thing, overworking team members—even with financial compensation—will likely take a toll on morale and quality.

"Even though team members are working longer hours, productivity can drop 60 percent, especially after six to eight weeks of overtime," Mr. Wessels says. "Then team members get burned out, jump ship to another project or leave the organization altogether."

Save the Team, Save the Schedule

Sometimes there's just no way to get a project back on track other than to involve an extra surge from team members, Mr. Sabry says.

One of the most traumatic scheduling complications of his career occurred when he was managing a project in the United Arab Emirates and then-president Sheikh Zayed bin Sultan Al Nahyan died. The entire country, including its government offices, immediately shut down for nearly two weeks.

Mr. Sabry leveraged the schedule compression technique to shorten the project schedule without minimizing scope, and employed fast-tracking to expedite certain project tasks by completing them simultaneously.

This involved team members putting in some extra hours. To maintain morale, he made sure to reward and recognize their efforts through bonuses, time off, certificates of achievement, and training opportunities.

"If I know we have a big push coming up, I might give the team a day or an afternoon off," Mr. Wessels says. "That's a strong incentive. People come back with more vigor and energy."

To ensure team morale stays intact as the schedule is restored, project managers must maintain clear lines of communication.

"Project leaders should inform the team of the recovery plan and keep them updated on the status," Mr. Monzón says.

During the schedule recovery period, project managers should discuss with team members what is needed and how each new task is going to get it done, Mr. Mosley adds.

Communication also involves getting out in the trenches, talking to team members and looking for clues that morale may be suffering.

"When you talk to team members, are they with you in the conversation and paying attention, or are they looking out the window and zoning out?" Mr. Mosley asks. "If they come in dragging in the morning and in the evening, you've got a problem."

Institute quality-control measures as the project gets back on track. That doesn't necessarily mean a large quality-assurance team must be hired, according to Mr. Mosley. "It starts with the team member, his or her supervisor, and the supervisor's supervisor," he says.

Quality monitoring should be conducted throughout the project life cycle—not just until the schedule is restored. Track deliverables to assure they meet specifications and requirements, as well as how often the same work must be repeated because of quality issues.

Finally, it never hurts to infuse some humor in the schedule recovery plan, Mr. Mosley advises. He managed a construction project for a national power provider in Florida, USA that was running behind schedule, largely due to bad weather. The project team hadn't taken into account rain drainage issues at the work site, and it became flooded.

"The project sponsor came down for a monthly meeting and told me that 'Not even a bucketful of fairy dust could get this project back on schedule,'" he says. To keep up team morale, he bought a keychain depicting Tinker Bell, the fairy from *Peter Pan*, and hung it on the wall.

The team set about modifying the site layout to keep it dry. In the end, the project came back in a month ahead of schedule.

"I took the picture of the Tinker Bell keychain, framed it and presented it to the project sponsor," Mr. Mosley says.

Most of the time, though, there's nothing funny about project schedule delays. In an effort to salvage the schedule, project managers can inadvertently kill their team's energy and toss quality out the door.

But that doesn't have to be the case, Mr. Mosley says.

Just keep it simple. "Focus your corrective measure on what is wrong and what you can affect," he advises. "It may be an issue beyond the scope of what you can address. Once you figure out what the issue is, then you can look for workarounds."

Questions

1. List all the tips in the article for avoiding scheduling delays.
2. List all the methods for recovering in the article from scheduling delays.
3. In the sidebar "Prevention Is the Best Medicine," which strategy seems the most important? Which is second most important? Why?
4. The article states that stakeholders push to start the project work quickly rather than spend the time planning. What would this have resulted in for the earlier PMIP "Massachusetts' Instant Bridges" sidebar?

CHAPTER **9**

Resource Allocation

 PMBOK

6.4

In the previous chapter, we looked at a special type of resource allocation problem, that of allocating time among project tasks, better known as *scheduling*. Now we consider the impact on the schedule of the allocation of physical resources as well, a topic considered along with scheduling in **PMBOK**. The subject relates directly to the topic of scheduling because altering schedules can alter the need for resources and—just as important—alter the timing of resource needs. At any given time, the firm may have a fixed level of various resources available for its projects. The fixed resources might include labor-hours of various types of special professional or technical services, machine-hours of various types of machinery or instrumentation, specialized locations, and similar scarce resources needed for accomplishing project tasks. For example, if the need for some resource varies between 70 and 120 percent of resource capacity, then that resource will be underutilized (and wasted if no alternative use exists) at one point in the project and in insufficient supply at another. If the project schedule can be adjusted to smooth the use of the resource, it may be possible to avoid project delay and, at the same time, not saddle the project with the high cost of excess resources allocated "just to make sure."

This chapter addresses situations that involve resource problems. We discuss the trade-offs involved, the relationship between resource loading and leveling, and some of the approaches employed to solve allocation problems, including the Critical Path Method (CPM), Goldratt's "critical chain," and several other approaches to the problem of scheduling under conditions of resource scarcity. We begin with resource conflicts in a single project. Although CPM is not actually a resource allocation method, we include it here because we view time as a resource, and trade-offs between time and other resources are a major problem in resource management. Finally, we note the major impact that current project management software has had on the PM's ability—and willingness—to deal with resource loading and leveling.

Like the topic of scheduling discussed in the previous chapter, on the surface the topic of resource allocation may appear to be mainly tactical in nature. However, there are important strategic implications associated with effective resource allocation. For example, properly evaluating whether additional resources to complete a project on time or early can only be done by considering the strategic objectives of the organization and how the project supports these objectives. Additionally, the development of an organization's human resources is critical to its long-term competitive success. With this in mind, an important consideration for PMs is to ensure that project team members are allocated to project work such that ample time is available for their development to support both their current responsibilities and their broader development.

9.1 Critical Path Method—Crashing a Project

When it was first developed in 1958, CPM used activity-on-node (AON) notation and included a way of relating the project schedule to the level of physical resources allocated to the project. This allowed the PM to trade time for cost, or vice versa. In CPM, two activity times and two costs were often specified for each activity. The first time/

Project Management in Practice

Expediting Los Angeles Freeway Repairs after the Earthquake

Damage to be repaired in the earthquake's aftermath. © David Butow/Corbis/Getty Images

Some years ago, at 4:31 A.M., a 6.8-magnitude earthquake hit Los Angeles and collapsed large sections of four major freeways, snarling one million commuters in daily gridlock for the indefinite future. Clearly, solutions to this crisis were of the highest priority. "Caltrans," the California Department of Transportation, sprung into action with a three-pronged attack. First, they rushed into emergency response, fanning out to conduct visual inspections and close dangerous segments of the roads and freeways. Second, they initiated interim traffic management strategies for all closed segments, utilizing parallel streets and old bypass roads to expand their capacity, change their signage and striping, and redirect adjacent traffic including traffic signal timing. Last, they planned for speedy demolition and rebuilding of the damaged portions of the freeways. Time was all-important and Caltrans used every trade-off available to expedite the repairs which would normally take years to complete.

1. California's governor signed an Emergency Declaration allowing Caltrans to streamline its contracting proce-

dures so that RFPs, bids, and evaluations that usually took 4 months could be completed in 5 days.

2. Significant incentives/disincentives were built into the contracts, the incentive depending on the value of the construction under consideration. One firm spent heavily on overtime, extra equipment rentals, and bonuses to keep working 24 hours a day, rain or shine, and came in 74 days ahead of a contractual date of 140 days, thereby earning a $14.8 million bonus that became the talk of the town!

3. All resources of the Federal Highway Administration were made available to work with Caltrans.

4. "Force Account" contracting was employed for immediate selection of sole-source contractors. The contractor then began work immediately under the direction of a Caltrans Resident Engineer.

5. Major project management processes were initiated including disaster response and an earthquake recovery task force consisting of top executives in local and national governmental agencies.

6. Millions in additional funds were made available through Caltrans' Director, a declaration of a state of emergency by President Clinton, and eventually Congress.

Questions

1. **Of the six constraints, which were cost trade-offs and which were scope trade-offs?**

2. **In what way were the performance trade-offs made? That is, how did they affect performance?**

3. **What kinds of resource allocation approaches discussed in the chapter were used in this situation?**

Source: J. B. Baxter, "Responding to the Northridge Earthquake," *PM Network*, Vol. 8.

cost combination was called *normal*, and the second set was referred to as *crash*. Normal times are "normal" in the same sense as the *m* time estimate of the three times used in PERT. Crash times result from an attempt to expedite the activity by the application of additional resources—for example, overtime, special equipment, and additional staff or material.

It is standard practice with activity-on-arrow (AOA) and AON to estimate activity times under the assumption of resource loadings that are normal. To discuss a time requirement for any task without some assumption about the level of resources devoted to the task makes no real sense. At the same time, it does not make sense to insist on a full list of each and every resource that will be spent on each of the hundreds of activities that may comprise a network. Clearly, there must have been some prior decision about what resources would be devoted to each task, but much of the decision making is, in practice, relegated to the common methods of standard practice and rules of thumb. The allocation problem requires more careful consideration if it is decided to speed up the accomplishment of tasks and/or the total project. We need to know what additional resources it will take to shorten completion times for the various activities making up the project.

While standard practice and rules of thumb are sufficient for estimating the resource needs for normal progress, careful planning is critical when attempting to expedite (crash) a project. Crash plans that appear feasible when considered activity by activity may incorporate impossible assumptions about resource availability. For example, we may need to crash some activities on the Wild Horse Dam Project. To do so, we have all the labor and materials required, but we will need a tractor-driven crawler crane on the project site not later than the eighth of next month. Unfortunately, our crane will be in Decatur, Illinois, on that date. No local contractor has a suitable crane for hire. Can we hire one in Decatur or Springfield and bring ours here? And so it goes. When we expedite a project, we tend to create problems; and the solution to one problem often creates several more problems that require solutions.

Difficulties notwithstanding, the wise PM adopts the Scout's motto: "Be prepared." If deterministic time estimates are used, and if project deadlines are firm, there is a high likelihood that it will be necessary to crash the last few activities of most projects. The use of three probabilistic activity time estimates may reduce the chance that crashing will be needed because they include identification and estimation of risks and uncertainties that are sometimes forgotten or ignored when making deterministic time estimates. Even so, many things make crashing a way of life on some projects—things such as last-minute changes in client specifications, without permission to extend the project deadline by an appropriate increment, that is, scope creep. An example of one of the problems that commonly result from the use of deterministic time estimates can be seen in the boxed example that follows.

Consider the data in Table 9.1. First, we compute a cost/time slope for each activity that can be expedited (crashed). Slope is defined as follows:

$$\text{Slope} = \frac{\text{crash cost} - \text{normal cost}}{\text{crash time} - \text{normal time}}$$

that is, the cost per day of crashing a project. The slope is negative, indicating that as the time required for a project or task is decreased, the cost is increased. Note that activity c cannot be expedited. Table 9.2 shows the time/cost slopes for our example.

An implication of this calculation is that activities can be crashed in increments of 1 day (or one period). Often, this is not true. A given activity may have only two or three technically feasible durations. The "dollars per day" slope of such activities is relevant only if the whole crash increment is useful. For example, if an activity can be carried out in either 8 days or 4 days, with no feasible intermediate times, and if an uncrashable parallel path goes critical when the first activity is reduced from 8 down to 6 days, then the last

TABLE 9.1	An Example of Two-Time CPM		
Activity	**Precedence**	**Duration, Days (normal, crash)**	**Cost (normal, crash)**
a	—	3, 2	$40, 80
b	a	2, 1	20, 80
c	a	2, 2	20, 20
d*	a	4, 1	30, 120
e**	b	3, 1	10, 80

*Partial crashing allowed.
**Partial crashing *not* allowed.

TABLE 9.2	Activity Slopes–Cost per Period for Crashing
Activity	**Slope ($/day)**
a	$40/-1 = -40$
b	$60/-1 = -60$
c	—
d	$90/-3 = -30$
e	-70 (2 days)

2 days (to 4 days) of time reduction are useless. Of course, if the PM needs to complete the project 2 days earlier, reducing the duration of one activity by 4 days may be the easiest and cheapest way to do it. (And there are times when the PM may expedite activities that have little or no impact on the network's critical time, such as when the resources used must be made available to another project.)

One must remember that crashing a project may require a change in the technology with which something is done. In the language of economics, it is a change in the "production function." At other times, crashing may involve a relatively simple decision to increase groups of resources already being used. If the project, for instance, is to dig a ditch of a certain length and depth, we might add units of labor-shovel to shorten the time required. On the other hand, we might replace labor-shovel units with a Ditch Witch. Technological discontinuities in outcomes usually result. Different amounts of labor-shovel input may result in a job that takes anywhere from 1 to 3 days. Use of the Ditch Witch may require three hours. There may be no sensible combination of resources that would complete the job in, say, 6 hours. It is important to remember that when we change technology, we may also be changing the level of risk in carrying out the activity. In some cases, technology cannot be changed, and task duration is fixed. A 30-day toxicity test for a new drug requires 30 days—no more, no less.

Not only do changes in technology tend to produce discontinuities in outcomes, but they also tend to produce discontinuities in cost. As the technology is changed to speed a project, the relationship of input cost to activity duration is apt to jump as we move from less to more sophisticated production systems.

When crashing a project, our first task is to develop a table or graph of the cost of a project as a function of the project's various possible completion dates. Starting with the normal schedule for all project activities, crash selected activities, one at a time, to decrease project duration at the minimum additional cost. To crash a project, follow two simple principles: First, focus on the critical path(s) when trying to shorten the duration of a project, with the exception we noted above when a resource used by an activity not on the critical path is needed for another project. Crashing a noncritical activity will not influence project duration. Second, when shortening a project's duration, select the least expensive way to do it.

Given these guides, consider the network shown in Figure 9.1a that was constructed from the data in Table 9.1. It is easier to illustrate the impact of crashing on an AOA network than on an AON network, so we use that approach here. Also, we use dummy activities in this case not to illustrate precedence but to show time durations and slack on the time axis. As indicated in Tables 9.1 and 9.2, activity **d** can be partially crashed, but activity **e** involves a technological discontinuity and must take either 3 days to complete at $10 or 1 day at $80. In general, the impact of having such a technological discontinuity is that the best solution for crashing n days might not be part of the best solution for crashing $n + 1$ days. Rather, it may be best to crash the activity with the technological discontinuity at $n + 1$ days and not crash another activity that could be crashed for n days. This situation is illustrated in the discussion that follows.

The network's critical path is **a-b-e**, the project duration is 8 days, and the normal total cost is $120, as illustrated in the network of Figure 9.1a. The decision about which activities to crash depends on how much we need to reduce the duration of the project. To reduce the total network duration by 1 day, we must reduce the time required by one of the activities along the critical path. Inspecting Table 9.2 to see which critical activity can be reduced at the least cost, we find it is activity **a** which adds $40 to the project's current cost of $120. Activity **b** could be crashed at a cost of $60 or we could even crash **e** 2 days for a cost of $70. Of course, crashing **e** would only shorten the project duration by 1 day because when **e** is shortened, the path **a-d-dummy**, 7 days long, becomes the critical path and does not allow the project to be shortened to 6 days. Of the three options, crashing **a** is the lowest cost and therefore preferable (see Figure 9.1b). Notice that crashing **a** also shortens **a-d-dummy** and **a-c-dummy** by 1 day.

Suppose the project must be crashed by 2 days. What are the options? Reconsidering Table 9.2 and Figure 9.1a, we see that we could crash activity **e** for 2 days ($70), but path **a-d-dummy** (7-days' duration) must also be crashed at least 1 day. We choose **d** ($30/day) because it is cheaper than a ($40). The cost of crashing is $100, and the total project cost is $120 + $100 = $220. Alternatively, we could crash **a** and **b**, also for a cost of $100 ($40 + $60). Arbitrarily, we choose the latter option (Figure 9.1c).

Now suppose we wanted to crash the project by 3 days, from the original 8 days down to 5 days. Clearly **e** must be crashed by 2 days, costing $70, and **a** or **b** by a day. We choose **a**, the cheapest, for an additional $40. This leaves **d** to be crashed by 1 day for another $30, resulting in a total crashing cost of $140 and a project cost of $120 + $140 = $260 (Figure 9.1d). Note that we did not crash **b** this time, as we did for 6 days. This is due to the technological discontinuity in activity **e**.

Last, let us consider crashing the project by 4 days down to a project duration of 4 days. Since we crashed **e**, the technological discontinuity, to reach a 5-day duration, all the remaining activities can be incrementally crashed. Thus, we can simply inspect Figure 9.1d to see what else needs incremental crashing to reduce the project by another day. Notice in Figure 9.1d that **a-b-e** and **a-d-dummy** are both critical paths. Only **b** and **d** can still be crashed, so we crash each by 1 day for an additional cost beyond the 5-day schedule of Figure 9.1d of $60 + $30 = $90 for a total project cost of $260 + $90 = $350 (Figure 9.1e). Note that **c** is now critical so *all* activities are critical. Since the critical paths **a-b-e** and **a-c** are at their full extent of crashing, the project duration cannot be further reduced, even

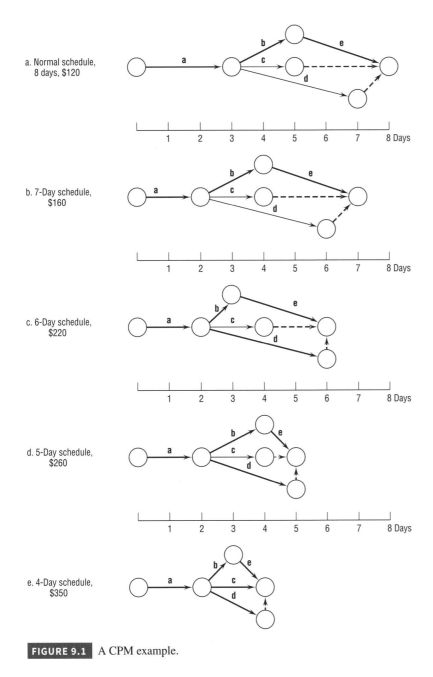

a. Normal schedule,
   8 days, $120

b. 7-Day schedule,
   $160

c. 6-Day schedule,
   $220

d. 5-Day schedule,
   $260

e. 4-Day schedule,
   $350

FIGURE 9.1 A CPM example.

though activity **d** could be crashed another day. Thus, Figure 9.1e is *not* the all-crash network although it equals the all-crash time schedule of four days.

Another approach to CPM would have been starting with an all-crash schedule costing $380 and "relaxing" the activities one at a time. Of course, the activities relaxed first should be those that do not extend the completion date of the project. In our example, this is possible because **d** does not need to be at 1 day and so could be extended by 1 day at a cost saving of $30 without altering the project's completion date. This can be seen in Figure 9.1e, where activity **d** is shown taking 2 days with a project cost of $350. Continuing in this manner and relaxing the most expensive activities first would eventually result in the all-normal schedule of 8 days and a cost of $120, as shown in Figure 9.1a.

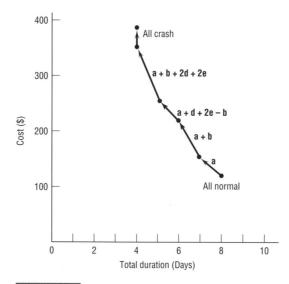

FIGURE 9.2 CPM cost-duration history.

Whether or not all this crashing is worthwhile is another matter. On the cost side, Figure 9.2 shows the time/cost relationship of crashing the project. On the benefit side, some projects have penalty clauses that make the parent organization liable for late delivery—and sometimes bonuses for early delivery. Starting at the right (all-normal) side of Figure 9.2, note that it becomes increasingly costly to squeeze additional time out of the project. Charts such as the one shown in Figure 9.2 are useful to the PM in exercising control over project duration and cost. They are particularly helpful in dealing with senior managers who may argue for early project completion dates with little understanding of the costs involved. Similarly, such data are of great benefit when clients plead for early delivery. If the client is willing to pay the cost of crashing, or if the firm is willing to subsidize the client, the PM can afford to listen with a sympathetic ear. (While we advise the PM to ignore overhead cost over which he or she has no control, it should be noted that indirect costs are often altered when a project is crashed.)

Some organizations have more than one level of crashing. Table 9.3 illustrates such a case. In this example, the firm has two distinct levels of expediting a project: *rush* and *blitz*. The differences in the precedence relationships between tasks are noted in Table 9.3, as are differences in resource commitments. The last two rows of Table 9.3 show the expected changes in cost and time if the project is expedited.

Fast-Tracking

Another way to expedite a project is known as "fast-tracking." This term has been applied mostly to construction projects, but the technique can be used in many other types of projects. It refers to overlapping the design and build phases of a project. Because design is usually completed before construction starts, overlapping the two activities will result in shortening the project duration. Beginning to build before design is completed might also, however, result in an increased number of change orders, subsequent loss of productivity, increased cost, and loss of time. Studies of construction projects revealed, however, that while there were more design changes in fast-tracked projects, the total number of project change orders was not significantly different than in similar projects that were not fast-tracked (Ibbs et al., 1998). Fast-tracking seems to be a reasonable way to expedite

TABLE 9.3   Official Pace of a Construction Project

Title	Normal	Rush	Blitz
Approved Project Definition	Full	Some abbreviations from normal pace	Only if needed for major management decisions, purchasing and design engineering
Study of Alternates	Reasonable	Quick study of major profitable items	Only those not affecting schedule
Engineering Design	Begins near end of Approved Project Definition	Begins when Approved Project Definition 50–75% complete	Concurrently with Approved Project Definition
Issue Engineering to Field	Usually 2–8 weeks lead time between issue and field erection to plan and purchase	Little lead time between issue and field erection	No lead time between issue and field erection
Purchasing	Begins in latter stages of Approved Project Definition	Rush purchase of all long delivery items. Many purchases on "advise price" basis	Done concurrently with Project Definition. Rush buy anything that will do job. Overorder and duplicate order to guarantee schedule
Premium Payments	Negligible	Some to break specific bottlenecks	As necessary to forestall any possible delays
Field Crew Strength	Minimum practical or optimum cost	Large crew with some spot overtime	Large crew; overtime and/or extra shifts
Cost Difference Compared with Normal Pace, as a Result of:			
— Design and Development	Base	5–10% more	15% and up
— Engineering and Construction Costs	Base	3–5% more	10% and up
Probable Time	Base	Up to 10% less	Up to 50% less

construction projects, as well as other types of projects when the early "build" or "carry out" steps are fairly routine and well understood. It is a partial use of the basic concept in phase-gate project management and is dependent on effective feedback and feedforward communication.

Solved Problem

Given the following network (time in days):

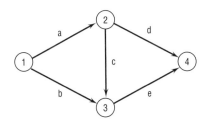

Activity	Crash Time, Cost	Normal Time, Cost	Partial Crashing?
a	3, $60	3, $60	No
b	6, 80	7, 30	Yes
c	2, 90	5, 50	No
d	5, 50	6, 30	No
e	2, 100	4, 40	Yes

Find the lowest cost to complete the project in 10 days.

Answer

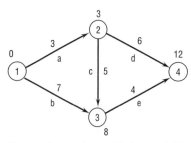

Current time and cost: 12 days and $210

Since the critical path is **a-c-e**, we only initially need to consider these three activities:

    a: cannot be crashed

    c: can cut 3 days at an extra cost of $40 but, due to **b**, only results in project completion by day 11. To reach 10 days, cut **b** by 1 day, total extra cost $90.

    e: can cut **e** by 2 days for an extra cost of $60 and results in project completion by day 10.

Thus, cut **e** by 2 days at a cost of $60.

9.2 | The Resource Allocation Problem

A shortcoming of the scheduling procedures covered in the previous chapter is that they do not address the issues of resource utilization and availability. The focus is on time rather than physical resources. Also, in the discussion that follows, it will not be sufficient to refer to resource usage simply as "costs." Instead, we must refer to individual types of labor, specific facilities, kinds of materials, individual pieces of equipment, and other discrete inputs that are relevant to an individual project but are limited in availability. In addition, we commonly must consider two types of resources: (1) those that are needed in a specific amount for an activity (e.g., 2 machine hours, 5 yards of cement, 12 labor days) and (2) those that are needed to accompany the labor for as long as the labor is used, such as a machine. This chapter will always clarify which type of these two types of resources we are considering at the time. Last, we must not forget that time itself is always a critical resource in project management, one that is unique because it can neither be inventoried nor renewed. **One cannot save time—one can only spend more or less of it.**

    The relationship between progress, time, and resource availability/usage is the major focus of this chapter. Schedules should be evaluated not merely in terms of meeting project milestones but also in terms of the timing and use of scarce resources. A fundamental measure of the PM's success in project management is the skill with which the trade-offs among scope,

Project Management in Practice

Thirty Days to Rescue

World Pictures/Photoshot

Global Healthcare Project (GHP) of California, USA, conducts various community projects in poor communities and regions across the globe. Previously, they had helped the residents of Pueblo Nuevo, Guatemala, set up a local pharmacy for their remote village in the northwest mountain highlands. Recently, the community again requested GHP's help in setting up an ambulance service since people couldn't reach a hospital when there was an emergency. GHP assembled a volunteer team of 22 university students to provide an ambulance, set up an emergency call system, and train some of the residents to act as EMTs (emergency medical technicians). However, the students could only be gone for 30 days, so this had to be a very fast project.

However, GHP found that the resource and infrastructure needs were overwhelming:

- There was no suitable vehicle in the community to buy and convert into an ambulance. Moreover, they wanted this project to be a "community-owned" effort with the community owning the ambulance and maintaining the system.

- The nearest hospital was 3 hours away down rough mountain terrain.

- There was no basic equipment available for the ambulance, not even oxygen tanks.

- Very few villagers had a driver's license nor the time to spend as an ambulance driver.

- Ongoing funding was needed for the ambulance and supplies and maintenance.

- Training the driver-EMTs faced problems of limited education and medical knowledge, as well as literacy, language, and other difficulties.

The first task for the project team upon arrival was to find and register the vehicle. They did locate an acceptable vehicle 4 hours away near the Mexican border, but it couldn't be registered in the name of the community without engaging a lawyer and going through a lot of paperwork. This was done, but it took almost the full 30 days. They equipped the vehicle with mountain terrain tires to handle the rough trails. They skipped trying to equip the ambulance with any equipment other than simple medical supplies. They eventually located three residents who had driver's licenses, could handle driving on mountain terrain, were trainable, and had the time to drive patients to the hospital. To secure ongoing funding, the community agreed to add a surtax on the pharmacy for the supplies and maintenance. The trainers threw out the training manual and instead just demonstrated emergency-response procedures. For the call system, GHP arranged for a satellite phone number that could always reach one of the three driver-EMTs.

As the team was preparing to depart, a young girl required emergency transport to the hospital near midnight and got there safely with the new phone-ambulance system,

a tribute to the efforts of the project team! The ambulance returned the next morning.

Questions

1. **What "lessons learned" could you suggest for GHP from this project for similar, future projects?**

2. **Does this project sound like a "mission impossible?" In what regards?**

3. **What would you suggest to GHP regarding overcoming the short time span for this kind of project?**

Source: J. Danko, "Rescue Squad," *PM Network*, Vol. 24.

---

time, and cost are managed. It is a continuous process of cost–benefit analysis: "I can shorten this project by a day at a cost of $400. Should I do it?" "If I buy 300 more hours of engineering time, I may be able to improve performance by 2 or 3 percent. Should I do it?" Of course, all such estimates are uncertain. What are the risks and how should we deal with them?

Occasionally, it is possible that some additional (useful) resources can be added at little or no cost to a project during a crisis period. At other times, some resources in abundant supply may be traded for scarce ones. Most of the time, however, these trades entail additional costs to the organization, so a primary responsibility for the PM is to make do with what is available.

The extreme points of the relationship between time use and resource use are as follows:

- **Time Limited:** The project must be finished by a certain time, using as few resources as possible. But it is time, not resource usage, that is critical.

- **Resource Limited:** The project must be finished as soon as possible, but without exceeding some specific level of resource usage or some general resource constraint.

The points between these two extremes represent time/resource-use trade-offs. As in Figure 9.2, they specify the times achievable at various resource levels. Equivalently, they specify the resources associated with various completion times. Clearly, the range of time or resource variability is limited.

Occasionally, both time and resources may be limited, but in this case the specifications cannot also be fixed. If all three variables—time, cost, scope (specifications)—are fixed, the system is "overdetermined." The PM has lost all flexibility to perform the trade-offs that are so necessary to the successful completion of projects. Of course, it is possible that all three variables might be fixed at levels that allowed the PM plenty of maneuvering room, but this is most unlikely. Far more likely, our PM acquaintances tell us, is the case in which senior management assigns budgets, schedules, and the scope without regard for the uncertainties of reality. It is the PM's responsibility, possibly with help from the project's champion, to warn senior management of the impropriety of such restrictions in spite of the chance that a senior manager might respond with "I'll get someone who can . . . !" If our advice seems a bit strong, we refer you to Jim McCarthy's Rule #25 (McCarthy, 1995, pp. 88–89): "Don't accept task dates, features, and resource dictates from managers unfamiliar with the task."

On occasion, it may be that one or more tasks in a project are *system-constrained*. A system-constrained task requires a fixed amount of time and known quantities of resources. Some industrial processes—heat treating, for instance—are system-constrained. The material must "cook" for a specified time to achieve the desired effect. More or less "cooking" will not help. When dealing with a system-constrained task or project, no trade-offs are possible. The only matter of interest in these cases is to make sure that the required resources are available when needed.

In the following sections, we discuss approaches for understanding and using these relationships in various project situations.

9.3 | Resource Loading

Resource loading describes the amounts of individual resources an existing schedule requires during specific time periods. Therefore, it is irrelevant whether we are considering a single work unit or several projects; the loads (requirements) of each resource type are simply listed as a function of time period. Resource loading gives a general understanding of the demands a project or set of projects will make on a firm's resources. It is an excellent guide for early, rough project planning. Obviously, it is also a first step in attempting to reduce excessive demands on certain resources, regardless of the specific technique used to reduce the demands. Again, we caution the PM to recognize that the use of resources on a project is often nonlinear. Much of the project management software does not recognize this fact.

If resources of a project are increased by X percent, the output of the project usually does not increase by X percent, and the time required for the project does not decrease by X percent. The output and time may not change at all, or may change by an amount seemingly not related to X. An increase of 20 percent in the number of notes played does not necessarily improve the quality of the music. Any time the resource base of a project is altered from standard practice, the risk that the project may not be successful is changed, often increased.

Given a WBS, deriving a resource-loading document is not difficult. Figure 6.4 (Chapter 6) shows part of a WBS for a "Career Day" at a college. The part of the WBS shown lists the personnel resources needed for each activity. (The hours required are included in the WBS, but were not printed in Figure 6.4.) Utilizing data in the WBS, MSP generated Figure 9.3, the resource usage calendar. Each of the human resources used in the project is listed, followed by the name of the activities in which the resource is used. The total hours of work for each resource called for by the WBS are shown together with the amount planned for each activity. The schedule for resource loading is derived and the loading is then shown for each resource for each week (or day or month) of the project. It should be clear that if the information in this calendar were entered into an Excel® spreadsheet along with estimates of the variability of resource times, Crystal Ball® could be used to simulate the resource loading for any or all of these resources.

An examination of Figure 9.3 shows that the secretary is overloaded during late May and early June. Assuming that there is only one secretary, during the week of May 30 he or she must work 17+ hours per day of a 7-day week (or 24 hours per 5-day week). This is apt to try the patience of the most determined and loyal employee. Graduate assistants are certainly considered slaves by their faculty masters, but are usually indentured for only 20 hours per week of servitude. Unless there are four GAs, the project will have problems. It is the job of the PM to deal with these problems, either by adding people or by changing the schedule in such a way that the demand for resources does not exceed resource capacities.

Because the project WBS is the source of information on activity precedences, durations, and resources requirements, it is the primary input for both the project schedule and its budget. The WBS links the schedule directly to specific demands for resources. Thus, the AOA network technique can be modified to generate time-phased resource requirements. A Gantt chart could be adapted, but the AOA diagram, particularly if modified to illustrate slacks as in Figure 9.1, will be helpful in the analysis used for resource leveling. Let us illustrate with the AON network used as an example in the previous chapter, but converted to an AOA diagram. The AOA network (from Table 8.2) is illustrated in Figure 9.4, and resource usage is illustrated for two hypothetical resources, A and B, on the arcs. The expected activity time is shown above the arc, and resource usage is shown in brackets just below the arc, with the use of A shown first and B second—for example, [5,3] would mean that five units of A and three units of B would be used on the activity represented by the

ID	Resource Name	Work	May					June					July			
			25	2	9	16	23	30	6	13	20	27	4	11	18	25
1	**Secretary**	**1,020 hrs**	24h	40h	40h	40h	88h	120h	102h	40h	40h	40h	40h	40h	40h	40h
	Print forms	240 hrs														
	Gather college particulars	160 hrs	24h	40h	40h	40h	16h									
	Print programs	240 hrs					24h	40h	40h	40h	40h	40h	16h			
	Advertise in college paper	200 hrs					24h	40h	36h	0h	0h	0h	24h	40h	36h	
	Organize posters	180 hrs					24h	40h	26h	0h	0h	0h	0h	0h	4h	40h
2	**Program Manager**	**1,440 hrs**	40h	40h	40h	16h	24h	40h	40h	40h	16h					
	Contact organizations	600 hrs	16h													
	Select guest speaker	560 hrs														
	Organize food	120 hrs	24h	40h	40h	16h										
	Contact faculty	60 hrs					24h	36h								
	Arrange facility for event	100 hrs						4h	40h	40h	16h					
3	**Office Manager**	**180 hrs**	24h	40h	40h	40h	16h				20h					
	Collect display information	160 hrs	24h	40h	40h	40h	16h									
	Transport materials	20 hrs									20h					
4	**Graduate Assistant**	**1,140 hrs**	24h	40h	40h	40h	64h	80h	80h	56h	40h	40h	16h			
	Print participants' certificates	320 hrs														
	Organize refreshments	280 hrs	24h	40h	40h	40h	40h	40h	40h	16h						
	Send invitations	80 hrs														
	Organize gift certificates	220 hrs														
	Arrange banner	200 hrs					24h	40h	40h	40h	40h	16h				
	Class announcements	40 hrs											24h	16h		
5	**Director**	**400 hrs**	24h	40h	40h	40h	40h	40h	40h	40h	40h	40h	16h			
	Organize liquor	400 hrs	24h	40h	40h	40h	40h	40h	40h	40h	40h	40h	16h			

FIGURE 9.3 Resource usage calendar for Career Day Project.

arc. Figure 9.5 shows the "calendarized" AOA diagram, similar to the familiar Gantt chart. Resource demands can now be summed by time period across all activities.

The loading diagram for resource A is illustrated in Figure 9.6a and that for resource B in Figure 9.6b. The loads are erratic and vary substantially over the duration of the project. Resource A, used in tasks **a**, **b**, and **c**, has a high initial demand that drops through

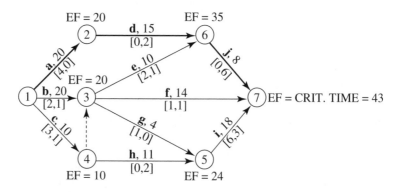

FIGURE 9.4 The AOA network of Table 8.2.

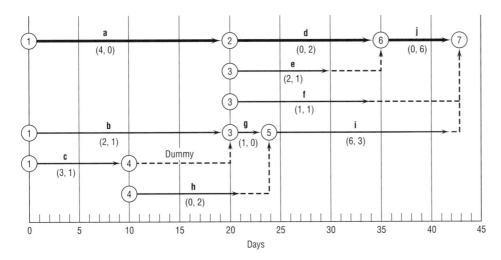

FIGURE 9.5 Modified AOA diagram showing activity slack and resource usage (from Figure 9.4).

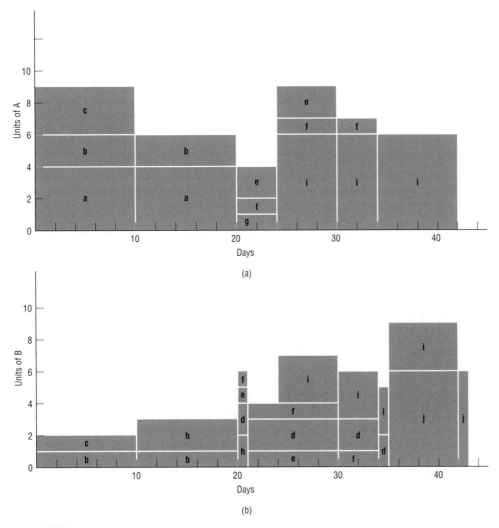

FIGURE 9.6 (a) Load diagram for resource A. (b) Load diagram for resource B.

the middle of the project and then climbs again. Resource B, on the other hand, has low initial use but increases as the project develops. The PM must be aware of the ebbs and flows of usage for each input resource throughout the life of the project. It is the PM's responsibility to ensure that the required resources, in the required amounts, are available when and where they are needed. In the next three sections, we will discuss how to meet this responsibility.

9.4 | Resource Leveling

In the preceding example, we noted that the project began with the heavy use of resource A, used smaller amounts during the middle of the project, and then continued with rising usage during the project's latter stages. Usage of B started low and rose throughout the project's life. Large fluctuations in the required loads for various resources are a normal occurrence—and are undesirable from the PM's point of view. Resource leveling aims to minimize the period-by-period variations in resource loading *by shifting tasks within their slack allowances*. The purpose is to create a smoother distribution of resource usage.

There are several advantages to smoother resource usage. First, much less hands-on management is required if the use of a given resource is nearly constant over its period of use. The PM can arrange to have the resource available when needed, can have the supplier furnish constant amounts, and can arrange for a backup supplier if advisable. Moreover, the PM can do this with little error. Second, if resource usage is level, the PM may be able to use a "just-in-time" inventory policy without much worry that the quantity delivered will be wrong. If the resource being leveled is people, leveling improves morale and results in fewer problems in the personnel and payroll offices because of increasing and decreasing labor levels.

Not only are there managerial implications to resource leveling, but there are also important cost implications. When resources are leveled, the associated costs also tend to be leveled. If resource use increases as time goes by, and if resources are shifted closer to the present by leveling, costs will be shifted in the same way. The opposite is true, of course, if resource usage is shifted to the future. Perhaps most important from a cost perspective is leveling employment throughout a project or task. For most organizations, the costs of hiring and layoff are quite significant. It is often less expensive to level labor requirements in order to avoid hiring and layoff, even if it means some extra wages will be paid. In any case, the PM must be aware of the cash flows associated with the project and of the means of shifting them in ways that are useful to the parent firm.

The basic procedure for resource leveling is straightforward. For example, consider the simple AOA network shown in Figure 9.7a. The activity time is shown above the arc, and resource usage (one resource, workers) is in brackets below the arc. Activities **a**, **b**, and **c** follow event 1, and all must precede event 4. Activity **a** requires two workers and takes 2 days, **b** requires two workers and takes 3 days, and **c** needs four workers and 5 days. (We addressed the problem of trade-offs between labor and activity time in the first section of this chapter.) If all these tasks are begun on their early start dates, the resource loading diagram appears as shown in Figure 9.7b, steps of decreasing labor demand varying from eight workers to four workers. If, however, task **b** is delayed for 2 days, the full length of its slack in this particular case, the resource loading diagram is smoothed, as shown in Figure 9.7c. The same result would have occurred if **b** were started as early as possible and task **a** were delayed until day 3.

Resource leveling is a procedure that can be used for almost all projects, whether or not resources are constrained. If the network is not too large and there are only a few

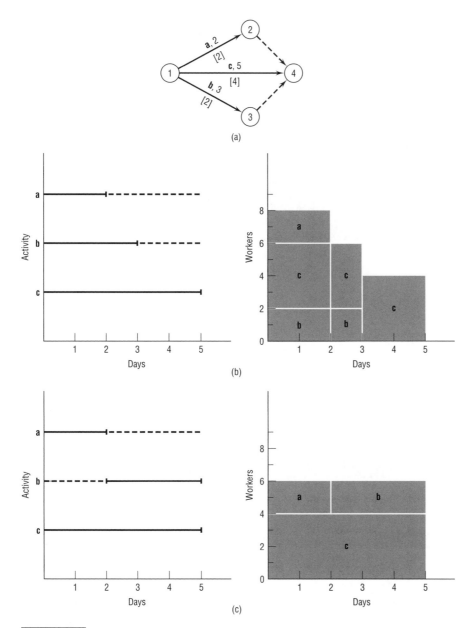

FIGURE 9.7   (a) The network. (b) Before resource leveling. (c) After resource leveling.

resources, the leveling process can be done manually. For larger networks and multiple resources, resource leveling becomes extremely complex, far beyond the power of manual solutions. Fortunately, a number of computer programs can handle most leveling problems efficiently.

Reconsider the load diagrams of Figure 9.6a and b. Assume it is desired to smooth the loading of resource B, which is particularly jagged. Both activities **e** and **f** can be delayed (**e** has 5 days of slack and **f** has 9). If we delay both for 1 day, we remove the peak on day 20 without increasing any of the other peaks (see Figure 9.8b). If we do this, however, it also alters the use of resource A and deepens the "valley" on day 20 (see Figure 9.8a). If we further delay **f** another 7 days in order to level the use of A

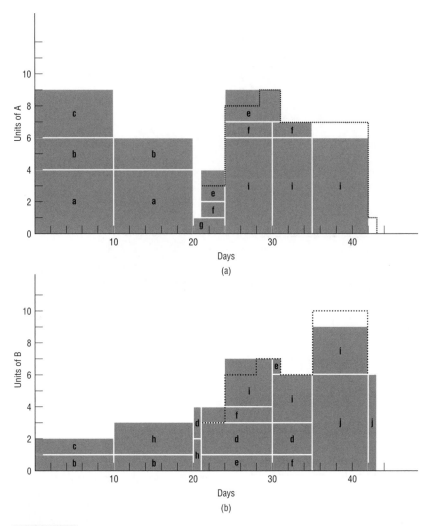

FIGURE 9.8 (a) Load diagram for resource A with activities e and f delayed by 1 day each. (b) Load diagram for resource B with activities e and f delayed by 1 day each.

toward the end of the project, we would deepen the valley between days 20 and 24, and the resultant use of A would be as shown by the dotted lines on Figure 9.8a. Activity **f** would begin on day 28 (and would become critical). The effect on the usage of B is easy to see (Figure 9.8b). The change would lower usage by one unit beginning on day 21 (remember that we have already delayed **f** by 1 day), and increase usage by one unit beginning on day 35, continuing to the end of the project. This action increases peak use of B from 9 to 10 units.

It is important to emphasize that if the network under consideration is more complex and the number of resources to be leveled is realistically large, a manual leveling process is out of the question. Computer-aided leveling is not only mandatory but also helpful because it allows the PM to experiment with various patterns of resource usage through simulation. In the next section, we raise the most general problem of minimizing resource usage while still achieving various completion dates—or the inverse problem, minimizing completion times while operating with specified limits on resources.

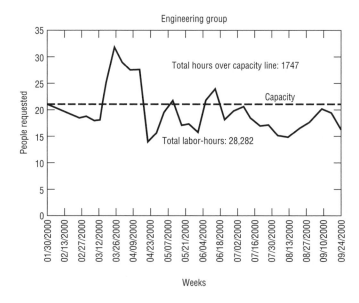

FIGURE 9.9 Thirty-four-week resource logging chart for a software engineering group.

Resource Loading/Leveling and Uncertainty

Figure 9.9 is a resource loading chart for a software engineering group in a large company, constructed by importing MSP resource loading information into an Excel® spreadsheet and then displaying it graphically. There are 21 engineers in the group, nominally scheduled to work 40 hours a week, resulting in a weekly capacity of

$$21 \times 40 = 840 \text{ labor-hours each week.}$$

The graph covers February through September, a period of 34 weeks. Thus, the total engineering capacity for the period shown is

$$34 \times 840 = 28,560 \text{ labor-hours.}$$

As shown, the total labor-hours required for the period is 28,282, so we see that there is excess capacity, a nice situation normally. However, there are two problems. As is clear in the loading chart, the demand for engineering labor is not evenly distributed throughout the period, hitting a major peak in the late March–early April time frame and then a few more times later in the period. This is counterbalanced by weeks throughout the time period where less-than-full capacity is required; however, this is not helpful since the engineers are employed for 40-hour weeks so the undercapacity times are wasted.

There are some alternatives used to address these kinds of situations. First, we can try to level the demand, moving some of it forward and some back, depending on our flexibility in this operating environment. Second, we can try to alter the supply of engineering hours, asking the engineers to trade off time between periods of overcapacity and periods of undercapacity. We might expend additional resources, bringing in contract engineers to handle the overload period, or subcontract the workload, but such suggestions would almost certainly be rejected by senior management because of security worries by our clients. Perhaps it would be cheaper to let the work be delayed a few weeks and try to catch up later. We will identify other ways of resolving this element of uneven demand a bit later.

But there is another problem with this situation, which is that we try not to schedule a scarce resource for more than 85–90 percent capacity. The reason is due to disruptions, emergencies, maintenance requirements, personnel issues, and simple inefficiency of any resource that is scheduled for full production over an extended time period. Let us consider the case of the engineers, in particular. Over this 34-week period that includes the summer, there will probably be most of the scheduled 2-week vacations (if not longer). If 15 engineers are scheduled for vacations during this period, that will remove 15×2 weeks $\times 40 = 1,200$ labor-hours from the capacity. In addition, there are three national holidays during this period: Memorial Day, the Fourth of July, and Labor Day, resulting in a further loss of $21 \times 3 \times 8$ hours $= 504$ hours. These two scheduled sets of events have now reduced our capacity to $28,560 - 1,200 - 504 = 26,856$ labor-hours, 5 percent less than the demand over the period.

What about unscheduled events and disruptions? Illnesses will surely occur in this long time frame. Furthermore, will the facilities, equipment, materials, and the work itself be ready for the engineers when they move to the next task? Will everything show up precisely when it is needed? Will there be no delays in the work preceding what the engineers are expected to do? Will there be no scope changes in the preceding work, thus delaying the succeeding tasks scheduled for the engineers? As you can see, we expect there to be "unexpected" delays for multiple reasons, hence the admonition to never schedule a resource for more than 85–90 percent of its capacity.

But what about manufacturing situations in which machines and processes are commonly run near capacity for extended durations? These situations are not projects but rather routine production environments, assembly lines, for example. New work is scheduled to arrive precisely when the previous work has been completed. Planning is extensive, maintenance is carefully scheduled, experience in what can go wrong is abundant, resources are carefully controlled and monitored, and so on. That is not the situation of projects, which by definition are nonroutine. Depending on experience, when planning routine types of manufacturing processes, we try to have line capacity just slightly in excess of our average demand for the line's output. This policy is a sure course to disaster when applied to project management.

Now, what do we do about our software engineers? As it happens, some groups of professionals, such as engineers, are employed with the understanding that there will be periods of overtime required (for which they are generally not paid) and periods when things will be slack and they are relatively free to come and go as they please. In reality, engineers often work 50–60 hours per week for extended periods, and if a prolonged period of insufficient work is available at the company, management may lay off some engineers. As can be seen, a workweek of, say, 55 hours $\times 21$ engineers $\times 34$ weeks $\times 85$ percent capacity $= 33,379$ labor-hours, more than sufficient for the 28,282 labor-hours required—but not much more than sufficient.

9.5 | Constrained Resource Scheduling

Far too often, PMs are surprised by resource constraints. The cause of this condition is usually the direct result of a failure to include resource availability in risk identification activities. The lack of a resource where and when it is needed can have many causes, but the most common causes are not difficult to identify and mitigate: failure of a supplier to produce and/or deliver, the assignment of the resource to another activity, and loss or theft of a resource. PMs often apply risk management techniques to resources known to be scarce, but neglect to consider the more common resources that usually cause the problems.

There are two fundamental approaches to constrained resource allocation problems: heuristics and optimization models. Heuristic approaches employ rules of thumb that have been found to work reasonably well in similar situations. They seek better solutions. Optimization approaches seek the best solutions but are far more limited in their ability to handle complex situations and large problems. We will discuss each separately.

Most software designed for project management will level resources and solve the problems of overscheduling resources. They require priority rules to establish which activities take precedence. The priority rules that the programs use vary somewhat, but most packages offer a choice. For example, reconsider the video project used to demonstrate MSP output forms in Chapter 8. We can include the resource requirement for each activity directly on the Gantt chart, as in Figure 9.10, but we can also show separate diagrams that illustrate the demand or "load" for each of the resources as in Figure 9.11. Figures 9.11 and 9.12 show a resource conflict for the producer and the resource leveling solution. Note the changes in the scheduled finish dates for the leveled solution.

Heuristic Methods

Heuristic approaches to constrained resource scheduling problems are in wide, general use for a number of reasons. First, they are the only feasible methods of attacking the large, nonlinear, complex problems that tend to occur in the real world of project management. Second, while the schedules that heuristics generate may not be optimal, they are usually quite good—certainly good enough for most purposes. Commercially available computer programs handle large problems and have had considerable use in industry. Further, modern simulation techniques allow the PM to develop many different schedules quickly and to determine which, if any, are significantly better than current practice. If a reasonable

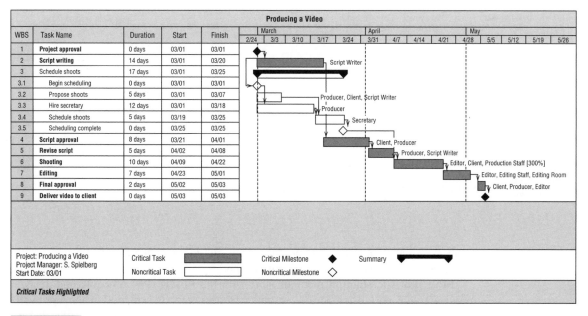

FIGURE 9.10   MSP Gantt chart of video project showing resource needs.

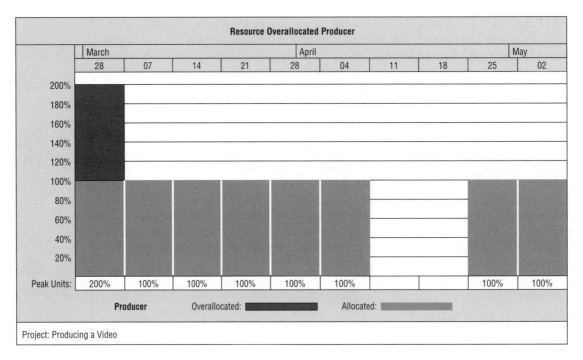

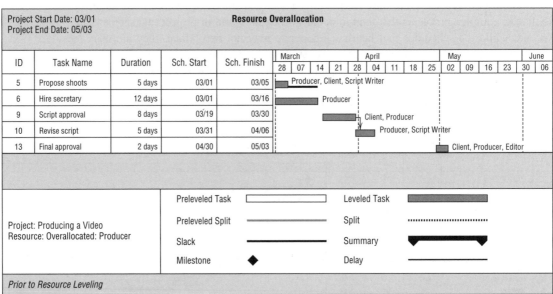

FIGURE 9.11 MSP load diagram showing resource conflict (producer used beyond capacity).

number of simulation runs fail to produce significant improvement, the PM can feel fairly confident that the existing solution is a good one.

Most heuristic solution methods start with the PERT/CPM schedule and analyze resource usage period by period, resource by resource. In a period when the available supply of a resource is exceeded, the heuristic examines the tasks in that period and allocates the scarce resource to them sequentially, according to some priority rule. The major difference among the heuristics is in the priority rules they use. Remember

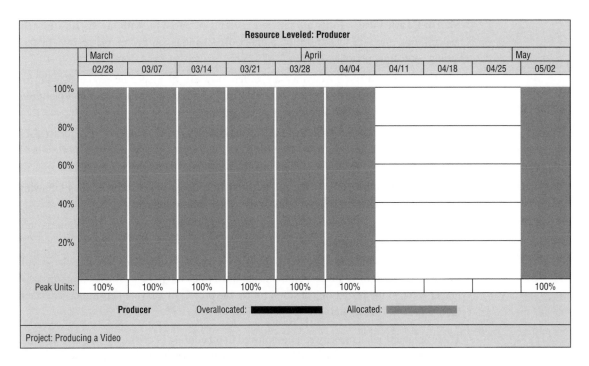

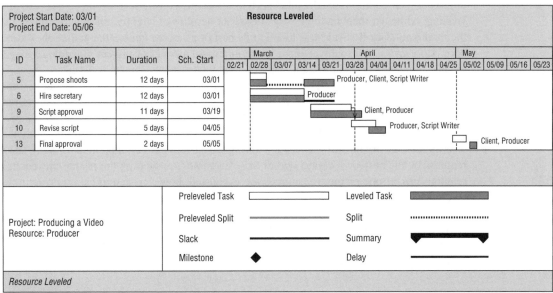

FIGURE 9.12 MSP rescheduling to level producer resource usage without exceeding capacity.

that the *technological necessities always take precedence*. Some of the most common priority rules are:

As Soon As Possible   The default rule for scheduling. This provides the general solution for critical path and time.

As Late As Possible   All activities are scheduled as late as possible without delaying the project. The usual purpose of this heuristic is to defer cash outflows as long as possible.

Shortest Task First   Tasks are ordered in terms of duration, with the shortest first. In general, this rule will maximize the number of tasks that can be completed by a system during some time period.

Most Resources First   Activities are ordered by use of a specific resource, with the largest user heading the list. The assumption behind this rule is that more important tasks usually place a higher demand on scarce resources.

Minimum Slack First   This heuristic orders activities by the amount of slack, least slack going first. (It is common, when using this rule, to break ties by using the shortest-task-first rule.)

Most Critical Followers   Tasks are arranged by number of critical activities following them. The ones with the greatest number of critical followers go first.

Most Successors   This is the same as the previous rule, except that all followers, not merely critical ones, are counted.

Arbitrary   Priorities are assigned to activities according to some rule not associated with task length, slack, or resource requirements. Such rules might be that tasks on projects of higher value to the parent organization (or for the project of a favored customer) are taken before those of lower value.

There are many such priority rules employed in scheduling heuristics. From time to time, researchers subject several of the more popular of the project management software programs to tests of their ability to handle tasks such as allocating constrained resources and resource leveling. Although their findings vary somewhat because of slightly different assumptions, the minimum-slack-first rule was found to be best or near-best quite often and rarely caused poor performance. It usually resulted in the minimum amount of project schedule slippage, the best utilization of facilities, and the minimum total system occupancy time.

As the scheduling heuristic operates, one of two events will result. The routine runs out of activities (for the current period) before it runs out of the resources, or it runs out of resources before all activities have been scheduled. (Rarely is the supply of resources precisely equal to the demand.) If the former occurs, the excess resources are left idle, assigned elsewhere in the organization as needed during the current period, or applied to future tasks required by the project—always within the constraints imposed by the proper precedence relationships. If one or more resources are exhausted, however, activities requiring those resources are slowed or delayed until the next period when resources can be reallocated. For example, if the minimum-slack-first rule is used, resources would be devoted to critical or nearly critical activities, delaying those with greater slack. Delay of an activity uses some of its slack, so the activity will have a better chance of receiving resources in the next period's allocation. Repeated delays move the activity higher and higher on the priority list.

Optimizing Methods

In the past several years, a wide range of attacks have been made on the problems of resource allocation and scheduling when resources are constrained. Some of these depend on sophisticated mathematical and/or graphical tools and may be quite powerful in what they can do. The methods to find an optimal solution to the constrained resource scheduling problem fall primarily into two categories: mathematical programming (linear programming, LP, for the most part) and enumeration. In the late 1960s and early 1970s, limited enumeration techniques were applied to the constrained resource problem with some success. Advances in LP techniques now allow LP to be used on large constrained resource scheduling problems. Other approaches have combined programming and enumeration methods.

Project Management in Practice

Benefits of Resource Constraining at Pennsylvania Electric

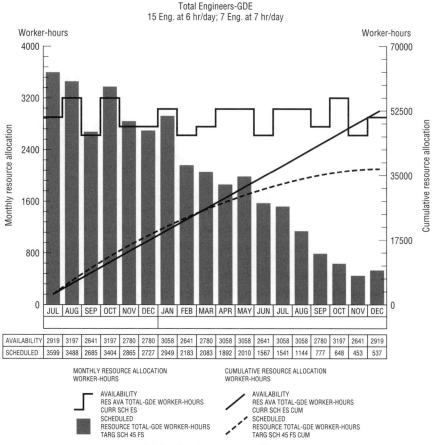

Total Engineers-GDE
15 Eng. at 6 hr/day; 7 Eng. at 7 hr/day

	JUL	AUG	SEP	OCT	NOV	DEC	JAN	FEB	MAR	APR	MAY	JUN	JUL	AUG	SEP	OCT	NOV	DEC
AVAILABILITY	2919	3197	2641	3197	2780	2780	3058	2641	2780	3058	3058	2641	3058	3058	2780	3197	2641	2919
SCHEDULED	3599	3488	2685	3404	2865	2727	2949	2183	2083	1892	2010	1567	1541	1144	777	648	453	537

MONTHLY RESOURCE ALLOCATION
WORKER-HOURS

CUMULATIVE RESOURCE ALLOCATION
WORKER-HOURS

AVAILABILITY
RES AVA TOTAL-GDE WORKER-HOURS
CURR SCH ES

SCHEDULED
RESOURCE TOTAL-GDE WORKER-HOURS
TARG SCH 45 FS

AVAILABILITY
RES AVA TOTAL-GDE WORKER-HOURS
CURR SCH ES CUM

SCHEDULED
RESOURCE TOTAL-GDE WORKER-HOURS
TARG SCH 45 FS CUM

Total engineering resource profile

Pennsylvania Electric Company, headquartered in Johnstown, PA, operates generating facilities with a capacity of 6950 megawatts to serve 547,000 customers over an area of 17,600 square miles. The Generation Division Planning Group is responsible for planning all maintenance and capital projects. In the early 1980s, the group used manual methods of planning with hand-drawn charts. Of course, planning is now computerized, which is faster, allows "what-if" analyses, and controls more than just the previously monitored critical path.

A special feature of the computerized system is its resource constraining module, which establishes labor requirements across all jobs. In the pilot program to test the new software, $300,000 was saved when it was discovered that a particular job could be done with 40 percent fewer mechanics than normally used and still complete the job on time.

After worker-hours are input to the program by activity, actual progress is monitored (see figure) and schedule and cost deviations are highlighted for management attention. This allows management to make adjustments to recover the

schedule, slow the project down, or acquire more funds to get the project back on schedule. Obviously, there are always some emergencies outside the plan that must be handled on an exception basis. But with this software, management knows what effect different actions will have on the basic plan and can thereby make the best use of available resources to handle the emergency with minimal impact on the plan.

Questions

1. **Why would the planning group use 40 percent more mechanics than necessary?**

2. **What does the availability in the chart represent? Why do the monthly values move up and down?**

3. **What does the scheduled amount represent? Why does it drop off toward the end? How can it exceed the availability?**

Source: A. J. Cantanese, "At Penelec, Project Management Is a Way of Life.," *Project Management Journal*, Vol. 21.

9.6 | Goldratt's Critical Chain

In the previous section, we showed that the problem of constrained resource scheduling of multiple projects could be reduced to the problem of scheduling activities using scarce resources in the case of a single project. However, the best-known attack on the resource-constrained scheduling problem is Goldratt's *Critical Chain* (1997). The celebrated author applies his Theory of Constraints to the constrained resource scheduling problem. The original focus of the Theory of Constraints to project management was the single project case, but it, too, is just as applicable to multiple projects.

If we consider all the comments we have heard about the problems PMs have to deal with on a daily basis, many are brought up over and over again. Further, it is interesting to note that these statements are made by PMs working in construction, manufacturing, software development, R&D, marketing, communications, maintenance, and so on and the list of industries could easily be extended. For example, the following issues are raised with high frequency, and this short list is only indicative, not nearly exhaustive.

- Senior management changes the project's scope without consultation, without warning, and without changing the budget or schedule.
- Project due dates are unrealistic and set with little regard given to availability of resources.
- There is no possible way of accomplishing a project without exceeding the given budget.
- Project workloads and due dates are set by the sales group, not by the nature of the projects and the level of resources needed.
- Project due dates are set unrealistically short as an "incentive" for people to work harder and faster.

It appears that these, and many other, problems are generic. They are independent of the area of application. Note that all of these issues concern trading off time, cost, and scope. To deal with the strong optimistic bias in many project schedules, let us consider just a few of the things that tend to create it.

1. **Thoughtless optimism**   Some PMs, apparently with a strong need to deny that lateness could be their fault, deal with every problem faced by their projects as strict exceptions, acts of chance that cannot be forecast and hence need not be the subject of planning. These individuals simply ignore risk management.

2. **Capacity should be set to equal demand**   Some senior managers refuse to recognize that projects are not assembly lines and are not subject to standard operations management line balancing methods. Refer back to Section 9.4, subsection "Resource Loading/Leveling and Uncertainty," for proof of the need for capacity to exceed demand for projects.

3. **The "Student Syndrome"**   This phrase is Goldratt's term for his view that students often delay starting school projects until the last possible moment. The same tendency is observed in projects where project team members delay the start of their work. The problem with delaying the start of a task is that obstacles are frequently not discovered until the work has been underway for some time. Delaying the start of a task diminishes the opportunity to cope with these unexpected obstacles and increases the risk of completing the work late.

4. **Multitasking to reduce idle time**   Consider a situation where there are two projects, A and B, each with three sequential activities and with you as the only resource

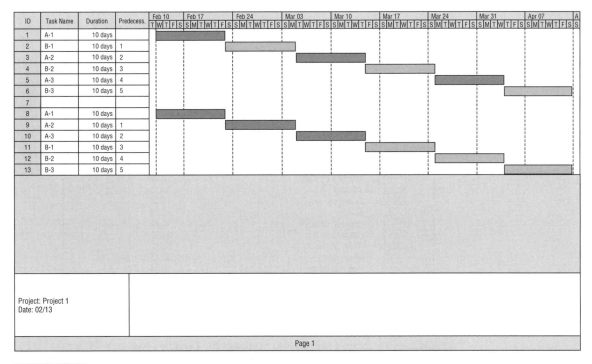

ID	Task Name	Duration	Predecess.
1	A-1	10 days	
2	B-1	10 days	1
3	A-2	10 days	2
4	B-2	10 days	3
5	A-3	10 days	4
6	B-3	10 days	5
7			
8	A-1	10 days	
9	A-2	10 days	1
10	A-3	10 days	2
11	B-1	10 days	3
12	B-2	10 days	4
13	B-3	10 days	5

Project: Project 1
Date: 02/13

Page 1

FIGURE 9.13 Effect of multitasking on project completion given fixed activity times.

required by both projects. Each activity requires 10 days. In Figure 9.13 see two Gantt charts for sequencing the activities in the two projects. In the first, switch from project A (dark) to project B (light) for each of the three activities, that is, carry out Activity 1 for project A, then Activity 1 for project B, then Activity 2 for A, and so forth. In the second sequence, complete project A before starting project B. In both cases, the total time required will be 60 days. In the second, note that project A is completed after 30 days and B after 60 days. In the first chart, however, Project A will be finished after 50 days and B after 60 days. While the total time required is the same, project A has been delayed for 20 days by the multitasking. Further, this ignores the startup time and loss in efficiency that often accompanies switching back and forth between tasks.

5. **Complexity of networks makes no difference**   Consider two different projects as seen in Figure 9.14. Assume that each activity requires 10 days and is known with certainty. Clearly, both projects are completed in 40 days though one is considerably more complex than the other. But let's get a bit more real. Assume that each activity is stochastic, with normally distributed times. The mean time is 10 days, and the standard deviation is 3 days. If we simulate the projects 500 times, we get the results shown in Tables 9.4 and 9.5. Table 9.4, covering the simulation of the simple network, shows (as we expected) a mean project completion time of about 40 days. Table 9.5 covers the simulation of the complex network, and its mean completion time is about 46 days. Complexity, uncertainty, and merging paths all join to make trouble.

6. **People need a reason to work hard**   Senior managers of our acquaintance have been known to argue that project workers—and they include PMs in that category—"always" have enough slack time in their

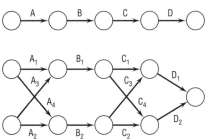

FIGURE 9.14 Two levels of 40-day network complexity.

TABLE 9.4　Project Simulation Statistics for Simple Network #1

Forecast: Completion Time Network #1

Edit　Preferences　View　Run　Help

Cell U3　　　　　　　　　　　**Statistics**

Statistic	Value
Trials	500
Mean	39.97
Median	40.23
Mode	—
Standard Deviation	5.85
Variance	34.18
Skewness	0.09
Kurtosis	2.86
Coeff. of Variability	0.15
Range Minimum	24.32
Range Maximum	56.97
Range Width	32.65
Mean Std. Error	0.26

TABLE 9.5　Project Simulation Statistics for Complex Network #2

Forecast: Completion Time Network #2

Edit　Preferences　View　Run　Help

Cell V3　　　　　　　　　　　**Statistics**

Statistic	Value
Trials	500
Mean	46.31
Median	46.25
Mode	—
Standard Deviation	4.53
Variance	20.51
Skewness	0.05
Kurtosis	2.78
Coeff. of Variability	0.10
Range Minimum	34.83
Range Maximum	59.02
Range Width	24.18
Mean Std. Error	0.20

activity duration estimates to make sure that they can complete the activities on time and "without too much sweat." Therefore, it makes some managerial sense to cut back on the time allowances until they can serve as an incentive to the project team. It has, however, long been known that for people with a high need for achievement, the maximum level of motivation is associated with only moderate, not high, levels of risk of failure.

7. **Game playing**　This is possibly the most common cause of late projects. It is certainly a major cause of frustration for anyone involved in a project. Senior managers, firm in the belief that project workers add extra time and resources to activity time and budget estimates in order to insure a safe and peaceful life on their portion of a project, routinely cut schedules and budgets. Project workers, suspecting that senior management will cut schedules and budgets without regard to any logic or reason, increase their schedules and budgets as much as they guess will be allowed. Each assumes that the other is not

to be trusted. The outcome is simple. Rather than practice careful risk management, each blames the other for any lateness or budget overage. As we noted in the "Aside" in Chapter 8, unbiased honesty in estimates on the part of both worker and manager is mandatory for any reasonable chance of on-schedule performance of projects.

Do Early Finishes and Late Finishes Cancel Out? So What?

One of the tacit assumptions of probabilistic networks is that early and late activity completions cancel out. This assumption might be sensible were it not for the matters listed in the previous subsection. Assume two activities, A and B. A is a predecessor of B. If activity A is late, then activity B will start late by whatever amount of lateness is bequeathed to it by A. Similarly, if in spite of all the forces tending to thwart such things, activity A finishes early, B will start early. The assumption, which is also a tacit assumption of both the analytical and simulation methods of finding a path's duration, is generally true for the first case, when A is late. But for the case when A is early, *the assumption is rarely true*. Unfortunately, a finish by A in less than its expected duration almost never translates to a start by B before its expected start time.

With a few exceptions, the fact that early finishes do not become early starts is ignored by most people involved with projects. Goldratt writes about the phenomenon (1997, Chapter 13 and elsewhere), and a few others have also briefly discussed the matter. There is a mild debate as to the reason for this deplorable condition. Goldratt feels that project workers will avoid admitting that an activity has been completed early out of fear that future time estimates will be cut.

Others point out that when the activity schedule is set, it is presumed that the activity will start immediately after the most likely finish date of its (latest) predecessor. The reason is simple—its resources will not be available until that date. There is also a logical explanation of why the start of a successor is usually delayed until its predetermined expected start time. Some say that project workers will not report finishes before the most likely duration. The logic of this position depends on an inherent distrust between project workers and senior management. If an early finish is reported, workers assume that the shorter-than-normal activity duration will be the expectation for similar activities in the future. Senior managers, the argument proceeds, do not really understand the uncertainty faced by project workers. Senior management will assume that if an activity can be finished early once, it can be finished early again, or that they were correct in their assumption that workers "pad" their time and resource estimates. The chance event of an early finish is, thus, used to substantiate a shortened duration estimate in the future.

There is also a logical explanation of why a successor activity does not receive resources until its predetermined expected start, which is, by definition, equal to the expected finish of the latest predecessor activity. A stochastic network has little in common with an assembly line; nonetheless, we find some managers attempting to delay the deployment of resources to a project as long as possible. If we agree to start a project as soon as its predecessors are completed, we must contemplate having the resources available and waiting well before the activity's expected start. Idle resources, however, are not acceptable to managers trained in a just-in-time view of the world. Assembly lines are reasonably predictable; projects are not.

A Common Chain of Events

According to Goldratt, the behaviors and practices discussed above lead to the following chain of events:

1. Assuming that activity times are known and that the paths are independent leads to underestimating the actual amount of time needed to complete the project.

2. Because the time needed to complete the project is underestimated, project team members tend to inflate their time estimates by some "safety" time.

3. Inflated time estimates lead to work filling available time, workers not reporting that a task has been completed early, and the ever-present student syndrome.

4. An important caveat is that the safety time is only visible to the project workers and is often misused.

5. Misused safety time results in missed deadlines and milestones.

6. Hidden safety time further complicates the PM's task of prioritizing project activities.

7. The lack of clear priorities likely results in poor multitasking.

8. Task durations increase as a result of poor multitasking.

9. Uneven demand on resources—some overloaded and others underloaded—may also occur as a result of poor multitasking.

10. In an effort to utilize all resources fully, more projects will be undertaken to make sure that no resources are underutilized.

11. Adding more projects further increases poor multitasking.

According to Goldratt, this chain of events leads to a vicious cycle. Specifically, as work continues to pile up, team members are pressured to do more poor multitasking. Increasing the amount of poor multitasking leads to longer activity times. Longer activity times lead to longer project completion times, which ultimately lead to more projects in the waiting line.

It might have occurred to you that one way to reverse this cycle would be to add more resources. According to Goldratt, however, the appropriate response is to reduce the number of projects assigned to each person in an effort to reduce the amount of bad multitasking. Incidentally, a simple way to measure the amount of bad multitasking is to calculate the difference between the time required to do the work for a task and the elapsed time actually required to complete the task.

Determining when to release projects into the system is the primary mechanism for ensuring that the right amount of work is assigned to each person. If projects are started too early, they simply add to the chaos and contribute to poor multitasking. On the other hand, if projects are started too late, key resources may go underutilized and projects will be inevitably delayed.

Consistent with his Theory of Constraints, Goldratt suggests that the key to resolving this trade-off is to schedule the start of new projects based on the availability of bottleneck (scarce) resources.

While properly scheduling the start of new projects does much to address the problems associated with poor multitasking, it does little to address the problem of setting unrealistic project deadlines and the accompanying response of inflated time estimates. Relying on elementary statistics, it can be easily shown that the amount of safety time needed to protect a particular path is less than the sum of the safety times required to protect the individual activities making up the path. The same approach is commonly used in inventory management where it can be shown that less safety stock is needed at a central warehouse to provide a certain service level than the amount of safety stock that would be required to provide this same service level if carried at multiple distributed locations.

Based on this insight, Goldratt suggests reducing the amount of safety time workers add to individual tasks and then adding some fraction of the safety time reduced back into the system as safety buffer for the entire project, called the *project buffer*. The amount of time each task is reduced depends on how much of a reduction is needed to get project team members to change their behavior. For example, the allotted time for tasks should be reduced to the point that the student syndrome is eliminated. Indeed, Goldratt suggests using activity durations where in fact there is a high probability that the task will not be finished on time.

The Critical Chain

Another limitation associated with traditional approaches to project management is that the dependency between resources and tasks is often ignored. More specifically, Goldratt argues that two activities scheduled to be carried out in parallel and using the same scarce resource are not independent as the traditional theory would assume.[1] If the supply of the scarce resource is not sufficient to allow both activities to be carried out simultaneously, then whichever of the two is given priority immediately lengthens the other activity's path but not its actual duration.

Assume that two parallel paths compose a project. One path consists of activities A_1 and **B** and the other path consists of activities A_2 and **C**. Activities A_1 and A_2 require the same scarce resource. Activities **B** and **C** use different resources. A_1 requires 7 days, A_2 requires 5 days, **B** needs 10 days, and **C** needs 6 days and thus, the path A_1-**B** is 17 days and the path A_2-**C** is 11 days. If there is not enough of the scarce resource to fund both **A** activities, they must be done sequentially. If A_1 is done first, A_2 cannot start until A_1 is complete, thereby adding 7 days to the A_2-**C** path, making it 18 days long and increasing the project finish date by 1 day. If A_2 is done first, 5 days will be added to the A_1-**B** path, making it 22 days, a 5-day increase over its original 17-day duration. If this problem seems familiar, it is. This is precisely the issue we dealt with when we examined the process of resource leveling in Section 9.4.

Using Goldratt's meaning of the word "dependent," the activities of a project can be ordered into paths based on their resource dependencies as well as on their technological precedence requirements. The longest of these paths of sequentially time-dependent activities is known as the "critical chain." A project, therefore, is composed of its critical chain and of noncritical chains that feed into it—see Figure 9.15. There are two sources of delay for the project. One comes from a delay of one or more activities in the critical chain. The second results from a delay in one or more of the activities on a noncritical or "feeder" chain because such delays could delay activities on the critical chain. A project buffer protects the critical chain, and feeding buffers protect the feeder paths. Resources used by activities on the critical chain are given priority so that they are available when required.

In the next chapter, we move to the ongoing implementation of the project and consider the project information systems used for monitoring progress, costs, scope, and so on. The chapter also describes some available computer packages for this function.

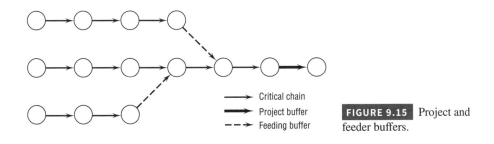

→ Critical chain
⟹ Project buffer
--→ Feeding buffer

FIGURE 9.15 Project and feeder buffers.

---

[1]The word "dependent" has two different meanings in this context. Two parallel activities using the same scarce resource depend on each other in the sense that the ability to *start* one depends on the existence of priorities indicating which of the two competing activities gets first use of the scarce resource. At the same time, they may be statistically independent, which means that the *duration* of one activity does not depend on the duration of the other.

Project Management in Practice

Architectural Associates, Inc.

Architectural Associates, Inc. (AAI) specializes in large, industrial, retail, and public projects, including shopping malls, manufacturing complexes, convention centers, and the like. The firm is considered to be one of the region's most effective and creative design studios. The entire space devoted to design is a single, open area and workstations are laid out in such a way as to encourage communication between individuals working on a common project.

A senior executive of AAI noticed that for the past year or two, the chance of bringing design projects in on time and on budget had decreased to the point where the only uncertainty was how late and how much over budget a project would be.

An examination of the workplace disclosed a large, green felt display board mounted on the wall where it was visible to the entire design staff. The board listed the names of individual designers and technicians vertically, and design contract numbers across the horizontal axis. The times allocated for work on each project by appropriate staff members were shown at the intersections of the rows and columns. The time estimates were made by senior managers, themselves architects, based on their experience. The individuals with direct responsibility for design work generally felt that the time estimates were reasonable.

The work process was studied and the following problem was revealed. If the design of the electrical systems involved in a plan was estimated to take 5 days, for example, the individual(s) responsible for the work planned it in such a way that it used the 5 days allowed. If a problem occurred on the first day, the worker(s) simply stayed late or speeded up work the next day in order to get back on schedule. Problems on the second day, and even on the third and fourth days were handled in the same way, by crashing the work. Problems occurring on the fifth day, however, could not be handled so easily and this part of the project would be late. Because most of the different systems (the mechanicals, landscape, etc.) were designed simultaneously and staffed to require about the same number of days (rather than being sequential), and because problems were very likely to arise late in the design process of at least one of the systems, the overall design project, which required all tasks to be completed on time, was almost invariably late.

In an attempt to solve the problem, a simple checkmark to show job assignments was substituted for time allocations on the green board. Additionally, senior management made normal, optimistic, and pessimistic time estimates for each task and calculated "TE," also used to help estimate project cost. These estimates, however, were not given to the design staff who were simply told to do the work involved as efficiently and effectively as they could. The result was that the degree to which actual task times were early or late increased slightly, but the average time required for the various tasks was decreased because task schedules were now designed for efficiency rather than to meet management's expectations.

Questions

1. Was the problem here one of those described in Critical Chain? Which one, if so?
2. Describe how the change effectively solved the problem.

Source: S. J. Mantel, Jr. Consulting project.

Summary

In this chapter we looked at the problem of allocating physical resources, both among the multiple activities of a project and among multiple projects. The continuous problem to the PM is finding the best trade-offs among resources, particularly time. We considered resource loading, allocation, and leveling and presented methods and concepts to aid in all these tasks.

Specific points made in the chapter were these:

- The CPM is a network constructed in the same manner as PERT, but it also considers the possibility of adding resources to tasks (crashing) to shorten their duration, thereby expediting the project. This can also be done with PERT.

- The resource allocation problem is concerned with determining the best trade-offs between available resources, including time, throughout the duration of a project.

- Resource loading is the process of calculating the total load from project tasks on each resource for each time period of the project's duration.

- Resource leveling is concerned with evening out the demand for various resources required in a project by shifting tasks within their slack allowances. The aid of a computer is mandatory for realistic projects.

- There are two basic approaches to addressing the constrained resources allocation problem:

— *Heuristic methods* are realistic approaches that may identify feasible solutions to the problem. They essentially use simple priority rules, such as shortest task first, to determine which task should receive resources and which task must wait.

— *Optimizing method*s, such as LP, find the best allocation of resources to tasks but are limited in the size of problems they can efficiently solve.

• Goldratt's "critical chain" is based on a behavioral analysis of projects and their management, and consists of using feeder buffers leading into the critical chain and a project buffer for the critical chain.

Glossary

Bottleneck   the resource(s) with limited capacity that restrict the rate of progress on the project

Critical Chain   The longest chain of activities in a project when no buffers are considered.

Cost/Time Slope   The ratio of the increased cost for expediting to the decreased amount of time for the activity.

Followers   The tasks that logically follow a particular task in time.

Heuristic   A formal process for solving a problem, like a rule of thumb, that results in an acceptable solution.

Mathematical Programming   A general term for certain mathematical approaches to solving constrained optimization problems, including linear programming, integer programming, and so on.

Predecessors   The tasks that logically precede a particular task in time.

Priority Rules   Formal methods, such as ratios, that rank items to determine which one should be next.

Project buffer   safety time taken from individual activities and added as buffer for the entire project

Resource Leveling   Approaches to even out the peaks and valleys of resource requirements so that a fixed amount of resources can be employed over time.

Resource Loading   The amount of resources of each kind that are to be devoted to a specific activity in a certain time period.

Student Syndrome   tendency to delay starting tasks until the last possible moment

Successors   See Followers.

Questions

Material Review Questions

1. Identify several resources that may need to be considered when scheduling projects.

2. What is resource loading? How does it differ from resource leveling?

3. What is an activity slope, and what does it indicate?

4. Name four priority rules. What priority rule is best overall? How would a firm decide which priority rule to use?

5. What are two methods for addressing the constrained resources allocation problem?

6. How does the task life cycle type affect our attempts to level the resource loads?

7. Describe the concept "critical chain" in your own words.

Class Discussion Questions

8. Why are large fluctuations in the demands for particular resources undesirable? What are the costs of resource leveling? How would a PM determine the "best" amount of leveling?

9. When might a firm choose to crash a project? What factors must be considered in making this decision?

10. Why is the impact of scheduling and resource allocation more significant in multiproject organizations?

11. How much should a manager know about a scheduling or resource allocation computer program to be able to use the output intelligently?

12. With the significantly increased power of today's computers, do you think the mathematical programming optimization approaches will become more popular?

13. Why is leveling of resources needed?

14. What are some implications of resource allocation when an organization is involved in several projects at once?

15. What are some of the indirect costs of crashing?

16. How might AON be used for strategic planning purposes?

17. List all the various ways that resources greatly increase scheduling complexity.

18. Goldratt suggests setting task durations so short there is a high probability they will not be done on time. What is his thinking here? Do you agree with him?

Exercises

1. Given the following network, determine the first activity to be crashed by the following priority rules:

   a. Shortest task first

   b. Minimum slack first

   c. Most critical followers

   d. Most successors

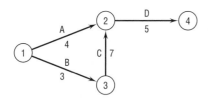

2. Using the network above and the additional information below, find

   a. The crash cost per day

   b. Which activities should be crashed to meet a project deadline of 13 days at minimum cost. Assume partial crashing is allowed.

Activity	Crash Time (days)	Crashed Cost (total)	Normal Time (days)	Normal Cost
A	3	$500	4	$300
B	1	325	3	250
C	4	550	7	400
D	3	250	5	150

3. Consider the following network for conducting a 2-week (10 working days) computer training class:

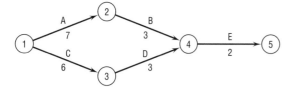

   a. Construct a schedule showing:

   ESs for all activities

   LSs for all activities

   Slacks for all activities

   Critical path

b. Given the following

Activity	Crash Time (days)	Crashed Cost (total)	Normal Time (days)	Normal Cost
A: Obtain instructor	4	$800	7	$500
B: Locate a room	2	350	3	200
C: Check costs	4	900	6	500
D: Room open?	1	500	3	200
E: Schedule class	1	550	2	300
		$3100		

   1. Find the crash cost per day.

   2. Which activities should be crashed to meet a project deadline of 10 days with a minimum cost? Assume partial crashing.

   3. Find the new cost.

   4. Is partial crashing an appropriate assumption in this kind of project?

4. Given the following highway rerouting project,

Activity	Immediate Predecessor	Activity Time (months)
A: Schedule crew	—	4
B: Schedule equipment	—	6
C: Plan new route	A	2
D: Costs meet budget?	B	6
E: Inform public	C, B	3
F: Put out signs	C, B	3
G: Begin rerouting	D, E	5

   a. Draw the network.

   b. Find the ESs, LSs, and slacks.

   c. Find the critical path.

   d. If the project has a 1 1/2-year deadline for reopening, should we consider crashing some activities? Explain.

5. Given the following network for a stock repurchase project with outside consulting resource demands, construct a modified Gantt AOA chart with resources and a resource load diagram. Suggest how to level the outside consulting load if you can split operations.

$$\text{code}: \frac{\text{activity}, \text{time}}{\text{resource units}}$$

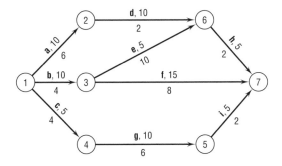

6. Consider the following activity information and the constraint that the project must be completed in 16 weeks.

Activity	Prec. Evt.	Suc. Evt.	TE (weeks)	Prec. Activ.
a	1	2	3	None
b	1	3	6	None
c	1	4	8	None
d	2	5	7	a
e	3	5	5	b
f	4	5	10	c
g	4	6	4	c
h	5	7	5	d,e,f
i	6	7	6	g

In addition, activities **c, f, h**, and **i** may be crashed as follows. Assume partial crashing.

Activity	Crash Time (weeks)	Additional Cost per Week
c	7	$40
f	6	20
h	2	10
I	3	30

Find the best schedule and its cost

7. The following data were obtained from a study of the times required to conduct a consumer test panel study:

Activity	Crash Schedule Time	Crash Schedule Cost	Normal Schedule Time	Normal Schedule Cost
1–2: City center	3	$6	5	$4
1–3: City northeast	1	5	5	3
2–4: City south	5	7	10	4
3–4: City southeast	2	6	7	4
2–6: City west	2	5	6	3
4–6: County east	5	9	11	6
4–5: County north	4	6	6	3
6–7: County south	1	4	5	2
5–7: County west	1	5	4	2

Note: Costs are given in thousands of dollars, time in weeks.

a. Find the all-normal schedule and cost.

b. Find the all-crash schedule and cost.

c. Find the total cost required to expedite all activities from all-normal (case a) to all-crash (case b).

d. Find the *least-cost* plan for the all-crash problem (b). Assume partial crashing.

8. Given the data in Exercise 7, determine the first activities to be crashed by the following priority rules:

a. Shortest task first

b. Most resources first (use normal cost as the basis)

c. Minimum slack first

d. Most critical followers

e. Most successors

9. Consider the project network below. Suppose the duration of both activities **A** and **D** can be reduced to 1 day, at a cost of $15 per day of reduction. Also, activities **E, G**, and **H** can be reduced in duration by 1 day at a cost of $25 per day of reduction. What is the least-cost approach to crash the project 2 days? What is the shortest "crashed" duration, the new critical path, and the cost of crashing?

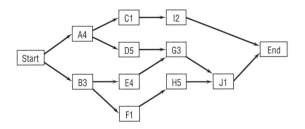

10. Given a network for an HR training project with normal times and crash times (in parentheses), find the cost-duration history. Assume indirect costs for facilities and equipment are $100 per day. The data are as follows:

Activity	Time Reduction, Direct Cost per Day
1–2: Obtain room	$30 first, $50 second
2–3: Select trainer	$80
3–4: Invite personnel	$25 first, $60 second
2–4: Check budget	$30 first, $70 second, $90 third

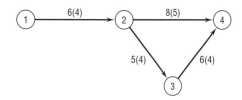

11. Reconsider Exercise 2, assuming a fixed overhead cost of $30 per day but no project deadline. What is the least-cost crash program? What if the overhead cost was $40? What if it was $60?

12. The network for shooting a TV commercial as shown in the table has a fixed cost of $90 per day, but money can be saved by shortening the project duration. Find the least-cost schedule.

Activity	Normal Time	Crash Time	Cost Increase (1st, 2nd, 3rd day)
1–2: Contract personnel	7	4	$30, 50, 70
2–3: Obtain stage props	9	6	40, 45, 65
1–3: Rent equipment	12	10	60, 60
2–4: Contract studio	11	9	35, 60
3–4: Set time and date	3	3	—

13. Given the following project to landscape a new building site,

Activity	Immediate Predecessor	Activity Duration (days)	Resource Used
A: Get plants	—	2	X, Y
B: Get flowers	A	2	X
C: Obtain soil	A	3	X
D: Obtain fertilizer	B, C	4	X, Y
E: Select labor	D	3	W, X
F: Set date	D	1	W, X, Y
G: Begin	E, F	2	X, Y

a. Draw a Gantt chart using MSP.

b. Find the critical path and project duration in days.

c. Given that each resource is assigned 100 percent to each task, identify the resource constraints.

d. Level the resources and determine the new project duration and critical path.

e. Identify what alternative solutions can be used to shorten the project duration and not overallocate the resources.

14. Assume that a resource used by activities **e**, **f**, **g**, and **h** in the figure below is scarce. To which activity would you assign the resource, based on the following rules?

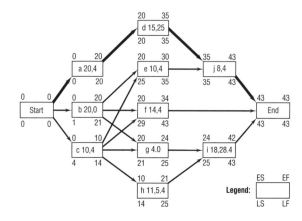

a. Minimum slack

b. Most successors

c. Most critical followers

d. Shortest task first

e. As late as possible

15. Given the following project (all times are in days):

Activity	Predecessor	Normal Time	Normal Cost	Crash Time	Crash Cost
a	—	5	$50	3	$150
b	—	4	40	2	200
c	b	7	70	6	160
d	a, c	2	20	1	50
e	a, c	3	30	—	—
f	b	8	80	5	290
g	d	5	50	4	100
h	e, f	6	60	3	180

a. Draw the network and find the critical path, time, and cost for an all-normal level of project activity.

b. Calculate the crash cost-per-day (all activities may be partially crashed).

c. Find the optimal way of getting an 18-day delivery time. What is the project cost?

d. Find the optimal way of getting a 16-day delivery time. What is the project cost?

e. Calculate the shortest delivery time for the project. What is the cost?

16. A simulation model was developed in Section 9.6 to illustrate the problem with assuming activity times were known with certainty. However, in the simulation analysis, the activity times were assumed to be normally distributed. Do you have any concerns with assuming that the activity times were normally distributed? Redo the simulation analysis using a BetaPERT distribution with parameters of 7, 10, and 15 for the optimistic, most likely, and pessimistic times estimates. How do the results compare with the results obtained using a normal distribution?

17. In Section 9.6 the consequences of not reporting early completion times were discussed. Modify the simulation model you created for Exercise 16 so that early completion of the tasks before the scheduled time of 10 days is not reported. Compare your results to the results obtained in Exercise 16.

Incidents For Discussion

Bryce Power Tool Company

Kevin Ertle is the director of information technology (IT) for the Bryce Power Tool Company. A decision was made recently to upgrade Bryce's legacy systems to a comprehensive ERP system. The president of Bryce has indicated that he expects the modernization program to result in a significant improvement in new product time to market. Ertle is concerned with the possibility that his department will not have adequate resources to support the upgrade. Kevin believes he has enough staff to handle the aggregate IT requirements, but he is not too sure he will be able to supply the proper IT personnel at the times and quantities requested by the company's project managers.

To complicate matters further, the upgrade will be under the control of four different business unit PMs. Each major market segment has been recognized as a separate business unit with the authority to select IT subsystems for their segment based on a schedule that makes sense for it. Kevin knows a little bit about resource allocation techniques. He remembers that one of the most effective allocation techniques is to work first on the activity with the minimum slack, so he has instructed his staff to approach any tasks they are assigned as members of a project team on that basis.

Questions

Is this technique a reasonable way to schedule the IT resources of Bryce? Why or why not? What complication is added by making this four separate projects?

Critical Care Hospital

Critical Care Hospital will be purchasing a CATSCAN (computerized axial tomography scanner) in the next 6 months. The CATSCAN equipment will be installed in the radiology department and will require a significant renovation for the area. The scanner will arrive in about 5 months, but the construction project cannot be started until the unit is set in place. This will result in a project length of approximately 12 months. The hospital estimates the equipment will generate an income of $25,000 per month and is therefore in a hurry to complete the project. The project manager feels he or she may be able to cut the time on some aspects of the project, but at an increased cost. He or she has decided, in an effort to make the best decision, to use a resource allocation version of CPM.

Questions

What information must the PM gather to use this method properly? How should he or she use this version of CPM to reduce the project time?

Continuing Integrative Class Project

Although the budget didn't allow for additional resources to speed up activities that fell behind schedule, you have some slack paths in the project where you can borrow people to help with problem activities. Based on the tasks that constitute the critical path, determine where you would borrow resources from if each task were to fall behind schedule, assuming other tasks stayed on schedule. (That is, you can't borrow people from a task that is at the beginning of the project to help with a critical path task that is at the end of the project.) Also develop a load diagram for each project team member. If there is an overload, level the resources.

Bibliography

Adler, P. S., A. Mandelbaum, V. Nguyen, and E. Schwerer. "Getting the Most Out of Your Product Development Process." *Harvard Business Review*, March–April 1996.

Goldratt, E. M. *Critical Chain*. Great Barrington, MA: North River, 1997.

Ibbs, C. W., S. A. Lee, and M. I. Li. "Fast-Tracking's Impact on Project Change." *Project Management Journal*, December 1998.

McCarthy, J. *Dynamics of Software Development*. Redmond, WA: Microsoft Press, 1995.

Piney, C. "Critical Path or Critical Chain: Combining the Best of Both." *PM Network*, December 2000.

Raz, T., R. Barnes, and D. Dvir. "A Critical Look at Critical Chain Project Management." *Project Management Journal*, December 2003.

Trietsch, D. "Why a Critical Path by Any Other Name Would Smell as Sweet." *Project Management Journal*, March 2005.

Weist, J. D. "A Heuristic Model for Scheduling Large Projects with Limited Resources." *Management Science*, February 1967.

Wheatley, M. "Future Perfect." *PM Network*, April 2004.

The following case describes the evolution of a new product and the project devised to take it to market. As well as discussing the issues of developing a work breakdown structure, network diagram, schedule, and resource loading diagrams for each of the involved departments, the case also brings up the issues of time–cost trade-offs, cash flows, and resource leveling.

Case

D. U. Singer Hospital Products Corp.   Herbert F. Spirer

D. U. Singer Hospital Products Corp. has done sufficient new product development at the research and development level to estimate a high likelihood of technical success for a product of assured commercial success: A long-term antiseptic. Management has instructed Singer's Antiseptic Division to make a market entry at the earliest possible time; they have requested a complete plan up to the startup of production. Marketing and other plans following startup of production are to be prepared separately after this plan has been completed.

Project responsibility is assigned to the division's Research and Development Group; Mike Richards, the project scientist who developed the product, is assigned responsibility for project management. Assistance will be required from other parts of the company: Packaging Task Force, R & D Group; Corporate Engineering; Corporate Purchasing; Hospital Products Manufacturing Group; Packaged Products Manufacturing Group.

Mike was concerned about the scope of the project. He knew from his own experience that a final formula had yet to be developed, although such development was really a "routine" function. The remaining questions had to do with color, odor, and consistency additives rather than any performance-related modification. Fortunately, the major regulatory issues had been resolved and he believed that submission of regulatory documentation would be followed by rapid approval as they already had a letter of approval contingent on final documentation.

But there were also issues in packaging that had to be resolved; development of the packaging design was one of his primary concerns at this time. Ultimately, there will have to be manufacturing procedures in accordance with corporate policies and standards: capital equipment selection and procurement, installation of this equipment and startup.

Mike was concerned about defining the project unambiguously. To that end, he obtained an interview with S. L. Mander, the group vice-president.

When he asked Mander where his responsibility should end, the executive turned the question back to him. Mike had been prepared for this and said that he would like to regard his part of the project as done when the production process could be turned over to manufacturing. They agreed that according to Singer practice, this would be when the manufacturing operation could produce a 95 percent yield of product (fully packaged) at a level of 80 percent of the full production goal of 10 million liters per year.

"But I want you to remember," said Mander, "that you must meet all current FDA, EPA, and OSHA regulations and you must be in compliance with our internal specification—the one I've got is dated September and is RD78/965. And you know that manufacturing now—quite rightly, I feel—insists on full written manufacturing procedures."

After this discussion, Mike felt that he had enough information about this aspect to start to pin down what had to be done to achieve these results. His first step in this effort was to meet with P. H. Docent, the director of research.

"You are naive if you think that you can just start right in finalizing the formula," said Docent. "You must first develop a product rationale (**a**).[2] This is a formally defined process according to company policy. Marketing expects inputs at this stage, manufacturing expects their voice to be heard, and you will have to have approvals from every unit of the company that is involved; all of this is reviewed by the Executive Committee. You should have no trouble if you do your homework, but expect to spend a good eight weeks to get this done."

"That certainly stretches things out," said Mike. "I expected to take 12 weeks to develop the ingredient formula (**b**) and you know that I can't start to establish product specifications (**c**) until the formula is complete. That's another three weeks."

"Yes, but while you are working on the product specifications you can get going on the regulatory documentation (**d**). Full internal specifications are not required for that work, but you can't start those documents until the formula is complete."

"Yes, and I find it hard to believe that we can push through both preparation of documents and getting approval in three weeks, but Environmental swears it can be done."

"Oh, it can be done in this case because of the preparatory work. Of course, I won't say that this estimate of three weeks is as certain as our other time estimates. All we need is a change of staff at the Agency and we are in trouble. But once you have both the specifications and the approval, you can immediately start on developing the production processing system (**g**)."

"Yes, and how I wish we could get a lead on that, but the designers say that there is too much uncertainty and they won't move until they have both specifications and regulatory documentation and approval. They are offering pretty fast response; six weeks from start to finish for the processing system."

"They are a good crew, Mike. And of course, you know that you don't have to delay on starting the packaging segment of this project. You can start developing the packaging concept (**e**) just as soon as the product rationale has been developed. If my experience is any judge, it will take a full eight weeks; you'll have to work to keep the process from running forever."

"But as soon as that is finished we can start on the design of the package and its materials (**f**), which usually takes about six weeks. Once that is done we can start developing the packaging system (**h**), which shouldn't take longer than eight weeks," concluded Mike. At this point he realized that although Docent would have general knowledge, he needed to talk directly to the director of manufacturing.

"The first step, which follows the completion of the development of processing and packaging systems," said the director of manufacturing, "is to do a complete study of the facilities and equipment requirements (**i**). You won't be able to get that done in less than four weeks. And that must precede the preparation of the capital equipment list (**j**) which should take about three-quarters as long. Of course, as soon as the development of both the process system and packaging system are completed, you could start on preparing the written manufacturing facilities procedures (**q**)."

"But," said Mike, "Can I really finish the procedures before I have installed the manufacturing facilities (**p**)?"

"No, quite right. What you can do is get the first phase done, but the last three of the ten weeks it will take to do that will have to wait for the installation of the manufacturing facilities."

"Then this means that I really have two phases for the writing, that which can be completed without the manufacturing facilities installation (**q**), and that which has to wait for them (**q'**)."

"True. Now you realize that the last thing you have to do after completing the procedures and installing the equipment and facilities is to run a pilot test (**r**) which will show that you have reached a satisfactory level?"

"Yes. Since that must include debugging, I've estimated a six-week period as adequate." The director of manufacturing assented. Mike continued, "What I'm not sure of is whether we can run all the installation tasks in parallel."

"You can let the purchase orders and carry out the procurement of process equipment (**k**), packaging equipment (**l**), and facilities (**m**) as soon as the capital equipment list is complete. The installation of each of these types of equipment and facilities can start as soon as the goods are on hand (**n, o, p**)."

"What do you estimate for the times to do these tasks?" asked Mike. The director of manufacturing estimated 18, 8, and 4 weeks for the purchasing phases for each of the subsystems in that order and four weeks for each of the installations. "Then I can regard my job as done with the delivery of the procedures and when I show my 95 percent yield," said Mike, and the director of manufacturing agreed, but reminded Mike that none of the purchasing cycles could start until the capital equipment list had been prepared and approved (**j**) which he saw as a three-week task.

The executive committee of D. U. Singer Hospital Products Corporation set a starting date for the project of March 10 and asked Mike to project a completion date with his submission of the plan. The committee's request implied that whatever date Mike came up with was acceptable, but Mike knew that he would be expected to show how to shorten the time to complete the project. However, his task in making the schedule was clear; he had to establish the resource requirements and deal with calendar constraints as best as he could.

To this end, Mike had to get an estimate of resources, which he decided to do by making a list of the activities and asking each group involved what was their level of employee input. The results of this survey are shown in Exhibit 1. For example, activity **a** takes 8 weeks and requires 12 worker-weeks from R&D, or an average of 1.5 workers for the entire 8-week duration of activity **a**.

For the purposes of overall planning, the accounting department told Mike that he could estimate a cost of $600 per week per employee. This would enable him to provide a cash flow forecast along with his plan, which the chief accountant said would be expected, something that Mike had not realized.

---

[2]Tasks which must be accounted for in a network plan are identified by lower-case alphabetic symbols in parentheses. Refer to Exhibit 1.

Activity	Packaging Task Force	R&D Group	Corp. Eng.	H-P Manuf.	Pack. Prod. Manuf.	Maint.	Purchasing	Material & Other Direct Charges
a—prod. rationale	1	12	1	1	2	0	0	$ 0
b—dev. formula	0	16	4	2	0	0	0	500
c—prod. spec.	1	6	3	1	1	0	1	0
d—reg. document	0	12	4	2	0	0	0	0
e—dev. pkg. concept	12	8	4	2	8	0	2	4000
f—design pkg.	12	2	3	0	3	0	3	2000
g—dev. proces. sys.	0	18	12	12	0	0	0	0
h—dev. pkg. sys.	24	8	8	0	8	0	2	0
i—study facil./eqpt. req.	0	4	16	2	2	0	0	0
j—capital equip. list	0	1	3	0	0	0	1	0
k—procure proces. eqpt.	0	1	1	1	0	0	7	40,000
l—procure pkg. eqpt.	1	0	1	0	1	0	9	160,000
m—procure facil.	0	0	1	1	1	1	6	30,000
n—install proces. eqpt.	0	2	4	8	0	4	1	4000
o—install pkg. eqpt.	2	0	4	0	8	4	1	8000
p—install mfg. facil.	0	0	5	5	5	10	1	6000
q,q'—written procedures	5	5	5	10	15	10	0	5000
r—pilot test	3	6	6	6	6	6	0	0

EXHIBIT 1 Labor Requirements (Worker-weeks).

Mike knew that it was customary at D. U. Singer to provide the following as parts of a plan to be submitted to the executive committee:

a. Statement of objectives

b. Work breakdown structure

c. An AON network

d. A determination of the critical path(s) and the duration along the path

e. An activity list, early-start schedule, and slack list. Assume that every activity begins at its early start, regardless of resource constraints.

f. A period labor requirements table for each group and the project as a whole

g. A cumulative labor requirements table for each group and the project as a whole. Include line graphs to illustrate the cumulative loads

h. A schedule based on the best leveling of labor requirements that could be achieved without lengthening project duration by more than 14 percent in calendar days

i. A cash flow requirements graph for the project, assuming that charges are uniformly distributed throughout the activity

Questions

1. Construct the nine elements of the plan identified above.

2. Analyze the plan for potential problems.

3. Analyze the plan for opportunities.

4. Should the executive committee approve the plan? Why or why not?

5. What alternatives might the executive committee suggest for analysis?

The following reading describes a project where the objectives were extremely complicated due to the wide variety of stakeholders. Yet the project team came in both under schedule and under budget.

Reading

Let The Games Begin—Now[3]   S. F. Gale

The lead-up to an Olympic event is often overshadowed by panicked project managers trying to finish stadiums on time or sponsors worried that funds will run out before the torch has even been lit.

Not so in London, England, where the bulk of the project work for the 2012 Olympic Games has come in ahead of schedule and what looks to be under budget.

Project teams are still working on minor details, such as landscaping, but major venues were completed and ready for use as of July, says Mike Szomjassy, president of the environmental services business group at CH2M Hill, Englewood, Colorado, USA, and former deputy program manager overseeing construction of venue infrastructure for the London Olympics projects. CH2M Hill partnered with two British firms, Laing O'Rourke and Mace, in a consortium called CLM Delivery Partner Ltd. to deliver the projects for the Olympic Delivery Authority (ODA). "The major venues were done almost a year ahead of the games, and we are forecast to come in about two billion pounds under the 9.3 billion pound budget," he says.

Mr. Szomjassy credits CLM's strong relationship with ODA. "They had a vision and they trusted us to deliver," he says.

To ensure that vision became reality, the team established a clearly defined scope, formal metrics, and an agreement from all contractors and stakeholders to meet their deadlines—or face stiff penalties.

"Commitments were made in the bid process that were incorporated into the design, rolled into the specs and turned into goals with very specific key performance indicators," Mr. Szomjassy says.

If the CLM exceeded expectations by coming in under budget or early, the team could share in the savings. But if it missed a deadline, or failed to deliver quality or sustainability goals, it was held financially accountable.

"One hundred percent of our fee was at risk based on our ability to meet the budget, schedule and other target requirements, including sustainability," he says. "Everyone knew that if they didn't fulfill expectations, they would be dinged."

That accountability didn't stop with the contractors and team members. If ODA stakeholders didn't meet their commitments or failed to warn the contractors of potential problems, they also risked having to absorb additional costs or lose a desired feature of the project. The stakeholders involved at the Aquatic Centre, for example, were late in agreeing to the specifications for key design criteria, including the diving area's configuration. The indecision could potentially lead to a construction delay, adding cost to that piece of the project.

CLM helped identify solutions with ODA to mitigate the impact to the project, but the stakeholders were accountable for the cost overrun where possible.

"That was an important part of the relationship," Mr. Szomjassy says. "We worked together to solve problems even when we weren't the ones held at fault."

Ready, Set, Go Green

The collaborative approach and culture of accountability adopted by CLM and ODA enabled the team to deliver the program on time and under budget. It also resulted in what could be the most socially responsible games yet.

"Legacy—what is left behind when the games are complete—is a huge component of the spirit of the Olympics," Mr. Szomjassy says. "For London, one of the key components of legacy was sustainability, in its very broadest sense."

The program's wide range of environmental and social goals includes:

- Recycling 90 percent of waste material on site.
- Hiring 15 percent of workers from surrounding economically depressed boroughs, 7 percent from the ranks of previously unemployed, and 15 percent from minority populations.
- Building a stadium that can be partially dismantled and reused elsewhere

"This comprehensive sustainability legacy was a significant energizing factor for London and the United Kingdom, helping to attract both public support and government funding because of the long-term benefits it would provide," Mr. Szomjassy says.

Olympic Feats

| 2005 | 2006 | 2007 | 2008 | 2009 | 2010 | 2011 | 2012 | 2013 |

Foundation — Strategic/business — Operational planning — Games readiness — Games time — Dissoluble

[3]Reprinted from *PM Network* with permission. Copyright Project Management Institute Inc.

Aligning all those social responsibility elements took serious planning. And while Mr. Szomjassy credits that work with helping make the program a success, Olympic program leaders initially faced criticism from the public for the extra time devoted to the planning phase. ODA and CLM agreed, however, that up-front due diligence would pay off, particularly when it came to managing tradeoffs to achieve sustainability objectives. "We always had to drive value for public funds," he says. "So we were constantly balancing cost and aspirational construction."

This balancing act led Olympic organizers to drop plans to offset the event's carbon emissions themselves, saving up to 2.7 million pounds, according to Bloomberg. Instead, the team hired energy giant BP's Target Neutral unit to offset the expected 34,000 tons of CO_2 generated through traveling to and from one project in each of the continents taking part in the sports event. The unit is also supporting a group of athletes to reduce and off-set their carbon footprint as they prepare for the games, as well as making specific offset offers to spectators, the general view-ing public and partner organizations.

Coaching the Entire Team

Project leaders worked closely with subcontractors to help them think creatively about how to achieve sustainability goals within the constraints of the job site. Olympic Park, for example, is in East London, with only two narrow access roads. But it's also intersected by three waterways and a rail system, so the team relied on those to ship 50 percent of materials in and out of the site. The move not only reduced traffic and congestion on the site, it also cut the use of fossil fuel.

"Contractors don't normally think about using water and rail, but on this project it was easier and cheaper," Mr. Szomjassy says. It also enabled them to prefabricate large pieces of the proj-ect off site for less cost, because they weren't constrained by the space limitations of truck transportation.

By planning ahead and considering each choice in the con-text of the broader program, project teams were able to engage the entire supply chain in finding the most cost-effective solu-tions, David Stubbs of the London Organizing Committee told *The Guardian* in August.

"That's how we have been able to turn around the percep-tion that sustainability costs more," he told the newspaper. "We have found that by making our requirements very clear up front, the market has responded. So we are getting some of our best deals from suppliers who are taking sustainability seriously, and our stance has helped draw in significantly stronger interest from commercial sponsors. This means an effective sustainabil-ity approach creates efficiencies, saves costs, and helps generate additional revenue."

Questions

1. The Olympic leaders faced harsh criticism for the "delay" in beginning work on the project. Have you read about this kind of response elsewhere? What is the message here?

2. What were the major factors in the success of this project?

3. What particularly creative solutions were taken when prob-lems seemed unsolvable?

CHAPTER 10

Monitoring and Information Systems

Our fundamental approach to the monitoring, evaluation, and control of projects is that these activities are, at base, the opposite sides of project selection and planning. The logic of selection, described in Chapter 2, dictates the components to be evaluated, and the details of planning expose the elements to be controlled. The ability to measure is prerequisite to either. Thus, all of the project's objectives as delineated in the project selection process must be examined and measures for each included in the monitoring system.

Monitoring the critical project measures as the project proceeds through its life cycle, such as by the Project Owner as described in Chapter 2, is required so projects can be realigned with the changing scope, or terminated, if necessary, and new projects initiated. We are finding that with the spread of project management to more strategic, complex, expensive, longer term, multistakeholder, and multi-organizational endeavors, scope changes almost always occur over the life of the project—it just happens. And the need for a project owner to monitor these changes and work with the sponsor and Project manager (PM) to oversee the alterations needed in the project to accommodate these shifts in the scope is paramount. More will be said about this in Chapters 11–13.

Many more evaluative measures are needed for the maintenance of a risk management system. Not only must the project performance be monitored, but the environment within which the project exists must also be observed and recorded. *Monitoring* is collecting, recording, and reporting information concerning any and all aspects of project performance that the PM, the project owner, or others in the organization wish to know. In our discussion, it is important to remember that monitoring, as an activity, should be kept distinct from controlling (which uses the data supplied by monitoring to bring actual performance into approximate congruence with planned performance), as well as from evaluation (through which judgments are made about the quality and effectiveness of project performance). In this chapter, we first expand on the nature of this link between planning and control, including a brief discussion of the various aspects of project performance that need to be monitored. We then examine some of the problems associated with monitoring a project.

This book is addressed to practicing PMs as well as students of project management. Students resist the idea that PMs do not have immediate access to accurate information on every aspect of the project. But PMs know that it is not always easy to find out what's going on when working on a project. Records are frequently out of date, incomplete, in error, or "somewhere else" when needed. Throughout the chapter, our primary concern is to ensure that all stakeholders in the project, and especially the project owner, have available, *on a timely basis*, the information needed to exercise effective control over the project and the uncertainties that impact on it. The other uses for monitoring (e.g., auditing, learning from past mistakes, or keeping senior management informed), important as they are, must be considered secondary to the control function when constructing the monitoring system.

One final note: In this chapter, we frequently refer to a "project owner," a "project sponsor," or even to the "office" responsible for monitoring. These individuals and groups do in fact exist on most large projects. On a small project, it is likely that the project owner is the same person as the project sponsor. That is, we are referring to *roles* needed in project management, not necessarily to different individuals.

10.1 The Planning–Monitoring–Controlling Cycle

Throughout this book, we have stressed the need to plan, check on progress, compare progress to the plan, and take corrective action if progress does not match the plan. The key things to be planned, monitored, and controlled are time (schedule), cost (budget), and scope (performance). These, after all, encompass the fundamental objectives of the project. However, we are finding that with more complex projects, scope is usually by far the most important of the three and invariably changes, sometimes substantially, as the project progresses. Hence, the need for the project owner to work closely with the sponsor and PM.

There is no doubt that some organizations do not spend sufficient time and effort on planning and controlling projects. It is far easier to focus on doing, especially because it appears to be more effective to "stop all the talk and get on with the work." We could cite firm after firm that incurred great expense (and major losses) because the planning process was inadequate for the tasks undertaken.

- A major construction project ran over budget by 63 percent and over schedule by 48 percent because the PM decided that, since "he had managed similar projects several times before, he knew what to do without going into all that detail that no one looks at anyway."

- A large industrial equipment supplier "took a bath" on a project designed to develop a new area of business because they applied the same planning and control procedures to the new area that they had used (successfully) on previous, smaller, less complex jobs.

- A computer store won a competitive bid to supply a computer, five terminals, and associated software to the Kansas City office of a national firm. Admittedly insufficient planning made the installation significantly late. Performance of the software was not close to specified levels. This botched job prevented the firm from being invited to bid on more than 20 similar installations planned by the client.

The planning (budgeting and scheduling) methods we propose "put the hassles up front." They require a significantly greater investment of time and energy early in the life of the project, but they significantly reduce the extent and cost of poor performance and time/cost overruns. Note that this is no guarantee of a trouble-free project, merely a decline in the risk of failure.

It is useful to perceive the control process as a *closed-loop* system, with revised plans and schedules (if warranted) following corrective actions. We delay a detailed discussion on control until the next chapter, but the planning–monitoring–controlling cycle is continuously in process until the project is completed. It is also useful to construct this process as an internal part of the organizational structure of the project, not something external to and imposed on it or, worse, in conflict with it. Finally, experience tells us that it is

Project Management in Practice

Using Project Management Software to Schedule the Olympic Games

Steve Powell/Getty Images

The XV Olympiad in Calgary involved nearly 2000 athletes from 57 countries in 129 competitive events, attracted over 1,500,000 spectators, was covered by over 5000 journalists, and was run by a staff of 600 professionals complemented by 10,000 volunteers. For those 600 responsible for organizing, planning, scheduling, coordinating, and handling the information requirements for the 16-day extravaganza, the task was overwhelming. The top managers of the organizing committee thus turned to a Computer-Based Project Planning and Scheduling (CBPPS) system for scheduling and managing the 30,000 tasks organized into 50 projects.

The goal for the Calgary Games was to provide the best games ever, but within the budget. The philosophy employed was to let each PM plan his/her own project but meet firm completion dates and budget limits. This made a lot of additional work for the upper managers since each project's reports and needs were different from every

other project's. However, two major features of the project helped make this a success: (1) knowing that the Games would happen on the scheduled date regardless of whether they were ready or not, and (2) being such a high-visibility, challenging project that demands exceptional focus on the task.

To schedule the entire Winter Games, the 129-event, 16-day Olympics was broken down into 15-minute periods, except for short-track speed skating, which was segmented into 1-minute intervals. There was a printout for every day by venue, minute by minute, and a complete set of drawings of every site, building, and room. Meticulous scheduling was necessary to ensure that the 2500 or so competitors, members of royalty, and government officials were at the right place at the right time. Support staff, including medical and security personnel, were also carefully scheduled for each event as crowds shifted from competition to competition. Transportation—600 buses—also had to be scheduled, oftentimes on short notice. The biggest concern was the weather, and sure enough, the Chinook winds forced the rescheduling of over 20 events, some of them twice!

Yet, the Calgary Games were the best yet and organized better than ever before. Moreover, as compared to the budget overruns of many other cities, this Olympiad was completed under budget!

Questions

1. **Why did they need drawings of every site, building, and room?**

2. **How do you think they did planning for the bad weather?**

3. **Was scheduling the difficult aspect of planning the games or the logistics?**

Source: R. G. Holland, "The XV Olympic Winter Games: A Case Study in Project Management," *PM Network*, Vol. 3.

---

also desirable, though not mandatory, that the planning–monitoring–controlling cycle be the normal way of life in the parent organization. What is good for the project is equally good for the parent firm. In any case, unless the PM has a smoothly operating monitoring/control system, it will be difficult to manage the project effectively. As we will describe in Chapter 11 on *controlling*, it is useful to specify up-front in the project plan what will happen—some contingency or agreed-upon action—in case, monitoring shows the project is not tracking as was expected. In Chapters 12 and 13, we will discuss research indicating that planning, monitoring, and control are clearly associated with project success.

Designing the Monitoring System

The first step in setting up any monitoring system is to identify the key factors to be controlled. Clearly, the PM wants to monitor scope, cost, and time but must define precisely which specific characteristics of scope, cost, and time should be controlled and then establish exact boundaries within which control should be maintained. There may also be other factors of importance worth noting at least at milestones or review points in the life of the project. For example, the number of labor hours used, the number or extent of process or output changes, the level of funder satisfaction, and similar items may be worthy of note on individual projects.

But the best sources of items to be monitored are the project work breakdown structure (WBS), change of scope orders, and the risk management plan. The WBS describes what is being done, when, and the planned level of resource usage for each task, work package, and work element in the project. Monitoring the risks found in the risk management plan keeps the PM and project team alert to specific risks and thus lowers the probability of surprises. The monitoring system is a direct connection between planning and control. If it does not collect and report information on some significant element of the plan, control can be faulty or missing. The WBS furnishes the key items that must be measured and reported to the control system, but it is not sufficient. For example, the PM might want to know about changes in the client's attitudes toward the project. Information on the morale of the project team might be useful in preparing for organizational or personnel changes on the project. These two latter items may be quite important but are not usually reflected in the project's WBS.

Unfortunately, it is common to focus monitoring activities on data that are easily gathered—rather than important—or to concentrate on "objective" measures that are easily defended at the expense of softer, more subjective data that may be more important to control. Above all, monitoring should concentrate primarily on measuring various facets of output rather than intensity of activity. It is crucial to remember that effective PMs are not primarily interested in how hard their project teams work. They are interested in achieving results.

The measurement of project performance usually poses the most difficult data gathering problem. There is a strong tendency to let project inputs serve as surrogate measures for output. If we have spent 50 percent of the budget (or of the scheduled time), we assume that we have also completed 50 percent of the project or reached 50 percent of our performance goal. If the item being referenced is a small work unit, it does not make a significant difference if we are wrong. If, however, the reference is to a task or to the entire project, the assumption of input/output proportionality (hereafter, the "proportionality rule") is often seriously misleading.

Further, it is common to specify performance to a level of precision that is both unnecessary and unrealistic or a level of lenience that is worthless. For example, a communications software project specified that a telephone "information" system had to locate a phone number and respond to the queries in 5 seconds or less. Is 5.1 seconds a failure? Does the specification mean 5 seconds or less every time or merely that response times should average 5 seconds or less? Is the specification satisfied if the response time is 5 seconds or less than 90 percent of the time?

The monitoring systems we describe in this chapter, however, focus mainly on time and cost as measures of performance, not scope (performance). While we are most certainly concerned with keeping the project "on spec," and do consider some of the problems of monitoring output, the subject is not fully developed here because the software designed to monitor projects is not constructed to deal with performance adequately.

Given all this, performance criteria, standards, and data collection procedures must be established for each of the factors to be measured. The criteria and data collection procedures are usually set up for the life of the project. The standards themselves, however, may not be constant over the project's life. They may change as a result of altered capabilities within the parent organization or a technological breakthrough made by the project team; but, perhaps more often than not, standards and criteria change because of factors that are not under the control of the PM. For example, they may be changed by the client. One client who had ordered a special piece of audio equipment altered performance specifications significantly when electronic parts became available that could filter out random noises. This is, of course, a change in scope, a serious matter that we discuss in detail later under the topic of "control."

Perhaps the most common error made when monitoring data is to gather information that is clearly related to project performance but has little or no probability of changing significantly from one collection period to the next. Prior to its breakup, the American Telephone and Telegraph Company used to collect monthly statistics on a very large number of indicators of operating efficiency. The extent of the collection was such that it filled a telephone-book-sized volume known as "Ma Bell's Green Book." For a great many of the indicators, the likelihood of a significant change from 1 month to the next was extremely small. When asked about the matter, one official remarked that the mere collection of the data kept the operating companies "on their toes." We feel that there are other, more positive and less expensive ways of motivating project personnel. Certainly, "collect everything" is inappropriate as a monitoring policy.

Therefore, the first task is to examine the WBS in order to extract scope, time, and cost goals. These goals should relate in some manner to each of the different levels of detail; that is, some should relate to the project, some to its tasks, some to the work packages, and so on. Data must be identified that measure achievement against these goals, and mechanisms designed that gather and store such data. If at least some of the data do not relate to the work unit level, no useful action is apt to be taken. In the end, it is the detailed work of the project that must be altered if any aspect of project performance is to be changed. A reading of the fascinating book *The Soul of a New Machine* (Kidder, 1981) reveals the crucial roles that organizational factors, interpersonal relationships, and managerial style still play in determining project success. Also of value is a paper by Mekhilef et al. (2005) that develops a method to find and analyze the ways in which individuals introduce dysfunction into decision processes.

Alderton (2013) suggests five telltale signs of project trouble it is wise to monitor.

1. **Muddy Waters:**   The project plan is often the starting point for project trouble, especially if it is unduly long or confusing in its goals, scope, deliverables, and processes. "The most common cause of troubled projects . . . is that the scope is not well defined or well understood." Vague or incomplete project requirements are a major red flag.

2. **Mysterious Stakeholders:**   Full and detailed stakeholder descriptions and analysis are key to avoiding late problems and delays. Incomplete documentation of all stakeholders is a major risk for any project. There should be two versions of the stakeholder description: A formal one that identifies who each one is, their role, how to reach them, and their preferred mode of communication. The other also includes whether they are a supporter of the project or a detractor, or perhaps a fence sitter, so the PM can anticipate any trouble that may occur later on and get to these people early to head it off.

3. **Unconstrained Constraints:**   Knowing how much leeway there is in your schedule and budget for each task, and where delays or cost overruns can be made up, keeps a project out of trouble. "If you don't have a detailed project schedule, the chance of the project failing increases exponentially." Milestones are especially important since they usually have the least give. Establish tolerance limits on each task, and intervene when they are exceeded.

4. **Suspicious Status Reports:**   Status reports that are unclear, inconsistent, late, or lack specific measures are a red flag for coming trouble. Vague or overly optimistic language such as "very soon" or "marginal increase" in costs also indicates trouble ahead.

5. **Discord and Drama:**   Unhappy team members can cause major trouble in the project, though hard to detect early on. Meeting minutes can show team members who are consistently missing, have low participation, or seem to have excessive objections and

complaints. The PM needs to be a coach and mentor for the team by establishing trust and respect within the team and an open and honest feedback environment. Create a positive team dynamic as soon as possible.

10.2 | Information Needs and Reporting

Everyone concerned with the project should be appropriately tied into the project reporting system (Back et al., 2001). The monitoring system ought to be constructed so that it addresses every level of management, but reports need not be of the same depth or at the same frequency for each level. Lower-level personnel have a need for detailed information about individual tasks and the factors affecting such tasks. Report frequency is usually high. For the senior management levels, overview reports describe progress in more aggregated terms with less individual task detail unless senior management has a special interest in a specific activity or task. Reports are issued less often. In both cases, the structure of the reports should reflect the WBS, with each managerial level receiving reports that allow the exercise of control at the relevant level. At times, it may be necessary to move information between organizations, as illustrated in Figure 10.1, as well as between managerial levels.

The proliferation of electronic mechanisms along with a wide array of software has made the process of collecting and disseminating information much faster and less arduous than previously. In addition to its use for conducting the routines of project management, the Internet is a rich source of information, including databases on almost anything, patent information, and technical aid for managing projects, to mention only a small fraction of readily available information. Many current project management software

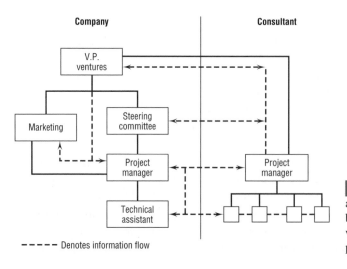

FIGURE 10.1 Reporting and information flows between organizations working on a common project.

packages allow easy connection to the Internet and e-mail to transmit information, charts, networks, and reports practically anywhere. The material can be altered or updated and returned to the sender with minimal effort beyond that needed to move the information to the next cubicle.

"E-mail is not to be used to pass on information or data. It should be used only for company business."

The Reporting Process

The relationship of project reports to the project WBS is the key to the determination of both report content and frequency. Reports must contain data relevant to the control of specific tasks that are being carried out according to a specific schedule. The frequency of reporting should be great enough to allow control to be exerted during or before the period in which the task is scheduled for completion. For example, efficacy tests of drugs do not produce rapid results in most cases. Thus, there is no reason for weekly (and perhaps not even monthly) reports on such tests. When test results begin to occur, more frequent reports and updates may be required.

In addition to the criterion that reports should be available in time to be used for project control, the timing of reports should generally correspond to the timing of project milestones. This means that project reports may not be issued periodically—excepting progress reports for senior management. There seems to be no logical reason, except for tradition, to issue weekly, monthly, quarterly, etc., reports. Few projects require attention so neatly consistent with the calendar. This must not be taken as advice to issue reports "every once in a while." Reports should be scheduled in the project plan. They should be issued on time. The report schedule, however, need not call for *periodic* reports.

The distribution of project reports depends on who is interested. For senior management, there may be only a few milestones, even in large projects. For the PM, there may be many critical points in the project schedule at which major decisions must be made, large changes in the resource base must be initiated, or key technical results achieved. Similar points relevant to lower levels relate to finer detail and occur with higher frequency. Individual senior managers have widely varying preferences in the frequency and content of reports they wish to see. The PM is well advised to supply them. But irrespective of the senior manager's wishes, the PM must make sure that relevant information about progress is always included—and reported in a way it cannot be overlooked. It is also counterproductive to delay reporting on a current or immediately potential crisis until the next routine report is due.

The nature of the monitoring reports should be consistent with the logic of the planning, budgeting, and scheduling systems. The primary purpose is, of course, to ensure achievement of the project plan through control. There is little reason to burden operating members of the project team with extensive reports on matters that are not subject to control—at least not by them. For example, overhead costs or the in-house rental costs of the project war room are simply not appropriate considerations for a team member who is supervising a research experiment in polymer chemistry or designing the advertising campaign for a new brand of coffee. The scheduling and resource usage columns of the project WBS will serve as the key to the design of project reports.

There are many benefits of detailed, timely reports delivered to the proper people. Among them are:

- Mutual understanding of the goals of the project
- Awareness of the progress of parallel activities and of the problems associated with coordination among activities

- Understanding the relationships of individual tasks to one another and to the overall project
- Early warning signals of potential problems and delays in the project
- Minimizing the confusion associated with change by reducing delays in communicating the change
- Higher visibility to top management, including attention directed to the immediate needs of the project
- Keeping the client and other interested outside parties up to date on project status, particularly regarding project costs, milestones, and deliverables

Report Types

"One day my boss asked me to submit a status report to him concerning a project I was working on. I asked him if tomorrow would be soon enough. He said, 'If I wanted it tomorrow, I would have waited until tomorrow to ask for it!' "

For the purposes of project management, we can consider three distinct types of reports: routine, exception, and special analysis. The routine reports are those issued on a regular basis; but, as we noted earlier, *regular* does not necessarily refer to the calendar. For senior management, the reports will usually be periodic and at major milestones, but for the PM and lower-level project personnel, critical events may be used to trigger routine reports. At times, it may be useful to issue routine reports on resource usage periodically, occasionally on a weekly or even daily basis.

Exception reports are useful in two cases. First, they are directly oriented to project management decision-making and should be distributed to the team members who will have prime responsibility for decisions or who have a clear "need to know." Second, they may be issued when a decision is made on an exception basis, and it is desirable to inform other managers as well as to document the decision—in other words, as part of a sensible procedure for protecting oneself. (PMs should be aware that overuse of exception reporting will be perceived by top management as sheep-like, overly cautious behavior.)

Special analysis reports are used to disseminate the results of special studies conducted as part of the project or as a response to special problems that arise during the project. Usually, they cover matters that may be of interest to other PMs or make use of analytic methods that might be helpful on other projects. Studies on the use of substitute materials, evaluation of alternative manufacturing processes, availability of external consultants, capabilities of new software, and descriptions of new governmental regulations are all typical of the kinds of subjects covered in special analysis reports. Distribution of these reports is usually made to anyone who might be interested.

Meetings

To celebrate his 50th birthday, columnist Dave Barry listed "25 things you will learn in 50 years of living." The sixteenth was "If you had to identify, in one word, the reason why the human race has not and never will achieve its full potential, that word would be 'meetings.'" For a large majority of PMs and workers, meetings are as welcome as bad checks or unmentionable diseases. There is no doubt that meetings of project teams are necessary and often helpful. The main complaints are that they are interminably long, come to no conclusions, and waste everyone's time. Indeed, a short commentary on how not to run a meeting is entitled, "Creative Time Wasting" (Nevison, 1995).

Thus far, we have implicitly assumed that "reports" were written and disseminated by hard copy, e-mail, or by Internet. Far more often, however, all three types of reports are delivered in face-to-face meetings or in telephone conference calls. Indeed, senior managers usually insist on face-to-face meetings for staying informed about project progress, and these meetings may touch on almost any subject relevant to the project (or not). Project review meetings can be either highly structured (see Knutson, 1996, for instance) or deceptively casual, but they are always important.

A large majority of project meetings do not concern senior management. They are project team meetings, occasionally including the client, and concern the day-to-day problems met on all projects. There is no particular reason that these meetings need to be conducted in a manner that is so dreaded by attendees. A few simple rules can remove most of the pain associated with project meetings.

- Use meetings for making group decisions or getting input for important problems. Avoid "show-and-tell" meetings, sometimes called "status and review meetings." If the latter type of meeting has been used to keep project team members informed about what others are doing on the project, insist that such information be communicated personally or electronically by the relevant individuals to the relevant individuals. Only when there is a clear need, such as informing senior management of the project's status, and it is difficult for team members to "get together" on their own, are status and review meetings appropriate.

- Have preset starting and stopping times as well as a written agenda. Stick with both, and above all, do not penalize those who show up on time by making them wait for those who are tardy.

- Make sure that you (and others) do your homework prior to the meeting. Be prepared!

- If you chair the meeting, take your own minutes. Reality (and the minutes become reality as soon as the meeting is over) is too important to be left to the most junior person present. Distribute the minutes as soon as possible after the meeting, no later than the next work day.

- Avoid attributing remarks or viewpoints to individuals in the minutes. Attribution makes people quite wary about what they say in meetings and damps creativity as well as controversy. In addition, do not report votes on controversial matters. It is, for example, inappropriate to report in the minutes that the project team voted to send a "Get Well" card to the boss; four yea and three nay.

- Avoid overly formal rules of procedure. A project meeting is not a parliament and is not the place for Robert's Rules of Order, though courtesy is always in order.

- If a serious problem or crisis arises, call a meeting for the purpose of dealing with that issue only. The stopping time for such meetings may be "When the problem has been solved." Some types of meetings should never be held at all. A large, diversified manufacturing firm holds monthly "status and review" meetings in each of its divisions at which the managers of all projects report to a Project Review Committee (PRC). The divisional PRCs are made up of senior managers. At least one, and we are told more than one, of the PRCs apparently models its meetings on "Hell Week" at a nearby university fraternity. Hazing and humiliating the PMs who must report to the committee is standard practice. The results are to be expected. Projects are managed defensively. Creativity is avoided. PMs spend time printing and distributing résumés. The best PMs do not stay long.

Antony Jay (1995) wrote a classic article in the *Harvard Business Review* on how to conduct a meeting. We recommend it highly.

Common Reporting Problems

There are three common difficulties in the design of project reports. First, there is usually too much detail, both in the reports themselves and in the input being solicited from workers. Unnecessary detail (or too frequent reporting) usually results in the reports not being read. In addition, it prevents project team members from finding the information they need. Furthermore, the demand for large quantities of highly detailed input information often results in careless preparation of the data, thereby casting doubt on the validity of reports based on such data. Finally, the preparation and inclusion of unnecessary detail are costly, at the very least.

A second major problem is the poor interface between the project information system and the parent firm's information system. In our experience, the PM may try to force a connection. It rarely works well. The parent organization's information system must serve as the definitional prototype for the project's information system. Obviously, different types of reports must be constructed for managing the project, but they can be built by using standard data, for the most part. The PM can feel free to add new kinds of data to the information base but cannot insist that costs, resource usage, and the like be reported in the project differently from how they are reported in the parent organization. (Clearly, this rule does not apply to information generated or requested by the PM for the purpose of project management.)

The project-oriented firm or the organization that simultaneously conducts a large number of projects can justify a customized project database and report system specifically tailored to its special needs. In such cases, the interface between the project information system and the organization's overall information system must be carefully designed to ensure that data are not lost or distorted when moving from one system to the other. It is also important to make sure that when cost/scope data are reported, the data represent appropriate time periods.

The third problem concerns a poor correspondence between the planning and the monitoring systems. If the monitoring system is not tracking information directly related to the project's plans, control is meaningless. This often happens when the firm's existing information system is used for monitoring without modifications specifically designed for project management. For example, an existing cost tracking system oriented to shop operations would be inappropriate for a project with major activities in the area of research and development. But as we just noted, the PM's problem is to fit standard information into a reporting and tracking system that is appropriate for the project.

The real message carried by project reports is in the comparison of actual activity to plan and of actual output to desired output. Variances are reported by the monitoring system, and responsibility for action rests with the project owner. Because the project plan is described in terms of scope, time, and cost, variances are reported for those same variables. Project variance reports usually follow the same format used by the accounting department, but at times, they may be presented differently.

10.3 | Earned Value Analysis

Thus far, our examples have covered monitoring for parts of projects. The monitoring of performance for the entire project is also crucial because performance is the *raison d'être* of the project. *Individual* task performance must be monitored carefully because the timing and coordination between individual tasks are important. But overall project performance is the crux of the matter and must not be overlooked. One way of measuring overall performance is by using an aggregate performance measure called *earned value* (EV).

The Earned Value Chart and Calculations

There is a considerable body of literature devoted to earned value. To note only a few of the available items, see Anbari (2003), the Flemming references, Hatfield (1996), Project Management Institute (2013), Kwak et al. (2012), and Singletary (1996). One must, however, exercise some care when reading any article on the subject. Various ratio index numbers have almost as many names (and hence, acronyms) as there are writers. Some authors take further license; see Brandon (1998) for instance, and also see the subsequent *Project Management Journal's* Correspondence column (September 1998, p. 53) for readers' reactions. We will adopt and stick to the **PMBOK** version of things but will also note the names and acronyms used by Microsoft's Project®.[1] Any other names/acronyms will be identified with the author(s). A history of earned value from its origin in PERT/Cost together with its techniques, advantages, and disadvantages is reported in a series in *PM Network* starting with Flemming et al. (1994).

7.4.2

A serious difficulty with comparing actual expenditures against budgeted or *baseline* expenditures for any given time period is that the comparison fails to take into account the amount of work accomplished relative to the cost incurred. The earned value of work performed (*value completed*) for those tasks in progress is found by multiplying the estimated percent physical completion of work for each task by the planned cost for those tasks. The result is the amount that should have been spent on the task thus far. This can then be compared with the actual amount spent.

Making an overall estimate of the percent completion of a project without careful study of each of its tasks and work units is not sensible—though some people make such estimates nonetheless. Instead, it is apparent that at any date during the life of a project, the following general condition exists: Some work units have been finished, and they are 100 percent complete; some work units have not yet been started, and they are 0 percent complete; other units have been started but are not yet finished, and for this latter group, we may estimate a percent completion.

As we said, estimating the "percent completion" of each task (or work package) is nontrivial. If the task is to write a piece of software, percent completion can be estimated as the number of lines of code written divided by the total number of lines to be written—given that the latter has been estimated. But what if the task is to test the software? We have run a known number of tests, but how many remain to be run?

There are several conventions used to aid in estimating percent completion:

- **The 50–50 rule.** Fifty percent completion is assumed when the task is begun, and the remaining 50 percent when the work is complete. This seems to be the most popular rule, probably because it is relatively fair and doesn't require the effort of attempting to estimate task progress. Since it gives credit for half the task as soon as it has begun, it is excessively generous at the beginning of tasks, but then doesn't give credit for the other half until the task is finally complete, so is excessively conservative toward the end of tasks, thereby tending to balance out on an overall basis.

- **The 0–100 percent rule.** This rule allows no credit for work until the task is complete. With this highly conservative rule, the project always seems to be

---

[1]Earlier versions of Microsoft Project® used a slightly different way to calculate earned value variances.

running late, until the very end of the project when it appears to suddenly catch up. Consequently, the earned value line will always lag the planned value (PV) line on the graph.

- **Critical input use rule.** This rule assigns task progress according to the amount of a critical input that has been used. Obviously, the rule is more accurate if the task uses this input in direct proportion to the true progress being made. For example, when building a house, the task of building the foundation could be measured by the cubic yards (or meters) of concrete poured, the task of framing the house could relate to the linear feet (meters) of lumber used, the roofing task could relate to the sheets of 4 x 8 foot plywood used, and the task of installing cabinets might be measured by the hours of skilled cabinet labor expended.

- **The proportionality rule.** This commonly used rule is also based on proportionalities, but uses time (or cost) as the critical input. It thus divides actual task time-to-date by the scheduled time for the task [or actual task cost-to-date by total budgeted task cost] to calculate percent complete. If desirable, this rule can be subdivided according to the subactivities within the task. For example, suppose that progress on a task is dependent on purchasing a large, expensive machine to do a long and difficult task, but just having the machine itself does not contribute to any substantial task progress. We could create a table or graph of the use of money relative to task progress, which would show a large amount of money being expended up front for the machine, but with little (or no) corresponding progress toward the completion of the task per se being made. This would then be followed by a continuing expenditure of a smaller stream of money (or time) to run the machine and finish the job, perhaps in direct proportion to the progress.

These rough guides to "percent completion" are not meant to be applied to the project as a whole, though sometimes they are, but rather to individual activities. For projects with few activities, rough measures can be misleading. For projects with a fairly large number of activities, however, the error caused by percent completion rules is such a small part of the total project time/cost that the errors are insignificant. More serious is the tendency to speak of an entire project as being "73 percent complete." In most cases, this has no real meaning—certainly not what is implied by the overly exact number. Some authors assume that making estimates of percent completion is simple (Brandon, 1998, p. 12, col. 2, for instance). The estimation task is difficult and arbitrary at best, which is why the 50–50, and other rules have been adopted.

A graph illustrating the concept of earned value such as that shown in Figure 10.2 can be constructed using the aforementioned rules and provides a basis for evaluating cost and scope to date. If the total value of the work accomplished is in balance with the planned (baseline) cost (i.e., minimal scheduling variance), as well as its actual cost (minimal cost variance), then top management has no particular need for a detailed analysis of individual tasks. Thus, the concept of earned value combines cost reporting and aggregate scope reporting into one comprehensive chart. The baseline cost to completion is indicated on the chart and referred to as the budget at completion (BAC). The actual cost to date can also be projected to completion, as will be shown further on, and is referred to as the estimated cost at completion (EAC).

We identify several variances on the EV chart following two primary guidelines: (1) A negative variance is "bad," and (2) the cost and schedule variances are calculated as the EV minus some other measure. Specifically, the *cost* (or sometimes the *spending*) *variance* (CV) is the difference between the amount of money we budgeted for the work that has been performed to date, that is, the EV and the actual cost of that work (AC). The *schedule variance* (SV) is the difference between the EV and the cost of the work we scheduled to be performed to date, or the PV. The *time variance* is the difference in the time

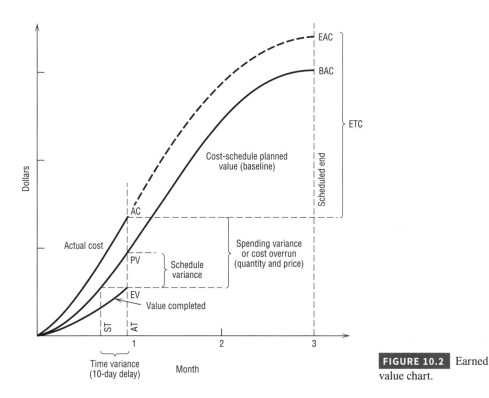

FIGURE 10.2   Earned value chart.

scheduled for the work that has been performed (ST) and the actual time used to perform it (AT).[2] In compact form,

$$EV - AC = \text{cost variance (CV, overrun is negative)}$$
$$EV - PV = \text{schedule variance (SV, behind is negative)}$$
$$ST - AT = \text{time variance (TV, delay is negative)}$$

Typically, variances are defined in such a way that they will be negative when the project is behind schedule and/or over cost. As we have noted, however, this practice is not universal either in the literature or in practice.

The variances are also often formulated as ratios rather than differences so that the CV becomes the Cost Performance Index (CPI) = EV/AC, the SV becomes the Schedule Performance Index (SPI) = EV/PV, and the time variance becomes the Time Performance Index (TPI) = ST/AT, where values less than 1.0 are "bad." Use of ratios is particularly helpful when an organization wishes to compare the performance of several projects (or PMs), or the same project over different time periods. As we just noted, however, the accuracy and usefulness of all these performance measures depend on the degree in which estimates of percent completion reflect reality.

Cost and schedule variances (or CPI and SPI) are very commonly used. A short example illustrates their application. Assume that operations on a work package were expected to cost $1,500 to complete the package. They were originally scheduled to have been finished today. At this point, however, we have actually expended $1,350, and we estimate that we have completed two-thirds of the work. What are the cost and schedule variances?

---

[2]A fourth variance can be found. It is the difference between the cost that the project budget says should have been expended to date (PV) and the actual cost incurred to date by the project (AC). PV − AC is what we call the *resource flow variance*. (Note that the resource flow variance is not a "cash flow" variance.)

$$\begin{aligned}
\text{cost variance} &= \text{EV} - \text{AC} \\
&= \$1,500(2/3) - 1,350 \\
&= -\$350 \\
\text{schedule variance} &= \text{EV} - \text{PV} \\
&= \$1,500(2/3) - 1,500 \\
&= -\$500 \\
\text{CPI} &= \text{EV}/\text{AC} \\
&= \$(1,500(2/3))/1,350 \\
&= 0.74 \\
\text{SPI} &= \text{EV}/\text{PV} \\
&= \$(1,500(2/3))/1,500 \\
&= .67
\end{aligned}$$

In other words, we are spending at a higher level than our budget plan indicates, and we are not as far along as we should be (i.e., we have not completed as much work as we should have). We can also use SPI to calculate the time variance TV if we realize that the scheduled time, ST, should conceptually be in proportion to (EV/PV): $\text{ST} = (\text{AT})(\text{EV}/\text{PV})$. Since $\text{TV} = \text{ST} - \text{AT}$, then $\text{TV} = (\text{AT})((\text{EV}/\text{PV}) - 1) = (\text{AT})(\text{SPI} - 1)$. (This can be derived through simple trigonometry.)

It is, of course, quite possible for one of the indicators to be favorable while the other is unfavorable. We might be ahead of schedule and behind in cost, or vice versa. There are six possibilities in total, all illustrated in Figure 10.3. The scenario shown in Figure 10.2, where both SV and CV are negative, is captured in arrangement *d* of Figure 10.3. The example immediately above, which also results in negative values of SV and CV, is arrangement *c* of Figure 10.3. Barr (and others) combines the two indexes, CPI and SPI, to make a type of "critical ratio" (described further in Chapter 11) called the Cost–Schedule Index (Barr, 1996, p. 32).

$$\begin{aligned}
\text{CSI} &= (\text{CPI})(\text{SPI}) \\
&= (\text{EV}/\text{AC})(\text{EV}/\text{PV}) \\
&= \text{EV}^2/(\text{AC})(\text{PV})
\end{aligned}$$

In our case,

$$\begin{aligned}
&= \$(1,500(2/3))^2/(1,350)(1,500) \\
&= \$1,000,000/2,025,000 \\
&= 0.49
\end{aligned}$$

As Barr writes, $\text{CSI} < 1$ is indicative of a problem.

One can continue the analysis to forecast the future of this work unit under the condition when no measures are taken to correct matters. The cost to complete the work unit can be estimated as the budgeted cost of the entire unit, less the EV to date, adjusted by the CPI to reflect the actual level of performance. The BAC in our example is \$1,500. The earned value to date (EV) is $\$1,500 \times 2/3 = \$1,000$. The estimated cost to complete (ETC), assuming the same cost efficiency level, can be projected as:

$$\begin{aligned}
\text{ETC} &= (\text{BAC} - \text{EV})/\text{CPI} \\
&= \$(1,500 - 1,000)/0.74 \\
&= \$676
\end{aligned}$$

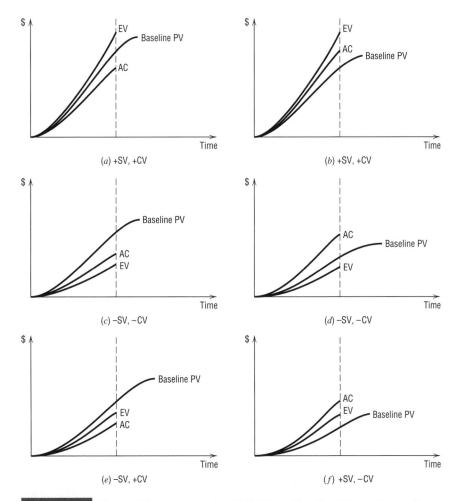

FIGURE 10.3 Six possible arrangements of AC, EV, and baseline PV resulting in four combinations of positive and negative schedule variance (SV) and cost variance (CV). (Figure 10.2 is arrangement *d*.)

The estimated EAC—and we use Barr's term (1996) rather than Microsoft's FAC (forecast at completion) or any of the many other names in the literature—is the amount expended to date (AC) plus the estimated cost to complete (ETC):

$$\begin{aligned} EAC &= ETC + AC \\ &= \$676 + 1,350 \\ &= \$2,026 \end{aligned}$$

rather than the original estimate of $1,500. For a complete description of this approach to estimating the total cost of a work unit, or a set of work units, see Barr (1996) and the Flemming and Koppelman works. We also could consider the ETC as a probabilistic number, and, given upper and lower bounds and an estimated distribution for ETC, we can easily apply simulation to find a distribution for EAC.

The **PMBOK** also considers two other ways to calculate ETC. If you assume that the team is now going to do all the future work at the originally budgeted rate, then $ETC = BAC - EV$. Another possible assumption is that the team will do all the future work at a rate that considers both the cost and schedule deviations to date, in which case $ETC = (BAC - EV)/(CPI)(SPI)$ or just $(BAC - EV)/CSI$. Recognize that if the team is behind schedule, this implies a crash schedule to catch up, which will further inflate the costs.

7.4.2.2

Note: The PV for each task would normally be known from the WBS and budget for the project tasks. However, when distributing PV over the scheduled time for a task (e.g., 3 weeks) for comparison to EV for monitoring purposes during the actual project, consideration should be given to how each task's EV is going to be determined. For example, if the PV is assumed to be generated in proportion to the time spent on the task, then the use of a 0–100 percent rule for EV will result in the project always appearing behind schedule. This is fine if the person monitoring the project understands that this difference of measurement methods is the cause of the "behind schedule" appearance. However, an alternative approach would be to distribute the PV for each task in the same manner that the EV is going to be measured for each task, and then the comparison of the EV to the PV will be more realistic.

Thus far, the focus has been on measuring performance on a work unit rather than on the project as a whole. Where dealing with a specific work unit, the estimates of costs and time can be fairly precise. Even the estimate of percent completion can be made without introducing too much error when using, as we did earlier, the proportionality rule. Given the relatively short time frame and relatively small cost compared to the whole project, errors are not apt to be significant. Random errors in estimating will tend to cancel out, and we can aggregate the work unit data into larger elements, for example, tasks or even the whole project. (Bias in estimating is, of course, a different matter.) Although the measurement error may be minimal, for most projects, there is still no sound basis for estimating percent completion of the project as a whole.

Even if this aggregation is feasible, the use of EV analysis for forecasting project schedules and costs does not mean that the forecasts will make it possible to correct malperformance. The case for remediation is not hopeful. In a study of more than 700 projects carried out under Department of Defense contracts, the chances of correcting a poorly performing project more than 15 percent complete were effectively nil (Flemming et al., 1996).

Project Management in Practice

Using Earned Value to Monitor Governmental Archiving and Records Costs

Governmental institutions are drowning in data, and doing their best to digitize all this data for not only current use but for future patrons in decades and even centuries to come. The challenge is immense—consider all the agencies such as courthouses, offices, universities, libraries, and at all levels: city, county, state, federal. Beyond this, there are about 4500 types of file formats to contend with—pdf, jpg, doc, mpeg, m4v, wpl, etc., as well as computer-aided designs and drawings and photos. Which ones should be standardized on and for which types of records? And what of the unknown future technologies—how will they access these obsolete, if not antique, formats?

In spite of the massive need, funding for the task is difficult to obtain given the many competing priorities. The U.S. National Archive and Records Administration (NARA) is conducting a project to preserve email message, memos, electronic documents and files created by government agencies. The budget could soar to as much as $1.4 billion over the project life cycle.

However, a Government Accountability Office (GAO) report on the project found that development costs could end up more than doubling for the project. The GAO blamed the cost overruns on the weak application of standard EV management principles and predicted that the situation wouldn't improve without their use: "Without more useful earned value data, NARA will remain unprepared to effectively oversee contractor performance and make realistic projections of program costs." The GAO report made 11 recommendations to NARA, including engaging senior NARA leadership and oversight officials to ensure that EV data are used for decision making.

Questions

1. The GAO report seemed to say that EV data was available but not actually used for decisions. What data do you imagine was being created?

2. Why do you think the EV data wasn't being used?

3. What use do you suspect is being made of EV data in the projects of other federal agencies? What about state, county, or city agencies?

Source: K. Hunsburger, "One for the Ages." *PM Network*, Vol. 25.

The study concludes that if the beginning of the project was underestimated and took longer and cost more than the plan indicated, there was little or no chance that the rest of the project would be estimated more accurately (p. 13ff). For relatively small deviations from plan, the PM may be able to do a lot of catching up.

If the EV chart shows a cost overrun or scope underrun, the PM must figure out what to do to get the system back on target. Options include such things as borrowing resources from activities performing better than expected, or holding a meeting of project team members to see if anyone can suggest solutions to the problems, or perhaps notifying the client that the project may be late or over budget. Of course, careful risk analysis at the beginning of the project can do a great deal to avoid the embarrassment of notifying the client and senior management of the bad news.

Example: Updating a Project's Earned Value

We use a simple example to illustrate the process of determining the baseline budget and interim EV and actual costs for a project. Table 10.1 presents the basic project information and updated information as of day 7 in the project. The planned AON diagram is shown in Figure 10.4, where path **a–c–e** is the critical path, with project completion expected at day 10. What has actually happened in the project is that the first activity, **a**, took 4 days instead of the planned 3 days to complete, delaying the start of both activities **b** and **c**. Activities **b** and **d** are proceeding as expected, except of course for their 1-day delay in initiation, but anyway, path **a–b–d** was not the critical path for the project.

Activities **a** and **b** are both completed, and their actual costs are shown in Table 10.1. (The costs to date for activities **c** and **d** are not known.) However, due to its delay, activity **a** cost $80 more than budgeted. Hence, the PM is trying to cut the costs of the remaining activities, and we see that activity **b** came in $30 under budget, which helps but does not fully offset the previous overrun.

TABLE 10.1   **Earned Value Example (today is day 7)**

Activity	Predecessors	Days Duration	Budget, $	Actual Cost, $
a	—	3	600	680
b	a	2	300	270
c	a	5	800	
d	b	4	400	
e	c	2	400	

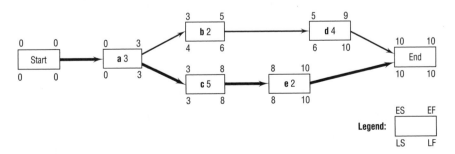

FIGURE 10.4   Example AON diagram.

Day

Activity	0	1	2	3	4	5	6	7	8	9	10
a		300		300							
b					150	150					
c					400				400		
d							200			200	
e										200	200
Total		300		300	550	150	200		400	400	200
Cum. Total		300	300	600	1150	1300	1500	1500	1900	2300	2500

FIGURE 10.5 Example baseline (PV) budget using the 50–50 rule.

The baseline budget (PV) (Figure 10.5) using the 50–50 rule is graphed in Figure 10.7 (solid line) where the BAC is listed as $2,500. The project's status and EV as of day 7 are given in Figure 10.6 and shown in Figure 10.7 as a dotted line. Included in the figure is the actual cost (AC, the dashed line in Figure 10.7) for the two completed activities. As shown in Figure 10.7, the SV is currently 0 and the CV is $1,500 − 950 = +550$.

But notice how these figures do not give a very accurate picture of project progress. The EV up to now has been trailing the baseline and has only caught up because the 50–50 rule doesn't have any activity beginning or ending at day 6; however, with expediting activity **c**, we may in fact be back on schedule by day 8. The CV, however, is highly affected by the fact that actual costs are not recorded until the activity is 100 percent complete, combined with the impact of the 50–50 rule. The result is that the baseline and EV cost figures will tend to converge when activities begin, but the actual costs will lag them considerably. Even though the proportionality rule would more accurately delay the aggregation of EV costs, there would still be a positive bias if the actual costs were not calculated until the activities were completed. It would be more accurate, but considerably more complex, to apportion actual costs according to percentage activity completion. These effects are illustrated further in some of the problems at the end of the chapter.

Day

Activity	0	1	2	3	4	5	6	7	8	9	10
a		300			300						
b						150	150				
c						400					
d								200			
e											
EV		300			300	550	150	200			
Cum. EV		300	300	300	600	1150	1300	1500			
Actual Cost					680		270				
Cum. AC		0	0	0	680	680	950	950			

FIGURE 10.6 Example status at day 7.

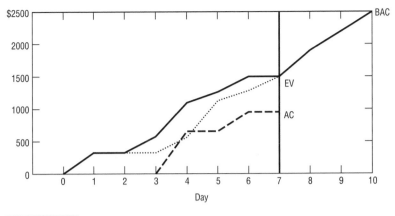

FIGURE 10.7 Example earned value chart at day 7.

MSP Variance and Earned Value Reports

Figure 10.8 shows an EV budget for the Career Day project described in Chapter 6. It includes all the budget, actual, and EV figures for each work package in the project, as well as projections at completion. The budget was generated as a standard report from MSP. (Similar reports are available through most other PC project management software packages.) Note that the project is reported on at the work package level. The first two tasks, *Contact Organizations* and *Banquet and Refreshments*, have been completed, and the third task, *Publicity and Promotion*, is currently underway. Note that in the first task, the fifth

Name	PV	EV	AC	Sch. Variance	Cost Variance	BAC	FAC	Variance
Contact Organizations	$3797.00	$3980.00	$3920.00	$183.00	$60.00	$3980.00	$3920.00	$60.00
Print forms	$645.00	$645.00	$645.00	$0.00	$0.00	$645.00	$645.00	$0.00
Contact organizations	$840.00	$840.00	$728.00	$0.00	$112.00	$840.00	$728.00	$112.00
Collect display information	$660.00	$660.00	$660.00	$0.00	$0.00	$660.00	$660.00	$0.00
Gather college particulars	$520.00	$520.00	$520.00	$0.00	$0.00	$520.00	$520.00	$0.00
Print programs	$687.00	$870.00	$922.00	$183.00	($52.00)	$870.00	$922.00	($52.00)
Print participants' certificates	$445.00	$445.00	$445.00	$0.00	$0.00	$445.00	$445.00	$0.00
Banquet and Refreshments	$1220.00	$1220.00	$1200.00	$0.00	$20.00	$1220.00	$1200.00	$20.00
Select guest speaker	$500.00	$500.00	$500.00	$0.00	$0.00	$500.00	$500.00	$0.00
Organize food	$325.00	$325.00	$325.00	$0.00	$0.00	$325.00	$325.00	$0.00
Organize liquor	$100.00	$100.00	$100.00	$0.00	$0.00	$100.00	$100.00	$0.00
Organize refreshments	$295.00	$295.00	$275.00	$0.00	$20.00	$295.00	$275.00	$20.00
Publicity and Promotion	$2732.00	$2297.75	$2039.00	($434.25)	$258.75	$3010.00	$2870.00	$140.00
Send invitations	$700.00	$700.00	$560.00	$0.00	$140.00	$700.00	$560.00	$140.00
Organize gift certificates	$330.00	$330.00	$330.00	$0.00	$0.00	$330.00	$330.00	$0.00
Arrange banner	$570.00	$570.00	$570.00	$0.00	$0.00	$570.00	$570.00	$0.00
Contact faculty	$280.00	$280.00	$280.00	$0.00	$0.00	$280.00	$280.00	$0.00
Advertise in college paper	$165.00	$82.50	$65.00	($82.50)	$17.50	$165.00	$165.00	$0.00
Class announcements	$99.00	$0.00	$0.00	($99.00)	$0.00	$220.00	$220.00	$0.00
Organize posters	$588.00	$335.25	$234.00	($252.75)	$101.25	$745.00	$745.00	$0.00
Facilities	$200.00	$0.00	$0.00	($200.00)	$0.00	$200.00	$200.00	$0.00
Arrange facility for event	$52.00	$0.00	$0.00	($52.00)	$0.00	$52.00	$52.00	$0.00
Transport materials	$148.00	$0.00	$0.00	($148.00)	$0.00	$148.00	$148.00	$0.00

Project: Career Day
Date: 3/24

◻ Critical   ——— Progress   ◆ Milestone
▨ Noncritical   ▽▽▽ Summary   ◇ Rolled up

FIGURE 10.8 MSP budget sheet for Career Day project (cf. Chapter 6).

work package, "Print Programs," finished early (PV < EV). The first four work packages under *Publicity and Promotion* have been completed, but the fifth and seventh are only partially finished. The sixth work package has not been started, nor has the fourth task, *Facilities*, been started. A compressed Gantt chart is shown on the right side.

The three columns of data on the right, BAC, FAC, and Variance, are "Budget at Completion," "Forecast at Completion" (same as EAC), and the Variance or difference between BAC and FAC. For all activities that have been completed, BAC = EV and FAC = AC. Note that the final variance is not calculated for tasks that are incomplete; see "Advertise in college paper" and "Organize posters," for example. *Advertise in college paper* is 50 percent complete, and *Organize posters* is 45 percent complete. That is, for *Advertise in college paper*, the EV of $82.50 is 50 percent of the BAC. Similarly for *Organize posters*, $335.25 is 45 percent of the BAC of $745.00. When the two work packages are completed, however, and if there is still a CV, then BAC and FAC will no longer be equal. For a completed work package, the cost variance EV − AC = BAC − FAC.

Milestone Reporting

We referred earlier to milestone reports. A typical example of such a report is shown in Figures 10.9 and 10.10. In this illustration, a sample network with milestones is shown, followed by a routine milestone report form. A model top management project status report is illustrated in the next chapter. When filled out, these reports show project status at a specific time. They serve to keep all parties up to date on what has been accomplished. If accomplishments are inadequate or late, these reports serve as starting points for remedial planning.

Figure 10.9 shows the network for a new product development project for a manufacturer. A steady flow of new products is an essential feature of this firm's business, and each new product is organized as a project as soon as its basic concept is approved by a project selection group. If we examine Figure 10.9 closely, we see that the sign-off control boxes at the top of the page correspond with sequences of events in the network. For example, look at the bottom line of the upper network in Figure 10.9. The design of this product requires a sculpture that is formed on an armature. The armature must be constructed, and the sculpture of the product completed and signed off. Note that the sculpture is used as a form for making models that are, in turn, used to make the prototype product. The completion of the sculpture is signed off in the next-to-last box in the lower line of boxes at the top of the page.

The upper network in Figure 10.9 is primarily concerned with product design, and the lower network with production. The expected times for various activities are noted on the network, along with the various operations that must be performed. Figure 10.10 is a summary milestone report. Each project has a series of steps that must be completed. Each has an original schedule that may be amended for use as a current schedule. Steps are completed in actual times. This form helps program managers coordinate several projects by trying to schedule the various steps to minimize the degree to which the projects interfere with one another by being scheduled for the same facilities at the same time.

Burnup and Burndown Charts

Burnup and *burndown* charts are relatively new additions to the PM's arsenal of tools to help monitor overall project progress. Their popularity stems from increased interest in Agile Project Management approaches as well their intuitive nature. A burndown chart is created with scope on the vertical axis and time on the horizontal axis. The remaining work that needs to be completed to finish the project at various points in time is plotted on

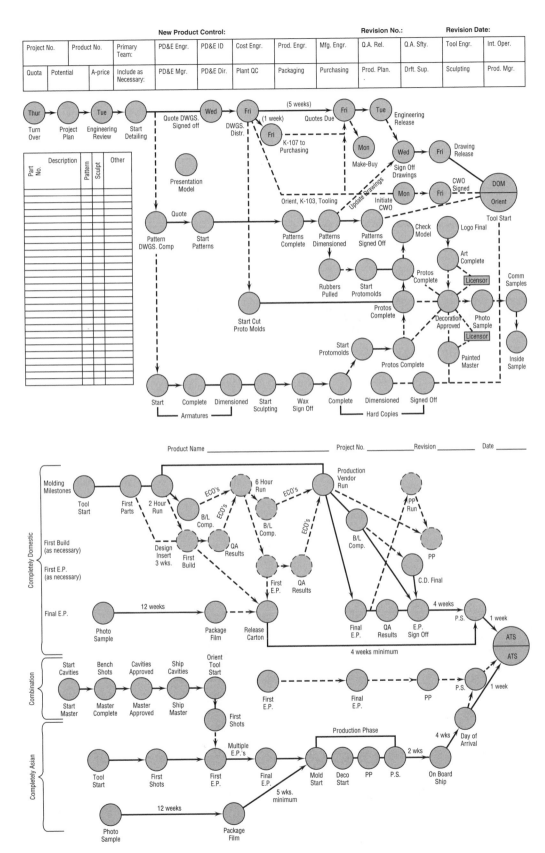

Project No.	Product No.	Primary Team:	PD&E Engr.	PD&E ID	Cost Engr.	Prod. Engr.	Mfg. Engr.	Q.A. Rel.	Q.A. Sfty.	Tool Engr.	Int. Oper.
Quota	Potential	A-price	Include as Necessary:	PD&E Mgr.	PD&E Dir.	Plant QC	Packaging	Purchasing	Prod. Plan.	Drft. Sup.	Sculpting	Prod. Mgr.

FIGURE 10.9   Sample project network with sign-off control.

NAME						PROJECT PLAN	ENGR. REVIEW	DESIGN REVIEW	QUOTE QUES.	PAT SCULP COMPL.	PAT SCULP COMPL	QUOTES DUE	MAKE BUY
PROJECT NO.	PRODUCT NO.	MFG SOURCE	TURNOVER		ORIGINAL								
A = PRICE	QUOTA	POTENTIAL			CURRENT								
					ACTUAL								

ENGR. RELEASE	PROJECT REVIEW	RELEASE DWGS.	TOOL START	PHOTO SAMPLES	INSIDE SAMPLES	PKG. FILM	INSTR. LAYOUT	INSTR. FILM ART	FINAL PARTS	FIRST EP	FINAL EP	EP SIGN- OFF	ORIENT PS	OBS	PROD. PILOT	PT SIGN- OFF	PROD. START	ATS

FIGURE 10.10 Milestone monitoring chart for Figure 10.9.

Project Management in Practice

Success through Earned Value at Texas Instruments

When Texas Instruments, Inc. wanted an imaging system designed for their Accounts Receivable department that would interface with their mainframe accounts receivable system, they turned to ViewStar Corporation to design it. Several leading edge technologies were desired, so ViewStar compiled the WBS from which to plan the budget and track actual spending. However, the planned budget exceeded the contract funds available. In order to match the overall budget to the contract funds, the budget for selected early-on tasks was arbitrarily reduced because top management wanted to win this contract.

As the contract progressed, the underbudgeted items showed up quickly in the EV chart, as illustrated next. Although funds were being expended at the planned rate, progress wasn't keeping up with the plan. However, with special attention to

meeting *only* key requirements for later project tasks, EV began to climb back toward plan. Near the very end of the project, the client asked for additional technology, which ViewStar easily provided in trade for Texas Instruments completing some of the high-earned-value production tasks themselves, thereby bringing the project in only 1 percent over budget.

Questions

1. Isn't arbitrarily reducing the available budget for tasks dangerous? What was ViewStar's probable strategic thinking here?
2. What would be the motivation of a project team that immediately falls behind schedule?
3. How did the trade late in the project between ViewStar and Texas Instruments probably operate?

Source: T. Ingram, "Client/Server, Imaging and Earned Value: A Success Story," *PM Network*, Vol. 9.

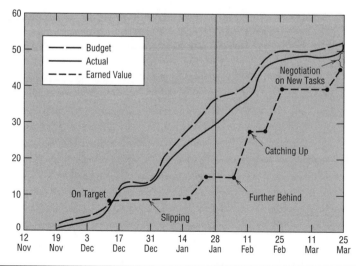

the chart, which creates a downward sloping line. The slope of the plotted line corresponds to the rate of progress with a steeper line being associated with a greater rate of progress. Based on an estimate of the future slope of the line, the time of projection completion can be estimated.

While a burnup chart contains the same axes as the burndown chart, two different lines are plotted on it. The first set of data plotted is the amount of work completed to date, and the second set of data is the total amount of work, including scope changes, yet to be completed. Both burnup and burndown charts provide the PM with a straightforward approach for monitoring and communicating overall project progress. The choice of one chart versus the other is a matter of personal preference.

The next section of this chapter, which considers computerized project management information systems (PMISs), contains several other examples of project reports.

Summary

In this chapter, we reviewed the monitoring function, relating it to project planning and control, and described its role in the project implementation process. The requirements for monitoring were discussed, in addition to data needs and reporting considerations. Finally, some techniques for monitoring progress were illustrated.

Specific points made in the chapter were:

- It is important that the planning–monitoring–controlling cycle be a closed-loop cycle based on the same structure as the parent system.

- The first task in designing the monitoring system is to identify the key factors in the project WBS to be monitored and to devise standards for them. The factors should concern results, rather than activities.

- Project reports are of three types: routine, exception, and special analysis.

- Project reports should include an amount of detail appropriate to the target level of management with a frequency appropriate to the need for control (i.e., probably not weekly or other such regular basis). More commonly, reports occur near milestone dates.

- Three common project reporting problems are too much detail, poor correspondence to the parent firm's reporting system, and a poor correspondence between the planning and monitoring systems.

- The EV chart depicts scheduled progress, actual cost, and actual progress (EV) to allow the determination of spending, schedule, and time variances.

Glossary

Computer Paralysis Excessive fascination or activity with the computer rather than the project itself such that the project suffers.

Cost (or Spending) Variance The budgeted cost of the work performed less the actual cost of the work performed.

Earned Value An approach for monitoring project progress that relies on the budgeted cost of activities completed to ascribe value.

Information Overload Having an excess of information so that the information desired is difficult to locate.

Monitor To keep watch in order to take action when progress fails to match plans.

Schedule Variance The budgeted cost of work completed less the budgeted cost of work scheduled at this time.

Time Variance The scheduled time for the work completed less the actual time.

Variance A deviation from plan or expectation.

Questions

Material Review Questions

1. Define *monitoring*. Are there any additional activities that should be part of the monitoring function?

2. Identify the key factors that need to be considered when setting up a monitoring system.

3. List some factors that would be difficult to monitor.

4. Describe routine reports and some problems with them.

5. What are the primary difficulties experienced in the design of project reports?

6. Describe the three variances of an EV chart and explain their significance.

7. Can you identify other symptoms of computer misuse besides those in Section 10.4?

8. What is the purpose of "earned value"? How would the progress of the project as a whole be calculated?

9. Describe the various ways that EV can be found.

Class Discussion Questions

10. Discuss the benefits of timely, appropriate, detailed information. How can a value be assigned to these characteristics?

11. What are the advantages for a PM of having a computerized system over a manual one? The disadvantages?

12. A more intensive, and extensive, monitoring system is needed in project management than in a functional organization. Why?

13. The EV chart is an attempt to put the three-dimensional concept of Figure 1.1 (see Chapter 1) into a two-dimensional format. Is it successful? What is missing?

14. How might a variance be traced back to its source?

15. Is it unethical, in an attempt to avoid a "shoot-the-messenger" response, to simply not mention bad news?

16. Which method of estimating EV seems the most accurate? Which one would you recommend? Why?

Exercises

1. Find the schedule and cost variances for a project that has an actual cost at month 22 of $540,000, a scheduled cost of $523,000, and an EV of $535,000.

2. A sales project at month 5 had an actual cost of $34,000, a planned cost of $42,000, and a value completed of $39,000. Find the cost and schedule variances and the CPI and SPI.

3. A software development project at day 70 exhibits an actual cost of $78,000 and a scheduled cost of $84,000. The software manager estimates a value completed of $81,000. What are the cost and schedule variances and CSI? Estimate the time variance.

4. A project to develop a county park has an actual cost in month 17 of $350,000, a planned cost of $475,000, and a value completed of $300,000. Find the cost and schedule variances and the three indexes.

5. A consulting project has an actual cost in month 10 of $23,000, a scheduled cost of $17,000, and a value completed of $20,000. Find the schedule and cost variances and the three indexes.

6. A project to develop technology training seminars is 5 days behind schedule at day 65. It had a planned cost of $735,000 for this point in time, but the actual cost is only $550,000. Estimate the schedule and cost variances. Re-estimate the variances if the actual cost had been $750,000.

7. Given an activity in an advertising project whose planned cost was $12,000 but actual cost to date is $10,000 so far and the value completed is only 70 percent, calculate the cost and schedule variances. Will the client be pleased or angry?

8. For the following test marketing project at week 6:

   a. Ignore the far right "% Complete" column, and using the 50–50 percent completion rule for PV and EV, calculate the cost, schedule, and time variances. Also calculate the CPI, SPI, CSI, and the ETC and EAC.

   b. Repeat the calculations in a, but now using the "% Complete" column. Assume that the PV values are based on time proportionality but the "% Complete" values for EV are from the workers actually doing the tasks.

Activity	Predecessors	Duration (weeks)	Budget, $	Actual Cost, $	% Complete
a: Build items	—	2	300	400	100
b: Supply stores	—	3	200	180	100
c: Create ad program	a	2	250	300	100
d: Schedule ads	a	5	600	400	20
e: Check sale results	b, c	4	400	200	20

9. At week 24 of a project to shoot a television commercial, what should the expenditures be? If the EV is right on schedule but the actual expenses are $9000, what are the cost and schedule variances? What are the three indexes, the ETC, and the EAC? Use the proportionality rule.

Activity	Pre-decessors	Duration (weeks)	Budget, $
a: Write script	—	6	900
b: Screen actors	—	6	1200
c: Select actors	a	6	1200
d: Contract studio	a	12	1800
e: Obtain props	b, c	14	1400
f: Schedule date	b, c, d	10	1500
g: Shoot commercial	d, e	16	800

10. Resolve Exercise 8b using MSP. Omit the calculations for CPI, SPI, and CSI.

11. Resolve the EV example of Table 10.1 by recomputing Figures 10.5 and 10.6 using the 0–100% rule.

12. Repeat Exercise 11 using the time proportionality rule and the following new data for % completion of each task: **a**: 100; **b**: 100; **c**: 80 (cost 600); **d**: 50 (cost 200); **e**: 0.

13. Draw an EV chart for the end of the first week (5 days) assuming the time proportionality rule for the project

illustrated in the following network diagram given the following costs and percentage completions:

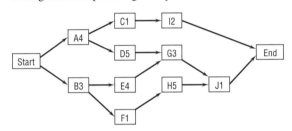

Activity	Budget, $	Actual, $	% Complete
A	600	400	100
B	300	450	100
C	150	100	100
D	750	60	10
E	400	150	30
F	100	50	100
G	200	0	0
H	400	0	0
I	100	0	0
J	100	0	0

14. The following project is at the end of its sixth week. Find the cost and schedule variances. Also find the CPI, SPI, ETC, and EAC for the project.

Activity	Predecessors	Duration (weeks)	Budget, $	Actual Cost, $	% Complete
a	—	2	300	400	100
b	—	3	200	180	100
c	a	2	250	300	100
d	a	5	600	400	20
e	b, c	4	400	200	20

Incidents For Discussion

Jackson Insurance and Title Company

Mark Suturana joined the Jackson Company 6 months ago. He is an experienced management information systems executive, who has been given the task of improving the responsiveness of Jackson's data processing group to the end user. After several months of investigation, Mark felt certain he understood the current situation clearly enough to proceed. First, approximately 90 percent of all end-user requests came to data processing (DP) in the form of a project, with the DP output either the final product of the project, or, more commonly, one step of a project. Accordingly, Mark felt he should initially direct his efforts toward integrating DP's approach to projects with the company's formal project management system.

It has been Mark's experience that most problems associated with DP projects revolve around poor project definition and inadequate participation by the end user during the system design phase. Typically, the end user does not become heavily involved in the project until the new system is ready to install. At that point, a great deal of work is required to adapt the system to meet end-user requirements. Mark decided to institute a procedure that put end-user cooperation and participation on the front end of the project. The idea was to define the objective and design of the system so thoroughly that implementation would become almost mechanical in nature rather than an introduction to the end user of "his or her new system."

Mark also recognized that something had to be done to control the programming quality of DP's output. A more effective front-end approach to DP projects would subject DP managers to more intense pressure to produce results within user's needs, including time constraints. Mark was concerned that the quality of the DP output would deteriorate under those conditions, especially given the lack of technical expertise on the part of end users and outside PMs. To solve this problem, Mark recommended the creation of a DP quality assurance (QA) manager who would approve the initial steps of the projects and review each additional step. The QA manager would have the authority to declare any step or portion of the output inadequate and to send it back to be reworked.

Question

Is this a good control system for DP? Why or why not? Does it also represent a good control point for company projects using DP to accomplish one portion of the project objective? What would be your answer if you were a non-DP PM? Might scope creep become a problem under this new system? If so, how should Mark control it?

The U.S. Army Corps of Engineers

The U.S. Army Corps of Engineers has contracted with a medium-size excavation firm to construct a small series of three earthen dams as part of a flood control project in North Carolina. For economic reasons, dams #1 and #2 have to be constructed at the same time and dam #3 can be built only after #1 and #2 are completed. There is also a very important scheduled completion date that has to be met (relating to next year's flood season). The project is being handled by Bryan Johnson, who has been with the company for about a year.

This is a new job for Bryan in that he had never before headed more than one project at a time. About 3 months into the building of dams #1 and #2, he began to notice an information problem. He had supervisors from dams #1 and #2 reporting to him, but he never knew how far along they were in relation to each other. Since dam #3 cannot be built until both dams are fully complete, he cannot tell if it will be started on time and therefore completed on time. Realizing that the situation was becoming serious, he began to wonder about how he could coordinate the projects. How could he tell where the projects were in relation to each other? How far were they *jointly* behind? Bryan's major problem was his inability to monitor and record the dual projects effectively.

Question

What would you recommend to Bryan?

Continuing Integrative Class Project

Devise a plan for monitoring the project tasks. Then create an EV table and chart to fill out as the project progresses. Unless outside resources are substantial, the main "costs" you will be tracking will be labor hours to complete the tasks. Generate the PV history for the project, the cumulative PV, and the EAC. Decide how you will determine the EV for the tasks as they progress. For example, worker estimates, 50–50, what?

Bibliography

Alderton, M. "The Case of the Troubled Project." *PM Network*, September 2013.

Anbari, F. T. "Earned Value Project Management Method and Extensions." *Project Management Journal*, December 2003.

Back, W. E., and K. A. Moreau. "Information Management Strategies for Project Management." *Project Management Journal*, March 2001.

Barr, Z. "Earned Value Analysis: A Case Study." *PM Network*, December 1996.

Brandon, D. M., Jr. "Implementing Earned Value Easily and Effectively." *Project Management Journal*, June 1998.

Evans, J. R., and W. M. Lindsay. *Management for Quality and Performance Excellence*, 9th ed. Florence, KY, 2012.

Flemming, Q. W., and J. M. Koppelman. *Earned Value Project Management*. Upper Darby, PA: Project Management Institute, 1996.

Flemming, Q. W., and J. M. Koppelman. "The Earned Value Body of Knowledge." *PM Network*, May 1996.

Flemming, Q. W., and J. M. Koppelman. "Forecasting the Final Cost and Schedule Results." *PM Network*, January 1996.

Flemming, Q. W., and J. M. Koppelman. "Taking Step Four with Earned Value: Establish the Project Baseline. *PM Network*, May 1995.

Flemming, Q. W., and J. M. Koppelman. "Taking Step Three with Earned Value: Estimate and Budget Resources." *PM Network*, January 1995.

Flemming, Q. W., and J. M. Koppelman "The 'Earned Value' Concept: Back to the Basics." *PM Network*, January 1994.

Hatfield, M. A. "The Case for Earned Value." *PM Network*, December 1996.

Jay, A. "How to Run a Meeting." *IEEE Engineering Management Review*, Winter 1995, reprinted from the *Harvard Business Review*, March–April 1976.

Kidder, T. *The Soul of a New Machine.* Boston: Little, Brown, 1981.

Knutson, J. "How to Prepare and Conduct a Project Review." *PM Network*, October 1996.

Kwak, Y. H. and F. T. Anbari. "History, Practices, and Future of Earned Value Management in Government: Perspectives from NASA." *Project Management Journal*, February 2012.

Levine, H. A. "PM Software Forum." *Project Management Journal*, 1987 in (all issues). See "Hints for Software Selection," June and December 1987.

Libratore, M. J., and B. Pollack-Johnson. "Factors Influencing the Usage and Selection of Project Management Software." *IEEE Transactions on Engineering Management*, May 2003.

Mekhilef, M., and J. S. Le Cardinal. "A Pragmatic Methodology to Capture and Analyse Decision Dysfunctions in Development Projects." *Technovation*, April 2005.

Nevison, J. M. "Creative Time Wasting." *PM Network*, November 1995.

Project Management Institute. *A Guide to the Project Management Body of Knowledge*, 5th ed. Newtown Square, PA: Project Management Institute, 2013.

Project Management Institute. *Software Survey.* Newtown Square, PA: Project Management Institute, 2001.

Singletary, N. "What's the Value of Earned Value?" *PM Network*, December 1996.

Thamhain, H. J. "The New Product Management Software and Its Impact on Management Style." *Project Management Journal*, August 1987.

The following case illustrates how easily a project can get into massive trouble when the funder changes policies, responsibilities, or managers on a project and the contractor fails to monitor and control these events. Because the terminology is rather specialized, it tends to mislead the reader into focusing on the technology instead of the crucial events happening on the project. There are also a great number of players in the project, and keeping them straight takes careful documentation. Finally, the case raises legitimate questions about how formally to manage and control a project that is in serious trouble when the funder is disposed to be informal and casual about activities, until it comes time to pay the bill.

Case

The Project Manager/Customer Interface[3]

E. Filliben and J. L. Colley, Jr.

Reggie Brown, B&W Nuclear Service Company's (BWNS) project manager for Nita Light and Power's Green Meadow

[3]Copyright The Darden Graduate Business School Foundation, Charlottesville, Virginia. Reprinted with permission.

plant, reflected on the dilemma that had plagued him for over a year. His team had completed an outage for Green Meadow over a year ago last October. The project was originally designed as a fixed-price contract. Delays and an expanded scope, however, forced the outage to be changed to a time-and-materials job with a final price that was significantly higher than the original contract price. Now it was December, well over a year after the completion of the outage, and the bill had still not been paid in full. Insisting that it was not responsible for the enormous overrun, the utility refused to pay what BWNS's Special Products and Integrated Services Division was charging. Brown knew that maintaining a good relationship with the customer had to take priority over getting the bill paid.

Background

The Special Products and Integrated Services Division (SPIS) had been working with Nita Light and Power (NLP) since 1983. Relations with the utility remained favorable since then as SPIS performed a wide variety of services for NLP. In the summer last year, NLP sought a fixed-price contract for work to be performed by SPIS. The focus of the work was the imminent Fall refueling outage and steam-generator inspection. SPIS representatives worked with the utility to develop the fixed-price contract, which totaled approximately $500,000. The contract assumed that SPIS crews would work on all three of the utility's generators concurrently.

There were, however, several early signs of potential problems. Reggie Brown had concerns about delays even before arriving on site in late August. He expected the badging process to take longer than the time allotted. Moreover, the SPIS team knew that it would need to relieve stress in the tight-radius U-bends (rows 1 and 2) and perform additional roll inspection, none of which was contemplated at the time of the original request. Representatives approached Stan Goodsen, NLP's site manager, at the end of summer and explained that the outage could not be completed under the original terms in light of anticipated delays and increased work scope. Goodsen asked for a budget and a schedule and gave the go-ahead for a time-and-materials billing.

Brown's fear of delay was realized. First, over Labor Day weekend, badging was completed and the equipment was staged as far as possible. The process of badging involved a series of tests, including site-security and health-physics qualification, psychological assessment, background check, fingerprinting, and drug screening. The utility did not want to accept SPIS's badging; it wanted to have its own separate process, which was quite time-consuming. Second, because of a delay in the chemical-channelhead decontamination, the three generators were not turned over to SPIS personnel on time. The first generator was turned over 10 days after the date promised. The second one was turned over 12 days later; the third, 9 days after that.

Recognizing that the cost of the work was going to exceed the contracted amount because of the utility's delay in turning over the generators, Brown, as project manager, made numerous attempts to clarify the situation early on and avert any problems down the road. First, he requested that some of the SPIS personnel be sent home while they were waiting for the other generators to become available. NLP officials refused, however, saying that the other two steam generators would be available shortly and that the field crew needed to be ready to go as soon as they were available. Second, Brown sent letters detailing the situation to the people identified on NLP's original purchase order as the utility's representatives. The only response was from on-site personnel like Goodsen, who gave repeated assurances that the SPIS contract had been switched to time-and-materials.

Initially, BWNS sent 40 engineers and technicians to start the work. When the project was in full swing, close to 100 BWNS personnel were on site. Although the original contract was for approximately $500,000 worth of work, the actual bill came to over $1,500,000. Some of the overrun was attributable to U-bend stress relief and added plug inspection, all part of the expanded scope. Much of the overrun, however, was caused by underutilization of the personnel who were on site waiting for initial access to the generators. The outage was completed 44 days after it began, 22 days longer than originally anticipated (see Exhibit 1).

Green Meadow Purchasing Procedures

Complicating the overrun situation was the fact that the utility was in the process of converting its purchasing procedures from a centralized to a decentralized program. The Contract Administrative Group, located at NLP's corporate headquarters, was originally responsible for all initial contract negotiations; all added–scope issues such as delays had formerly been handled by the on-site technical people. Over the years the entire purchasing process had been quite informal, however, especially given SPIS's long-term relationship with NLP. Some years ago, SPIS had, for example, completed a multimillion-dollar project at Green Meadow without any purchase order whatsoever. Now, under the new procedures, the individual generating plants would be responsible for handling the entire purchasing process. Unfortunately, SPIS was never adequately informed of the changes.

Under NPL's new procedures, Lou Mayhew was assigned to the on-site Contract Administration Group. He was to be SPIS's main contact for contract negotiations. Because the SPIS team had worked at Green Meadow on two previous outages and was not aware of the purchasing reorganization, it followed the same procedures it had used before. Although SPIS personnel knew that Mayhew existed because he had participated in the technical presentations for both previous outages, both of those purchase orders had been signed downtown at the central office. As there was no indication that the procedures had changed, the original purchase order was sent to the central office.

Timeline	
August 31:	Verbal okay from Goodsen to go with a time-and-materials arrangement.
September 1:	Utility shut down. All three generators scheduled to be delivered. None ready.
September 11:	First generator to SPIS.
September 23:	Memo from Goodsen confirming 8/31 authorization.
September 23:	Second generator to SPIS.
October 2:	Third generator to SPIS.
October 14:	Outage complete.

EXHIBIT 1 The Project Manager–Customer Interface.

The Invoice

After the outage was completed, a price estimate was compiled in November. It totaled $1,600,000; additional services, worth an estimated $350,000, were provided at no cost. The estimate was sent to Bill Jones, a technical specialist who was Stan Goodsen's boss, with a carbon copy to Mel Carter in Purchasing. NLP personnel's initial reaction was that the estimate looked fine; because the utility had caused the considerable delay, SPIS was entitled to full reimbursement.

The release of the invoice estimate was followed by a meeting on site in February. Several representatives from SPIS sat down with Stan Goodsen and some technicians from the utility and presented them with an initial invoice for the outage. Throughout the process, SPIS's on-site personnel dealt extensively with Goodsen. Mayhew had been invited to the meeting but did not attend. Green Meadow's technical personnel agreed to accept the invoice "as is." With NLP's input, the actual bill was sent in February to Carter in the central office.

The utility usually paid its bills within 60 days. After 90 days, Reggie Brown still had not heard anything and was starting to get nervous. He recognized, however, that the bill had been sent with volumes of paper work, including the site sheets that had been signed daily by Goodsen, and he was sure that the utility's billing department was simply bogged down with paper work. Nevertheless, Brown decided to call the utility and inquire about the delay; he was assured that there was "no problem."

The utility eventually did send some money. By this October, SPIS had received a total of $1.2 million. Then, on October 17, Roger Roberts, regional sales manager for SPIS, received a letter from utility Vice President Rus Clemons requesting a meeting. On October 26, Roberts and Jacqueline Doyle, manager of Contract Management, traveled to the Green Meadow plant for a meeting. Reggie Brown, on a field assignment, was unable to attend. Neither Roberts nor Doyle knew quite what to expect.

The Negotiations

On the 26th, Roberts and Doyle met with three NLP officials, Sly Simmons, Lou Mayhew, and Mayhew's boss, Rick James. The committee from the utility informed the SPIS team that, because the original agreement had been a fixed-price contract, not only would the utility not pay any more money toward the $1.6 million SPIS said it owed, but also that BWNS owed Nita Light and Power $300,000 plus interest for the amount NLP had overpaid to date. Shocked, Roberts and Doyle responded with the memo from Stan Goodsen that converted the fixed-price contract to one for time and materials. Mayhew simply kept repeating one sentence, "The price is too high." From 9:00 a.m. to 2:00 p.m., in an extremely frustrating exchange, all that was accomplished was that the group finally agreed that the contract was on a time-and-materials basis. Once that agreement was reached, however, Mayhew alleged that SPIS had loaded the project with people.

The same group met again on November 9. At that meeting, Doyle and Roberts laid out the staffing proposal that was originally accepted by Green Meadow. Then they compared it with the job's actual staffing numbers, which were within two people

of the projections. Doyle then pointed out that the promised production rate, 20 tubes per hour, was also met, as corroborated by the site sheets. The problem leading to the large overrun was the delay in the utility's relinquishment of the generators. During this meeting, Doyle and Roberts also presented NLP officials with an invoice for $250,000 to cover some of the $350,000 in expenses that were never charged on the first invoice, bringing the total cost of the outage to roughly $1,850,000.

Because they believed that much of the impasse thus far was due to the lack of technical understanding of the commercial representatives NLP sent to negotiate, Doyle, Roberts, and Brown requested that Green Meadow's technical people be included in a third meeting. The technical people had agreed to accept the initial invoice "as is." All subsequent negotiations were conducted with commercial representatives, that is, the Contract Administration Group. These meetings were frustrating because the business group did not have a solid understanding of the technical aspects of the project and was, therefore, unsympathetic to SPIS's reasoning. During the third meeting, the utility's business representatives purportedly made a phone call to the technical people. SPIS later found out from on-site personnel, however, that the call was merely for show and that no attempt was made to include the technical group. Very little was resolved during the third meeting. The utility's technical and commercial people never met together to discuss the invoice.

In December, $650,000 was outstanding on the bill ($1,850,000 in total charges − $1,200,000 previously paid). NLP officials offered $400,000, bringing SPIS's total received to $1.6 million. In deciding how to handle the shortfall, Doyle knew she had to balance the competing interests of maximizing profit and nurturing this long-term customer relationship.

Long-Term Ramifications

The overrun had other serious ramifications for SPIS's relationship with Green Meadow. NLP's next project was a five-outage package worth approximately $8 million. For this package, Green Meadow proposed all new terms and conditions that strongly favored the utility. Following its proposal of other terms and conditions, SPIS received no response for almost 18 months. Doyle and Brown started pushing Mayhew and James, who essentially responded, "Take it or leave it." In February, SPIS went all out with its proposal for the five-outage package. Its proposal won the technical staff's recommendation and also offered the best price. Green Meadow decided not to award a contract for all five at once, however, but rather to award the contract for the first (April) outage only. Despite the SPIS proposal's technical and price advantages, NLP awarded the outage to Westinghouse because the latter agreed to the utility's terms and conditions.

Word in the industry was that Westinghouse had performed well on the April outage, coming in 8 hours ahead of schedule. Westinghouse did, however, contest $1 million after completing the outage.

Given the events of the past year, Doyle and Brown knew that SPIS faced an uphill battle for the remaining four outages. They reflected on the lessons they had learned and wondered how they could apply them in order to put the relationship with Nita Light and Power back on track.

Advice for Project Managers

In reflecting on SPIS's experience with NLP, Jacqueline Doyle provided some advice for project managers.

It is crucial to know who is the authorized agent on site for the utility. I thought Goodsen was authorized. He obviously was not. Always find out who needs to know about progress and deviations from plans. Keep that person informed.

Given the long-standing practice in the industry, it would not have been feasible to stop work in the middle. Building a relationship with the utility over the years means that you agree to work things out as partners. Invoices on a daily or at least weekly basis would have been a good idea in this case.

The biggest lesson, though, was to send documentation to, and to communicate with, the commercial personnel on a regular basis. This communication can be complicated by the tension that often exists between technical people and commercial people. So even though day-to-day communication with the on-site technical group appears congenial, one person should be appointed to communicate with the business managers.

Doyle also cited the following responsibilities of project management:

- Know who the decision makers are
- Ask the right questions of the right people
- Control the customer
- Get money for work performed
- Persevere

Questions

1. What did Brown and BWNS do well in this situation? What could have been done better?

2. What factors outside Brown's control interfered with his efforts to work with the utility?

3. What skills does it take to be an effective interface with the customer? Has this project been successful for BWNS?

4. In what ways did the project scope change? How can a company control scope change when the customer is so casual about the project, until it comes time to pay the bill?

5. Is the customer always right? Do you think any of the "common reporting problems" described at the end of Section 10.2 may have occurred here?

6. Should BWNS try to win back NLP's business *at this time*? How could BWNS eventually win back NLP's business?

The following reading describes the symptoms that upper managers need to monitor to make sure that the projects under their responsibility don't get off track. Too often, these managers abdicate project responsibility to the PM; yet, what could be more important than the success of strategic projects to keep or make the organization competitive? The article describes three major ways of monitoring projects; through the available metrics and clear symptoms, through meetings and milestones, and via an open-door culture.

Reading

Raise The Red Flags[4] S. A. Swanson

In businesses large and small, the executive suite carries an overwhelming list of responsibilities. When a company is trying to stay competitive—or just stay afloat—it's rare for CEOs, CIOs, and other executives to have a firm grasp on the day-to-day developments affecting the projects in their portfolio.

And that's a big mistake, given that the execution of strategic projects has a dramatic effect on an organization's success.

"One of the biggest pitfalls we have seen top executives make is abdicating their leadership role to the project management team," says Rick Warter, practice director at the San Francisco, California, USA office of Point B, a management consulting firm whose services include setting up project management offices (PMOs) for organizations. "The 'C-suite'

has to stay involved to reinforce what the business value of the project is."

When executives finally learn that a project is about to go off the rails, it can be too late to avert a crisis. But there are steps that upper management can take to facilitate communication with project teams—and to raise red flags in the early stages of a project's life cycle.

Sometimes Numbers Lie

Start by having an enterprise portfolio project management information system in place to ensure that relevant details are captured for all projects—in particular, those deemed necessary for achieving strategic corporate goals, says Bassam Samman, PMP, CEO and founder of CMCS, a portfolio and project management consultancy in Dubai, United Arab Emirates. "This will enable executives to have a single version of the truth of the status of all of those projects and thus do their own business intelligence analysis."

[4]Reprinted from *PM Network* with permission. Copyright Project Management Institute Inc.

Getting at the real truth behind project status is no easy task, though. For instance, critical-path method scheduling will provide important indicators of a project's health, but those indicators can be manipulated, Mr. Samman says.

Case in point: David Walton, founder and managing director of Bestoutcome, a project management consultancy in Slough, Berkshire, England, assessed the progress of a new e-commerce platform. While reviewing the project governance documentation, Mr. Walton found that the project manager had kept all status indicators at "green."

"This was despite a mutinous team, constantly missed deadlines, a poor-performing supplier and a constantly changing scope," he says.

It's common for executives to focus only on projects with obvious warning signs while ignoring the others. But there's a growing trend among executives to carefully review all projects, even those with excellent status reports, Mr. Samman says.

A savvy executive will also ask project teams to track the time spent on high-level tasks. It's a good indicator of where trouble areas may be occurring, says Joan Bever, managing director of the technology PMO at media conglomerate Tribune Company, Chicago, Illinois, USA.

"For instance, in some of our interactive development projects, we noticed there was not enough time spent in quality assurance testing," she says. "As a result, some of the product releases were experiencing a lot of bugs or didn't perform properly when faced with high-volume activity."

On the flip side, if the hours spent in a particular iteration are high, it may hint that the project is running behind schedule or is about to go over budget, Ms. Bever adds.

Other indicators of impending trouble can include the number of scope changes, budget variance and amount of labor spent managing the project, Mr. Warter says.

It's essential to look beyond those metrics, too, though. When tracking the progress of projects, a common error executives make is "getting lost in the numbers," Mr. Warter says. "It is more important to engage in a conversation with your project management team on how the project is going and what outcomes you are trying to achieve."

He advocates that executives conduct regular "360-degree reviews" of projects. Look beyond the triple constraints to external threats, strategic alignment and business readiness trends.

By analyzing that broader organizational context, executives can get a clearer indication of how a project is truly progressing, Mr. Warter says.

His company has gone through this exercise with many of its healthcare and financial services clients who are implementing core IT systems. In one case, the review allowed a CFO to turn an estimated one-year delay into a 3-month delay by allowing her to prioritize and resolve key issues the project was facing, he says.

Make Meetings and Milestones Work

At Conifer Health Solutions, a healthcare consultancy in Frisco, Texas, USA, vice president and CIO Chris Dyler makes sure there are frequent measurable milestones—every 6 weeks, at most.

"In my experience, projects end up in these troublesome positions because of a lack of succinctly defined success criteria, or because of lengthy timelines that do not quickly deliver measureable results," he says.

Even with the best project management and delivery team in place, projects that span more than 6 weeks without measurable results can easily find themselves in trouble, Mr. Tyler attests.

As an executive with little time to stay in tune with the day-to-day activities of a project, he says the most effective approach is to ensure the project has a work breakdown structure that facilitates meaningful status updates: "Factoring shorter milestones into the plan will likely increase costs of the overall project. But it will better allow for the agility needed to sustain accurate direction of the project, and alignment with the more fluid corporate strategies that are required to successfully run most companies today."

Ask the project manager probing questions that drive the necessary discussions to get at the root of any problems. Choose these questions wisely though; the most common mistake senior executives make is not asking the right ones, Mr. Walton says.

- Is there anything that keeps the project team up at night?
- Are there roadblocks you can help remove?
- How is the sponsor handling his or her role?
- How are you keeping stakeholders engaged and supportive?
- If it was your money, would you still do this project?
- How much contingency is left in terms of money and time?

A True Open-Door Culture

Although regular meetings are important, the ultimate goal is to have a project team that shares challenges as soon as they arise. You don't want them just waiting for a monthly update or steering committee meeting.

"Work with your team to create an escalation plan for executives when key issues arise, so you can be aware of trouble areas more quickly," Ms. Bever says. "To let a week expire without action is costly and demoralizing to a project team."

To create an environment where employees feel comfortable speaking up when something goes wrong, executives must do more than pay lip service to an open-door policy. Take an honest look at the culture that exists at your organization. Are employees receiving subtle messages that encourage them to camouflage red flags?

"Inevitably, projects have problems," Ms. Bever says. And when those problems arise, the executives' response sets the tone for how well the project team will keep them informed of future dilemmas.

"Some executives who have not been involved in projects before expect everything to be delivered on time and within budget," Mr. Walton says. "Projects deal with the future and uncertainty, and this is an unrealistic expectation."

If a project member is berated—or fired—for communicating problems on a project, the team will be reluctant to deliver additional bad news. That, in turn, leaves considerably less reaction time for resolving problems.

The Tribune Company, for one, made a concerted effort to create an environment where timely updates, both good and bad, were encouraged and expected, according to Ms. Bever.

"We actually started to celebrate some of our failures," she says. "We wanted the project team to understand that it is okay to make mistakes once in a while, because we were spending too much time on contingency planning and not enough time on delivering projects. Many of our project teams were paralyzed on projects due to the 'what-if' scenario mapping. A good balance of both good judgment and risk-taking was required to deliver on more projects and to move to our company ahead."

In addition, top executives need to remind the project team of their critical role in the organization.

"It's all about communication," Mr. Samman says. "They need to make it clear to the project team that they depend on the performance of those projects for making strategic decisions."

Make sure everyone understands the organization's vision and strategy—and that there are clear expectations for how projects must support those main objectives.

"When the project team has a clear understanding of the project expectations and priorities, it can keep executives informed on the particular facets that affect project budget, scope or delivery time," Ms. Bever says.

The key is getting that critical information when you need it most—before trouble occurs.

Questions

1. What period of time does the article imply becomes too long to monitor and correct a project that has gone off the tracks? Why?

2. Were you surprised at the critical questions suggested to managers for their PMs?

3. Explain why the top manager's reaction to a project problem is so important.

4. What's the danger for a manager in just monitoring a project's summary statistics, metrics, and status "indicators"?

5. Describe what a low level of time spent on a crucial task may indicate. What problems might a high level indicate?

CHAPTER 11

Project Control

In the previous chapter, we described the monitoring and information gathering process that would help the Project Manager (PM), the project owner, and the sponsor control the project. Control is the last element in the implementation cycle of planning–monitoring–controlling. Information is collected about system performance, compared with the desired (or planned) level, and action taken if actual and desired performance differ enough that the controller (manager) wishes to decrease the difference. Note that reporting performance, comparing the differences between desired and actual performance levels, and accounting for why such differences exist are all parts of the control process. In essence, control is the *act* of reducing the difference between plan and reality.

Although this chapter is primarily directed to the exercise of control by the PM, we must note that the project owner, or other project overseer reporting to upper management, also has a project control function. The aim of the project is to help achieve some strategic objective of the organization; thus, the project owner or project council charged with overseeing the project, must appraise the continuing value of the project in achieving those objectives. Using the information gained from monitoring the project, as well as information concerning changes in the organizational goals, resources, and strategy, this group may need to take some form of action (control) regarding the project, such as redirecting it, getting it back on track, or perhaps even terminating it.

A special kind of control is exercised through risk management. The group responsible for risk management, be it the project owner, the PMO, or a specific group devoted to the subject, may exert its actions on the project but also may act on the environment, the major source of risk for the project. As you will see, a great many of the things that can go wrong with project scope, cost, or schedule are the result of uncertainty. And the lion's share of the uncertainty has its source in systems that lie outside the project, its environment. When feasible, the group may act on these outside systems to decrease or remove threats to the project, but often they are beyond the group's influence. All that can be done is to act on the project in order to mitigate or counteract or enhance the actions of these external systems. In our opinion, far too little attention is given to risk identification and management.

As has been emphasized throughout this book, control is focused on three elements of a project—scope, cost, and time. The PM is constantly concerned with these three aspects of the project. Is the project delivering what it promised to deliver, or more? Is it making delivery at or below the promised cost? Is it making delivery at or before the promised time? It is strangely easy to lose sight of these fundamental targets, especially in large projects with a wealth of detail and a great number of subprojects. Large projects develop their own momentum and tend to get out of hand, going their own way independent of the wishes of the PM and the intent of the proposal.

Think, for a moment, of a few things that can cause a project to require the control of scope, costs, or time.

Scope

Unexpected technical problems arise.

Insurmountable technical difficulties are present.

Quality or reliability problems occur.

Client requires changes in system specifications.

Interfunctional complications and conflicts arise.

Technological breakthroughs affect the project.

Intrateam conflicts arise on interpretation of specifications, or solutions to technical problems.

Market changes increase or decrease the project's value.

Cost

Technical difficulties require more resources.

The scope of the work increases.

Initial bids or estimates were too low.

Reporting was poor or untimely. Budgeting was inadequate.

Corrective control was not exercised in time.

Input price changes occurred.

Time

Technical difficulties took longer than planned to solve.

Initial time estimates were optimistic.

Task sequencing was incorrect.

Required inputs of material, personnel, or equipment were unavailable when needed.

Necessary preceding tasks were incomplete.

Funder-generated change orders required rework.

Governmental regulations were altered.

These are only a few of the relatively "mechanistic" problems that can occur. Actually, there are no purely mechanistic problems on projects. All problems have a human element, too. For example, humans, by action or inaction, set a chain of events in motion that leads to a failure to budget adequately, creates a quality problem, leads the project down a technically difficult path, or fails to note a change in government regulations. If, by chance, some of these or other things happen (as a result of human action or not), humans are affected by them. Frustration, pleasure, determination, hopelessness, anger, and many other emotions arise during the course of a project. They affect the work of the individuals who feel them—for better or worse. It is over this welter of confusion, emotion, fallibility, and general cussedness that the PM tries to exert control.

Control is a necessary and inherent part of life in any organization. It is not helpful to think of control as coercive, though, at times, it may be. We prefer to think of control as the maintenance of ethical, goal-directed behavior. The PM is always subject to such eternal verities as the law of gravity, and the brute fact that the exercise of managerial control will result in distorting the behavior of subordinates. The job of the PM is to set controls that will encourage those behaviors/results that are deemed desirable and discourage those that are not. By and large, people respond to the goal-directedness of control systems in one of three general ways: (1) by active and positive participation and goal seeking; (2) by passive participation in order to avoid loss; and (3) by active but negative participation and resistance—usually not active resistance to the goal, but failure to undertake those activities that will result in goal achievement. Which of the three responses a given individual exhibits depends on several variables, including things such as the specific control mechanism used, the nature of the goal being sought, and the individual's basic tolerance for being controlled.

All of these problems, always indeterminate combinations of the human and mechanistic subsystems, call for intervention and control by the project owner and PM. There are infinite "slips 'twixt cup and lip'," especially in projects where the technology or the deliverables are new and unfamiliar, and PMs, like most managers, find control is a difficult function to perform. There are several reasons why this is so. One of the main reasons is that PMs, again like most managers, do not discover problems. Managers discover what has come to be known as a "mess." A "mess" is a general condition of a system that, when viewed by a manager, leads to a statement that begins, %#^@*&+#!" and goes downhill from there. It is the discovery of a mess that leads the PM to the conclusion that there is a problem(s) lurking somewhere around.

In systems as complex as projects, the task of defining the problem(s) is formidable, and thus knowing what to control is not a simple task. Another reason, control is difficult is because, in spite of an almost universal need to blame some person for any trouble, it is often almost impossible to know if a problem resulted from human error or from the random application of Murphy's Law. PMs also find it tough to exercise control because the project team, even on large projects, is an "in-group." It is "we," while outsiders are "they." It is usually hard to criticize friends or subject them to control. Further, many PMs see control as an ad hoc process. Each need to exercise control is seen as a unique event, rather than as one instance of an ongoing and recurring process. Whitten (1995) offers the observation that projects are drifting out of control if the achievement of milestones is being threatened. He also offers some guidelines on how to resolve this problem and bring the project back in control.

Because control of projects is such a mixture of feeling and fact, of human and mechanism, of causation and random chance, we must approach the subject in an extremely orderly way. In this chapter, we start by examining the general purposes of control. Then we consider the basic structure of the process of control. We do this by describing control theory in the form of a cybernetic control loop. While most projects offer little opportunity for the actual application of automatic feedback loops, this system provides us with a comprehensive but reasonably simple illustration of all the elements necessary to control any system. From this model, we then turn to the types of control that are most often applied to projects. The design of control systems is discussed as are the impacts that various types of controls tend to have on the humans being controlled. The specific requirement of "balance" in a control system is also covered, as are two special control problems: control of creative activities, and control of change.

All in all, it is our opinion that of all the major tasks of project management, control is the least understood. Most PMs are ill-at-ease while in the role of exercising control. Many seem to associate the notion of disciplinarian with control. A few simple suggestions might help. Avoid heavily criticizing people for actions they know (now) are wrong. A simple reminder will do. Avoid criticizing people in public under any circumstances. Recall, from time to time, that the people working for you are reasonably bright and almost never act out of malice—unless you have just violated the immediately preceding rule. Above all, remember that placing blame does not fix the problem. Fix first, blame later—if you still have the energy and "simply must."

Project Management in Practice

Regaining Control of Nuclear Fusion

Ben Margot / AP Photo

In 1996, the U.S. Dept. of Energy (DOE) initiated a project to build a National Ignition Facility (NIF) to help learn how to achieve a controlled, self-sustaining nuclear fusion reaction known as "ignition." The facility would require a 500,000-square-foot area to house 192 laser beams directed by mirrors mounted on a 10-story tall structure onto the center of a 33-foot-diameter concrete-shielded target chamber. The deadline was September 2001.

However, unexpected risks stymied the effort. First, El Niño rains flooded the worksite the following year. After construction resumed, workers then uncovered a 16,000-year-old mammoth, requiring an archaeological team to come on-site to excavate "Niffy," as they called him. But more importantly, two other factors stopped progress completely in 1999: (1) Laser installation was much more complex and demanded much higher cleanliness standards than could be provided. (2) Inadequate systems engineering greatly underestimated the engineering complexity and scope of the project.

To regain control, the DOE developed a new baseline with a bottom-up reassessment of costs, schedules, risks, and contingencies, which then had to be approved by the DOE and the U.S. congress. These estimates were then reviewed by outside scientific and technical experts to validate their accuracy. To ensure the project's performance at the level of best practice, the DOE adopted PMBOK standards and, in particular, an earned value system of cost and schedule management. After approval, 12,000 contracts were awarded to over 8,000 vendors, representing an almost $2 billion effort to complete the NIF, which proceeded smoothly to completion in 2009. The month after completion NIF successfully fired a 192-beam laser shot delivering 1.1 megajoules of infrared energy to the center of the target chamber, an historic level of energy all concentrated in a few billionths of a second.

The successful turnaround and control of the NIF project is attributed to the strategic use of project management principles, and resulted in the NIF winning the PMI 2010 Project of the Year award.

Questions

1. Why do you think the complexity of the task was so greatly underestimated?

2. Why weren't standard project management principles used from the start, do you suppose?

3. Based on the material in the chapter, what type of control did they employ here: cybernetic, go/no-go, or post-control? Justify your answer.

4. What tools from the chapter would have been useful to them in this project?

Source: K. Hunsberger, "Sparking Ignition," *PM Network*, Vol. 24.

11.1 | The Fundamental Purposes of Control

The two fundamental objectives of control are as follows:

1. The regulation of results through the alteration of activities.
2. The stewardship of organizational assets.

Most discussions of the control function are focused on regulation. The PM needs to be equally attentive to both regulation and conservation. Because the main body of this chapter (and much of the next) concerns the PM as regulator, let us emphasize the conservationist role here. The PM must guard the physical assets of the organization, its human resources, and its financial resources. The processes for conserving these three different kinds of assets are different.

Physical Asset Control

Physical asset control requires control of the *use* of physical assets. It is concerned with asset maintenance, whether preventive or corrective. At issue, also is the timing of maintenance or replacement as well as the quality of maintenance. Some years ago, a New England brewery purchased the abandoned and obsolete brewing plant of a newly defunct competitor. A PM was put in charge of this old facility with the instruction that the plant should be completely "worn out" over the next 5-year period, but that it should be fully operational in the meantime. This presented an interesting problem: the controlled deterioration of a plant while at the same time maintaining as much of its productive capability as possible. Clearly, both objectives could not be achieved simultaneously, but the PM met the spirit of the project quite well.

Physical inventory, whether equipment or material, must also be controlled. It must be received, inspected (or certified), and possibly stored prior to use. Records of all incoming shipments must be carefully validated so that payment to suppliers can be authorized. With the exploding growth of outsourcing (even within projects) and the development of supply chains, both domestic and global, the difficulties of physical asset control have grown enormously. The proper design and operation of supply chains, known as supply chain management, or SCM (see Meredith et al., 2013, Chapter 7; Lee, 2003), is imperative to business as well as project success these days. The same precautions applied to goods from external suppliers must also be applied to suppliers from inside the organization. Even details such as the project library, project coffee maker, project office furniture, and all the other minor bits and pieces must be counted, maintained, and conserved.

Human Resource Control

Stewardship of human resources requires controlling and maintaining the growth and development of people. Projects provide particularly fertile ground for cultivating people. Because projects are unique, differing one from another in many ways, it is possible for people working on projects to gain a wide range of experience in a reasonably short time.

While the measurement of physical resource conservation is accomplished through standard audit procedures, the measurement of human resource conservation is far more difficult. Devices such as employee appraisals, personnel performance indices, and screening methods for appointment, promotion, and retention are not particularly satisfactory devices for ensuring that the conservation function is being properly handled. The accounting profession has worked for some years on the development of *human resource accounting*, and while the effort has produced some interesting ideas, human resource accounting is not well accepted by the accounting profession.

Financial Resource Control

Though accountants have not succeeded in developing acceptable methods for human resource accounting, their work on techniques for the conservation (and regulation) of financial resources has most certainly resulted in excellent tools for financial control.

The techniques of financial control, both conservation and regulation, are well known. They include current asset controls, and project budgets as well as capital investment controls. These controls are exercised through a series of analyses and audits conducted by the accounting/controller function for the most part. Representation of this function on the project team is mandatory. The structure of the techniques applied to projects does not differ appreciably from those applied to the general operation of the firm, but the context within which they are applied is quite different. One reason for the differences is that the project is accountable to an outsider—an external client, or another division of the parent firm, or both at the same time.

The importance of proper conformance to both organizational and client control standards in financial practice and record keeping cannot be overemphasized. The parent organization, through its agent, the PM, is responsible for the conservation and proper *use of* resources owned by the client or owned by the parent and charged to the client. Clients will insist on, and the courts will require the practice of, *due diligence* in the exercise of such responsibility. While some clients may not be aware of this responsibility on the part of firms with whom they contract, the government is most certainly aware of it. In essence, due diligence requires that the organization proposing a project conduct a reasonable investigation, verification, and disclosure, in language that is understandable, of every material fact relevant to the firm's ability to conduct the project, and to omit nothing where such omission might ethically mislead the client. It is not possible to define, in some general way, precisely what might be required for any given project. The firm should, however, make sure that it has legal counsel competent to aid it in meeting this responsibility.

One final note on the conservationist role of the controller—the mind-set of the conservationist is often antithetical to the mind-set of the PM, whose attention is focused on the *use* of resources rather than their *conservation*. The conservationist reminds one of the fabled librarian who is happiest when all the books are ordered neatly on the library shelves. The PM, often the manager and controller at one and the same time, is subject to this conflict and has no choice but to live with it. The warring attitudes must be merged and compromised as best they can.

11.2 | Three Types of Control Processes

The process of controlling a project (or any system) is far more complex than simply waiting for something to go wrong and then, if possible, fixing it. We must decide at what points in the project we will try to exert control, what is to be controlled, how it will be measured, how much deviation from plan will be tolerated before we act, what kinds of interventions should be used, and how to spot and correct potential deviations before they occur. In order to keep these and other such issues sorted out, it is helpful to begin a consideration of control with a brief exposition on the theory of control.

No matter what our purpose in controlling a project, there are three basic types of control mechanisms we can use: "cybernetic" control, go/no-go control, and postcontrol. In this section, we will describe these three types and briefly discuss the information requirements of each. While few cybernetic control systems are used for project control, we will describe them here because they clearly delineate the elements that must be present in *any* control system, as well as the information requirements of control systems.

Project Management in Practice

Extensive Controls for San Francisco's Metro Turnback Project

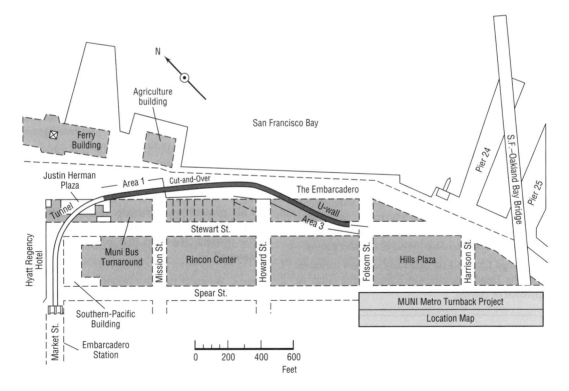

By the late 1990s, transportation in San Francisco's financial district, an area built over loose fill, which had once been part of the bay, had become a serious problem. The addition of the Bay Area Rapid Transit (BART), plus the usual buses, metro, cabs, and commuting traffic made for severe congestion in the district. To provide relief, the city launched the MUNI Metro Turnback Project to increase capacity and provide for future expansion. The 11-year planned project consisted of building a pair of twin tunnels 18 feet in diameter and a sixth of a mile long under the busiest street in San Francisco, connected to a

Given the decisions about what to control, the information requirements of a cybernetic controller are easy to describe, if not to meet. First, the PM must define precisely what characteristics of an output (interim output or final output) are to be controlled. Second, standards must be set for each characteristic. Third, sensors must be acquired that will measure those characteristics at the desired level of precision. Fourth, these measurements must be compared to a "standard" signal. Fifth, the difference between the two is sent to the decision maker, which, if it is sufficiently large, then transmits a signal to the effector that causes the operating system to react in a way that will counteract the deviation from standard.

Perhaps the most difficult task in creating a cybernetic control system is setting the standards for each element of output we wish to control. For some things, a single standard with a range of error that can be tolerated might be appropriate. In most cases, however, the standards must be set by the PM and/or the client and/or senior management about what is acceptable output at each stage of a project. These standards are a common subject for negotiation between the interested parties.

The Critical Ratio (CR, described in the next section) and Earned Value analysis (EV, in Chapter 10) can both be used in cybernetic control systems. For example, the cost and schedule variance indices (CPI and SPI) can be entered as standards and specific deviations from the desired cost/schedule results to date can be used to trigger an investigation and resulting control of the relevant process. Deviations from a desired level of CR might be used similarly.

Knowledge of cybernetic control is important because all control systems are merely variants, extensions, or nonautomatic modifications of such controls. Because most projects have relatively few mechanistic elements that can be subjected to classic cybernetic controls, this concept of control is best applied to tracking the system and automatically notifying the PM when things threaten to get out of control.

Human response to steering controls tends to be positive. Steering controls are usually viewed as helpful rather than as a source of unwelcome pressure if the controlees perceive themselves as able to perform inside the prescribed limits. Contrary to the popular song, it is not the "impossible dream" that motivates goal-seeking behavior, but rather a moderately good chance of success. Of course, response to steering control is dependent on the individual's acceptance of the goal as appropriate. Indeed, no control system is acceptable if the objective of control is not acceptable.

Go/No-Go Controls

Go/no-go controls take the form of testing to see if some specific precondition has been met. Most of the control in project management, if it exists at all, falls into this category. This type of control can be used on almost every aspect of a project. For many facets of the project's scope, cost, and time, it is sufficient to know that the predetermined specifications have been met. Certain characteristics of output may be required to fall within precisely determined limits if the output is to be accepted by the client. In regard to time and cost, there may be penalties associated with nonconformance with the approved plans. Penalty clauses that make late (or too early) delivery costly for the producer are often included in the project contract. Cost overruns may be shared with the client or borne by the project. Some contracts arrange for the first $X of cost overrun to be shared by client and producer, with any further overrun being the producer's responsibility. The number and type of go/no-go controls on a project are limited only by the imagination and desire of the contracting parties.

The project plan, budget, and schedule are all control documents, so the PM has a predesigned control system complete with prespecified milestones as natural control checkpoints. Extra milestones can also be inserted, such as special reviews to make sure the project is still on course to meet its return on investment goals, or whatever else might be involved in a continue/terminate decision. Control can be exercised at any level of detail that is supported by detail in the plans, budgets, and schedules. The parts of a new jet engine, for instance, are individually checked for quality conformance. These are go/no-go controls. The part passes or it does not, and every part must pass its own go/no-go test before being used in an engine. Similarly, computer programs are tested for bugs. The program passes its tests or it does not.

Go/no-go controls operate only when and if the controller uses them. In many cases, go/no-go controls function periodically, at regular, preset intervals. The intervals are usually determined by clock, calendar, or the operating cycles of some machine system. Such periodicity makes it easy to administer a control system, but it often allows errors to be compounded before they are detected. Things begin to go awry just after a quarterly progress check, for instance, and by the time the next quarterly check is made, some items may be seriously out of control. Project milestones typically do not occur at neat, periodic intervals; thus, *controls should be linked to the actual plans and to the occurrence of real events, not simply to the calendar*. Senior management should review reports on all projects at reasonably frequent intervals.

The PM must keep abreast of all aspects of the project, directly or through deputies. Competent functional managers understand the importance of *follow-up*, and the PM's work provides no exception. Control is best exerted while there is still time for corrective action. To this end, the PM should establish an *early warning system* so that potential problems can be exposed and dealt with before they turn into full-fledged disasters. One way to construct such an early warning system is to set up a project forecast data sheet. On this sheet, outputs or progress are forecast by period. Actual output or progress is then checked against the forecast, period by period. Sometimes projects, especially information system projects, get "stuck" in their progress, absorbing large quantities of resources but yielding no progress or value. Keil et al. (2010) call these "black hole" projects and offer a variety of suggestions to help turn them around.

As we have said before, for an early warning system to work, it must be clear that the messenger who brings bad news will not be shot and that anyone caught sweeping problems and mistakes under the rug will be. As we have also said before, the most important rule for any subordinate is the Prime Law of Life on a project: Never let the boss be surprised! Controls have a tendency to terrorize the insecure and to induce high anxiety in everyone else. The result is avoidance, and avoidance is exactly what the PM cannot tolerate. Unless deviation from plan is discovered, it cannot be corrected. Therefore, a spirit of trust between superior and subordinate at all levels of the project is a prime requisite for the effective application of control.

Response to go/no-go controls tends to be neutral or negative. The reason appears to be related to the inherent nature of this type of control system. With go/no-go control systems, "barely good enough" results are just as acceptable as "perfect" results. The control system itself makes it difficult for the worker to take pride in high-quality work because the system does not recognize gradations of quality. In addition, it is all too common to be rather casual about setting the control limits for a go/no-go control; the limits should be very carefully set. While go/no-go control is the most frequent type of control exercised on projects, the impact of such control on the project team seems, to us, to be less negative because *project team performance* is the primary focus of control rather than specific items of work performed by individuals.

Phase-Gated Processes   One form of go/no-go control that has gained popularity is that of phase-gated processes (also known as stage gates, toll gates, quality gates, and so on). Rather than waiting until the project is completed, and then finding out that it doesn't achieve the objectives of the organization, the phase-gate process controls the project at

various points throughout its life cycle to make sure it remains on course and of value to the organization. This process is most commonly used for new product/service development projects where it is important to constantly evaluate the match between the changing, dynamic market and the changing nature of the new product/service under development. At the launch of the new development project, a series of "gates" are planned, whereby the project cannot continue with funding until each gate has been successfully passed.

In addition to being commonly applied in new product/service development projects, phase gates are also commonly employed in process improvement projects. For example, in the Six Sigma DMAIC (Define-Measure-Analyze-Improve-Control) methodology, each of the five phases serves as a project milestone, which in turn is frequently used as a tollgate to the next phase. More specifically, the progress and outcomes associated with the process improvement project are evaluated at the end of each phase to assess the merits of permitting the project to move on to the next phase. The extent to which organizational resources will continue to be allocated to the project is typically assessed at these milestones as well.

Although often placed at natural project milestones, there may be more or fewer gates than milestones, but the purpose is different—milestones are natural "end-of-phase" points within a project, whereas gates are meant to catch problems early on. The initial gates tend to be conceptual and performance-based, while the latter are more market oriented, such as whether we should commit to producing this prototype for the mass market. Figure 11.3 shows one PowerPoint slide from a presentation to senior management using a "quality-gate" system for reporting progress on the firm's projects.

Milestone Tracking
CRS-J3

Quality Gate Milestone Tracking		Q9	Q8	Q7	Q6	Q5	Q4	Q3	Q2	Q1
		Business Review	Req'ts	HLD	Release Commit	Iteration Planning	Handoff to Test	Test Complete	Perf Results	GA
Products/Programs										
CRS-J3	Std Interval		5/14	7/9	8/6		11/5	12/31	12/31	11/14
	Commit		5/14	6/4	7/9					
	Revised			6/8	7/22					
	Actual		5/14	6/8						
% Over (Under) Plan			0.0%	13.3%	0.0%		0.0%	0.0%	0.0%	0.0%
Developers: 3			Testers: 0		Architects: 2		July Dev, Test, Arch	3	8	2

- **Quality Gate 8 approved on 05/14**
- **Successfully completed the Design Documents and Annotated MRD**
- **Quality Gate 7 approved on 06/08**
- **Quality Gate 6 is targeted for 07/22 (original 07/09 – Delay is due to the COMMCO work planning)**
- **Revised Targets:**
  - Gate 4 – 08/25
  - Gate 1 – 10/13
  - Customer Commit – 10/14

Operations Update – Engineering
6/15
Page 16

FIGURE 11.3 A quality-gate application.

The criteria for passing each gate are developed in the project planning stage. There is a wide range of reasons for terminating a project midstream; for example, most of the benefits have already been achieved and further expenditures aren't justified, or the market potential of the project has changed substantially. Other possible reasons easily come to mind: critical personnel have left the organization, the project life cycle costs have gotten out of hand, a competitor has already come out with a better product at a cheaper price, and so on.

We recommend above that senior managers should review reports on all projects at frequent intervals. In actual practice, reporting on the progress of each project in terms of the project's phase gates appears to be a uniquely helpful approach for senior managers.

Discovery-Driven Planning and Learning Plans Another more recent type of go/no-go control has been proposed by McGrath et al. (1995) and Rice et al. (2008), which reverses the evaluation process. Instead of trying to determine whether the project is achieving the numbers it needs to at this stage of the project, it looks at how valid the initial assumptions now appear to be regarding the project: the market, the funder's needs, the progress that has been made, performance expected in the future, costs to date and expected at completion, schedule to date and expected at completion, and so on. An assumptions checklist for each stage is prepared with the most critical assumptions first and when the project reaches that stage, the assumptions are checked for validity. If a critical assumption is not met, the project must be replanned or the assumptions revised as appropriate. If no plan can satisfy all the revised assumptions, the project is terminated.

Information Requirements for Go/No-Go Controls Most of the input information needed to operate go/no-go project control has already been referenced directly or implied by the previous discussion. The project proposal, plans, specifications, schedules, and budgets (complete with approved change orders) contain all the information needed to apply go/no-go controls to the project. Milestones are often key events that serve as a focus for ongoing control activity. These milestones are the project's deliverables in the form of in-process output or final output. If the milestones occur on time, on budget, and at the planned level of quality, the PM and senior management can take comfort from the fact that things are proceeding properly.

Except for a few important projects, senior managers usually neither keep up with the day-to-day or week-to-week progress of work nor should they try. Senior management does, however, need a monthly or quarterly status review for all projects. The project status report contains a list of the important milestones for each project together with the status of each. If many of the projects are similar—such as construction projects or marketing projects, for example—the milestones will be of similar type, and one table can show the status of several projects in spite of the fact that each milestone may not be applicable to each and every project. The Elanco Animal Health Company, a division of Eli Lilly and Company, uses such a report. A generalized version of Elanco's Project Status Report is shown in Figure 11.4. The Gantt chart (see Chapter 8) is also a convenient way to present senior managers with information on project status.

The PM should ensure that the status reports given to senior management contain information that is current enough to be actionable (and always as accurate as required for control). Some firms are now putting such control information on the Internet to make it instantly available to all parties on a worldwide basis. Some guidelines for this approach are given in Seesing (1996). The PM is well advised to insist that status reports make clear implications of specific conditions where those implications might be overlooked—or not understood—by senior managers. If meetings between senior management and PMs are used to report project status and progress, it is critical to remember that the process employed in such meetings should not be punitive or intimidating. As we pointed out in Chapter 10, punitive meetings do far more damage than good.

Task	Project #1	Project #2	Project #3
Priorities set	C	C	C
PM selected	C	C	C
Key members briefed on RFP	C	C	C
Proposal sent	C	C	C
Proposal accepted as negotiated	C	C	C
Preliminary design developed	C	W/10	C
Design accepted	C	W/12	C
Software developed	C	NS/NR	N/A
Product test design	C	W/30	W/15
Manufacturing scheduled	C	NS/HR	W/8
Tools, jigs, fixtures designed	W/1	NS/HR	W/2
Tools, jigs, fixtures delivered	W/2	NS/HR	W/8
Production complete	NS/HR	NS/HR	NS/HR
Product test complete	NS/HR	NS/HR	NS/HR
Marketing sign-off on product	NS/HR	NS/HR	NS/HR

Notes:

N/A—Not applicable   W—Work in progress (number refers to month required)   NS—Not started

C—Completed   NR—Need resources   HR—Have resources

FIGURE 11.4   Sample project status report.

Postcontrol

Postcontrols (also known as postperformance controls or reviews, or postproject controls or reviews) are applied after the fact. One might draw parallels between postcontrol and "locking the barn after the horse has been stolen," but postcontrol is not a vain attempt to alter what has already occurred. Instead, it is a full recognition of George Santayana's observation that "Those who cannot remember the past are condemned to repeat it." Cybernetic and go/no-go controls are directed toward accomplishing the goals of an ongoing project. Postcontrol is directed toward improving the chances for *future* projects to meet their goals. The **PMBOK** recognizes the value of what is called "Organizational Process Assets" (OPA), and in the Project Time Management chapter there states: "Organizational Process Assets . . . include lessons learned knowledge base containing historical information regarding activities lists used by previous similar projects." (See Project Management Institute, 2013.)

2.1.4; 6.2.1.4

Postcontrols are seen as much the same as a report card. Whether reaction to postcontrol is positive, neutral, or negative seems to depend on the "grade" received. In cases where a series of similar projects must be undertaken, postcontrols are regarded as helpful in planning for future work, but considerable care must be devoted to ensuring that controls are consistent with changing environmental conditions. Changes in project management methods resulting from changes suggested and tested by the PMO are seen as very helpful, particularly if they result from project worker involvement. Postcontrol is applied through a relatively formal document that is usually constructed with four distinct sections.

The Project Objectives   The postcontrol report will contain a description of the objectives of the project. Usually, this description is taken from the project proposal, and the entire proposal often appears as an appendix to the postcontrol report. As reported here, project objectives include the effects of all change orders issued and approved during the project.

Because actual project performance depends in part on uncontrollable events (strikes, weather, failure of trusted suppliers, sudden loss of key employees, and other acts of God), the key initial assumptions made about risks during preparation of the project budget and schedule should be noted in this section. A certain amount of care must be taken in reporting these assumptions. They should not be written with a tone that makes them appear to be excuses for poor performance. At the same time, it is useful to remember that brevity is a virtue when writing postcontrol reports on routine projects unless the uncontrollable events are apt to occur with some frequency. While it is clearly the prerogative, if not the duty, of every PM to protect him- or herself politically, he or she should do so in moderation to be effective.

Milestones, Gates, and Budgets   This section of the postcontrol document starts with a full report of project performance against the planned schedule and budget. This can be prepared by combining and editing the various project status reports made during the project's life. Significant deviations of actual schedule and budget from planned schedule and budget should be highlighted. Explanations of why these deviations occurred will be offered in the next section of the postcontrol report.

The Final Report on Project Results   When significant variations of actual from planned project performance are indicated, no distinction should be made between favorable and unfavorable variations. Like the tongue that invariably goes to the sore tooth, project managers tend to focus their attention on trouble. While this is quite natural, it leads to complete documentation on why some things went wrong and little or no documentation on why some things went particularly well. Both sides, the good and the bad, should be chronicled here.

Recommendations for Performance and Process Improvement   The culmination of the postcontrol report is a set of recommendations covering the ways that future projects can be improved. Many of the explanations appearing in the previous sections are related to one-time happenings—sickness, weather, strikes, or the appearance of a new technology—these are not apt to affect future projects, although other, different one-time events may affect them. But some of the deviations from plan were caused by happenings that are very likely to recur. Examples of recurring problems might be a chronically late supplier, a generally noncooperative functional department, a habitually optimistic cost estimator, or a highly negative project team member. Provision for such things can be factored into future project plans, thereby adding to predictability and control. This is risk identification and management in practice. We cannot overemphasize the importance of this section. It is the critical element of the OPA.

Just as important, the process of organizing and conducting projects can be improved by recommending the continuation of managerial methods and organizational systems that appear to be effective, together with the alteration of practices and procedures that do not. In this way, the conduct of projects will become smoother, just as the likelihood of achieving good results, on time and on cost, is increased. In thinking about the ways to improve the management of future projects, it is essential to remember that we need not wait for the next generation of projects to introduce more effective methods for managing projects. We can usually introduce them when they are discovered, after clearing them with the PMO or whatever body controls the organization's project management protocol. Project management is a steadily evolving science. Thoughtful PMs and project workers help it evolve.

Postcontrol can have a considerable impact on the way projects are run. A large, market-driven company in consumer household products developed new products through projects that were organized in matrix form, but had a functional tie to the marketing division. PMs were almost always chosen from the marketing area. Members of the project team who represented R&D had argued that they should be given a leadership role, particularly early in the project's life. Marketing resisted this suggestion on the grounds that R&D

people were not market oriented, did not know what would sell, and were mainly interested in pursuing their own "academic" interests. After reading the perennial R&D request in a postcontrol report, the program manager of one product line decided to reorganize a project as requested by R&D. The result was not merely a successful project, but was the first in a series of related projects based on extensions of ideas generated by an R&D group not restricted to work on the specific product sought by marketing. Following this successful experiment, project organization was modified to include more input from R&D at an earlier stage of the project.

There is no need to repeat the information requirements for postcontrol here. It should be noted, however, that we have not discussed the postcontrol audit, a full review and audit of all aspects of the project. This is covered in Chapter 12. The postcontrol report is a major source of input for the postcontrol audit.

11.3 | The Design of Control Systems

Irrespective of the type of control used, there are some important questions to be answered when designing any control system: Who sets the standards? Will they achieve the project's goals? What output, activities, behaviors should be monitored? How timely must the monitoring be? How great must a difference between standard and actual be before it becomes actionable? What are the most appropriate actions for each situation? What rewards and penalties can be used? Who should take what action?

In addition to being sensible, a good control system should also possess some other characteristics.

- The system should be flexible. Where possible, it should be able to react to and report unforeseen changes in system performance.
- The system should be cost-effective. The cost of control should never exceed the value of control. One study (Heywood et al., 1996) has found that the cost of control in projects ranges from as much as 5 percent of total project costs for small projects to less than 1 percent for very large projects.
- The control system must be truly useful and satisfy the real needs of the project.
- The system must operate in an ethical manner.
- The system must operate in a timely manner. Problems must be reported while there is still time to do something about them and before they become large enough to destroy the project.
- Sensors and monitors should be sufficiently accurate and precise to control the project within limits that are truly functional for the client and the parent organization.
- The system should be as simple as possible to operate.
- The control system should be easy to maintain. Further, the control system should signal if it goes out of order.
- Control systems should be fully documented when installed, and the documentation should include a complete training program in system operation.

No matter how designed, all control systems we have described use feedback as a control process. Let us now consider some more specific aspects of control. To a large extent, the PM is trying to anticipate problems or catch them just as they begin to occur. The PM wants to keep the project out of trouble because upper management often bases their continuing funding decision on a milestone or stage-gate review of the project. If all is not going well, other technological alternatives may be recommended; or if things are going badly, the project may be terminated. Thus, the PM must monitor and control the project quite closely. Burba (2013) suggests setting the limits on various measures of project progress, as well as the actions that will be taken if these limits are breached, ahead of time such as in the Project Charter.

The control of scope, cost, and time usually requires different input data. To control scope, the PM may need specific documentation such as engineering change notices, test results, quality checks, rework tickets, scrap rates, and maintenance activities. Of particular importance here is carefully controlling any changes, usually increases, in scope due to *scope creep*: the natural inclination of the funder to change the deliverables as they obtain better information about their needs over time. Scope creep is not always the fault of the funder, however; sometimes the team members themselves, in an effort to do their best work, unwittingly increase the scope of the project. The PM must be constantly on guard to identify such changes. We will have more to say about this shortly.

For cost control, the manager compares budgets to actual cash flows, purchase orders, labor hour charges, amount of overtime worked, absenteeism, accounting variance reports, accounting projections, income reports, cost exception reports, and the like. To control the schedule, the PM examines benchmark reports, periodic activity and status reports, exception reports, AOA or AON networks, Gantt charts, the project schedule, EV graphs, and probably reviews the WBS.

The PM may find a particular activity perplexing or not understand why it is taking longer than it should or costing more than expected. An audit would provide the data to explain the unusual nature of the discrepancy. The PM may choose to do the audit or have the organization's accountant perform the work.

A large variety of new tools have recently become available for the control of projects such as benchmarking, quality function deployment, stage-gate processing, self-directed teams, the design-build approach, and so on. Thamhain (1996) describes these tools and offers suggestions for selecting and implementing them according to individual circumstances of the project.

Some of the most important analytic tools available for the PM to use in controlling the project are variance analysis and trend projection, both of which were discussed in Chapter 10. The essence of these tools is shown in Figure 11.5. A budget, plan, or expected growth curve of time or cost for some task is plotted. Then actual values are plotted as a dashed line as the work is actually finished. At each point in time, a new projection from the actual data is used to forecast what will occur in the future if the PM does not intervene. Based on this projection, the manager can decide if there is a problem, what action alternatives exist, what they will cost and require, and what they will achieve. Trend projection charts can even be used for combined scope/cost/time charts, as illustrated in Figure 11.6.

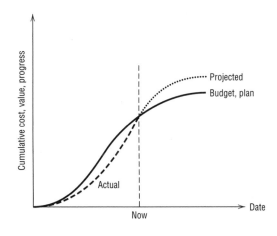

FIGURE 11.5 Trend projection.

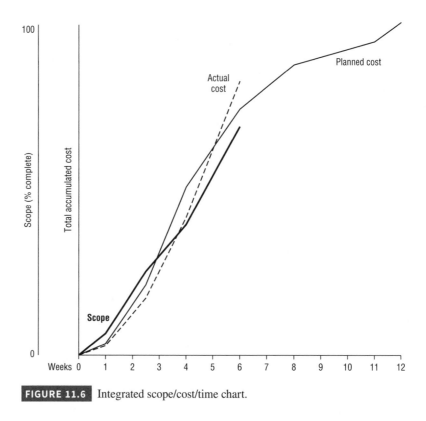

FIGURE 11.6 Integrated scope/cost/time chart.

Critical Ratio Control Charts

On occasion, it may be worthwhile, particularly on large projects, for the PM to calculate a set of CRs for all project activities. The CR is

$$(\text{actual progress}/\text{scheduled progress}) \times (\text{budgeted cost}/\text{actual cost})$$

The CR is made up of two parts—the ratio of actual progress to scheduled progress and the ratio of budgeted cost to actual cost. *Caeteris paribus*, to quote any economist whoever lived,[1] a ratio of actual to scheduled progress greater than 1 is "good." If the ratio is less than 1, it is "bad." Similarly with the ratio of budgeted to actual cost—never forgetting *caeteris paribus*. Assuming moderately accurate measures for each element of each ratio (an assumption that rivals *caeteris paribus* for its *chutzpa*), the CR is a good measure of the general health of the project. Note that the CR is the product of the two separate ratios. This way of combining the two underlying ratios weights them equally, allowing a "bad" ratio for one part to be offset by an equally "good" ratio in the other. The PM may or may not agree that this results in a valid measure of project "health."

Consider Table 11.1. We can see that the first task is behind schedule but also has a correspondingly lower cost, which is below budget. Hence, even though the project is running late, the CR shows no problems. If lateness is, in fact, no problem for this activity, the PM need take no action. The second task is on budget but its physical progress is lagging. Even if there is slack in the activity, the budget will probably be overrun. The third task is on

---

[1] For those who have never been blessed with a course in economics, this Latin phrase means "other things being equal." The phrase is the economist's equivalent of the physicist's frictionless plane. It does not and cannot exist in fact.

Project Management in Practice

Tracking Scope Creep: A Project Manager Responds

Dear Editor:

The two-part *Scope Creep* article in the Winter and Spring issues of *Today's Engineer* presented an interesting case study. The engineering-only solution, however, misses the bigger issue—lack of a formal project management process. It is unfortunate that the need for formal project management is omitted from the article. A formal project management process is the cornerstone of on-time and on-schedule projects. Such a process includes:

- A formal project plan development process
- A tracking system capable of providing variance analysis data
- Managing project scope, schedule, and resource changes throughout the project life cycle.

This case study depicts an all-too-familiar scenario:

1. An engineer is selected as PM—usually with no formal project management training.

2. The project team is composed of primarily engineers—marketing and other functional organizations are viewed as project outsiders, rather than team members, and do not participate in the planning process.

3. Project objectives and deliverables are poorly defined—usually by engineering—including only engineering deliverables.

4. A comprehensive work breakdown structure, task completion criteria, and network diagram are nonexistent—progress measurement is therefore somewhat arbitrary and difficult to ascertain.

5. Task duration estimates are probably determined by someone other than the task owner—making estimates invalid.

6. The project schedule is pasted together to look good and match target dates—missing the opportunity to use critical path method (CPM) to develop a credible schedule.

7. Resource requirements, including people and budget, are guesses—usually without the benefit of using a comprehensive CPM-developed preliminary schedule.

8. A risk management plan does not exist—most project risks are treated as surprises.

9. The project plan is not validated and baselined by the project sponsor—missing the opportunity to obtain team and sponsor commitment prior to implementation.

10. A formal project tracking and change management system does not exist—impossible to track a project without a plan to measure progress against and to manage changes.

Project management, like engineering, is a discipline that must be learned. Project management is not for everyone. It requires a different skill set than, say, engineering or marketing.

Questions

1. **Comment on the role of the engineer as an "accidental" PM.**

2. **Which numbered item in the list leads, do you think, to scope creep?**

Source: J. Sivak, "Scope Creep: A Project Manager Responds," ©IEEE. Reprinted with permission from *Today's Engineer*, Vol. 1.

TABLE 11.1	(Actual Progress/Scheduled Progress) × (Budgeted Cost/Actual Cost)								
Task Number	Actual Progress		Scheduled Progress		Budgeted Cost		Actual Cost		Critical Ratio
1	(2	/	3)	×	(3	/	2)	=	1.00
2	(2	/	3)	×	(6	/	6)	=	0.67
3	(3	/	3)	×	(4	/	6)	=	0.67
4	(3	/	2)	×	(6	/	6)	=	1.50
5	(3	/	3)	×	(6	/	4)	=	1.50

schedule, but cost is running higher than budget, creating another probable cost overrun. The fourth task is on budget but ahead of schedule. A cost saving may result. Finally, the fifth task is on schedule and is running under budget, another probable cost saving.

Tasks 4 and 5 have CRs greater than 1 and might not concern some PMs, but the thoughtful manager wants to know why they are doing so well (and the PM may also want to check the information system to validate the unexpectedly favorable findings). The second and third activities need attention, and the first task may need attention also. The PM may set some CR control limits intuitively. The PM may also wish to set different control limits on different activities, controlling progress in the critical path more closely than on paths with high slack.

The CR can also be used with EVs, bearing in mind that "progress" in EV nomenclature is expressed in monetary units, and we only have three measures instead of four. Clearly, actual progress is EV, scheduled progress is PV, and actual cost is AC. But what then is budgeted cost? Logically, this would be planned value, but if we use PV for budgeted cost, we wind up with the same dilemma we had for Task 1 in Table 11.1: Although the project was substantially late, the CR indicated that everything was fine. It is preferable to use EV and then the CR does show that there is a problem. As a result, the CR becomes precisely the cost schedule index, CSI.

The use of EV for budgeted cost doesn't completely solve the possibility of a misleading CR, unfortunately. There can still be instances where the EV is less than the planned value (a problem!) but the actual cost is so much less than the planned value that the critical ratio is still greater than 1, or where the actual cost exceeds the planned value (a problem) but the EV sufficiently exceeds the planned value that the CR is again greater than 1.

Charts can be used to monitor and control the project through the use of these ratios; Figure 11.7 shows an example. Note that the PM will ignore CRs in some ranges and that the ranges are not necessarily symmetric around 1.0. Different types of tasks may have different control limits. Control charts can also be used to aid in controlling costs (Figure 11.8), work force levels, and other project parameters.

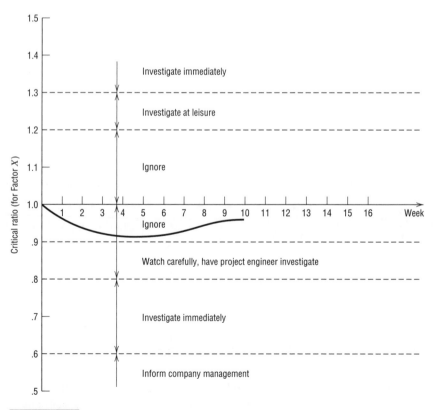

FIGURE 11.7 Critical ratio control limits.

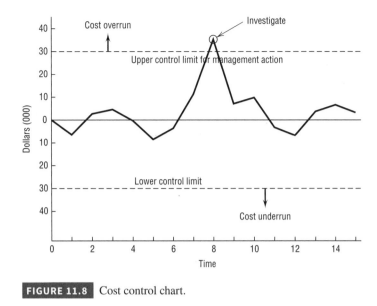

FIGURE 11.8 Cost control chart.

Benchmarking

Another addition to the arsenal of project control tools is *benchmarking*, or making comparisons to "best in class" practices across organizations. Benchmarking controls the project management *process* rather than the project itself. This concept is explained and demonstrated in many relevant publications (see, e.g., Byrne, 1999; Thamhain, 1996). One case study (Gupta et al., 1997) points out the importance of including the customer's perceptions in the benchmarking study or else the data may be accurate but not give the firm any insight into why customers don't recognize their top-level quality. A benchmarking study (Ibbs et al., 1998) to generate input for the Project Management Maturity Model measured project processes, tools, techniques, and practices across a range of industries, the six life-cycle phases, and the nine knowledge areas of the **PMBOK**. Graphs were then generated to show the distribution of scores in these industries across the various factors.

Table 3.1

Another study (Toney, 1997) benchmarked Fortune 500 firms in terms of best practices and key success factors for projects being conducted in functional organizations. The conclusions of the study were reported in four major areas, as described next. These areas are typically the responsibility of the PMO.

- **Promoting the benefits of project management**   Have the PM report to a senior executive with multifunctional authority. Identify and nurture senior officers who champion project management. Conduct training in project management. Participate in project management benchmarking forums. Partner with educational and professional project management organizations. Use a variety of sources to communicate the strategic benefits of project management to senior management.

- **Personnel**   Pay for project management skills and taking on high-risk projects through bonuses, stock options, and other incentives. Employ team-based pay. Create job descriptions and career paths for PMs. Develop a checklist for PM selection and evaluation criteria. Offer PM development programs. Design PM retention programs. Offer advanced training and continuing education for PMs. Design a broadly based PM evaluation process based on project skills, funder satisfaction, negotiation skills, and so on.

- **Methodology**   Standardize the organization's project management methods. Integrate the project management processes. Develop project management into a core competence of the organization. Develop a standard process for change management. Develop a standard process for conflict management.

- **Results of project management**   Measure project performance and the strategic impact of the project on the organization. Link the strategic portfolio elements with the tactical project elements to realize the true benefits. Measure the value received from the project. Measure the riskiness of the project. As Mihalic (2013, p. 5) notes: "We need to develop solid performance metrics that focus on measuring the 'outcome' and business benefit of projects (i.e., meeting strategic goals), not just their executable (tactical) 'output.'" Identify the lessons learned from the project.

We are adding another "best practice" to be handled by the PMO:

- **On-course improvement in project management practices**   When improvements are suggested to the current project management protocol, the PMO should review them immediately and, if approved, institute them as soon as possible.

11.4   Control of Change and Scope Creep

In earlier chapters, we discussed the fact that the original plans for projects are almost certain to be changed before the projects are completed. Project changes, we noted earlier, result from three basic causes: (1) uncertainty about the technology on which the work of the project or its output is based; (2) an increase in the knowledge base or sophistication of the client/user leading to scope creep; and (3) a modification of the rules applying to the process of carrying out the project or to its output. All three of these causes are especially common in software projects, where scope creep is legendary. When either the process or output of a project is changed, there is almost always a concomitant change in the budget and/or schedule. For example, the lead contractor on the Dallas Cowboys' new Cowboys Stadium, the largest domed stadium in the world, experienced 1,500 scope changes during construction, all oriented toward enhancing the fans' experience (Hunsberger, 2010). Since there were over 250 subcontractors building the new stadium, all of whom had to be coordinated, retasked, and rescheduled, these changes resulted in major increases in the budget, which were even further exacerbated by the constraint that the project could *not* be delayed!

Conversations in recent years with more than 500 PMs have convinced us that coping with changes and changing priorities is perceived as the most important single problem facing the PM—or if not the most important, certainly the most irritating. When a senior financial officer of a toy manufacturing firm makes an offhand, negative comment about the color of a toy, and triggers a "total redesign" of the toy, thereby invalidating an already approved design, schedule, and budget, the PM and the design artist may consider murder. (It is probable that a knowledgeable jury would find such action justifiable.)

Our casual, open-ended question was "What kind of problem arising on projects bugs you the most?" Coping with change (scope design, schedule, personnel, resources, etc.) had the largest response in our open-ended query. Adding support to this view, a "Voices on Project Management" poll of project managers by PMI (2012, p. 7) asking what the #1 reason projects fail resulted in 37 percent saying scope creep/changing requirements, 20 percent saying inadequate stakeholder involvement, and 16 percent saying insufficient sponsor or executive support. Similarly, in a study of risk classes, frequency, and impact on project performance, Thamhain (2013) found that changing project requirements was not only the most frequent risk class but also had the most impact on project performance. Changes in the market or funder needs was a close second.

The most common changes are those due to the natural tendency of the client and project team members to try to improve the product or service. New demands and scope requirements become apparent to the client, which were not realized at the time of project initiation. Hunsberger (2011) agrees and attributes scope creep to just two reasons: (1) stakeholders only being consulted at the beginning of the project and (2) requirements changing due to new information about the needs of the project. New technologies become available or better ideas occur to the team as work progresses. As noted earlier, the later these changes are made in the project, the more difficult and costly they are to complete. Burba (2013) recommends that PMs frame the project in such a way that sponsors and clients can see for themselves what the trade-offs of a desired scope change are. Instead of telling the client "No," say "Sure, we can change the design. I'll get back to you with the schedule and budget impact of this change." Without control, a continuing accumulation of little changes can have a major negative impact on the project's schedule and cost.

Leffingwell (1997) suggests that interaction between the project team and the funder should be regularized by partnering. The funder may then take some official responsibility for helping to manage project scope. When the funder is a part of the parent organization, the problem is often more difficult. Jealousy, mistrust, and conflict among departments (e.g., the traditional battle between marketing and engineering) leads to uncontrolled scope creep and to inevitable delays and budget overruns (Gibson, 1998).

There is, however, no insurance against the risks associated with project changes. Total quality management and employee involvement will help if both the deliverable and the process by which it is to be produced are carefully studied by thoughtful teams that represent the interests of the major stakeholders in any project: the client, senior management, the project team, and the community. Since prevention of change is not possible, the PM's best hope seems to lie in controlling the process by which change is introduced and accomplished. Control of change is, therefore, one of the primary concerns of risk management. Heerkens (2014) cautions, however, that all project changes should be financially justified in terms of the positive economic benefits of the proposed change compared to the increased cost and delay in the project. That is, it isn't just a decision by the client, even if he or she is willing to pay for the change; it needs to be examined very carefully by the sponsor as well in terms of the change in strategic benefits and timing of those benefits for everyone.

Control of scope creep is accomplished with a formal *change control system*, which, in some industries, is a part of their *configuration management system* responsible for integrating and coordinating changes throughout the systems development cycle. The purpose of the formal change control system is to

- review all requested changes to the project (both content and procedures)
- identify all task impacts
- translate these impacts into project scope, cost, and schedule
- evaluate the benefits and costs of the requested changes
- identify alternative changes that might accomplish the same ends
- accept or reject the requested changes
- communicate the changes to all concerned parties
- ensure that the changes are implemented properly
- prepare monthly reports that summarize all changes to date and their project impacts

Project Management in Practice

Major Scope Creep in Boston's "Big Dig"

Robert Spencer/The New York Times/Redux Pictures

Boston's "Big Dig" highway/tunnel project is considered to be one of the largest, most complex, and technologically challenging highway projects in U.S. history. In early 2003, Boston's "Big Dig," originally expected to cost less than $3 billion, was declared complete after two decades and over $14 billion for planning and construction. This project was clearly one that offered little value to the city if it wasn't completed, so it continued far past what planners thought was a worthwhile investment, primarily because the federal government was paying 85 percent of its cost. With an estimated benefit of $500 million per year in reduced congestion, pollution, accidents, fuel costs, and lateness, but a total investment cost of $14.6 billion (a 470 percent cost overrun), it is expected to take 78 years to pay its costs back. The overrun is attributed to two major factors: (1) A major underestimate of the initial project scope, typical of government projects, and (2) lack of control, particularly costs, including conflicts of interest between the public and private sectors. One clear lesson from the project has been that unless the state and local governments are required to pay at least half the cost of these megaprojects, there won't be serious local deliberation of their pros and cons.

Questions

1. **What elements of the project do you think escalated about 400 percent?**

2. **What do you expect the outcome would have been if the city had been required to pay half the costs?**

Source: S. Abrams, "The Big Dig," *Kennedy School Bulletin*, Spring 2003, pp. 30–35; Project Management Institute, "Digging Deep," *PM Network*, Vol. 18.

The following simple guidelines, applied with reasonable rigor, can be used to establish an effective change control procedure. The guidelines can also be integrated into the risk management system as a way to manage the risks imposed by scope creep.

1. All project contracts or agreements must include a description of how requests for a change in the project's plan, budget, schedule, and/or deliverables will be introduced and processed.

2. Once a project is approved, any change in the project will be in the form of a *change order* that will include a description of the agreed-upon change together with any changes in the plan, budget, schedule, and/or deliverables that result from the change. For any but minor changes, a risk identification and analysis study should be performed. In order to study the potential impact of change, it is often possible to conduct a simulation study.

3. The PM must be consulted on all desired changes prior to the preparation and approval of the change order. The PM's approval, however, is not required.

4. Changes must be approved, in writing, by the client's agent as well as by an appropriate representative of senior management of the firm responsible for carrying out the project.

5. Once the change order has been completed and approved, the project plan should be amended to reflect the change, and the change order becomes a part of the project plan.

The process of controlling change is not complicated. If the project is large, a change control board needs to be constituted. This is a group representing all interested parties that processes all requests for change. For the typical small- or medium-sized project, however, the problem of handling change need not be complex. The main source of trouble is that too many PMs, in an attempt to avoid anything that smacks of bureaucracy, adopt an informal process of handling requests for change. Misunderstanding often arises from this informality, and the PM finds that the project becomes committed to deliver a changed output of extended scope, but will have to swallow the additional cost involved, and will have to scramble to meet the old, unchanged schedule.

The problems associated with dealing with change orders informally are particularly severe in the case of software and information system projects. The severity of the problem of dealing with change in software projects, it seems to us, is caused by two interrelated factors. First, software and information systems experts too often fail to explain adequately to the client the real nature of the systems they develop. Second, clients too often fail to make an adequate effort to understand the systems that become the lifeblood for their organizations. The development of *Agile* approaches for managing IT projects, or the use of the formal process for change suggested above, should help to reduce the degree of misunderstanding and disappointment.

A senior executive at a large industrial firm that carries out many projects each year sees control in a slightly different light. Noting that differences between plan and reality usually represent problems for project managers, he remarked: "If you are solving problems faster than they are arriving to be solved, you have the project under control. If not, you haven't."

Difficult as it may be, control is an important part of the PM's job on every project. Perhaps the most helpful advice we can give the PM is, in the language of the 1970s, to "hang loose." One effective PM of our acquaintance tells his project team, "I will not accept crises after 4:30 P.M. You are limited to one crisis per day. Crises are not cumulative. If

Project Management in Practice

Better Control of Development Projects at Johnson Controls

The Automotive Systems Group of Johnson Controls was having trouble controlling their product development programs with each project being managed differently, disagreements about who was responsible for what, projects failing because of rapid company growth, and new employees having trouble fitting into the culture. For a solution, they went to their most experienced and successful PMs and condensed their knowledge into four detailed procedures for managing projects. Because these procedures are now common to all projects, they can be used to train new employees, standardize practices, create a common language, tie together different company functions, create common experiences, act as implicit job descriptions, and create a positive overall project management culture.

The first procedure is project approval for authorizing the expenditure of funds and use of resources. The sales department must first provide a set of product/market information, including financial data, project scope, critical dates, and engineering resource requirements before management will approve the project. Thus, projects are now scrutinized much more closely before work is started and money spent—when more questions are asked and more people are involved, better decisions tend to be made.

The second procedure is the statement-of-work, identifying agreements, and assumptions for the project. Here, both the customer and top management must sign off before product design work begins, thereby reducing misunderstandings regarding not only product specifications, prices, and milestones but also intangible product requirements, explicit exclusions, and generic performance targets. Maintaining this documentation over the life of the project has helped avoid problems caused by late product changes from the customer, particularly for 3- to 5-year projects where the personnel rotate off the project. Customers have, however, been slow to agree to this level of documentation because it limits their ability to change timing, prices, and specifications late in the program when they are more knowledgeable about their needs.

The third procedure is the work breakdown structure, consisting of nine critical life-cycle phases running from definition through production. Included in each of these nine phases are four key elements: the tasks, the timing of each task, the responsible individuals, and the meeting dates for simultaneous engineering (a formalized procedure at Johnson Controls).

The fourth procedure is a set of management reviews, crucial to successful project completion. Both the content and timing of these reviews are specified in advance and progression to the next phase of a project cannot occur until senior management has approved the prespecified requirements, objectives, and quality criteria for that phase. The procedure also specifies questions that must be answered and work that must be reviewed by senior management.

Through the use of these procedures, which are updated and improved with each new project experience, the learning that occurs in the organization is captured and made useful for future projects.

Questions

1. **Summarize the unique way Johnson achieved control over their projects.**

2. **How did "scope creep" enter the projects in the past? Which procedure is now directed at controlling this effect?**

3. **Which of the four procedures is probably most critical to successful projects?**

4. **What is the term used in the chapter for the senior management review described in the fourth procedure?**

Source: W. D. Reith and D. B. Kandt, "Project Management at a Major Automotive Seating Supplier," *Project Management Journal*, Vol. 22.

you don't get yours in today, you do not get two tomorrow." All this is said, of course, with good humor. Team members understand that the PM is not serious, but his projects seem to progress with exceptional smoothness. Crises do occur from time to time, but everyone on the team works to prevent them by applying control in an effective and timely manner.

Controlling Creative Activities

Some brief attention should be paid to the special case of controlling research and development projects, design projects, and similar processes that depend intimately on the creativity of individuals and teams. First, the more creativity involved, the greater the degree of uncertainty surrounding outcomes. Second, too much control tends to inhibit creativity. But neither of these dicta can be taken without reservation. Control is necessarily neither the enemy of creativity nor, popular myth to the contrary, does creative activity imply complete uncertainty. While the exact outcomes of creative activity may be more or less uncertain, the process of getting the outcome is usually not uncertain. If the potential payoff for the creative activity is high, the need for careful risk management is also high.

In order to control creative projects, the PM must adopt one or some combination of three general approaches to the problem: (1) process review, (2) personnel reassignment, and (3) control of input resources.

Process Review   The process review focuses on the process of reaching outcomes rather than on the outcomes per se. Because the outcomes are partially dependent on the process used to achieve them, uncertain though they may be, the *process* is subjected to control. For example, in research projects, the researcher cannot be held responsible for the outcome of the research, but can most certainly be held responsible for adherence to the research proposal, the budget, and the schedule. The process is controllable even if the precise results are not.

Control should be instituted at each project milestone, an obvious opportunity for phase-gate controls. If research results are not as expected or desired, milestones provide a convenient opportunity to assess the state of progress, the value of accomplishment to date, the probability of valuable results in the future, and the desirability of changes in the research design. Again, the object of control is to ensure that the research design is sound and is being carried out as planned or amended. The review process should be participative. Unilateral judgments from the superior are not apt to be accepted or effective. Care must be taken not to overstress method as opposed to result. Method is controllable, and should be controlled, but results are still what count.

Personnel Reassignment This type of control is straightforward—individuals who are productive are kept; those who are not are moved to other jobs or to other organizations. Problems with this technique can arise because it is easy to create an elite group. While the favored few are highly motivated to further achievement, everyone else tends to be demotivated. It is also important not to apply control with too fine an edge. While it is not particularly difficult to identify those who fall in the top and bottom quartiles of productivity, it is usually quite hard to make clear distinctions between people in the middle quartiles.

Control of Input Resources In this case, the focus is on efficiency. The ability to manipulate input resources carries with it considerable control over output. Obviously, efficiency is not synonymous with creativity, but the converse is equally untrue—creativity is not synonymous with the extravagant use of resources.

The results flowing from creative activity tend to arrive in batches. Considerable resource expenditure may occur with no visible results, but then, seemingly all of a sudden, many outcomes may be delivered. The milestones for application of resource control must therefore be chosen with great care. The controller who decides to withhold resources just before the fruition of a research project is apt to become an ex-controller.

Sound judgment argues for some blend of these three approaches when controlling creative projects. The first and third approaches concentrate on process because process is observable and can be affected. But process is not the matter of moment; results are. The second approach requires us to measure (or at least to recognize) output when it occurs. This is often quite difficult. Thus, the wise PM will use all three approaches: checking process and method, manipulating resources, and culling those who cannot or do not produce.

In the next chapter, we initiate the project closure part of the text, beginning with evaluation and auditing. This topic is closely related to the postcontrol topics in this chapter.

Summary

As the final subject in the project implementation part of the text, this chapter described the project control process in the planning–monitoring–controlling cycle. The need for control was discussed, and the three types available were described. Then the design of control systems was addressed, including management's role, achieving the proper balance, and attaining control of creative activity as well as handling changes.

- Control is directed to scope, cost, and time.

- The two fundamental purposes of control are to regulate results through altering activity and to conserve the organization's physical, human, and financial assets.

- The three main types of control processes are cybernetic, go/no-go, and postcontrol.

- The postcontrol report contains four sections:
  - Project objectives
  - Milestones and budgets
  - Final project results
  - Recommendations for improvement
- The trend projection curve, CRs, and the control chart are useful control tools.

- Control systems have a close relationship to motivation and should be well-balanced; that is, cost-effective, appropriate to the desired end results, and not overdone.
- Three approaches to the control of creativity are process review, personnel reassignment, and control of inputs.
- The most irritating problem facing a PM is the control of change.

Glossary

Champion   A person with organizational clout who takes on personal responsibility (though not usually day-to-day management) for the successful completion of a project for the organization.

Control   Assuring that reality meets expectations or plans. Usually involves the process of keeping actions within limits to assure that certain outcomes will in fact happen.

Control Chart   A chart of a measure of performance—commonly a quality characteristic—over time, showing how it changes compared to a desired mean and upper and lower limits.

Critical Ratio   A ratio of progress (actual/scheduled) times a cost ratio (budgeted/actual).

Cybernetic   An automatic control system containing a negative feedback loop.

Early Warning System   A monitoring system that forewarns the PM if trouble arises.

Go/No-Go   Initially, a type of gauge that quickly tells an inspector if an object's dimension is within certain limits. In the case of project management, this can be any measure that allows a manager to decide whether to continue, change, or terminate an activity or a project.

Questions

Material Review Questions

1. What is the purpose of control? To what is it directed?
2. What are the three main types of control system? What questions should a control system answer?
3. What tools are available to the PM to use in controlling a project? Identify some characteristics of a good control system.
4. What is the mathematical expression for the CR? What does it tell a manager?
5. How is creativity controlled?
6. What are go/no-go controls?
7. What is a champion?
8. Describe a cybernetic control system.
9. What should the postcontrol report include?
10. How should change be controlled?
11. Describe the phase-gate process.

Class Discussion Questions

12. How might the PM integrate the various control tools into a project control system?
13. How could a negative feedback control system be implemented in project management to anticipate client problems?

14. How does the EV approach achieve the objective of the trend projection curve in Figure 11.5?
15. What other project parameters besides schedule and cost might a control chart be used for? How would their limits be set?
16. Control systems are sometimes classified into two categories, preventive and feedback. How do the three types of systems described in the chapter relate to these two categories?
17. How do internal and external controls differ?
18. What are some difficulties encountered when attempting project control?
19. How might the information required for control systems be collected?
20. How might the information collected through the control system be used on subsequent projects?
21. How does the control of creative projects differ from the control of ordinary projects?
22. Where might ethical issues arise for a PM in the stewardship of the company's resources?
23. Why is the control of change such a difficult problem for a PM? How might a change control system help?
24. Give a numeric example where using the CSI as the CR would be misleading.

Exercises

1. Given the following information, calculate the CRs, and indicate which activities are on target and which need to be investigated. Comment on the situation for each of the activities.

Activity	Actual Progress	Scheduled Progress	Budgeted Cost	Actual Cost
A	2 days	2 days	$40	$35
B	4 days	6 days	$30	$40
C	1 day	3 days	$50	$70
D	3 days	2 days	$25	$25

2. Calculate the CRs for the following activities and indicate which activities are probably on target and which need to be investigated. Comment on each activity.

Activity	Actual Progress	Scheduled Progress	Budgeted Cost	Actual Cost
A	4 days	4 days	$60	$40
B	3 days	2 days	$50	$50
C	2 days	3 days	$30	$20
D	1 day	1 day	$20	$30
E	2 days	4 days	$25	$25

3. Given the following information about a showroom renovation, which activities are on time, which are early, and which are behind schedule?

Activity	Budgeted Cost	Actual Cost	Critical Ratio
A: Plan changes	$60	$40	1.0
B: Solicit bids	$25	$50	0.5
C: Select contractor	$45	$30	1.5
D: Schedule date	$20	$20	1.5
E: Start renovation	$50	$50	0.67

4. Design and plot a CR for a computer installation project that had planned constant, linear progress from 0 to an EV of 200 over a 100-day duration. In fact, progress for the first 20 days has been: 2, 3, 4, 6, 7, 9, 12, 14, 15, 17, 20, 21, 21, 22, 24, 26, 27, 29, 31, 33. What can you conclude about this project?

5. Design and plot a CR for a website project that has planned constant, linear spending from 0 to a total of 1000 over a 100-day duration. In fact, daily spending for the first 15 days has been: 11, 10, 9, 10, 11, 12, 11, 9, 8, 9, 10, 12, 14, 11, 7. What can you conclude about this project?

6. Industrial Building, Inc., has two project teams installing virtually identical, four-story commercial buildings for a funder in two separate cities. Both projects have a planned daily cost of 100 and a planned daily EV of 100. The first 6 days for each team have progressed as follows:

Day	Team A: Earned Value	Team B: Earned Value	A: Cost	B: Cost
1	90	90	95	95
2	92	88	98	94
3	94	95	101	102
4	98	101	106	109
5	104	89	116	99
6	112	105	126	118

Compare the two projects in terms of general progress and according to CRs.

7. Samson Building, Ltd., is also constructing an identical building for the same funder as in Exercise 6 and has the following EVs and costs for the first 6 days: EV: 90, 88, 95, 101, 89, 105; Cost: 92, 88, 93, 98, 85, 100. Compare this project to the two in Exercise 6.

8. The following information (in AOA format) concerns progress at day 40 of an Internet marketing project. Determine if the project is in control based on time and cost to date. If not, what is the cost overage or underage?

Activity	Days Duration	Budget	Actual Cost	% Completed
1–2: Contact sites	10	300	250	100
2–3: Solicit costs	8	400	450	100
2–4: Design ads	12	350	380	100
4–3: Evaluate budget	0	0	0	—
3–5: Shoot ads	18	405	400	70
5–6: Place ads	16	450	—	0

9. Determine if the following test marketing project at week 6 is in control. If not, what is out of control? If it is in control, are both budget and schedule in control?

Activity	Prede-cessors	Dura-tion (weeks)	Budget, $	Actual Cost, $	% Completed
a: Build items	—	2	300	400	100
b: Supply stores	—	3	200	180	100
c: Create ad program	a	2	250	300	100
d: Schedule ads	a	5	600	400	20
e: Check sale results	b, c	4	400	200	20

10. At week 24 of a project to shoot a television commercial, the PM is worried about her budget since costs have risen to $7,500. Is there a cost overage? If so, how much is it? Is the schedule ahead or behind? Overall, does the project appear to be in control?

Activity	Prede-cessors	Duration (weeks)	Budget, $	% Completed
a: Write script	—	6	900	100
b: Screen actors	—	6	1,200	100
c: Select actors	a	6	1,200	100
d: Contract studio	a	12	1,800	100
e: Obtain props	b, c	14	1,400	100
f: Schedule date	b, c, d	10	1,500	40
g: Shoot commercial	d, e	16	800	0

Incidents For Discussion

Speciality Service, Inc.

Speciality Service, Inc., is a field computer repair operation serving the small commercial industry in seven states. Speciality Service has one operation in each state, and they vary in size from 50 to 240 employees. A disturbing trend has been developing for the last couple of years that Speciality Service management wishes to stop. The incidence of tardiness and absenteeism is on the increase. Both are extremely disruptive in a custom packing operation. Speciality Service is nonunion in all seven locations, and since management wants to keep this situation, it wants a careful, low-key approach to the problem. Jason Horn, assistant personnel manager, has been appointed PM to recommend a solution. All seven operations managers have been assigned to work with him on this problem.

Jason has had no problem interfacing with the operations managers. They have very quickly agreed that three steps must be taken to solve the problem:

1. Institute a uniform daily attendance report that is summarized weekly and forwarded to the main office. (Current practice varies from location to location, but comments on attendance are normally included in monthly operations reports.)

2. Institute a uniform disciplinary policy, enforced in a uniform manner.

3. Initiate an intensive employee education program to emphasize the importance of good attendance.

The team has further decided that the three-point program should be tested before a final recommendation is presented. They have decided to test the program at one location for 2 months. Jason wishes to control and evaluate the test by having the daily attendance report transmitted to him directly at headquarters, from which he will make the final decision on whether to present the program in its current format or not.

Questions

Does this monitoring and control method appear adequate? What are the potential problems?

Night Tran Construction Company

Night Tran Construction Company specializes in building small power plants, mostly for utility companies. The company was awarded a contract approximately 2 years ago to build such a power plant. The contract stated a project duration of 3 years, after which a 1 percent penalty would be invoked for each additional month of construction. Project records indicate the utility plan is only 50 percent completed and is encountering continuing problems. The owner of Night Tran Company, concerned over the potential losses, investigated the project and found the following: There was an excessive number of engineering design changes; there was a high work rejection rate; and the project was generally understaffed. As a result, she directed the PM to develop a better system of project control and present this method to the board members in 1 week.

Questions

If you were the PM, what characteristics would you be looking for in the new control system? Will a new control system be adequate for the problem? Will it control scope creep? Explain.

Continuing Integrative Class Project

Decide what type of control system you plan to use for the project and describe it—you may wish to use subteam leaders in the control process if you have them. Then design a CR control

chart for the project that you will use as the project progresses. Once again, the costs will probably be the labor hours put in by members of the class. How will you determine actual progress?

Bibliography

Burba, D. "The Complexity Equation." *PM Network*, November 2013.

Byrne, J. "Project Management: How Much Is Enough?" *PM Network*, February 1999.

Gibson, L. "*Project Scope Creep.*" Today's Engineer, Spring 1998.

Gupta, V. K., and D. J. Graham. "A Customer-Driven Quality Improvement and Management Project at Diamond Offshore Drilling." *Project Management Journal*, September 1997.

Hajek, V. G. *Management of Engineering Projects.* New York: McGraw Hill, 1977.

Heerkens, G. R. "The Cost of Change." *PM Network*, January 2014.

Heywood, G. E., and T. J. Allen. "Project Controls: How Much Is Enough?" *PM Network*, November 1996.

Hunsberger, K. "The Best of the Best." *PM Network*, September 2010.

Hunsberger, K. "Change Is Good." *PM Network*, February 2011.

Ibbs, C. W., and Y.-H. Kwak. "Benchmarking Project Management Organizations." *PM Network*, February 1998.

Keil, M., and M. Mähring. "Is Your Project Turning into a Black Hole?" *California Management Review*, Fall 2010.

Lee, H. L. "Aligning Supply Chain Strategies with Product Uncertainties." *IEEE Engineering Management Review*, 2nd Qtr. 2003.

Leffingwell, D. "Engage! Involve the Customer to Manage Scope." *PM Network*, August 1997.

McGrath, R. G., and I. Macmillan, "Discovery-Driven Planning." *Harvard Business Review*, July–August 1995.

Meredith, J. R., and S. M. Shafer. *Operations Management for MBAs*, 5th ed. New York: Wiley, 2013.

Mihalic, J. "From the Board: Leading the Way with Thought Leadership." *PMI Today*, September 2013.

Project Management Institute. *A Guide to the Project Management Body of Knowledge*, 5th ed. Newtown Square, PA: Project Management Institute, 2013.

Project Management Institute. "Q&A: On Track." *PM Network*, October 2002.

Rice, M. P., G. C. O'Connor, and R. Pierantozzi. "Implementing a Learning Plan to Counter Project Uncertainty." *MIT Sloan Management Review*, Winter 2008.

Seesing, P. R. "Distributing Project Control Database Information on the World Wide Web." *PM Network*, October 1996.

Thamhain, H. J. "Best Practices for Controlling Technology-Based Projects." *Project Management Journal*, December 1996.

Thamhain, H. J. "Managing Risks in Complex Projects." *Project Management Journal*, April 2013.

Toney, F. "What the *Fortune* 500 Know about PM Best Practices." *PM Network*, February 1997.

Voices on Project Management. "Poll: What Is the No. 1 Reason Projects Fail?" *PM Network*, May 2012.

Whitten, N. "Managing Priorities Effectively." *PM Network*, July 1995.

The following case continues the Project Manager/Customer Interface case from the previous chapter, exploring issues about the lack of control in that project. Jacqueline Doyle, manager of Contract Management, remains concerned with how the project grew from $500,000 to almost $2 million without her knowledge, and especially how she was drawn into a divisive meeting with the client without knowing ahead of time what the meeting was about.

Case

The Project Manager/Customer
Interface (B)   Jack R. Meredith

Jacqueline Doyle, Manager of Contract Management for BWNS, was having second thoughts about their recent contract dispute

with NLP over the Green Meadow plant outage contract. She had recently issued a memo to project management hoping to avoid such future problems by listing their responsibilities as including the following: (1) Know who the decisions makers are; (2) ask the right questions of the right people; (3) control the customer; (4) get money for work performed; and (5) persevere. However, upon reflection, she wasn't confident these vague responsibilities would be sufficient to avoid similar problems in the future, or in some cases even actionable. She thus decided to consult some reference books on the topic of managerial control of projects, taking some notes as she read.

She was first interested in the way changes occurred in the execution of the project plan due to unexpected changes in the scope of what was to be done and when. She read that this was called "scope creep," and was defined as follows: "The natural inclination of the client (or sometimes project team members) to change the deliverables as they obtain better information about their needs over time." She also found out that there are three common causes of scope creep: (1) Uncertainty about the technology involved in the project; (2) an increase in the knowledge of the client or user about their needs; and (3) A change in the agreed-upon rules of the project.

Jacqueline then wondered how to exercise control over these kinds of unanticipated changes. She found a book on project control that said there were three major types of control that could be exercised in projects: cybernetic, a type of automatic control based on feedback; go/no-go controls, such as phase-gates at various milestones throughout the project; and last, postcontrol, to avoid problems in the future, which she recognized as precisely what she was doing. The book indicated that some incidents that affect the scope are clearly one-time events that, although difficult to predict, can frequently be mitigated by actions preceding the project. Jacqueline was intrigued by some of the techniques the book suggested such as adding time or cost buffers to the project, monitoring potential incidents for their impending occurrence, or through specific exclusions in the contract such as descoping contingencies. However, many events that appear to be one-time occurrences may in fact have been anticipated early on by careful attention to the past actions of the client, potential subcontractors, the likely project team, the PM, the project owner, the sponsor, and other such stakeholders.

Jacqueline found the idea of monitoring project progress in real time to be interesting, rather than discovering problems later on after it was too late to rectify them. The book suggested a few different measures that could be used. One overall measure to indicate potential problems was a "critical ratio" defined as the actual over scheduled progress times the budgeted over actual cost which, if less than 1, indicated problems in the project. However, this ratio can be misleading if the actual cost or schedule looks good but the other measure is bad. To dig further into what the problem is, the book recommended individual variance analyses on both cost and schedule, or simply a projection of the final budget at completion. She decided to ask Reggie Brown about the feasibility of doing this.

Since Jacqueline was in charge of contracts, the idea of adding contingency language to all project contracts in the future seemed to her to be an easy and excellent way to avoid conflicts with BWNS's clients, as long as they weren't perceived as harming the clients' interests. Thinking back to the NLP contract, a

major delaying event in that project was the late delivery of the generators by NLP to SPIS, which could have been anticipated and a clause inserted in the contract. A primary assumption in the contract was that the generators would be delivered on time, but suppose they weren't? Another assumption was that NLP would accept SPIS' badging process, but they insisted on using their own process, which also delayed the project. Clearly, future contracts would have to be carefully reviewed for unspecified assumptions and then either contingency measures added for each of them or monitoring to avoid their occurrence. But what if a client, anticipating a problem, asked to change the contract before the project was completed, which could circumvent the contingency measures? Jacqueline realized that a "change control" section would be needed in future contracts specifying how requested changes by either party regarding things such as schedule, cost, or deliverables would be handled. Any proposed changes would have to be studied by both parties, perhaps a compromise reached, and then signed off by the appropriate officials of both the client and the contractor.

Last, Jacqueline was irritated that she and Roberts went into a meeting with a client without having a clue what the meeting was for because the PM was on a field assignment and couldn't be reached. She wondered why she hadn't been alerted to the fact that there had been a problem with this project. Here she consulted books on managerial communications and also project information systems. As she took notes, she came up with three likely possibilities. One was that the information may have been in her reports but was buried in details that weren't noticeable. Another was that the monitoring systems she relied on at BWNS weren't appropriate for tracking projects, or perhaps individual project plans. The information systems book indicated a third possibility—that the project's and BWNS's information systems didn't work together and information about projects got lost at the upper management level. She decided that she needed to look further into these three possibilities.

Questions

1. Would you consider the scope changes in the case to be "scope creep"?

2. Are each of the scope changes one of the three basic causes of change in projects? If so, which one and why?

3. Would you recommend any of the go/no-go control types for BWNS? If so, how would you suggest they implement these controls?

4. Do you suspect that any of the three common reporting problems Jacqueline found were occurring? Can you find evidence in the case to support your suspicions?

5. Jacqueline is trying to solve two problems: Avoiding conflicts with clients and learning about potential problems early on when they can be solved. What would you suggest for each one from what she has learned?

6. What else would you recommend to Jacqueline?

The following article describes the installation of a PMO at Ford to improve the delivery and success of projects. In contrast to the chapter, the article shows how to control projects by design rather than by correction.

Reading

Ford Motor Co.: Electrical/Electronic Systems Engineering[2]   H. R. Kerzner

Ford Motor, Co. has revenues of $147 billion and 224,000 employees worldwide. The Electrical/Electronic Systems Engineering department develops electrical systems valued at $800 to $1,000 at cost to more than 80 vehicle programs. The department consists of approximately 740 staff resources, with electrical program management teams comprising about twenty-five engineering resources each.

The Electrical/Electronic Systems Engineering department has four functional engineering areas, each with its own chief engineer:

1. North America Truck
2. North America Car
3. Commodity and Application Engineering
4. E/E Software and Modeling

This department is aligned with the product creation mission of Ford—"Great Products . . . More Products . . . Faster"—that outlines the priorities for the department:

- Improve quality
- Improve quality (intentionally repeated)
- Develop exciting products
- Achieve competitive cost and revenue
- Build relationships

Additionally, Ford's Electrical/Electronic Systems Engineering department has aligned with the company's key focus areas for department communication and processes. To "intensify communications," the department stresses the following:

- Communicate consistently
- Focus on vital few priorities
- Keep the message simple
- Help people prioritize
- Remove barriers

The department also emphasizes that each team member should improve working processes by simplifying, stabilizing, standardizing, setting cadence, and sustaining.

By using these principles across all product development commodities, the department has achieved a reduction in engineering errors, as well as higher engineer engagement.

Overall Best Practices

Examining project management at Ford revealed three best practices. First is Ford's executive sponsorship of an Electrical/Electronic Systems Engineering project management office. This office standardizes project management and engineering processes across its internal functional areas and the electrical program management team. It also acts as a single governance board for the project management office framework. The department's directors, chiefs, and the electrical business planning and technology office participate in the governance board through weekly project management meetings to provide support and shift priorities as required.

Second, professional project managers consult on the implementation, execution, and maintenance of the project management office, as well as assisting with the transfer of project management knowledge for the organization.

Additionally, the Electrical/Electronic Systems Engineering department has internalized project management as a discipline in engineering and provided training to the entire organization, with follow-up auditing processes in place for implemented projects. It has always been Ford's intent for engineers to develop competencies in the area and build an in-house project management discipline.

Managing Resistance

Transferring the leadership and ownership of project management from professional managers to the engineering division has allowed further entrenching of the organization's goal of increasing project management maturity and has produced positive results.

Senior-level managers in the organization expect 100 percent compliance with the project management tools and methodologies developed by the project management office and approved by the governance board. They approached the changes as sustained continuous improvement and took the time to listen to comments and criticism from the people in the framework, which resulted in less overall resistance than was expected.

Another method used by the Electrical/Electronic Systems Engineering department to counter resistance was to design the project management office framework around stakeholder participation. All organization personnel can participate in the project management office tools and methodology discussions at the management level, as well as the project management office working level meetings. This level of participation in the organization helps build the best practice process.

Driving Consistency in Project Management

Project Definition

The Electrical/Electronic Systems Engineering project management office acts as the central project manager to standardize projects. The office engages defined projects that usually have a short time frame with a clearly defined scope and a

454 CHAPTER 11 Project Control

clear allocation of resources. Long-term technical or business planning projects are handled outside of the project management office. Although these projects may interact with the office, it does not directly manage them.

Project Management Organization/Methodology

The Electrical/Electronic Systems Engineering department's project management office compromises three levels.

1. **The governance board of executive directors and engineering chiefs**. This small body prioritizes projects according to the corporate scorecard. The group includes two executive directors and four engineering chiefs and set the tone for the department's overall level of project management excellence.

2. **Stakeholders**. This group includes members of the department that participate either regularly or sporadically in approved projects, usually as subject matter experts. These resources provide technical knowledge regarding the various engineering disciplines and tools.

3. **Professional project managers**. These staff members are from the project management-consulting firm retained by the department. Their duties include participating in cascaded/prioritized projects, developing project execution plans and work plans, performing audit processes, and facilitating team formation and execution of deliverables in a specified timeline and scope as approved by the governance board. The professional project managers also developed a change management process for updating existing project management tools on an as-needed basis.

The professional firm of Pcubed Inc. is considered the owner of the project management methodology employed at Ford Motor Company. This methodology is aligned with the Project Management Body of Knowledge (PMBOK Guide), PMI, and PM Berkeley Maturity models, which are the recognized industry standards. The approach comprises three phases.

1. **Discover and define** The objective during this phase is to assess the overall health and baseline project management process.

2. **Develop and deliver** The Phase 2 objective is to develop and pilot the recommended solutions to address the needs identified in Phase 1.

3. **Deploy and drive** The last objective is to ensure solutions are fully implemented across the department.

Project Managers/Teams

Five to eight full-time professional project managers staff the Electrical/Electronic Systems Engineering project management office per quarter, depending on the project needs. The project management office reports its general project scope recommendations or issues to the Electrical/Electronic Systems Engineering department business office manager prior to those recommendations/issues being elevated to the governance board review process, where they are then reviewed by directors and engineering chiefs.

The relationship between the project management office and the functional areas is clearly structured, with the project management office as the focal point for all project management processes. The functional teams do not have the authority to influence or overrule the directives managed by the project management office. In 2004, the project management office began to work with the Electrical/Electronic Systems Engineering department to identify resources that will participate in an increased capacity based on the job families for engineers with project management responsibilities.

The composition of a typical Electric/Electronic Systems Engineering department project team and the corresponding roles and responsibilities include the following:

- **The project manager** This person leads the project execution plan development. This also includes gathering the necessary resources, as well as defining the scope, deliverables, and time line for the project.

- **The stakeholders** Usually they are subject-matter experts who provide feedback about the project deliverables.

- **The governance board** The board reviews the progress of the project and gives the necessary approval or rejections for recommendations.

In some instances, the stakeholders take the lead role, and the project management office acts as coordinator or facilitator.

Currently, the Electric/Electronic Systems Engineering department identifies resources and potential leaders using the individual development plan, a tool completed by the department's engineers. Resources identified for advance training take on permanent leadership roles in the organization. Some of these resources will have only part-time responsibilities for project management, and others will be used full-time to manage the project management office.

To maintain the structure necessary for consistent project delivery while allowing for changing circumstances, the project management office and the governance board review projects' status monthly and make any necessary recommendations. Stakeholders also meet monthly for change control of project management tools and processes. This is the formal change control process for any methodology improvements to existing projects. The project scope can be modified as necessary to manage changes to the original project assumptions. The suggested revisions are always reviewed by the top two levels of the project management structure (governance board and stakeholder team), and any revisions are taken from their directions.

Ford used the Berkeley Project Management Maturity Model to quantify the needs assessment results across the project management disciplines and the project life cycle. Level one of the Berkeley Maturity Model is the ad hoc stage, where no formal procedures or plans to execute exist and where project management techniques are applied inconsistently, if at all. Level two is the planned stage, where informal and incomplete processes are used, and planning and management of projects depend primarily on individuals. Level three is the managed stage, where project management processes demonstrate systematic planning and control and where cross-functional teams are becoming integrated. Level four of the model is the integrated stage. Here, project management processes are formal, integrated, and fully implemented. Lastly, level five is the sustained stage, which involves continuous improvement of the project management process. At the project management office launch in 2003, the Electrical/Electronic Systems Engineering department had a maturity level rating of 1.85, aligning with the average maturity level of most organizations, which is between level one and two.

At the end of 2003, after the implementation of the project management office and achievement of an organized approach, an informal review of the organization's processes moved the rating to 3.0. To continue increasing its maturity level in 2004, the department's governance board began internalizing the effort to transfer project management knowledge by using technical maturity models, which provide training models, individual development plans, and core training and education online sources in department project management processes. The goal of the department is to internalize competency and to approach project management broadly.

Project Management Strategy

The Electrical/Electronic Systems Engineering department has two primary strategies for selecting project management office projects:

1. Base selection on the corporate scorecard objectives for the given calendar year.
2. Base selection on the underlying goal of increasing the department's project management maturity.

The project management strategy aligns with the corporate strategic plan by placing top priority on selecting a project based on its ability to meet the corporate scorecard objectives (i.e., improving the product creation process and engineering disciplines). Other criteria can also include the ability to improve work-related efficiency, standardize reports and processes to improve clarity of data for decision making at the senior level, and realign the organization cross-functionally to increase project synergies.

The department's approach to project management has been used to achieve the strategic objectives of the organization in the following ways:

- The project management office had input into the corporate-level development of the engineering quality operating system. The office also had responsibility for building electrical assessment health charts by system and commodity levels, training the Electrical/Electronic Systems Engineering organization to integrate new corporate reporting tools, implementing an auditing process to ensure proper compliance with procedure, and reporting the efficiency of the organization to senior leadership.
- The department worked toward realigning the sourcing process with the finance department, catalogued issues via the engineering quality operation system reporting system, and gained the support of the finance department in a joint partnership to improve the supplier sourcing process.

- The department also maintained continuous improvement projects in product development, such as participating in corporate objectives as they pertain to the processes to improve product creation (e.g., improving time to market and the quality of the product launch).

Resource Assignment

Electrical/Electronic Systems Engineering ensures that adequate project resources are devoted to the upfront project phases (project initiation and planning) by defining project execution plans one month prior to the project kick-off. This plan details the scope, timeline, and required resources. Once the governance board approves the plan, it ensures that sufficient organization resources are enabled, and the project management office matches projects to the skill sets of individual project managers.

To effectively manage geographically dispersed or global project teams, the department uses a clearly defined communication plan, including the scope, timeline, resources, and the necessary communication tools that can facilitate a global meeting such as eRoom or Pictel. It is also important to form the project team early and clearly define the objectives, as well as outline regular status-reporting meetings. Cultural differences that might arise during the project are managed by best practices training. For example, the project leader might make recommendations to the team for specific communication plans, the formality of meetings, or conduct, and might negotiate work-related differences and scope disagreements.

Project Management Professionalism/Training

As discussed previously, advanced project managers in the Electrical/Electronic Systems Engineering department are identified through individual development plans as part of the technical maturity model for project management. Resources identified for advanced training will take on permanent leadership roles in the department, which usually consists of managing projects or the project management office.

Training needs for project managers are also identified by comparing the results of the completed individual personal development plans to the technical maturity model for project management. Resources requiring user/expert level skills will be trained by a variety of sources:

- Current professional project managers assigned to train them on project management office operations
- Web-based training or seminar training provided by Ford on core project management disciplines
- Specialized courses developed by the department along with Ford Motor Co. on project management processes, tools, and methodologies

Structuring and Negotiating Project Scope

Professional project managers in the project management office initially prepare the project scope based on a discovery phase approach. The scope is outlined in a project execution plan against the project requirements, timeline, and resources required. Process changes must go through the formal change control process, as outlined earlier, that begins at the monthly stakeholder meeting. Scope changes related to resources are first reviewed with the manager of electrical technology and operations. The governance board must then review the proposed changes before giving its approval or rejection. An adjustment of resources is then made as necessary to meet the approved changes to the scope.

Maintaining Consistency in Project Management Delivery

Overall, the department identifies a number of important ways that it maintains consistency in project management delivery:

- Project management tools, processes, and methods in the department are standardized.
- The project management office institutionalizes approved new processes through training of the organization.
- The project management office audits the correct use of new tools and processes.
- Monthly change control actions are taken to improve gaps.
- Processes are available to the organization through the use of eRoom documentation storage.
- Ongoing organization training and project management pocket cards for engineers are provided.

Building Project Portfolios by Prioritizing Projects

In Ford's portfolio management approach, projects are ranked based on the priorities identified by the governance board using the corporate scorecard. Initially, the scopes of the various projects are high level, and the project managers review all requested projects and define the scope with the department's business operations manager. In 2004, the organization performed an assessment of this approach and plans to make assessments a biannual process.

Allocation of Resources

As previously outlined, the Electrical/Electronic Systems Engineering department allocates resources to projects based on the project priority, scope, and available resources. If reassignment of resources is necessary because of changes to the project or the personnel, then proposed changes are reviewed and approved by the governance board and department's business office manager. However, the final decision on prioritization of projects lies with the department's governance board.

The allocation of development funds or resources to different project types, business areas, market sectors, or product lines again depends on the corporate scorecard objectives are cascaded by the governance board to the project management office, which develops high-level project plans that the governance board then reviews for approval. To ensure sufficient resources are available for projects, the governance board conducts monthly reviews to monitor strict adherence to the scope management of projects, as well as manage any over-allocation of resources.

The job of ensuring that low-value projects are terminated before consuming resources is primarily that of the project management office's project manager, governance board, and the Electrical/Electronic Systems Engineering department's

business manager. The feedback on value achievement from these sources is provided monthly. Additionally, a periodic formal project management office survey is administered by the Electrical/Electronic Systems Engineering department's business operations planning group to the department to rank the effectiveness and use of project management office tools, processes, and project outcomes. The results of the survey are reviewed with the project management office and the governance board to identify areas of improvement and capture lessons learned.

To enhance ongoing management decisions using the project portfolio, Ford uses the engineering quality operating system reporting system to quantitatively measure the success of program delivery across the North American engineering community, including electrical/electronic commodity and deliverables to the program level. This measurement system is designed to review the history and also present the status of progress across the vehicle programs. The project management office has worked on various projects that have facilitated the communication of these status results in a more streamlined manner to help decision-making capabilities. For example, the Electrical/Electronic Systems Engineering department will prioritize "red issues" and track any red issue closures in a database. These progress reports against the closure of red issues are reviewed as high as the vice president level.

Measuring Project Delivery and End Results

Ford uses the engineering quality operating system to measure the success of its projects in the engineering community. Its integrator reporting system captures the status of projects and can report these findings up to the system and program levels.

Additionally, the metrics or measures used by the project management office are mostly qualitative and can include completed deliverables assigned to the project or feedback by the user community or other outside sources.

The department's business operations planning department manages all financial aspects of the Electrical/Electronic Systems Engineering project cost. The department's business operations planning manager found the project management approach the most cost effective for managing projects in a large organization. This approach has driven 5 percent efficiency in the operating costs for the electrical area of the company.

The collection of project data is managed by the project management office and can come from various sources, such as the engineering quality operating system health charts (project status reports) or work plans. Data integrity is managed by periodic auditing of the functional engineering team's adherence to the organization's tools and processes. The results of the audit are reported to the chief engineers examine the auditing reports to drive 100 percent compliance through the organization.

To make data informational and useful, the organization analyzes various types of data with the following frequency:

- Trend analysis of engineering quality operating system health charts is done twice monthly.
- Timing analysis on work plans is conducted monthly and reported to the electrical program management team.

- Updates to the engineering quality operating system integrator are conducted monthly, but tracking of red issues is conducted on a weekly basis.

Additionally, the following reporting methods or mechanisms are used in the organization:

- The Web-based engineering quality operating system assessment provides red/yellow/green health charts for the commodity and system-level teams.
- Work plans are maintained on eRooms for easy access to project timing data and deliverables.
- Tracking of red issues conducted via a tracking database and a trend analysis is performed on this data.

Decision makers in the organization act on the reported metric data in different ways. The governance board conducts reviews of the engineering quality operating system red-status items across the organization for two hours every week and provides feedback to the managers on action items. The timing reviews are held bimonthly at the system level to review commodity development and testing status. Issues arising from these reviews are elevated to the chief engineers, who actively manage the red issues to green status.

To ensure that the project-related measures add value to the organization, the Electrical/Electronic Systems Engineering department can point to improvements in performance. The quality of the red/yellow/green status at various vehicle program milestones has been steadily improving since 2003. The organization acknowledges an effort to minimize projects in the yellow status. Corrective action plans are for the purpose of changing a commodity status to green, not to merely improve it from red to yellow. The Web-based engineering quality operating system assesses milestones deliverables using the red/yellow/green status and provides managers with immediate issue elevation.

Accountability/Authority

Because project managers execute governance-board-approved projects, team members know they are expected to participate and meet project objectives. Project managers are given the authority to elevate issues or roadblocks that arise during the life of the project to the governance board for any needed feedback or assistance. The overall authority granted to project managers is commensurate with their level of authority.

The roles and responsibilities for project managers are in the process of being mapped into the Electrical/Electronic Systems Engineering job families. At the manager level, however, achievement and technical excellence is recognized and rewarded by senior management.

In terms of future objectives, the project management office has outlined the following effort to continue to improve the Electrical/Electronic Systems Engineering department's project management maturity:

- Develop a technical maturity model for project management to provide training and organizational structure to transfer project management roles and responsibilities and/or competencies.

- Migrate commodity engineering quality operating system assessment summaries to the integrator and audit/coach/mentor commodity teams on the integrator.
- Continue to expand electrical program management teams and commodity-in-a-box tools and processes.
- Lead electrical work stream development in new product development system.

Greatest Measurement Challenges

The primary measurement challenge for Ford's Electrical/Electronic Systems Engineering department was the length of time it took managers to realize that the project management office approach was necessary for project management processes to improve.

As discussed previously, the current auditing processes used by the project management office to measure project delivery typically address quality issues, whereas the project management change control process in the department allows for ongoing improvement to tools and processes, as well as the management of scope changes. Flexibility in these measurement systems has been important in achieving a higher rate of successful project outcomes. Additionally, process training surveys are conducted with team members after the rolling out of a new process or tool to gather feedback and to identify areas of improvement.

Final Comments and Thoughts
Learning from Project Management Missteps

Even with a strong effort to engage personnel, the objectives of the project management office were not initially clearly understood in the Electrical/Electronic Systems Engineering organization. Because most personnel had not previously experienced a working project management office, incorrect assumptions were sometimes made regarding its scope, roles, and responsibilities. It took the project management office some time to get the entire organization aligned on its value and the most effective method for execution of projects. The participation of the stakeholder board was key to the eventual acceptance of the project management office, along with constant communication.

To summarize, the Electrical/Electronic Systems Engineering department's project manage office's project execution plans were developed and reviewed and then approved by the governance board to clearly define the quarterly project management office objectives, scope, and resource allocation. These plans were made available to the organization via the eRoom and also reviewed at the manager level. Any overextending of project management resources or changes in project scope are routinely reviewed by the governance board at the monthly status review. After one year, the department had developed an effective working relationship with the project management office and had accepted the accompanying project management tools and methodologies.

Questions

1. Compare how Ford Motor Co. is trying to control their projects with the methods listed in the chapter.

2. What were the three organizational levels in their PMO?

3. What are the five stages of project management maturity in the Berkeley model? At what stage was Ford in 2003? What stage after installation of the PMO?

4. Whose job was it to decide the value of projects before they used up excessive resources and terminate them?

5. The chapter talks about the difficulties of working with outside clients and stakeholders. How did Ford avoid these problems?

6. What measures does the Engineering Quality Operating System use to measure project success?

7. Did the PMO installation go smoothly? Describe.

8. Who is responsible for overseeing projects and changes in their scope?

9. Contrast the way that Ford selected projects with the PPM approach in Chapter 2.

CHAPTER 12

Project Auditing

In the previous chapter, we discussed postcontrol. Postcontrol cannot change the past, but it tries to capture the essence of project successes and failures so that future projects can benefit from past experiences. **PMBOK** refers to this as "lessons learned," a topic addressed in Chapter 8 on Quality. To benefit from past experiences implies that one understands them, and understanding requires evaluation. But project evaluation is not limited to after-the-fact analysis. While the project as a whole is evaluated when it has been completed (the basis for postcontrols), project evaluation should be conducted at a number of points during the life cycle, for instance at major phase gates, and especially if there is a crisis or major problem in the project.

8.3.3.8

A particularly useful vehicle for evaluation (but by no means the only one) is the *project audit*, a more or less formal inquiry into any aspect of the project. We associate the word *audit* with a detailed examination of financial matters, but a project audit is highly flexible and may focus on whatever matters senior management desires. Because the projects an organization initiates support its strategy, which in turn supports its overall competitiveness, proactively determining how a project is performing through periodic project audits provides timely insights into the project that can be leveraged to further increase the odds of successful project completion. Thus, from a strategic perspective, project audits play an important role by helping ensure project success, which subsequently translates into improved competitive success.

Note that there are also other types of audits such as *ethics audits*, which can be helpful when employing project management in an organization. For example, as Schaefer et al. (1998, p. 40) note, "Ethics is not a matter of right or wrong; it is a process by which an organization evaluates decisions," a process that is most certainly relevant to project management! And in addition to project audits, there are also other kinds of project evaluations, such as project *reviews*[1]; see also Sangameswaran (1995) for more details.

The term *evaluate* means to set the value of or appraise. Project evaluation appraises the progress and performance of a project compared to that project's planned progress and performance, or compared to the progress and performance of other, similar projects. The comparison is made by measuring the project against several different types of standards. The evaluation also supports any management decisions required for the project. Therefore, the evaluation must be conducted and presented in a manner and format that assure management that all pertinent data have been considered. The evaluation of a project must have credibility in the eyes of the management group for whom it is performed and also in the eyes of the project team on whom it is performed. Accordingly, the project evaluation must be just as carefully constructed and controlled as the project itself.

In this chapter, we describe the project audit/review/evaluation, its various forms and purposes, and some typical problems encountered in conducting an audit/evaluation.

---

[1]The reading "An Assessment of Postproject Reviews" at the end of this chapter examines four such evaluations and summarizes the pros and cons of conducting such evaluations.

12.1 Purposes of Evaluation—Goals of the System

Certainly, the major element in the evaluation of a project is its "success." In a study of a variety of different kinds and sizes of industrial projects (Shenhar et al., 1997), 127 project managers (PMs) identified 13 factors constituting four independent dimensions of project success, from their perspective as PMs. The first and most straightforward dimension is the project's *efficiency* in meeting both the budget and the schedule. This has been the primary focus of our discussion of project management and control thus far, meeting the time, cost, and scope objectives of the project. The second and most complex dimension is that of *funder impact/satisfaction*. This dimension includes meeting the project's technical and operational specifications but also includes factors relating to loyalty and repurchase: fulfilling the funder's needs, actual use by the customer, solving a major operational problem of the funder, and the perennial challenge of funder satisfaction.

The third dimension is *business/direct success*, measured here primarily in terms of level of commercial success and market share. For internal projects, however, the factors might include such measures as yields, cycle times, processing steps, and quality. The last dimension, somewhat more difficult and nebulous to ascertain, is *future potential*. This includes factors relating to opening a new market, developing a new line of products or services, or if an internal project, developing a new technology, skills, or competences. Next, we will note some additional dimensions for evaluating projects that go beyond those discussed by Shenhar et al. (1997).

Beyond the straightforward considerations of project success, another primary purpose of evaluation is to help translate the achievement of the project's goals into a contribution to the parent organization's goals. To do this, all facets of the project are studied in order to identify and understand the project's strengths and weaknesses. It is the equivalent of an application of Six Sigma or TQM to project management. The result is a set of recommendations for improvements that can help both ongoing and future projects to:

- Identify problems earlier
- Clarify scope, cost, and time relationships
- Improve project performance
- Locate opportunities for future technological advances
- Evaluate the quality of project management
- Reduce costs
- Improve the process of risk identification and management
- Speed up the achievement of results
- Identify mistakes, remedy them, and avoid them in the future
- Provide information to the client
- Reconfirm the organization's interest in and commitment to the project

For brevity, we will refer to the stated project objectives, including funder satisfaction, as the project's "direct goals." They ignore, however, many costs and benefits to the project, to its team members, and to the parent organization that are not overtly established as objectives, such as the preceding list of project improvements. Evaluation often makes recommendations that relate to these ancillary, unplanned but important contributions to the project and its parent. Some examples of recommendations concerning these "ancillary goals" include attempts to:

- Improve understanding of the ways in which projects may be of value to the organization
- Improve the processes for organizing and managing projects, better known as the firm's project management "maturity"
- Provide information and experience for entering new markets
- Provide a congenial environment in which project team members can work creatively together
- Identify organizational strengths and weaknesses in project-related personnel, general management, and decision-making techniques and systems
- Identify and improve the response to risk factors in the firm's use of projects
- Allow access to project policy decision-making by external stakeholders
- Improve the way projects contribute to the professional growth of project team members
- Identify project personnel who have high potential for managerial leadership

The identification of ancillary goals is a difficult and politically delicate task. Although the adjective "ancillary" is not a sufficient descriptor, it is the best single word we could find. Synonyms are "helpful," "subsidiary," "accessory," and the like, and we have all these things in mind. In addition, the ancillary goals are usually not overtly identified. Interviews with the individuals in charge of making decisions about projects will help to expose the ancillary goals that the firm is seeking by supporting the project. But for the most part, they are "hidden" by accident, not by purpose. Finding them often requires deductive reasoning. Organizational decisions and behaviors imply goals, often very specific goals, that are simply not spelled out anywhere in the organizational manuals. For example, most executives desire to operate their organizations in such a way that people enjoy the work they do and enjoy working together, but only occasionally do firms publish such statements. Few firms would disavow this objective; they simply do not *overtly* subscribe to it. Even so, this particular objective affects the decisions made in almost every firm we know.

At times, however, ancillary goals and the stakeholders that support them can be readily identified. Some examples are: goals that govern the treatment of animals that may be involved in a project, goals that demand highly specific processing of information about a project output (e.g., pharmaceutical drugs), or goals that control the production processes associated with a project (e.g., antipollution). Whether clearly identified or not, and whether measured or not, ancillary goals affect decisions made on all projects.

A reasonable attempt to identify as many goals as possible is valuable. Frequently, recognition of an ancillary goal is required to understand why certain decisions on projects are made. The desire to identify individuals who have high potential for leadership may explain why a given person with relatively little experience is given a specific project responsibility. Ancillary goals add several additional dimensions to project evaluation.

There are tough problems associated with finding the ancillary goals of a project. First, and probably the most important, is the obvious fact that one cannot measure performance against an unknown goal. Therefore, if a goal is not openly acknowledged, project team members need not fear that their performance can be weighed and found wanting. The result is that goals appearing in the project proposal must be recognized and are a source of some anxiety in members of the project team. But "unwritten" goals can often be ignored. Again, ancillary goals are rarely disclaimed; they are merely not mentioned.

Whether or not anxiety about meeting ancillary goals is deserved is not relevant. Particularly in this era of corporate "restructuring," anxiety is present. It is heightened by the fear that an evaluation may not be conducted "fairly," with proper emphasis on what is being accomplished rather than stressing shortcomings. If the self-image of the project team is very strong, this barrier to finding ancillary goals of the project may be weak, but it is never absent.

A second problem arises during attempts to find the ancillary goals of a project. Individuals pursue their own ends while working for organizations. At times, however, people may be unwilling to admit to personal goals—goals they may see as not entirely consistent with organizational objectives. For example, a person may seek to join a project in order to learn a new skill, one that increases that person's employment mobility. At times, the scientific direction taken by R&D projects is as much a function of the current interest areas of the scientists working on the project as it is the scientific need of the project. While such purposes are not illegitimate or unethical, they are rarely admitted.

A third problem arises through lack of trust. Members of a project team are never quite comfortable in the presence of an auditor/evaluator. If the auditor/evaluator is an "outsider"—anyone who cannot be identified as a project team member—there is fear that "we won't be understood." While such fears are rarely specific, they are nonetheless real. If the auditor/evaluator is an "insider," fear focuses on the possibility that the insider has some hidden agenda, is seeking some personal advantage at the expense of the "rest of us." The motives of insider and outsider alike are distrusted. As a result, project team members have little or no incentive to be forthcoming about their individual or project ancillary goals.

Finally, a fourth problem exists. Projects, similarly to all organizations that serve human ends, are multipurposed. The diverse set of direct and ancillary, project, and individual goals do not bear clear, organizationally determined (or accepted) priorities. Various members of the project team may have quite different ideas about which purposes are most important, which come next in line, and which are least important. In the absence of direct questions about the matter, no one has to confront the issue of who is right and who is wrong. As long as the goals and priorities are not made explicit, project team members can agree on *what* things should be done without necessarily agreeing (or even discussing) *why* those things should be done. Thus, if some of the project's objectives are not openly debated, each member can tolerate the different emphases of fellow team members. No one is forced to pick and choose or even to discuss such matters with coworkers.

All in all, the task of finding the ancillary goals of a project is difficult. Most evaluations simply ignore them, but the PM is well advised to take a keen interest in this area, and to request that evaluations include ancillary goals, the project's and the parent organization's, if not those of individuals. Even though one must usually be satisfied with rough, qualitative measures of ancillary-goal achievement, the information can be valuable. It may provide insight into such questions as: What sorts of things motivate people to join and work on projects? What sorts of rewards are most effective in eliciting maximum effort from project personnel? What are the major concerns of specific individuals working on the project?

In Chapter 5, we alluded to the importance of the project management "war room" (office, PMO) as a meeting place for the project team, a display area for the charts that show the project's progress, a central repository for project files and reports, and an office for the PM and other project administrators. The war room is also the "clubhouse" for the project team members and serves an important ancillary goal. It is to the project what the local pub was to "that old gang of mine." The camaraderie associated with a successful, well-run project provides great satisfaction to team members. The PMO, therefore, fills an emotional need as well as meeting its more mundane, direct administrative goals. The best PMOs (Baker, 2007) also, however, offer the best project leadership in the organization and are proud of it, enjoying strong executive support and the admiration of others in the organization who would love to be a part of this future-oriented, well-run learning team.

12.2 The Project Audit

The project audit is a thorough examination of the management of a project, its methodology and procedures, its records, its properties, its budgets and expenditures, and its degree of completion. It may deal with the project as a whole or only with a part of the project. The formal report may be presented in various formats but should, at a minimum, contain comments on the following points:

1. **Current status of the project.**   Does the work actually completed match the planned level of completion?

2. **Future status.**   Are significant schedule/cost/scope changes likely? If so, indicate the nature of the changes.

3. **Status of crucial tasks.**   What progress has been made on tasks that could decide the success or failure of the project?

4. **Risk assessment.**   What is the potential for project failure or monetary loss?

5. **Information pertinent to other projects.**   What lessons learned from the project being audited can be applied to other projects being undertaken by the organization?

6. **Limitations of the audit.**   What assumptions or limitations affect the data in the audit?

Note that the project audit is not a financial audit. The audit processes are similar in that each represents a careful investigation of the subject of the audit, but the outputs of these processes are quite different. The principal distinction between the two is that the financial audit has a limited scope. It concentrates on the use and preservation of the organization's assets. The project audit is far broader in scope and may deal with the project as

Project Management in Practice

Lessons from Auditing 110 Client/Server and Open Systems Projects

In an 11-year audit of 110 client/server and open systems projects, one auditor boiled the differences between success and failure down to four foundational concepts.

1. **Objectivity regarding scope, budget, deadlines, and solution design.**   Lack of objectivity in these areas is one of the basic causes of project failure. Decisions concerning the business case for initiating the project and establishing all of its parameters need to be scrutinized for bias and inadequate diligence.

2. **Experienced people at all levels in the project.**   Having experienced people on both the client side and the contractor side helps in a number of areas: maintaining a cooperative, problem-solving attitude, enforcing milestones and deliverables, using professional project management techniques, and maintaining continuous user involvement.

3. **Authority matched with responsibility.**   Since a project is usually established with a certain scope but limited budget and schedule, the PM needs to have the authority to make trade-offs between these objectives. This level of authority needs to be present on both the client side and the contractor side.

4. **Accountability sufficient to ensure that all parties perform as promised or are definitely held responsible.**   Accountability needs to be thoroughly detailed in the original contracts and purchase orders. It should include details concerning the project champion, the original estimator, suppliers, the client team and users, and the contractor team. Keeping projects short, such as under 6 months, keeps from diluting accountability through personnel turnover.

Questions

1. **Which of the four concepts is the most important, in your opinion?**

2. **Elaborate on item 3.**

3. **What lessons might you have expected that do not seem to be included?**

Source: T. Ingram, "Client/Server and Imaging: On Time, On Budget, As Promised," *PM Network*, Vol. 9.

TABLE 12.1 **Comparison of Financial Audits with Project Audits**

	Financial Audits	Project Audits
Status	Confirms status of business in relation to accepted standard	Must create basis for, and confirm, status on each project
Predictions	Company's state of economic well-being	Future status of project
Measurement	Mostly in financial terms	Financial terms plus schedule, progress, resource usage, status of ancillary goals
Record-keeping system	Format dictated by legal regulations and professional standards	No standard system, uses any system desired by individual organization or dictated by contract
Existence of information system	Minimal records needed to start audit	No records exist, data bank must be designed and used to start audit
Recommendations	Usually few or none, often restricted to management of accounting system	Often required, and may cover any aspect of the project or its management
Qualifications to the audit report	Customary to qualify statements if conditions dictate, but strong managerial pressure not to do so	Qualifications focus on shortcomings of audit process (e.g., lack of technical expertise, lack of funds or time)

a whole or any component or set of components of the project. Table 12.1 lists the primary differences between financial and project audits.

While the project audit may be concerned with any aspect of project management, it is not a traditional management audit. Management audits are primarily aimed at ensuring that the organization's management systems are in place and operative. The project audit goes beyond this. Among other things, it is meant to ensure that the project is being *appropriately* managed. Some managerial systems apply fairly well to all projects: for example, the techniques of planning, scheduling, budgeting, and so forth. On the other hand, some management practices should differ with different types of projects. See Sangameswaran (1995) and Corbin et al. (2001) for some guidance on auditing do's and don'ts.

We maintain that software projects are not *significantly* different from other types of projects. We stand on that position, but we also note that they possess some unique characteristics worthy of recognition and response, thus the rise of agile management for projects with uncertain scope. For example, computer-based projects are ordinarily very labor-intensive while many manufacturing projects, for instance, are highly capital-intensive. A thoughtful manager will simply not adopt the same managerial approach to each. The need for and value of a participative style (Six Sigma, TQM, employee involvement, etc.) are well established in the case of labor-intensive projects where problems are often ill-structured. If the project is capital-intensive and characterized by well-structured problems, the need for and value of a participative style are *relatively* diminished. (The reader must not read these statements as degrading the value of participative management. It is simply more valuable and relevant in some cases than others.)

To sum up, the management audit looks at managerial systems and their use. The project audit studies the financial, managerial, and technical aspects of the project as an integrated set applied to a specific project in a specific organizational environment.

Depth of the Audit

There are several practical constraints that may limit the depth of the project auditor's investigation. Time and money are two of the most common (and obvious) limits on the depth of investigation and level of detail presented in the audit report. Of course, there are costs associated with the audit/evaluation process over and above the usual costs of the professional and clerical time used in conducting the audit. Accumulation, storage, and maintenance of auditable data are important cost elements. Remember that such storage may be critically important in meeting the test of "due diligence" noted in Chapter 11. (Remember, too, that destruction of business data may be illegal under certain circumstances.)

Also serious, but less quantifiable, are two often overlooked costs. First, no matter how skilled the evaluator, an audit/evaluation process is always distracting to those working on the project. No project is completely populated with individuals whose self-esteem is so high that evaluation is greeted without anxiety. Worry about the outcome of the audit tends to produce an excessive level of self-protective activity, which, in turn, lowers the level of activity devoted to the project. Second, if the evaluation report is not written with a "constructive" tone, project morale will suffer.[2] Depending on the severity of the drop in morale, work on the project may receive a serious setback.

It is logical to vary the depth of the investigation depending on circumstances and needs unique to each project. While an audit can be performed at any level the organization wishes, four distinct levels are easily recognized and widely used: the general audit, the detailed audit, the technical audit, and the risk audit. The general audit is normally most constrained by time and resources and is usually a brief review of the project, touching lightly on the six concerns noted earlier. A typical detailed audit is conducted when a follow-up to the general audit is required. This tends to occur when the general audit has disclosed an unacceptable level of risk or malperformance in some part(s) of the project.

At times, the detailed audit cannot investigate problems at a satisfactory technical level because the auditor does not possess the technical knowledge needed. In such cases, a technical audit is required. Technical audits are normally carried out by a qualified technician under the direct guidance of the project auditor. In the case of very advanced or secret technology, it may be difficult to find qualified technical auditors inside the organization. In such cases, it is not uncommon for the firm to use academic consultants who have signed the appropriate nondisclosure documents. Although not a hard and fast rule, the technical audit is usually the most detailed.

While general, detailed, and technical audits are typically initiated by the organization, the PM has the responsibility for performing risk audits at appropriate points in the execution of the project. Addressed in **PMBOK**, risk audits are used to investigate the effectiveness with which project risks are identified and managed. Since risk audits are the responsibility of the PM, they can be incorporated into routine project meetings or performed as independent stand-alone activities.

11.6.2.2

Timing of the Audit

Given that all projects of significant size or importance should be audited, the first audits are usually done early in the project's life. The sooner a problem is discovered, the easier it is to deal with. Early audits are often focused on the technical issues in order to make sure that key technical problems have been solved or are under competent attack.

---

[2]The evaluator is well advised to remember two fundamental principles: (1) Constructive criticism does not feel all that constructive to the criticizee; and (2) Fix first, then blame—if you have any energy left.

Ordinarily, audits done later in the life cycle of a project are of less immediate value to the project but are of more value to the parent organization. As the project develops, technical issues are less likely to be matters of concern. Conformity to the schedule and budget becomes the primary interest. Management issues are major matters of interest for audits made late in the project's life (e.g., disposal of equipment or reallocation of project personnel).

Postproject audits are conducted with several basic objectives in mind. First, a postproject audit is often a legal necessity because the client specified such an audit in the contract. Second, the postproject audit is a major part of the Postproject Report, which is, in turn, the main source of managerial feedback to the parent firm. Third, the postproject audit is needed to account for all project property and expenditures.

Additional observations on the timing and value of audits are shown in Table 12.2.

Format and Use of the Audit Report

The type of project being audited and the uses for which the audit is intended dictate some specifics of the audit report format. Within any particular organization, however, it is useful to establish a general format to which all audit reports must conform. This makes it possible for PMs, auditors, and organizational management all to have the same understanding of, and expectations for, the audit report as a communication device. If the audit report is to serve as a communication device, there must also be a predetermined distribution list for such documents. When distribution is highly restricted, the report is almost certain to become the focus for interpersonal and intergroup conflict and tension.

While a few PMs insist on a complicated format for evaluation reports tailored to their individual projects, the simpler and more straightforward the format, the better. The information should be arranged so as to facilitate the comparison of predicted versus actual results. Significant deviations of actual from predicted results should be highlighted and explained in a set of comments. This eases the reader's work and tends to keep questions focused on important issues rather than trivia. This arrangement also reduces the likelihood that senior managers will engage in "fishing expeditions," searching for something "wrong"

TABLE 12.2   **Timing and Value of Project Audits/Evaluations**

Project Stage	Value
Initiation	Significant value if audit takes place early—prior to 25 percent completion of initial planning stage
Feasibility study	Very useful, particularly the technical audit
Preliminary plan/schedule budget	Very useful, particularly for setting measurement standards to ensure conformance with standards
Baseline schedule	Less useful, plan frozen, flexibility of team limited
Evaluation of data by project team	Marginally useful, team defensive about findings
Implementation	More or less useful, depending on importance of project methodology to successful implementation
Postproject	More or less useful, depending on applicability of findings to future projects

in every piece of data and sentence of the report. Once again, we would remind PMs of the dictum "Never let the boss be surprised."

Negative comments about individuals or groups associated with the project should be avoided. Write the report in a clear, professional, unemotional style, and restrict its content to information and issues that are relevant to the project. The following items cover the *minimum* information that should be contained in the audit report.

1. **Introduction**   This section contains a description of the project to provide a framework of understanding for the reader. Project objectives (direct goals) must be clearly delineated. If the objectives are complex, it may be useful to include explanatory parts of the project proposal as an addendum to the report.

2. **Current Status**   Status should be reported as of the time of the audit and, among other things, should include the following measures of performance:

   Cost: This section compares actual costs to budgeted costs. The time periods for which the comparisons are made should be clearly defined. As noted in Chapter 7, the report should focus on the *direct* charges made to the project. If it is also necessary to show project *total* costs, complete with all overheads, this cost data should be presented in an *additional* set of tables.

   Schedule: Performance in terms of planned events or milestones should be reported (see Figures 10.15 and 11.5 as examples). Completed portions of the project should be clearly identified, and the percent completion should be reported on all unfinished tasks for which estimates are possible. Make sure that the method used for estimating percent completion does not mislead readers (c.f. Section 10.3).

   Scope: This section compares work completed with resources expended. Earned value charts or tables (see Figures 10.7 and 10.13) may be used for this purpose if desired, but they may lack the appropriate level of detail. The requirement here is for information that will help to pinpoint problems with specific tasks or sets of tasks. Based on this information, projections regarding the timing and amounts of remaining planned expenditures are made.

   Quality: Whether or not this is a critical issue depends on the type of project being audited. Quality is a measure of the degree to which the output of a system conforms to prespecified characteristics. For some projects, the prespecified characteristics are so loosely stated that conformity is not much of an issue. At times, a project may produce outputs that far exceed original specifications. For instance, a project might require a subsystem that meets certain minimum standards. The firm may already have produced such a subsystem—one that meets standards well in excess of the current requirements. It may be efficient, with no less effectiveness, to use the previously designed system with its excess performance. If there is a detailed quality specification associated with the project, this section of the report may have to include a full review of the quality control procedures, along with full disclosure of the results of quality tests conducted to date.

3. **Future Project Status**   This section contains the auditor's conclusions regarding progress together with recommendations for any changes in technical approach, schedule, or budget that should be made in the remaining tasks. Except in unusual circumstances, for example, when results to date distinctly indicate the undesirability of some preplanned task, the auditor's report should consider only work that has already been completed or is well under way. No assumptions should be made about technical problems that are still under investigation at the time of the audit. Project audit/evaluation reports are not appropriate documents in which to rewrite the project proposal.

4. **Critical Management Issues**   All issues that the auditor feels require close monitoring by senior management should be included in this section, along with a brief explanation of the relationships between these issues and the objectives of the project. A brief discussion of time/cost/scope trade-offs will give senior management useful input information for decisions about the future of the project.

5. **Risk Management**   This section should contain a review of major risks associated with the project and their projected impact on project time/cost/scope. If alternative decisions exist that may significantly alter future risks, they can be noted at this point in the report. Once again, we note that the audit report is not the proper place to second-guess those who wrote the project proposal. The Postproject Report, on the other hand, will often contain sections on the general subject of "If only we knew then what we know now."

6. **Caveats, Limitations, and Assumptions**   This section of the report may be placed at the end or may be included as a part of the introduction. The auditor is responsible for the accuracy and timeliness of the report, but senior management still retains full responsibility for the interpretation of the report and for any action(s) based on the findings. For that reason, the auditor should specifically include a statement covering any limitations on the accuracy or validity of the report.

Responsibilities of the Project Auditor/Evaluator

First and foremost, the auditor should "tell the truth." This statement is not so simplistic as it might appear. It is a recognition of the fact that there are various levels of truth associated with any project. The auditor must approach the audit in an objective and ethical manner and assume responsibility for what is included and excluded from consideration in the report. Awareness of the biases of the several parties interested in the project—including the auditor's own biases—is essential, but extreme care is required if the auditor wishes to compensate for such biases. (A note that certain information *may* be biased is usually sufficient.) Areas of investigation outside the auditor's area of technical expertise should be acknowledged, and assistance sought when necessary. The auditor/evaluator must maintain political and technical independence during the audit and treat all materials gathered as confidential until the audit is formally released.

Walker et al. (1980) develop an even stronger case for the "independence" of the auditor. They argue that independence is essential for management's ability to assemble information that is both timely and accurate. They also list the following steps for carrying out an audit:

- Assemble a small team of experienced experts
- Familiarize the team with the requirements of the project
- Audit the project on site
- After completion, debrief the project's management
- Produce a written report according to a prespecified format
- Distribute the report to the PM and project team for their response
- Follow up to see if the recommendations have been implemented

If senior management and the project team are to take the audit/evaluation seriously, all information must be presented in a credible manner. The accuracy of data should be carefully checked, as should all calculations. The determination of what information to include and exclude is one that cannot be taken lightly. Finally, the auditor should engage in a continuing evaluation of the auditing process in a search for ways to improve the effectiveness, efficiency, and value of the process.

12.3 | The Project Audit Life Cycle

Thus far, we have considered the project audit and project evaluation as if they were one and the same. In most ways they are. The audit contains an evaluation, and an evaluator must conduct some sort of audit. Let us now consider the audit as a formal document required by contract with the client. If the client is the federal government, the nature of the project audit is more or less precisely defined, as is the audit process.

Project Management in Practice

Auditing a Troubled Project at Atlantic States Chemical Laboratories

Atlantic States Chemical Laboratories (ASCL) received a contract from an entrepreneurial firm, Oretec, to conduct a unique type of chemical analysis on special alloys they had created in their own laboratories in the interest of identifying potentially successful commercial alloys. The contract emphasized quality of the effort and speed of continuing laboratory analyses. The contract duration would be open-ended, with payment at the monthly rate of $100,000. The liaison officer from Oretec would have access to ASCL's laboratory work for observation.

As work progressed, the liaison officer became more involved in the project, pressuring the team to alter their approach and skip the usual repeat-verification procedures in the interest of time. On two occasions, the ASCL team devised an analysis indicating that a commercially successful product could be produced. The liaison officer was gratified with the effort and asked for suggestions on how to produce the product commercially. However, tests at Oretec indicated that these approaches would not work. As the project midpoint passed, the pressure for more and faster analyses increased even more, with the liaison officer becoming more belligerent and difficult to please. Soon thereafter, the president of ASCL received a letter from Oretec voicing a number of complaints and terminating the contract effective immediately. Puzzled by the unexpected displeasure of their client with no indication of trouble on the project from internal sources, the president requested a comprehensive audit of the project.

The audit reported the following:

1. **Overview Points:**
   o The original approach to the project was sound but was altered by the client's liaison officer; nevertheless, significant findings were still made.
   o The analyses themselves were conducted properly.
   o There were several analytical successes during the project (each identified).
   o Commercialization was not ASCL's responsibility but the client's, even if ASCL suggested some possible processes.

   o There was excessive involvement of the liaison officer in the management of the project, including frequent changes of direction.
   o Ongoing project management decisions and changes were not documented by ASCL, nor communicated to the client.

2. **Analysis of Client's Criticism**   (about half of the criticisms were valid, details described).

3. **Further Points of Note:**
   o The commercialization processes proposed by ASCL have, in fact, been successfully used in similar instances. The client's tests indicating their unacceptability are incorrect.
   o The reports provided by ASCL and criticized by the client as incomplete were redirected by the liaison officer to be prepared quickly and informally. The reports of project analysis success would not have been understandable to the client's management, only to technical personnel or the liaison officer.
   o ASCL management gave insufficient guidance/support to the project leader in his relations with the client.

4. **Recommendation:**   Establish a formal procedure for identifying high-risk projects at the contract stage and then monitor them carefully for deviations from plan. The factors contributing to making this a high-risk project were inadequate funding, insufficient time, low chance of success, an unsophisticated client, and excessive access to ongoing project activities by the client.

Questions

1. Was this a good use of the audit concept?
2. What was the major problem in this project?
3. In spite of the recommendation, ASCL had already had a "problem project" list and system in place. Why do you think it may not have caught this particular project? Will the new procedure do any better?

Source: J. Meredith, consulting project.

As the project itself, the audit has a *life cycle* composed of an orderly progression of well-defined events. There are six of these events.

1. **Project Audit Initiation**   This step involves starting the audit process, defining the purpose and scope of the audit, and gathering sufficient information to determine the proper audit methodology.

2. **Project Baseline Definition**   This phase of the cycle normally consists of identifying the performance areas to be evaluated, determining standards for each area through benchmarking or some other process, ascertaining management performance expectations for each area, and developing a program to measure and assemble the requisite information.

   Occasionally, no convenient standards exist or can be determined through benchmarking. For example, a commodity pricing model was developed as part of a large marketing project. No baseline data existed that could serve to help evaluate the model. Because the commodity was sold by open bid, the firm used its standard bidding procedures. The results formed baseline data against which the pricing model could be tested on an "as if" basis. Table 12.3 shows the results of one such test. CCC is the firm, and the contracts on which it bid *and won*, together with the associated revenues (mine net price × tonnage), are shown. Similar information is displayed for Model C, which was used on an "as if" basis, so the Model C Revenue column shows those bids the model *would have won*, had it actually been used.

3. **Establishing an Audit Database**   Once the baseline standards are established, execution of the audit begins. The next step is to create a database for use by the audit team. For example, consider the database required by the CCC pricing model test in Table 12.3. Depending on the purpose and scope of the audit, the database might include information needed for assessment of project organization, management and control, past and current project status, schedule performance, cost performance, and output quality, as well as plans for the future of the project. The information may vary from a highly technical description of performance to a behaviorally based description of the interaction of project team members.

   Because the purpose and scope of audits vary widely from one project to another and for different times on any given project, the audit database is frequently quite extensive. The required database for project audits should be specified in the project master plan. If this is done, the necessary information will be available when needed. Nonetheless, it is important to avoid collecting "anything that might be useful," since this can place extraordinary information collection and storage requirements on the project.

4. **Preliminary Analysis of the Project**   After standards are set and data collected, judgments are made. Some auditors eschew judgment on the grounds that such a delicate but weighty responsibility must be reserved to senior management. But judgment often requires a fairly sophisticated understanding of the technical aspects of the project, and/or of statistics and probability, subjects that may elude some managers. In such an event, the auditor must analyze the data and then present the analysis to managers in ways that communicate the real meaning of the audit's findings. It is the auditor's duty to brief the PM on all findings and judgments *before* releasing the audit report. The purpose of the audit is to improve the project being audited as well as to improve the entire process of managing projects. It is not intended as a device to embarrass the PM.

5. **Audit Report Preparation**   This part of the audit life cycle includes the preparation of the audit report, organized by whatever format has been selected for use. A set of recommendations, together with a plan for implementing them, is also a part of the audit report. If the recommendations go beyond normal practices of the

TABLE 12.3 Performance against Baseline Data

| | | | | Bid Performance for Model "C" | | |
| | | Award | | | | |
Destination	Tonnage	CCC Bid	Model "C" Bid	Mine Net Price	CCC Revenue	Model "C" Revenue
D1-2	3800		X	$4.11		$15,618
D1-7	1600		X	3.92		6,272
D2-7	1300		X	4.11		5,343
D3-2	700		X	5.13		3,591
D3-3	500	X		5.22	$2,610	
D3-4	600		X	5.72		3,432
D3-5	1200		X	5.12		6,144
D3-6	1000		X	5.83		5,830
D4-6	700		X	4.88		3,416
D4-8	600		X	5.34		3,204
D5-1	500	X		3.54	1,770	
D6-1	1000	X	X	4.02–3.92	4,020	3,920
D6-2	900	X		4.35	3,915	
D6-5	200	X		3.75	750	
D6-6	800		X	3.17		2,536
D7-5	1600		X	5.12		8,192
D7-8	2600		X	5.29		13,754
D8-2	1600	X	X	4.83	7728	7,728
D8-3	2400		X	4.32		10,368
				Total revenue	$20,793	$99,348
				Total tonnage	4700	21,500
				Average mine net	$4.42	$4.62

organization, they will need support from the policy-making level of management. This support should be sought and verified *before* the recommendations are published. If support is not forthcoming, the recommendations should be modified until satisfactory. Figure 12.1 is one page of an extensive and detailed set of recommendations that resulted from an evaluation project conducted by a private social service agency.

6. **Project Audit Termination** As with the project itself, after the audit has accomplished its designated task, the audit process should be terminated. When the final report and recommendations are released, there will be a review of the audit process. This is done in order to improve the methods for conducting the audit. When the review is finished, the audit is truly complete and the audit team should be formally disbanded.

> *Final Report, Agency Evaluation, Sub-Committee II*
> *Physical Plant, Management of Office, Personnel Practices*
>
> ### Summary of Recommendations
>
> Recommendations which require Board action.
>
> 1. The Board of _____ should continue its efforts to obtain additional funds for our salary item.
> 2. The cost of Blue Cross and Blue Shield insurance coverage on individual employees should be borne by _____.
>
> Recommendations which can be put into effect by *Presidential Order* to committees, staff, or others.
>
> 3. The House Committee should activate, with first priority, the replacement of the heating/air conditioning system. Further, this committee should give assistance and support to the Secretary to the Executive Director in maintenance and repair procedures.
> 4. A professional library should be established even if part time workers must share space to accomplish this.
> 5. Our insurance needs should be re-evaluated.
> 6. All activities related to food at meetings should be delegated to someone other than the Secretary to the Executive Director.
> 7. Majority opinion—positions of Administrative Assistant and Bookkeeper will need more time in the future. Minority opinion—positions of Administrative Assistant, Bookkeeper, and Statistical Assistant should be combined.
> 8. The Personnel Practices Committee should review job descriptions of Bookkeeper and Statistical Assistant and establish salary ranges for those two positions and that of the Administrative Assistant.
> 9. Dialogue among the Executive Director, his secretary, and the Administrative Assistant should continue in an effort to streamline office procedures and expedite handling of paperwork.
> 10. The written description of the Personnel Practices Committee should include membership of a representative of the nonprofessional staff.
> 11. The Personnel Practices Committee should study, with a view toward action, the practice of part-time vs. full-time casework staff.

FIGURE 12.1   Sample recommendations for a social service agency.

12.4 Some Essentials of an Audit/Evaluation

For an audit/evaluation (hereafter, simply a/e) to be conducted with skill and precision, for it to be credible and generally acceptable to senior management, to the project team, and to the client, several essential conditions must be met. The a/e team must be properly selected, all records and files must be accessible, and free contact with project members must be preserved.

The A/E Team

The choice of the a/e team is critical to the success of the entire process. It may seem unnecessary to note that team members should be selected because of their ability to contribute to the a/e procedure, but sometimes members are selected merely because they are available. The size of the team will generally be a function of the size and complexity of the project. For a small project, one person can often handle all the tasks of the a/e, but for a large project, the team may require representatives from several different constituencies. Typical areas that might furnish a/e team members are:

- The project itself, including the PM, the project owner, and the project sponsor
- The PMO, or Program Office manager
- The accounting/controller department
- Technical specialty areas
- The funder
- The marketing department
- Senior management
- Purchasing/asset management
- The personnel department
- The legal/contract administration department

The main role of the a/e team is to conduct a thorough and complete examination of the project or some prespecified aspect of the project. The team must determine which items should be brought to management's attention. It should report information and make recommendations in such a way as to maximize the utility of its work. The team is responsible for constructive observations and advice based on the training and experience of its members. Members must be aloof from personal involvement with conflicts among project team staff and from rivalries between projects. The a/e is a highly disciplined process, and all team members must willingly and sincerely subject themselves to that discipline.

Access to Records

In order for the a/e team to be effective, it must have free access to all information relevant to the project. This may present some problems on government projects that may be classified for reasons of national security. In such cases, a subgroup of the a/e team may be formed from qualified ("cleared") individuals.

Most of the information needed for an a/e will come from the project team's records and those of the Project Management Office, and/or from various departments such as accounting, personnel, and purchasing. Obviously, gathering the data is the responsibility of the a/e team, and this burden should not be passed on to the project management team, though the project team is responsible for collecting the usual data on the project and keeping project records up-to-date during the project's life.

In addition to the formal records of the project, some of the most valuable information comes from documents that predate the project—for example, correspondence with the funder that led to the RFP, minutes of the Project Selection Committee, and minutes of senior management committees that decided to pursue a specific area of technical interest. Clearly, project status reports, relevant technical memoranda, change orders, information about project organization and management methods, and financial and resource usage information are also important. The a/e team may have to extract much of these data from other documents because the required information is often not in the form needed. Data collection is time-consuming, but careful work is absolutely necessary for an effective, credible a/e.

As information is collected, it must be organized and filed in a systematic way. Systematic methods need to be developed for separating out useful information. Most important, stopping rules are needed to prevent data collection and processing from continuing far past the point of diminishing returns. Priorities must be set to ensure that important analyses are undertaken before those of lesser import. In addition, safeguards are needed against duplication of efforts. The careful development of forms and procedures will help to standardize the process as much as possible.

Access to Project Personnel and Others

Contact between a/e team members and project team members, or between the a/e team and other members of the organization who have knowledge of the project, should be free. One exception is contact between the a/e team and the funder; such contacts are *not made without clearance* from senior management. This restriction would hold even when the funder is represented on the audit team and should also hold for in-house clients.

In any case, there are several rules that should be followed when contacting project personnel. Care must be taken to avoid misunderstandings between a/e team members and project team members. Project personnel should always be made aware of the in-progress a/e. Critical comments should be avoided. Particularly serious is the practice of delivering on-the-spot, off-the-cuff opinions and remarks that may not be appropriate or represent the consensus opinion of the a/e team.

The a/e team will undoubtedly encounter political opposition during its work. If the project is a subject of political tension, attempts will most certainly be made by the opposing sides to co-opt (or repudiate) the a/e team. As much as possible, they should avoid becoming involved. At times, information may be given to a/e team members in confidence. Discreet attempts should be made to confirm such information through nonconfidential sources. If it cannot be confirmed, it should not be used. The auditor/evaluator must protect the sources of confidential information and must not become a conduit for unverifiable criticism of the project.

12.5 | Measurement

Measurement is an integral part of the a/e process. Many issues of what and how to measure have been discussed in earlier chapters, particularly in Chapter 2. Several aspects of a project that should be measured are obvious and, fortunately, rather easy to measure. For the most part, it is not difficult to know if and when a milestone has been completed. We can directly observe the fact that a building foundation has been poured, that all required materials for a corporate annual report have been collected and delivered to the printer, or that all contracts have been let for the rehabilitation of an apartment complex. At times, of course, milestone completion may not be quite so evident. It may be difficult to tell when a chemical experiment is finished, and it is almost impossible to tell when a complex computer program is finally "bug free." Largely, however, milestone completion can be measured adequately.

Similarly, performance against planned budget and schedule usually poses no major measurement problems. We may be a bit uncertain whether or not a "nine-day" scheduled completion time should include weekend days, but most organizations adopt conventions to ease these minor counting problems. Measuring the actual expenditures against the planned budget is a bit trickier and depends on an in-depth understanding of the procedures used by the accounting department. It is common to imbue cost data with higher levels of reality and precision than is warranted.

When the objectives of a project have been stated in terms of profits, rates of return, or discounted cash flows, as in the financial selection models discussed in Chapter 2, measurement problems may be more obstinate. The problem does not often revolve around the accounting conventions used, though if those conventions have not been clearly established in advance, there may be bitter arguments about what costs are appropriately assigned to the individual project being evaluated. A far more difficult task is the determination of what revenues should be assigned to the project.

Assume, for example, that a drug firm creates a project for the development of a new drug and simultaneously sets up a project to develop and implement a marketing strategy for the potential new drug and two existing allied drugs. Assume further that the entire program is successful and large amounts of revenue are generated. How much revenue should be assigned to the credit of the drug research project? How much to the marketing project? Within the marketing project, how much should go to each of the subprojects for the individual drugs? If the entire program is treated as one project, the problem is less serious; but R&D and marketing are in different functional areas of the parent organization, and each may be evaluated on the basis of its contribution to the parent firm's profitability. The year-end bonuses of divisional managers are determined in part (often in large part) by the profitability of the units they manage. Figure 12.2 illustrates project baseline data established for a new product. This figure shows the use of multiple measures including

PRODUCT _____   DATE _____

MARKET _____

DATE OF FIRST SALE: U.S. _____

O.U.S. _____

	1ST YEAR			2ND YEAR			3RD YEAR			4TH YEAR			5TH YEAR			TOTAL		
	MIN	B.E.*	MAX	MIN	B.E.	MAX	MIN	B.E.	MAX	MIN	B.E.	MAX	MIN	B.E.	MAX	MIN	B.E.	MAX
1. Total Market Size:																		
2. Expected Market Share:																		
3. Kg or Units:																		
4. Est. Selling Price:																		
5. Gross Sales:																		
6. Est. COPS %:																		
7. Gross Margin %:																		
8. Est. Marketing Expense %:																		
9. Marketing Margin %:																		
10. Loss on Profit from other Products List:																		
11. Est. Profit:																		
12. Development Expenses:																		
13. Capital Expenditures:																		

*Best estimate.

FIGURE 12.2 Baseline marketing data for a new product.

price, unit sales, market share, development costs, capital expenditures, and other measures of performance.

There is no theoretically acceptable solution to such measurement problems, but there are politically acceptable solutions. All the cost/revenue allocation decisions must be made when the various projects are initiated. If this is done, the battles are fought "up front," and the equity of cost/revenue allocations ceases to be so serious an issue. As long as allocations are made by a formula, major conflict is avoided—or, at least, mitigated.

If multiobjective scoring models rather than financial models are being used for project selection, measurement problems are somewhat exacerbated. There are more elements to measure, some of which are objective and measured with relative ease. But some elements are subjective and require reasonably standard measurement techniques if the measures are to be reliable. Interview and questionnaire methods for gathering data must be carefully constructed and carried out if the project scores are to be taken seriously. Criteria weights and scoring procedures should be decided at the start of the project.

A Note to the Auditor/Evaluator

A kindly critic and colleague uses what he calls the "rules of engagement" to explain to his students how to schedule interviews, conduct interviews, get copies, limit the scope of activities, and handle the many mundane tasks included in auditing/evaluating projects. While the phrase "rules of engagement" seems a bit warlike to us, we do have some similar advice for the auditor/evaluator.

Above all else, the a/e needs "permission to enter the system." It is difficult to describe precisely what is meant by that phrase, but every experienced auditor or evaluator will know. Senior management can assign an individual to the job of heading an audit/evaluation team, but this does not automatically imply that project personnel will accept that person as a legitimate a/e. There will be several indicators if the a/e is not accepted. Phone calls from the a/e will be returned only at times when the a/e is not available. Requests for information will be politely accepted, but little or no information will be forthcoming—though copious, sincere apologies and semibelievable excuses will be. Interviews with project team members will be strangely without content. Attempts to determine the project's ancillary goals will be unsuccessful, as will attempts to get team members to discuss intrateam conflict. Everyone will be quite pleasant, but somehow promises of cooperation do not turn into fact. Always, there are good excuses and looks of wide-eyed innocence.

If the a/e is reasonably likable and maintains a calm, relaxed attitude, the project team generally begins to extend limited trust. The usual first step is to allow the a/e qualified access to information about the project. Missing information from the official project files is suddenly found. The a/e has then been given tentative permission to enter the system. If the a/e deals gently with this information, neither ignoring nor stressing the project's shortcomings while recognizing and appreciating the project's strengths, trust will be extended, and the permission to enter the system will no longer be tentative.

Trust building is a slow and delicate process that is easily thwarted. The a/e needs to understand the politics of the project team and the interpersonal relationships among its members and must deal with this confidential knowledge respectfully. On this base is trust built and meaningful audit/evaluation constructed. There is an almost universal propensity for the a/e to mimic Jack Webb's Sgt. Friday on the old Dragnet TV show—"Just give me the facts, ma'am." It is not that simple, nor are any processes involving human beings that simple.

In the next chapter, we move into the final state of the project management process, termination. There we will look at when to terminate a project and the various ways to conduct the termination.

Summary

This chapter initiated our discussion of the final part of the text, project termination. A major concluding step in the termination process is the evaluation of the project process and results, otherwise known as an audit. Here we looked at the purposes of evaluation and what it should encompass: the audit process and measurement considerations, the demands placed on the auditor, and the construction and design of the final report.

Specific points made in the chapter are:

- The purposes of the evaluation are both goal-directed, aiding the project in achieving its objectives, and also aimed at achieving unspecified, sometimes hidden, yet firmly held, ancillary objectives.

- The audit report should contain at least the current status of the project, the expected future status, the status of crucial tasks, a risk assessment, information pertinent to other projects, and any caveats and limitations.

- Audit depth and timing are critical elements of the audit because, for example, it is much more difficult to alter the project based on a late audit than an early audit.

- The difficult responsibility of the auditor is to be honest in fairly presenting the audit results. This may even require data interpretation on occasion.

- The audit life cycle includes audit initiation, project baseline definition, establishing a database, preliminary project analysis, report preparation, and termination.

- Several essential conditions must be met for a credible audit: a credible a/e team, sufficient access to records, and sufficient access to personnel.

- Measurement, particularly of revenues, is a special problem.

Glossary

Audit A formal inquiry into some issue or aspect of a system.

Baseline A standard for performance, commonly established early on for later comparisons.

Evaluate To set a value for or appraise.

Risk Analysis An evaluation of the likely outcomes of a policy and their probability of occurrence, usually conducted to compare two or more scenarios or policies.

Questions

Material Review Questions

1. Give some examples of ancillary project objectives.

2. When should an audit be conducted during a project? Is there a "best" time?

3. What occurs in each stage of the audit life cycle?

4. What items should be included in the audit status report?

5. What access is required for an accurate audit?

6. Why is measurement a particular problem in auditing?

7. What is a "baseline"?

8. What is the purpose of a risk analysis?

9. What are the essential conditions of a credible audit?

Class Discussion Questions

10. In a typical project, do you feel frequent brief evaluations or periodic major evaluations are better in establishing control? Why?

11. Do you think that project evaluations cost-justify themselves?

12. What steps can be taken to ease the perceived threat to team members of an external evaluation?

13. What feedback, if any, should the project team get from the evaluation?

14. During the project audit, a tremendous amount of time can be wasted if a systematic method of information handling is not adopted. Briefly explain how this systematic method may be developed.

15. "Evaluation of a project is another means of project control." Comment.
16. Why is it better to rely on several sources of information than just a few?
17. What could be some advantages and disadvantages of the following sources of information: (a) charts, (b) written reports, and (c) firsthand observation?
18. Why is it important to use outside auditors rather than inside auditors who would be more familiar with the company and the project?
19. What kinds of reports might be sent to funders?
20. What would you identify as the ethical responsibilities of an auditor?
21. Given the great variety of items for an auditor to evaluate, what should the PM do given that the project evaluation basis was clearly laid out in the project plan? What about ancillary goals?

Incidents For Discussion

Gerkin Pension Services

Dana Lasket was the PM of a project with the objective of determining the feasibility of moving a significant portion of Gerkin's computing capacity to another geographical location. Project completion was scheduled for 28 weeks. Dana had the project team motivated, and at the end of the twentieth week, the project was on schedule.

The next week, during a casual lunch conversation, Dana discovered that the vice-president of finance had serious doubts about the validity of the assumptions the team was using to decide which computers should be relocated.

Dana tried to convince him that he was wrong during two follow-up meetings, with no success. In fact, the more they talked, the more convinced the vice-president became that Dana was wrong. The project was too far along to change any assumptions without causing significant delays. In addition, the vice-president was likely to inherit the responsibility for implementing any approved plans for the new location. For those reasons, Dana felt it was essential to resolve the disagreement before the scheduled completion of the project. Dana requested a project auditor be assigned to audit the project, paying special attention to the assumptions made to identify the computers to be moved.

Questions

Is this a good use of the audit technique? Will it be helpful here? Why or why not?

General Ship Building Company

General Ship Building has a contract with the Department of the Navy to build three new aircraft carriers over the next 5 years. During the construction of the first ship, the PM formed an auditing team to audit the construction process for the three ships. After picking the audit team members, he requested that they develop a set of minimum requirements for the projects and use this as a baseline in the audit. While reviewing the contract documents, an auditing team member discovered a discrepancy between the contract minimum requirements and the Navy's minimum requirements. Based on his findings, he has told the PM that he has decided to contact the local Navy contract office and inform them of the problem.

Questions

If you were the PM, how would you handle this situation? How can a funder be assured of satisfactory contract completion?

Continuing Integrative Class Project

At this point (or perhaps if a special problem has arisen in the project), the Instructor should have the project audited. Possible auditors include members of the class who have finished their project tasks, the Historian, the Instructor himself or herself, or someone outside the project. Follow the guidelines in the chapter for conducting the audit. An alternative is to show how the Historian's report relates to a full-blown post-project evaluation.

Bibliography

Baker, B. "In Common." *Project Management Journal*, September 2007.

Corbin, D., R. Cox, R. Hamerly, and K. Knight. "Project Management of Project Reviews." *PM Network*, March 2001.

Sangameswaran, A. "A Key to Effective Independent Project Reviews." *PM Network*, April 1995.

Schaefer, A. G., and A. J. Zaller. "The Ethics Audit for Nonprofit Organizations." *PM Network*, April 1998.

Shenhar, A. J., O. Levy, and D. Dvir, "Mapping the Dimensions of Project Success." *Project Management Journal*, June 1997.

Walker, M. G., and R. Bracey. "Independent Auditing As Project Control." *Datamation*, March 1980.

The following case concerns a multiphase U.S. Army missile development program. The first phase was difficult, and six consecutive flight tests ended in failure, with the contractor paying millions of dollars in fines for the failures. However, the next two tests were successful, and the Pentagon decided to skip a third planned test and move directly to the next phase of the program—Engineering and Manufacturing Development. Before doing so, however, an audit of the program's progress to date was requested of the U.S. Government Accountability Office. The case reports the underlying problems revealed by the audit and the lessons learned by the program managers.

Case

Theater High Altitude Area Defense (THAAD):

Five Failures and Counting (B)[3]   Tom Cross, Alan Beckenstein, and Tim Laseter

It was July 2004. John West and Joy Adams had been through a lot since the THAAD program had begun in 1992. Eleven THAAD flight tests had been conducted in the Program Definition and Risk Reduction (PDRR) Phase. After six initial failures, the first successful missile-to-missile intercept of a ballistic missile target was achieved on June 10, 1999, during Flight Test 10. West and Adams reflected on the contract lessons they had learned.

GAO Study—June 1999

Studies conducted by both Department of Defense and independent sources identified the following underlying problems in the THAAD program:

- The program's compressed flight-test schedule did not allow for adequate ground testing, and as a result, officials could not detect problems prior to flight tests. The schedule also left insufficient time for preflight testing, postflight analysis, and corrective action.

- The requirement to be able to quickly deploy an early prototype system diverted the contractor and government project management's attention away from the normal interceptor development process and resulted in interceptors that were not equipped with sufficient instruments to provide optimum test data.

- Quality assurance received insufficient emphasis and resources during the time of component production, resulting in unreliable components.

- The contract for developing the interceptor was a cost-plus-fixed-fee contract, a contract type that placed all of the program's financial risk on the government and did not include provisions that could be used to hold the contractor accountable for less than optimum performance.

Flight-test failures had been caused primarily by manufacturing defects rather than problems with advanced technology. These failures prevented the army from demonstrating that it could reliably employ the "hit-to-kill" technology critical to THAAD's success. The restructured program addressed each of the program's four underlying problems. It

- lengthened the flight-test schedule and increased ground testing

- removed the requirement for the deployable, early prototype interceptors

- increased the contractor's quality emphasis, including its commitment, leadership, and quality assurance staffing

- modified the cost-plus-fixed-fee contract to provide performance-based incentives and penalties and introduced a degree of competition into the program.

[3]Reprinted by permission Copyright by the University of Virginia Darden School foundation, Charlottesville, VA.

Despite these changes, the reliability of the remaining flight-test interceptors remained a concern because most components were produced when the contractor's quality assurance system was inadequate.

Contract Performance Lessons Learned

- The THAAD PDRR missiles had not yet demonstrated any military capability. Acquiring a significant number of missiles from the current design to support a contingency deployment concept was unwise. The hardware for the remaining missiles had been built and procured several years before, and only minor changes or upgrades could be made to the existing hardware. Until new hardware was built that incorporated the necessary design changes and improved manufacturing, product assurance, and test processes, there was no reason to expect any significant improvement in the THAAD missile's performance.

- Stable program funding and guidance was essential for program success. That was especially true with a complex "cutting-edge" technology program such as THAAD. Pressures to quickly field a prototype, budget cuts, program restructuring, and the misapplication of the principles of acquisition reform all strongly influenced the programmatic decisions. The Program Management Office and contractor made tradeoffs that were necessary to meet a budget and a schedule driven by the requirement for early deployment of the User Operational Evaluation System.

- Improved component level design, qualification testing, quality control processes, and product assurance and testing procedures in the manufacturing of the interceptor were needed. Improved component level quality testing to confirm both design and reliability would greatly enhance the reliability and provide increased confidence in the integrated missile subsystems and system.

- More thorough ground and hardware-in-the-loop simulation testing of the THAAD missile assembly, and especially the seeker, needed to be performed. Due to the strong DOT&E influence, the Program Management Office had chartered a team to review the contractor and government hardware-in-the-loop testing capabilities. The team would provide recommendations on where improvements were needed to permit testing of end-to-end integrated missiles and to test critical subsystems (e.g., divert attitude control system, seeker, avionics package, etc.).

Contract Administration Lessons Learned

- A solid teaming environment (Battle Rhythm concept) early in the program life cycle, including all THAAD stakeholders (DCMA, THAAD Program Office (TPO), the prime contractor, and subcontractors) was critical to solving potential problems prior to any major milestone/funding decision points. This resulted in a proactive, solution-oriented business environment, where issues were identified with real-time resolution.

- Prime contractor DCMA Commander needed to participate actively in the Award Fee process, and THAAD stakeholders needed to participate in the Award Fee process, to address the then current program risk factors as determined by the Award Fee Board, to focus contractor risk mitigation efforts to reduce program risk, and to ensure overall mission success.

- Utilization of an electronic data management system to provide all players real-time information of all aspects of the program, from basic contract modifications to IPT minutes to program matrices, which had been paramount to the Battle Rhythm initiative success.

The THAAD program entered the engineering and manufacturing development (EMD) phase in 2000, with the award of a $3.8 billion contract to Lockheed Martin Space Systems Company. West and Adams had used the contract lessons learned and incorporated unique incentives into the EMD contract (Exhibit 1).

Between 2000 and 2003, THAAD engineers reworked the entire system and fixed many of its inherent problems and redundancies. In May 2004, production of 16 flight test missiles began at Lockheed Martin's new production facilities in Pike County, Alabama. Flight testing of the EMD system was scheduled to begin in early 2005 and continue till 2009. The system was expected to enter low-rate production, to support initial operating capability (IOC) in 2007.

Then in the development phase, THAAD was implementing a block development strategy designed to get the THAAD system into the hands of our soldiers as quickly as possible, using the latest technology in the most affordable manner. Each two-year block (Block 2004, 2006, and 2008) built on and integrated with the capabilities of the predecessor block. The program continued to refine and mature the system design to ensure that the element performed to an acceptable standard and could be produced efficiently and maintained. This would be accomplished by continuing current component design and development activities, robust ground tests, and quality assurance programs. Flight-testing would resume in late 2004 at White Sands Missile Range, transitioning to the Pacific Missile Range Facility in Hawaii in 2006 to test against representative threat systems.

Questions

1. Do you think this was a financial audit, a project audit, or a management audit? Why?

2. Was the purpose of the audit to exert cybernetic control, go/no-go control, or postproject control? Explain.

Army Acquisition Reform *Newsletter*

Special Incentives for Successful Flight Tests
in THAAD Award Fee Contract

The Theater High Altitude Area Defense (THAAD) Engineering and Manufacturing Development (EMD) contract for $3.8 billion was awarded to Lockheed Martin Space Systems Company, Missile and Space Operations (LMSSC/M&SO), Sunnyvale, CA, on June 28, 2000. The THAAD EMD contract is an award fee type contract. The functional performance areas are technical, management, schedule and cost.

Emphasis was placed on the importance of successful flight tests occurring on schedule and within cost by including in the contract an award fee pool with special incentives for successful flight test intercepts for the first two flight attempts at White Sands Missile Range (WSMR) and Kwajalein Missile Range (KMR). If Lockheed Martin achieves a successful intercept within the first two attempts at WSMR, they will receive $25M in award fee. However, if they are unsuccessful after the first attempt, LM will share $15M of the contract cost. If Lockheed Martin achieves a successful intercept within the first two attempts at KMR, they will receive $25M in award fee. However, if they are unsuccessful after the first attempt, LM will share $20M of the contract cost. The clause identifies technical parameters that must be met during each of the first two flight tests at both ranges.

The use of the alpha contracting process for development of the scope of work (SOW) and the integrated Master Plan and Master Schedule as well as proposal preparation/evaluation provided the government with a best value contract. The Integrated Master Plan (IMP) provides the process narratives, events and criteria for the EMD program. The Integrated Master Schedule (IMS) provides the detail tasks and schedule for implementing the IMP. Both of these documents were developed during the alpha contracting process, substantially reducing the normal negotiation time and promoting a better understanding of the EMD requirements and the contractor-proposed approach to meeting these requirements.

EXHIBIT 1   Army Acquisition Reform Newsletter.

3. Given the comments in the case, do you surmise that the reason for the audit was to improve future projects or to ascertain the reasons for not meeting the project's goals, and if the latter, its direct goals or ancillary goals?

4. Do you think the GAO was the best choice for an audit team? Would it have the trust of the project personnel?

5. Given the minimal elements of a project audit present in Section 12.2, which element(s) would have been primary to the audit team? Why? Which section would have contained the "underlying problems" reported in the case?

The following reading shows that project audits and evaluations help further knowledge concerning good project practice and improving the understanding of those in the organization about neighboring functions. However, most current audits/evaluations appear to be shallow, based on naive assumptions, and remedies for project difficulties tend to be superficial. Yet, audits and evaluations were important learning experiences and are undervalued in organizations in terms of the insights they can provide about good project management.

Reading

An Assessment of Postproject Reviews[4]   J. S. Busby

Potential Benefits

Many organizations set out to do postproject reviews, and for some compelling reasons:

- People do not automatically learn from their own experience, even as isolated individuals. They have to test new experiences against their existing knowledge and revise that knowledge in order to learn. A good example is learning about people. You can encounter a person on several occasions, but you do not learn from these occasions in any profound sense until you make a decision about the person (Eraut, 1994). It is at this point that you assemble the different experiences you have had and draw some coherent conclusions. The upshot is that, if you want to learn from experience, you consciously have to reflect on it.

- The knowledge of what occurred is usually dispersed among several people. We do many things, especially in organizations, where outcomes are not directly observable. (We might not know, for instance, how readily users of our new product design adapt to the demands made on them.) Therefore, we need to consult other people to know the outcomes of our performance.

- The knowledge needed to diagnose outcomes is similarly dispersed among several people. For instance, people commonly make wrong assumptions about why others fail in their duties, and these misconceptions need to be corrected if reasonable remedies are to be identified for such failings. So, again, if we want to learn from experience, we must do so collectively.

- Dissemination matters, often critically. Organizations are rarely so specialized that every task of type X always goes to individual A. Some organizations seem to arrange things in such a way that tasks always go to the people least qualified to do them. Therefore, what one person learns from doing a project needs to be disseminated to others who might fill similar roles in the future. And, of course, this dissemination does not happen as a matter of course. Repeated errors are a characteristic of organizational life. Learning from experience within an organization has to be a public, recorded activity.

In some organizations, retrospective reviews are a natural and integral part of their operations; these include organizations that are highly regarded, such as military air forces (Lipshitz, Popper, & Oz, 1996).

Potential Drawbacks

The reality is, however, that postproject reviews are often curtailed and sometimes fall into complete disuse. Even when they are enthusiastically conducted, their outcomes are poorly disseminated. The reasons for this neglect include:

- They take time. This is especially a problem in project-oriented firms since project managers want to minimize costs allocated to their projects (particularly toward the end), and the beneficiaries of postproject reviews are future projects, not current ones.

- Reviews involve looking back over events that project participants are likely to feel cynical or embarrassed about. Looking forward to new work is more appealing.

- Maintaining social relationships typically matters more to most people than accurate diagnoses of isolated events. People can be reluctant to engage in activity that might lead to blame, criticism or recrimination (Argyris, 1977).

- Many people think that experience is a necessary and sufficient teacher in its own right. According to this point of view, if you have an experience you will necessarily learn from it, and if you have not had the experience you will not learn from someone else who has. We tried to suggest above this is not so, but many people believe it is and are predisposed against postproject reviews. So the question is, given cogent reasons on both sides, should we conduct postproject reviews? And how should we conduct them?

The Study

Four postproject review meetings were studied in three companies. All the projects involved in the study had values of several hundred thousand to a few million dollars, and all involved extensive engineering design and development activity. All three companies supplied capital equipment to industrial users, although they came from different sectors: one in electrical equipment, one in a coating plant, and one in precision product machinery. One of the companies had a policy of always running postproject reviews, but the other two did so only intermittently.

Discourse analyses of the postproject review meetings were performed (Stubbs, 1983). This kind of analysis involves a detailed inspection of what took place in the meetings. It means dividing up the transcripts into small speech units—typically sentences—and working out the structure of the conversation that these sentences comprise in general rather than particular terms. The advantage of discourse analysis is that it gives a detailed and comprehensive picture of what actually takes place, and generates fairly clear evidence for any conclusions you draw. The drawback is that it is very time-consuming and one cannot cover very many situations. Therefore, the observations we discuss later in the paper are based on clear evidence, but we cannot

[4]Reprinted from *Project Management Journal*, with permission, Copyright Project Management Institute, Inc.

claim you would see the same thing in postproject reviews in other organizations.

How Did People Learn?

The first thing of interest was how people, collectively, went about learning from project reviews.

Dialectic Argument

First, the participants commonly resorted to a dialectic form of argument. One person would voice an explanation of something, another would come back with a contradictory explanation, and someone would find a third explanation that incorporated both the previous ones, that is a case of thesis, antithesis, and synthesis. For instance, in one case the participants were trying to explain why a handover meeting had been missed. One person thought another party had simply ignored a request to participate, the other party argued that it had received inadequate notice of the meeting, and the synthesis was simply that the two parties had insufficient knowledge of the others' time constraints. This kind of argument reflects the common fact that there are several sides to an event, and no one person alone has enough information to consider all sides of the argument. One person can argue one case, another can argue the opposite, and the meeting can reach a conclusion about where the best explanation lies.

Event Rehearsal

Second, a lot of mental rehearsal, or replay, of event sequences occurred. For example, a common case involved participants recalling their interactions with clients about successive changes to design requirements. This kind of replay is a natural process because one of the tests of whether A caused B is whether it preceded it, and building up a picture of event sequences therefore helps us infer why things happened the way they did. That said, there are two caveats. The first is that, despite the importance of time and deadlines during the projects, the review participants verbally rehearsed event sequences but did not put times against those events. (There were a couple of exceptions to this.) And second, precedence is only a partial indication of causality and people are susceptible to inferring causality when none exists (Tversky & Kahneman, 1982).

Mental Simulation

The third thing that was observed was that a kind of mental simulation was very common. This simulation almost always took the form of working out what would have happened had people's practices been different. For instance, in one case, the review participants reasoned about how the outcome would have been different had they used a different supplier. This kind of simulation used the informal, mental models that the participants had about how one event caused another. So, in the case of reasoning about the use of a different supplier, one participant would make a statement about how using the alternative supplier would have meant a greater need for coordinating effort. And another participant then argued that this would have led to a missed deadline since there was no available staff to provide this effort.

Simulation is somewhat similar to replay, except that it involved hypothetical events rather than actual ones. The extent of this simulation is significant in several ways. For a start,

working forward from doing something to its result, called *causal reasoning*, is something we know that people instinctively prefer to the opposite, *diagnostic reasoning* (Tversky & Kahneman, 1982). Diagnostic reasoning involves working back from some result to the action that caused it. People generally have less facility with diagnostic reasoning than with causal reasoning. Causal reasoning can also be more acceptable socially because it avoids the question of who did what, concentrating instead on what would happen if someone did something else. The result of this, unfortunately, is a lack of deep diagnosis. Instead of tracing back the chain, or network, of causes and effects, people jump to possible remedies and work forward to simulate their results.

It would be wrong to paint simulation as a wholly misguided strategy, however. In particular, there is a side benefit, in that it can help you learn from very few examples. If you have very small numbers of experiences from which to reason, maybe just one, it is hard to draw dependable conclusions. By simulating what would have happened had things been a little different you can effectively broaden the sample of experiences from which to draw conclusions (March, Sproull, & Tamuz, 1991).

Review Structure

The reviews that were observed differed in their general structure. In the two firms for which reviews were new, the structure of the review matched the structure of the project. The chairmen divided up the project into roughly chronological stages, asked people to say how successful the outcomes were, and encouraged them to work out why the less successful ones turned out so. In the firm that had had experience with running reviews, the chairman asked people to compile individual lists of good and bad things they had observed about the project, and then encouraged the participants to group these under a set of common headings. This structure had been adopted because the organization had found with the chronological approach that the reviews lasted too long. In our observations, the discussion processes that took place, and the effectiveness of the reviews, seemed to be unrelated to the overall structure. The successes and failings seemed to be common to the different structures. It was also observed that the intended structure of the reviews was easily sidetracked. Events are so densely interconnected that participants often had to move from one topic to another to reconstruct what happened because they realized in examining the first topic that another was more important.

The one characteristic that differentiated the reviews, in a way that seemed to matter, was the presence of outsiders. The chairman of one review had invited managers of new projects to attend the review, which was an important way of disseminating the results. There was no apparent evidence that the presence of outsiders inhibited the working of the review, but it did mean that the outsiders obtained quite a profound understanding of what had succeeded and failed on the project under review. They not only saw the headlines but also saw the reasoning that led up to the review's conclusions and got a sense of the context in which the project had taken place. Such a sense of context is usually vital in gaining a meaningful understanding of how things succeed or fail.

Historical References

Our next observation is concerned with how review participants referred to history. In principle, historical references should be central to the diagnostic process. You cannot know whether an event on a single project (like an earthquake or a bankruptcy) is unique, frequent, or systemic unless you examine other completed projects. In fact, there were few historical references; only six were made in 12 hours of review meetings. Those that there were had three different functions:

1. Using historical events as evidence for some explanation of events.

2. Demonstrating that there had been some change in the firm by contrasting recent events with historical ones.

3. Explaining people's behavior. (For example, people historically had become used to working in a particular way and carried on working in that way even when it became less appropriate.)

There were *no* historical references that simply helped people understand whether events on the project being reviewed were systemic. You could therefore argue that, as a means of learning from a specific experience, the postproject reviews failed to draw effectively on broader experience.

What Did People Learn?

As might be expected, some of the learning that took place involved disseminating knowledge of both successful and unsuccessful practices. For example, in one review, the project managers of new projects were able to hear about the consequences of having a single individual exercising both technical and managerial roles. It was evidently a poor practice. It is impossible to know, of course, if these managers of new projects would actually reproduce those practices in similar circumstances. So we can only say that there has been dissemination of what is called "propositional" knowledge, knowledge that, essentially, you can articulate but not necessarily practice.

Some of the knowledge that was learned was not so much task knowledge as knowledge that helped social relationships. For example, people would find out how hard others' jobs were, understand how severe were the constraints others operated under, and how hard it could be for others to be helpful. Knowing other people's points of view is an important kind of knowledge for effective members of organizations, and evidently it is not always learned during normal working activity.

Another important kind of knowledge was complexity. For example, there were several instances where individual participants had thought they had known why some event had happened, but in the reviews found out the explanation was far more clouded. The case of a late handover meeting illustrated this: everyone had had different ideas about why it had been late, but all turned out to be oversimplified. Individuals had each attributed the delay to a single cause, whereas the reality turned out to be a complex combination of several causes. Although this kind of learning, or really *unlearning*, is as good as any other, people feel less happy about it. It makes their models of their world less definite and more complicated. And it usually means that, contrary to what they might have thought, many problems do not have straightforward remedies.

How Well Did People Learn?

The next question addressed in the analysis was how well the learning process went in the reviews. Although it might seem unfair to do so, our approach was to look for flaws and limitations in the reasoning process that took place. It is unfair in that it might wrongly give the impression that the general level of learning was poor. We did it because it is easier to identify problems than successes. It also gives clues to how the reviews can be improved.

Attribution Problems

First, the reviews demonstrated *attribution bias*. One manifestation of attribution bias is that the participants in a process tend to overemphasize the role of the environment and underemphasize their own involvement when explaining results. You could expect review meetings to tend to blame factors beyond the participants' control and parties not represented at the reviews for problems during the project. Our observations indicated a strong tendency to explain problems by referring to other parties. On only two occasions did an individual admit an error or a need to change a way of working. This said, occasionally a participant would say something like "Okay, the customer was the problem, but was there anything we could have done?" It is characteristic of most successful individuals and firms to have an "internal locus of control"; that is, to believe that events are within their control, for then they devote effort to exerting control. It is therefore important to ask what could have been done to remedy a problem, even if you believe it had external causes.

Excessive Concreteness

It is hard to provide objective evidence but the analysis at least suggested that review participants were too narrowly specific in their diagnoses. For instance, locating a piece of equipment in a place where it was hard to install and maintain was diagnosed as a slip. No attempt was made to determine whether it reflected a more general difficulty with visualizing installation and maintenance problems during equipment design. Too much specificity means missing bigger problems, tackling intermediate rather than basic causes, and implementing remedies that are too elaborate. There were very few examples of generalization during the review—very few occasions when participants asked something like "Is this a case of a bigger problem?" or "Are we missing something bigger?"

Overall, review participants were therefore too concrete in their diagnoses. The inevitable result is strictly *incremental learning:* learning by small revisions to current knowledge rather than wholesale replacements of it. The result of persistently incremental learning is an inability to react to large changes in the environment. We had no indication that any of the firms currently faced such large changes, but most organizations face them at some time and becoming habituated to incremental learning means they will be ill-placed to cope with large changes.

Shallow Diagnosis

Another characteristic of the reviews was an absence of deep diagnosis. It was mentioned in the previous section that the participants preferred causal reasoning (reasoning forward from cause to effect) to diagnostic reasoning (effect to cause). They were also very reluctant to ask others for diagnoses. No one, during the course of the reviews, asked a diagnostic "why"; they only asked clarifying "whys," as in "why was it poor?" meaning "in what way was it poor?" rather than "what were the causes of it being poor?" The explanation in the last section for the absence of diagnosis was cognitive, involving the preferred styles with which individuals reason. One could probably add social convention. Participants could well have been reluctant to ask others why they had done something because they were reluctant to sour their relationships with them. Sacrificing the truth about a single event that is now beyond correction may be necessary in order to maintain good relationships with a person you might have to work with in the future.

Organizations like the ones studied here also strongly promote the norm of being constructive: managers prefer people who "come to them with solutions, not problems," and it is virtually an automatic response when asked about the value of criticism to say it is important "provided it is constructive." This norm means that people will draw back from exploring the causation behind a problem unless they know they can provide a solution; not so much because they are intrinsically reluctant to criticize but because they know it does not look good to others in the organization to criticize gratuitously.

Lack of Data

A further issue that emerged from the analysis was the lack of reference to objective outcome data, especially costs and time scales that would not have been hard to collect from the firms' records. In some cases participants spent much time trying to recall when things in fact happened. In other cases, there was obvious uncertainty about how well the project had performed financially. Both conditions could have been answered easily by a little research into the record. Given that these outcomes are so central to most people's ideas about project success, it could be argued that such outcomes should be central to the review process. There was one occasion in which costs were available and were an important part of the review. This involved remediation costs: that is, the costs needed to put right errors or problems in preceding parts of the project. Even there, though, the figures were not clear-cut because the accounting basis that underlay them was unknown to the participants. In one sense, accounting conventions are irrelevant to diagnoses of project problems, but, when one does not know what they are, it is hard to know how big were the problems one actually encountered.

In fact, far more references were made during the reviews to practices than to outcomes. Instead of examining how far, say, costs deviated from budget and working out why, most of the time people examined how they worked and whether they could have done better. This seems to be putting the cart before the horse, and one could put this down to the mainly technical participants showing too little concern with business matters. But there are reasons to be concerned more with practices than outcomes. First, outcomes such as financial performance are determined jointly by project members' activities and the environment they work in. This means that poor financial performance does not necessarily indicate poor practices. It also means that the thing project members have most direct control over is their practices, not project outcomes. Thus, they have a natural incentive to examine practices rather than outcomes. Second, global outcomes of complex undertakings like projects generally provide poor feedback when they are composed of many different kinds of activities. It is like trying to learn a complex skill such as driving by being told only how long your complete journey took. For the review participants, project costs and timings were not especially helpful indicators of how well they performed their tasks (even if they are obviously informative to senior project managers).

Interpretation Errors

Even when outcomes were referred to, people sometimes appeared to make interpretation errors. For instance, in one case it turned out that the siting of a piece of equipment was poor because it made maintenance of the equipment difficult. The equipment was small, of low value, and needed relatively little maintenance, so the problem was dismissed as being very minor and led to no further discussion. We would say, however, that this easy dismissal makes the error of assuming that minor outcomes reflect minor causes. The question of maintainability is important for customers in industrial plant industries, sometimes critical. This interpretative error suggested that the organization's engineers had too little awareness of the issue, perhaps through a lack of training, a lack of formal process, or a lack of knowledge transfer among different engineers. None of this was explored. Naturally, organizations with limited time and resources pay most attention to big outcomes, not small ones. The danger of doing so in an unthinking way is that one misses big issues simply because, on isolated occasions, they happen not to have big outcomes. However, later the outcome might be major and adverse; good learning stimulated by a minor adverse outcome could pay big dividends in the future.

How Worthwhile Was It?

After the reviews had taken place, participants were interviewed, for about 10 minutes each, and the researcher spoke informally to members of the other reviews immediately after they had finished. None of the participants dismissed them as worthless, but none gave the reviews unqualified support. There was skepticism in particular about any prospect that the reviews would actually make a difference. Part of this skepticism undoubtedly lay in people's cynicism about organizations, conditioned by long experience of managerial activities that led to no obvious improvement. But part of it lay in the unconvincing nature of the remedies that were explored in the reviews. Two of the reviews were distinctly hurried toward the end, so remedies received only superficial treatment. Yet, even in the others, remedies were not analyzed, only proposed and briefly contested. Side-effects were not explored and implementation was not planned. At best, there was only an acknowledgment in one of the reviews that someone would have to go away and plan the remedies in more detail. Given that organizational interventions invariably have unfavorable side-effects, and that their implementation is generally protracted and messy, people will naturally be skeptical about remedies that receive only glancing attention.

In all then, a number of limitations in the learning process existed during the course of the reviews. In previous sections the neglect of history, the lack of generalization, and the lack of any profound diagnosis was mentioned. The superficial treatment given to remedies has just been mentioned. However, it was also evident from the analyses that these reviews had a number of important functions:

- They gave people a chance to demonstrate their concern with the organization's objectives.

- They helped people correct misconceptions they had learned in the course of normal project activity.

- They gave people the chance to explain and justify their actions in a way that was not always open to them during the project.

- They suggested available practices that had not been realized by those who might have used them.

- They promoted collective remedies and engendered feelings of commitment to them. Remedies were sometimes dismissed for their superficiality, as explained, but at least they were voiced collectively.

- The reviews had an important disseminating function, although this requires sharing the review results with outsiders. Most review participants who have worked on the project under the microscope say things like "I already knew X." But typically it does not occur to them to go around other projects telling people about X—maybe because they do not realize X matters to others, did not know they knew X until it was pointed out, or were just too busy to think about anything to do with X. Whatever the case, postproject reviews (provided you invite along outsiders) helped X get out. We found, however, that people generally underestimated the dissemination function of postproject reviews.

What Should You Do?

The Shortfalls

The three greatest shortfalls in the reviews that were studied were that people were overspecific, ahistorical, and undiagnostic. Being too specific in your learning actually refers to two different things. One way to be too specific is to have too narrow a view of the process you are learning about. If you think of an engineering project just in terms of what the project manager can affect, for instance, you will not question whether there is something to be learned about, say, the process of assigning project managers. The other way to be too specific is to view what you are learning about too literally. If it turns out that a product fails because a wall thickness of a designed part was insufficient, you could diagnose this as a failure to specify adequate wall thickness. You could go on to add something to your codes of practice that says all wall thickness should be checked

with the chief engineer. But you could go to a more general level and diagnose this as a failure among designers to understand the extremes of operating duty that their products have to meet. You might then think of remedies to do with giving designers greater exposure to customers using their products. Both types of over-specificity cause learning to be less effective than it should be. Therefore, the messages are try to learn about the bigger system, not just day-to-day activities, and try to think of particular failings as examples of more general types of failing.

How much do people think about history? The answer seems to be "not much," since only six references of any kind to historical experience occurred throughout the reviews. The big problem of *not* referring to history is that you will not learn what types of problems are unique and what types are characteristic or systemic. Also, you will have an excessive confidence in any remedies you plan. But, having said this, the way you use history is not clear cut. There are two common aphorisms about learning from history that seem to contradict each other: one is "There is nothing new under the sun" and the other is "History never repeats itself." The first suggests that knowing history is essential because the future will resemble it. The second suggests that knowing history is dangerous because you can be trapped into believing that the future will be the same as the past. The important point is to look at history at the right level of generality. Your next product development will be unique because in all its detail it will differ in many respects from previous developments. At the same time, you simply would not be able to do it if it were wholly unique. You still have to go through very similar processes, deal with very similar *kinds* of objects, and so on.

Finally, true diagnosis was mostly absent. Why, given the extent to which people are encouraged to adopt cause-effect analysis, fishbone diagrams, problem-solving devices, and so on, do they not practice causal diagnosis? As with other matters, you can take your explanation either from individual psychology or from organizational behavior. The psychological explanation has to do with the distinction between causal reasoning and diagnostic reasoning that was mentioned earlier. Individuals simply seem to find it easier to reason from cause to effect than vice versa. The organizational explanation is that most people regard it as a social requirement to avoid direct criticism of one another, especially if they have to maintain some kind of long-term relationship. Most people are not going to sacrifice good long-term relationships for the sake of one or two accurate diagnoses of events that cannot be undone. And they have probably reached their own, private diagnosis of events anyway, and do not see a need for a collective diagnosis. The fact that the collective diagnosis could be better than their private one may not even occur to them. Moreover, it is a social norm to be constructive—emphasizing the search for better ways rather than the diagnosis of a bad way. Unfortunately, the consequence of all this very reasonable avoidance of deep diagnosis is shallow understanding and, most likely, wrong remedies that treat symptoms rather than causes. Ineffective post mortems, like ineffectual people, avoid conflict in the name of long-term ends, but ultimately sacrifice long-term ends for short-term comfort. Getting an organization to do the opposite (pursue long-term ends and endure a lack of short-term comfort) is ultimately a test of leadership, of moral courage, persuasiveness, and will.

Recommendations

We would recommend the following "watchwords" for review chairpersons:

1. Encourage deep diagnosis. Use cause-effect diagrams if they are likely to help.

2. Encourage attention to history. Ask whether similar things have occurred historically.

3. Encourage the examination of the bigger system beyond the immediate confines of the project.

4. Discourage glib categorization. There is little that cannot be put down to "communications problems" in complex projects, but categorizing something this way is only a starting point to the diagnosis, not a finishing point. It is easy to put down as a communications problem, for example, two people making different assumptions about who has responsibility for a particular action. A proper diagnosis would examine how different assumptions arise and why they persist even when they lead to errors.

5. Plan remedies properly by examining side-effects and thinking through the implementation. If this has to be the subject of a second meeting, then so be it. Chairpeople need to have the maturity to realize that suggested but unplanned remedies will simply deepen review participants' cynicism.

6. Invite key outsiders to postproject reviews to assist in dissemination. In one of the reviews we studied, managers of new projects were invited, and this was probably far more effective at dissemination than written summaries would have been. Written summaries tend to be written from one person's standpoint, so one often does not know how contentious certain issues were. And these summaries often lack the detail that adopting a new practice depends on.

Most people would probably count such practices as common sense. It is therefore important to be aware that such practices often failed to materialize—even among the highly intelligent, knowledgeable, and thoughtful people who ran the reviews we studied.

Summary

Overall, in the light of this study, we would come out strongly in favor of postproject reviews (provided you do not call them "post mortems"). We could spot flaws in the ones we saw, but they were still valuable. And most of the organizations we worked with had not run them before, so judging them by the first-of-kind would not be reasonable. This study, while limited, points the direction for additional research in this important area of project management.

References

Argyris, C. (1977, September–October). Double loop learning in organizations. *Harvard Business Review*, 115–125.

Eraut, M. (1994). *Developing Professional Knowledge and Competence* (p. 51). London: Falmer Press.

Lipshitz, R., Popper, M., and Oz, S. (1996). Building learning organizations: The design and implementation of organizational learning mechanisms. *Journal of Applied Behavioral Science*, 32(3), 292–305.

March, J. G., Sproull, L. S., and Tamuz, M. (1991). Learning from samples of one or fewer. *Organization Science*, 2(1), 1–13.

Stubbs, M. (1983). *Discourse Analysis.* Oxford: Basil Blackwell.

Tversky, A., and Kahneman, D. (1982). Causal schemas in judgments under uncertainty. In D. Kahneman, P. Slovic, & A. Tversky (Eds.), *Judgment under Uncertainty: Heuristics and Biases* (pp. 117–128). Cambridge University Press.

Questions

1. Why do you think organizations tend to ignore postproject evaluations?

2. How could the concept of making such evaluations mandatory be implemented?

3. Evaluate their advice for conducting postproject evaluations.

4. How does an understanding of how people learn affect project audits and evaluations?

5. How can an auditor/evaluator avoid the shortfalls described in the article?

6. Summarize the author's recommendations.

CHAPTER 13

Project Closure and Benefits Realization

As it must to all things, closure comes to every project. At times, project death is quick and clean, but more often it is a long process; and there are times when it is practically impossible to establish that death has occurred. The skill with which closure, or a condition we might call "near closure," is managed has a great deal to do with the quality of life after the project. The closure stage of the project rarely has much impact on technical success or failure, but it has a great deal to do with residual attitudes toward the project—the "taste left in the mouth" of the client, senior management, and the project team. It also has a great deal to do with learning about the things that lead to success—or failure.

At this point, the joy of discovery is past. Problems have been solved, bypassed, lived with, or ignored. Implementation plans have been carried out. The client is delighted, angry, or reasonably satisfied. In construction-type projects where the project cadre remains intact, the closure issue is eased because the team moves on to another challenge. For nonrecurring projects, the issue is far more akin to the breakup of a family. While the members of the family may be on the best of terms, they must now separate, go their individual ways, divide or dispose of the family property, and make plans for individual survival. Unless the project life was only a few weeks or a few months, the change is stressful. For projects organized as weak matrices, there will be only a few individuals, perhaps only the project manager (PM), who "belong" to the project. This may represent an even more stressful situation than the breakup of a large project family because there is little or no peer group for support.

The process of closure is never easy, always complicated, and, as much as we might wish to avoid it, almost always inevitable. The problem is how to accomplish one of the several levels of what is meant by project closure with a minimum of trouble and administrative dislocation.

In this chapter, we examine the variety of conditions that may be generally referred to as *project closure*. We then view some decision-aiding models that can assist an organization in making the shutdown decision. This requires us to return to the subject of evaluation and discuss indicators of success and failure in projects. We also discuss some procedures that decrease the pain of closure and others that reduce the administrative problems that often arise after projects have been closed. We look into the typical causes of closure, and finally note that the preparation of a project history is an integral part of the closure process.

But closing the project is not the end of the story. Just because the bridge has been built or the software installed and the PM moved on to the next project, does not mean that the benefits desired from this project will automatically appear. Much more still may be involved on the part of the project owner before the project becomes a success. These tasks are covered in the Benefits Realization section following the discussion of project closure.

13.1 | The Varieties of Project Closure

For our purposes, a project can be said to be closed when work on the substance of the project has ceased or slowed to the point that further progress on the project is no longer possible, when the project has been indefinitely delayed, when its resources have been deployed to other projects, or when project personnel (especially the PM) become *personae non gratae* with senior management and in the company lunchroom. There may seem to be a spark of life left, but resuscitation to a healthy state is most unlikely. On rare occasions, projects are reborn to a new, glorious existence (Baker, 1997). But such rebirth is not expected, and project team members who "hang on to the bitter end" have allowed optimism to overcome wisdom. The PM must understand that the ancient naval tradition that the captain should go down with the ship does not serve the best interests of the Navy, the crew, the ship, and most certainly not the captain.

On the other hand, the captain must not, rat-like, flee the "ship" at the first sign of trouble. In the next section of this chapter, we note many of the signs and signals that indicate that the project may be in real trouble. At this point, it is appropriate to consider the ways in which a project can be closed. There are four fundamentally different ways to close out a project: extinction, addition, integration, and starvation.

Closure by Extinction

The project is stopped. It may end because it has been successful and achieved its goals: The new product has been developed and handed over to the client, or the software has been installed and is running at the client's facility.

The project may also be stopped because it is unsuccessful or has been superseded: The new drug failed its efficacy tests; there are better/faster/cheaper/prettier alternatives available; or it will cost too much and take too long to get the desired performance. Changes in the external environment can kill projects as well. The explosion of the Challenger stopped a number of space shuttle projects overnight. More recently, extraordinary cost escalation in the technology and materials associated with automotive racing caused the ruling bodies of both Formula 1 and Indy-car racing to stop (and even repeal) specific technological changes in their respective venues.

A special case of closure by extinction is "termination by murder."[1] There are all sorts of murders. They range from political assassination to accidental projecticide. When senior executives vie for promotion, projects for which the loser is champion are apt to suffer. Corporate mergers often make certain projects redundant or irrelevant. NCR was forced to cancel several projects following its merger into AT&T, and probably several more when NCR was later unmerged.

Two important characteristics of termination by murder, premeditated or not, are the suddenness of the project demise and the lack of obvious signals that death is imminent.

When a decision is made to close a project by extinction, the most noticeable event is that all activity on the *substance* of the project ceases. A great deal of organizational activity, however, remains to be done. Arrangements must be made for the orderly release of project team members and their reassignment to other activities if they are to remain in the parent organization. The property, equipment, and materials belonging to the project must be disbursed according to the dictates of the project contract or in accord with the established procedures of the parent organization. Finally, the Project Final Report, also known as the *project history*, must be prepared. These subjects will be covered in greater detail later in this chapter.

---

[1]The authors thank Professor Emeritus Samuel G. Taylor (University of Wyoming) for noting this special case of termination by murder.

Closure by Addition

Most projects are "in-house," that is, carried out by the project team for use in the parent organization. If a project is a major success, it may be closed by institutionalizing it as a formal part of the parent organization. NCR Corporation (prior to its merger and demerger with AT&T), for example, used this method of transforming a project into a division of the firm and then, if real economic stability seems assured, into an independent subsidiary. Essentially, the same process occurs when a university creates an academic department out of what originally was a few courses in an existing department. For example, most software engineering and/or information systems departments began by reorganizing an engineering or business school "subspecialty" into a full-fledged department.

When the project is made a more or less full-fledged member of the parent, it lives its first years in a protected status—carrying less than an "adult" share of overhead cost. As the years pass, however, the child is expected gradually to assume the economic responsibilities of full adulthood.

When project success results in closure by addition, the transition is strikingly different from closeout by extinction. In both cases, the project ceases to exist, but there the similarity stops. Project personnel, property, and equipment are often simply transferred from the dying project to the newly born division. The metamorphosis from project to department, to division, and even to subsidiary is accompanied by budgets and administrative practices that conform to standard procedure in the parent firm, by demands for contribution profits, by the probable decline of political protection from the project's corporate "champion," indeed by a greater exposure to all the usual stresses and strains of regular, routine, day-to-day operations.

It is not uncommon, however, for some of the more adventurous members of the project team to request transfers to other projects or to seek the chance to start new projects. Project life is exciting, and some team members are uncomfortable with what they perceive to be the staid, regulated existence of the parent organization. The change from project to division brings with it a sharply diminished sense of freedom.

This transition poses a difficult time for the PM, who must see to it that the shift is made smoothly. In Part I of this book, and especially in Chapter 3, we referred repeatedly to the indispensable requirement of political sensitivity in the PM. The transition from project to division demands a superior level of political sensitivity for successful accomplishment. Projects lead a sheltered life, for all the risks they run. The regular operating divisions of a firm are subjected to the daily infighting that seems, in most firms, to be a normal result of competition between executives.

Closure by Integration

This method of closing a project is the most common way of dealing with successful projects and the most complex. The property, equipment, material, personnel, and functions of the project are distributed among the existing elements of the parent organization. The output of the project becomes a standard part of the operating systems of the parent or client.

In some cases, the problems of in-house integration are relatively minor. The project team that installed a new piece of software instructed the information systems division in its operation and maintenance, and then departed, probably left only minor problems behind it, problems familiar to experienced IS managers. If the installation was an enterprise-wide system with numerous modules, then the complexities of integration are apt to be more severe. In general, the problems of integration are inversely related to the level of experience that the parent organization (or client) has had with: (1) the technology being integrated and (2) the successful integration of other projects, regardless of technology.

Project Management in Practice

Nucor's Approach to Closure by Addition

Nucor, one of the early steel "minimills," is a highly entrepreneurial firm with a compound growth rate of 23 percent per year. In 1987, its sales were $851 million with an executive staff of only 19 monitoring the operations of 23 plants and 4600 employees. As part of its strategy, Nucor decided to move into the flat rolled steel market, the largest market for steel products. They thus initiated the construction of a major plant in Crawfordsville, Indiana, which would comprise over 20 percent of their total assets.

As another part of its strategy, Nucor does its own construction management, with most of the construction team then transitioning into permanent positions in the newly constructed plant. In this case, four managers started the conceptual team for the new facility and then brought in 19 other people from outside the company to form the rest of the construction team, none of them ever having built a steel mill before. The manager on the conceptual team for the new plant was the lead person on the site determination team and became the general manager of the facility. The field shift superintendents on the construction project will have permanent managerial responsibility for the melt shop, the hot mill, and the cold mill. The engineers will become supervisors in the mill. Even the secretary/clerk will have a position in the new facility.

Nucor also relies heavily on the services and capabilities of its suppliers in the construction process, since they are such a small firm. But it also reflects Nucor's "lean and mean" philosophy. In this case, the only error the construction team made was underestimating the engineering time required from suppliers, the time coming in at about double the estimate. Even so, the engineering costs (and probably most other labor costs, too) apparently only ran about 20 percent of what it historically costs to build this type of steel facility!

Questions

1. Why would Nucor have thought they could build a new steel mill with one-tenth the engineering resources it normally requires?

2. What characteristics of this project closure made it a closure by addition?

3. What other ways could Nucor have closed this project? What terms would you give these approaches?

Source: R. Kimball, "Nucor's Strategic Project," *Project Management Journal*, Vol. 19.

Most problems of closure by addition are also present when the project is integrated. In the case of integration, the project may not be viewed as a competitive interloper, but the project personnel being moved into established units of the parent organization will be so viewed. In addition, the project, which flourished so well in its protected existence as a project, may not be quite so healthy in the chill atmosphere of the "real world." The individuals who nurtured the project may have returned to their respective organizational divisions and may have new responsibilities. They tend to lose their fervid interest in the "old" project.

Following is a list of a few of the more important aspects of the transition from project to integrated operation that must be considered when the project functions are distributed.

1. **Personnel**   Where will the project team go? Will it remain a team? If the functions that the team performed are still needed, who will do them? If ex-team members are assigned to a new project, under what conditions or circumstances might they be temporarily available for help on the old project?

2. **Manufacturing**   Is training complete? Are input materials and the required facilities available? Does the production system layout have to be replanned? Did the change create new bottlenecks or line-of-balance problems? Are new operating or control procedures needed? Is the new operation integrated into the firm's computer systems?

3. **Accounting/Finance**   Have the project accounts been closed and audited? Do the new department budgets include the additional work needed by the project? Have the new accounts been created and account numbers been distributed? Have all project property and equipment been distributed according to the contract or established agreements?

4. **Engineering**   Are all drawings complete and on file? Are operating manuals and change procedures understood? Have training programs been altered appropriately for new employees? Have maintenance schedules been adjusted for the change? Do we have a proper level of "spares" in stock?

5. **Information Systems/Software**   Has the new system been thoroughly tested? Is the software properly documented and are "comments" complete? Is the new system fully integrated with current systems? Have the potential users been properly trained to use the new system?

6. **Marketing**   Is the sales department aware of the change? Is marketing in agreement about lead times? Is marketing comfortable with the new line? Is the marketing strategy ready for implementation?

7. **Purchasing, Distribution, Legal, etc.**   Are all these and other functional areas aware of the change? Has each made sure that the transition from project to standard operation has been accomplished within standard organizational guidelines and that standard administrative procedures have been installed?

8. **Risk Identification and Management**   Most of the questions and conditions noted in items 1–7 represent risks for successful integration. They should be handled similarly to any other risks the project has faced, subjected to analysis, and dealt with accordingly.

Closure by Starvation

There is a fourth type of project closure, although strictly speaking, it is not a "closure" at all. It is "slow starvation by budget decrement." Almost anyone who has been involved with projects over a sufficient period of time to have covered a business recession has had to cope with budget cuts. Budget cuts, or decrements, are not rare. Because they are common, they are sometimes used to mask a project closure.

There may be a number of reasons why senior management does not wish to close an unsuccessful or obsolete project. In some firms, for example, it is politically dangerous to admit that one has championed a failure, and closing a project that has not accomplished its goals is an admission of failure. In such a case, the project budget might receive a deep cut—or a series of small cuts—large enough to prevent further progress on the project and to force the reassignment of many project team members. In effect, the project is closed, but the project still exists as a legal entity complete with sufficient staff to maintain some sort of presence such as an administrative assistant who issues a project "no-progress" report each year. In general, it is considered bad manners to inquire into such projects or to ask why they are still "on the books."

13.2 When to Close a Project

The decision to shut down a project early, by whatever method, is difficult. As we emphasized in Chapter 4, projects tend to develop a life of their own—a life seemingly independent of whether or not the project is successful. In an early article on the subject of terminating R&D projects, Buell (1967) suspected that the main reason why so little information was available on the subject was that it was hard to spell out specific guidelines and standards for the decision. He expressed strong doubts about the ability to "wrap everything up in a neat set of quantitative mathematical expressions" and then went on to develop an extensive set of questions that, if answered, should lead management to a decision. While these questions were aimed at R&D projects, they have wide, general applicability. Paraphrased and slightly modified to broaden and extend them beyond R&D projects, they are:

- Is the project still consistent with organizational goals?
- Is it practical? Useful?
- Is management sufficiently enthusiastic about the project to support its implementation?
- Is the scope of the project consistent with the organization's financial strength?
- Is the project consistent with the notion of a "balanced" program in all areas of the organization's technical interests? In "age?" In cost?
- Does the project have the support of all the departments (e.g., finance, manufacturing, marketing, IT, and legal) needed to implement it?
- Is organizational project support being spread too thin?
- Is support of this individual project sufficient for success?
- Does this project represent too great an advance over current technology? Too small an advance?
- Is the project team still innovative, or has it gone stale?
- Can the new knowledge be protected by patent, copyright, or trade secret?
- Could the project be farmed out without loss of quality?
- Is the current project team properly qualified to continue the project?
- Does the organization have the required skills to achieve full implementation or exploitation of the project?
- Has the subject area of the project already been "thoroughly plowed?"
- Has the project lost its key person or champion?
- Is the project team enthusiastic about success?
- Can the potential results be purchased or subcontracted more efficiently than developed in-house?
- Does it seem likely that the project will achieve the minimum goals set for it? Is it still profitable? Timely?

Project Management in Practice

Twelve Hospital Handoff Projects

When construction on the new Norton Brownsboro Hospital in Louisville, Kentucky, was 7 months from completion, it was time to start the transition from project to smooth operations. Previously, to help set up the patient processes, subject matter experts from other Norton facilities were brought in for consultation, particularly in regard to how patients would want the processes to work. As one example, rather than the usual waiting-line patient registration system, patients register themselves at kiosks.

Since 700 new hires for the hospital had to learn how to operate 51 information systems on 13 technologies, 12 projects were set up to train them. To help with the training, the operations people were brought in early to facilitate a smooth transition and hear any concerns or needs from the new hires. In a hospital, project failure and closure are not an option since lives are constantly at stake. As it happened, the projects finished on schedule and the hospital opened by its due date and almost $3 million under budget.

Questions

1. **How much attention do you think is usually given to the handoff from a project team to an ongoing staff?**

2. **Would you classify this as a closure by addition, by integration, or by extinction? Why?**

Source: K. Hunsberger, "The Best of the Best." *PM Network*, Vol. 24.

We could add many other such questions to Buell's list. For instance:

- Has the project been obviated by technical advances or new products/services developed elsewhere?
- Is the output of the product still cost-effective? Has its risk level changed significantly?
- Is it time to integrate or add the project as a part of the regular, ongoing operation of the parent organization?
- Would we support the project if it were proposed today at the time and cost required to complete it?
- Are there better alternative uses for the funds, time, and personnel devoted to the project?
- Has a change in the environment altered the need for the project's output?

Such questions clearly overlap, and the list could easily be extended further. Even in the 1960s, the reasons for shutting down projects early was more frequently due to economic and market conditions than to technical factors. And since then, economic and market conditions have become even more difficult with globalization and greater competition, while our project management knowledge has increased to help make projects successful more often. Compared to the great level of research and thought concerning the project selection decision before the 1980s (see also Chapter 2), there has been relatively little research published on the closure decision. But even this bit was more than the work devoted to defining project success.

As interest in project closure increased in the mid-1980s, interest in understanding project success also rose. Pinto (2013) surveyed experienced PMs and found 10 factors that the managers felt to be critical to successful project implementation (see Table 13.1). Jiang et al. (1996) surveyed information system "business professionals" on the relative importance of the Pinto critical success factors and came to roughly similar conclusions. More recently, Zou et al. (2014) surveyed industry practitioners experienced in public–private partnership projects and found that the top two critical success factors were, again, commitment and participation of senior executives, and clearly defining the objectives to be achieved through the project. In addition, Zou et al. measured the current importance

TABLE 13.1	**Critical Success Factors in Order of Importance**

1. *Project Mission*—Initial clearly defined goals and general directions.
2. *Top-Management Support*—Willingness of top management to provide the necessary resources and authority/power for project success.
3. *Project Schedule/Plan*—A detailed specification of the individual action steps for project implementation.
4. *Client Consultation*—Communication, consultation, and active listening to all impacted parties.
5. *Personnel*—Recruitment, selection, and training of the necessary personnel for the project team.
6. *Technical Tasks*—Availability of the required technology and expertise to accomplish the specific technical action steps.
7. *Client Acceptance*—The act of "selling" the final project to its ultimate intended users.
8. *Monitoring and Feedback*—Timely provision of comprehensive control information at each stage in the implementation process.
9. *Communication*—The provision of an appropriate network and necessary data to all key actors in the project implementation.
10. *Trouble-shooting*—Ability to handle unexpected crises and deviations from plan.

Source: Pinto (2013).

these factors had and the importance they should have and found them to be currently undervalued by about a third. And finally, they measured the practitioners' perceptions of the difficulty of improving these two measures and found that senior management commitment and participation were by far the most difficult to improve and clarifying the objectives was only slightly less difficult.

Baker et al. (1983) looked at similar factors associated with R&D project success and failure. A particularly important finding of Baker et al. is that the *factors associated with project success are different for different industries*. Baker's work was restricted to R&D projects, but the Pinto study covered many different types of projects. They found that the success-related factors differed between fundamentally different types of projects—between R&D and construction projects, for example. At the very least, the factors and their relative importance are idiosyncratic to the industry, to the project type, and, we suggest, possibly to the firm.

Out of this work came some models that could be used to predict project success or failure, based on certain project characteristics or practices. Pinto et al. (1990) reported on factors that were associated with project failure. The factors differed for the type of project involved (R&D vs. construction), for the project's position in the life cycle, as well as for the precise way in which "failure" was defined. In addition, Green et al. (1993) found that a poor fit with the firm's existing technological expertise and/or with its existing marketing area and channels was a good early predictor of project closure.

In the face of this diversity of success factors, it is interesting to note that there are relatively few fundamental reasons why some projects fail to produce satisfactory answers to Buell's questions about early closures of projects.

1. **A Project Organization Is Not Required**   The use of the project form of organization was inappropriate for this particular task or in this particular environment. The parent organization must understand the conditions that require instituting a project.

2. **Insufficient Support from Senior Management**   Projects invariably develop needs for resources that were not originally allocated. Arguments between functional departments over the command of such resources are very common. Without the direct support of a champion in senior management, the project is almost certain to lose the resource battle.

3. **Naming the Wrong Person as Project Manager**   This book is testimony to the importance of the PM. A common mistake is to appoint an individual with excellent technical skills but weak managerial skills or training as PM.

4. **Poor Planning**   This is a very common cause of project failure. In the rush to get the substance of the project under way, competent planning is neglected. In such cases, crisis management becomes a way of life, difficulties and errors are compounded, and the project slowly gets farther behind schedule and over budget. Indeed, careful planning is associated with success in almost all empirical research on project success—Tom Peter's "Ready, Fire, Aim" to the contrary notwithstanding. Not only is proper planning often cited as a *success factor*, lack of planning is cited as a *cause of failure* (Black, 1996).

These, and a few other reasons, are the base causes of most project failures. The specific causes of failure, for the most part, derive from these fundamental items. For example,

- No use was made of earlier project Final Reports that contained a number of recommendations for operating projects in the future.
- Time/cost estimates were not prepared by those who had responsibility for doing the work.
- Starting late, the PM jumped into the tasks without adequate planning.
- Project personnel were moved without adjusting the schedule or were reassigned during slow periods and then were unavailable when needed.

- Project auditors/evaluators were reluctant to conduct careful, detailed meaningful evaluations.
- The project was allowed to continue in existence long after it had ceased to make cost-effective progress.
- Evaluations failed to determine why problems were arising during the early phases of the project life cycle due to inadequate, or no, risk assessment and management.

All these causes of failure underline the need for careful evaluation at all stages of the project. But at the same time, it is most important to note that the lion's share of the attention given to the closure issue is focused on the failing project. It is equally or more important to close successful projects at the right time and by proper methods. One rarely mentioned problem affecting many organizations is the inability or unwillingness of successful PMs working on successful projects to "let their projects go." This is a particularly difficult problem for in-house projects. The PM (and team) simply will not release the project to the tender care of the client department. An outstanding technical specialist and manager conducting communications projects was released from employment simply because he or she insisted on maintaining semipermanent control of projects that had essentially been completed, but which were not released to the users because they "needed further testing" or "fine-tuning."

In addition, little consideration has been given to *how* the closure decision is made and *who* makes it. We feel that a broadly based committee of reasonably senior executives is probably the best. The broad organizational base of the committee is needed to diffuse and withstand the political pressure that accompanies all closures—successes and failures alike. To the extent possible, the criteria used by the closure committee should be written and explained in some detail. It is, however, important to write the criteria in such a way that the committee is not frozen into a mechanistic approach to a decision. There are times when hunches should be followed (or rejected) and blind faith should be respected (or ignored). It depends on whose hunches and faith are under consideration (Baker, 1997).

A reviewer of this book noted that we had covered a great many "technical" reasons for closing projects, but had not said that many projects are closed for "nontechnical" reasons. There are several nontechnical reasons why projects are closed, but almost always these closures seem to be associated with conflict, even when the conflict is anticipated at the beginning of the project.

Political closures We mentioned this type of project demise when discussing termination by murder. These closures are typically the result of conflict among senior managers, one of whom may be terminated along with the project.

Cross-cultural closures Multinational projects sometimes fail because the different cultural groups do not/cannot communicate well, or because their working styles do not/cannot mesh. See Chapter 3 for other examples. The conflicts arise when poor communication or diverse working styles cause the different cultures to compete for ascendancy or to engage in win/lose negotiations. The same cross-cultural forces operate when different disciplines, for example, marketing and engineering, develop precisely the same problems.

Senescence closures There are projects that pass away simply because senior managers, the project champion, the PM, and even key project workers lose interest in the project. The project has neither failed nor succeeded. It simply exists. Meanwhile, other new exciting ideas are being projectized. The organization's attention (and resources) is being directed elsewhere. The conflict between the old and the new may not be active. The senescent project simply gives way to the new.

13.3 The Closure Process

The closure process has two distinct parts. First is the decision whether or not to close. Second, if the decision is to close out the project, the decision must be carried out.

The Decision Process

Decision-aiding models for the closure decision fall into three generic categories. First, there are models that base the decision on the degree to which the project qualifies against a set of factors generally held to be associated with successful (or failed) projects. Second, there are models that base the decision on the degree to which the project meets the goals and objectives set for it. Third, there are projects that have fallen far enough behind their schedules and planned progress that the cost to complete them is no longer justifiable.

In terms of the first model, Starke (2012) points out that it is easy for PMs to get caught up in the momentum of work and not stop for a second to question whether the work

---

Project Management in Practice

Terminating the Superconducting Super Collider Project

"The giant tunnels for the super collider are prepared first."
(John Bird Photography)

When the U.S. Congress pulled the plug on the Superconducting Super Collider (SSC) project, it ended 11 years of work costing over $2 billion dollars and threw 2000 people out of work. The objective of the planned $11 billion SSC was to accelerate subatomic particles within a 54-mile underground circular chamber to almost the speed of light and smash them together at energies of 40 trillion electronic volts. The benefits to society of these experiments were unclear, some maintaining they could have been enormous, but others, including members of Congress, were less sure.

The project also suffered from an identity crisis. It was not clear if this was to be a U.S. "first" in basic science or a "world" science project, funded in its early stages by a $1 billion commitment from other nations. Although the costs of the SSC had ballooned, the main reason it was shut down was that it lost its political support.* Although the SSC scientists and backers had rallied good will among universities, schools, and scientific meetings, the potential benefits of the project never reached the President and his administration, where it only enjoyed lukewarm support at best. When a $4 trillion budget deficit appeared likely, the SSC project was sacrificed.

Questions

1. **Which of the various forms of closure was this?**

2. **The authors of this article maintain that politics is an important element of project implementation. Do you agree? Was this project shut down through "political" means?**

Source: B. Baker and R. Menon, "Politics and Project Performance: The Fourth Dimension of Project Management," *PM Network*, Vol. 9.

....

*The authors of this book believe that the loss of political support was because Texas was the only state that would directly gain from the project.

itself is still justified. Clearly, if it seems apparent that the project will not be completed in terms of its scope, cost, and schedule, it should be reconsidered and either restructured or shut down. However, this should also be recommended if the PM senses that the project no longer aligns with the strategic value objectives of the organization, where "Value" = Benefits/(Cost + Schedule). In that case, the PM should attempt to find alternatives to recommend that could leverage the investment to date but provide value through a more strategically relevant project.

Kumar et al. (1996) noted that project selection models are not appropriate for the project closure decision. The argument is that the data requirements for selection models are too large and costly. They also argue that the evaluation of factors in project selection models may change as projects are evaluated at different stages in their life cycles. They noted that the probability of technical success of a project is usually estimated to be close to 1.0 early in the life cycle, but lower during later stages when the technical problems are known. This, they say, would bias decisions in favor of new projects and against ongoing ones.

However, the first argument is generally untrue of those selection models actually being used, which are typically of modest size. As we have remarked elsewhere in this book, the uncertainty associated with most projects is not concerned with whether or not the project objective is technically achievable, but rather with the time and cost required to achieve it. The fact that selection criteria may change between the time that the project is started and the time it is judged for possible shutdown is not a relevant criticism of the use of a selection model. Indeed, whatever the source of the criteria for closure, they should be determined by the organization's policy at the time the decision is made—not judged by the policy of some prior time.

Adopting the position that sunk costs are not relevant to current investment decisions, we hold that the primary criterion for project continuance or closure is *whether or not the organization is willing to invest the estimated time and cost required to complete the project, given the project's current status and current expected outcome.* We emphasize that this criterion can be applied to any project.

Shafer et al. (1989) developed a project closure decision support system (DSS) based on a constrained weighted factor scoring model (see Chapter 2). The capabilities of most popular spreadsheets allow direct modeling of the scoring model, allow customized menus, and allow decision makers to adapt and enhance the model as they gain experience in the use of the DSS. The decision criteria, constraints, weights, and environmental data are unique to each organization, as are the specifics of using this (or any) decision model. A detailed discussion of various potential decision rules that might be useful with such a model can be found in Shafer et al. (1989). Figure 13.1 illustrates the structure of this model.

The Implementation Process

Once it has been decided to close a project, the process by which it will be terminated must be implemented. The actual closure can be planned and orderly or a simple hatchet job. The former is apt to have significantly better results, and so we suggest that the closure process be planned, budgeted, and scheduled just as is done for any other phase of the project life cycle. Such a project is illustrated in Figure 13.2. Archibald (1992) has prepared an extensive checklist of items covering the closeout of both the administrative and substantive parts of the project (see Figure 13.3).

In some organizations, the processing of the project closeout is conducted under the direct supervision of the PM, but this often raises dilemmas. For many PMs, closure signals the end of their reign as project leader. If the PM has another project to lead, the issue may not be serious; but if there is no other project and if the PM faces a return to a staid life in a functional division, there may be a great temptation to stretch out the shutdown process.

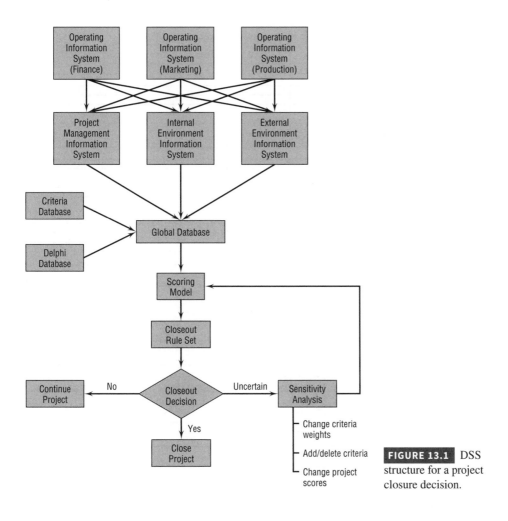

FIGURE 13.1   DSS structure for a project closure decision.

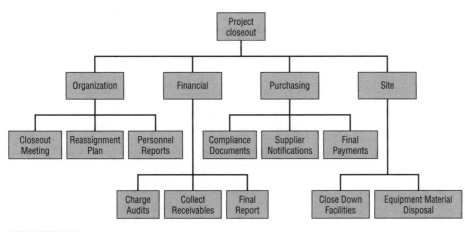

FIGURE 13.2   Design for project closure.

An examination of Figure 13.3 shows that implementing closure is a complex process. Note that in Figure 13.3 such items as A-4, B-4, C-3, and G-2, among many others, are actually small projects. It is all too easy, at this final stage of the game, to give this mountain of paperwork a "lick and a promise"—easy, but foolish. Someone must handle all

Item No.	Task Description	Required		Required Date	Assigned Responsibility	Priority	Notes Reference
		Yes	No				
A.	*Project Office (PO) and Project Team (PT) Organization*						
1.	Conduct project closeout meeting						
2.	Establish PO and PT release and reassignment plan						
3.	Carry out necessary personnel actions						
4.	Prepare personal performance evaluation on each PO and PT member						
B.	*Instructions and Procedures* *Issues Instructions for:*						
1.	Termination of PO and PT						
2.	Closeout of all work orders and contracts						
3.	Termination of reporting procedures						
4.	Preparation of final report(s)						
5.	Completion and disposition of project file						
C.	*Financial*						
1.	Close out financial documents and records						
2.	Audit final charges and costs						
3.	Prepare final project financial report(s)						
4.	Collect receivables						
D.	*Project Definition*						
1.	Document final approved project scope						
2.	Prepare final project breakdown structure and enter into project file						
E.	*Plans, Budgets, and Schedules*						
1.	Document actual delivery dates of all contractual deliverable end items						
2.	Document actual completion dates of all other contractual obligations						
3.	Prepare final project and task status reports						
F.	*Work Authorization and Control*						
1.	Close out all work orders and contracts						
G.	*Project Evaluation and Control*						
1.	Assure completion of all action assignments						
2.	Prepare final evaluation report(s)						
3.	Conduct final review meeting						
4.	Terminate financial, manpower, and progress reporting procedures						
H.	*Management and Customer Reporting*						
1.	Submit final report to customer						
2.	Submit final report to management						
I.	*Marketing and Contract Administration*						
1.	Compile all final contract documents with revision, waivers, and related correspondence						
2.	Verify and document compliance with all contractual terms						
3.	Compile required proof of shipment and customer acceptance documents						
4.	Officially notify customer of contract completion						
5.	Initiate and pursue any claims against customer						
6.	Prepare and conduct defense against claims by customer						
7.	Initiate public relations announcements re. contract completion						
8.	Prepare final contract status report						
J.	*Extension-New Business*						
1.	Document possibilities for project or contract extensions, or other related new business						
2.	Obtain commitment for extension						
K.	*Project Records Control*						
1.	Complete project file and transmit to designated manager						
2.	Dispose of other project records as required by established procedures						
L.	*Purchasing and Subcontracting* For each Purchase Order and Subcontract:						
1.	Document compliance and completion						
2.	Verify final payment and proper accounting to project						
3.	Notify vendor/contractor of final completion						
M.	*Engineering Documentation*						
1.	Compile and store all engineering documentation						
2.	Prepare final technical report						
N.	*Site Operations*						
1.	Close down site operations						
2.	Dispose of equipment and material						

FIGURE 13.3　Checklist for project closure.

Source: Archibald (1992).

the bureaucratic tasks, and if the PM leaves many loose ends, he or she will rapidly get a reputation for being slipshod, a characterization not associated with career success.

The PM also has another option, to ignore the closeout process entirely. The evaluation has already been conducted, and praise or censure has been delivered. Rather than deal with closure, the PM may let the project administrator handle things. Project team members may well have similar feelings and reactions and may seek new jobs or affiliations before the project actually ends, thereby dragging out some final tasks interminably.

Special *closure managers* are sometimes useful in completing the long and involved process of shutting down a project. In such cases, the PM is transferred to another project or reassigned to a functional "home." The closure manager does not have to deal with substantive project tasks and therefore may be a person familiar with the administrative requirements of closure and the environment within which the project will be operating (if it continues to live). If personnel performance evaluations are required, and they usually are, they must be prepared by the PM or whoever supervised the work of each individual team member, not by a specially appointed closure manager.

If technical knowledge is required during the closure process, a member of the project team may be upgraded and assigned responsibility for the shutdown. This "promotion" is often a motivator and will provide development experience for the team member.

The primary duties of the closure manager are encompassed in the following nine general tasks:

1. Ensure completion of the work, including tasks performed by subcontractors.
2. Notify the client of project completion, and ensure that delivery (and installation) is accomplished. Acceptance of the project must be acknowledged by the client.
3. Ensure that documentation is complete, including a terminal evaluation of the project deliverables and preparation of the project's final report, including any lessons learned from the administration and management of the project.
4. Clear for final billings, and oversee preparation of the final invoices sent to the client.
5. Redistribute personnel, materials, equipment, and any other resources to the appropriate places.
6. Clear project with legal counsel or consultant. File for patents if appropriate. Record and archive all "nondisclosure" documents.
7. Determine what records (manuals, reports, and other paperwork) to keep. Ensure that such documents are stored in the proper places and that responsibility for document retention is turned over to the parent organization's archivist.
8. Ascertain any product support requirements (e.g., spares, service), decide how such support will be delivered, and assign responsibility.
9. Oversee the closing of the project's books.

It is likely that tasks 1 to 3 will be handled by the regular PM immediately before the project closure process is started. If the closure manager must handle these tasks, technical support will almost certainly be needed. Of course, many of the tasks on this list will be quite simple if the project is not large, but even with small- or medium-sized projects, the PM should make sure that all items are covered. For routine projects, for example, maintenance, simplified checklists are helpful.

Item 5 on this list deserves some amplification. The PM can do a great deal to reduce the problems of closure by dealing with these issues well before the actual closure process begins. Arrangements for the distribution and disposal of property and equipment belonging to the project should be included in the charter and/or in the contract with the client. Obviously, this does not stop all arguments, but it does soften the conflicts. Dealing with project personnel is more difficult.

Most PMs delay the personnel reassignment/release issue as long as possible for three main reasons: a strong reluctance to face the interpersonal conflicts that might arise when new assignments and layoffs are announced; worry that people will lose interest and stop work on the project as soon as it becomes known that closure is being considered; or concern—particularly in the case of a standalone project organization—that team members will try to avoid death by stretching out the work as far as possible.

As long as the PM has access to the functional managers' ears, any team member who "quits work" before the project is completed or stalls by stretching out tasks or creating task extensions would be subject to the usual sanctions of the workplace. The PM should make it quite clear that retirement while still on-the-job and tenure-for-life are equally unacceptable.

The first problem results when project leadership is held by a managerially weak PM. The height of weakness is demonstrated when the PM posts a written list of reassignments and layoffs on the project's bulletin board late Friday afternoon and then leaves for a long weekend. A more useful course of action is to speak with project members individually or in small groups, let them know about plans for closure, and offer to consult with each in order to aid in the reassignment process or to assist in finding new work. If layoffs are involved, the use of an outplacement organization is very helpful. (A preliminary announcement to the entire project team is in order because the interviews may cover several weeks or months.) It is almost impossible to keep shutdown plans a secret, and to confront the matter immediately tends to minimize rumors.

In a large project, of course, the PM will not be able to conduct personal interviews except with a few senior assistants. The project's personnel officer, or a representative from the parent firm's personnel department, can serve instead. This may seem like an unnecessary service to the team members, but a reputation of "taking care of one's people" is an invaluable aid to the PM when recruiting for the next project.

Termination by murder makes it very difficult to follow these suggestions about dealing with project personnel. The project's death often occurs with so little warning that the PM learns of the fact at the same time as the project team—or, as sometimes happens, learns about it from a member of the project team.

There is little the PM can do in such a case except to try to minimize the damage. The team should be assembled as rapidly as possible and informed, to the best of the PM's ability, about what has happened. At this point, the PM should start the reassignment/release process.

Items 6 and 7 on our list, and several items in Figure 13.3 (cf. particularly sections I, K, L, and M), concern retention of project-related documents in the parent organization's archives. There are several reasons why document retention may be critically important. Following the completion of the project, the project's parent organization and the client may differ in their recollection of precisely what was promised as output—recall that agreements about the deliverables, including all change orders, must be in writing and signed off by all affected parties. They may differ in their recollection of precisely how nondisclosure agreements were worded.

The problem can be avoided by ensuring that the documents retained do not include material previously identified as being "confidential." Most nondisclosure agreements require that confidential material be so labeled. If the inclusion of confidential information in project documents is mandatory for clarity or other pertinent reasons, it is sometimes possible to include it with the prior written permission of the discloser, usually conditioned that the project documents not be disclosed to a competitor, or pursuant to a court order, without immediate notice to the discloser so it can get a suitable court order protecting the confidential information. Finally, the parent organization and client may differ in their understanding of precisely what was approved or not approved at various stages of the project's life. Indeed, maintenance of sign-off records at each of the phase gates of a project life

Project Management in Practice

When You Have to Kill a Project

It takes courage to kill a project, but sometimes you know it has to be done. Some common symptoms of a failing project are ill-defined initial requirements, constant changes in scope, excessive changes in resources and personnel, and extreme stress/tension over anticipated changes. Yet, a project may have followed the "book" and done everything right, but still need to be terminated. This was the case with a project in the United Kingdom, where the client was highly committed to the project, contributing time, resources, and prompt decisions. The scope was clear, completion criteria agreed upon, the budget and timeframe acceptable to all. Early on, however, an unavoidable scope change had to be made, requiring a 20 percent increase in time and a 10 percent increase in cost, agreed to by the client.

As the project approached the end of the first phase, it was clear that the quality and schedule were both deteriorating, as indicated in progress reports to both the client and senior management. A quick review showed that the results were not going to be acceptable. With the agreement of the PM, an outside Expert was called in to review the effort to date and make a recommendation. Then a joint meeting was held with the Expert, the PM, the Program Manager, and the primary contractor where it was decided that the best thing to do was to work together to complete phase one and then terminate the project, with a clean handover to another team to tackle phase two.

Although disappointing to everyone, the close and frequent communications of both progress and concerns throughout the project with upper management and the client, offered in timely, digestible amounts, reduced their expectations and protected the client from a surprise at the end. Honest, consistent communication throughout the project life cycle resulted in improved trust, integrity, and confidence in the vendor and their team.

Questions

1. **What are your thoughts about doing everything right and the project still failing?**

2. **Does the admonition "Never surprise the boss!" now make more sense? Why?**

3. **Do you think the scope change at the beginning was the problem here, or was there going to be a problem anyway?**

Source: S. Somani, "Anatomy of a Failed Project." *PM Network*, Vol. 24.

---

cycle are critical for the parent organization because it relies on the approval of the current stage before investing the resources required to work on the next stage.[2] We strongly advise that the organization's attorney be consulted on matters of document retention.

13.4 The Final Report—A Project History

Good project management systems have a memory, the Organization Process Assets. A key element of this memory is the Project Final Report. The final report is not another evaluation, though it may be an input to such, and/or for postproject control; rather, it is the history of the project. It is a chronicle of the life and times of the project, a compendium of what went right and what went wrong, of who served the project in what capacity, of what was done to create the substance of the project, of how it was managed. We learn from experience only if the experience is preserved and studied (Whitten, 1999). **PMBOK** emphasizes the importance of keeping and reviewing past experience as prelude to new experience.

2.1.4

The elements that should be covered in the final report are listed next. When considering these elements, it is also beneficial to consider where the source materials can be found. For the most part, the required information is contained in the project master plan,

---

[2]We thank T. D. Mantel, Esq., an attorney familiar with the legalities of document retention, for portions of this paragraph.

a document that includes the charter, the WBS, all budgets, schedules, change orders, and updates of the aforementioned. In addition to the master plan, all project audits and evaluations contain required input data. Almost everything else required by the final report is reflective, based on the thoughts of the PM and others involved in the project. There is little problem in knowing where the needed documents should be kept—in the project's files. Making sure that they are, in fact, there and that they are, in fact, up to date is a serious concern.

The precise organization of the final report is not a matter of great concern; the content is. Some are organized chronologically, while others feature sections on the technical and administrative aspects of the project. Some are written in a narrative style, and some contain copies of all project reports strung together with short commentaries. What matters is that several subjects should be addressed, one way or another, in the final report.

1. **Project Performance**　A key element of the report is a comparison of what the project achieved (the terminal evaluation) with what the project tried to achieve (the project proposal). This comparison may be quite extensive and should include explanations of all significant deviations of actual from plan. A final earned value discussion can also be helpful. Because the final report is not a formal evaluation, it can reflect the best judgment of the PM on why the triumphs and failures occurred. This comparison should be followed with a set of recommendations for future projects dealing with like or similar technical matters.

2. **Administrative Performance**　The substantive side of the project usually gets a great deal of attention, while the administrative side is often ignored until administrative problems occur. There is also a strong tendency on the part of almost everyone to treat the "pencil pushers" with grudging tolerance, at best. The administration of a project cannot solve technical problems, but it can enable good technology to be implemented (or prevent it). Administrative practices should be reviewed, and those that worked particularly well or poorly should be highlighted. It is important, when possible, to report the reasons why some specific practice was effective or ineffective. If poor administration is to be avoided and good practices adopted, it is necessary to understand why some things work well and others do not in the environment of a particular organization. This becomes the basis for the recommendations that accompany the discussion.

3. **Organizational Structure**　Each of the organizational forms used for projects has its own unique set of advantages and disadvantages. The final report should include comments on the ways the structure aided or impeded the progress of the project. If it appears that a modification to the accepted form of project organization—or a change to a different basic organizational form—might be helpful for project management, such a recommendation should be made. Obviously, recommendations should be accompanied by detailed explanations and rationales.

4. **Project and Administrative Teams**　On occasion, individuals who are competent and likable as individuals do not perform well as members of a team when a high level of interpersonal communication and cooperation is required. A confidential section of the final report may be directed to a senior personnel officer of the parent organization, recommending that such individuals not be assigned to future projects. Similarly, the PM may recommend that individuals or groups who are particularly effective when operating as a team be kept together on future projects or when reassigned to the firm's regular operations.

5. **Techniques of Project Management**　The outcome of the project is so dependent on the skill with which the forecasting, planning, budgeting, scheduling, resource allocation, risk management, and control are handled that attention must be given to checking on the way these tasks were accomplished. If the forecasts, budgets, and schedules

were not reasonably accurate, recommendations for improved methods should be made. The techniques used for planning, control, and risk management should also be subject to scrutiny.

For each element covered in the final report, recommendations for changing current practice should be made and defended. Insofar as is possible, the implications of each potential change should be noted. Commonly ignored, but equally important, are comments and recommendations about those aspects of the project that worked unusually well. Most projects, project teams, and PMs develop informal procedures that speed budget preparation, ease the tasks of scheduling, improve forecasts, and the like. The final report is an appropriate repository for such knowledge. Once reported, they can be tested and, if generally useful, can be added to the parent organization's list of approved project management methods.

The fundamental purpose of the final report is to improve future projects, hence its value in postproject control. It is ultimately focused on the project itself and on the process by which the project was conducted. Data on the project and its outcomes are available in the many interim reports, audits, and evaluations conducted during the project's life. But data on the process come largely from the PM's recollections. To ensure that significant issues are included, the PM should keep a diary. The PM's diary is not an official project document, but rather an informal collection of thoughts, reflections, and commentaries on project happenings. Such a diary tends to be a rich source of unconventional wisdom when written by a thoughtful PM. It may also be a great source of learning for a young, aspiring PM. Above all, it keeps ideas from "getting lost" amid the welter of activity on the project.

Occasionally, the project diary serves a purpose not originally intended. A PM working for a Minnesota highway construction company made a habit of keeping a project diary, mostly for his or her own interest and amusement. The firm was sued as the result of an accident on a road under construction. The plaintiff alleged that the highway shoulder was not complete nor was it marked "Under Construction" at the time of the accident. The PM's diary noted daily progress on the road, and it showed that the relevant piece of the road had been completed several days prior to the accident. The company successfully defended its position. All company PMs keep diaries now. A vice president of the firm mentioned that they are the same type of diary his high-school-aged daughter uses.

13.5 | Benefits Realization

Now that the project execution effort has been completed, the PO, sponsor, and the PM will have to close it out by seeing that the project personnel, equipment, and remaining resources are properly transferred to their correct locations and uses. If this was a project closure by addition, these resources may in fact stay with the project output, including possibly the personnel, for utilization within the organization. Nevertheless, there may still be contractual and legal documents and payments that need to be completed, administrative affairs to attend to, and final reports to be written.

Next, the official benefits realization stage begins for the PO. Of course, the PO has been preparing for this stage throughout the execution of the project by working with the appropriate functional manager and other users of the project outputs. As we noted earlier, the PO may in fact *be* the functional manager, if the project was intended for this function. Still, there probably are other users of the project outputs, either on a regular or on an intermittent basis. There are three primary phases to this final stage of the project. The first phase is the biggest and involves implementing the project's outputs as they were intended. The second phase is the handoff to the functional manager to assure that the benefits that have been obtained will continue to be realized. And the third phase is the routine use of the outputs where the PO writes the final report on the implementation for the funder and council.

Implementing the proper use of the outputs is a difficult task. It is often the case that the intended customers/users of the outputs don't want to change the procedures they have been using, which are comfortable and routine for them, in order to take on the difficult tasks of learning new procedures and risking the chance that they won't be able to understand this new method and how to properly do their job. This is commonly known as "resistance." That is especially the case if they haven't been involved in designing the new system or even been informed about the change until it was dumped on them. Another danger is that they will use the new system for a while and then slowly revert back to their previous system, which may well have been less work for them. That is, often a new system may be better overall for the company but is more work for some employees. All of these behavioral issues are even more difficult if the new system involves technology that is complex and confusing for the employees, especially computers.

There are other reasons as well for employees to resist adopting a new system. Many times it simply doesn't work as it is supposed to, so the firm ends up reverting to the old system. Then all that training and hassle and time spent have been just a bothersome waste. Other times, a new manager arrives and doesn't agree that this system is worth the trouble. Or a new top executive/administrator arrives and has a different idea of how the organization should operate and terminate funding for the new system.

As a result of all these potential pitfalls, it is mandatory that the PO begin the preparation for this stage well beforehand, when the project is being executed. But the preparation may need to be adjusted as the project plan changes, which presents other problems for the PO. For example, there is the possibility that the customer training may begin too early, before the new system is fully operational and debugged. Then if the system has to be drastically changed, it is likely that the training will have to be redone as well, which tends to drive the users nuts! It is no wonder that their response is: "I'll start the training *after* you've figured out what the final system is going to be."

As the PO is preparing the customers for the implementation of the new system, there are many tools available, the main one typically being training. However, there may also be education classes, motivational events such as tours of other organizations that use a similar system, and other ways of engaging and motivating these intended users. Beyond training in new procedures, though, there may also be new responsibilities for the customers or reorganizations of the work groups or departments. All this adds to the headaches for the PO, so it is no wonder that it is so difficult to obtain the intended benefits from a "successfully completed" project.

The next phase is the handoff to the functional manager if the PO isn't that person. All of the aforementioned dangers and difficulties apply in this phase as well, although the functional manager has typically been involved in all the training and other activities that the users have experienced, and even more involving administration, oversight, human resources, and general management. Beyond this, however, the PO needs to be sure that at some point in the future, the users don't slip back into old habits and routines, so the handoff will be a slow one. For example, it is common with new technology implementations in manufacturing for the PO to stay around until production reaches 80 percent utilization with the new system. It is also well recognized that when a new system is installed, there is an immediate drop in productivity, but then productivity slowly starts to rise back up, eventually returning to its previous level, and then (if the new system is well designed) improving even further and gaining the benefits desired by the funder.

And at some point in the last, routine use phase, the PO's job is complete. It may be when the system reaches 80 percent of the benefits expected, or more, or less, depending on the organization and situation. However, at some point, the PO has to be satisfied that the benefits eventually desired will, in fact, continue to occur. Similarly to the Sydney, Australia Opera House, the worldwide familiarity and admiration of the structure took years after completion to develop.

13.6 Afterword

It is common for students to ask, "Does anybody really use this stuff?"—sometimes in less-polite language. Over the years, there has been considerable academic research devoted to answering that question; see, for example, Ibbs and Kwak, (2000). As we noted in this chapter, there has also been much research on understanding the causes of project success and failure. Comparatively little work has investigated the degree to which specific project management practices are associated with project success. Research helping to close that gap in knowledge has been conducted by Papke-Shields and her coauthors (2010). The remainder of this section reports on their work.

A survey was conducted with responses from 142 active project managers. The frequency of use of each project management practice associated with each **PMBOK** knowledge area was scored on a five-point scale (never, seldom, sometimes, frequently, always). The use of time management techniques was the highest with a score of 4.03 for the average of seven time-related practices (project schedule and updates, baseline schedule, PERT/Gantt charts, activity lists, duration estimates, and updates). Risk had the lowest average score with an average of 2.79 for the six related practices (risk management plan, contingency plan, risk register, quantitative risk analysis, register updates, and pre-planned responses).

In addition to time and risk, the other **PMBOK** knowledge areas surveyed were: integration, scope, cost, quality, human resources, communication, procurement, and status review. All knowledge areas had average practice-usage levels above the level reported for risk.

Project success was measured across three levels: low, moderate, and high. For all project management practice areas, the average use was higher in the high success group than in the low success group. Taken as a group, the practices had a significant impact on the difference between high and low success ratings. Further, the practices in each of the knowledge areas account for the differences in success.

The answer to the question at the beginning of this section is: Yes, the management practices are being used.

> *Respondents reported that PM practices associated with time, scope, and cost were widely used; practices associated with integration, HR, and procurement were used somewhat less; and finally, practices related to communication, quality, and risk tend to be used least frequently. (Papke-Shields et al. 2010, p. 659).*

An unasked, but implied question follows the first question, "So what?" The answer is that "the use of practices across all knowledge areas varied significantly between the 'low' and 'high' success groups." (Op. cit.)

Project managers do use this stuff, and it helps.

Summary

At last, we come to the completion of our project—closure. In this chapter we looked at the ways in which projects can be closed, how to decide if a project should be closed, the closure process, and the preparation of the Project Final Report.

Specific points made in the chapter were these:

- A project can be closed in one of four ways: extinction, addition, integration, or starvation.

- Making a decision to shut down a project before its completion is difficult, but a number of factors can be of help in reaching a conclusion.
- Most projects fail because of one or more of the following reasons:
  - Inappropriate use of the project form of organization
  - Insufficient top-management support
  - Naming the wrong PM
  - Poor planning
- Studies have shown that the factors associated with project success are different for different industries and the various types of projects.
- Success-related factors, or any factors management wishes, can be used in closure decision models.
- Special closure managers are often used, and needed, for closing out projects. This task, consisting of eight major duties, is a project in itself.
- The Project Final Report incorporates the process knowledge gained from the project. In addition to preservation of project records, the Final Report embodies the experience from which we learn. It should include:
  - Project performance comments
  - Administrative performance comments
  - Organizational structure comments
  - Personnel suggestions, possibly a confidential section
- Although the official technical aspects of the project may be finished, the job of assuring that the desired benefits from the project can still be a major endeavor.

Glossary

Benefit Realization   The tasks facing the project owner in order to achieve the benefits desired from the project.

Budget Decrement   A reduction in the amount of funds for an activity.

Closure by Addition   Bringing the project into the organization as a separate, ongoing entity.

Closure by Extinction   The end of all activity on a project without extending it in some form, such as by inclusion or integration.

Closure by Integration   Bringing the project activities into the organization and distributing them among existing functions.

Closure by Starvation   Cutting a project's budget sufficiently to stop progress without actually killing the project.

Closure Manager   An administrator responsible for wrapping up the administrative details of a project.

Resistance   When an employee opposes a change in their work procedures.

Termination by Murder   Terminating a project suddenly and without warning, usually for a cause not related to the project's purpose.

Questions

Material Review Questions

1. List and briefly describe the ways projects may be closed.
2. What problems may occur if the PM does not have a follow-on project when the current project nears closeout?
3. What are the primary duties of a closure manager?
4. Upon closure of a project, what happens to the information gathered throughout the course of the project?
5. What is a budget decrement?
6. Identify the four reasons for project closure.
7. What does the Project Final Report include?
8. What factors are considered most important in the decision to close a project?
9. What issues should be considered when using the closure-by-integration method?
10. What are the tasks involved for the PO when attempting to obtain the benefits desired from the project?
11. How can the PO overcome employee "resistance?"

Class Discussion Questions

12. Discuss the impact, both positive and negative, of closure on the project team members. How might the negative impact be lessened?
13. If the actual closure of a project becomes a project in itself, what are the characteristics of this project? How is it different from other projects?
14. Discuss some reasons why a Project Final Report, when completed, should be permanently retained by the firm.
15. What elements of the closure process may be responsible for making a project unsuccessful?

16. What are some characteristics of a good closure manager?
17. How might one choose which closure method to use?
18. Why might a failing project not be closed?
19. How can shutdown for reasons other than achievement of project goals be avoided?
20. What must the PM do in planning, scheduling, monitoring, and closing out the project?
21. Which of the four major types of closures are Political? Cross-Cultural? Senescence?
22. Would you suspect that most projects are closed for "non-technical" reasons? Why or why not?
23. How would you decide when the benefits have been "permanently" achieved in the Routine phase?
24. If the functional manager is lukewarm on the change involved with the project, what would you do to help get him or her on board?

Incidents For Discussion

Electrical Broom and Supply Co

IMSCO began manufacturing and distributing electrical brooms to industrial customers 43 years ago. Mr. Bretting, President of IMSCO, has been toying with the idea of using IMSCO's manufacturing and distribution expertise to begin making and selling consumer products. He has already decided that he cannot sell any of his current products to consumers. In addition, if IMSCO is going to go through the trouble of developing consumer markets, Mr. Bretting feels very strongly that their first product should be something new and innovative that will help establish their reputation. He thinks that the expertise required to develop a new product exists within the company, but no one has any real experience in organizing or managing such a project. Fortunately, Mr. Bretting is familiar with a local consulting firm that has a good reputation and track record of leading companies through projects such as this, so he contacted them.

Three months into the project, Mr. Bretting contacted the program manager/consultant and mentioned that he was worried about the amount of risk involved in trying to introduce such an innovative consumer product with his current organization. He was worried that the project was oriented too strongly toward R&D and did not consider related business problems in enough depth. (This was a complete about-face from his feelings three months earlier, when he had approved the first plan submitted with no changes.)

Mr. Bretting suggested that the consultant modify the existing project to include the introduction of a "me-too" consumer product before IMSCO's new product was defined and tested. Mr. Bretting thought that some experience with a "me-too"

product would provide IMSCO management with valuable experience and would improve later performance with the new product. He allowed the R&D portion of the project to continue concurrently, but the "me-too" phase would have top priority as far as resources were concerned. The consultant said she would think about it and contact him next week.

Questions

If you were the consultant, what would you recommend to Mr. Bretting? Would you continue the relationship?

Excel Electronics

Excel Electronics is nearing completion of a three-year project to develop and produce a new pocket Phone-Fax-Internet device (PFI). The PFI is no larger than a cigarette pack but has all the power and features of full sized devices. The assembly line and all the production facilities will be completed in six months and the first units will begin production in seven months. The plant manager believes it is time to begin winding the project down. He or she has three methods in mind for closing the project: extinction, addition, and integration, but he or she is not sure which method would be best.

Questions

Which of the three methods would you recommend, and why? Would you expect resistance of the employees to implementing this project? Why or why not? If the plant manager is the PO for this project, what will his or her duties be for assuring benefit realization?

Continuing Integrative Class Project

It is time to close the project. Decide what form of closure will be appropriate for this project and what the closure duties should include. (Perhaps a party?) How should the project results be distributed? Where will the project workers go next? How can the PM and team be sure that the results of the project will achieve the benefits envisioned at the start?

Finally, craft the project history report and specifically address the following topics:

- Assessment of the project's performance: Contrast what the project achieved with the original project goals. What recommendations would you make for future projects to help ensure they achieve high levels of performance?

- Assessment of administrative performance: Again, include recommendations for future projects that would mitigate administrative problems encountered in completing the project and best practices to continue.

- Assessment of the project management techniques employed: What project management techniques proved to be especially effective and should be continued in future projects? Were there any techniques that were not used that in hindsight would have been useful? Are there any modifications you would make to the techniques used in future projects?

- Suggest changes that would have been helpful at the beginning, and throughout, this project.

Bibliography

Archibald, R. D. *Managing High Technology Programs and Projects*, 4th ed. New York: Wiley, 1992.

Baker, B. "Great Expectations." *PM Network*, May 1997.

Baker, N. R., S. G. Green, A. S. Bean, W. Blank, and S. K. Tadisina. "Sources of First Suggestion and Project Success/Failure in Industrial Research." *Proceedings, Conference on the Management of Technological Innovation*, Washington, D.C., 1983.

Black, K. "Causes of Project Failure: A Survey of Professional Engineers." *PM Network*, November 1996.

Buell, C. K. "When to Terminate a Research and Development Project." *Research Management*, July 1967.

Green, S. G., M. A. Welsh, and G. E. Dehler. "Red Flags at Dawn or Predicting Project Terminations at Start Up." *Research Technology Management*, May–June 1993.

Hussain, R., and S. Wearne. "Problems and Needs of Project Management in the Process and Other Industries." *Transactions of the Institution of Chemical Engineers, Part A*, Apr. 2005.

Ibbs, C., and Y. Kwak, "Assessing Project Management Maturity: An Empirical Assessment." *Project Management Journal*, 2000.

Jiang, J. J., G. Klein, and J. Balloun. "Ranking of System Implementation Success Factors." *Project Management Journal*, December 1996.

Kumar, V., A. N. S. Persaud, and U. Kumar. "To Terminate or Not—An Ongoing R&D Project: A Managerial-Dilemma." *IEEE Transactions on Engineering Management*, August 1996.

Papke-Shields, K. E., C. Beise, and J. Quan. "Do Project Managers Practice What They Preach, and Does It Matter to Project Success?" *International Journal of Project Management*, 2010.

Pinto, J. K., and S. J. Mantel, Jr. "The Causes of Project Failure." *IEEE Transactions on Engineering Management*, November 1990.

Pinto, J. K. *Project Management: Achieving Competitive Advantage*, 3rd ed. Upper Saddle River, NJ: Pearson, 2013.

Project Management Institute, *A Guide to the Project Management Body of Knowledge (PMBOK®)*, 5th ed. Newtown Square, PA: Project Management Institute, 2013.

Shafer, S. M., and S. J. Mantel, Jr. "A Decision Support System for the Project Termination Decision." *Project Management Journal*, June 1989.

Starke, S. "Going Against the Grain." *PM Network*, July 2012.

Whitten, N. "Are You Learning from Project to Project?" *PM Network*, March 1999.

Zou, W., M. Kumaraswamy, J. Chung, and J. Wong. "Identifying the Critical Success Factors for Relationship Management in PPP Projects." *International Journal of Project Management*, 32/2, 2014.

Author Index

Subject Index